The
NEW TESTAMENT
and the
BOOK OF PSALMS

NEW INTERNATIONAL
VERSION

The
NEW TESTAMENT
and the
BOOK OF PSALMS

NEW INTERNATIONAL
VERSION

HODDER AND STOUGHTON
LONDON SYDNEY AUCKLAND TORONTO

The Holy Bible, New International Version
Copyright © 1978 by New York International Bible Society
First published in Great Britain 1979
This edition 1983

The New Testament, New International Version
© 1973 by New York Bible Society International
© 1978 by New York International Bible Society

The Book of John
© 1970 by New York International Bible Society

British Library Cataloguing in Publication Data

[Bible. English. New International Version.
Selections. 1983] New Testament and Psalms.
I. New Testament and Psalms
   220.5'2   BS195.157
ISBN 0 340 33837 7

PREFACE

THE NEW INTERNATIONAL VERSION of the Holy Bible is a completely new translation made by many scholars working directly from the Greek.

The New International Version had its beginning in 1965, when, after many years of exploratory study, a group of biblical scholars met in Chicago and concurred in the need for a new translation of the Holy Scriptures. This group, though not made up of official church representatives, was nevertheless transdenominational in character. Their conclusion was subsequently endorsed by a large gathering of Christian leaders from many denominations in North America. Final responsibility for the new version was delegated to a body of fifteen, the Committee on Bible Translation, composed for the most part of biblical specialists from universities, colleges and theological seminaries. In 1967 the New York International Bible Society generously undertook financial sponsorship of the project—a sponsorship that has made it possible to enlist the help of many distinguished scholars. The fact that participants from the United States, Canada, England, Australia and New Zealand worked together gives the project its international scope. That they were from various denominations, including Anglican, Baptist, Brethren, Church of Christ, Episcopal, Lutheran, Mennonite, Methodist, Nazarene, Presbyterian, Reformed and other churches, safeguards it from sectarian bias.

Because the distinctive nature of the New International Version is derived so largely from the working procedures, an explanation of these is in order. The translation of each book was assigned to a team of scholars. Next, an Intermediate Editorial Committee revised the initial translation, with constant reference to the Greek. Their work then went to a General Editorial Committee, which rechecked it in

PREFACE

relation to the Greek and made another thorough revision. This revision in turn was carefully reviewed by the Committee on Bible Translation, which made further changes and then issued the final version. In this way the entire New Testament underwent three revisions, during each of which the translation was examined for its faithfulness to the original Greek and for its English style.

A sensitive feeling for style does not always go with scholarship in biblical languages. Accordingly the Committee on Bible Translation submitted the developing version to a number of literary consultants. Two of them read every word of the completed New Testament twice—once before and once after the last major revision—making invaluable suggestions. During the process, it was also tested for clarity and idiom by various kinds of people—young and old, educated and uneducated, ministers and laymen.

The Greek text used in the work of translation was an eclectic one. No other piece of ancient literature has so much manuscript support as does the New Testament. Where existing texts differ, the translators made their choice of readings in accord with sound principles of textual criticism. Footnotes call attention to places where there is uncertainty about what constitutes the original text. These have been introduced by the phrase "Some MSS add (or omit or read)."

As in all translations of the Scriptures, the precise meaning of the original text could not in every case be determined. In important instances of this kind, footnotes introduced by "Or" suggest an alternate rendering of the text. In the translation itself, brackets are occasionally used to indicate words or phrases supplied for clarification.

Certain convictions and aims have guided the translators. They are all committed to the full authority and complete trustworthiness of the Scriptures, which they believe to be God's Word in written form. They are agreed that the Bible contains the answer to man's deepest needs and sets forth the way to his eternal well-being. Therefore their first concern has been the accuracy of the translation and its fidelity to the thought of the New Testament writers. While they have weighed the significance of the lexical and grammatical details of the Greek text, they have striven for more than a word-for-word translation. Because thought patterns and syntax differ from language to language, faithful communication of the meaning of the writers of the New Testament demands frequent modifications in sentence structure and constant regard for the contextual meanings of words.

Concern for clarity of style—that it should be idiomatic without being idiosyncratic, contemporary without being dated—has also motivated the translators and their consultants. They have consistently aimed at simplicity of expression, with sensitive attention to the connotation and sound of the chosen word. At the same time, they have endeavoured to avoid a sameness of style in order to reflect the varied styles and moods of the New Testament writers. These aims the translators and consultants have tried to embody in language that will speak not only to people today but also to those of future decades. And they trust that the wide use of the New International Version will encourage the wholesome practice of memorising Scripture.

Among the languages of the world, English stands first in international use. The translators of this version, coming as they do from major English-speaking nations, have sought to recognise the world-wide character of the language by avoiding overt Americanisms on the one hand and overt Anglicisms on the other hand.

As for the omission of the pronouns "thou," "thee," and "thine" in reference to the Deity, the translators remind the reader that to retain these archaisms (along with the strange verb forms, such as *doest*, *wouldest* and *hadst*) would have violated their aim of faithful translation. The Greek text uses no special pronouns to express reverence for God and Christ. Scripture is not enhanced by keeping, as a special mode of addressing Deity, forms that in the days of the King James Bible were simply the regular pronouns and verbs used in everyday speech, whether referring to God or to man.

Like all translations of the Bible, made as they are by

PREFACE

imperfect men, this one undoubtedly falls short of its aims. Yet we are grateful to God for the extent to which he has enabled us to realise our aims and for the strength he has given us to complete this part of our task. We offer this version of the New Testament to him in whose name and for whose glory it has been made. We pray that it will lead many into a better understanding of the Holy Scriptures and a fuller knowledge of Jesus Christ the Incarnate Word, of whom the Scriptures so faithfully testify.

The Committee on Bible Translation

Names of the translators and editors may be secured from the New York International Bible Society, 144 Tices Lane, East Brunswick, New Jersey 08816, U.S.A.

CONTENTS

THE BOOKS OF THE NEW TESTAMENT

THE
NEW TESTAMENT

Matthew

The Genealogy of Jesus

1 A record of the genealogy of Jesus Christ the son of David, the son of Abraham:

² Abraham was the father of Isaac,
Isaac the father of Jacob,
Jacob the father of Judah and
his brothers,
³ Judah the father of Perez and
Zerah, whose mother was
Tamar,
Perez the father of Hezron,
Hezron the father of Ram,
⁴ Ram the father of Amminadab,
Amminadab the father of
Nahshon,
Nahshon the father of Salmon,
⁵ Salmon the father of Boaz,
whose mother was Rahab,
Boaz the father of Obed, whose
mother was Ruth,
Obed the father of Jesse,
⁶ and Jesse the father of King
David.

David was the father of
Solomon, whose mother had
been Uriah's wife,
⁷ Solomon the father of
Rehoboam,
Rehoboam the father of Abijah,
Abijah the father of Asa,
⁸ Asa the father of Jehoshaphat,
Jehoshaphat the father of Joram,
Joram the father of Uzziah,
⁹ Uzziah the father of Jotham,
Jotham the father of Ahaz,
Ahaz the father of Hezekiah,
¹⁰ Hezekiah the father of
Manasseh,
Manasseh the father of Amon,
Amon the father of Josiah,
¹¹ and Josiah the father of Jeconiah*a* and his brothers at the
time of the exile to Babylon.

¹² After the exile to Babylon:
Jeconiah was the father of
Shealtiel,
Shealtiel the father of
Zerubbabel,
¹³ Zerubbabel the father of Abiud,
Abiud the father of Eliakim,
Eliakim the father of Azor,
¹⁴ Azor the father of Zadok,
Zadok the father of Akim,
Akim the father of Eliud,
¹⁵ Eliud the father of Eleazar,
Eleazar the father of Matthan,
Matthan the father of Jacob,
¹⁶ and Jacob the father of Joseph,
the husband of Mary, of whom
was born Jesus, who is called
Christ.

¹⁷ Thus there were fourteen generations in all from Abraham to David, fourteen from David to the exile to Babylon, and fourteen from the exile to the Christ.*b*

The Birth of Jesus Christ

¹⁸ This is how the birth of Jesus Christ came about. His mother Mary was pledged to be married to Joseph, but before they came together, she was found to be with child through the Holy Spirit. ¹⁹ Because Joseph her husband was a righteous man and did not want to expose her to public disgrace, he had in mind to divorce her quietly.

---

*a*11 That is, Jehoiachin; also in verse 12
*b*17 Or *Messiah*. "The Christ" (Greek) and "the Messiah" (Hebrew) both mean "the Anointed One".

1

20But after he had considered this, an angel of the Lord appeared to him in a dream and said, "Joseph son of David, do not be afraid to take Mary home as your wife, because what is conceived in her is from the Holy Spirit. 21She will give birth to a son, and you are to give him the name Jesus,c because he will save his people from their sins."

22All this took place to fulfil what the Lord had said through the prophet: 23"The virgin will be with child and will give birth to a son, and they will call him Immanuel"d— which means, "God with us."

24When Joseph woke up, he did what the angel of the Lord had commanded him and took Mary home as his wife. 25But he had no union with her until she gave birth to a son. And he gave him the name Jesus.

The Visit of the Magi

2 After Jesus was born in Bethlehem in Judea, during the time of King Herod, Magia from the east came to Jerusalem 2and asked, "Where is the one who has been born king of the Jews? We saw his star in the eastb and have come to worship him."

3When King Herod heard this he was disturbed, and all Jerusalem with him. 4When he had called together all the people's chief priests and teachers of the law, he asked them where the Christc was to be born. 5"In Bethlehem in Judea," they replied, "for this is what the prophet has written:

6 "But you, Bethlehem, in the land of Judah,
    are by no means least among the rulers of Judah;
for out of you will come a ruler
    who will be the shepherd of my people Israel.'d

7Then Herod called the Magi secretly and found out from them the exact time the star had appeared. 8He sent them to Bethlehem and said, "Go and make a careful search for the child. As soon as you find him, report to me, so that I too may go and worship him."

9After they had heard the king, they went on their way, and the star they had seen in the easte went ahead of them until it stopped over the place where the child was. 10When they saw the star, they were overjoyed. 11On coming to the house, they saw the child with his mother Mary, and they bowed down and worshipped him. Then they opened their treasures and presented him with gifts of gold and of incense and of myrrh. 12And having been warned in a dream not to go back to Herod, they returned to their country by another route.

The Escape to Egypt

13When they had gone, an angel of the Lord appeared to Joseph in a dream. "Get up," he said, "take the child and his mother and escape to Egypt. Stay there until I tell you, for Herod is going to search for the child to kill him."

14So he got up, took the child and his mother during the night and left for Egypt, 15where he stayed until the death of Herod. And so was fulfilled what the Lord had said through the prophet: "Out of Egypt I called my son."f

16When Herod realised that he had been outwitted by the Magi, he was furious, and he gave orders to kill all the boys in Bethlehem and its vicinity who were two years old and under, in accordance with the time he had learned from the Magi. 17Then what was said through the prophet Jeremiah was fulfilled:

18"A voice is heard in Ramah,
    weeping and great mourning,
Rachel weeping for her children
    and refusing to be comforted,
    because they are no more."g

---

c21 *Jesus* is the Greek form of *Joshua*, which means the LORD *saves.*
d23 Isaiah 7:14   a1 Traditionally *Wise Men*   b2 Or *star when it rose*
c4 Or *Messiah*   d6 Micah 5:2   e 9 Or *seen when it rose*
f15 Hosea 11:1   g18 Jer. 31:15

The Return to Nazareth

19After Herod died, an angel of the Lord appeared in a dream to Joseph in Egypt 20and said, "Get up, take the child and his mother and go to the land of Israel, for those who were trying to take the child's life are dead."

21So he got up, took the child and his mother and went to the land of Israel. 22But when he heard that Archelaus was reigning in Judea in place of his father Herod, he was afraid to go there. Having been warned in a dream, he withdrew to the district of Galilee, 23and he went and lived in a town called Nazareth. So was fulfilled what was said through the prophets: "He will be called a Nazarene."

John the Baptist Prepares the Way

3 In those days John the Baptist came, preaching in the Desert of Judea 2and saying, "Repent, for the kingdom of heaven is near." 3This is he who was spoken of through the prophet Isaiah:

"A voice of one calling in the
    desert,
'Prepare the way for the Lord,
    make straight paths for him.' "a

4John's clothes were made of camel's hair, and he had a leather belt round his waist. His food was locusts and wild honey. 5People went out to him from Jerusalem and all Judea and the whole region of the Jordan. 6Confessing their sins, they were baptised by him in the Jordan River.

7But when he saw many of the Pharisees and Sadducees coming to where he was baptising, he said to them: "You brood of vipers! Who warned you to flee from the coming wrath? 8Produce fruit in keeping with repentance. 9And do not think you can say to yourselves, 'We have Abraham as our father.' I tell you that out of these stones God can raise up children for Abraham. 10The axe is already at the root of the trees, and every tree that does not produce good fruit will be cut down and thrown into the fire.

11"I baptise you withb water for repentance. But after me will come one who is more powerful than I, whose sandals I am not fit to carry. He will baptise you with the Holy Spirit and with fire. 12His winnowing fork is in his hand, and he will clear his threshing-floor, gathering the wheat into his barn and burning up the chaff with unquenchable fire."

The Baptism of Jesus

13Then Jesus came from Galilee to the Jordan to be baptised by John. 14But John tried to deter him, saying, "I need to be baptised by you, and do you come to me?"

15Jesus replied, "Let it be so now; it is proper for us to do this to fulfil all righteousness." Then John consented.

16As soon as Jesus was baptised, he went up out of the water. At that moment heaven was opened, and he saw the Spirit of God descending like a dove and lighting on him. 17And a voice from heaven said, "This is my Son, whom I love; with him I am well pleased."

The Temptation of Jesus

4 Then Jesus was led by the Spirit into the desert to be tempted by the devil. 2After fasting for forty days and forty nights, he was hungry. 3The tempter came to him and said, "If you are the Son of God, tell these stones to become bread."

4Jesus answered, "It is written: 'Man does not live on bread alone, but on every word that comes from the mouth of God.'a"

5Then the devil took him to the holy city and had him stand on the highest point of the temple. 6"If you are the Son of God," he said, "throw yourself down. For it is written:

" 'He will command his angels
        concerning you,
    and they will lift you up in their
        hands,

a3 Isaiah 40:3   b11 Or in   a4 Deut. 8:3

3

so that you will not strike your foot
against a stone.'b'"

7Jesus answered him, "It is also
written: 'Do not put the Lord your
God to the test.'c'"

8Again, the devil took him to a very
high mountain and showed him all
the kingdoms of the world and their
splendour. 9"All this I will give you,"
he said, "if you will bow down and
worship me."

10Jesus said to him, "Away from
me, Satan! For it is written: 'Worship
the Lord your God, and serve him
only.'d'"

11Then the devil left him, and
angels came and attended him.

Jesus Begins to Preach

12When Jesus heard that John had
been put in prison, he returned to
Galilee. 13Leaving Nazareth, he went
and lived in Capernaum, which was
by the lake in the area of Zebulun
and Naphtali—14to fulfil what was
said through the prophet Isaiah:

15"Land of Zebulun and land of
    Naphtali,
   the way to the sea, along the
     Jordan,
   Galilee of the Gentiles—
16the people living in darkness
   have seen a great light;
 on those living in the land of the
     shadow of death
   a light has dawned."e

17From that time on Jesus began to
preach, "Repent, for the kingdom of
heaven is near."

The Calling of the First Disciples

18As Jesus was walking beside the
Sea of Galilee, he saw two brothers,
Simon called Peter and his brother
Andrew. They were casting a net into
the lake, for they were fishermen.
19"Come, follow me," Jesus said, "and
I will make you fishers of men." 20At
once they left their nets and followed
him.

21Going on from there, he saw two
other brothers, James son of Zebedee
and his brother John. They were in a

boat with their father Zebedee, preparing their nets. Jesus called them,
22and immediately they left the boat
and their father and followed him.

Jesus Heals the Sick

23Jesus went throughout Galilee,
teaching in their synagogues, preaching the good news of the kingdom,
and healing every disease and sickness among the people. 24News about
him spread all over Syria, and people
brought to him all who were ill with
various diseases, those suffering
severe pain, the demon-possessed,
the epileptics and the paralytics, and
he healed them. 25Large crowds from
Galilee, the Decapolis,f Jerusalem,
Judea and the region across the Jordan followed him.

The Beatitudes

5 Now when he saw the crowds,
 he went up on a mountainside
and sat down. His disciples came to
him, 2and he began to teach them,
saying:

3 "Blessed are the poor in spirit,
   for theirs is the kingdom of
     heaven.
4 Blessed are those who mourn,
   for they will be comforted.
5 Blessed are the meek,
   for they will inherit the earth.
6 Blessed are those who hunger and
     thirst for righteousness,
   for they will be filled.
7 Blessed are the merciful,
   for they will be shown mercy.
8 Blessed are the pure in heart,
   for they will see God.
9 Blessed are the peacemakers,
   for they will be called sons of
     God.
10Blessed are those who are
     persecuted because of
     righteousness,
   for theirs is the kingdom of
     heaven.

11"Blessed are you when people
insult you, persecute you and falsely
say all kinds of evil against you
because of me. 12Rejoice and be glad,

b6 Psalm 91:11,12   c7 Deut. 6:16   d10 Deut. 6:13
e16 Isaiah 9:1,2   f25 That is, the Ten Cities

because great is your reward in heaven, for in the same way they persecuted the prophets who were before you.

Salt and Light

13"You are the salt of the earth. But if the salt loses its saltiness, how can it be made salty again? It is no longer good for anything, except to be thrown out and trampled by men.

14"You are the light of the world. A city on a hill cannot be hidden. 15Neither do people light a lamp and put it under a bowl. Instead they put it on its stand, and it gives light to everyone in the house. 16In the same way, let your light shine before men, that they may see your good deeds and praise your Father in heaven.

The Fulfilment of the Law

17"Do not think that I have come to abolish the Law or the Prophets; I have not come to abolish them but to fulfil them. 18I tell you the truth, until heaven and earth disappear, not the smallest letter, not the least stroke of a pen, will by any means disappear from the Law until everything is accomplished. 19Anyone who breaks one of the least of these commandments and teaches others to do the same will be called least in the kingdom of heaven, but whoever practises and teaches these commands will be called great in the kingdom of heaven. 20For I tell you that unless your righteousness surpasses that of the Pharisees and the teachers of the law, you will certainly not enter the kingdom of heaven.

Murder

21"You have heard that it was said to the people long ago, 'Do not murder,[a] and anyone who murders will be subject to judgment.' 22But I tell you that anyone who is angry with his brother[b] will be subject to judgment. Again, anyone who says to his brother, 'Raca,'[c] is answerable to the Sanhedrin. But anyone who says,

'You fool!' will be in danger of the fire of hell.

23"Therefore, if you are offering your gift at the altar and there remember that your brother has something against you, 24leave your gift there in front of the altar. First go and be reconciled to your brother; then come and offer your gift.

25"Settle matters quickly with your adversary who is taking you to court. Do it while you are still with him on the way, or he may hand you over to the judge, and the judge may hand you over to the officer, and you may be thrown into prison. 26I tell you the truth, you will not get out until you have paid the last penny.[d]

Adultery

27"You have heard that it was said, 'Do not commit adultery.'[e] 28But I tell you that anyone who looks at a woman lustfully has already committed adultery with her in his heart. 29If your right eye causes you to sin, gouge it out and throw it away. It is better for you to lose one part of your body than for your whole body to be thrown into hell. 30And if your right hand causes you to sin, cut it off and throw it away. It is better for you to lose one part of your body than for your whole body to go into hell.

Divorce

31"It has been said, 'Anyone who divorces his wife must give her a certificate of divorce.'[f] 32But I tell you that anyone who divorces his wife, except for marital unfaithfulness, causes her to commit adultery, and anyone who marries a woman so divorced commits adultery.

Oaths

33"Again, you have heard that it was said to the people long ago, 'Do not break your oath, but keep the oaths you have made to the Lord.' 34But I tell you, Do not swear at all: either by heaven, for it is God's throne; 35or by the earth, for it is his

---

a21 Exodus 20:13
b22 Some manuscripts *brother* without cause
d26 Greek *kodrantes*   e27 Exodus 20:14
c22 An Aramaic term of contempt
f31 Deut. 24:1

footstool; or by Jerusalem, for it is the city of the Great King. 36And do not swear by your head, for you cannot make even one hair white or black. 37Simply let your 'Yes' be 'Yes', and your 'No', 'No'; anything beyond this comes from the evil one.

An Eye for an Eye

38"You have heard that it was said, 'Eye for eye, and tooth for tooth.'8 39But I tell you, Do not resist an evil person. If someone strikes you on the right cheek, turn to him the other also, 40And if someone wants to sue you and take your tunic, let him have your cloak as well. 41If someone forces you to go one mile, go with him two miles. 42Give to the one who asks you, and do not turn away from the one who wants to borrow from you.

Love for Enemies

43"You have heard that it was said, 'Love your neighbourh and hate your enemy.' 44But I tell you: Love your enemiesi and pray for those who persecute you, 45that you may be sons of your Father in heaven. He causes his sun to rise on the evil and the good, and sends rain on the righteous and the unrighteous. 46If you love those who love you, what reward will you get? Are not even the tax collectors doing that? 47And if you greet only your brothers, what are you doing more than others? Do not even pagans do that? 48Be perfect, therefore, as your heavenly Father is perfect.

Giving to the Needy

6 "Be careful not to do your 'acts of righteousness' before men, to be seen by them. If you do, you will have no reward from your Father in heaven.

2"So when you give to the needy, do not announce it with trumpets, as the hypocrites do in the synagogues and on the streets, to be honoured by men. I tell you the truth, they have received their reward in full. 3But when you give to the needy, do not let your left hand know what your right hand is doing, 4so that your giving may be in secret. Then your Father, who sees what is done in secret, will reward you.

Prayer

5"But when you pray, do not be like the hypocrites, for they love to pray standing in the synagogues and on the street corners to be seen by men. I tell you the truth, they have received their reward in full. 6When you pray, go into your room, close the door and pray to your Father, who is unseen. Then your Father, who sees what is done in secret, will reward you. 7And when you pray, do not keep on babbling like pagans, for they think they will be heard because of their many words. 8Do not be like them, for your Father knows what you need before you ask him.

9"This is how you should pray:

" 'Our Father in heaven,
   hallowed be your name,
10your kingdom come,
   your will be done
      on earth as it is in heaven.
11Give us today our daily bread.
12Forgive us our debts,
   as we also have forgiven our
      debtors.
13And lead us not into temptation,
   but deliver us from the evil one.'a

14For if you forgive men when they sin against you, your heavenly Father will also forgive you. 15But if you do not forgive men their sins, your Father will not forgive your sins

Fasting

16"When you fast, do not look sombre as the hypocrites do, for they disfigure their faces to show men they are fasting. I tell you the truth, they have received their reward in full. 17But when you fast, put oil on your

---

g38 Exodus 21:24; Lev. 24:20 and Deut. 19:21
h43 Lev. 19:18
i44 Some late manuscripts enemies, bless those who curse you, do good to those who hate you
a13 Or from evil; some late manuscripts one, / for yours is the kingdom and the power and the glory for ever. Amen.

head and wash your face, 18so that it will not be obvious to men that you are fasting, but only to your Father, who is unseen; and your Father, who sees what is done in secret, will reward you.

Treasures in Heaven

19"Do not store up for yourselves treasures on earth, where moth and rust destroy, and where thieves break in and steal. 20But store up for yourselves treasures in heaven, where moth and rust do not destroy, and where thieves do not break in and steal. 21For where your treasure is, there your heart will be also.

22"The eye is the lamp of the body. If your eyes are good, your whole body will be full of light. 23But if your eyes are bad, your whole body will be full of darkness. If then the light within you is darkness, how great is that darkness!

24"No-one can serve two masters. Either he will hate the one and love the other, or he will be devoted to the one and despise the other. You cannot serve both God and Money.

Do Not Worry

25"Therefore I tell you, do not worry about your life, what you will eat or drink; or about your body, what you will wear. Is not life more important than food, and the body more important than clothes? 26Look at the birds of the air; they do not sow or reap or store away in barns, and yet your heavenly Father feeds them. Are you not much more valuable than they? 27Who of you by worrying can add a single hour to his life?b

28"And why do you worry about clothes? See how the lilies of the field grow. They do not labour or spin. 29Yet I tell you that not even Solomon in all his splendour was dressed like one of these. 30If that is how God clothes the grass of the field, which is here today and tomorrow is thrown into the fire, will he not much more clothe you, O you of little faith? 31So do not worry, saying, 'What shall we eat?' or 'What shall we drink?' or

'What shall we wear?' 32For the pagans run after all these things, and your heavenly Father knows that you need them. 33But seek first his kingdom and his righteousness, and all these things will be given to you as well. 34Therefore do not worry about tomorrow, for tomorrow will worry about itself. Each day has enough trouble of its own.

Judging Others

7 "Do not judge, or you too will be judged. 2For in the same way you judge others, you will be judged, and with the measure you use, it will be measured to you.

3"Why do you look at the speck of sawdust in your brother's eye and pay no attention to the plank in your own eye? 4How can you say to your brother, 'Let me take the speck out of your eye,' when all the time there is a plank in your own eye? 5You hypocrite, first take the plank out of your own eye, and then you will see clearly to remove the speck from your brother's eye.

6"Do not give dogs what is sacred; do not throw your pearls to pigs. If you do, they may trample them under their feet, and then turn and tear you to pieces.

Ask, Seek, Knock

7"Ask and it will be given to you; seek and you will find; knock and the door will be opened to you. 8For everyone who asks receives; he who seeks finds; and to him who knocks, the door will be opened.

9"Which of you, if his son asks for bread, will give him a stone? 10Or if he asks for a fish, will give him a snake? 11If you, then, though you are evil, know how to give good gifts to your children, how much more will your Father in heaven give good gifts to those who ask him! 12In everything, do to others what you would have them do to you, for this sums up the Law and the Prophets.

The Narrow and Wide Gates

13"Enter through the narrow gate.

b27 Or single cubit to his height

7

For wide is the gate and broad is the road that leads to destruction, and many enter through it. ¹⁴But small is the gate and narrow the road that leads to life, and only a few find it.

A Tree and Its Fruit

¹⁵"Watch out for false prophets. They come to you in sheep's clothing, but inwardly they are ferocious wolves. ¹⁶By their fruit you will recognise them. Do people pick grapes from thornbushes, or figs from thistles? ¹⁷Likewise every good tree bears good fruit, but a bad tree bears bad fruit. ¹⁸A good tree cannot bear bad fruit, and a bad tree cannot bear good fruit. ¹⁹Every tree that does not bear good fruit is cut down and thrown into the fire. ²⁰Thus, by their fruit you will recognise them.

²¹"Not everyone who says to me, 'Lord, Lord,' will enter the kingdom of heaven, but only he who does the will of my Father who is in heaven. ²²Many will say to me on that day, 'Lord, Lord, did we not prophesy in your name, and in your name drive out demons and perform many miracles?' ²³Then I will tell them plainly, 'I never knew you. Away from me, you evildoers!'

The Wise and Foolish Builders

²⁴"Therefore everyone who hears these words of mine and puts them into practice is like a wise man who built his house on the rock. ²⁵The rain came down, the streams rose, and the winds blew and beat against that house; yet it did not fall, because it had its foundation on the rock. ²⁶But everyone who hears these words of mine and does not put them into practice is like a foolish man who built his house on sand. ²⁷The rain came down, the streams rose, and the winds blew and beat against that house, and it fell with a great crash."

²⁸When Jesus had finished saying these things, the crowds were amazed at his teaching, ²⁹because he taught as one who had authority, and not as their teachers of the law.

The Man With Leprosy

8 When he came down from the mountainside, large crowds followed him. ²A man with leprosy^a came and knelt before him and said, "Lord, if you are willing, you can make me clean."

³Jesus reached out his hand and touched the man. "I am willing," he said. "Be clean!" Immediately he was cured^b of his leprosy. ⁴Then Jesus said to him, "See that you don't tell anyone. But go, show yourself to the priest and offer the gift Moses commanded, as a testimony to them."

The Faith of the Centurion

⁵When Jesus had entered Capernaum, a centurion came to him, asking for help. ⁶"Lord," he said, "my servant lies at home paralysed and in terrible suffering."

⁷Jesus said to him, "I will go and heal him."

⁸The centurion replied, "Lord, I do not deserve to have you come under my roof. But just say the word, and my servant will be healed. ⁹For I myself am a man under authority, with soldiers under me. I tell this one, 'Go,' and he goes; and that one, 'Come,' and he comes. I say to my servant, 'Do this,' and he does it."

¹⁰When Jesus heard this, he was astonished and said to those following him, "I tell you the truth, I have not found anyone in Israel with such great faith. ¹¹I say to you that many will come from the east and the west, and will take their places at the feast with Abraham, Isaac and Jacob in the kingdom of heaven. ¹²But the subjects of the kingdom will be thrown outside, into the darkness, where there will be weeping and gnashing of teeth."

¹³Then Jesus said to the centurion, "Go! It will be done just as you believed it would." And his servant was healed at that very hour.

Jesus Heals Many

¹⁴When Jesus came into Peter's house, he saw Peter's mother-in-law

---

^{a}2 The Greek word was used for various diseases affecting the skin—not necessarily leprosy.
^{b}3 Greek made clean

lying in bed with a fever. 15He touched her hand and the fever left her, and she got up and began to wait on him.

16When evening came, many who were demon-possessed were brought to him, and he drove out the spirits with a word and healed all the sick. 17This was to fulfil what was spoken through the prophet Isaiah:

"He took up our infirmities
and carried our diseases."c

The Cost of Following Jesus

18When Jesus saw the crowd around him, he gave orders to cross to the other side of the lake. 19Then a teacher of the law came to him and said, "Teacher, I will follow you wherever you go."

20Jesus replied, "Foxes have holes and birds of the air have nests, but the Son of Man has no place to lay his head."

21Another man, one of his disciples, said to him, "Lord, first let me go and bury my father."

22But Jesus told him, "Follow me, and let the dead bury their own dead."

Jesus Calms the Storm

23Then he got into the boat and his disciples followed him. 24Without warning, a furious storm came up on the lake, so that the waves swept over the boat. But Jesus was sleeping. 25The disciples went and woke him, saying, "Lord, save us! We're going to drown!"

26He replied, "You of little faith, why are you so afraid?" Then he got up and rebuked the winds and the waves, and it was completely calm.

27The men were amazed and asked, "What kind of man is this? Even the winds and the waves obey him!"

*The Healing of Two
Demon-Possessed Men*

28When he arrived at the other side in the region of the Gadarenes,d two demon-possessed men coming from the tombs met him. They were so violent that no-one could pass that way. 29"What do you want with us, Son of God?" they shouted. "Have you come here to torture us before the appointed time?"

30Some distance from them a large herd of pigs was feeding. 31The demons begged Jesus, "If you drive us out, send us into the herd of pigs."

32He said to them, "Go!" So they came out and went into the pigs, and the whole herd rushed into the steep bank into the lake and died in the water. 33Those tending the pigs ran off, went into the town and reported all this, including what had happened to the demon-possessed men. 34Then the whole town went out to meet Jesus. And when they saw him, they pleaded with him to leave their region.

Jesus Heals a Paralytic

9 Jesus stepped into a boat, crossed over and came to his own town. 2Some men brought to him a paralytic, lying on a mat. When Jesus saw their faith, he said to the paralytic, "Take heart, son; your sins are forgiven."

3At this, some of the teachers of the law said to themselves, "This fellow is blaspheming!"

4Knowing their thoughts, Jesus said, "Why do you entertain evil thoughts in your hearts? 5Which is easier: to say, 'Your sins are forgiven,' or to say, 'Get up and walk'? 6But so that you may know that the Son of Man has authority on earth to forgive sins...." Then he said to the paralytic, "Get up, take your mat and go home." 7And the man got up and went home. 8When the crowd saw this, they were filled with awe; and they praised God, who had given such authority to men.

The Calling of Matthew

9As Jesus went on from there, he saw a man named Matthew sitting at the tax collector's booth. "Follow me," he told him, and Matthew got up and followed him.

10While Jesus was having dinner at

c17 Isaiah 53:4   d28 Some manuscripts *Gergesenes*; others *Gerasenes*

Matthew's house, many tax collectors and "sinners" came and ate with him and his disciples. 11When the Pharisees saw this, they asked his disciples, "Why does your teacher eat with tax collectors and 'sinners'?"

12On hearing this, Jesus said, "It is not the healthy who need a doctor, but the sick. 13But go and learn what this means: 'I desire mercy, not sacrifice.'*a* For I have not come to call the righteous, but sinners."

Jesus Questioned About Fasting

14Then John's disciples came and asked him, "How is it that we and the Pharisees fast, but your disciples do not fast?"

15Jesus answered, "How can the guests of the bridegroom mourn while he is with them? The time will come when the bridegroom will be taken from them; then they will fast.

16"No-one sews a patch of unshrunk cloth on an old garment, for the patch will pull away from the garment, making the tear worse. 17Neither do men pour new wine into old wineskins. If they do, the skins will burst, the wine will run out and the wineskins will be ruined. No, they pour new wine into new wineskins, and both are preserved."

A Dead Girl and a Sick Woman

18While he was saying this, a ruler came and knelt before him and said, "My daughter has just died.*b* But come and put your hand on her, and she will live." 19Jesus got up and went with him, and so did his disciples.

20Just then a woman who had been subject to bleeding for twelve years came up behind him and touched the edge of his cloak. 21She said to herself, "If I only touch his cloak, I will be healed."

22Jesus turned and saw her. "Take heart, daughter," he said, "your faith has healed you." And the woman was healed from that moment.

23When Jesus entered the ruler's house and saw the flute players and the noisy crowd, 24he said, "Go away.

The girl is not dead but asleep." But they laughed at him. 25After the crowd had been put outside, he went in and took the girl by the hand, and she got up. 26News of this spread through all that region.

Jesus Heals the Blind and Dumb

27As Jesus went on from there, two blind men followed him, calling out, "Have mercy on us, Son of David!"

28When he had gone indoors, the blind men came to him, and he asked them, "Do you believe that I am able to do this?"

"Yes, Lord," they replied.

29Then he touched their eyes and said, "According to your faith will it be done to you"; 30and their sight was restored. Jesus warned them sternly, "See that no-one knows about this." 31But they went out and spread the news about him all over that region.

32While they were going out, a man who was demon-possessed and could not talk was brought to Jesus. 33And when the demon was driven out, the man who had been dumb spoke. The crowd was amazed and said, "Nothing like this has ever been seen in Israel."

34But the Pharisees said, "It is by the prince of demons that he drives out demons."

The Workers Are Few

35Jesus went through all the towns and villages, teaching in their synagogues, preaching the good news of the kingdom and healing every disease and sickness. 36When he saw the crowds, he had compassion on them, because they were harassed and helpless, like sheep without a shepherd. 37Then he said to his disciples, "The harvest is plentiful but the workers are few. 38Ask the Lord of the harvest, therefore, to send out workers into his harvest field."

Jesus Sends Out the Twelve

10 He called his twelve disciples to him and gave them authority to drive out evil*a* spirits and to

*a*13 Hosea 6:6   *b*18 Or *daughter is now dying*
*a*1 Greek *unclean*

heal every disease and sickness.

²These are the names of the twelve apostles: first, Simon (who is called Peter) and his brother Andrew; James son of Zebedee, and his brother John; ³Philip and Bartholomew; Thomas and Matthew the tax collector; James son of Alphaeus, and Thaddaeus; ⁴Simon the Zealot and Judas Iscariot, who betrayed him.

⁵These twelve Jesus sent out with the following instructions: "Do not go among the Gentiles or enter any town of the Samaritans. ⁶Go rather to the lost sheep of Israel. ⁷As you go, preach this message: 'The kingdom of heaven is near.' ⁸Heal the sick, raise the dead, cleanse those who have leprosy,b drive out demons. Freely you have received, freely give. ⁹Do not take along any gold or silver or copper in your belts; ¹⁰take no bag for the journey, or extra tunic, or sandals or a staff; for the worker is worth his keep.

¹¹"Whatever town or village you enter, search for some worthy person there and stay at his house until you leave. ¹²As you enter the home, give it your greeting. ¹³If the home is deserving, let your peace rest on it; if it is not, let your peace return to you. ¹⁴If anyone will not welcome you or listen to your words, shake the dust off your feet when you leave that home or town. ¹⁵I tell you the truth, it will be more bearable for Sodom and Gomorrah on the day of judgment than for that town.

¹⁶"I am sending you out like sheep among wolves. Therefore be as shrewd as snakes and as innocent as doves. ¹⁷But be on your guard against men; they will hand you over to the local councils and flog you in their synagogues. ¹⁸On my account you will be brought before governors and kings as witnesses to them and to the Gentiles. ¹⁹But when they arrest you, do not worry about what to say or how to say it. At that time you will be given what to say, ²⁰for it will not be you speaking, but the Spirit of your

Father speaking through you.

²¹"Brother will betray brother to death, and a father his child; children will rebel against their parents and have them put to death. ²²All men will hate you because of me, but he who stands firm to the end will be saved. ²³When you are persecuted in one place, flee to another. I tell you the truth, you will not finish going through the cities of Israel before the Son of Man comes.

²⁴"A student is not above his teacher, nor a servant above his master. ²⁵It is enough for the student to be like his teacher, and the servant like his master. If the head of the house has been called Beelzebub,c how much more the members of his household!

²⁶"So do not be afraid of them. There is nothing concealed that will not be disclosed, or hidden that will not be made known. ²⁷What I tell you in the dark, speak in the daylight; what is whispered in your ear, proclaim from the housetops. ²⁸Do not be afraid of those who kill the body but cannot kill the soul. Rather, be afraid of the one who can destroy both soul and body in hell. ²⁹Are not two sparrows sold for a penny?d Yet not one of them will fall to the ground apart from the will of your Father. ³⁰And even the very hairs of your head are all numbered. ³¹So don't be afraid; you are worth more than many sparrows.

³²"Whoever acknowledges me before men, I will also acknowledge him before my Father in heaven. ³³But whoever disowns me before men, I will disown him before my Father in heaven.

³⁴"Do not suppose that I have come to bring peace to the earth. I did not come to bring peace, but a sword. ³⁵For I have come to turn

" 'a man against his father,
  a daughter against her mother,
a daughter-in-law against her
  mother-in-law—
³⁶ a man's enemies will be the

---

b8 The Greek word was used for various diseases affecting the skin—not necessarily leprosy.
c25 Greek Beezeboul or Beelzeboul   d29 Greek an assarion

MATTHEW 10:37

37"Anyone who loves his father or mother more than me is not worthy of me; anyone who loves his son or daughter more than me is not worthy of me; 38and anyone who does not take his cross and follow me is not worthy of me. 39Whoever finds his life will lose it, and whoever loses his life for my sake will find it.

40"He who receives you receives me, and he who receives me receives the one who sent me. 41Anyone who receives a prophet because he is a prophet will receive a prophet's reward, and anyone who receives a righteous man because he is a righteous man will receive a righteous man's reward. 42And if anyone gives a cup of cold water to one of these little ones because he is my disciple, I tell you the truth, he will certainly not lose his reward."

Jesus and John the Baptist

11 After Jesus had finished instructing his twelve disciples, he went on from there to teach and preach in the towns of Galilee.[a]

2When John heard in prison what Christ was doing, he sent his disciples 3to ask him, "Are you the one who was to come, or should we expect someone else?"

4Jesus replied, "Go back and report to John what you hear and see: 5The blind receive sight, the lame walk, those who have leprosy[b] are cured, the deaf hear, the dead are raised, and the good news is preached to the poor. 6Blessed is the man who does not fall away on account of me."

7As John's disciples were leaving, Jesus began to speak to the crowd about John: "What did you go out into the desert to see? A reed swayed by the wind? 8If not, what did you go out to see? A man dressed in fine clothes? No, those who wear fine clothes are in kings' palaces. 9Then what did you go out to see? A prophet? Yes, I tell you, and more than a prophet. 10This is the one about whom it is written:

" 'I will send my messenger ahead of you,
who will prepare your way before you.'[c]

11I tell you the truth: Among those born of women there has not risen anyone greater than John the Baptist; yet he who is least in the kingdom of heaven is greater than he. 12From the days of John the Baptist until now, the kingdom of heaven has been forcefully advancing, and forceful men lay hold of it. 13For all the Prophets and the Law prophesied until John. 14And if you are willing to accept it, he is the Elijah who was to come. 15He who has ears, let him hear.

16"To what can I compare this generation? They are like children sitting in the market-places and calling out to others:

17" 'We played the flute for you,
and you did not dance;
we sang a dirge,
and you did not mourn.'

18For John came neither eating nor drinking, and they say, 'He has a demon.' 19The Son of Man came eating and drinking, and they say, 'Here is a glutton and a drunkard, a friend of tax collectors and "sinners".' But wisdom is proved right by her actions."

Woe on Unrepentant Cities

20Then Jesus began to denounce the cities in which most of his miracles had been performed, because they did not repent. 21"Woe to you, Korazin! Woe to you, Bethsaida! If the miracles that were performed in you had been performed in Tyre and Sidon, they would have repented long ago in sackcloth and ashes. 22But I tell you, it will be more bearable for Tyre and Sidon on the day of judgment than for you. 23And you, Capernaum, will you be lifted up to the

e36 Micah 7:6
a1 Greek in their towns
b5 The Greek word was used for various diseases affecting the skin—not necessarily leprosy.
c10 Mal. 3:1

12

skies? No, you will go down to the depths.d If the miracles that were performed in you had been performed in Sodom, it would have remained to this day. 24But I tell you that it will be more bearable for Sodom on the day of judgment than for you."

Rest for the Weary

25At that time Jesus said, "I praise you, Father, Lord of heaven and earth, because you have hidden these things from the wise and learned, and revealed them to little children. 26Yes, Father, for this was your good pleasure.

27"All things have been committed to me by my Father. No-one knows the Son except the Father, and no-one knows the Father except the Son and those to whom the Son chooses to reveal him.

28"Come to me, all you who are weary and burdened, and I will give you rest. 29Take my yoke upon you and learn from me, for I am gentle and humble in heart, and you will find rest for your souls. 30For my yoke is easy and my burden is light."

Lord of the Sabbath

12 At that time Jesus went through the cornfields on the Sabbath. His disciples were hungry and began to pick some ears of corn and eat them. 2When the Pharisees saw this, they said to him, "Look! Your disciples are doing what is unlawful on the Sabbath."

3He answered, "Haven't you read what David did when he and his companions were hungry? 4He entered the house of God, and he and his companions ate the consecrated bread—which was not lawful for them to do, but only for the priests. 5Or haven't you read in the Law that on the Sabbath the priests in the temple desecrate the day and yet are innocent? 6I tell you that onea greater than the temple is here. 7If you had known what these words mean, 'I desire mercy, not sacrifice,'b you

would not have condemned the innocent. 8For the Son of Man is Lord of the Sabbath."

9Going on from that place, he went into their synagogue, and 10a man with a shrivelled hand was there. Looking for a reason to accuse Jesus, they asked him, "Is it lawful to heal on the Sabbath?"

11He said to them, "If any of you has a sheep and it falls into a pit on the Sabbath, will you not take hold of it and lift it out? 12How much more valuable is a man than a sheep! Therefore it is lawful to do good on the Sabbath."

13Then he said to the man, "Stretch out your hand." So he stretched it out and it was completely restored, just as sound as the other. 14But the Pharisees went out and plotted how they might kill Jesus.

God's Chosen Servant

15Aware of this, Jesus withdrew from that place. Many followed him, and he healed all their sick, 16warning them not to tell who he was. 17This was to fulfil what was spoken through the prophet Isaiah:

18"Here is my servant whom I have chosen,
the one I love, in whom I delight;
I will put my Spirit on him,
and he will proclaim justice to the nations.
19He will not quarrel or cry out;
no-one will hear his voice in the streets.
20A bruised reed he will not break,
and a smouldering wick he will not snuff out,
till he leads justice to victory.
21 In his name the nations will put their hope."c

Jesus and Beelzebub

22Then they brought him a demon-possessed man who was blind and dumb, and Jesus healed him, so that he could both talk and see. 23All the people were astonished and said, "Could this be the Son of David?"

d23 Greek Hades   a6 Or something; also in verses 41 and 42   b7 Hosea 6:6
c21 Isaiah 42:1-4

13

²⁴But when the Pharisees heard this, they said, "It is only by Beelzebub,ᵈ the prince of demons, that this fellow drives out demons."

²⁵Jesus knew their thoughts and said to them, "Every kingdom divided against itself will be ruined, and every city or household divided against itself will not stand. ²⁶If Satan drives out Satan, he is divided against himself. How then can his kingdom stand? ²⁷And if I drive out demons by Beelzebub, by whom do your people drive them out? So then, they will be your judges. ²⁸But if I drive out demons by the Spirit of God, then the kingdom of God has come upon you.

²⁹"Or again, how can anyone enter a strong man's house and carry off his possessions unless he first ties up the strong man? Then he can rob his house.

³⁰"He who is not with me is against me, and he who does not gather with me scatters. ³¹And so I tell you, every sin and blasphemy will be forgiven men, but the blasphemy against the Spirit will not be forgiven. ³²Anyone who speaks a word against the Son of Man will be forgiven, but anyone who speaks against the Holy Spirit will not be forgiven, either in this age or in the age to come.

³³"Make a tree good and its fruit will be good, or make a tree bad and its fruit will be bad, for a tree is recognised by its fruit. ³⁴You brood of vipers, how can you who are evil say anything good? For out of the overflow of the heart the mouth speaks. ³⁵The good man brings good things out of the good stored up in him, and the evil man brings evil things out of the evil stored up in him. ³⁶But I tell you that men will have to give account on the day of judgment for every careless word they have spoken. ³⁷For by your words you will be acquitted, and by your words you will be condemned."

The Sign of Jonah

³⁸Then some of the Pharisees and teachers of the law said to him,

"Teacher, we want to see a miraculous sign from you."

³⁹He answered, "A wicked and adulterous generation asks for a miraculous sign! But none will be given it except the sign of the prophet Jonah. ⁴⁰For as Jonah was three days and three nights in the belly of a huge fish, so the Son of Man will be three days and three nights in the heart of the earth. ⁴¹The men of Nineveh will stand up at the judgment with this generation and condemn it; for they repented at the preaching of Jonah, and now one greater than Jonah is here. ⁴²The Queen of the South will rise at the judgment with this generation and condemn it; for she came from the ends of the earth to listen to Solomon's wisdom, and now one greater than Solomon is here.

⁴³"When an evilᵉ spirit comes out of a man, it goes through arid places seeking rest and does not find it. ⁴⁴Then it says, 'I will return to the house I left.' When it arrives, it finds the house unoccupied, swept clean and put in order. ⁴⁵Then it goes and takes with it seven other spirits more wicked than itself, and they go in and live there. And the final condition of that man is worse than the first. That is how it will be with this wicked generation."

Jesus' Mother and Brothers

⁴⁶While Jesus was still talking to the crowd, his mother and brothers stood outside, wanting to speak to him. ⁴⁷Someone told him, "Your mother and brothers are standing outside, wanting to speak to you."ᶠ

⁴⁸He replied, "Who is my mother, and who are my brothers?" ⁴⁹Pointing to his disciples, he said, "Here are my mother and my brothers. ⁵⁰For whoever does the will of my Father in heaven is my brother and sister and mother."

The Parable of the Sower

13 That same day Jesus went out of the house and sat by the

ᵈ24 Greek Beezeboul or Beelzeboul; also in verse 27
ᵉ43 Greek unclean   ᶠ47 Some manuscripts do not have verse 47.

lake. ²Such large crowds gathered round him that he got into a boat and sat in it, while all the people stood on the shore. ³Then he told them many things in parables, saying: "A farmer went out to sow his seed. ⁴As he was scattering the seed, some fell along the path, and the birds came and ate it up. ⁵Some fell on rocky places, where it did not have much soil. It sprang up quickly, because the soil was shallow. ⁶But when the sun came up, the plants were scorched, and they withered because they had no root. ⁷Other seed fell among thorns, which grew up and choked the plants. ⁸Still other seed fell on good soil, where it produced a crop—a hundred, sixty or thirty times what was sown. ⁹He who has ears, let him hear."

¹⁰The disciples came to him and asked, "Why do you speak to the people in parables?"

¹¹He replied, "The knowledge of the secrets of the kingdom of heaven has been given to you, but not to them. ¹²Whoever has will be given more, and he will have an abundance. Whoever does not have, even what he has will be taken from him. ¹³This is why I speak to them in parables:

"Though seeing, they do not see;
though hearing, they do not hear
or understand.'

¹⁴In them is fulfilled the prophecy of Isaiah:

" 'You will be ever hearing but
never understanding;
you will be ever seeing but never
perceiving.
¹⁵For this people's heart has become
calloused;
they hardly hear with their ears,
and they have closed their eyes.
Otherwise they might see with their
eyes,
hear with their ears,
understand with their hearts
and turn, and I would heal them.'ᵃ

¹⁶"But blessed are your eyes because they see, and your ears because they

ᵃ15 Isaiah 6:9,10

hear. ¹⁷For I tell you the truth, many prophets and righteous men longed to see what you see but did not see it, and to hear what you hear but did not hear it.

¹⁸"Listen then to what the parable of the sower means: ¹⁹When anyone hears the message about the kingdom and does not understand it, the evil one comes and snatches away what was sown in his heart. This is the seed sown along the path. ²⁰What was sown on rocky places is the man who hears the word and at once receives it with joy. ²¹But since he has no root, he lasts only a short time. When trouble or persecution comes because of the word, he quickly falls away. ²²What was sown among the thorns is the man who hears the word, but worries of this life and the deceitfulness of wealth choke it, making it unfruitful. ²³But what was sown on good soil is the man who hears the word and understands it. He produces a crop, yielding a hundred, sixty or thirty times what was sown."

The Parable of the Weeds

²⁴Jesus told them another parable: "The kingdom of heaven is like a man who sowed good seed in his field. ²⁵But while everyone was sleeping, his enemy came and sowed weeds among the wheat, and went away. ²⁶When the wheat sprouted and formed heads, then the weeds also appeared.

²⁷"The owner's servants came to him and said, 'Sir, didn't you sow good seed in your field? Where did the weeds come from?'

²⁸" 'An enemy did this,' he replied.

"The servants asked him, 'Do you want us to go and pull them up?'

²⁹" 'No,' he answered, 'because while you are pulling the weeds, you may root up the wheat with them. ³⁰Let both grow together until the harvest. At that time I will tell the harvesters: First collect the weeds and tie them in bundles to be burned, then gather the wheat and bring it into my barn.' "

The Parables of the Mustard Seed and the Yeast

31He told them another parable: "The kingdom of heaven is like a mustard seed, which a man took and planted in his field. 32Though it is the smallest of all your seeds, yet when it grows, it is the largest of garden plants and becomes a tree, so that the birds of the air come and perch in its branches."

33He told them still another parable: "The kingdom of heaven is like yeast that a woman took and mixed into a large amountb of flour until it worked all through the dough."

34Jesus spoke all these things to the crowd in parables; he did not say anything to them without using a parable. 35So was fulfilled what was spoken through the prophet:

"I will open my mouth in
     parables,
  I will utter things hidden since
     the creation of the world."c

The Parable of the Weeds Explained

36Then he left the crowd and went into the house. His disciples came to him and said, "Explain to us the parable of the weeds in the field."

37He answered, "The one who sowed the good seed is the Son of Man. 38The field is the world, and the good seed stands for the sons of the kingdom. The weeds are the sons of the evil one, 39and the enemy who sows them is the devil. The harvest is the end of the age, and the harvesters are angels.

40"As the weeds are pulled up and burned in the fire, so it will be at the end of the age. 41The Son of Man will send out his angels, and they will weed out of his kingdom everything that causes sin and all who do evil. 42They will throw them into the fiery furnace, where there will be weeping and gnashing of teeth. 43Then the righteous will shine like the sun in the kingdom of their Father. He who has ears, let him hear.

The Parables of the Hidden Treasure and the Pearl

44"The kingdom of heaven is like treasure hidden in a field. When a man found it, he hid it again, and then in his joy went and sold all he had and bought that field.

45"Again, the kingdom of heaven is like a merchant looking for fine pearls. 46When he found one of great value, he went away and sold everything he had and bought it.

The Parable of the Net

47"Once again, the kingdom of heaven is like a net that was let down into the lake and caught all kinds of fish. 48When it was full, the fishermen pulled it up on the shore. Then they sat down and collected the good fish in baskets, but threw the bad away. 49This is how it will be at the end of the age. The angels will come and separate the wicked from the righteous 50and throw them into the fiery furnace, where there will be weeping and gnashing of teeth."

51"Have you understood all these things?" Jesus asked.

"Yes," they replied.

52He said to them, "Therefore every teacher of the law who has been instructed about the kingdom of heaven is like the owner of a house who brings out of his storeroom new treasures as well as old."

A Prophet Without Honour

53When Jesus had finished these parables, he moved on from there. 54Coming to his home town, he began teaching the people in their synagogue, and they were amazed. "Where did this man get this wisdom and these miraculous powers?" they asked. 55"Isn't this the carpenter's son? Isn't his mother's name Mary, and aren't his brothers James, Joseph, Simon and Judas? 56Aren't all his sisters with us? Where then did this man get all these things?" 57And they took offence at him.

But Jesus said to them, "Only in his home town and in his own house is a

b33 Greek *three satas* (probably about ½ bushel or 22 litres)
c35 Psalm 78:2

prophet without honour."

58And he did not do many miracles there because of their lack of faith.

John the Baptist Beheaded

14 At that time Herod the tetrarch heard the reports about Jesus, 2and he said to his attendants, "This is John the Baptist; he has risen from the dead! That is why miraculous powers are at work in him."

3Now Herod had arrested John and bound him and put him in prison because of Herodias, his brother Philip's wife, 4for John had been saying to him: "It is not lawful for you to have her." 5Herod wanted to kill John, but he was afraid of the people, because they considered him a prophet.

6On Herod's birthday the daughter of Herodias danced for them and pleased Herod so much 7that he promised with an oath to give her whatever she asked. 8Prompted by her mother, she said, "Give me here on a platter the head of John the Baptist." 9The king was distressed, but because of his oaths and his dinner guests, he ordered that her request be granted 10and had John beheaded in the prison. 11His head was brought in on a platter and given to the girl, who carried it to her mother. 12John's disciples came and took his body and buried it. Then they went and told Jesus.

Jesus Feeds the Five Thousand

13When Jesus heard what had happened, he withdrew by boat privately to a solitary place. Hearing of this, the crowds followed him on foot from the towns. 14When Jesus landed and saw a large crowd, he had compassion on them and healed their sick.

15As evening approached, the disciples came to him and said, "This is a remote place, and it's already getting late. Send the crowds away, so that they can go to the villages and buy themselves some food."

16Jesus replied, "They do not need to go away. You give them something to eat."

17"We have here only five loaves of bread and two fish," they answered.

18"Bring them here to me," he said. 19And he directed the people to sit down on the grass. Taking the five loaves and the two fish and looking up to heaven, he gave thanks and broke the loaves. Then he gave them to the disciples, and the disciples gave them to the people. 20They all ate and were satisfied, and the disciples picked up twelve basketfuls of broken pieces that were left over. 21The number of those who ate was about five thousand men, besides women and children.

Jesus Walks on the Water

22Immediately Jesus made the disciples get into the boat and go on ahead of him to the other side, while he dismissed the crowd. 23After he had dismissed them, he went up into the hills by himself to pray. When evening came, he was there alone, 24but the boat was already a considerable distance*a* from land, buffeted by the waves because the wind was against it.

25During the fourth watch of the night Jesus went out to them, walking on the lake. 26When the disciples saw him walking on the lake, they were terrified. "It's a ghost," they said, and cried out in fear.

27But Jesus immediately said to them: "Take courage! It is I. Don't be afraid."

28"Lord, if it's you," Peter replied, "tell me to come to you on the water."

29"Come," he said.

Then Peter got down out of the boat and walked on the water to Jesus. 30But when he saw the wind, he was afraid and, beginning to sink, cried out, "Lord, save me!"

31Immediately Jesus reached out his hand and caught him. "You of little faith," he said, "why did you doubt?"

32And when they climbed into the boat, the wind died down. 33Then those who were in the boat worshipped him, saying, "Truly you are the Son of God."

a24 Greek many stadia

34When they had crossed over, they landed at Gennesaret. 35And when the men of that place recognised Jesus, they sent word to all the surrounding country. People brought all their sick to him 36and begged him to let the sick just touch the edge of his cloak, and all who touched him were healed.

Clean and Unclean

15 Then some Pharisees and teachers of the law came to Jesus from Jerusalem and asked, 2"Why do your disciples break the tradition of the elders? They don't wash their hands before they eat!"

3Jesus replied, "And why do you break the command of God for the sake of your tradition? 4For God said, 'Honour your father and mother'*a* and 'Anyone who curses his father or mother must be put to death.'*b* 5But you say that if a man says to his father or mother, 'Whatever help you might otherwise have received from me is a gift devoted to God,' 6he is not to 'honour his father'*c* with it. Thus you nullify the word of God for the sake of your tradition. 7You hypocrites! Isaiah was right when he prophesied about you:

8" 'These people honour me with
      their lips,
    but their hearts are far from me.
9They worship me in vain;
      their teachings are but rules
      taught by men.'*d*"

10Jesus called the crowd to him and said, "Listen and understand. 11What goes into a man's mouth does not make him 'unclean', but what comes out of his mouth, that is what makes him 'unclean'."

12Then the disciples came to him and asked, "Do you know that the Pharisees were offended when they heard this?"

13He replied, "Every plant that my heavenly Father has not planted will be pulled up by the roots. 14Leave them; they are blind guides.*e* If a blind man leads a blind man, both will fall into a pit."

15Peter said, "Explain the parable to us."

16"Are you still so dull?" Jesus asked them. 17"Don't you see that whatever enters the mouth goes into the stomach and then out of the body? 18But the things that come out of the mouth come from the heart, and these make a man 'unclean'. 19For out of the heart come evil thoughts, murder, adultery, sexual immorality, theft, false testimony, slander. 20These are what make a man 'unclean'; but eating with unwashed hands does not make him 'unclean'."

The Faith of the Canaanite Woman

21Leaving that place, Jesus withdrew to the region of Tyre and Sidon. 22A Canaanite woman from that vicinity came to him, crying out, "Lord, Son of David, have mercy on me! My daughter is suffering terribly from demon-possession."

23Jesus did not answer a word. So his disciples came to him and urged him, "Send her away, for she keeps crying out after us."

24He answered, "I was sent only to the lost sheep of Israel."

25The woman came and knelt before him. "Lord, help me!" she said.

26He replied, "It is not right to take the children's bread and toss it to their dogs."

27"Yes, Lord," she said, "but even the dogs eat the crumbs that fall from their masters' table."

28Then Jesus answered, "Woman, you have great faith! Your request is granted." And her daughter was healed from that very hour.

Jesus Feeds the Four Thousand

29Jesus left there and went along the Sea of Galilee. Then he went up into the hills and sat down. 30Great crowds came to him, bringing the lame, the blind, the crippled, the dumb and many others, and laid them at his feet; and he healed them.

*a*4 Exodus 20:12; Deut. 5:16   *b*4 Exodus 21:17; Lev. 20:9
*c*6 Some manuscripts *father or his mother*
*d*9 Isaiah 29:13
*e*14 Some manuscripts *guides of the blind*

31The people were amazed when they saw the dumb speaking, the crippled made well, the lame walking and the blind seeing. And they praised the God of Israel.

32Jesus called his disciples to him and said, "I have compassion for these people; they have already been with me three days and have nothing to eat. I do not want to send them away hungry, or they may collapse on the way."

33His disciples answered, "Where could we get enough bread in this remote place to feed such a crowd?"

34"How many loaves do you have?" Jesus asked.

"Seven," they replied, "and a few small fish."

35He told the crowd to sit down on the ground. 36Then he took the seven loaves and the fish, and when he had given thanks, he broke them and gave them to the disciples, and they in turn to the people. 37They all ate and were satisfied. Afterwards the disciples picked up seven basketfuls of broken pieces that were left over. 38The number of those who ate was four thousand, besides women and children. 39After Jesus had sent the crowd away, he got into the boat and went to the vicinity of Magadan.

The Demand for a Sign

16 The Pharisees and Sadducees came to Jesus and tested him by asking him to show them a sign from heaven.

2He replied,*a* "When evening comes, you say, 'It will be fair weather, for the sky is red,' 3and in the morning, 'Today it will be stormy, for the sky is red and overcast.' You know how to interpret the appearance of the sky, but you cannot interpret the signs of the times. 4A wicked and adulterous generation looks for a miraculous sign, but none will be given it except the sign of Jonah." Jesus then left them and went away.

The Yeast of the Pharisees and Sadducees

5When they went across the lake, the disciples forgot to take bread. 6"Be careful," Jesus said to them. "Be on your guard against the yeast of the Pharisees and Sadducees."

7They discussed this among themselves and said, "It is because we didn't bring any bread."

8Aware of their discussion, Jesus asked, "You of little faith, why are you talking among yourselves about having no bread? 9Do you still not understand? Don't you remember the five loaves for the five thousand, and how many basketfuls you gathered? 10Or the seven loaves for the four thousand, and how many basketfuls you gathered? 11How is it you don't understand that I was not talking to you about bread? But be on your guard against the yeast of the Pharisees and Sadducees." 12Then they understood that he was not telling them to guard against the yeast used in bread, but against the teaching of the Pharisees and Sadducees.

Peter's Confession of Christ

13When Jesus came to the region of Caesarea Philippi, he asked his disciples, "Who do people say the Son of Man is?"

14They replied, "Some say John the Baptist; others say Elijah; and still others, Jeremiah or one of the prophets."

15"But what about you?" he asked. "Who do you say I am?"

16Simon Peter answered, "You are the Christ,*b* the Son of the living God."

17Jesus replied, "Blessed are you, Simon son of Jonah, for this was not revealed to you by man, but by my Father in heaven. 18And I tell you that you are Peter,*c* and on this rock I will build my church, and the gates of Hades*d* will not overcome it.*e* 19I will give you the keys of the kingdom

---

*a*2 Some early manuscripts do not have the rest of verse 2 and all of verse 3.   *b*16 Or *Messiah*; also in verse 20   *c*18 *Peter* means *rock.*   *d*18 Or *hell*   *e*18 Or *not prove stronger than it*

19

of heaven; whatever you bind on earth will be bound in heaven, and whatever you loose on earth will be loosed in heaven." 20Then he warned his disciples not to tell anyone that he was the Christ.

Jesus Predicts His Death

21From that time on Jesus began to explain to his disciples that he must go to Jerusalem and suffer many things at the hands of the elders, chief priests and teachers of the law, and that he must be killed and on the third day be raised to life.

22Peter took him aside and began to rebuke him. "Never, Lord!" he said. "This shall never happen to you!"

23Jesus turned and said to Peter, "Out of my sight, Satan! You are a stumbling block to me; you do not have in mind the things of God, but the things of men."

24Then Jesus said to his disciples, "If anyone would come after me, he must deny himself and take up his cross and follow me. 25For whoever wants to save his life/ will lose it, but whoever loses his life for me will find it. 26What good will it be for a man if he gains the whole world, yet forfeits his soul? Or what can a man give in exchange for his soul? 27For the Son of Man is going to come in his Father's glory with his angels, and then he will reward each person according to what he has done. 28I tell you the truth, some who are standing here will not taste death before they see the Son of Man coming in his kingdom."

The Transfiguration

17 After six days Jesus took with him Peter, James and John the brother of James, and led them up a high mountain by themselves. 2There he was transfigured before them. His face shone like the sun, and his clothes became as white as the light. 3Just then there appeared before them Moses and Elijah, talking with Jesus.

4Peter said to Jesus, "Lord, it is good for us to be here. If you wish, I will put up three shelters—one for you, one for Moses and one for Elijah."

5While he was still speaking, a bright cloud enveloped them, and a voice from the cloud said, "This is my Son, whom I love; with him I am well pleased. Listen to him!"

6When the disciples heard this, they fell face down to the ground, terrified. 7But Jesus came and touched them. "Get up," he said. "Don't be afraid." 8When they looked up, they saw no-one except Jesus.

9As they were coming down the mountain, Jesus instructed them, "Don't tell anyone what you have seen, until the Son of Man has been raised from the dead."

10The disciples asked him, "Why then do the teachers of the law say that Elijah must come first?"

11Jesus replied, "To be sure, Elijah comes and will restore all things. 12But I tell you, Elijah has already come, and they did not recognise him, but have done to him everything they wished. In the same way the Son of Man is going to suffer at their hands." 13Then the disciples understood that he was talking to them about John the Baptist.

The Healing of an Epileptic Boy

14When they came to the crowd, a man approached Jesus and knelt before him. 15"Lord, have mercy on my son," he said. "He is an epileptic and is suffering greatly. He often falls into the fire or into the water. 16I brought him to your disciples, but they could not heal him."

17"O unbelieving and perverse generation," Jesus replied, "how long shall I stay with you? How long shall I put up with you? Bring the boy here to me." 18Jesus rebuked the demon, and it came out of the boy, and he was healed from that moment.

19Then the disciples came to Jesus in private and asked, "Why couldn't we drive it out?"

20He replied, "Because you have so little faith. I tell you the truth, if you

/25 The Greek word means either life or soul; also in verse 26.

have faith as small as a mustard seed, you can say to this mountain, 'Move from here to there' and it will move. Nothing will be impossible for you."[a]

22When they came together in Galilee, he said to them, "The Son of Man is going to be betrayed into the hands of men. 23They will kill him, and on the third day he will be raised to life." And the disciples were filled with grief.

The Temple Tax

24After Jesus and his disciples arrived in Capernaum, the collectors of the two-drachma tax came to Peter and asked, "Doesn't your teacher pay the temple tax?"[b]

25"Yes, he does," he replied.

When Peter came into the house, Jesus was the first to speak. "What do you think, Simon?" he asked. "From whom do the kings of the earth collect duty and taxes—from their own sons or from others?"

26"From others," Peter answered.

"Then the sons are exempt," Jesus said to him. 27"But so that we may not offend them, go to the lake and throw out your line. Take the first fish you catch; open its mouth and you will find a four-drachma coin. Take it and give it to them for my tax and yours."

The Greatest in the Kingdom of Heaven

18 At that time the disciples came to Jesus and asked, "Who is the greatest in the kingdom of heaven?"

2He called a little child and had him stand among them. 3And he said: "I tell you the truth, unless you change and become like little children, you will never enter the kingdom of heaven. 4Therefore, whoever humbles himself like this child is the greatest in the kingdom of heaven. 5And whoever welcomes a little child like this in my name welcomes me.

6"But if anyone causes one of these little ones who believe in me to sin, it

would be better for him to have a large millstone hung around his neck and to be drowned in the depths of the sea. 7Woe to the world because of the things that cause people to sin! Such things must come, but woe to the man through whom they come! 8If your hand or your foot causes you to sin, cut it off and throw it away. It is better for you to enter life maimed or crippled than to have two hands or two feet and be thrown into eternal fire. 9And if your eye causes you to sin, gouge it out and throw it away. It is better for you to enter life with one eye than to have two eyes and be thrown into the fire of hell.

The Parable of the Lost Sheep

10"See that you do not look down on one of these little ones. For I tell you that their angels in heaven always see the face of my Father in heaven.[a]

12"What do you think? If a man owns a hundred sheep, and one of them wanders away, will he not leave the ninety-nine on the hills and go to look for the one that wandered off? 13And if he finds it, I tell you the truth, he is happier about that one sheep than about the ninety-nine that did not wander off. 14In the same way your Father in heaven is not willing that any of these little ones should be lost.

A Brother Who Sins Against You

15"If your brother sins against you,[b] go and show him his fault, just between the two of you. If he listens to you, you have won your brother over. 16But if he will not listen, take one or two others along, so that 'every matter may be established by the testimony of two or three witnesses.'[c] 17If he refuses to listen to them, tell it to the church; and if he refuses to listen even to the church, treat him as you would a pagan or a tax collector.

18"I tell you the truth, whatever you bind on earth will be bound in

---

[a]20 Some manuscripts you. [b]But this kind does not go out except by prayer and fasting.
[b]24 Greek the two drachmas   [a]10 Some manuscripts heaven. 11The Son of Man came to save what was lost.
[b]15 Some manuscripts do not have against you.   [c]16 Deut. 19:15

21

heaven, and whatever you loose on earth will be loosed in heaven.

19"Again, I tell you that if two of you on earth agree about anything you ask for, it will be done for you by my Father in heaven. 20For where two or three come together in my name, there am I with them."

The Parable of the Unmerciful Servant

21Then Peter came to Jesus and asked, "Lord, how many times shall I forgive my brother when he sins against me? Up to seven times?"

22Jesus answered, "I tell you, not seven times, but seventy-seven times.d

23"Therefore, the kingdom of heaven is like a king who wanted to settle accounts with his servants. 24As he began the settlement, a man who owed him ten thousand talentse was brought to him. 25Since he was not able to pay, the master ordered that he and his wife and his children and all that he had be sold to repay the debt.

26"The servant fell on his knees before him. 'Be patient with me,' he begged, 'and I will pay back everything.' 27The servant's master took pity on him, cancelled the debt and let him go.

28"But when that servant went out, he found one of his fellow servants who owed him a hundred denarii.f He grabbed him and began to choke him. 'Pay back what you owe me!' he demanded.

29"His fellow servant fell to his knees and begged him, 'Be patient with me, and I will pay you back.'

30"But he refused. Instead, he went off and had the man thrown into prison until he could pay the debt. 31When the other servants saw what had happened, they were greatly distressed and went and told their master everything that had happened.

32"Then the master called the servant in. 'You wicked servant,' he said,

'I cancelled all that debt of yours because you begged me to. 33Shouldn't you have had mercy on your fellow servant just as I had on you?' 34In anger his master turned him over to the jailers until he should pay back all he owed.

35"This is how my heavenly Father will treat each of you unless you forgive your brother from your heart."

Divorce

19 When Jesus had finished saying these things, he left Galilee and went into the region of Judea to the other side of the Jordan. 2Large crowds followed him, and he healed them there.

3Some Pharisees came to him to test him. They asked, "Is it lawful for a man to divorce his wife for any and every reason?"

4"Haven't you read," he replied, "that at the beginning the Creator 'made them male and female',a 5and said, 'For this reason a man will leave his father and mother and be united to his wife, and the two will become one flesh'b? 6So they are no longer two, but one. Therefore what God has joined together, let man not separate."

7"Why then," they asked, "did Moses command that a man give his wife a certificate of divorce and send her away?"

8Jesus replied, "Moses permitted you to divorce your wives because your hearts were hard. But it was not this way from the beginning. 9I tell you that anyone who divorces his wife, except for marital unfaithfulness, and marries another woman commits adultery."

10The disciples said to him, "If this is the situation between a husband and wife, it is better not to marry."

11Jesus replied, "Not everyone can accept this teaching, but only those to whom it has been given. 12For some are eunuchs because they were born that way; others were made that way

d22 Or seventy times seven
f28 That is, a few pounds
e24 That is, over a million pounds
a4 Gen. 1:27
b5 Gen. 2:24

by men; and others have renounced marriage[c] because of the kingdom of heaven. The one who can accept this should accept it."

The Little Children and Jesus

13Then little children were brought to Jesus for him to place his hands on them and pray for them. But the disciples rebuked those who brought them.

14Jesus said, "Let the little children come to me, and do not hinder them, for the kingdom of heaven belongs to such as these." 15When he had placed his hands on them, he went on from there.

The Rich Young Man

16Now a man came up to Jesus and asked, "Teacher, what good thing must I do to get eternal life?"

17"Why do you ask me about what is good?" Jesus replied. "There is only One who is good. If you want to enter life, obey the commandments."

18"Which ones?" the man enquired.

Jesus replied, " 'Do not murder, do not commit adultery, do not steal, do not give false testimony, 19honour your father and mother,[d] and 'love your neighbour as yourself.'[e]"

20"All these I have kept," the young man said. "What do I still lack?"

21Jesus answered, "If you want to be perfect, go, sell your possessions and give to the poor, and you will have treasure in heaven. Then come, follow me."

22When the young man heard this, he went away sad, because he had great wealth.

23Then Jesus said to his disciples, "I tell you the truth, it is hard for a rich man to enter the kingdom of heaven. 24Again I tell you, it is easier for a camel to go through the eye of a needle than for a rich man to enter the kingdom of God."

25When the disciples heard this, they were greatly astonished and asked, "Who then can be saved?"

26Jesus looked at them and said, "With man this is impossible, but with God all things are possible."

27Peter answered him, "We have left everything to follow you! What then will there be for us?"

28Jesus said to them, "I tell you the truth, at the renewal of all things, when the Son of Man sits on his glorious throne, you who have followed me will also sit on twelve thrones, judging the twelve tribes of Israel. 29And everyone who has left houses or brothers or sisters or father or mother or children or fields for my sake will receive a hundred times as much and will inherit eternal life. 30But many who are first will be last, and many who are last will be first.

The Parable of the Workers in the Vineyard

20 "For the kingdom of heaven is like a landowner who went out early in the morning to hire men to work in his vineyard. 2He agreed to pay them a denarius for the day and sent them into his vineyard.

3"About the third hour he went out and saw others standing in the market-place doing nothing. 4He told them, 'You also go and work in my vineyard, and I will pay you whatever is right.' 5So they went.

"He went out again about the sixth hour and the ninth hour and did the same thing. 6About the eleventh hour he went out and found still others standing around. He asked them, 'Why have you been standing here all day long doing nothing?'

7" 'Because no-one has hired us,' they answered.

"He said to them, 'You also go and work in my vineyard.'

8"When evening came, the owner of the vineyard said to his foreman, 'Call the workers and pay them their wages, beginning with the last ones hired and going on to the first.'

9"The workers who were hired about the eleventh hour came and each received a denarius. 10So when those came who were hired first, they expected to receive more. But each

---

[c]12 Or have made themselves eunuchs
[d]19 Exodus 20:12–16; Deut. 5:16–20   [e]19 Lev. 19:18

one of them also received a denarius. [11]When they received it, they began to grumble against the landowner. [12]"These men who were hired last worked only one hour," they said, 'and you have made them equal to us who have borne the burden of the work and the heat of the day.'

[13]"But he answered one of them, 'Friend, I am not being unfair to you. Didn't you agree to work for a denarius? [14]Take your pay and go. I want to give the man who was hired last the same as I gave you. [15]Don't I have the right to do what I want with my own money? Or are you envious because I am generous?'

[16]"So the last will be first, and the first will be last."

Jesus Again Predicts His Death

[17]Now as Jesus was going up to Jerusalem, he took the twelve disciples aside and said to them, [18]"We are going up to Jerusalem, and the Son of Man will be betrayed to the chief priests and the teachers of the law. They will condemn him to death [19]and will turn him over to the Gentiles to be mocked and flogged and crucified. On the third day he will be raised to life!"

A Mother's Request

[20]Then the mother of Zebedee's sons came to Jesus with her sons and, kneeling down, asked a favour of him.

[21]"What is it you want?" he asked.

She said, "Grant that one of these two sons of mine may sit at your right and the other at your left in your kingdom."

[22]"You don't know what you are asking," Jesus said to them. "Can you drink the cup I am going to drink?"

"We can," they answered.

[23]Jesus said to them, "You will indeed drink from my cup, but to sit at my right or left is not for me to grant. These places belong to those for whom they have been prepared by my Father."

[24]When the ten heard about this, they were indignant with the two brothers. [25]Jesus called them together and said, "You know that the rulers of the Gentiles lord it over them, and their high officials exercise authority over them. [26]Not so with you. Instead, whoever wants to become great among you must be your servant, [27]and whoever wants to be first must be your slave—[28]just as the Son of Man did not come to be served, but to serve, and to give his life as a ransom for many."

Two Blind Men Receive Sight

[29]As Jesus and his disciples were leaving Jericho, a large crowd followed him. [30]Two blind men were sitting by the roadside, and when they heard that Jesus was going by, they shouted, "Lord, Son of David, have mercy on us!"

[31]The crowd rebuked them and told them to be quiet, but they shouted all the louder, "Lord, Son of David, have mercy on us!"

[32]Jesus stopped and called them. "What do you want me to do for you?" he asked.

[33]"Lord," they answered, "we want our sight."

[34]Jesus had compassion on them and touched their eyes. Immediately they received their sight and followed him.

The Triumphal Entry

21 As they approached Jerusalem and came to Bethphage on the Mount of Olives, Jesus sent two disciples, [2]saying to them, "Go to the village ahead of you, and at once you will find a donkey tied there, with her colt by her. Untie them and bring them to me. [3]If anyone says anything to you, tell him that the Lord needs them, and he will send them right away."

[4]This took place to fulfil what was spoken through the prophet:

[5]"Say to the Daughter of Zion,
'See, your king comes to you,
gentle and riding on a donkey,
on a colt, the foal of a donkey.' " [a]

[6]The disciples went and did as

[a]5 Zech. 9:9

Jesus had instructed them. [7]They brought the donkey and the colt, placed their cloaks on them, and Jesus sat on them. [8]A very large crowd spread their cloaks on the road, while others cut branches from the trees and spread them on the road. [9]The crowds that went ahead of him and those that followed shouted,

"Hosanna[b] to the Son of David!"

"Blessed is he who comes in the name of the Lord!"[c]

"Hosanna[b] in the highest!"

[10]When Jesus entered Jerusalem, the whole city was stirred and asked, "Who is this?"

[11]The crowds answered, "This is Jesus, the prophet from Nazareth in Galilee."

Jesus at the Temple

[12]Jesus entered the temple area and drove out all who were buying and selling there. He overturned the tables of the money changers and the benches of those selling doves. [13]"It is written," he said to them, " 'My house will be called a house of prayer,'[d] but you are making it a 'den of robbers'.[e]"

[14]The blind and the lame came to him at the temple, and he healed them. [15]But when the chief priests and the teachers of the law saw the wonderful things he did and the children shouting in the temple area, "Hosanna to the Son of David," they were indignant.

[16]"Do you hear what these children are saying?" they asked him.

"Yes," replied Jesus, "have you never read,

" 'From the lips of children and infants
you have ordained praise'?[f]"

[17]And he left them and went out of the city to Bethany, where he spent the night.

The Fig-Tree Withers

[18]Early in the morning, as he was on his way back to the city, he was hungry. [19]Seeing a fig-tree by the road, he went up to it but found nothing on it except leaves. Then he said to it, "May you never bear fruit again!" Immediately the tree withered.

[20]When the disciples saw this, they were amazed. "How did the fig-tree wither so quickly?" they asked.

[21]Jesus replied, "I tell you the truth, if you have faith and do not doubt, not only can you do what was done to the fig-tree, but also you can say to this mountain, 'Go, throw yourself into the sea,' and it will be done. [22]If you believe, you will receive whatever you ask for in prayer."

The Authority of Jesus Questioned

[23]Jesus entered the temple courts, and, while he was teaching, the chief priests and the elders of the people came to him. "By what authority are you doing these things?" they asked. "And who gave you this authority?"

[24]Jesus replied, "I will also ask you one question. If you answer me, I will tell you by what authority I am doing these things. [25]John's baptism—where did it come from? Was it from heaven, or from men?"

They discussed it among themselves and said, "If we say, 'From heaven', he will ask, 'Then why didn't you believe him?' [26]But if we say, 'From men'—we are afraid of the people, for they all hold that John was a prophet."

[27]So they answered Jesus, "We don't know."

Then he said, "Neither will I tell you by what authority I am doing these things.

The Parable of the Two Sons

[28]"What do you think? There was a man who had two sons. He went to the first and said, 'Son, go and work today in the vineyard.'

---

[b]9 A Hebrew expression meaning "Save!" which became an exclamation of praise; also in verse 15
[c]9 Psalm 118:26   [d]13 Isaiah 56:7   [e]13 Jer. 7:11   [f]16 Psalm 8:2

29"'I will not,' he answered, but later he changed his mind and went.

30"Then the father went to the other son and said the same thing. He answered, 'I will, sir,' but he did not go.

31"Which of the two did what his father wanted?"

"The first," they answered.

Jesus said to them, "I tell you the truth, the tax collectors and the prostitutes are entering the kingdom of God ahead of you. 32For John came to you to show you the way of righteousness, and you did not believe him, but the tax collectors and the prostitutes did. And even after you saw this, you did not repent and believe him.

The Parable of the Tenants

33"Listen to another parable: There was a landowner who planted a vineyard. He put a wall around it, dug a winepress in it and built a watchtower. Then he rented the vineyard to some farmers and went away on a journey. 34When the harvest time approached, he sent his servants to the tenants to collect his fruit.

35"The tenants seized his servants; they beat one, killed another, and stoned a third. 36Then he sent other servants to them, more than the first time, and the tenants treated them the same way. 37Last of all, he sent his son to them. 'They will respect my son,' he said.

38"But when the tenants saw the son, they said to each other, 'This is the heir. Come, let's kill him and take his inheritance.' 39So they took him and threw him out of the vineyard and killed him.

40"Therefore, when the owner of the vineyard comes, what will he do to those tenants?"

41"He will bring those wretches to a wretched end," they replied, "and he will rent the vineyard to other tenants, who will give him his share of the crop at harvest time."

42Jesus said to them, "Have you never read in the Scriptures:

"'The stone the builders rejected
has become the capstone;g
the Lord has done this,
and it is marvellous in our eyes'h?

43"Therefore I tell you that the kingdom of God will be taken away from you and given to a people who will produce its fruit. 44He who falls on this stone will be broken to pieces, but he on whom it falls will be crushed."i

45When the chief priests and the Pharisees heard Jesus' parables, they knew he was talking about them. 46They looked for a way to arrest him, but they were afraid of the crowd because the people held that he was a prophet.

The Parable of the Wedding Banquet

22 Jesus spoke to them again in parables, saying: 2"The kingdom of heaven is like a king who prepared a wedding banquet for his son. 3He sent his servants to those who had been invited to the banquet to tell them to come, but they refused to come.

4"Then he sent some more servants and said, 'Tell those who have been invited that I have prepared my dinner: My oxen and fattened cattle have been slaughtered, and everything is ready. Come to the wedding banquet.'

5"But they paid no attention and went off—one to his field, another to his business. 6The rest seized his servants, ill-treated them and killed them. 7The king was enraged. He sent his army and destroyed those murderers and burned their city.

8"Then he said to his servants, 'The wedding banquet is ready, but those I invited did not deserve to come. 9Go to the street corners and invite to the banquet anyone you find.' 10So the servants went out into the streets and gathered all the people they could find, both good and bad, and the wedding hall was filled with guests.

11"But when the king came in to see the guests, he noticed a man there

g42 Or cornerstone   h42 Psalm 118:22,23   i44 Some manuscripts do not have verse 44.

who was not wearing wedding clothes. 12'Friend,' he asked, 'how did you get in here without wedding clothes?' The man was speechless.

13"Then the king told the attendants, 'Tie him hand and foot, and throw him outside, into the darkness, where there will be weeping and gnashing of teeth.'

14"For many are invited, but few are chosen."

Paying Taxes to Caesar

15Then the Pharisees went out and laid plans to trap him in his words. 16They sent their disciples to him along with the Herodians. "Teacher," they said, "we know you are a man of integrity and that you teach the way of God in accordance with the truth. You aren't swayed by men, because you pay no attention to who they are. 17Tell us then, what is your opinion? Is it right to pay taxes to Caesar or not?"

18But Jesus, knowing their evil intent, said, "You hypocrites, why are you trying to trap me? 19Show me the coin used for paying the tax." They brought him a denarius, 20and he asked them, "Whose portrait is this? And whose inscription?"

21"Caesar's," they replied.

Then he said to them, "Give to Caesar what is Caesar's, and to God what is God's."

22When they heard this, they were amazed. So they left him and went away.

Marriage at the Resurrection

23That same day the Sadducees, who say there is no resurrection, came to him with a question. 24"Teacher," they said, "Moses told us that if a man dies without having children, his brother must marry the widow and have children for him. 25Now there were seven brothers among us. The first one married and died, and since he had no children, he left his wife to his brother. 26The same thing happened to the second and third brother, right on down to

the seventh. 27Finally, the woman died. 28Now then, at the resurrection, whose wife will she be of the seven, since all of them were married to her?"

29Jesus replied, "You are in error because you do not know the Scriptures or the power of God. 30At the resurrection people will neither marry nor be given in marriage; they will be like the angels in heaven. 31But about the resurrection of the dead—have you not read what God said to you, 32'I am the God of Abraham, the God of Isaac, and the God of Jacob'a? He is not the God of the dead but of the living."

33When the crowds heard this, they were astonished at his teaching.

The Greatest Commandment

34Hearing that Jesus had silenced the Sadducees, the Pharisees got together. 35One of them, an expert in the law, tested him with this question: 36"Teacher, which is the greatest commandment in the Law?"

37Jesus replied: "Love the Lord your God with all your heart and with all your soul and with all your mind.'b 38This is the first and greatest commandment. 39And the second is like it: 'Love your neighbour as yourself.'c 40All the Law and the Prophets hang on these two commandments."

Whose Son Is the Christ?

41While the Pharisees were gathered together, Jesus asked them, 42"What do you think about the Christ?d Whose son is he?"

"The son of David," they replied.

43He said to them, "How is it then that David, speaking by the Spirit, calls him 'Lord'? For he says,

44"'The Lord said to my Lord:
  "Sit at my right hand
  until I put your enemies
    under your feet." 'e

45If then David calls him 'Lord', how can he be his son?" 46No-one could say a word in reply, and from that day on no-one dared to ask him any more questions.

a32 Exodus 3:6   b37 Deut. 6:5   c39 Lev. 19:18
d42 Or Messiah   e44 Psalm 110:1

Seven Woes

23 Then Jesus said to the crowds and to his disciples: ²"The teachers of the law and the Pharisees sit in Moses' seat. ³So you must obey them and do everything they tell you. But do not do what they do, for they do not practise what they preach. ⁴They tie up heavy loads and put them on men's shoulders, but they themselves are not willing to lift a finger to move them.

⁵"Everything they do is done for men to see: They make their phylacteries⁰ wide and the tassels of their prayer shawls long; ⁶they love the place of honour at banquets and the most important seats in the synagogues; ⁷they love to be greeted in the market-places and to have men call them 'Rabbi'.

⁸"But you are not to be called 'Rabbi', for you have only one Master and you are all brothers. ⁹And do not call anyone on earth 'father', for you have one Father, and he is in heaven. ¹⁰Nor are you to be called 'teacher', for you have one Teacher, the Christ.ᵇ ¹¹The greatest among you will be your servant. ¹²For whoever exalts himself will be humbled, and whoever humbles himself will be exalted.

¹³"Woe to you, teachers of the law and Pharisees, you hypocrites! You shut the kingdom of heaven in men's faces. You yourselves do not enter, nor will you let those enter who are trying to.ᶜ

¹⁵"Woe to you, teachers of the law and Pharisees, you hypocrites! You travel over land and sea to win a single convert, and when he becomes one, you make him twice as much a son of hell as you are.

¹⁶"Woe to you, blind guides! You say, 'If anyone swears by the temple, it means nothing; but if anyone swears by the gold of the temple, he is bound by his oath.' ¹⁷You blind fools! Which is greater: the gold, or the temple that makes the gold sacred? ¹⁸You also say, 'If anyone swears by the altar, it means nothing; but if anyone swears by the gift on it, he is bound by his oath.' ¹⁹You blind men! Which is greater: the gift, or the altar that makes the gift sacred? ²⁰Therefore, he who swears by the altar swears by it and by everything on it. ²¹And he who swears by the temple swears by it and by the one who dwells in it. ²²And he who swears by heaven swears by God's throne and by the one who sits on it.

²³"Woe to you, teachers of the law and Pharisees, you hypocrites! You give a tenth of your spices—mint, dill and cummin. But you have neglected the more important matters of the law—justice, mercy and faithfulness. You should have practised the latter, without neglecting the former. ²⁴You blind guides! You strain out a gnat but swallow a camel.

²⁵"Woe to you, teachers of the law and Pharisees, you hypocrites! You clean the outside of the cup and dish, but inside they are full of greed and self-indulgence. ²⁶Blind Pharisee! First clean the inside of the cup and dish, and then the outside also will be clean.

²⁷"Woe to you, teachers of the law and Pharisees, you hypocrites! You are like whitewashed tombs, which look beautiful on the outside but on the inside are full of dead men's bones and everything unclean. ²⁸In the same way, on the outside you appear to people as righteous but on the inside you are full of hypocrisy and wickedness.

²⁹"Woe to you, teachers of the law and Pharisees, you hypocrites! You build tombs for the prophets and decorate the graves of the righteous. ³⁰And you say, 'If we had lived in the days of our forefathers, we would not have taken part with them in shedding the blood of the prophets.' ³¹So

---

ᵒ5 That is, boxes containing Scripture verses, which were worn on the forehead and arms   ᵇ10 Or *Messiah*
ᶜ13 Some manuscripts *to.* ¹⁴*Woe to you, teachers of the Law and Pharisees, you hypocrites! You devour widows' houses and for a show make lengthy prayers. Therefore you will be punished more severely.*

you testify against yourselves that you are the descendants of those who murdered the prophets. 32Fill up, then, the measure of the sin of your forefathers!

33"You snakes! You brood of vipers! How will you escape being condemned to hell? 34Therefore I am sending you prophets and wise men and teachers. Some of them you will kill and crucify; others you will flog in your synagogues and pursue from town to town. 35And so upon you will come all the righteous blood that has been shed on earth, from the blood of righteous Abel to the blood of Zechariah son of Berakiah, whom you murdered between the temple and the altar. 36I tell you the truth, all this will come upon this generation.

37"O Jerusalem, Jerusalem, you who kill the prophets and stone those sent to you, how often I have longed to gather your children together, as a hen gathers her chicks under her wings, but you were not willing. 38Look, your house is left to you desolate. 39For I tell you, you will not see me again until you say, 'Blessed is he who comes in the name of the Lord.'d"

Signs of the End of the Age

24 Jesus left the temple and was walking away when his disciples came up to him to call his attention to its buildings. 2"Do you see all these things?" he asked. "I tell you the truth, not one stone here will be left on another; every one will be thrown down."

3As Jesus was sitting on the Mount of Olives, the disciples came to him privately. "Tell us," they said, "when will this happen, and what will be the sign of your coming and of the end of the age?"

4Jesus answered: "Watch out that no-one deceives you. 5For many will come in my name, claiming, 'I am the Christ,'a and will deceive many. 6You will hear of wars and rumours of wars, but see to it that you are not alarmed. Such things must happen, but the end is still to come. 7Nation will rise against nation, and kingdom against kingdom. There will be famines and earthquakes in various places. 8All these are the beginning of birth-pains.

9"Then you will be handed over to be persecuted and put to death, and you will be hated by all nations because of me. 10At that time many will turn away from the faith and will betray and hate each other, 11and many false prophets will appear and deceive many people. 12Because of the increase of wickedness, the love of most will grow cold, 13but he who stands firm to the end will be saved. 14And this gospel of the kingdom will be preached in the whole world as a testimony to all nations, and then the end will come.

15"So when you see standing in the holy place 'the abomination that causes desolation',b spoken of through the prophet Daniel—let the reader understand—16then let those who are in Judea flee to the mountains. 17Let no-one on the roof of his house go down to take anything out of the house. 18Let no-one in the field go back to get his cloak. 19How dreadful it will be in those days for pregnant women and nursing mothers! 20Pray that your flight will not take place in winter or on the Sabbath. 21For then there will be great distress, unequalled from the beginning of the world until now—and never to be equalled again. 22If those days had not been cut short, no-one would survive, but for the sake of the elect those days will be shortened. 23At that time if anyone says to you, 'Look, here is the Christ!' or, 'There he is!' do not believe it. 24For false Christs and false prophets will appear and perform great signs and miracles to deceive even the elect—if that were possible. 25See, I have told you ahead of time.

26"So if anyone tells you, 'There he is, out in the desert,' do not go out; or, 'Here he is, in the inner rooms,' do not believe it. 27For as the lightning

d39 Psalm 118:26   a5 Or *Messiah*; also in verse 23   b15 Daniel 9:27; 11:31; 12:11

comes from the east and flashes to the west, so will be the coming of the Son of Man. 28Wherever there is a carcass, there the vultures will gather.

29"Immediately after the distress of those days

" 'the sun will be darkened,
and the moon will not give its
light;
the stars will fall from the sky,
and the heavenly bodies will be
shaken.'c

30"At that time the sign of the Son of Man will appear in the sky, and all the nations of the earth will mourn. They will see the Son of Man coming on the clouds of the sky, with power and great glory. 31And he will send his angels with a loud trumpet call, and they will gather his elect from the four winds, from one end of the heavens to the other.

32"Now learn this lesson from the fig-tree: As soon as its twigs get tender and its leaves come out, you know that summer is near. 33Even so, when you see all these things, you know that itd is near, right at the door. 34I tell you the truth, this generatione will certainly not pass away until all these things have happened. 35Heaven and earth will pass away, but my words will never pass away.

The Day and Hour Unknown

36"No-one knows about that day or hour, not even the angels in heaven, nor the Son,f but only the Father. 37As it was in the days of Noah, so it will be at the coming of the Son of Man. 38For in the days before the flood, people were eating and drinking, marrying and giving in marriage, up to the day Noah entered the ark; 39and they knew nothing about what would happen until the flood came and took them all away. That is how it will be at the coming of the Son of Man. 40Two men will be in the field; one will be taken and the other left. 41Two women will be grinding with a hand mill; one will be taken and the other left.

42"Therefore keep watch, because you do not know on what day your Lord will come. 43But understand this: If the owner of the house had known at what time of night the thief was coming, he would have kept watch and would not have let his house be broken into. 44So you also must be ready, because the Son of Man will come at an hour when you do not expect him.

45"Who then is the faithful and wise servant, whom the master has put in charge of the servants in his household to give them their food at the proper time? 46It will be good for that servant whose master finds him doing so when he returns. 47I tell you the truth, he will put him in charge of all his possessions. 48But suppose that servant is wicked and says to himself, 'My master is staying away a long time,' 49and he then begins to beat his fellow servants and to eat and drink with drunkards. 50The master of that servant will come on a day when he does not expect him and at an hour he is not aware of. 51He will cut him to pieces and assign him a place with the hypocrites, where there will be weeping and gnashing of teeth.

The Parable of the Ten Virgins

25 "At that time the kingdom of heaven will be like ten virgins who took their lamps and went out to meet the bridegroom. 2Five of them were foolish and five were wise. 3The foolish ones took their lamps but did not take any oil with them. 4The wise, however, took oil in jars along with their lamps. 5The bridegroom was a long time in coming, and they all became drowsy and fell asleep.

6"At midnight the cry rang out: 'Here's the bridegroom! Come out to meet him!'

7"Then all the virgins woke up and trimmed their lamps. 8The foolish ones said to the wise, 'Give us some of your oil; our lamps are going out.'

9" 'No,' they replied, 'there may not be enough for both us and you. Instead, go to those who sell oil and

c29 Isaiah 13:10; 34:4   d33 Or he   e34 Or race
f36 Some manuscripts do not have nor the Son.

buy some for yourselves.'

¹⁰"But while they were on their way to buy the oil, the bridegroom arrived. The virgins who were ready went in with him to the wedding banquet. And the door was shut.

¹¹"Later the others also came. 'Sir! Sir!' they said. 'Open the door for us!'

¹²"But he replied, 'I tell you the truth, I don't know you.'

¹³"Therefore keep watch, because you do not know the day or the hour.

The Parable of the Talents

¹⁴"Again, it will be like a man going on a journey, who called his servants and entrusted his property to them. ¹⁵To one he gave five talents*a* of money, to another two talents, and to another one talent, each according to his ability. Then he went on his journey. ¹⁶The man who had received the five talents went at once and put his money to work and gained five more. ¹⁷So also, the one with the two talents gained two more. ¹⁸But the man who had received the one talent went off, dug a hole in the ground and hid his master's money.

¹⁹"After a long time the master of those servants returned and settled accounts with them. ²⁰The man who had received the five talents brought the other five. 'Master,' he said, 'you entrusted me with five talents. See, I have gained five more.'

²¹"His master replied, 'Well done, good and faithful servant! You have been faithful with a few things; I will put you in charge of many things. Come and share your master's happiness!'

²²"The man with the two talents also came. 'Master,' he said, 'you entrusted me with two talents; see, I have gained two more.'

²³"His master replied, 'Well done, good and faithful servant! You have been faithful with a few things; I will put you in charge of many things. Come and share your master's happiness!'

²⁴"Then the man who had received the one talent came. 'Master,' he said, 'I knew that you are a hard man,

harvesting where you have not sown and gathering where you have not scattered seed. ²⁵So I was afraid and went out and hid your talent in the ground. See, here is what belongs to you.'

²⁶"His master replied, 'You wicked, lazy servant! So you knew that I harvest where I have not sown and gather where I have not scattered seed? ²⁷Well then, you should have put my money on deposit with the bankers, so that when I returned I would have received it back with interest.

²⁸"'Take the talent from him and give it to the one who has the ten talents. ²⁹For everyone who has will be given more, and he will have an abundance. Whoever does not have, even what he has will be taken from him. ³⁰And throw that worthless servant outside, into the darkness, where there will be weeping and gnashing of teeth.'

The Sheep and the Goats

³¹"When the Son of Man comes in his glory, and all the angels with him, he will sit on his throne in heavenly glory. ³²All the nations will be gathered before him, and he will separate the people one from another as a shepherd separates the sheep from the goats. ³³He will put the sheep on his right and the goats on his left.

³⁴"Then the King will say to those on his right, 'Come, you who are blessed by my Father; take your inheritance, the kingdom prepared for you since the creation of the world. ³⁵For I was hungry and you gave me something to eat, I was thirsty and you gave me something to drink, I was a stranger and you invited me in, ³⁶I needed clothes and you clothed me, I was sick and you looked after me, I was in prison and you came to visit me.'

³⁷"Then the righteous will answer him, 'Lord, when did we see you hungry and feed you, or thirsty and give you something to drink? ³⁸When did we see you a stranger and invite you in, or needing clothes and clothe

a15 A talent was worth several hundred pounds.

you? ³⁹When did we see you sick or in prison and go to visit you?'

⁴⁰"The King will reply, 'I tell you the truth, whatever you did for one of the least of these brothers of mine, you did for me.'

⁴¹"Then he will say to those on his left, 'Depart from me, you who are cursed, into the eternal fire prepared for the devil and his angels. ⁴²For I was hungry and you gave me nothing to eat, I was thirsty and you gave me nothing to drink, I was a stranger and you did not invite me in, I needed clothes and you did not clothe me, I was sick and in prison and you did not look after me.'

⁴⁴"They also will answer, 'Lord, when did we see you hungry or thirsty or a stranger or needing clothes or sick or in prison, and did not help you?'

⁴⁵"He will reply, 'I tell you the truth, whatever you did not do for one of the least of these, you did not do for me.'

⁴⁶"Then they will go away to eternal punishment, but the righteous to eternal life."

The Plot Against Jesus

26 When Jesus had finished saying all these things, he said to his disciples, ²"As you know, the Passover is two days away—and the Son of Man will be handed over to be crucified."

³Then the chief priests and the elders of the people assembled in the palace of the high priest, whose name was Caiaphas, ⁴and they plotted to arrest Jesus in some sly way and kill him. ⁵"But not during the Feast," they said, "or there may be a riot among the people."

Jesus Anointed at Bethany

⁶While Jesus was in Bethany in the home of a man known as Simon the Leper, ⁷a woman came to him with an alabaster jar of very expensive perfume, which she poured on his head as he was reclining at the table.

⁸When the disciples saw this, they were indignant. "Why this waste?" they asked. ⁹"This perfume could

have been sold at a high price and the money given to the poor."

¹⁰Aware of this, Jesus said to them, "Why are you bothering this woman? She has done a beautiful thing to me. ¹¹The poor you will always have with you, but you will not always have me. ¹²When she poured this perfume on my body, she did it to prepare me for burial. ¹³I tell you the truth, wherever this gospel is preached throughout the world, what she has done will also be told, in memory of her."

Judas Agrees to Betray Jesus

¹⁴Then one of the Twelve—the one called Judas Iscariot—went to the chief priests ¹⁵and asked, "What are you willing to give me if I hand him over to you?" So they counted out for him thirty silver coins. ¹⁶From then on Judas watched for an opportunity to hand him over.

The Lord's Supper

¹⁷On the first day of the Feast of Unleavened Bread, the disciples came to Jesus and asked, "Where do you want us to make preparations for you to eat the Passover?"

¹⁸He replied, "Go into the city to a certain man and tell him, 'The Teacher says: My appointed time is near. I am going to celebrate the Passover with my disciples at your house.'" ¹⁹So the disciples did as Jesus had directed them and prepared the Passover.

²⁰When evening came, Jesus was reclining at the table with the Twelve. ²¹And while they were eating, he said, "I tell you the truth, one of you will betray me."

²²They were very sad and began to say to him one after the other, "Surely not I, Lord?"

²³Jesus replied, "The one who has dipped his hand into the bowl with me will betray me. ²⁴The Son of Man will go just as it is written about him. But woe to that man who betrays the Son of Man! It would be better for him if he had not been born."

²⁵Then Judas, the one who would betray him, said, "Surely not I, Rabbi?"

Jesus answered, "Yes, it is you."[a]

26While they were eating, Jesus took bread, gave thanks and broke it, and gave it to his disciples, saying, "Take and eat; this is my body."

27Then he took the cup, gave thanks and offered it to them, saying, "Drink from it, all of you. 28This is my blood of the[b] covenant, which is poured out for many for the forgiveness of sins. 29I tell you, I will not drink of this fruit of the vine from now on until that day when I drink it anew with you in my Father's kingdom."

30When they had sung a hymn, they went out to the Mount of Olives.

Jesus Predicts Peter's Denial

31Then Jesus told them, "This very night you will all fall away on account of me, for it is written:

" 'I will strike the shepherd,
    and the sheep of the flock will be
    scattered.'[c]

32But after I have risen, I will go ahead of you into Galilee."

33Peter replied, "Even if all fall away on account of you, I never will."

34"I tell you the truth," Jesus answered, "this very night, before the cock crows, you will disown me three times."

35But Peter declared, "Even if I have to die with you, I will never disown you." And all the other disciples said the same.

Gethsemane

36Then Jesus went with his disciples to a place called Gethsemane, and he said to them, "Sit here while I go over there and pray." 37He took Peter and the two sons of Zebedee along with him, and he began to be sorrowful and troubled. 38Then he said to them, "My soul is overwhelmed with sorrow to the point of death. Stay here and keep watch with me."

39Going a little farther, he fell with his face to the ground and prayed, "My Father, if it is possible, may this cup be taken from me. Yet not as I will, but as you will."

40Then he returned to his disciples and found them sleeping. "Could you men not keep watch with me for one hour?" he asked Peter. 41"Watch and pray so that you will not fall into temptation. The spirit is willing, but the body is weak."

42He went away a second time and prayed, "My Father, if it is not possible for this cup to be taken away unless I drink it, may your will be done."

43When he came back, he again found them sleeping, because their eyes were heavy. 44So he left them and went away once more and prayed the third time, saying the same thing.

45Then he returned to the disciples and said to them, "Are you still sleeping and resting? Look, the hour is near, and the Son of Man is betrayed into the hands of sinners. 46Rise, let us go! Here comes my betrayer!"

Jesus Arrested

47While he was still speaking, Judas, one of the Twelve, arrived. With him was a large crowd armed with swords and clubs, sent from the chief priests and the elders of the people. 48Now the betrayer had arranged a signal with them: "The one I kiss is the man; arrest him." 49Going at once to Jesus, Judas said, "Greetings, Rabbi!" and kissed him.

50Jesus replied, "Friend, do what you came for."[d]

Then the men stepped forward, seized Jesus and arrested him. 51With that, one of Jesus' companions reached for his sword, drew it out and struck the servant of the high priest, cutting off his ear.

52"Put your sword back in its place," Jesus said to him, "for all who draw the sword will die by the sword. 53Do you think I cannot call on my Father, and he will at once put at my disposal more than twelve legions of angels? 54But how then would the Scriptures be fulfilled that say it must happen in this way?"

*a*25 Or "You yourself have said it."   *b*28 Some manuscripts the new   *c*31 Zech. 13:7
*d*50 Or "Friend, why have you come?"

33

55At that time Jesus said to the crowd, "Am I leading a rebellion, that you have come out with swords and clubs to capture me? Every day I sat in the temple courts teaching, and you did not arrest me. 56But this has all taken place that the writings of the prophets might be fulfilled." Then all the disciples deserted him and fled.

Before the Sanhedrin

57Those who had arrested Jesus took him to Caiaphas, the high priest, where the teachers of the law and the elders had assembled. 58But Peter followed him at a distance, right up to the courtyard of the high priest. He entered and sat down with the guards to see the outcome.

59The chief priests and the whole Sanhedrin were looking for false evidence against Jesus so that they could put him to death. 60But they did not find any, though many false witnesses came forward.

Finally two came forward 61and declared, "This fellow said, 'I am able to destroy the temple of God and rebuild it in three days.' "

62Then the high priest stood up and said to Jesus, "Are you not going to answer? What is this testimony that these men are bringing against you?" 63But Jesus remained silent.

The high priest said to him, "I charge you under oath by the living God: Tell us if you are the Christ,e the Son of God."

64"Yes, it is as you say," Jesus replied. "But I say to all of you: In the future you will see the Son of Man sitting at the right hand of the Mighty One and coming on the clouds of heaven."

65Then the high priest tore his clothes and said, "He has spoken blasphemy! Why do we need any more witnesses? Look, now you have heard the blasphemy. 66What do you think?"

"He is worthy of death," they answered.

67Then they spat in his face and struck him with their fists. Others

slapped him 68and said, "Prophesy to us, Christ. Who hit you?"

Peter Disowns Jesus

69Now Peter was sitting out in the courtyard, and a servant girl came to him. "You also were with Jesus of Galilee," she said.

70But he denied it before them all. "I don't know what you're talking about," he said.

71Then he went out to the gateway, where another girl saw him and said to the people there, "This fellow was with Jesus of Nazareth."

72He denied it again, with an oath: "I don't know the man!"

73After a little while, those standing there went up to Peter and said, "Surely you are one of them, for your accent gives you away."

74Then he began to call down curses on himself and he swore to them, "I don't know the man!"

Immediately a cock crowed. 75Then Peter remembered the word Jesus had spoken: "Before the cock crows, you will disown me three times." And he went outside and wept bitterly.

Judas Hangs Himself

27 Early in the morning, all the chief priests and the elders of the people came to the decision to put Jesus to death. 2They bound him, led him away and turned him over to Pilate, the governor.

3When Judas, who had betrayed him, saw that Jesus was condemned, he was seized with remorse and returned the thirty silver coins to the chief priests and the elders. 4"I have sinned," he said, "for I have betrayed innocent blood."

"What is that to us?" they replied. "That's your responsibility."

5So Judas threw the money into the temple and left. Then he went away and hanged himself.

6The chief priests picked up the coins and said, "It is against the law to put this into the treasury, since it is blood money." 7So they decided to use the money to buy the potter's field as a burial place for foreigners.

e63 Or Messiah; also in verse 68

8That is why it has been called the Field of Blood to this day. 9Then what was spoken by Jeremiah the prophet was fulfilled: "They took the thirty silver coins, the price set on him by the people of Israel, 10and they used them to buy the potter's field, as the Lord commanded me."[a]

Jesus Before Pilate

11Meanwhile Jesus stood before the governor, and the governor asked him, "Are you the king of the Jews?"

"Yes, it is as you say," Jesus replied.

12When he was accused by the chief priests and the elders, he gave no answer. 13Then Pilate asked him, "Don't you hear how many things they are accusing you of?" 14But Jesus made no reply, not even to a single charge—to the great amazement of the governor.

15Now it was the governor's custom at the Feast to release a prisoner chosen by the crowd. 16At that time they had a notorious prisoner, called Barabbas. 17So when the crowd gathered, Pilate asked them, "Which one do you want me to release to you: Barabbas, or Jesus who is called Christ?" 18For he knew it was out of envy that they had handed Jesus over to him.

19While Pilate was sitting on the judge's seat, his wife sent him this message: "Don't have anything to do with that innocent man, for I have suffered a great deal today in a dream because of him."

20But the chief priests and the elders persuaded the crowd to ask for Barabbas and to have Jesus executed.

21"Which of the two do you want me to release to you?" asked the governor.

"Barabbas," they answered.

22"What shall I do, then, with Jesus who is called Christ?" Pilate asked.

They all answered, "Crucify him!"

23"Why? What crime has he committed?" asked Pilate.

But they shouted all the louder, "Crucify him!"

24When Pilate saw that he was getting nowhere, but that instead an uproar was starting, he took water and washed his hands in front of the crowd. "I am innocent of this man's blood," he said. "It is your responsibility!"

25All the people answered, "Let his blood be on us and on our children!"

26Then he released Barabbas to them. But he had Jesus flogged, and handed him over to be crucified.

The Soldiers Mock Jesus

27Then the governor's soldiers took Jesus into the Praetorium and gathered the whole company of soldiers round him. 28They stripped him and put a scarlet robe on him, 29and then wove a crown of thorns and set it on his head. They put a staff in his right hand and knelt in front of him and mocked him. "Hail, King of the Jews!" they said. 30They spat on him, and took the staff and struck him on the head again and again. 31After they had mocked him, they took off the robe and put his own clothes on him. Then they led him away to crucify him.

The Crucifixion

32As they were going out, they met a man from Cyrene, named Simon, and they forced him to carry the cross. 33They came to a place called Golgotha (which means The Place of the Skull). 34There they offered him wine to drink, mixed with gall; but after tasting it, he refused to drink it. 35When they had crucified him, they divided up his clothes by casting lots.[b] 36And sitting down, they kept watch over him there. 37Above his head they placed the written charge against him: THIS IS JESUS, THE KING OF THE JEWS. 38Two robbers were crucified with him, one on his right and one on his left. 39Those who passed by hurled insults at him, shaking their heads 40and saying, "You who are going to destroy the temple and build it in three days, save yourself! Come

[a]10 Zech. 11:12,13; Jer. 32:6-9
[b]35 A few late manuscripts lots that the word spoken by the prophet might be fulfilled: "They divided my garments among themselves and cast lots for my clothing." (Psalm 22:18)

35

down from the cross, if you are the Son of God!"

[41]In the same way the chief priests, the teachers of the law and the elders mocked him. [42]"He saved others," they said, "but he can't save himself! He's the king of Israel! Let him come down now from the cross, and we will believe in him. [43]He trusts in God. Let God rescue him now if he wants him, for he said, 'I am the Son of God.'" [44]In the same way the robbers who were crucified with him also heaped insults on him.

The Death of Jesus

[45]From the sixth hour until the ninth hour darkness came over all the land. [46]About the ninth hour Jesus cried out in a loud voice, "*Eloi, Eloi,*[c] *lama sabachthani?*"—which means, "My God, my God, why have you forsaken me?"[d]

[47]When some of those standing there heard this, they said, "He's calling Elijah."

[48]Immediately one of them ran and got a sponge. He filled it with wine vinegar, put it on a stick, and offered it to Jesus to drink. [49]But the rest said, "Leave him alone. Let's see if Elijah comes to save him."

[50]And when Jesus had cried out again in a loud voice, he gave up his spirit.

[51]At that moment the curtain of the temple was torn in two from top to bottom. The earth shook and the rocks split. [52]The tombs broke open and the bodies of many holy people who had died were raised to life. [53]They came out of the tombs, and after Jesus' resurrection they went into the holy city and appeared to many people.

[54]When the centurion and those with him who were guarding Jesus saw the earthquake and all that had happened, they were terrified, and exclaimed, "Surely he was the Son[e] of God!"

[55]Many women were there, watching from a distance. They had followed Jesus from Galilee to care for

his needs. [56]Among them were Mary Magdalene, Mary the mother of James and Joseph, and the mother of Zebedee's sons.

The Burial of Jesus

[57]As evening approached, there came a rich man from Arimathea, named Joseph, who had himself become a disciple of Jesus. [58]Going to Pilate, he asked for Jesus' body, and Pilate ordered that it be given to him. [59]Joseph took the body, wrapped it in a clean linen cloth, [60]and placed it in his own new tomb that he had cut out of the rock. He rolled a big stone in front of the entrance to the tomb and went away. [61]Mary Magdalene and the other Mary were sitting there across from the tomb.

The Guard at the Tomb

[62]The next day, the one after Preparation Day, the chief priests and the Pharisees went to Pilate. [63]"Sir," they said, "we remember that while he was still alive that deceiver said, 'After three days I will rise again.' [64]So give the order for the tomb to be made secure until the third day. Otherwise, his disciples may come and steal the body and tell the people that he has been raised from the dead. This last deception will be worse than the first."

[65]"Take a guard," Pilate answered. "Go, make the tomb as secure as you know how." [66]So they went and made the tomb secure by putting a seal on the stone and posting the guard.

The Resurrection

28 After the Sabbath, at dawn on the first day of the week, Mary Magdalene and the other Mary went to look at the tomb.

[2]There was a violent earthquake, for an angel of the Lord came down from heaven and, going to the tomb, rolled back the stone and sat on it. [3]His appearance was like lightning, and his clothes were white as snow. [4]The guards were so afraid of him that they shook and became like dead men.

[c]46 Some manuscripts *Eli, Eli*   [d]46 Psalm 22:1
[e]54 Or *a son*

5The angel said to the women, "Do not be afraid, for I know that you are looking for Jesus, who was crucified. 6He is not here; he has risen, just as he said. Come and see the place where he lay. 7Then go quickly and tell his disciples: 'He has risen from the dead and is going ahead of you into Galilee. There you will see him.' Now I have told you."

8So the women hurried away from the tomb, afraid yet filled with joy, and ran to tell his disciples. 9Suddenly Jesus met them. "Greetings," he said. They came to him, clasped his feet and worshipped him. 10Then Jesus said to them, "Do not be afraid. Go and tell my brothers to go to Galilee; there they will see me."

The Guards' Report

11While the women were on their way, some of the guards went into the city and reported to the chief priests everything that had happened. 12When the chief priests had met with the elders and devised a plan, they gave the soldiers a large sum of money, 13telling them, "You are to say, 'His disciples came during the night and stole him away while we were asleep.' 14If this report gets to the governor, we will satisfy him and keep you out of trouble." 15So the soldiers took the money and did as they were instructed. And this story has been widely circulated among the Jews to this very day.

The Great Commission

16Then the eleven disciples went to Galilee, to the mountain where Jesus had told them to go. 17When they saw him, they worshipped him; but some doubted. 18Then Jesus came to them and said, "All authority in heaven and on earth has been given to me. 19Therefore go and make disciples of all nations, baptising them in*a* the name of the Father and of the Son and of the Holy Spirit, 20and teaching them to obey everything I have commanded you. And surely I will be with you always, to the very end of the age."

a19 Or into; see Acts 8:16; 19:5; Rom. 6:3; I Cor. 1:13; 10:2 and Gal. 3:27.

Mark

John the Baptist Prepares the Way

1 The beginning of the gospel about Jesus Christ, the Son of God.*a*

²It is written in Isaiah the prophet:

"I will send my messenger ahead
    of you,
    who will prepare your way"*b*—
³"a voice of one calling in the
    desert,
    'Prepare the way for the Lord,
    make straight paths for him.' "*c*

⁴And so John came, baptising in the desert region and preaching a baptism of repentance for the forgiveness of sins. ⁵The whole Judean countryside and all the people of Jerusalem went out to him. Confessing their sins, they were baptised by him in the Jordan River. ⁶John wore clothing made of camel's hair, with a leather belt round his waist, and he ate locusts and wild honey. ⁷And this was his message: "After me will come one more powerful than I, the thongs of whose sandals I am not worthy to stoop down and untie. ⁸I baptise you with*d* water, but he will baptise you with the Holy Spirit."

The Baptism and Temptation of Jesus

⁹At that time Jesus came from Nazareth in Galilee and was baptised by John in the Jordan. ¹⁰As Jesus was coming up out of the water, he saw heaven being torn open and the Spirit descending on him like a dove. ¹¹And a voice came from heaven: "You are my Son, whom I love; with you I am well pleased."

¹²At once the Spirit sent him out into the desert, ¹³and he was in the desert for forty days, being tempted by Satan. He was with the wild animals, and angels attended him.

The Calling of the First Disciples

¹⁴After John was put in prison, Jesus went into Galilee, proclaiming the good news of God. ¹⁵"The time has come," he said. "The kingdom of God is near. Repent and believe the good news!"

¹⁶As Jesus walked beside the Sea of Galilee, he saw Simon and his brother Andrew casting a net into the lake, for they were fishermen. ¹⁷"Come, follow me," Jesus said, "and I will make you fishers of men." ¹⁸At once they left their nets and followed him.

¹⁹When he had gone a little farther, he saw James son of Zebedee and his brother John in a boat, preparing their nets. ²⁰Without delay he called them, and they left their father Zebedee in the boat with the hired men and followed him.

Jesus Drives Out an Evil Spirit

²¹They went to Capernaum, and when the Sabbath came, Jesus went into the synagogue and began to teach. ²²The people were amazed at his teaching, because he taught them as one who had authority, not as the teachers of the law. ²³Just then a man in their synagogue who was possessed by an evil*e* spirit cried out, ²⁴"What do you want with us, Jesus of Nazareth? Have you come to destroy us? I know who you are—the Holy One of God!"

*a*1 Some manuscripts do not have *the Son of God.*   *b*2 Mal. 3:1   *c*3 Isaiah 40:3
*d*8 Or *in*   *e*23 Greek *unclean*; also in verses 26 and 27

25"Be quiet!" said Jesus sternly. "Come out of him!" 26The evil spirit shook the man violently and came out of him with a shriek.

27The people were all so amazed that they asked each other, "What is this? A new teaching—and with authority! He even gives orders to evil spirits and they obey him." 28News about him spread quickly over the whole region of Galilee.

Jesus Heals Many

29As soon as they left the synagogue, they went with James and John to the home of Simon and Andrew. 30Simon's mother-in-law was in bed with a fever, and they told Jesus about her. 31So he went to her, took her hand and helped her up. The fever left her and she began to wait on them.

32That evening after sunset the people brought to Jesus all the sick and demon-possessed. 33The whole town gathered at the door, 34and Jesus healed many who had various diseases. He also drove out many demons, but he would not let the demons speak because they knew who he was.

Jesus Prays in a Solitary Place

35Very early in the morning, while it was still dark, Jesus got up, left the house and went off to a solitary place, where he prayed. 36Simon and his companions went to look for him, 37and when they found him, they exclaimed: "Everyone is looking for you!"

38Jesus replied, "Let us go somewhere else—to the nearby villages—so that I can preach there also. That is why I have come." 39So he travelled throughout Galilee, preaching in their synagogues and driving out demons.

A Man With Leprosy

40A man with leprosy[f] came to him and begged him on his knees, "If you are willing, you can make me clean." 41Filled with compassion, Jesus reached out his hand and touched the man. "I am willing," he said. "Be

clean!" 42Immediately the leprosy left him and he was cured.

43Jesus sent him away at once with a strong warning: 44"See that you don't tell this to anyone. But go, show yourself to the priest and offer the sacrifices that Moses commanded for your cleansing, as a testimony to them." 45Instead he went out and began to talk freely, spreading the news. As a result, Jesus could no longer enter a town openly but stayed outside in lonely places. Yet the people still came to him from everywhere.

Jesus Heals a Paralytic

2 A few days later, when Jesus again entered Capernaum, the people heard that he had come home. 2So many gathered that there was no room left, not even outside the door, and he preached the word to them. 3Some men came, bringing to him a paralytic, carried by four of them. 4Since they could not get him to Jesus because of the crowd, they made an opening in the roof above Jesus and, after digging through it, lowered the mat the paralysed man was lying on. 5When Jesus saw their faith, he said to the paralytic, "Son, your sins are forgiven."

6Now some teachers of the law were sitting there, thinking to themselves, 7"Why does this fellow talk like that? He's blaspheming! Who can forgive sins but God alone?"

8Immediately Jesus knew in his spirit that this was what they were thinking in their hearts, and he said to them, "Why are you thinking these things? 9Which is easier: to say to the paralytic, 'Your sins are forgiven,' or to say, 'Get up, take your mat and walk'? 10But that you may know that the Son of Man has authority on earth to forgive sins. . . ." He said to the paralytic, 11"I tell you, get up, take your mat and go home." 12He got up, took his mat and walked out in full view of them all. This amazed everyone and they praised God, saying, "We have never seen anything like this!"

f40 The Greek word was used for various diseases affecting the skin—not necessarily leprosy.

39

The Calling of Levi

13Once again Jesus went out beside the lake. A large crowd came to him, and he began to teach them. 14As he walked along, he saw Levi son of Alphaeus sitting at the tax collector's booth. "Follow me," Jesus told him, and Levi got up and followed him.

15While Jesus was having dinner at Levi's house, many tax collectors and "sinners" were eating with him and his disciples, for there were many who followed him. 16When the teachers of the law who were Pharisees saw him eating with the "sinners" and tax collectors, they asked his disciples: "Why does he eat with tax collectors and 'sinners'?"

17On hearing this, Jesus said to them, "It is not the healthy who need a doctor, but the sick. I have not come to call the righteous, but sinners."

Jesus Questioned About Fasting

18Now John's disciples and the Pharisees were fasting. Some people came and asked Jesus, "How is it that John's disciples and the disciples of the Pharisees are fasting, but yours are not?"

19Jesus answered, "How can the guests of the bridegroom fast while he is with them? They cannot, so long as they have him with them. 20But the time will come when the bridegroom will be taken from them, and on that day they will fast.

21"No-one sews a patch of unshrunk cloth on an old garment. If he does, the new piece will pull away from the old, making the tear worse. 22And no-one pours new wine into old wineskins. If he does, the wine will burst the skins, and both the wine and the wineskins will be ruined. No, he pours new wine into new wineskins."

Lord of the Sabbath

23One Sabbath Jesus was going through the cornfields, and as his disciples walked along, they began to pick some ears of corn. 24The Pharisees said to him, "Look, why are they doing what is unlawful on the Sabbath?"

25He answered, "Have you never read what David did when he and his companions were hungry and in need? 26In the days of Abiathar the high priest, he entered the house of God and ate the consecrated bread, which is lawful only for priests to eat. And he also gave some to his companions."

27Then he said to them, "The Sabbath was made for man, not man for the Sabbath. 28So the Son of Man is Lord even of the Sabbath."

3 Another time he went into the synagogue, and a man with a shrivelled hand was there. 2Some of them were looking for a reason to accuse Jesus, so they watched him closely to see if he would heal him on the Sabbath. 3Jesus said to the man with the shrivelled hand, "Stand up in front of everyone."

4Then Jesus asked them, "Which is lawful on the Sabbath: to do good or to do evil, to save life or to kill?" But they remained silent.

5He looked round at them in anger and, deeply distressed at their stubborn hearts, said to the man, "Stretch out your hand." He stretched it out, and his hand was completely restored. 6Then the Pharisees went out and began to plot with the Herodians how they might kill Jesus.

Crowds Follow Jesus

7Jesus withdrew with his disciples to the lake, and a large crowd from Galilee followed. 8When they heard all he was doing, many people came to him from Judea, Jerusalem, Idumea, and the regions across the Jordan and around Tyre and Sidon. 9Because of the crowd he told his disciples to have a small boat ready for him, to keep the people from crowding him. 10For he had healed many, so that those with diseases were pushing forward to touch him. 11Whenever the evil*a* spirits saw him, they fell down before him and cried out, "You are the Son of God." 12But

*a*11 Greek *unclean*; also in verse 30

he gave them strict orders not to tell who he was.

The Appointing of the Twelve Apostles

13Jesus went up into the hills and called to him those he wanted, and they came to him. 14He appointed twelve—designating them apostles[b]— that they might be with him and that he might send them out to preach 15and to have authority to drive out demons. 16These are the twelve he appointed: Simon (to whom he gave the name Peter); 17James son of Zebedee, and his brother John (to them he gave the name Boanerges, which means Sons of Thunder); 18Andrew, Philip, Bartholomew, Matthew, Thomas, James son of Alphaeus, Thaddaeus, Simon the Zealot 19and Judas Iscariot, who betrayed him.

Jesus and Beelzebub

20Then Jesus entered a house, and again a crowd gathered, so that he and his disciples were not even able to eat. 21When his family heard about this, they went to take charge of him, for they said, "He is out of his mind." 22And the teachers of the law who came down from Jerusalem said, "He is possessed by Beelzebub![c] By the prince of demons he is driving out demons."

23So Jesus called them and spoke to them in parables: "How can Satan drive out Satan? 24If a kingdom is divided against itself, that kingdom cannot stand. 25If a house is divided against itself, that house cannot stand. 26And if Satan opposes himself and is divided, he cannot stand; his end has come. 27In fact, no-one can enter a strong man's house and carry off his possessions unless he first ties up the strong man. Then he can rob his house. 28I tell you the truth, all the sins and blasphemies of men will be forgiven. 29But whoever blasphemes against the Holy Spirit will never be forgiven; he is guilty of an eternal sin."

30He said this because they were saying, "He has an evil spirit."

Jesus' Mother and Brothers

31Then Jesus' mother and brothers arrived. Standing outside, they sent someone in to call him. 32A crowd was sitting around him, and they told him, "Your mother and brothers are outside looking for you."

33"Who are my mother and my brothers?" he asked.

34Then he looked at those seated in a circle around him and said, "Here are my mother and my brothers! 35Whoever does God's will is my brother and sister and mother."

The Parable of the Sower

4 On another occasion Jesus began to teach by the lake. The crowd that gathered round him was so large that he got into a boat and sat in it out on the lake, while all the people were along the shore at the water's edge. 2He taught them many things by parables, and in his teaching said: 3"Listen! A farmer went out to sow his seed. 4As he was scattering the seed, some fell along the path, and the birds came and ate it up. 5Some fell on rocky places, where it did not have much soil. It sprang up quickly, because the soil was shallow. 6But when the sun came up, the plants were scorched, and they withered because they had no root. 7Other seed fell among thorns, which grew up and choked the plants, so that they did not bear grain. 8Still other seed fell on good soil. It came up, grew and produced a crop, multiplying thirty, sixty, or even a hundred times."

9Then Jesus said, "He who has ears to hear, let him hear."

10When he was alone, the Twelve and the others around him asked him about the parables. 11He told them, "The secret of the kingdom of God has been given to you. But to those on the outside everything is said in parables 12so that,

" 'they may be ever seeing but
never perceiving,
and ever hearing but never
understanding;

b14 Some manuscripts do not have *designating them apostles*.
c22 Greek *Beezeboul* or *Beelzeboul*

41

otherwise they might turn and be forgiven!'*"

13Then Jesus said to them, "Don't you understand this parable? How then will you understand any parable? 14The farmer sows the word. 15Some people are like seed along the path, where the word is sown. As soon as they hear it, Satan comes and takes away the word that was sown in them. 16Others, like seed sown on rocky places, hear the word and at once receive it with joy. 17But since they have no root, they last only a short time. When trouble or persecution comes because of the word, they quickly fall away. 18Still others, like seed sown among thorns, hear the word; 19but the worries of this life, the deceitfulness of wealth and the desires for other things come in and choke the word, making it unfruitful. 20Others, like seed sown on good soil, hear the word, accept it, and produce a crop — thirty, sixty or even a hundred times what was sown."

A Lamp on a Stand

21He said to them, "Do you bring in a lamp to put it under a bowl or a bed? Instead, don't you put it on its stand? 22For whatever is hidden is meant to be disclosed, and whatever is concealed is meant to be brought out into the open. 23If anyone has ears to hear, let him hear."

24"Consider carefully what you hear," he continued. "With the measure you use, it will be measured to you—and even more. 25Whoever has will be given more; whoever does not have, even what he has will be taken from him."

The Parable of the Growing Seed

26He also said, "This is what the kingdom of God is like. A man scatters seed on the ground. 27Night and day, whether he sleeps or gets up, the seed sprouts and grows, though he does not know how. 28All by itself the soil produces corn—first the stalk, then the ear, then the full kernel in the ear. 29As soon as the grain is ripe,

he puts the sickle to it, because the harvest has come."

The Parable of the Mustard Seed

30Again he said, "What shall we say the kingdom of God is like, or what parable shall we use to describe it? 31It is like a mustard seed, which is the smallest seed you plant in the ground. 32Yet when planted, it grows and becomes the largest of all garden plants, with such big branches that the birds of the air can perch in its shade."

33With many similar parables Jesus spoke the word to them, as much as they could understand. 34He did not say anything to them without using a parable. But when he was alone with his own disciples, he explained everything.

Jesus Calms the Storm

35That day when evening came, he said to his disciples, "Let us go over to the other side." 36Leaving the crowd behind, they took him along, just as he was, in the boat. There were also other boats with him. 37A furious squall came up, and the waves broke over the boat, so that it was nearly swamped. 38Jesus was in the stern, sleeping on a cushion. The disciples woke him and said to him, "Teacher, don't you care if we drown?"

39He got up, rebuked the wind and said to the waves, "Quiet! Be still!" Then the wind died down and it was completely calm.

40He said to his disciples, "Why are you so afraid? Do you still have no faith?"

41They were terrified and asked each other, "Who is this? Even the wind and the waves obey him!"

The Healing of a Demon-Possessed Man

5 They went across the lake to the region of the Gerasenes.* 2When Jesus got out of the boat, a man with an evil* spirit came from the tombs to meet him. 3This man lived in the

*12 Isaiah 6:9,10   *1 Some manuscripts Gadarenes; other manuscripts Gergesenes
*2 Greek unclean; also in verses 8 and 13

tombs, and no-one could bind him any more, not even with a chain. 4For he had often been chained hand and foot, but he tore the chains apart and broke the irons on his feet. No-one was strong enough to subdue him. 5Night and day among the tombs and in the hills he would cry out and cut himself with stones.

6When he saw Jesus from a distance, he ran and fell on his knees in front of him. 7He shouted at the top of his voice, "What do you want with me, Jesus, Son of the Most High God? Swear to God that you won't torture me!" 8For Jesus was saying to him, "Come out of this man, you evil spirit!"

9Then Jesus asked him, "What is your name?"

"My name is Legion," he replied, "for we are many." 10And he begged Jesus again and again not to send them out of the area.

11A large herd of pigs was feeding on the nearby hillside. 12The demons begged Jesus, "Send us among the pigs; allow us to go into them." 13He gave them permission, and the evil spirits came out and went into the pigs. The herd, about two thousand in number, rushed down the steep bank into the lake and were drowned.

14Those tending the pigs ran off and reported this in the town and countryside, and the people went out to see what had happened. 15When they came to Jesus, they saw the man who had been possessed by the legion of demons, sitting there, dressed and in his right mind; and they were afraid. 16Those who had seen it told the people what had happened to the demon-possessed man—and told about the pigs as well. 17Then the people began to plead with Jesus to leave their region.

18As Jesus was getting into the boat, the man who had been demon-possessed begged to go with him. 19Jesus did not let him, but said, "Go home to your family and tell them how much the Lord has done for you, and how he has had mercy on you." 20So the man went away and began to tell in

the Decapolis[c] how much Jesus had done for him. And all the people were amazed.

A Dead Girl and a Sick Woman

21When Jesus had again crossed over by boat to the other side of the lake, a large crowd gathered round him. While he was by the lake, 22one of the synagogue rulers, named Jairus, came there. Seeing Jesus, he fell at his feet 23and pleaded earnestly with him, "My little daughter is dying. Please come and put your hands on her so that she will be healed and live." 24So Jesus went with him.

A large crowd followed and pressed around him. 25And a woman was there who had been subject to bleeding for twelve years. 26She had suffered a great deal under the care of many doctors and had spent all she had, yet instead of getting better she grew worse. 27When she heard about Jesus, she came up behind him in the crowd and touched his cloak, 28because she thought, "If I just touch his clothes, I will be healed." 29Immediately her bleeding stopped and she felt in her body that she was freed from her suffering.

30At once Jesus realised that power had gone out from him. He turned around in the crowd and asked, "Who touched my clothes?"

31"You see the people crowding against you," his disciples answered, "and yet you can ask, 'Who touched me?'"

32But Jesus kept looking around to see who had done it. 33Then the woman, knowing what had happened to her, came and fell at his feet and, trembling with fear, told him the whole truth. 34He said to her, "Daughter, your faith has healed you. Go in peace and be freed from your suffering."

35While Jesus was still speaking, some men came from the house of Jairus, the synagogue ruler. "Your daughter is dead," they said. "Why bother the teacher any more?"

36Ignoring what they said, Jesus

c20 That is, the Ten Cities

told the synagogue ruler, "Don't be afraid; just believe."

[37]He did not let anyone follow him except Peter, James and John the brother of James. [38]When they came to the home of the synagogue ruler, Jesus saw a commotion, with people crying and wailing loudly. [39]He went in and said to them, "Why all this commotion and wailing? The child is not dead but asleep." [40]But they laughed at him.

After he put them all out, he took the child's father and mother and the disciples who were with him, and went in where the child was. [41]He took her by the hand and said to her, "*Talitha koum!*" (which means, "Little girl, I say to you, get up!"). [42]Immediately the girl stood up and walked around (she was twelve years old). At this they were completely astonished. [43]He gave strict orders not to let anyone know about this, and told them to give her something to eat.

A Prophet Without Honour

6 Jesus left there and went to his home town, accompanied by his disciples. [2]When the Sabbath came, he began to teach in the synagogue, and many who heard him were amazed.

"Where did this man get these things?" they asked. "What's this wisdom that has been given him, that he even does miracles! [3]Isn't this the carpenter? Isn't this Mary's son and the brother of James, Joses, Judas and Simon? Aren't his sisters here with us?" And they took offence at him.

[4]Jesus said to them, "Only in his home town, among his relatives and in his own house is a prophet without honour." [5]He could not do any miracles there, except lay his hands on a few sick people and heal them. [6]And he was amazed at their lack of faith.

Jesus Sends Out the Twelve

Then Jesus went round teaching from village to village. [7]Calling the Twelve to him, he sent them out two

by two and gave them authority over evil[a] spirits.

[8]These were his instructions: "Take nothing for the journey except a staff—no bread, no bag, no money in your belts. [9]Wear sandals but not an extra tunic. [10]Whenever you enter a house, stay there until you leave that town. [11]And if any place will not welcome you or listen to you, shake the dust off your feet when you leave, as a testimony against them."

[12]They went out and preached that people should repent. [13]They drove out many demons and anointed many sick people with oil and healed them.

John the Baptist Beheaded

[14]King Herod heard about this, for Jesus' name had become well known. Some were saying,[b] "John the Baptist has been raised from the dead, and that is why miraculous powers are at work in him."

[15]Others said, "He is Elijah."

And still others claimed, "He is a prophet, like one of the prophets of long ago."

[16]But when Herod heard this, he said, "John, the man I beheaded, has been raised from the dead!"

[17]For Herod himself had given orders to have John arrested, and he had him bound and put in prison. He did this because of Herodias, his brother Philip's wife, whom he had married. [18]For John had been saying to Herod, "It is not lawful for you to have your brother's wife." [19]So Herodias nursed a grudge against John and wanted to kill him. But she was not able to, [20]because Herod feared John and protected him, knowing him to be a righteous and holy man. When Herod heard John, he was greatly puzzled;[c] yet he liked to listen to him.

[21]Finally the opportune time came. On his birthday Herod gave a banquet for his high officials and military commanders and the leading men of Galilee. [22]When the daughter of Herodias came in and danced, she pleased Herod and his dinner guests.

The king said to the girl, "Ask me

[a]7 Greek *unclean* [b]14 Some early manuscripts *He was saying* [c]20 Some early manuscripts *he did many things*

for anything you want, and I'll give it to you." 23And he promised her with an oath, "Whatever you ask I will give you, up to half my kingdom."

24She went out and said to her mother, "What shall I ask for?"

"The head of John the Baptist," she answered.

25At once the girl hurried in to the king with the request: "I want you to give me right now the head of John the Baptist on a platter."

26The king was greatly distressed, but because of his oaths and his dinner guests, he did not want to refuse her. 27So he immediately sent an executioner with orders to bring John's head. The man went, beheaded John in the prison, 28and brought back his head on a platter. He presented it to the girl, and she gave it to her mother. 29On hearing of this, John's disciples came and took his body and laid it in a tomb.

Jesus Feeds the Five Thousand

30The apostles gathered round Jesus and reported to him all they had done and taught. 31Then, because so many people were coming and going that they did not even have a chance to eat, he said to them, "Come with me by yourselves to a quiet place and get some rest."

32So they went away by themselves in a boat to a solitary place. 33But many who saw them leaving recognised them and ran on foot from all the towns and got there ahead of them. 34When Jesus landed and saw a large crowd, he had compassion on them, because they were like sheep without a shepherd. So he began teaching them many things.

35By this time it was late in the day, so his disciples came to him. "This is a remote place," they said, "and it's already very late. 36Send the people away so that they can go to the surrounding countryside and villages and buy themselves something to eat."

37But he answered, "You give them something to eat."

They said to him, "That would take

d37 Greek take two hundred denarii

eight months of a man's wages!d Are we to go and spend that much on bread and give it to them to eat?"

38"How many loaves do you have?" he asked. "Go and see."

When they found out, they said, "Five—and two fish."

39Then Jesus directed them to have all the people sit down in groups on the green grass. 40So they sat down in groups of hundreds and fifties. 41Taking the five loaves and the two fish and looking up to heaven, he gave thanks and broke the loaves. Then he gave them to his disciples to set before the people. He also divided the two fish among them all. 42They all ate and were satisfied, 43and the disciples picked up twelve basketfuls of broken pieces of bread and fish. 44The number of the men who had eaten was five thousand.

Jesus Walks on the Water

45Immediately Jesus made his disciples get into the boat and go on ahead of him to Bethsaida, while he dismissed the crowd. 46After leaving them, he went into the hills to pray.

47When evening came, the boat was in the middle of the lake, and he was alone on land. 48He saw the disciples straining at the oars, because the wind was against them. About the fourth watch of the night he went out to them, walking on the lake. He was about to pass by them, 49but when they saw him walking on the lake, they thought he was a ghost. They cried out, 50because they all saw him and were terrified.

Immediately he spoke to them and said, "Take courage! It is I. Don't be afraid." 51Then he climbed into the boat with them, and the wind died down. They were completely amazed, 52for they had not understood about the loaves; their hearts were hardened.

53When they had crossed over, they landed at Gennesaret and anchored there. 54As soon as they got out of the boat, people recognised Jesus. 55They ran throughout that whole region and carried the sick on mats to wherever

45

they heard he was. 56And everywhere he went—into villages, towns or countryside—they placed the sick in the market-places. They begged him to let them touch even the edge of his cloak, and all who touched him were healed.

Clean and Unclean

7 The Pharisees and some of the teachers of the law who had come from Jerusalem gathered round Jesus and 2saw some of his disciples eating food with "unclean"—that is, ceremonially unwashed—hands. 3[The Pharisees and all the Jews do not eat unless they give their hands a ceremonial washing, holding to the tradition of the elders. 4When they come from the market-place they do not eat unless they wash. And they observe many other traditions, such as the washing of cups, pitchers and kettles.*a*]

5So the Pharisees and teachers of the law asked Jesus, "Why don't your disciples live according to the tradition of the elders instead of eating their food with 'unclean' hands?"

6He replied, "Isaiah was right when he prophesied about you hypocrites; as it is written:

" 'These people honour me with
     their lips,
   but their hearts are far from me.
7They worship me in vain;
     their teachings are but rules
       taught by men.'*b*

8You have let go of the commands of God and are holding on to the traditions of men."

9And he said to them: "You have a fine way of setting aside the commands of God in order to observe*c* your own traditions! 10For Moses said, 'Honour your father and mother,'*d* and, 'Anyone who curses his father or mother must be put to death.'*e* 11But you say that if a man says to his father or mother: 'Whatever help you might otherwise have received from me is Corban' (that is, a gift devoted

to God), 12then you no longer let him do anything for his father or mother. 13Thus you nullify the word of God by your tradition that you have handed down. And you do many things like that."

14Again Jesus called the crowd to him and said, "Listen to me, everyone, and understand this. 15Nothing outside a man can make him 'unclean' by going into him. Rather, it is what comes out of a man that makes him 'unclean'."*f*

17After he had left the crowd and entered the house, his disciples asked him about this parable. 18"Are you so dull?" he asked. "Don't you see that nothing that enters a man from the outside can make him 'unclean'? 19For it doesn't go into his heart but into his stomach, and then out of his body." (In saying this, Jesus declared all foods "clean".)

20He went on: "What comes out of a man is what makes him 'unclean'. 21For from within, out of men's hearts, come evil thoughts, sexual immorality, theft, murder, adultery, 22greed, malice, deceit, lewdness, envy, slander, arrogance and folly. 23All these evils come from inside and make a man 'unclean'."

The Faith of a Syro-Phoenician Woman

24Jesus left that place and went to the vicinity of Tyre.*g* He entered a house and did not want anyone to know it; yet he could not keep his presence secret. 25In fact, as soon as she heard about him, a woman whose little daughter was possessed by an evil*h* spirit came and fell at his feet. 26The woman was a Greek, born in Syrian Phoenicia. She begged Jesus to drive the demon out of her daughter.

27"First let the children eat all they want," he told her, "for it is not right to take the children's bread and toss it to their dogs."

28"Yes, Lord," she replied, "but

---

*a*4 Some early manuscripts *pitchers, kettles and dining couches*   *b*6,7 Isaiah 29:13
*c*9 Some manuscripts *set up*   *d*10 Exodus 20:12; Deut. 5:16   *e*10 Exodus 21:17; Lev. 20:9
*f*15 Some early manuscripts *'unclean'.* *16If anyone has ears to hear, let him hear.*
*g*24 Many early manuscripts *Tyre and Sidon*   *h*25 Greek *unclean*

even the dogs under the table eat the children's crumbs."

29Then he told her, "For such a reply, you may go; the demon has left your daughter."

30She went home and found her child lying on the bed, and the demon gone.

The Healing of a Deaf and Dumb Man

31Then Jesus left the vicinity of Tyre and went through Sidon, down to the Sea of Galilee and into the region of the Decapolis.*i* 32There some people brought a man to him who was deaf and could hardly talk, and they begged him to place his hand on the man.

33After he took him aside, away from the crowd, Jesus put his fingers into the man's ears. Then he spat and touched the man's tongue. 34He looked up to heaven and with a deep sigh said to him, "*Ephphatha!*" (which means, "Be opened!"). 35At this, the man's ears were opened, his tongue was loosened and he began to speak plainly.

36Jesus commanded them not to tell anyone. But the more he did so, the more they kept talking about it. 37People were overwhelmed with amazement. "He has done everything well," they said. "He even makes the deaf hear and the dumb speak."

Jesus Feeds the Four Thousand

8 During those days another large crowd gathered. Since they had nothing to eat, Jesus called his disciples to him and said, 2"I have compassion for these people; they have already been with me three days and have nothing to eat. 3If I send them home hungry, they will collapse on the way, because some of them have come a long distance."

4His disciples answered, "But where in this remote place can anyone get enough bread to feed them?"

5"How many loaves do you have?" Jesus asked.

"Seven," they replied.

i31 That is, the Ten Cities

6He told the crowd to sit down on the ground. When he had taken the seven loaves and given thanks, he broke them and gave them to his disciples to set before the people, and they did so. 7They had a few small fish as well; he gave thanks for them also and told the disciples to distribute them. 8The people ate and were satisfied. Afterwards the disciples picked up seven basketfuls of broken pieces that were left over. 9About four thousand men were present. And having sent them away, 10he got into the boat with his disciples and went to the region of Dalmanutha.

11The Pharisees came and began to question Jesus. To test him, they asked him for a sign from heaven. 12He sighed deeply and said, "Why does this generation ask for a miraculous sign? I tell you the truth, no sign will be given to it." 13Then he left them, got back into the boat and crossed to the other side.

The Yeast of the Pharisees and Herod

14The disciples had forgotten to bring bread, except for one loaf they had with them in the boat. 15"Be careful," Jesus warned them. "Watch out for the yeast of the Pharisees and that of Herod."

16They discussed this with one another and said, "It is because we have no bread."

17Aware of their discussion, Jesus asked them: "Why are you talking about having no bread? Do you still not see or understand? Are your hearts hardened? 18Do you have eyes but fail to see, and ears but fail to hear? And don't you remember? 19When I broke the five loaves for the five thousand, how many basketfuls of pieces did you pick up?"

"Twelve," they replied.

20"And when I broke the seven loaves for the four thousand, how many basketfuls of pieces did you pick up?"

They answered, "Seven."

21He said to them, "Do you still not understand?"

The Healing of a Blind Man at Bethsaida

22They came to Bethsaida, and some people brought a blind man and begged Jesus to touch him. 23He took the blind man by the hand and led him outside the village. When he had spat on the man's eyes and put his hands on him, Jesus asked, "Do you see anything?"

24He looked up and said, "I see people; they look like trees walking around."

25Once more Jesus put his hands on the man's eyes. Then his eyes were opened, his sight was restored, and he saw everything clearly. 26Jesus sent him home, saying, "Don't go into the village."[a]

Peter's Confession of Christ

27Jesus and his disciples went on to the villages around Caesarea Philippi. On the way he asked them, "Who do people say I am?"

28They replied, "Some say John the Baptist; others say Elijah; and still others, one of the prophets."

29"But what about you?" he asked. "Who do you say I am?"

Peter answered, "You are the Christ."[b]

30Jesus warned them not to tell anyone about him.

Jesus Predicts His Death

31He then began to teach them that the Son of Man must suffer many things and be rejected by the elders, chief priests and teachers of the law, and that he must be killed and after three days rise again. 32He spoke plainly about this, and Peter took him aside and began to rebuke him.

33But when Jesus turned and looked at his disciples, he rebuked Peter. "Out of my sight, Satan!" he said. "You do not have in mind the things of God, but the things of men."

34Then he called the crowd to him along with his disciples and said: "If anyone would come after me, he must deny himself and take up his cross and follow me. 35For whoever wants to save his life[c] will lose it, but whoever loses his life for me and for the gospel will save it. 36What good is it for a man to gain the whole world, yet forfeit his soul? 37Or what can a man give in exchange for his soul? 38If anyone is ashamed of me and my words in this adulterous and sinful generation, the Son of Man will be ashamed of him when he comes in his Father's glory with the holy angels."

9 And he said to them, "I tell you the truth, some who are standing here will not taste death before they see the kingdom of God come with power."

The Transfiguration

2After six days Jesus took Peter, James and John with him and led them up a high mountain, where they were all alone. There he was transfigured before them. 3His clothes became dazzling white, whiter than anyone in the world could bleach them. 4And there appeared before them Elijah and Moses, who were talking with Jesus.

5Peter said to Jesus, "Rabbi, it is good for us to be here. Let us put up three shelters—one for you, one for Moses and one for Elijah." 6(He did not know what to say, they were so frightened.)

7Then a cloud appeared and enveloped them, and a voice came from the cloud: "This is my Son, whom I love. Listen to him!"

8Suddenly, when they looked round, they no longer saw anyone with them except Jesus.

9As they were coming down the mountain, Jesus gave them orders not to tell anyone what they had seen until the Son of Man had risen from the dead. 10They kept the matter to themselves, discussing what "rising from the dead" meant.

11And they asked him, "Why do the teachers of the law say that Elijah must come first?"

a26 Some manuscripts Don't go and tell anyone in the village
b29 Or Messiah. "The Christ" (Greek) and "the Messiah" (Hebrew) both mean "the Anointed One".
c35 The Greek word means either life or soul; also in verse 36.

12Jesus replied, "To be sure, Elijah does come first, and restores all things. Why then is it written that the Son of Man must suffer much and be rejected? 13But I tell you, Elijah has come, and they have done to him everything they wished, just as it is written about him."

The Healing of a Boy With an Evil Spirit

14When they came to the other disciples, they saw a large crowd around them and the teachers of the law arguing with them. 15As soon as all the people saw Jesus, they were overwhelmed with wonder and ran to greet him.

16"What are you arguing with them about?" he asked.

17A man in the crowd answered, "Teacher, I brought you my son, who is possessed by a spirit that has robbed him of speech. 18Whenever it seizes him, it throws him to the ground. He foams at the mouth, gnashes his teeth and becomes rigid. I asked your disciples to drive out the spirit, but they could not."

19"O unbelieving generation," Jesus replied, "how long shall I stay with you? How long shall I put up with you? Bring the boy to me."

20So they brought him. When the spirit saw Jesus, it immediately threw the boy into a convulsion. He fell to the ground and rolled around, foaming at the mouth.

21Jesus asked the boy's father, "How long has he been like this?"

"From childhood," he answered. 22"It has often thrown him into fire or water to kill him. But if you can do anything, take pity on us and help us."

23" 'If you can'?" said Jesus. "Everything is possible for him who believes."

24Immediately the boy's father exclaimed, "I do believe; help me overcome my unbelief!"

25When Jesus saw that a crowd was running to the scene, he rebuked the evila spirit. "You deaf and dumb spirit," he said, "I command you,

come out of him and never enter him again."

26The spirit shrieked, convulsed him violently and came out. The boy looked so much like a corpse that many said, "He's dead." 27But Jesus took him by the hand and lifted him to his feet, and he stood up.

28After Jesus had gone indoors, his disciples asked him privately, "Why couldn't we drive it out?"

29He replied, "This kind can come out only by prayer."b

30They left that place and passed through Galilee. Jesus did not want anyone to know where they were, 31because he was teaching his disciples. He said to them, "The Son of Man is going to be betrayed into the hands of men. They will kill him, and after three days he will rise." 32But they did not understand what he meant and were afraid to ask him about it.

Who Is the Greatest?

33They came to Capernaum. When he was in the house, he asked them, "What were you arguing about on the road?" 34But they kept quiet because on the way they had argued about who was the greatest.

35Sitting down, Jesus called the Twelve and said, "If anyone wants to be first, he must be the very last, and the servant of all."

36He took a little child and had him stand among them. Taking him in his arms, he said to them, 37"Whoever welcomes one of these little children in my name welcomes me; and whoever welcomes me does not welcome me but the one who sent me."

Whoever Is Not Against Us Is for Us

38"Teacher," said John, "we saw a man driving out demons in your name and we told him to stop, because he was not one of us."

39"Do not stop him," Jesus said. "No-one who does a miracle in my name can in the next moment say anything bad about me, 40for whoever is not against us is for us. 41I tell you the truth, anyone who gives you a cup

a25 Greek unclean   b29 Some manuscripts prayer and fasting

of water in my name because you belong to Christ will certainly not lose his reward.

Causing to Sin

42"And if anyone causes one of these little ones who believe in me to sin, it would be better for him to be thrown into the sea with a large millstone tied around his neck. 43If your hand causes you to sin, cut it off. It is better for you to enter life maimed than with two hands to go into hell, where the fire never goes out.c 45And if your foot causes you to sin, cut it off. It is better for you to enter life crippled than to have two feet and be thrown into hell.d 47And if your eye causes you to sin, pluck it out. It is better for you to enter the kingdom of God with one eye than to have two eyes and be thrown into hell, 48where

" 'their worm does not die,
and the fire is not quenched.'e

49Everyone will be salted with fire.

50"Salt is good, but if it loses its saltiness, how can you make it salty again? Have salt in yourselves, and be at peace with each other."

Divorce

10 Jesus then left that place and went into the region of Judea and across the Jordan. Again crowds of people came to him, and as was his custom, he taught them.

2Some Pharisees came and tested him by asking, "Is it lawful for a man to divorce his wife?"

3"What did Moses command you?" he replied.

4They said, "Moses permitted a man to write a certificate of divorce and send her away."

5"It was because your hearts were hard that Moses wrote you this law," Jesus replied. 6"But at the beginning of creation God 'made them male and female'.a 7"For this reason a man will leave his father and mother and be

united to his wife,b 8and the two will become one flesh.'c So they are no longer two, but one. 9Therefore what God has joined together, let man not separate."

10When they were in the house again, the disciples asked Jesus about this. 11He answered, "Anyone who divorces his wife and marries another woman commits adultery against her. 12And if she divorces her husband and marries another man, she commits adultery."

The Little Children and Jesus

13People were bringing little children to Jesus to have him touch them, but the disciples rebuked them. 14When Jesus saw this, he was indignant. He said to them, "Let the little children come to me, and do not hinder them, for the kingdom of God belongs to such as these. 15I tell you the truth, anyone who will not receive the kingdom of God like a little child will never enter it." 16And he took the children in his arms, put his hands on them and blessed them.

The Rich Young Man

17As Jesus started on his way, a man ran up to him and fell on his knees before him. "Good teacher," he asked, "what must I do to inherit eternal life?"

18"Why do you call me good?" Jesus answered. "No-one is good—except God alone. 19You know the commandments: 'Do not murder, do not commit adultery, do not steal, do not give false testimony, do not defraud, honour your father and mother.'d"

20"Teacher," he declared, "all these I have kept since I was a boy."

21Jesus looked at him and loved him. "One thing you lack," he said. "Go, sell everything you have and give to the poor, and you will have treasure in heaven. Then come, follow me."

22At this the man's face fell. He

---

c43 Some manuscripts out, "where/'their worm does not die, / and the fire is not quenched.'
d45 Some manuscripts hell, "where/ 'their worm does not die,/ and the fire is not quenched.'
e48 Isaiah 66:24   a6 Gen. 1:27   b7 Some early manuscripts do not have and be united to his wife.
c8 Gen. 2:24   d19 Exodus 20:12–16; Deut. 5:16–20

went away sad, because he had great wealth.

23Jesus looked around and said to his disciples, "How hard it is for the rich to enter the kingdom of God!"

24The disciples were amazed at his words. But Jesus said again, "Children, how hard it ise to enter the kingdom of God! 25It is easier for a camel to go through the eye of a needle than for a rich man to enter the kingdom of God."

26The disciples were even more amazed, and said to each other, "Who then can be saved?"

27Jesus looked at them and said, "With man this is impossible, but not with God; all things are possible with God."

28Peter said to him, "We have left everything to follow you!"

29"I tell you the truth," Jesus replied, "no-one who has left home or brothers or sisters or mother or father or children or fields for me and the gospel 30will fail to receive a hundred times as much in this present age (homes, brothers, sisters, mothers, children and fields—and with them, persecutions) and in the age to come, eternal life. 31But many who are first will be last, and the last first."

Jesus Again Predicts His Death

32They were on their way up to Jerusalem, with Jesus leading the way, and the disciples were astonished, while those who followed were afraid. Again he took the Twelve aside and told them what was going to happen to him. 33"We are going up to Jerusalem," he said, "and the Son of Man will be betrayed to the chief priests and teachers of the law. They will condemn him to death and will turn him over to the Gentiles, 34who will mock him and spit on him, flog him and kill him. Three days later he will rise."

The Request of James and John

35Then James and John, the sons of Zebedee, came to him. "Teacher," they said, "we want you to do for us whatever we ask."

36"What do you want me to do for you?" he asked.

37They replied, "Let one of us sit at your right and the other at your left in your glory."

38"You don't know what you are asking," Jesus said. "Can you drink the cup I drink or be baptised with the baptism I am baptised with?"

39"We can," they answered.

Jesus said to them, "You will drink the cup I drink and be baptised with the baptism I am baptised with, 40but to sit at my right or left is not for me to grant. These places belong to those for whom they have been prepared."

41When the ten heard about this, they became indignant with James and John. 42Jesus called them together and said, "You know that those who are regarded as rulers of the Gentiles lord it over them, and their high officials exercise authority over them. 43Not so with you. Instead, whoever wants to become great among you must be your servant, 44and whoever wants to be first must be slave of all. 45For even the Son of Man did not come to be served, but to serve, and to give his life as a ransom for many."

Blind Bartimaeus Receives His Sight

46Then they came to Jericho. As Jesus and his disciples, together with a large crowd, were leaving the city, a blind man, Bartimaeus (that is, the Son of Timaeus), was sitting by the roadside begging. 47When he heard that it was Jesus of Nazareth, he began to shout, "Jesus, Son of David, have mercy on me!"

48Many rebuked him and told him to be quiet, but he shouted all the more, "Son of David, have mercy on me!"

49Jesus stopped and said, "Call him."

So they called to the blind man, "Cheer up! On your feet! He's calling you." 50Throwing his cloak aside, he jumped to his feet and came to Jesus.

51"What do you want me to do for you?" Jesus asked him.

The blind man said, "Rabbi, I want to see."

e24 Some manuscripts is for those who trust in riches

52"Go," said Jesus, "your faith has healed you." Immediately he received his sight and followed Jesus along the road.

The Triumphal Entry

11 As they approached Jerusalem and came to Bethphage and Bethany at the Mount of Olives, Jesus sent two of his disciples, 2saying to them, "Go to the village ahead of you, and just as you enter it, you will find a colt tied there, which no-one has ever ridden. Untie it and bring it here. 3If anyone asks you, 'Why are you doing this?' tell him, 'The Lord needs it and will send it back here shortly.' "

4They went and found a colt outside in the street, tied at a doorway. As they untied it, 5some people standing there asked, "What are you doing, untying that colt?" 6They answered as Jesus had told them to, and the people let them go. 7When they brought the colt to Jesus and threw their cloaks over it, he sat on it. 8Many people spread their cloaks on the road, while others spread branches they had cut in the fields. 9Those who went ahead and those who followed shouted,

"Hosanna!"*a*

"Blessed is he who comes in the name of the Lord!"*b*

10"Blessed is the coming kingdom of our father David!"

"Hosanna in the highest!"

11Jesus entered Jerusalem and went to the temple. He looked around at everything, but since it was already late, he went out to Bethany with the Twelve.

Jesus Clears the Temple

12The next day as they were leaving Bethany, Jesus was hungry. 13Seeing in the distance a fig-tree in leaf, he went to find out if it had any fruit. When he reached it, he found nothing but leaves, because it was not the season for figs. 14Then he said to the tree, "May no-one ever eat fruit from you again." And his disciples heard him say it.

15On reaching Jerusalem, Jesus entered the temple area and began driving out those who were buying and selling there. He overturned the tables of the money changers and the benches of those selling doves, 16and would not allow anyone to carry merchandise through the temple courts. 17And as he taught them, he said, "Is it not written:

" 'My house will be called
a house of prayer for all
nations'*c*?

But you have made it 'a den of robbers'.*d*"

18The chief priests and the teachers of the law heard this and began looking for a way to kill him, for they feared him, because the whole crowd was amazed at his teaching.

19When evening came, they*e* went out of the city.

The Withered Fig-Tree

20In the morning, as they went along, they saw the fig-tree withered from the roots. 21Peter remembered and said to Jesus, "Rabbi, look! The fig-tree you cursed has withered!"

22"Have*f* faith in God," Jesus answered. 23"I tell you the truth, if anyone says to this mountain, 'Go, throw yourself into the sea,' and does not doubt in his heart but believes that what he says will happen, it will be done for him. 24Therefore I tell you, whatever you ask for in prayer, believe that you have received it, and it will be yours. 25And when you stand praying, if you hold anything against anyone, forgive him, so that your Father in heaven may forgive you your sins."*g*

---

a9 A Hebrew expression meaning "Save!" which became an exclamation of praise; also in verse 10.
b9 Psalm 118:25,26   *c17* Isaiah 56:7   *d17* Jer. 7:11   *e19* Some early manuscripts *he*
f22 Some early manuscripts *If you have*
g25 Some manuscripts *sins. 26But if you do not   forgive, neither will your Father who is in heaven forgive your sins.*

The Authority of Jesus Questioned

27They arrived again in Jerusalem, and while Jesus was walking in the temple courts, the chief priests, the teachers of the law and the elders came to him. 28"By what authority are you doing these things?" they asked. "And who gave you authority to do this?"

29Jesus replied, "I will ask you one question. Answer me, and I will tell you by what authority I am doing these things. 30John's baptism—was it from heaven, or from men? Tell me!"

31They discussed it among themselves and said, "If we say, 'From heaven,' he will ask, 'Then why didn't you believe him?' 32But if we say, 'From men'...." (They feared the people, for everyone held that John really was a prophet.)

33So they answered Jesus, "We don't know."

Jesus said, "Neither will I tell you by what authority I am doing these things."

The Parable of the Tenants

12 He then began to speak to them in parables: "A man planted a vineyard. He put a wall around it, dug a pit for the winepress and built a watchtower. Then he rented the vineyard to some farmers and went away on a journey. 2At harvest time he sent a servant to the tenants to collect from them some of the fruit of the vineyard. 3But they seized him, beat him and sent him away empty-handed. 4Then he sent another servant to them; they struck this man on the head and treated him shamefully. 5He sent still another, and that one they killed. He sent many others; some of them they beat, others they killed.

6"He had one left to send, a son, whom he loved. He sent him last of all, saying, 'They will respect my son.'

7"But the tenants said to one another, 'This is the heir. Come, let's kill him, and the inheritance will be ours.' 8So they took him and killed him, and threw him out of the vineyard.

9"What then will the owner of the vineyard do? He will come and kill those tenants and give the vineyard to others. 10Haven't you read this scripture:

" 'The stone the builders rejected
    has become the capstone;*a*
11the Lord has done this,
    and it is marvellous in our
    eyes'*b*?"

12Then they looked for a way to arrest him because they knew he had spoken the parable against them. But they were afraid of the crowd; so they left him and went away.

Paying Taxes to Caesar

13Later they sent some of the Pharisees and Herodians to Jesus to catch him in his words. 14They came to him and said, "Teacher, we know you are a man of integrity. You aren't swayed by men, because you pay no attention to who they are; but you teach the way of God in accordance with the truth. Is it right to pay taxes to Caesar or not? 15Should we pay or shouldn't we?"

But Jesus knew their hypocrisy. "Why are you trying to trap me?" he asked. "Bring me a denarius and let me look at it." 16They brought the coin, and he asked them, "Whose portrait is this? And whose inscription?"

"Caesar's," they replied.

17Then Jesus said to them, "Give to Caesar what is Caesar's and to God what is God's."

And they were amazed at him.

Marriage at the Resurrection

18Then the Sadducees, who say there is no resurrection, came to him with a question. 19"Teacher," they said, "Moses wrote for us that if a man's brother dies and leaves a wife but no children, the man must marry the widow and have children for his brother. 20Now there were seven brothers. The first one married and died without leaving any children. 21The second one married the widow, but he also died, leaving no child. It was the same with the third. 22In fact,

---

*a*10 Or *cornerstone*   *b*11 Psalm 118:22,23

53

none of the seven left any children. Last of all, the woman died too. 23At the resurrection*c* whose wife will she be, since the seven were married to her?"

24Jesus replied, "Are you not in error because you do not know the Scriptures or the power of God? 25When the dead rise, they will neither marry nor be given in marriage; they will be like the angels in heaven. 26Now about the dead rising—have you not read in the book of Moses, in the account of the bush, how God said to him, 'I am the God of Abraham, the God of Isaac, and the God of Jacob'*d*? 27He is not the God of the dead, but of the living. You are badly mistaken!"

The Greatest Commandment

28One of the teachers of the law came and heard them debating. Noticing that Jesus had given them a good answer, he asked him, "Of all the commandments, which is the most important?"

29"The most important one," answered Jesus, "is this: 'Hear, O Israel, the Lord our God, the Lord is one.*e* 30Love the Lord your God with all your heart and with all your soul and with all your mind and with all your strength.'*f* 31The second is this: 'Love your neighbour as yourself.'*g* There is no commandment greater than these."

32"Well said, teacher," the man replied. "You are right in saying that God is one and there is no other but him. 33To love him with all your heart, with all your understanding and with all your strength, and to love your neighbour as yourself is more important than all burnt offerings and sacrifices."

34When Jesus saw that he had answered wisely, he said to him, "You are not far from the kingdom of God." And from then on no-one dared ask him any more questions.

Whose Son Is the Christ?

35While Jesus was teaching in the temple courts, he asked, "How is it that the teachers of the law say that the Christ*h* is the son of David? 36David himself, speaking by the Holy Spirit, declared:

" 'The Lord said to my Lord:
  "Sit at my right hand
  until I put your enemies
    under your feet." '*i*

37David himself calls him 'Lord'. How then can he be his son?"

The large crowd listened to him with delight.

38As he taught, Jesus said, "Watch out for the teachers of the law. They like to walk around in flowing robes and be greeted in the market-places, 39and have the most important seats in the synagogues and the places of honour at banquets. 40They devour widows' houses and for a show make lengthy prayers. Such men will be punished most severely."

The Widow's Offering

41Jesus sat down opposite the place where the offerings were put and watched the crowd putting their money into the temple treasury. Many rich people threw in large amounts. 42But a poor widow came and put in two very small copper coins,*j* worth only a fraction of a penny.*k*

43Calling his disciples to him, Jesus said, "I tell you the truth, this poor widow has put more into the treasury than all the others. 44They all gave out of their wealth; but she, out of her poverty, put in everything—all she had to live on."

Signs of the End of the Age

13 As he was leaving the temple, one of his disciples said to him, "Look, Teacher! What massive stones! What magnificent buildings!"

2"Do you see all these great buildings?" replied Jesus. "Not one stone here will be left on another; every one will be thrown down."

3As Jesus was sitting on the Mount of Olives opposite the temple, Peter,

*c*23 Some manuscripts resurrection, when men rise from the dead,   *d*26 Exodus 3:6
*e*29 Or the Lord our God is one Lord   *f*30 Deut. 6:4,5   *g*31 Lev. 19:18
*h*35 Or Messiah   *i*36 Psalm 110:1   *j*42 Greek two lepta   *k*42 Greek kodrantes

James, John and Andrew asked him privately, 4"Tell us, when will these things happen? And what will be the sign that they are all about to be fulfilled?"

5Jesus said to them: "Watch out that no-one deceives you. 6Many will come in my name, claiming, 'I am he,' and will deceive many. 7When you hear of wars and rumours of wars, do not be alarmed. Such things must happen, but the end is still to come. 8Nation will rise against nation, and kingdom against kingdom. There will be earthquakes in various places, and famines. These are the beginning of birth-pains.

9"You must be on your guard. You will be handed over to the local councils and flogged in the synagogues. On account of me you will stand before governors and kings as witnesses to them. 10And the gospel must first be preached to all nations. 11Whenever you are arrested and brought to trial, do not worry beforehand about what to say. Just say whatever is given you at the time, for it is not you speaking, but the Holy Spirit.

12"Brother will betray brother to death, and a father his child. Children will rebel against their parents and have them put to death. 13All men will hate you because of me, but he who stands firm to the end will be saved.

14"When you see 'the abomination that causes desolation'a standing where itb does not belong—let the reader understand—then let those who are in Judea flee to the mountains. 15Let no-one on the roof of his house go down or enter the house to take anything out. 16Let no-one in the field go back to get his cloak. 17How dreadful it will be in those days for pregnant women and nursing mothers! 18Pray that this will not take place in winter, 19because those will be days of distress unequalled from the beginning, when God created the world, until now—and never to be equalled again. 20If the Lord had not

cut short those days, no-one would survive. But for the sake of the elect, whom he has chosen, he has shortened them. 21At that time if any-one says to you, 'Look, here is the Christ!'c or, 'Look, there he is!' do not believe it. 22For false Christs and false prophets will appear and perform signs and miracles to deceive the elect—if that were possible. 23So be on your guard; I have told you everything ahead of time.

24"But in those days, following that distress,

" 'the sun will be darkened,
   and the moon will not give its
      light;
25the stars will fall from the sky,
   and the heavenly bodies will be
      shaken.'d

26"At that time men will see the Son of Man coming in clouds with great power and glory. 27And he will send his angels and gather his elect from the four winds, from the ends of the earth to the ends of the heavens.

28"Now learn this lesson from the fig-tree: As soon as its twigs get tender and its leaves come out, you know that summer is near. 29Even so, when you see these things happening, you know that it is near, right at the door. 30I tell you the truth, this generatione will certainly not pass away until all these things have happened. 31Heaven and earth will pass away, but my words will never pass away.

The Day and Hour Unknown

32"No-one knows about that day or hour, not even the angels in heaven, nor the Son, but only the Father. 33Be on guard! Be alert!f You do not know when that time will come. 34It's like a man going away: He leaves his house in charge of his servants, each with his assigned task, and tells the one at the door to keep watch.

35"Therefore keep watch because you do not know when the owner of the house will come back—whether in the evening, or at midnight, or when the cock crows, or at dawn. 36If

---

a14 Daniel 9:27; 11:31; 12:11   b14 Or he; also in verse 29   c21 Or Messiah
d25 Isaiah 13:10; 34:4   e30 Or race   f33 Some manuscripts alert and pray

he comes suddenly, do not let him find you sleeping. ³⁷What I say to you, I say to everyone: 'Watch!' "

Jesus Anointed at Bethany

14 Now the Passover and the Feast of Unleavened Bread were only two days away, and the chief priests and the teachers of the law were looking for some sly way to arrest Jesus and kill him. ²"But not during the Feast," they said, "or the people may riot."

³While he was in Bethany, reclining at the table in the home of a man known as Simon the Leper, a woman came with an alabaster jar of very expensive perfume, made of pure nard. She broke the jar and poured the perfume on his head.

⁴Some of those present were saying indignantly to one another, "Why this waste of perfume? ⁵It could have been sold for more than a year's wages*ª* and the money given to the poor." And they rebuked her harshly.

⁶"Leave her alone," said Jesus. "Why are you bothering her? She has done a beautiful thing to me. ⁷The poor you will always have with you, and you can help them any time you want. But you will not always have me. ⁸She did what she could. She poured perfume on my body beforehand to prepare me for my burial. ⁹I tell you the truth, wherever the gospel is preached throughout the world, what she has done will also be told, in memory of her."

¹⁰Then Judas Iscariot, one of the Twelve, went to the chief priests to betray Jesus to them. ¹¹They were delighted to hear this and promised to give him money. So he watched for an opportunity to hand him over.

The Lord's Supper

¹²On the first day of the Feast of Unleavened Bread, when it was customary to sacrifice the Passover lamb, Jesus' disciples asked him, "Where do you want us to go and make preparations for you to eat the Passover?"

¹³So he sent two of his disciples, telling them, "Go into the city, and a man carrying a jar of water will meet you. Follow him. ¹⁴Say to the owner of the house he enters, 'The Teacher asks: Where is my guest room, where I may eat the Passover with my disciples?' ¹⁵He will show you a large upper room, furnished and ready. Make preparations for us there."

¹⁶The disciples left, went into the city and found things just as Jesus had told them. So they prepared the Passover.

¹⁷When evening came, Jesus arrived with the Twelve. ¹⁸While they were reclining at the table eating, he said, "I tell you the truth, one of you will betray me—one who is eating with me."

¹⁹They were saddened, and one by one they said to him, "Surely not I?"

²⁰"It is one of the Twelve," he replied, "one who dips bread into the bowl with me. ²¹The Son of Man will go just as it is written about him. But woe to that man who betrays the Son of Man! It would be better for him if he had not been born."

²²While they were eating, Jesus took bread, gave thanks and broke it, and gave it to his disciples, saying, "Take it; this is my body."

²³Then he took the cup, gave thanks and offered it to them, and they all drank from it.

²⁴"This is my blood of the*ᵇ* covenant, which is poured out for many," he said to them. ²⁵"I tell you the truth, I will not drink again of the fruit of the vine until that day when I drink it anew in the kingdom of God."

²⁶When they had sung a hymn, they went out to the Mount of Olives.

Jesus Predicts Peter's Denial

²⁷"You will all fall away," Jesus told them, "for it is written:

" ' I will strike the shepherd,
    and the sheep will be scattered.'*ᶜ*

²⁸But after I have risen, I will go ahead of you into Galilee."

²⁹Peter declared, "Even if all fall away, I will not."

³⁰"I tell you the truth," Jesus answered, "today—yes, tonight—

ª5 Greek than three hundred denarii   *ᵇ24 Some manuscripts the new*   *ᶜ27 Zech. 13:7* before the cock crows twice[d] you yourself will disown me three times."

³¹But Peter insisted emphatically, "Even if I have to die with you, I will never disown you." And all the others said the same.

Gethsemane

³²They went to a place called Gethsemane, and Jesus said to his disciples, "Sit here while I pray." ³³He took Peter, James and John along with him, and he began to be deeply distressed and troubled. ³⁴"My soul is overwhelmed with sorrow to the point of death," he said to them. "Stay here and keep watch."

³⁵Going a little farther, he fell to the ground and prayed that if possible the hour might pass from him. ³⁶"Abba,[e] Father," he said, "everything is possible for you. Take this cup from me. Yet not what I will, but what you will."

³⁷Then he returned to his disciples and found them sleeping. "Simon," he said to Peter, "are you asleep? Could you not keep watch for one hour? ³⁸Watch and pray so that you will not fall into temptation. The spirit is willing, but the body is weak."

³⁹Once more he went away and prayed the same thing. ⁴⁰When he came back, he again found them sleeping, because their eyes were heavy. They did not know what to say to him.

⁴¹Returning the third time, he said to them, "Are you still sleeping and resting? Enough! The hour has come. Look, the Son of Man is betrayed into the hands of sinners. ⁴²Rise! Let us go! Here comes my betrayer!"

Jesus Arrested

⁴³Just as he was speaking, Judas, one of the Twelve, appeared. With him was a crowd armed with swords and clubs, sent from the chief priests, the teachers of the law, and the elders.

⁴⁴Now the betrayer had arranged a signal with them: "The one I kiss is the man; arrest him and lead him away under guard." ⁴⁵Going at once to Jesus, Judas said, "Rabbi!" and kissed him. ⁴⁶Then the men seized Jesus and arrested him. ⁴⁷Then one of those standing near drew his sword and struck the servant of the high priest, cutting off his ear.

⁴⁸"Am I leading a rebellion," said Jesus, "that you have come out with swords and clubs to capture me? ⁴⁹Every day I was with you, teaching in the temple courts, and you did not arrest me. But the Scriptures must be fulfilled." ⁵⁰Then everyone deserted him and fled.

⁵¹A young man, wearing nothing but a linen garment, was following Jesus. When they seized him, ⁵²he fled naked, leaving his garment behind.

Before the Sanhedrin

⁵³They took Jesus to the high priest, and all the chief priests, elders and teachers of the law came together. ⁵⁴Peter followed him at a distance, right into the courtyard of the high priest. There he sat with the guards and warmed himself at the fire.

⁵⁵The chief priests and the whole Sanhedrin were looking for evidence against Jesus so that they could put him to death, but they did not find any. ⁵⁶Many testified falsely against him, but their statements did not agree.

⁵⁷Then some stood up and gave this false testimony against him: ⁵⁸"We heard him say, 'I will destroy this man-made temple and in three days will build another, not made by man.' " ⁵⁹Yet even then their testimony did not agree.

⁶⁰Then the high priest stood up before them and asked Jesus, "Are you not going to answer? What is this testimony that these men are bringing against you?" ⁶¹But Jesus remained silent and gave no answer.

Again the high priest asked him, "Are you the Christ,[f] the Son of the Blessed One?"

⁶²"I am," said Jesus. "And you will see the Son of Man sitting at the right

---

[d]30 Some early manuscripts do not have twice.
[f]61 Or Messiah

[e]36 Aramaic for Father

hand of the Mighty One and coming on the clouds of heaven."

63The high priest tore his clothes. "Why do we need any more witnesses?" he asked. 64"You have heard the blasphemy. What do you think?"

They all condemned him as worthy of death. 65Then some began to spit at him; they blindfolded him, struck him with their fists, and said, "Prophesy!" And the guards took him and beat him.

Peter Disowns Jesus

66While Peter was below in the courtyard, one of the servant girls of the high priest came by. 67When she saw Peter warming himself, she looked closely at him.

"You also were with that Nazarene, Jesus," she said.

68But he denied it. "I don't know or understand what you're talking about," he said, and went out into the entrance.8

69When the servant girl saw him there, she said again to those standing around, "This fellow is one of them." 70Again he denied it.

After a little while, those standing near said to Peter, "Surely you are one of them, for you are a Galilean."

71He began to call down curses on himself, and he swore to them, "I don't know this man you're talking about."

72Immediately the cock crowed the second time.h Then Peter remembered the word Jesus had spoken to him: "Before the cock crowsi you will disown me three times." And he broke down and wept.

Jesus Before Pilate

15 Very early in the morning, the chief priests, with the elders, the teachers of the law and the whole Sanhedrin, reached a decision. They bound Jesus, led him away and turned him over to Pilate.

2"Are you the king of the Jews?" asked Pilate.

"Yes, it is as you say," Jesus replied.

3The chief priests accused him of many things. 4So again Pilate asked him, "Aren't you going to answer? See how many things they are accusing you of."

5But Jesus still made no reply, and Pilate was amazed.

6Now it was the custom at the Feast to release a prisoner whom the people requested. 7A man called Barabbas was in prison with the insurrectionists who had committed murder in the uprising. 8The crowd came up and asked Pilate to do for them what he usually did.

9"Do you want me to release to you the king of the Jews?" asked Pilate, 10knowing it was out of envy that the chief priests had handed Jesus over to him. 11But the chief priests stirred up the crowd to have Pilate release Barabbas instead.

12"What shall I do, then, with the one you call the king of the Jews?" Pilate asked them.

13"Crucify him!" they shouted.

14"Why? What crime has he committed?" asked Pilate.

But they shouted all the louder, "Crucify him!"

15Wanting to satisfy the crowd, Pilate released Barabbas to them. He had Jesus flogged, and handed him over to be crucified.

The Soldiers Mock Jesus

16The soldiers led Jesus away into the palace (that is, the Praetorium) and called together the whole company of soldiers. 17They put a purple robe on him, then wove a crown of thorns and set it on him. 18And they began to call out to him, "Hail, King of the Jews!" 19Again and again they struck him on the head with a staff and spat on him. Falling on their knees, they worshipped him. 20And when they had mocked him, they took off the purple robe and put his own clothes on him. Then they led him out to crucify him.

The Crucifixion

21A certain man from Cyrene,

868 Some early manuscripts *entrance and the cock crowed*
h72 Some early manuscripts do not have *the second time.*
i72 Some early manuscripts do not have *twice.*

Simon, the father of Alexander and Rufus, was passing by on his way in from the country, and they forced him to carry the cross. 22They brought Jesus to the place called Golgotha (which means The Place of the Skull). 23Then they offered him wine mixed with myrrh, but he did not take it. 24And they crucified him. Dividing up his clothes, they cast lots to see what each would get.

25It was the third hour when they crucified him. 26The written notice of the charge against him read: THE KING OF THE JEWS. 27They crucified two robbers with him, one on his right and one on his left.[a] 29Those who passed by hurled insults at him, shaking their heads and saying, "So! You who are going to destroy the temple and build it in three days, 30come down from the cross and save yourself!" 31In the same way the chief priests and the teachers of the law mocked him among themselves. "He saved others," they said, "but he can't save himself! 32Let this Christ,[b] this King of Israel, come down now from the cross, that we may see and believe." Those crucified with him also heaped insults on him.

The Death of Jesus

33At the sixth hour darkness came over the whole land until the ninth hour. 34And at the ninth hour Jesus cried out in a loud voice, *"Eloi, Eloi, lama sabachthani?"*—which means, "My God, my God, why have you forsaken me?"[c]

35When some of those standing near heard this, they said, "Listen, he's calling Elijah."

36One man ran, filled a sponge with wine vinegar, put it on a stick, and offered it to Jesus to drink. "Leave him alone now. Let's see if Elijah comes to take him down," he said.

37With a loud cry, Jesus breathed his last.

38The curtain of the temple was torn in two from top to bottom. 39And when the centurion, who stood there in front of Jesus, heard his cry and[d] saw how he died, he said, "Surely this man was the Son[e] of God!"

40Some women were watching from a distance. Among them were Mary Magdalene, Mary the mother of James the younger and of Joses, and Salome. 41In Galilee these women had followed him and cared for his needs. Many other women who had come up with him to Jerusalem were also there.

The Burial of Jesus

42It was Preparation Day (that is, the day before the Sabbath). So as evening approached, 43Joseph of Arimathea, a prominent member of the Council, who was himself waiting for the kingdom of God, went boldly to Pilate and asked for Jesus' body. 44Pilate was surprised to hear that he was already dead. Summoning the centurion, he asked him if Jesus had already died. 45When he learned from the centurion that it was so, he gave the body to Joseph. 46So Joseph bought some linen cloth, took down the body, wrapped it in the linen, and placed it in a tomb cut out of rock. Then he rolled a stone against the entrance of the tomb. 47Mary Magdalene and Mary the mother of Joses saw where he was laid.

The Resurrection

16 When the Sabbath was over, Mary Magdalene, Mary the mother of James, and Salome bought spices so that they might go to anoint Jesus' body. 2Very early on the first day of the week, just after sunrise, they were on their way to the tomb 3and they asked each other, "Who will roll the stone away from the entrance of the tomb?"

4But when they looked up, they saw that the stone, which was very large, had been rolled away. 5As they entered the tomb, they saw a young man dressed in a white robe sitting on the right side, and they were alarmed.

---

a27 Some manuscripts left, 28and the scripture was fulfilled which says, "He was counted with the lawless ones" (Isaiah 53:12)   *b32 Or Messiah*   *c34 Psalm 22:1*
d39 Some manuscripts do not have heard his cry and.   *e39 Or a son*

6"Don't be alarmed," he said. "You are looking for Jesus the Nazarene, who was crucified. He has risen! He is not here. See the place where they laid him. 7But go, tell his disciples and Peter, 'He is going ahead of you into Galilee. There you will see him, just as he told you.' "

8Trembling and bewildered, the women went out and fled from the tomb. They said nothing to anyone, because they were afraid.

[The two most reliable early manuscripts do not have Mark 16:9–20.]

9When Jesus rose early on the first day of the week, he appeared first to Mary Magdalene, out of whom he had driven seven demons. 10She went and told those who had been with him and who were mourning and weeping. 11When they heard that Jesus was alive and that she had seen him, they did not believe it.

12Afterwards Jesus appeared in a different form to two of them while they were walking in the country.

13These returned and reported it to the rest; but they did not believe them either.

14Later Jesus appeared to the Eleven as they were eating; he rebuked them for their lack of faith and their stubborn refusal to believe those who had seen him after he had risen.

15He said to them, "Go into all the world and preach the good news to all creation. 16Whoever believes and is baptised will be saved, but whoever does not believe will be condemned. 17And these signs will accompany those who believe: In my name they will drive out demons; they will speak in new tongues; 18they will pick up snakes with their hands; and when they drink deadly poison, it will not hurt them at all; they will place their hands on sick people, and they will get well."

19After the Lord Jesus had spoken to them, he was taken up into heaven and he sat at the right hand of God. 20Then the disciples went out and preached everywhere, and the Lord worked with them and confirmed his word by the signs that accompanied it.

Luke

Introduction

1 Many have undertaken to draw up an account of the things that have been fulfilled[a] among us, 2just as they were handed down to us by those who from the first were eye-witnesses and servants of the word. 3Therefore, since I myself have carefully investigated everything from the beginning, it seemed good also to me to write an orderly account for you, most excellent Theophilus, 4so that you may know the certainty of the things you have been taught.

The Birth of John the Baptist Foretold

5In the time of Herod king of Judea there was a priest named Zechariah, who belonged to the priestly division of Abijah; his wife Elizabeth was also a descendant of Aaron. 6Both of them were upright in the sight of God, observing all the Lord's commandments and regulations blamelessly. 7But they had no children, because Elizabeth was barren; and they were both well on in years.

8Once when Zechariah's division was on duty and he was serving as priest before God, 9he was chosen by lot, according to the custom of the priesthood, to go into the temple of the Lord and burn incense. 10And when the time for the burning of incense came, all the assembled worshippers were praying outside.

11Then an angel of the Lord appeared to him, standing at the right side of the altar of incense. 12When Zechariah saw him, he was startled and was gripped with fear. 13But the angel said to him: "Do not be afraid, Zechariah; your prayer has been heard. Your wife Elizabeth will bear you a son, and you are to give him the name John. 14He will be a joy and delight to you, and many will rejoice because of his birth, 15for he will be great in the sight of the Lord. He is never to take wine or other fermented drink, and he will be filled with the Holy Spirit even from birth.[b] 16Many of the people of Israel will he bring back to the Lord their God. 17And he will go on before the Lord, in the spirit and power of Elijah, to turn the hearts of the fathers to their children and the disobedient to the wisdom of the righteous—to make ready a people prepared for the Lord."

18Zechariah asked the angel, "How can I be sure of this? I am an old man and my wife is well on in years."

19The angel answered, "I am Gabriel. I stand in the presence of God, and I have been sent to speak to you and to tell you this good news. 20And now you will be silent and not able to speak until the day this happens, because you did not believe my words, which will come true at their proper time."

21Meanwhile, the people were waiting for Zechariah and wondering why he stayed so long in the temple. 22When he came out, he could not speak to them. They realised he had seen a vision in the temple, for he kept making signs to them but remained unable to speak.

23When his time of service was completed, he returned home. 24After this his wife Elizabeth became pregnant and for five months remained in

---

*a*1 Or been surely believed   *b*15 Or from his mother's womb

61

seclusion. 25"The Lord has done this for me," she said. "In these days he has shown his favour and taken away my disgrace among the people."

The Birth of Jesus Foretold

26In the sixth month, God sent the angel Gabriel to Nazareth, a town in Galilee, 27to a virgin pledged to be married to a man named Joseph, a descendant of David. The virgin's name was Mary. 28The angel went to her and said, "Greetings, you who are highly favoured! The Lord is with you."

29Mary was greatly troubled at his words and wondered what kind of greeting this might be. 30But the angel said to her, "Do not be afraid, Mary, you have found favour with God. 31You will be with child and give birth to a son, and you are to give him the name Jesus. 32He will be great and will be called the Son of the Most High. The Lord God will give him the throne of his father David, 33and he will reign over the house of Jacob for ever; his kingdom will never end."

34"How will this be," Mary asked the angel, "since I am a virgin?"

35The angel answered, "The Holy Spirit will come upon you, and the power of the Most High will overshadow you. So the holy one to be born will be called*c* the Son of God. 36Even Elizabeth your relative is going to have a child in her old age, and she who was said to be barren is in her sixth month. 37For nothing is impossible with God."

38"I am the Lord's servant," Mary answered. "May it be to me as you have said." Then the angel left her.

Mary Visits Elizabeth

39At that time Mary got ready and hurried to a town in the hill country of Judah, 40where she entered Zechariah's home and greeted Elizabeth. 41When Elizabeth heard Mary's greeting, the baby leaped in her womb, and Elizabeth was filled with the Holy Spirit. 42In a loud voice she exclaimed: "Blessed are you among women, and blessed is the child you will bear! 43But why am I so favoured, that the mother of my Lord should come to me? 44As soon as the sound of your greeting reached my ears, the baby in my womb leaped for joy. 45Blessed is she who has believed that what the Lord has said to her will be accomplished!"

Mary's Song

46And Mary said:

"My soul praises the Lord
47 and my spirit rejoices in God my
        Saviour,
48for he has been mindful
    of the humble state of his
        servant.
    From now on all generations will
        call me blessed,
49   for the Mighty One has done
        great things for me—
    holy is his name.
50His mercy extends to those who
        fear him,
    from generation to generation.
51He has performed mighty deeds
        with his arm;
    he has scattered those who are
        proud in their inmost thoughts.
52He has brought down rulers from
        their thrones
    but has lifted up the humble.
53He has filled the hungry with good
        things
    but has sent the rich away
        empty.
54He has helped his servant Israel,
    remembering to be merciful
55to Abraham and his descendants
        for ever,
    even as he said to our fathers."

56Mary stayed with Elizabeth for about three months and then returned home.

The Birth of John the Baptist

57When it was time for Elizabeth to have her baby, she gave birth to a son. 58Her neighbours and relatives heard that the Lord had shown her great mercy, and they shared her joy.

59On the eighth day they came to circumcise the child, and they were

c35 Or So the child to be born will be called holy,

going to name him after his father Zechariah, 60but his mother spoke up and said, "No! He is to be called John."

61They said to her, "There is no-one among your relatives who has that name."

62Then they made signs to his father, to find out what he would like to name the child. 63He asked for a writing tablet, and to everyone's astonishment he wrote, "His name is John." 64Immediately his mouth was opened and his tongue was loosed, and he began to speak, praising God. 65The neighbours were all filled with awe, and throughout the hill country of Judea people were talking about all these things. 66Everyone who heard this wondered about it, asking, "What then is this child going to be?" For the Lord's hand was with him.

Zechariah's Song

67His father Zechariah was filled with the Holy Spirit and prophesied:

68"Praise be to the Lord, the God of Israel,
  because he has come and has redeemed his people.
69He has raised up a horn*d* of salvation for us
  in the house of his servant David
70(as he said through his holy prophets of long ago),
71salvation from our enemies
  and from the hand of all who hate us—
72to show mercy to our fathers
  and to remember his holy covenant,
73 the oath he swore to our father Abraham:
74to rescue us from the hand of our enemies,
  and to enable us to serve him without fear
75 in holiness and righteousness before him all our days.

76And you, my child, will be called a prophet of the Most High;
for you will go on before the Lord to prepare the way for him,
77to give his people the knowledge of salvation
  through the forgiveness of their sins,
78because of the tender mercy of our God,
  by which the rising sun will come to us from heaven
79to shine on those living in darkness and in the shadow of death,
to guide our feet into the path of peace."

80And the child grew and became strong in spirit; and he lived in the desert until he appeared publicly to Israel.

The Birth of Jesus

2 In those days Caesar Augustus issued a decree that a census should be taken of the entire Roman world. (2This was the first census that took place while Quirinius was governor of Syria.) 3And everyone went to his own town to register.

4So Joseph also went up from the town of Nazareth in Galilee to Judea, to Bethlehem the town of David, because he belonged to the house and line of David. 5He went there to register with Mary, who was pledged to be married to him and was expecting a child. 6While they were there, the time came for the baby to be born, 7and she gave birth to her first-born, a son. She wrapped him in cloths and placed him in a manger, because there was no room for them in the inn.

The Shepherds and the Angels

8And there were shepherds living out in the fields near by, keeping watch over their flocks at night. 9An angel of the Lord appeared to them, and the glory of the Lord shone around them, and they were terrified. 10But the angel said to them, "Do not be afraid. I bring you good news of great joy that will be for all the

---

*d*69 *Horn here symbolises strength.*

people. 11Today in the town of David a Saviour has been born to you; he is Christ[a] the Lord. 12This will be a sign to you: You will find a baby wrapped in cloths and lying in a manger."

13Suddenly a great company of the heavenly host appeared with the angel, praising God and saying,

14"Glory to God in the highest,
   and on earth peace to men on
     whom his favour rests."

15When the angels had left them and gone into heaven, the shepherds said to one another, "Let's go to Bethlehem and see this thing that has happened, which the Lord has told us about."

16So they hurried off and found Mary and Joseph, and the baby, who was lying in the manger. 17When they had seen him, they spread the word concerning what had been told them about this child, 18and all who heard it were amazed at what the shepherds said to them. 19But Mary treasured up all these things and pondered them in her heart. 20The shepherds returned, glorifying and praising God for all the things they had heard and seen, which were just as they had been told.

Jesus Presented in the Temple

21On the eighth day, when it was time to circumcise him, he was named Jesus, the name the angel had given him before he had been conceived.

22When the time of their purification according to the Law of Moses had been completed, Joseph and Mary took him to Jerusalem to present him to the Lord 23(as it is written in the Law of the Lord, "Every first-born male is to be consecrated to the Lord"[b], 24and to offer a sacrifice in keeping with what is said in the Law of the Lord: "a pair of doves or two young pigeons".[c]

25Now there was a man in Jerusalem called Simeon, who was righteous and devout. He was waiting for the consolation of Israel, and the Holy Spirit was upon him. 26It had been revealed to him by the Holy Spirit that he would not die before he had seen the Lord's Christ. 27Moved by the Spirit, he went into the temple courts. When the parents brought in the child Jesus to do for him what the custom of the Law required, 28Simeon took him in his arms and praised God, saying,

29"Sovereign Lord, as you have
   promised,
  you now dismiss[d] your servant in
   peace.
30For my eyes have seen your
   salvation,
31 which you have prepared in the
   sight of all people,
32a light for revelation to the
   Gentiles
  and for glory to your people
   Israel."

33The child's father and mother marvelled at what was said about him. 34Then Simeon blessed them and said to Mary, his mother: "This child is destined to cause the falling and rising of many in Israel, and to be a sign that will be spoken against, 35so that the thoughts of many hearts will be revealed. And a sword will pierce your own soul too."

36There was also a prophetess, Anna, the daughter of Phanuel, of the tribe of Asher. She was very old; she had lived with her husband seven years after her marriage, 37and then was a widow until she was eighty-four.[e] She never left the temple but worshipped night and day, fasting and praying. 38Coming up to them at that very moment, she gave thanks to God and spoke about the child to all who were looking forward to the redemption of Jerusalem.

39When Joseph and Mary had done everything required by the Law of the Lord, they returned to Galilee to their own town of Nazareth. 40And the child grew and became strong; he was filled with wisdom, and the grace of God was upon him.

[a]11 Or *Messiah*. "The Christ" (Greek) and "the Messiah" (Hebrew) both mean "the Anointed One"; also in verse 26.   [b]23 Exodus 13:2,12   [c]24 Lev. 12:8
[d]29 Or *promised, / now dismiss*   [e]37 Or *widow for eighty-four years*

The Boy Jesus at the Temple

41Every year his parents went to Jerusalem for the Feast of the Passover. 42When he was twelve years old, they went up to the Feast, according to the custom. 43After the Feast was over, while his parents were returning home, the boy Jesus stayed behind in Jerusalem, but they were unaware of it. 44Thinking he was in their company, they travelled on for a day. Then they began looking for him among their relatives and friends. 45When they did not find him, they went back to Jerusalem to look for him. 46After three days they found him in the temple courts, sitting among the teachers, listening to them and asking them questions. 47Everyone who heard him was amazed at his understanding and his answers. 48When his parents saw him, they were astonished. His mother said to him, "Son, why have you treated us like this? Your father and I have been anxiously searching for you."

49"Why were you searching for me?" he asked. "Didn't you know I had to be in my Father's house?" 50But they did not understand what he was saying to them.

51Then he went down to Nazareth with them and was obedient to them. But his mother treasured all these things in her heart. 52And Jesus grew in wisdom and stature, and in favour with God and men.

John the Baptist Prepares the Way

3 In the fifteenth year of the reign of Tiberius Caesar—when Pontius Pilate was governor of Judea, Herod tetrarch of Galilee, his brother Philip tetrarch of Iturea and Traconitis, and Lysanias tetrarch of Abilene—2during the high priesthood of Annas and Caiaphas, the word of God came to John son of Zechariah in the desert. 3He went into all the country around the Jordan, preaching a baptism of repentance for the forgiveness of sins. 4As is written in the book of the words of Isaiah the prophet:

"A voice of one calling in the desert,
'Prepare the way for the Lord,
    make straight paths for him.
5Every valley shall be filled in,
    every mountain and hill made low.
The crooked roads shall become straight,
    the rough ways smooth.
6And all mankind will see God's salvation.' "a

7John said to the crowds coming out to be baptised by him, "You brood of vipers! Who warned you to flee from the coming wrath? 8Produce fruit in keeping with repentance. And do not begin to say to yourselves, 'We have Abraham as our father.' For I tell you that out of these stones God can raise up children for Abraham. 9The axe is already at the root of the trees, and every tree that does not produce good fruit will be cut down and thrown into the fire."

10"What should we do then?" the crowd asked.

11John answered, "The man with two tunics should share with him who has none, and the one who has food should do the same."

12Tax collectors also came to be baptised. "Teacher," they asked, "what should we do?"

13"Don't collect any more than you are required to," he told them.

14Then some soldiers asked him, "And what should we do?"

He replied, "Don't extort money and don't accuse people falsely—be content with your pay."

15The people were waiting expectantly and were all wondering in their hearts if John might possibly be the Christ.b 16John answered them all, "I baptise you withc water. But one more powerful than I will come, the thongs of whose sandals I am not worthy to untie. He will baptise you with the Holy Spirit and with fire. 17His winnowing fork is in his hand to clear his

a6 Isaiah 40:3-5   b15 Or Messiah   c16 Or in

threshing floor and to gather the wheat into his barn, but he will burn up the chaff with unquenchable fire." [18]And with many other words John exhorted the people and preached the good news to them.

[19]But when John rebuked Herod the tetrarch because of Herodias, his brother's wife, and all the other evil things he had done, [20]Herod added this to them all: He locked John up in prison.

The Baptism and Genealogy of Jesus

[21]When all the people were being baptised, Jesus was baptised too. And as he was praying, heaven was opened [22]and the Holy Spirit descended on him in bodily form like a dove. And a voice came from heaven: "You are my Son, whom I love; with you I am well pleased."

[23]Now Jesus himself was about thirty years old when he began his ministry. He was the son, so it was thought, of Joseph,

the son of Heli, [24]the son of Matthat,
the son of Levi, the son of Melki,
the son of Jannai, the son of Joseph,
[25]the son of Mattathias, the son of Amos,
the son of Nahum, the son of Esli,
the son of Naggai, [26]the son of Maath,
the son of Mattathias, the son of Semein,
the son of Josech, the son of Joda,
[27]the son of Joanan, the son of Rhesa,
the son of Zerubbabel, the son of Shealtiel,
the son of Neri, [28]the son of Melki,
the son of Addi, the son of Cosam,
the son of Elmadam, the son of Er,
[29]the son of Joshua, the son of Eliezer,
the son of Jorim, the son of Matthat,
the son of Levi, [30]the son of Simeon,

the son of Judah, the son of Joseph,
the son of Jonam, the son of Eliakim,
[31]the son of Melea, the son of Menna,
the son of Mattatha, the son of Nathan,
the son of David, [32]the son of Jesse,
the son of Obed, the son of Boaz,
the son of Salmon,[d] the son of Nahshon,
[33]the son of Amminadab, the son of Ram,[e]
the son of Hezron, the son of Perez,
the son of Judah, [34]the son of Jacob,
the son of Isaac, the son of Abraham,
the son of Terah, the son of Nahor,
[35]the son of Serug, the son of Reu,
the son of Peleg, the son of Eber,
the son of Shelah, [36]the son of Cainan,
the son of Arphaxad, the son of Shem,
the son of Noah, the son of Lamech,
[37]the son of Methuselah, the son of Enoch,
the son of Jared, the son of Mahalaleel,
the son of Cainan, [38]the son of Enos,
the son of Seth, the son of Adam,
the son of God.

The Temptation of Jesus

4 Jesus, full of the Holy Spirit, returned from the Jordan and was led by the Spirit in the desert, [2]where for forty days he was tempted by the devil. He ate nothing during those days, and at the end of them he was hungry.

[3]The devil said to him, "If you are the Son of God, tell this stone to become bread."

[4]Jesus answered, "It is written: 'Man does not live on bread alone.'[a]"

[5]The devil led him up to a high place and showed him in an instant

[d]32 Some early manuscripts *Sala*
[e]33 Some manuscripts *Amminadab, the son of Admin, the son of Arni;* other manuscripts vary widely.
[a]4 Deut. 8:3

all the kingdoms of the world. 6And he said to him, "I will give you all their authority and splendour, for it has been given to me, and I can give it to anyone I want to. 7So if you worship me, it will all be yours."

8Jesus answered, "It is written: 'Worship the Lord your God and serve him only.'b"

9The devil led him to Jerusalem and had him stand on the highest point of the temple. "If you are the Son of God," he said, "throw yourself down from here. 10For it is written:

" 'He will command his angels
    concerning you
    to guard you carefully;
11they will lift you up in their hands,
    so that you will not strike your
    foot against a stone.'c"

12Jesus answered, "It says: 'Do not put the Lord your God to the test.'d"

13When the devil had finished all this tempting, he left him until an opportune time.

Jesus Rejected at Nazareth

14Jesus returned to Galilee in the power of the Spirit, and news about him spread through the whole countryside. 15He taught in their synagogues, and everyone praised him.

16He went to Nazareth, where he had been brought up, and on the Sabbath day he went into the synagogue, as was his custom. And he stood up to read. 17The scroll of the prophet Isaiah was handed to him. Unrolling it, he found the place where it is written:

18"The Spirit of the Lord is on me,
    because he has anointed me
    to preach good news to the poor.
He has sent me to proclaim
    freedom for the prisoners
    and recovery of sight for the
    blind,
to release the oppressed,
19 to proclaim the year of the Lord's
    favour."e

20Then he rolled up the scroll, gave it back to the attendant and sat down. The eyes of everyone in the synagogue were fastened on him, 21and he began by saying to them, "Today this scripture is fulfilled in your hearing."

22All spoke well of him and were amazed at the gracious words that came from his lips. "Isn't this Joseph's son?" they asked.

23Jesus said to them, "Surely you will quote this proverb to me: 'Physician, heal yourself! Do here in your home town what we have heard that you did in Capernaum.' "

24"I tell you the truth," he continued, "no prophet is accepted in his home town. 25I assure you that there were many widows in Israel in Elijah's time, when the sky was shut for three and a half years and there was a severe famine throughout the land. 26Yet Elijah was not sent to any of them, but to a widow in Zarephath in the region of Sidon. 27And there were many in Israel with leprosyf in the time of Elisha the prophet, yet not one of them was cleansed—only Naaman the Syrian."

28All the people in the synagogue were furious when they heard this. 29They got up, drove him out of the town, and took him to the brow of the hill on which the town was built, in order to throw him down the cliff. 30But he walked right through the crowd and went on his way.

Jesus Drives Out an Evil Spirit

31Then he went down to Capernaum, a town in Galilee, and on the Sabbath began to teach the people. 32They were amazed at his teaching, because his message had authority.

33In the synagogue there was a man possessed by a demon, an evilg spirit. He cried out at the top of his voice, 34"Ha! What do you want with us, Jesus of Nazareth? Have you come to destroy us? I know who you are—the Holy One of God!"

b8 Deut. 6:13   c11 Psalm 91:11,12
d12 Deut. 6:16   e19 Isaiah 61:1,2
f27 The Greek word was used for various diseases affecting the skin—not necessarily leprosy.
g33 Greek unclean; also in verse 36

35"Be quiet!" Jesus said sternly. "Come out of him!" Then the demon threw the man down before them all and came out without injuring him.

36All the people were amazed and said to each other, "What is this teaching? With authority and power he gives orders to evil spirits and they come out!" 37And the news about him spread throughout the surrounding area.

Jesus Heals Many

38Jesus left the synagogue and went to the home of Simon. Now Simon's mother-in-law was suffering from a high fever, and they asked Jesus to help her. 39So he bent over her and rebuked the fever, and it left her. She got up at once and began to wait on them.

40When the sun was setting, the people brought to Jesus all who had various kinds of sickness, and laying his hands on each one, he healed them. 41Moreover, demons came out of many people, shouting, "You are the Son of God!" But he rebuked them and would not allow them to speak, because they knew he was the Christ.h

42At daybreak Jesus went out to a solitary place. The people were looking for him and when they came to where he was, they tried to keep him from leaving them. 43But he said, "I must preach the good news of the kingdom of God to the other towns also, because that is why I was sent." 44And he kept on preaching in the synagogues of Judea.i

The Calling of the First Disciples

5 One day as Jesus was standing by the Lake of Gennesaret,a with the people crowding round him and listening to the word of God, 2he saw at the water's edge two boats, left there by the fishermen, who were washing their nets. 3He got into one of the boats, the one belonging to Simon, and asked him to put out a little from shore. Then he sat down

and taught the people from the boat.

4When he had finished speaking, he said to Simon, "Put out into deep water, and let downb the nets for a catch."

5Simon answered, "Master, we've worked hard all night and haven't caught anything. But because you say so, I will let down the nets."

6When they had done so, they caught such a large number of fish that their nets began to break. 7So they signalled their partners in the other boat to come and help them, and they came and filled both boats so full that they began to sink.

8When Simon Peter saw this, he fell at Jesus' knees and said, "Go away from me, Lord; I am a sinful man!" 9For he and all his companions were astonished at the catch of fish they had taken, 10and so were James and John, the sons of Zebedee, Simon's partners.

Then Jesus said to Simon, "Don't be afraid; from now on you will catch men." 11So they pulled their boats up on shore, left everything and followed him.

The Man With Leprosy

12While Jesus was in one of the towns, a man came along who was covered with leprosy.c When he saw Jesus, he fell with his face to the ground and begged him, "Lord, if you are willing, you can make me clean."

13Jesus reached out his hand and touched the man. "I am willing," he said. "Be clean!" And immediately the leprosy left him.

14Then Jesus ordered him, "Don't tell anyone, but go, show yourself to the priest and offer the sacrifices that Moses commanded for your cleansing, as a testimony to them."

15Yet the news about him spread all the more, so that crowds of people came to hear him and to be healed of their sicknesses. 16But Jesus often withdrew to lonely places and prayed.

h41 Or *Messiah*
i44 Or *the land of the Jews*; some manuscripts *Galilee*
a1 That is, Sea of Galilee   b4 The Greek verb is plural.
c12 The Greek word was used for various diseases affecting the skin—not necessarily leprosy.

Jesus Heals a Paralytic

17One day as he was teaching, Pharisees and teachers of the law, who had come from every village of Galilee and from Judea and Jerusalem, were sitting there. And the power of the Lord was present for him to heal the sick. 18Some men came carrying a paralytic on a mat and tried to take him into the house to lay him before Jesus. 19When they could not find a way to do this because of the crowd, they went up on the roof and lowered him on his mat through the tiles into the middle of the crowd, right in front of Jesus.

20When Jesus saw their faith, he said, "Friend, your sins are forgiven."

21The Pharisees and the teachers of the law began thinking to themselves, "Who is this fellow who speaks blasphemy? Who can forgive sins but God alone?"

22Jesus knew what they were thinking and asked, "Why are you thinking these things in your hearts? 23Which is easier: to say, 'Your sins are forgiven,' or to say, 'Get up and walk'? 24But that you may know that the Son of Man has authority on earth to forgive sins. . . ." He said to the paralysed man, "I tell you, get up, take your mat and go home." 25Immediately he stood up in front of them, took what he had been lying on and went home praising God. 26Everyone was amazed and gave praise to God. They were filled with awe and said, "We have seen remarkable things today."

The Calling of Levi

27After this, Jesus went out and saw a tax collector by the name of Levi sitting at his tax booth. "Follow me," Jesus said to him, 28and Levi got up, left everything and followed him.

29Then Levi held a great banquet for Jesus at his house, and a large crowd of tax collectors and others were eating with them. 30But the Pharisees and the teachers of the law who belonged to their sect complained to his disciples, "Why do you eat and drink with tax collectors and 'sinners'?"

31Jesus answered them, "It is not the healthy who need a doctor, but the sick. 32I have not come to call the righteous, but sinners to repentance."

Jesus Questioned About Fasting

33They said to him, "John's disciples often fast and pray, and so do the disciples of the Pharisees, but yours go on eating and drinking."

34Jesus answered, "Can you make the guests of the bridegroom fast while he is with them? 35But the time will come when the bridegroom will be taken from them; in those days they will fast."

36He told them this parable: "No-one tears a patch from a new garment and sews it on an old one. If he does, he will have torn the new garment, and the patch from the new will not match the old. 37And no-one pours new wine into old wineskins. If he does, the new wine will burst the skins, the wine will run out and the wineskins will be ruined. 38No, new wine must be poured into new wineskins. 39And no-one after drinking old wine wants the new, for he says, 'The old is better.' "

Lord of the Sabbath

6 One Sabbath Jesus was going through the cornfields, and his disciples began to pick some ears of corn, rub them in their hands and eat the grain. 2Some of the Pharisees asked, "Why are you doing what is unlawful on the Sabbath?"

3Jesus answered them, "Have you never read what David did when he and his companions were hungry? 4He entered the house of God, and taking the consecrated bread, he ate what is lawful only for priests to eat. And he also gave some to his companions." 5Then Jesus said to them, "The Son of Man is Lord of the Sabbath."

6On another Sabbath he went into the synagogue and was teaching, and a man was there whose right hand was shrivelled. 7The Pharisees and the teachers of the law were looking for a reason to accuse Jesus, so they watched him closely to see if he would heal on the Sabbath. 8But Jesus knew what they were thinking and said to the man with the shrivelled hand, "Get up and stand in front of everyone." So he got up and stood there.

9Then Jesus said to them, "I ask you, which is lawful on the Sabbath: to do good or to do evil, to save life or to destroy it?"

10He looked round at them all, and then said to the man, "Stretch out your hand." He did so, and his hand was completely restored. 11But they were furious and began to discuss with one another what they might do to Jesus.

The Twelve Apostles

12One of those days Jesus went out into the hills to pray, and spent the night praying to God. 13When morning came, he called his disciples to him and chose twelve of them, whom he also designated apostles: 14Simon (whom he named Peter), his brother Andrew, James, John, Philip, Bartholomew, 15Matthew, Thomas, James son of Alphaeus, Simon who was called the Zealot, 16Judas son of James, and Judas Iscariot, who became a traitor.

Blessings and Woes

17He went down with them and stood on a level place. A large crowd of his disciples was there and a great number of people from all over Judea, from Jerusalem, and from the sea-coast of Tyre and Sidon, 18who had come to hear him and to be healed of their diseases. Those troubled by evila spirits were cured, 19and the people all tried to touch him, because power was coming from him and healing them all.

20Looking at his disciples, he said:

"Blessed are you who are poor,
  for yours is the kingdom of God.
21Blessed are you who hunger now,
  for you will be satisfied.
Blessed are you who weep now,
  for you will laugh.
22Blessed are you when men hate you,

when they exclude you and insult you
and reject your name as evil,
  because of the Son of Man.

23"Rejoice in that day and leap for joy, because great is your reward in heaven. For that is how their fathers treated the prophets.

24"But woe to you who are rich,
  for you have already received your comfort.
25Woe to you who are well fed now,
  for you will go hungry.
Woe to you who laugh now,
  for you will mourn and weep.
26Woe to you when all men speak well of you,
  for that is how their fathers treated the false prophets.

Love for Enemies

27"But I tell you who hear me: Love your enemies, do good to those who hate you, 28bless those who curse you, pray for those who ill-treat you. 29If someone strikes you on one cheek, turn to him the other also. If someone takes your cloak, do not stop him from taking your tunic. 30Give to everyone who asks you, and if anyone takes what belongs to you, do not demand it back. 31Do to others as you would have them do to you.

32"If you love those who love you, what credit is that to you? Even 'sinners' love those who love them. 33And if you do good to those who are good to you, what credit is that to you? Even 'sinners' do that. 34And if you lend to those from whom you expect repayment, what credit is that to you? Even 'sinners' lend to 'sinners', expecting to be repaid in full. 35But love your enemies, do good to them, and lend to them without expecting to get anything back. Then your reward will be great, and you will be sons of the Most High, because he is kind to the ungrateful and wicked. 36Be merciful, just as your Father is merciful.

Judging Others

37"Do not judge, and you will not

---

a18 Greek *unclean*

be judged. Do not condemn, and you will not be condemned. Forgive, and you will be forgiven. 38Give, and it will be given to you. A good measure, pressed down, shaken together and running over, will be poured into your lap. For with the measure you use, it will be measured to you."

39He also told them this parable: "Can a blind man lead a blind man? Will they not both fall into a pit? 40A student is not above his teacher, but everyone who is fully trained will be like his teacher.

41"Why do you look at the speck of sawdust in your brother's eye and pay no attention to the plank in your own eye? 42How can you say to your brother, 'Brother, let me take the speck out of your eye,' when you yourself fail to see the plank in your own eye? You hypocrite, first take the plank out of your eye, and then you will see clearly to remove the speck from your brother's eye.

A Tree and Its Fruit

43"No good tree bears bad fruit, nor does a good tree bear good fruit. 44Each tree is recognised by its own fruit. People do not pick figs from thorn-bushes, or grapes from briers. 45The good man brings good things out of the good stored up in his heart, and the evil man brings evil things out of the evil stored up in his heart. For out of the overflow of his heart his mouth speaks.

The Wise and Foolish Builders

46"Why do you call me, 'Lord, Lord,' and do not do what I say? 47I will show you what he is like who comes to me and hears my words and puts them into practice. 48He is like a man building a house, who dug down deep and laid the foundation on rock. When the flood came, the torrent struck that house but could not shake it, because it was well built. 49But the one who hears my words and does not put them into practice is like a man who built a house on the ground without a foundation. The moment the torrent struck that house, it collapsed and its destruction was complete."

The Faith of the Centurion

7 When Jesus had finished saying all this in the hearing of the people, he entered Capernaum. 2There a centurion's servant, whom his master valued highly, was sick and about to die. 3The centurion heard of Jesus and sent some elders of the Jews to him, asking him to come and heal his servant. 4When they came to Jesus, they pleaded earnestly with him, "This man deserves to have you do this, 5because he loves our nation and has built our synagogue." 6So Jesus went with them.

He was not far from the house when the centurion sent friends to say to him: "Lord, don't trouble yourself, for I do not deserve to have you come under my roof. 7That is why I did not even consider myself worthy to come to you. But say the word, and my servant will be healed. 8For I myself am a man under authority, with soldiers under me. I tell this one, 'Go,' and he goes; and that one, 'Come', and he comes. I say to my servant, 'Do this', and he does it."

9When Jesus heard this, he was amazed at him, and turning to the crowd following him, he said, "I tell you, I have not found such great faith even in Israel." 10Then the men who had been sent returned to the house and found the servant well.

Jesus Raises a Widow's Son

11Soon afterwards, Jesus went to a town called Nain, and his disciples and a large crowd went along with him. 12As he approached the town gate, a dead person was being carried out—the only son of his mother, and she was a widow. And a large crowd from the town was with her. 13When the Lord saw her, his heart went out to her and he said, "Don't cry."

14Then he went up and touched the coffin, and those carrying it stood still. He said, "Young man, I say to you, get up!" 15The dead man sat up and began to talk, and Jesus gave him back to his mother.

16They were all filled with awe and praised God. "A great prophet has appeared among us," they said. "God

71

has come to help his people." [17]This news about Jesus spread throughout Judea[a] and the surrounding country.

Jesus and John the Baptist

[18]John's disciples told him about all these things. Calling two of them, [19]he sent them to the Lord to ask, "Are you the one who was to come, or should we expect someone else?"

[20]When the men came to Jesus, they said, "John the Baptist sent us to you to ask, 'Are you the one who was to come, or should we expect someone else?' "

[21]At that very time Jesus cured many who had diseases, sicknesses and evil spirits, and gave sight to many who were blind. [22]So he replied to the messengers, "Go back and report to John what you have seen and heard: The blind receive sight, the lame walk, those who have leprosy[b] are cured, the deaf hear, the dead are raised, and the good news is preached to the poor. [23]Blessed is the man who does not fall away on account of me."

[24]After John's messengers left, Jesus began to speak to the crowd about John: "What did you go out into the desert to see? A reed swayed by the wind? [25]If not, what did you go out to see? A man dressed in fine clothes? No, those who wear expensive clothes and indulge in luxury are in palaces. [26]But what did you go out to see? A prophet? Yes, I tell you, and more than a prophet. [27]This is the one about whom it is written:

" 'I will send my messenger ahead of you,
who will prepare your way before you.'[c]

[28]I tell you, among those born of women there is no-one greater than John; yet the one who is least in the kingdom of God is greater than he."

[29](All the people, even the tax collectors, when they heard Jesus' words, acknowledged that God's way was right, because they had been baptised by John. [30]But the Pharisees and experts in the law rejected God's purpose for themselves, because they had not been baptised by John.)

[31]"To what, then, can I compare the people of this generation? What are they like? [32]They are like children sitting in the market-place and calling out to each other:

" 'We played the flute for you,
and you did not dance;
we sang a dirge,
and you did not cry.'

[33]For John the Baptist came neither eating bread nor drinking wine, and you say, 'He has a demon.' [34]The Son of Man came eating and drinking, and you say, 'Here is a glutton and a drunkard, a friend of tax collectors and "sinners".' [35]But wisdom is proved right by all her children."

Jesus Anointed by a Sinful Woman

[36]Now one of the Pharisees invited Jesus to have dinner with him, so he went to the Pharisee's house and reclined at the table. [37]When a woman who had lived a sinful life in that town learned that Jesus was eating at the Pharisee's house, she brought an alabaster jar of perfume, [38]and as she stood behind him at his feet weeping, she began to wet his feet with her tears. Then she wiped them with her hair, kissed them and poured perfume on them.

[39]When the Pharisee who had invited him saw this, he said to himself, "If this man were a prophet, he would know who is touching him and what kind of woman she is—that she is a sinner."

[40]Jesus answered him, "Simon, I have something to tell you."

"Tell me, teacher," he said.

[41]"Two men owed money to a certain money-lender. One owed him five hundred denarii,[d] and the other fifty. [42]Neither of them had the money to pay him back, so he cancelled the debts of both. Now which of them will love him more?"

---

[a]17 Or the land of the Jews
[b]22 The Greek word was used for various diseases affecting the skin—not necessarily leprosy.
[c]27 Mal. 3:1 [d]41 A denarius was a coin worth about a day's wages.

⁴³Simon replied, "I suppose the one who had the bigger debt cancelled."

"You have judged correctly," Jesus said.

⁴⁴Then he turned towards the woman and said to Simon, "Do you see this woman? I came into your house. You did not give me any water for my feet, but she wet my feet with her tears and wiped them with her hair. ⁴⁵You did not give me a kiss, but this woman, from the time I entered has not stopped kissing my feet. ⁴⁶You did not put oil on my head, but she has poured perfume on my feet. ⁴⁷Therefore, I tell you, her many sins have been forgiven — for she loved much. But he who has been forgiven little loves little."

⁴⁸Then Jesus said to her, "Your sins are forgiven."

⁴⁹The other guests began to say among themselves, "Who is this who even forgives sins?"

⁵⁰Jesus said to the woman, "Your faith has saved you; go in peace."

The Parable of the Sower

8 After this, Jesus travelled about from one town and village to another, proclaiming the good news of the kingdom of God. The Twelve were with him, ²and also some women who had been cured of evil spirits and diseases: Mary (called Magdalene) from whom seven demons had come out; ³Joanna the wife of Chuza, the manager of Herod's household; Susanna; and many others. These women were helping to support them out of their own means.

⁴While a large crowd was gathering and people were coming to Jesus from town after town, he told this parable: ⁵"A farmer went out to sow his seed. As he was scattering the seed, some fell along the path; it was trampled on, and the birds of the air ate it up. ⁶Some fell on rock, and when it came up, the plants withered because they had no moisture. ⁷Other seed fell among thorns, which grew up with it and choked the plants.

⁸Still other seed fell on good soil. It came up and yielded a crop, a hundred times more than was sown."

When he said this, he called out, "He who has ears to hear, let him hear."

⁹His disciples asked him what this parable meant. ¹⁰He said, "The knowledge of the secrets of the kingdom of God has been given to you, but to others I speak in parables, so that,

" 'though seeing, they may not see; though hearing, they may not understand.'ᵃ

¹¹"This is the meaning of the parable: The seed is the word of God. ¹²Those along the path are the ones who hear, and then the devil comes and takes away the word from their hearts, so that they cannot believe and be saved. ¹³Those on the rock are the ones who receive the word with joy when they hear it, but they have no root. They believe for a while, but in the time of testing they fall away. ¹⁴The seed that fell among thorns stands for those who hear, but as they go on their way they are choked by life's worries, riches and pleasures, and they do not mature. ¹⁵But the seed on good soil stands for those with a noble and good heart, who hear the word, retain it, and by persevering produce a crop.

A Lamp on a Stand

¹⁶"No-one lights a lamp and hides it in a jar or puts it under a bed. Instead, he puts it on a stand, so that those who come in can see the light. ¹⁷For there is nothing hidden that will not be disclosed, and nothing concealed that will not be known or brought out into the open. ¹⁸Therefore consider carefully how you listen. Whoever has will be given more; whoever does not have, even what he thinks he has will be taken from him."

Jesus' Mother and Brothers

¹⁹Now Jesus' mother and brothers came to see him, but they were not

ᵃ10 Isaiah 6:9

able to get near him because of the crowd. 20Someone told him, "Your mother and brothers are standing outside, wanting to see you."

21He replied, "My mother and brothers are those who hear God's word and put it into practice."

Jesus Calms the Storm

22One day Jesus said to his disciples, "Let's go over to the other side of the lake." So they got into a boat and set out. 23As they sailed, he fell asleep. A squall came down on the lake, so that the boat was being swamped, and they were in great danger.

24The disciples went and woke him, saying, "Master, Master, we're going to drown!"

He got up and rebuked the wind and the raging waters; the storm subsided, and all was calm. 25"Where is your faith?" he asked his disciples.

In fear and amazement they asked one another, "Who is this? He commands even the winds and the water, and they obey him."

The Healing of a Demon-possessed Man

26They sailed to the region of the Gerasenes,[b] which is across the lake from Galilee. 27When Jesus stepped ashore, he was met by a demon-possessed man from the town. For a long time this man had not worn clothes or lived in a house, but had lived in the tombs. 28When he saw Jesus, he cried out and fell at his feet, shouting at the top of his voice, "What do you want with me, Jesus, Son of the Most High God? I beg you, don't torture me!" 29For Jesus had commanded the evil[c] spirit to come out of the man. Many times it had seized him, and though he was chained hand and foot and kept under guard, he had broken his chains and had been driven by the demon into solitary places.

30Jesus asked him, "What is your name?"

"Legion," he replied, because many

demons had gone into him. 31And they begged him repeatedly not to order them to go into the Abyss.

32A large herd of pigs was feeding there on the hillside. The demons begged Jesus to let them go into them, and he gave them permission. 33When the demons came out of the man, they went into the pigs, and the herd rushed down the steep bank into the lake and was drowned.

34When those tending the pigs saw what had happened, they ran off and reported this in the town and countryside, 35and the people went out to see what had happened. When they came to Jesus, they found the man from whom the demons had gone out, sitting at Jesus' feet, dressed and in his right mind; and they were afraid. 36Those who had seen it told the people how the demon-possessed man had been cured. 37Then all the people of the region of the Gerasenes asked Jesus to leave them, because they were overcome with fear. So he got into the boat and left.

38The man from whom the demons had gone out begged to go with him, but Jesus sent him away, saying, 39"Return home and tell how much God has done for you." So the man went away and told all over the town how much Jesus had done for him.

A Dead Girl and a Sick Woman

40Now when Jesus returned, a crowd welcomed him, for they were all expecting him. 41Just then a man named Jairus, a ruler of the synagogue, came and fell at Jesus' feet, pleading with him to come to his house 42because his only daughter, a girl of about twelve, was dying.

As Jesus was on his way, the crowds almost crushed him. 43And a woman was there who had been subject to bleeding for twelve years,[d] but no-one could heal her. 44She came up behind him and touched the edge of his cloak, and immediately her bleeding stopped.

45"Who touched me?" Jesus asked.

[b]26 Some manuscripts Gadarenes; other manuscripts Gergesenes; also in verse 37
[c]29 Greek unclean
[d]43 Many manuscripts years, and she had spent all she had on doctors

When they all denied it, Peter said, "Master, the people are crowding and pressing against you."

46But Jesus said, "Someone touched me; I know that power has gone out from me."

47Then the woman, seeing that she could not go unnoticed, came trembling and fell at his feet. In the presence of all the people, she told why she had touched him and how she had been instantly healed. 48Then he said to her, "Daughter, your faith has healed you. Go in peace."

49While Jesus was still speaking, someone came from the house of Jairus, the synagogue ruler. "Your daughter is dead," he said. "Don't bother the teacher any more."

50Hearing this, Jesus said to Jairus, "Don't be afraid; just believe, and she will be healed."

51When he arrived at the house of Jairus, he did not let anyone go in with him except Peter, John and James, and the child's father and mother. 52Meanwhile, all the people were wailing and mourning for her. "Stop wailing," Jesus said. "She is not dead but asleep."

53They laughed at him, knowing that she was dead. 54But he took her by the hand and said, "My child, get up!" 55Her spirit returned, and at once she stood up. Then Jesus told them to give her something to eat. 56Her parents were astonished, but he ordered them not to tell anyone what had happened.

Jesus Sends Out the Twelve

9 When Jesus had called the Twelve together, he gave them power and authority to drive out all demons and to cure diseases, 2and he sent them out to preach the kingdom of God and to heal the sick. 3He told them: "Take nothing for the journey—no staff, no bag, no bread, no money, no extra tunic. 4Whatever house you enter, stay there until you leave that town. 5If people do not welcome you, shake the dust off your feet when you leave their town, as a testimony against them." 6So they set out and went from village to village,

preaching the gospel and healing people everywhere.

7Now Herod the tetrarch heard about all that was going on. And he was perplexed, because some were saying that John had been raised from the dead, 8others that Elijah had appeared, and still others that one of the prophets of long ago had come back to life. 9But Herod said, "I beheaded John. Who, then, is this I hear such things about?" And he tried to see him.

Jesus Feeds the Five Thousand

10When the apostles returned, they reported to Jesus what they had done. Then he took them with him and they withdrew by themselves to a town called Bethsaida, 11but the crowds learned about it and followed him. He welcomed them and spoke to them about the kingdom of God, and healed those who needed healing.

12Late in the afternoon the Twelve came to him and said, "Send the crowd away so they can go to the surrounding villages and countryside and find food and lodging, because we are in a remote place here."

13He replied, "You give them something to eat."

They answered, "We have only five loaves of bread and two fish—unless you want us to go and buy food for all this crowd." 14(About five thousand men were there.)

But he said to his disciples, "Make them sit down in groups of about fifty each." 15The disciples did so, and everybody sat down. 16Taking the five loaves and the two fish and looking up to heaven, he gave thanks and broke them. Then he gave them to the disciples to set before the people. 17They all ate and were satisfied, and the disciples picked up twelve basketfuls of broken pieces that were left over.

Peter's Confession of Christ

18Once when Jesus was praying in private and his disciples were with him, he asked them, "Who do the crowds say I am?"

19They replied, "Some say John the Baptist; others say Elijah; and still others, that one of the prophets of long ago has come back to life."

[20]"But what about you?" he asked. "Who do you say I am?"

Peter answered, "The Christ[a] of God."

[21]Jesus strictly warned them not to tell this to anyone. [22]And he said, "The Son of Man must suffer many things and be rejected by the elders, chief priests and teachers of the law, and he must be killed and on the third day be raised to life."

[23]Then he said to them all: "If anyone would come after me, he must deny himself and take up his cross daily and follow me. [24]For whoever wants to save his life will lose it, but whoever loses his life for me will save it. [25]What good is it for a man to gain the whole world, and yet lose or forfeit his very self? [26]If anyone is ashamed of me and my words, the Son of Man will be ashamed of him when he comes in his glory and in the glory of the Father and of the holy angels. [27]I tell you the truth, some who are standing here will not taste death before they see the kingdom of God."

The Transfiguration

[28]About eight days after Jesus said this, he took Peter, John and James with him and went up onto a mountain to pray. [29]As he was praying, the appearance of his face changed, and his clothes became as bright as a flash of lightning. [30]Two men, Moses and Elijah, [31]appeared in glorious splendour, talking with Jesus. They spoke about his departure, which he was about to bring to fulfilment at Jerusalem. [32]Peter and his companions were very sleepy, but when they became fully awake, they saw his glory and the two men standing with him. [33]As the men were leaving Jesus, Peter said to him, "Master, it is good for us to be here. Let us put up three shelters—one for you, one for Moses and one for Elijah." (He did not know what he was saying.)

[34]While he was speaking, a cloud appeared and enveloped them, and they were afraid as they entered the cloud. [35]A voice came from the cloud, saying, "This is my Son, whom I have chosen; listen to him." [36]When the voice had spoken, they found that Jesus was alone. The disciples kept this to themselves, and told no-one at that time what they had seen.

The Healing of a Boy With an Evil Spirit

[37]The next day, when they came down from the mountain, a large crowd met him. [38]A man in the crowd called out, "Teacher, I beg you to look at my son, for he is my only child. [39]A spirit seizes him and he suddenly screams; it throws him into convulsions so that he foams at the mouth. It scarcely ever leaves him and is destroying him. [40]I begged your disciples to drive it out, but they could not."

[41]"O unbelieving and perverse generation," Jesus replied, "how long shall I stay with you and put up with you? Bring your son here."

[42]Even while the boy was coming, the demon threw him to the ground in a convulsion. But Jesus rebuked the evil[b] spirit, healed the boy and gave him back to his father. [43]And they were all amazed at the greatness of God.

While everyone was marvelling at all that Jesus did, he said to his disciples, [44]"Listen carefully to what I am about to tell you: The Son of Man is going to be betrayed into the hands of men." [45]But they did not understand what this meant. It was hidden from them, so that they did not grasp it, and they were afraid to ask him about it.

Who Will Be the Greatest?

[46]An argument started among the disciples as to which of them would be the greatest. [47]Jesus, knowing their thoughts, took a little child and had him stand beside him. [48]Then he said to them, "Whoever welcomes this little child in my name welcomes me; and whoever welcomes me welcomes

[a]20 Or Messiah   [b]42 Greek unclean

the one who sent me. For he who is least among you all—he is the greatest."

49"Master," said John, "we saw a man driving out demons in your name and we tried to stop him, because he is not one of us."

50"Do not stop him," Jesus said, "for whoever is not against you is for you."

Samaritan Opposition

51As the time approached for him to be taken up to heaven, Jesus resolutely set out for Jerusalem, 52and he sent messengers on ahead. They went into a Samaritan village to get things ready for him, 53but the people there did not welcome him, because he was heading for Jerusalem. 54When the disciples James and John saw this, they asked, "Lord, do you want us to call fire down from heaven to destroy them?"*c* 55But Jesus turned and rebuked them, 56and*d* they went to another village.

The Cost of Following Jesus

57As they were walking along the road, a man said to him, "I will follow you wherever you go."

58Jesus replied, "Foxes have holes and birds of the air have nests, but the Son of Man has no place to lay his head."

59He said to another man, "Follow me."

But the man replied, "Lord, first let me go and bury my father."

60Jesus said to him, "Let the dead bury their own dead, but you go and proclaim the kingdom of God."

61Still another said, "I will follow you, Lord; but first let me go back and say good-bye to my family."

62Jesus replied, "No-one who puts his hand to the plough and looks back is fit for service in the kingdom of God."

Jesus Sends Out the Seventy-two

10 After this the Lord appointed seventy-two*a* others and sent

them two by two ahead of him to every town and place where he was about to go. 2He told them, "The harvest is plentiful, but the workers are few. Ask the Lord of the harvest, therefore, to send out workers into his harvest field. 3Go! I am sending you out like lambs among wolves. 4Do not take a purse or bag or sandals; and do not greet anyone on the road.

5"When you enter a house, first say, 'Peace to this house.' 6If a man of peace is there, your peace will rest on him; if not, it will return to you. 7Stay in that house, eating and drinking whatever they give you, for the worker deserves his wages. Do not move around from house to house.

8"When you enter a town and are welcomed, eat what is set before you. 9Heal the sick who are there and tell them, 'The kingdom of God is near you.' 10But when you enter a town and are not welcomed, go into its streets and say, 11'Even the dust of your town that sticks to our feet we wipe off against you. Yet be sure of this: The kingdom of God is near.' 12I tell you, it will be more bearable on that day for Sodom than for that town.

13"Woe to you, Korazin! Woe to you, Bethsaida! For if the miracles that were performed in you had been performed in Tyre and Sidon, they would have repented long ago, sitting in sackcloth and ashes. 14But it will be more bearable for Tyre and Sidon at the judgment than for you. 15And you, Capernaum, will you be lifted up to the skies? No, you will go down to the depths.*b*

16"He who listens to you listens to me; he who rejects you rejects me; but he who rejects me rejects him who sent me."

17The seventy-two returned with joy and said, "Lord, even the demons submit to us in your name."

18He replied, "I saw Satan fall like lightning from heaven. 19I have given

c54 Some manuscripts them, even as Elijah did
d55,56 Some manuscripts them. And he said, "You do not know what kind of spirit you are of, for the Son of Man did not come to destroy men's lives, but to save them." 56And
a1 Some manuscripts seventy; also in verse 17
b15 Greek Hades

you authority to trample on snakes and scorpions and to overcome all the power of the enemy; nothing will harm you. [20]However, do not rejoice that the spirits submit to you, but rejoice that your names are written in heaven."

[21]At that time Jesus, full of joy through the Holy Spirit, said, "I praise you, Father, Lord of heaven and earth, because you have hidden these things from the wise and learned, and revealed them to little children. Yes, Father, for this was your good pleasure.

[22]"All things have been committed to me by my Father. No-one knows who the Son is except the Father, and no-one knows who the Father is except the Son and those to whom the Son chooses to reveal him."

[23]Then he turned to his disciples and said privately, "Blessed are the eyes that see what you see. [24]For I tell you that many prophets and kings wanted to see what you see but did not see it, and to hear what you hear but did not hear it."

The Parable of the Good Samaritan

[25]On one occasion an expert in the law stood up to test Jesus. "Teacher," he asked, "what must I do to inherit eternal life?"

[26]"What is written in the Law?" he replied. "How do you read it?"

[27]He answered: " 'Love the Lord your God with all your heart and with all your soul and with all your strength and with all your mind';[c] and, 'Love your neighbour as yourself.'[d]"

[28]"You have answered correctly," Jesus replied. "Do this and you will live."

[29]But he wanted to justify himself, so he asked Jesus, "And who is my neighbour?"

[30]In reply Jesus said: "A man was going down from Jerusalem to Jericho, when he fell into the hands of robbers. They stripped him of his clothes, beat him and went away, leaving him half-dead. [31]A priest hap-

pened to be going down the same road, and when he saw the man, he passed by on the other side. [32]So too, a Levite, when he came to the place and saw the man, passed by on the other side. [33]But a Samaritan, as he travelled, came where the man was; and when he saw him, he took pity on him. [34]He went to him and bandaged his wounds, pouring on oil and wine. Then he put the man on his own donkey, brought him to an inn and took care of him. [35]The next day he took out two silver coins[e] and gave them to the innkeeper. 'Look after him,' he said, 'and when I return, I will reimburse you for any extra expense you may have.'

[36]"Which of these three do you think was a neighbour to the man who fell into the hands of robbers?"

[37]The expert in the law replied, "The one who had mercy on him."

Jesus told him, "Go and do likewise."

At the Home of Martha and Mary

[38]As Jesus and his disciples were on their way, he came to a village where a woman named Martha opened her home to him. [39]She had a sister called Mary, who sat at the Lord's feet listening to what he said. [40]But Martha was distracted by all the preparations that had to be made. She came to him and asked, "Lord, don't you care that my sister has left me to do the work by myself? Tell her to help me!"

[41]"Martha, Martha," the Lord answered, "you are worried and upset about many things, [42]but only one thing is needed.[f] Mary has chosen what is better, and it will not be taken away from her."

Jesus' Teaching on Prayer

11 One day Jesus was praying in a certain place. When he finished, one of his disciples said to him, "Lord, teach us to pray, just as John taught his disciples."

[c]27 Deut. 6:5   [d]27 Lev. 19:18   [e]35 Greek two denarii
[f]42 Some manuscripts but few things are needed–or only one

²He said to them, "When you pray, say:

" 'Father,[a]
hallowed be your name,
your kingdom come.[b]
³Give us each day our daily bread.
⁴Forgive us our sins,
    for we also forgive everyone who
        sins against us.[c]
And lead us not into temptation.' "[d]

⁵Then he said to them, "Suppose one of you has a friend, and he goes to him at midnight and says, 'Friend, lend me three loaves of bread, ⁶because a friend of mine on a journey has come to me, and I have nothing to set before him.'

⁷"Then the one inside answers, 'Don't bother me. The door is already locked, and my children are with me in bed. I can't get up and give you anything.' ⁸I tell you, though he will not get up and give him the bread because he is his friend, yet because of the man's persistence he will get up and give him as much as he needs.

⁹"So I say to you: Ask and it will be given to you; seek and you will find; knock and the door will be opened to you. ¹⁰For everyone who asks receives; he who seeks finds; and to him who knocks, the door will be opened.

¹¹"Which of you fathers, if your son asks for[e] a fish, will give him a snake instead? ¹²Or if he asks for an egg, will give him a scorpion? ¹³If you then, though you are evil, know how to give good gifts to your children, how much more will your Father in heaven give the Holy Spirit to those who ask him!"

Jesus and Beelzebub

¹⁴Jesus was driving out a demon that was mute. When the demon left, the man who had been dumb spoke, and the crowd was amazed. ¹⁵But some of them said, "By Beelzebub,[f]

the prince of demons, he is driving out demons." ¹⁶Others tested him by asking for a sign from heaven.

¹⁷Jesus knew their thoughts and said to them: "Any kingdom divided against itself will be ruined, and a house divided against itself will fall. ¹⁸If Satan is divided against himself, how can his kingdom stand? I say this because you claim that I drive out demons by Beelzebub. ¹⁹Now if I drive out demons by Beelzebub, by whom do your followers drive them out? So then, they will be your judges. ²⁰But if I drive out demons by the finger of God, then the kingdom of God has come to you.

²¹"When a strong man, fully armed, guards his own house, his possessions are safe. ²²But when someone stronger attacks and overpowers him, he takes away the armour in which the man trusted and divides up the spoils.

²³"He who is not with me is against me, and he who does not gather with me, scatters.

²⁴"When an evil[g] spirit comes out of a man, it goes through arid places seeking rest and does not find it. Then it says, 'I will return to the house I left.' ²⁵When it arrives, it finds the house swept clean and put in order. ²⁶Then it goes and takes seven other spirits more wicked than itself, and they go in and live there. And the final condition of that man is worse than the first."

²⁷As Jesus was saying these things, a woman in the crowd called out, "Blessed is the mother who gave you birth and nursed you."

²⁸He replied, "Blessed rather are those who hear the word of God and obey it."

The Sign of Jonah

²⁹As the crowds increased, Jesus said, "This is a wicked generation. It asks for a miraculous sign, but none

---

[a]2 Some manuscripts Our Father in heaven
[b]2 Some manuscripts come. May your will be done on earth as it is in heaven.
[c]4 Greek everyone who is indebted to us
[d]4 Some manuscripts temptation but deliver us from the evil one
[e]11 Some manuscripts for bread, will give him a stone; or if he asks for
[f]15 Greek Beezeboul or Beelzeboul; also in verses 18 and 19
[g]24 Greek unclean

will be given it except the sign of Jonah. 30For as Jonah was a sign to the Ninevites, so also will the Son of Man be to this generation. 31The Queen of the South will rise at the judgment with the men of this generation and condemn them, for she came from the ends of the earth to listen to Solomon's wisdom, and now oneh greater than Solomon is here. 32The men of Nineveh will stand up at the judgment with this generation and condemn it, for they repented at the preaching of Jonah, and now one greater than Jonah is here.

The Lamp of the Body

33"No-one lights a lamp and puts it in a place where it will be hidden, or under a bowl. Instead he puts it on its stand, so that those who come in may see the light. 34Your eye is the lamp of your body. When your eyes are good, your whole body also is full of light. But when they are bad, your body also is full of darkness. 35See to it, then, that the light within you is not darkness. 36Therefore, if your whole body is full of light, and no part of it dark, it will be completely lighted, as when the light of a lamp shines on you."

Six Woes

37When Jesus had finished speaking, a Pharisee invited him to eat with him; so he went in and reclined at the table. 38But the Pharisee, noticing that Jesus did not first wash before the meal, was surprised.

39Then the Lord said to him, "Now then, you Pharisees clean the outside of the cup and dish, but inside you are full of greed and wickedness. 40You foolish people! Did not the one who made the outside make the inside also? 41But give what is inside the dishi to the poor, and everything will be clean for you.

42"Woe to you Pharisees, because you give God a tenth of your mint, rue and all other kinds of garden herbs, but you neglect justice and the love of God. You should have practised the latter without leaving the

former undone.

43"Woe to you Pharisees, because you love the most important seats in the synagogues and greetings in the market-places.

44"Woe to you, because you are like unmarked graves, which men walk over without knowing it."

45One of the experts in the law answered him, "Teacher, when you say these things, you insult us also."

46Jesus replied, "And you experts in the law, woe to you, because you load people down with burdens they can hardly carry, and you yourselves will not lift one finger to help them.

47"Woe to you, because you build tombs for the prophets, and it was your forefathers who killed them. 48So you testify that you approve of what your forefathers did; they killed the prophets, and you build their tombs. 49Because of this, God in his wisdom said, 'I will send them prophets and apostles, some of whom they will kill and others they will persecute.' 50Therefore this generation will be held responsible for the blood of all the prophets that has been shed since the beginning of the world, 51from the blood of Abel to the blood of Zechariah, who was killed between the altar and the sanctuary. Yes, I tell you, this generation will be held responsible for it all.

52"Woe to you experts in the law, because you have taken away the key to knowledge. You yourselves have not entered, and you have hindered those who were entering."

53When Jesus left there, the Pharisees and the teachers of the law began to oppose him fiercely and to besiege him with questions, 54waiting to catch him in something he might say.

Warnings and Encouragements

12 Meanwhile, when a crowd of many thousands had gathered, so that they were trampling on one another, Jesus began to speak first to his disciples, saying: "Be on your guard against the yeast of the Pharisees, which is hypocrisy. 2There is

h31 Or something; also in verse 32   i41 Or what you have

80

nothing concealed that will not be disclosed, or hidden that will not be made known. 3What you have said in the dark will be heard in the daylight, and what you have whispered in the ear in the inner rooms will be proclaimed from the housetops.

4"I tell you, my friends, do not be afraid of those who kill the body and after that can do no more. 5But I will show you whom you should fear: Fear him who, after the killing of the body, has power to throw you into hell. Yes, I tell you, fear him. 6Are not five sparrows sold for two pennies?[a] Yet not one of them is forgotten by God. 7Indeed, the very hairs of your head are all numbered. Don't be afraid; you are worth more than many sparrows.

8"I tell you, whoever acknowledges me before men, the Son of Man will also acknowledge him before the angels of God. 9But he who disowns me before men will be disowned before the angels of God. 10And everyone who speaks a word against the Son of Man will be forgiven, but anyone who blasphemes against the Holy Spirit will not be forgiven.

11"When you are brought before synagogues, rulers and authorities, do not worry about how you will defend yourselves or what you will say, 12for the Holy Spirit will teach you at that time what you should say."

The Parable of the Rich Fool

13Someone in the crowd said to him, "Teacher, tell my brother to divide the inheritance with me."

14Jesus replied, "Man, who appointed me a judge or an arbiter between you?" 15Then he said to them, "Watch out! Be on your guard against all kinds of greed; a man's life does not consist in the abundance of his possessions."

16And he told them this parable: "The ground of a certain rich man produced a good crop. 17He thought to himself, 'What shall I do? I have no place to store my crops.'

18"Then he said, 'This is what I'll do. I will tear down my barns and build bigger ones, and there I will store all my grain and my goods. 19And I'll say to myself, "You have plenty of good things laid up for many years. Take life easy; eat, drink and be merry." '

20"But God said to him, 'You fool! This very night your life will be demanded from you. Then who will get what you have prepared for yourself?'

21"This is how it will be with anyone who stores up things for himself but is not rich towards God."

Do Not Worry

22Then Jesus said to his disciples: "Therefore I tell you, do not worry about your life, what you will eat; or about your body, what you will wear. 23Life is more than food, and the body more than clothes. 24Consider the ravens: They do not sow or reap, they have no storeroom or barn; yet God feeds them. And how much more valuable you are than birds! 25Who of you by worrying can add a single hour to his life?[b] 26Since you cannot do this very little thing, why do you worry about the rest?

27"Consider how the lilies grow. They do not labour or spin. Yet I tell you, not even Solomon in all his splendour was dressed like one of these. 28If that is how God clothes the grass of the field, which is here today, and tomorrow is thrown into the fire, how much more will he clothe you, O you of little faith! 29And do not set your heart on what you will eat or drink; do not worry about it. 30For the pagan world runs after all such things, and your Father knows that you need them. 31But seek his kingdom, and these things will be given to you as well.

32"Do not be afraid, little flock, for your Father has been pleased to give you the kingdom. 33Sell your possessions and give to the poor. Provide purses for yourselves that will not wear out, a treasure in heaven that will not be exhausted, where no thief comes near and no moth destroys. 34For where your treasure is, there

---

a6 Greek two assaria   b25 Or single cubit to his height

your heart will be also.

Watchfulness

35"Be dressed ready for service and keep your lamps burning, 36like men waiting for their master to return from a wedding banquet, so that when he comes and knocks they can immediately open the door for him. 37It will be good for those servants whose master finds them watching when he comes. I tell you the truth, he will dress himself to serve, will have them recline at the table and will come and wait on them. 38It will be good for those servants whose master finds them ready, even if he comes in the second or third watch of the night. 39But understand this: If the owner of the house had known at what hour the thief was coming, he would not have let his house be broken into. 40You also must be ready, because the Son of Man will come at an hour when you do not expect him."

41Peter asked, "Lord, are you telling this parable to us, or to everyone?"

42The Lord answered, "Who then is the faithful and wise manager, whom the master puts in charge of his servants to give them their food allowance at the proper time? 43It will be good for that servant whom the master finds doing so when he returns. 44I tell you the truth, he will put him in charge of all his possessions. 45But suppose the servant says to himself, 'My master is taking a long time in coming,' and he then begins to beat the menservants and womenservants and to eat and drink and get drunk. 46The master of that servant will come on a day when he does not expect him and at an hour he is not aware of. He will cut him to pieces and assign him a place with the unbelievers.

47"That servant who knows his master's will and does not get ready or does not do what his master wants will be beaten with many blows. 48But the one who does not know and does things deserving punishment will be beaten with few blows. From

c59 Greek *lepton*

everyone who has been given much, much will be demanded; and from the one who has been entrusted with much, much more will be asked.

Not Peace but Division

49"I have come to bring fire on the earth, and how I wish it were already kindled! 50But I have a baptism to undergo, and how distressed I am until it is completed! 51Do you think I came to bring peace on earth? No, I tell you, but division. 52From now on there will be five in one family divided against each other, three against two and two against three. 53They will be divided, father against son and son against father, mother against daughter and daughter against mother, mother-in-law against daughter-in-law and daughter-in-law against mother-in-law."

Interpreting the Times

54He said to the crowd: "When you see a cloud rising in the west, immediately you say, 'It's going to rain,' and it does. 55And when the south wind blows, you say, 'It's going to be hot,' and it is. 56Hypocrites! You know how to interpret the appearance of the earth and the sky. How is it that you don't know how to interpret this present time?

57"Why don't you judge for yourselves what is right? 58As you are going with your adversary to the magistrate, try hard to be reconciled to him on the way, or he may drag you off to the judge, and the judge turn you over to the officer, and the officer throw you into prison. 59I tell you, you will not get out until you have paid the last penny."c

Repent or Perish

13 Now there were some present at that time who told Jesus about the Galileans whose blood Pilate had mixed with their sacrifices. 2Jesus answered, "Do you think that these Galileans were worse sinners than all the other Galileans because they suffered this way? 3I tell you, no!

But unless you repent, you too will all perish. 4Or those eighteen who died when the tower in Siloam fell on them—do you think they were more guilty than all the others living in Jerusalem? 5I tell you, no! But unless you repent, you too will all perish."

6Then he told this parable: "A man had a fig-tree, planted in his vineyard, and he went to look for fruit on it, but did not find any. 7So he said to the man who took care of the vineyard, 'For three years now I've been coming to look for fruit on this fig-tree and haven't found any. Cut it down! Why should it use up the soil?'

8" 'Sir,' the man replied, 'leave it alone for one more year, and I'll dig round it and fertilise it. 9If it bears fruit next year, fine! If not, then cut it down.' "

A Crippled Woman Healed on the Sabbath

10On a Sabbath Jesus was teaching in one of the synagogues, 11and a woman was there who had been crippled by a spirit for eighteen years. She was bent over and could not straighten up at all. 12When Jesus saw her, he called her forward and said to her, "Woman, you are set free from your infirmity." 13Then he put his hands on her, and immediately she straightened up and praised God.

14Indignant because Jesus had healed on the Sabbath, the synagogue ruler said to the people, "There are six days for work. So come and be healed on those days, not on the Sabbath."

15The Lord answered him, "You hypocrites! Doesn't each of you on the Sabbath untie his ox or donkey from the stall and lead it out to give it water? 16Then should not this woman, a daughter of Abraham, whom Satan has kept bound for eighteen long years, be set free on the Sabbath day from what bound her?"

17When he said this, all his opponents were humiliated, but the people were delighted with all the wonderful things he was doing.

The Parables of the Mustard Seed and the Yeast

18Then Jesus asked, "What is the kingdom of God like? What shall I compare it to? 19It is like a mustard seed, which a man took and planted in his garden. It grew, became a tree, and the birds of the air perched in its branches."

20Again he asked, "What shall I compare the kingdom of God to? 21It is like yeast that a woman took and mixed into a large amount*a* of flour until it worked all through the dough."

The Narrow Door

22Then Jesus went through the towns and villages, teaching as he made his way to Jerusalem. 23Someone asked him, "Lord, are only a few people going to be saved?"

He said to them, 24"Make every effort to enter through the narrow door, because many, I tell you, will try to enter and will not be able to. 25Once the owner of the house gets up and closes the door, you will stand outside knocking and pleading, 'Sir, open the door for us.'

"But he will answer, 'I don't know you or where you come from.'

26"Then you will say, 'We ate and drank with you, and you taught in our streets.'

27"But he will reply, 'I don't know you or where you come from. Away from me, all you evildoers!'

28"There will be weeping there, and gnashing of teeth, when you see Abraham, Isaac and Jacob and all the prophets in the kingdom of God, but you yourselves thrown out. 29People will come from east and west and north and south, and will take their places at the feast in the kingdom of God. 30Indeed there are those who are last who will be first, and first who will be last."

Jesus' Sorrow for Jerusalem

31At that time some Pharisees came to Jesus and said to him, "Leave this place and go somewhere else. Herod

a21 Greek three satas (probably about ½ bushel or 22 litres)

wants to kill you."

32He replied, "Go tell that fox, 'I will drive out demons and heal people today and tomorrow, and on the third day I will reach my goal.' 33In any case, I must keep going today and tomorrow and the next day—for surely no prophet can die outside Jerusalem!

34"O Jerusalem, Jerusalem, you who kill the prophets and stone those sent to you, how often I have longed to gather your children together, as a hen gathers her chicks under her wings, but you were not willing! 35Look, your house is left to you desolate. I tell you, you will not see me again until you say, 'Blessed is he who comes in the name of the Lord.'b"

Jesus at a Pharisee's House

14 One Sabbath, when Jesus went to eat in the house of a prominent Pharisee, he was being carefully watched. 2There in front of him was a man suffering from dropsy. 3Jesus asked the Pharisees and experts in the law, "Is it lawful to heal on the Sabbath or not?" 4But they remained silent. So taking hold of the man, he healed him and sent him away.

5Then he asked them, "If one of you has a sona or an ox that falls into a well on the Sabbath day, will you not immediately pull him out?" 6And they had nothing to say.

7When he noticed how the guests picked the places of honour at the table, he told them this parable: 8"When someone invites you to a wedding feast, do not take the place of honour, for a person more distinguished than you may have been invited. 9If so, the host who invited both of you will come and say to you, 'Give this man your seat.' Then, humiliated, you will have to take the least important place. 10But when you are invited, take the lowest place, so that when your host comes, he will say to you, 'Friend, move up to a better place.' Then you will be honoured in the presence of all your fellow guests. 11For everyone who exalts himself will be humbled, and he who humbles himself will be exalted."

12Then Jesus said to his host, "When you give a luncheon or dinner, do not invite your friends, your brothers or relatives, or your rich neighbours; if you do, they may invite you back and so you will be repaid. 13But when you give a banquet, invite the poor, the crippled, the lame, the blind, 14and you will be blessed. Although they cannot repay you, you will be repaid at the resurrection of the righteous."

The Parable of the Great Banquet

15When one of those at the table with him heard this, he said to Jesus, "Blessed is the man who will eat at the feast in the kingdom of God."

16Jesus replied: "A certain man was preparing a great banquet and invited many guests. 17At the time of the banquet he sent his servant to tell those who had been invited, 'Come, for everything is now ready.'

18"But they all alike began to make excuses. The first said, 'I have just bought a field, and I must go and see it. Please excuse me.'

19"Another said, 'I have just bought five yoke of oxen, and I'm on my way to try them out. Please excuse me.'

20"Still another said, 'I have just got married, so I can't come.'

21"The servant came back and reported this to his master. Then the owner of the house became angry and ordered his servant, 'Go out quickly into the streets and alleys of the town and bring in the poor, the crippled, the blind and the lame.'

22" 'Sir,' the servant said, 'what you ordered has been done, but there is still room.'

23"Then the master told his servant, 'Go out to the roads and country lanes and make them come in, so that my house will be full. 24I tell you, not one of those men who were invited will

b35 Psalm 118:26
a5 Some manuscripts donkey

get a taste of my banquet.' "

The Cost of Being a Disciple

25Large crowds were travelling with Jesus, and turning to them he said: 26"If anyone comes to me and does not hate his father and mother, his wife and children, his brothers and sisters—yes, even his own life— he cannot be my disciple. 27And anyone who does not carry his cross and follow me cannot be my disciple.

28"Suppose one of you wants to build a tower. Will he not first sit down and estimate the cost to see if he has enough money to complete it? 29For if he lays the foundation and is not able to finish it, everyone who sees it will ridicule him, 30saying, 'This fellow began to build and was not able to finish.'

31"Or suppose a king is about to go to war against another king. Will he not first sit down and consider whether he is able with ten thousand men to oppose the one coming against him with twenty thousand? 32If he is not able, he will send a delegation while the other is still a long way off and will ask for terms of peace. 33In the same way, any of you who does not give up everything he has cannot be my disciple.

34"Salt is good, but if it loses its saltiness, how can it be made salty again? 35It is fit neither for the soil nor for the manure heap; it is thrown out.

"He who has ears to hear, let him hear."

The Parable of the Lost Sheep

15 Now the tax collectors and "sinners" were all gathering round to hear him. 2But the Pharisees and the teachers of the law muttered, "This man welcomes sinners, and eats with them."

3Then Jesus told them this parable: 4"Suppose one of you has a hundred sheep and loses one of them. Does he not leave the ninety-nine in the open country and go after the lost sheep until he finds it? 5And when he finds it, he joyfully puts it on his shoulders 6and goes home. Then he calls his friends and neighbours together and says, 'Rejoice with me; I have found my lost sheep.' 7I tell you that in the same way there is more rejoicing in heaven over one sinner who repents than over ninety-nine righteous persons who do not need to repent.

The Parable of the Lost Coin

8"Or suppose a woman has ten silver coins*a* and loses one. Does she not light a lamp, sweep the house and search carefully until she finds it? 9And when she finds it, she calls her friends and neighbours together and says, 'Rejoice with me; I have found my lost coin.' 10In the same way, I tell you, there is rejoicing in the presence of the angels of God over one sinner who repents."

The Parable of the Lost Son

11Jesus continued: "There was a man who had two sons. 12The younger one said to his father, 'Father, give me my share of the estate.' So he divided his property between them.

13"Not long after that, the younger son got together all he had, set off for a distant country and there squandered his wealth in wild living. 14After he had spent everything, there was a severe famine in that whole country, and he began to be in need. 15So he went and hired himself out to a citizen of that country, who sent him to his fields to feed pigs. 16He longed to fill his stomach with the pods that the pigs were eating, but no-one gave him anything.

17"When he came to his senses, he said, 'How many of my father's hired men have food to spare, and here I am starving to death! 18I will set out and go back to my father and say to him: Father, I have sinned against heaven and against you. 19I am no longer worthy to be called your son; make me like one of your hired men.' 20So he got up and went to his father.

"But while he was still a long way off, his father saw him and was filled with compassion for him; he ran to

*a*8 Greek ten drachmas, each worth about a day's wages

his son, threw his arms around him and kissed him.

21"The son said to him, 'Father, I have sinned against heaven and against you. I am no longer worthy to be called your son.'[b]

22"But the father said to his servants, 'Quick! Bring the best robe and put it on him. Put a ring on his finger and sandals on his feet. 23Bring the fattened calf and kill it. Let's have a feast and celebrate. 24For this son of mine was dead and is alive again; he was lost and is found.' So they began to celebrate.

25"Meanwhile, the older son was in the field. When he came near the house, he heard music and dancing. 26So he called one of the servants and asked him what was going on. 27'Your brother has come,' he replied, 'and your father has killed the fattened calf because he has him back safe and sound.'

28"The older brother became angry and refused to go in. So his father went out and pleaded with him. 29But he answered his father, 'Look! All these years I've been slaving for you and never disobeyed your orders. Yet you never gave me even a young goat so I could celebrate with my friends. 30But when this son of yours who has squandered your property with prostitutes comes home, you kill the fattened calf for him!'

31"'My son,' the father said, 'you are always with me, and everything I have is yours. 32But we had to celebrate and be glad, because this brother of yours was dead and is alive again; he was lost and is found.'"

The Parable of the Shrewd Manager

16 Jesus told his disciples: "There was a rich man whose manager was accused of wasting his possessions. 2So he called him in and asked him, 'What is this I hear about you? Give an account of your management, because you cannot be manager any longer.'

3"The manager said to himself, 'What shall I do now? My master is taking away my job. I'm not strong enough to dig, and I'm ashamed to beg— 4I know what I'll do so that, when I lose my job here, people will welcome me into their houses.'

5"So he called in each one of his master's debtors. He asked the first, 'How much do you owe my master?'

6"'Eight hundred gallons[a] of olive oil,' he replied.

"The manager told him, 'Take your bill, sit down quickly, and make it four hundred.'

7"Then he asked the second, 'And how much do you owe?'

"'A thousand bushels[b] of wheat,' he replied.

"He told him, 'Take your bill and make it eight hundred.'

8"The master commended the dishonest manager because he had acted shrewdly. For the people of this world are more shrewd in dealing with their own kind than are the people of the light. 9I tell you, use worldly wealth to gain friends for yourselves, so that when it is gone, you will be welcomed into eternal dwellings.

10"Whoever can be trusted with very little can also be trusted with much, and whoever is dishonest with very little will also be dishonest with much. 11So if you have not been trustworthy in handling worldly wealth, who will trust you with true riches? 12And if you have not been trustworthy with someone else's property, who will give you property of your own?

13"No servant can serve two masters. Either he will hate the one and love the other, or he will be devoted to the one and despise the other. You cannot serve both God and Money."

14The Pharisees, who loved money, heard all this and were sneering at Jesus. 15He said to them, "You are the ones who justify yourselves in the eyes of men, but God knows your

---

b21 Some early manuscripts *son. Make me like one of your hired men.*
a6 Greek *one hundred batous* (probably about 3 kilolitres)
b7 Greek *one hundred korous* (probably about 35 kilolitres)

hearts. What is highly valued among men is detestable in God's sight.

16"The Law and the Prophets were proclaimed until John. Since that time, the good news of the kingdom of God is being preached, and everyone is forcing his way into it. 17It is easier for heaven and earth to disappear than for the least stroke of a pen to drop out of the Law.

18"Anyone who divorces his wife and marries another woman commits adultery, and the man who marries a divorced woman commits adultery.

The Rich Man and Lazarus

19"There was a rich man who was dressed in purple and fine linen and lived in luxury every day. 20At his gate was laid a beggar named Lazarus, covered with sores 21and longing to eat what fell from the rich man's table. Even the dogs came and licked his sores.

22"The time came when the beggar died and the angels carried him to Abraham's side. The rich man also died and was buried. 23In hell,c where he was in torment, he looked up and saw Abraham far away, with Lazarus by his side. 24So he called to him, 'Father Abraham, have pity on me and send Lazarus to dip the tip of his finger in water and cool my tongue, because I am in agony in this fire.'

25"But Abraham replied, 'Son, remember that in your lifetime you received your good things, while Lazarus received bad things, but now he is comforted here and you are in agony. 26And besides all this, between us and you a great chasm has been fixed, so that those who want to go from here to you cannot, nor can anyone cross over from there to us.'

27"He answered, 'Then I beg you, father, send Lazarus to my father's house, 28for I have five brothers. Let him warn them, so that they will not also come to this place of torment.'

29"Abraham replied, 'They have Moses and the Prophets; let them

listen to them.'

30" 'No father Abraham,' he said, 'but if someone from the dead goes to them, they will repent.'

31"He said to him, 'If they do not listen to Moses and the Prophets, they will not be convinced even if someone rises from the dead.' "

Sin, Faith, Duty

17 Jesus said to his disciples: "Things that cause people to sin are bound to come, but woe to that person through whom they come. 2It would be better for him to be thrown into the sea with a millstone tied round his neck than for him to cause one of these little ones to sin. 3So watch yourselves.

"If your brother sins, rebuke him, and if he repents, forgive him. 4If he sins against you seven times in a day, and seven times comes back to you and says, 'I repent,' forgive him."

5The apostles said to the Lord, "Increase our faith!"

6He replied, "If you have faith as small as a mustard seed, you can say to this mulberry tree, 'Be uprooted and planted in the sea,' and it will obey you.

7"Suppose one of you had a servant ploughing or looking after the sheep. Would he say to the servant when he comes in from the field, 'Come along now and sit down to eat'? 8Would he not rather say, 'Prepare my supper, get yourself ready and wait on me while I eat and drink; after that you may eat and drink'? 9Would he thank the servant because he did what he was told to do? 10So you also, when you have done everything you were told to do, should say, 'We are unworthy servants; we have only done our duty.' "

Ten Healed of Leprosy

11Now on his way to Jerusalem, Jesus travelled along the border between Samaria and Galilee. 12As he was going into a village, ten men who had leprosya met him. They

c23 Greek *Hades*
a12 The Greek word was used for various diseases affecting the skin—not necessarily leprosy.

stood at a distance ¹³and called out in a loud voice, "Jesus, Master, have pity on us!"

¹⁴When he saw them, he said, "Go, show yourselves to the priests." And as they went, they were cleansed.

¹⁵One of them, when he saw he was healed, came back, praising God in a loud voice. ¹⁶He threw himself at Jesus' feet and thanked him—and he was a Samaritan.

¹⁷Jesus asked, "Were not all ten cleansed? Where are the other nine? ¹⁸Was no-one found to return and give praise to God except this foreigner?" ¹⁹Then he said to him, "Rise and go; your faith has made you well."

The Coming of the Kingdom of God

²⁰Once, having been asked by the Pharisees when the kingdom of God would come, Jesus replied, "The kingdom of God does not come visibly, ²¹nor will people say, 'Here it is,' or 'There it is,' because the kingdom of God is within[b] you."

²²Then he said to his disciples, "The time is coming when you will long to see one of the days of the Son of Man, but you will not see it. ²³Men will tell you, 'There he is!' or 'Here he is!' Do not go running off after them. ²⁴For the Son of Man in his day[c] will be like the lightning, which flashes and lights up the sky from one end to the other. ²⁵But first he must suffer many things and be rejected by this generation.

²⁶"Just as it was in the days of Noah, so also will it be in the days of the Son of Man. ²⁷People were eating, drinking, marrying and being given in marriage up to the day Noah entered the ark. Then the flood came and destroyed them all.

²⁸"It was the same in the days of Lot. People were eating and drinking, buying and selling, planting and building. ²⁹But the day Lot left Sodom, fire and sulphur rained down from heaven and destroyed them all.

³⁰"It will be just like this on the day

the Son of Man is revealed. ³¹On that day no-one who is on the roof of his house, with his goods inside, should go down to get them. Likewise, no-one in the field should go back for anything. ³²Remember Lot's wife! ³³Whoever tries to keep his life will lose it, and whoever loses his life will preserve it. ³⁴I tell you, on that night two people will be in one bed; one will be taken and the other left. ³⁵Two women will be grinding grain together; one will be taken and the other left."[d]

³⁷"Where, Lord?" they asked.

He replied, "Where there is a dead body, there the vultures will gather."

The Parable of the Persistent Widow

18 Then Jesus told his disciples a parable to show them that they should always pray and not give up. ²He said: "In a certain town there was a judge who neither feared God nor cared about men. ³And there was a widow in that town who kept coming to him with the plea, 'Grant me justice against my adversary.'

⁴"For some time he refused. But finally he said to himself, 'Even though I don't fear God or care about men, ⁵yet because this widow keeps bothering me, I will see that she gets justice, so that she won't eventually wear me out with her coming!'"

⁶And the Lord said, "Listen to what the unjust judge says. ⁷And will not God bring about justice for his chosen ones, who cry out to him day and night? Will he keep putting them off? ⁸I tell you, he will see that they get justice, and quickly. However, when the Son of Man comes, will he find faith on the earth?"

The Parable of the Pharisee and the Tax Collector

⁹To some who were confident of their own righteousness and looked down on everybody else, Jesus told this parable: ¹⁰"Two men went up to the temple to pray, one a Pharisee and the other a tax collector. ¹¹The

---

b21 Or among   c24 Some manuscripts do not have in his day.
d35 Some manuscripts left. ³⁶Two men will be in the field; one will be taken and the other left.

Pharisee stood up and prayed about[a] himself: 'God, I thank you that I am not like all other men—robbers, evildoers, adulterers—or even like this tax collector. 12I fast twice a week and give a tenth of all I get.'

13"But the tax collector stood at a distance. He would not even look up to heaven, but beat his breast and said, 'God, have mercy on me, a sinner.'

14"I tell you that this man, rather than the other, went home justified before God. For everyone who exalts himself will be humbled, and he who humbles himself will be exalted."

The Little Children and Jesus

15People were also bringing babies to Jesus to have him touch them. When the disciples saw this, they rebuked them. 16But Jesus called the children to him and said, "Let the little children come to me, and do not hinder them, for the kingdom of God belongs to such as these. 17I tell you the truth, anyone who will not receive the kingdom of God like a little child will never enter it."

The Rich Ruler

18A certain ruler asked him, "Good teacher, what must I do to inherit eternal life?"

19"Why do you call me good?" Jesus answered. "No-one is good—except God alone. 20You know the commandments: 'Do not commit adultery, do not murder, do not steal, do not give false testimony, honour your father and mother.'[b]

21"All these I have kept since I was a boy," he said.

22When Jesus heard this, he said to him, "You still lack one thing. Sell everything you have and give to the poor, and you will have treasure in heaven. Then come, follow me."

23When he heard this, he became very sad, because he was a man of great wealth. 24Jesus looked at him and said, "How hard it is for the rich to enter the kingdom of God! 25Indeed, it is easier for a camel to go through the eye of a needle than for a rich man to enter the kingdom of God."

26Those who heard this asked, "Who then can be saved?"

27Jesus replied, "What is impossible with men is possible with God."

28Peter said to him, "We have left all we had to follow you!"

29"I tell you the truth," Jesus said to them, "no-one who has left home or wife or brothers or parents or children for the sake of the kingdom of God 30will fail to receive many times as much in this age and, in the age to come, eternal life."

Jesus Again Predicts His Death

31Jesus took the Twelve aside and told them, "We are going up to Jerusalem, and everything that is written by the prophets about the Son of Man will be fulfilled. 32He will be turned over to the Gentiles. They will mock him, insult him, spit on him, flog him and kill him. 33On the third day he will rise again."

34The disciples did not understand any of this. Its meaning was hidden from them, and they did not know what he was talking about.

A Blind Beggar Receives His Sight

35As Jesus approached Jericho, a blind man was sitting by the roadside begging. 36When he heard the crowd going by, he asked what was happening. 37They told him, "Jesus of Nazareth is passing by."

38He called out, "Jesus, Son of David, have mercy on me!"

39Those who led the way rebuked him and told him to be quiet, but he shouted all the more, "Son of David, have mercy on me!"

40Jesus stopped and ordered the man to be brought to him. When he came near, Jesus asked him, 41"What do you want me to do for you?"

"Lord, I want to see," he replied.

42Jesus said to him, "Receive your sight; your faith has healed you." 43Immediately he received his sight and followed Jesus, praising God.

---

[a]11 Or to
[b]20 Exodus 20:12-16; Deut. 5:16-20

When all the people saw it, they also praised God.

Zacchaeus the Tax Collector

19 Jesus entered Jericho and was passing through. [2]A man was there by the name of Zacchaeus; he was a chief tax collector and was wealthy. [3]He wanted to see who Jesus was, but being a short man he could not, because of the crowd. [4]So he ran ahead and climbed a sycamore-fig tree to see him, since Jesus was coming that way.

[5]When Jesus reached the spot, he looked up and said to him, "Zacchaeus, come down immediately. I must stay at your house today." [6]So he came down at once and welcomed him gladly.

[7]All the people saw this and began to mutter, "He has gone to be the guest of a 'sinner.'"

[8]But Zacchaeus stood up and said to the Lord, "Look, Lord! Here and now I give half of my possessions to the poor, and if I have cheated anybody out of anything, I will pay back four times the amount."

[9]Jesus said to him, "Today salvation has come to this house, because this man, too, is a son of Abraham. [10]For the Son of Man came to seek and to save what was lost."

The Parable of the Ten Minas

[11]While they were listening to this, he went on to tell them a parable, because he was near Jerusalem and the people thought that the kingdom of God was going to appear at once. [12]He said: "A man of noble birth went to a distant country to have himself appointed king and then to return. [13]So he called ten of his servants and gave them ten minas.[a] 'Put this money to work,' he said, 'until I come back.'

[14]"But his subjects hated him and sent a delegation after him to say, 'We don't want this man to be our king.'

[15]"He was made king, however, and returned home. Then he sent for the servants to whom he had given

---

[a]13 A mina was about three months' wages.

the money, in order to find out what they had gained with it.

[16]"The first one came and said, 'Sir, your mina has earned ten more.'

[17]"'Well done, my good servant!' his master replied. 'Because you have been trustworthy in a very small matter, take charge of ten cities.'

[18]"The second came and said, 'Sir, your mina has earned five more.'

[19]"His master answered, 'You take charge of five cities.'

[20]"Then another servant came and said, 'Sir, here is your mina; I have kept it laid away in a piece of cloth. [21]I was afraid of you, because you are a hard man. You take out what you did not put in and reap what you did not sow.'

[22]"His master replied, 'I will judge you by your own words, you wicked servant! You knew, did you, that I am a hard man, taking out what I did not put in, and reaping what I did not sow? [23]Why then didn't you put my money on deposit, so that when I came back, I could have collected it with interest?'

[24]"Then he said to those standing by, 'Take his mina away from him and give it to the one who has ten minas.'

[25]"'Sir,' they said, 'he already has ten!'

[26]"He replied, 'I tell you that to everyone who has, more will be given, but as for the one who has nothing, even what he has will be taken away. [27]But those enemies of mine who did not want me to be a king over them—bring them here and kill them in front of me.'"

The Triumphal Entry

[28]After Jesus had said this, he went on ahead, going up to Jerusalem. [29]As he approached Bethphage and Bethany at the hill called the Mount of Olives, he sent two of his disciples, saying to them, [30]"Go to the village ahead of you, and as you enter it, you will find a colt tied there, which no-one has ever ridden. Untie it and bring it here. [31]If anyone asks you, 'Why are you untying it?' tell him,

'The Lord needs it.' "

³²Those who were sent ahead went and found it just as he had told them. ³³As they were untying the colt, its owners asked them, "Why are you untying the colt?"

³⁴They replied, "The Lord needs it."

³⁵They brought it to Jesus, threw their cloaks on the colt and put Jesus on it. ³⁶As he went along, people spread their cloaks on the road.

³⁷When he came near the place where the road goes down the Mount of Olives, the whole crowd of disciples began joyfully to praise God in loud voices for all the miracles they had seen:

³⁸"Blessed is the king who comes in the name of the Lord!"[b]

"Peace in heaven and glory in the highest!"

³⁹Some of the Pharisees in the crowd said to Jesus, "Teacher, rebuke your disciples!"

⁴⁰"I tell you," he replied, "if they keep quiet, the stones will cry out."

⁴¹As he approached Jerusalem and saw the city, he wept over it ⁴²and said, "If you, even you, had only known on this day what would bring you peace—but now it is hidden from your eyes. ⁴³The days will come upon you when your enemies will build an embankment against you and encircle you and hem you in on every side. ⁴⁴They will dash you to the ground, you and the children within your walls. They will not leave one stone on another, because you did not recognise the time of God's coming to you."

Jesus at the Temple

⁴⁵Then he entered the temple area and began driving out those who were selling. ⁴⁶"It is written," he said to them, " 'My house will be a house of prayer';[c] but you have made it 'a den of robbers'.[d]"

⁴⁷Every day he was teaching at the temple. But the chief priests, the teachers of the law and the leaders among the people were trying to kill him. ⁴⁸Yet they could not find any way to do it, because all the people hung on his words.

The Authority of Jesus Questioned

20 One day as he was teaching the people in the temple courts and preaching the gospel, the chief priests and the teachers of the law, together with the elders, came up to him. ²"Tell us by what authority you are doing these things," they said. "Who gave you this authority?"

³He replied, "I will also ask you a question. Tell me, ⁴John's baptism—was it from heaven, or from men?"

⁵They discussed it among themselves and said, "If we say, 'From heaven', he will ask, 'Why didn't you believe him?' ⁶But if we say, 'From men', all the people will stone us, because they are persuaded that John was a prophet."

⁷So they answered, "We don't know where it was from."

⁸Jesus said, "Neither will I tell you by what authority I am doing these things."

The Parable of the Tenants

⁹He went on to tell the people this parable: "A man planted a vineyard, rented it to some farmers and went away for a long time. ¹⁰At harvest time he sent a servant to the tenants so they would give him some of the fruit of the vineyard. But the tenants beat him and sent him away empty-handed. ¹¹He sent another servant, but that one also they beat and treated shamefully and sent away empty-handed. ¹²He sent still a third, and they wounded him and threw him out.

¹³"Then the owner of the vineyard said, 'What shall I do? I will send my son, whom I love; perhaps they will respect him.'

¹⁴"But when the tenants saw him, they talked the matter over. 'This is the heir,' they said. 'Let's kill him, and the inheritance will be ours.' ¹⁵So they threw him out of the vineyard

---

[b]38 Psalm 118:26   [c]46 Isaiah 56:7   [d]46 Jer. 7:11

and killed him.

"What then will the owner of the vineyard do to them? ¹⁶He will come and kill those tenants and give the vineyard to others."

When the people heard this, they said, "May this never be!"

¹⁷Jesus looked directly at them and asked, "Then what is the meaning of that which is written:

" 'The stone the builders rejected
has become the capstone'ᵃ,ᵇ?

¹⁸Everyone who falls on that stone will be broken to pieces, but he on whom it falls will be crushed."

¹⁹The teachers of the law and the chief priests looked for a way to arrest him immediately, because they knew he had spoken this parable against them. But they were afraid of the people.

Paying Taxes to Caesar

²⁰Keeping a close watch on him, they sent spies, who pretended to be honest. They hoped to catch Jesus in something he said so that they might hand him over to the power and authority of the governor. ²¹So the spies questioned him: "Teacher, we know that you speak and teach what is right, and that you do not show partiality but teach the way of God in accordance with the truth. ²²Is it right for us to pay taxes to Caesar or not?"

²³He saw through their duplicity and said to them, ²⁴"Show me a denarius. Whose portrait and inscription are on it?"

²⁵"Caesar's," they replied.

He said to them, "Then give to Caesar what is Caesar's, and to God what is God's."

²⁶They were unable to trap him in what he had said there in public. And astonished by his answer, they became silent.

The Resurrection and Marriage

²⁷Some of the Sadducees, who say there is no resurrection, came to Jesus with a question. ²⁸"Teacher," they said, "Moses wrote for us that if a man's brother dies and leaves a wife but no children, the man must marry the widow and have children for his brother. ²⁹Now there were seven brothers. The first one married a woman and died childless. ³⁰The second and ³¹then the third married her, and in the same way the seven died, leaving no children. ³²Finally, the woman died too. ³³Now then, at the resurrection whose wife will she be, since the seven were married to her?"

³⁴Jesus replied, "The people of this age marry and are given in marriage. ³⁵But those who are considered worthy of taking part in that age and in the resurrection from the dead will neither marry nor be given in marriage, ³⁶and they can no longer die; for they are like the angels. They are God's children, since they are children of the resurrection. ³⁷But in the account of the bush, even Moses showed that the dead rise, for he calls the Lord 'the God of Abraham, and the God of Isaac, and the God of Jacob',ᶜ ³⁸He is not the God of the dead, but of the living, for to him all are alive."

³⁹Some of the teachers of the law responded, "Well said, teacher!" ⁴⁰And no-one dared to ask him any more questions.

Whose Son Is the Christ?

⁴¹Then Jesus said to them, "How is it that they say the Christᵈ is the Son of David? ⁴²David himself declares in the Book of Psalms:

" 'The Lord said to my Lord:
"Sit at my right hand
⁴³until I make your enemies
a footstool for your feet." 'ᵉ

⁴⁴David calls him 'Lord'. How then can he be his son?"

⁴⁵While all the people were listening, Jesus said to his disciples, ⁴⁶"Beware of the teachers of the law. They like to walk around in flowing robes and love to be greeted in the market-places and have the most important seats in the synagogues and

---

ᵃ17 Or cornerstone   ᵇ17 Psalm 118:22   ᶜ37 Exodus 3:6   ᵈ41 Or Messiah
ᵉ43 Psalm 110:1

the places of honour at banquets. 47They devour widows' houses and for a show make lengthy prayers. Such men will be punished most severely."

The Widow's Offering

21 As he looked up, Jesus saw the rich putting their gifts into the temple treasury. 2He also saw a poor widow put in two very small copper coins.*a* 3"I tell you the truth," he said, "this poor widow has put in more than all the others. 4All these people gave their gifts out of their wealth; but she out of her poverty put in all she had to live on."

Signs of the End of the Age

5Some of his disciples were remarking about how the temple was adorned with beautiful stones and with gifts dedicated to God. But Jesus said, 6"As for what you see here, the time will come when not one stone will be left on another; every one of them will be thrown down."

7"Teacher," they asked, "when will these things happen? And what will be the sign that they are about to take place?"

8He replied: "Watch out that you are not deceived. For many will come in my name, claiming, 'I am he,' and 'The time is near.' Do not follow them. 9When you hear of wars and revolutions, do not be frightened. These things must happen first, but the end will not come right away."

10Then he said to them: "Nation will rise against nation, and kingdom against kingdom. 11There will be great earthquakes, famines and pestilences in various places, and fearful events and great signs from heaven.

12"But before all this, they will lay hands on you and persecute you. They will deliver you to synagogues and prisons, and you will be brought before kings and governors, and all on account of my name. 13This will result in your being witnesses to them. 14But make up your mind not to worry beforehand how you will defend yourselves. 15For I will give

you words and wisdom that none of your adversaries will be able to resist or contradict. 16You will be betrayed by parents, brothers, relatives and friends, and they will put some of you to death. 17All men will hate you because of me. 18But not a hair of your head will perish. 19By standing firm you will save yourselves.

20"When you see Jerusalem surrounded by armies, you will know that its desolation is near. 21Then let those who are in Judea flee to the mountains, let those in the city get out, and let those in the country not enter the city. 22For this is the time of punishment in fulfilment of all that has been written. 23How dreadful it will be in those days for pregnant women and nursing mothers! There will be great distress in the land and wrath against this people. 24They will fall by the sword and will be taken as prisoners to all the nations. Jerusalem will be trampled on by the Gentiles until the times of the Gentiles are fulfilled.

25"There will be signs in the sun, moon and stars. On the earth, nations will be in anguish and perplexity at the roaring and tossing of the sea. 26Men will faint from terror, apprehensive of what is coming on the world, for the heavenly bodies will be shaken. 27At that time they will see the Son of Man coming in a cloud with power and great glory. 28When these things begin to take place, stand up and lift up your heads, because your redemption is drawing near."

29He told them this parable: "Look at the fig-tree and all the trees. 30When they sprout leaves, you can see for yourselves and know that summer is near. 31Even so, when you see these things happening, you know that the kingdom of God is near.

32"I tell you the truth, this generation*b* will certainly not pass away until all these things have happened. 33Heaven and earth will pass away, but my words will never pass away.

34"Be careful, or your hearts will be weighed down with dissipation, drunkenness and the anxieties of life,

*a*2 Greek two lepta   *b*32 Or race

93

and that day will close on you unexpectedly like a trap. 35For it will come upon all those who live on the face of the whole earth. 36Be always on the watch, and pray that you may be able to escape all that is about to happen, and that you may be able to stand before the Son of Man."

37Each day Jesus was teaching at the temple, and each evening he went out to spend the night on the hill called the Mount of Olives, 38and all the people came early in the morning to hear him at the temple.

Judas Agrees to Betray Jesus

22 Now the Feast of Unleavened Bread, called the Passover, was approaching, 2and the chief priests and the teachers of the law were looking for some way to get rid of Jesus, for they were afraid of the people. 3Then Satan entered Judas, called Iscariot, one of the Twelve. 4And Judas went to the chief priests and the officers of the temple guard and discussed with them how he might betray Jesus. 5They were delighted and agreed to give him money. 6He consented, and watched for an opportunity to hand Jesus over to them when no crowd was present.

The Last Supper

7Then came the day of Unleavened Bread on which the Passover lamb had to be sacrificed. 8Jesus sent Peter and John, saying, "Go and make preparations for us to eat the Passover."

9"Where do you want us to prepare for it?" they asked.

10He replied, "As you enter the city, a man carrying a jar of water will meet you. Follow him to the house that he enters, 11and say to the owner of the house, 'The Teacher asks: Where is the guest room, where I may eat the Passover with my disciples?' 12He will show you a large upper room, all furnished. Make preparations there."

13They left and found things just as Jesus had told them. So they prepared the Passover.

14When the hour came, Jesus and

a31 The Greek is plural.

his apostles reclined at the table. 15And he said to them, "I have eagerly desired to eat this Passover with you before I suffer. 16For I tell you, I will not eat it again until it finds fulfilment in the kingdom of God."

17After taking the cup, he gave thanks and said, "Take this and divide it among you. 18For I tell you I will not drink again of the fruit of the vine until the kingdom of God comes."

19And he took bread, gave thanks and broke it, and gave it to them, saying, "This is my body given for you; do this in remembrance of me."

20In the same way, after the supper he took the cup, saying, "This cup is the new covenant in my blood, which is poured out for you. 21But the hand of him who is going to betray me is with mine on the table. 22The Son of Man will go as it has been decreed, but woe to that man who betrays him." 23They began to question among themselves which of them it might be who would do this.

24Also a dispute arose among them as to which of them was considered to be greatest. 25Jesus said to them, "The kings of the Gentiles lord it over them; and those who exercise authority over them call themselves Benefactors. 26But you are not to be like that. Instead, the greatest among you should be like the youngest, and the one who rules like the one who serves. 27For who is greater, the one who is at the table or the one who serves? Is it not the one who is at the table? But I am among you as one who serves. 28You are those who have stood by me in my trials. 29And I confer on you a kingdom, just as my Father conferred one on me, 30so that you may eat and drink at my table in my kingdom and sit on thrones, judging the twelve tribes of Israel.

31"Simon, Simon, Satan has asked to sift you*a* as wheat. 32But I have prayed for you, Simon, that your faith may not fail. And when you have turned back, strengthen your brothers."

33But he replied, "Lord, I am ready

to go with you to prison and to death."

[34]Jesus answered, "I tell you, Peter, before the cock crows today, you will deny three times that you know me."

[35]Then Jesus asked them, "When I sent you without purse, bag or sandals, did you lack anything?"

"Nothing," they answered.

[36]He said to them, "But now if you have a purse, take it, and also a bag; and if you don't have a sword, sell your cloak and buy one. [37]It is written: 'And he was numbered with the transgressors';[b] and I tell you that this must be fulfilled in me. Yes, what is written about me is reaching its fulfilment."

[38]The disciples said, "See, Lord, here are two swords."

"That is enough," he replied.

Jesus Prays on the Mount of Olives

[39]Jesus went out as usual to the Mount of Olives, and his disciples followed him. [40]On reaching the place, he said to them, "Pray that you will not fall into temptation." [41]He withdrew about a stone's throw beyond them, knelt down and prayed, [42]"Father, if you are willing, take this cup from me; yet not my will, but yours be done." [43]An angel from heaven appeared to him and strengthened him. [44]And being in anguish, he prayed more earnestly, and his sweat was like drops of blood falling to the ground.[c]

[45]When he rose from prayer and went back to the disciples, he found them asleep, exhausted from sorrow. [46]"Why are you sleeping?" he asked them. "Get up and pray so that you will not fall into temptation."

Jesus Arrested

[47]While he was still speaking a crowd came up, and the man who was called Judas, one of the Twelve, was leading them. He approached Jesus to kiss him, [48]but Jesus asked him, "Judas, are you betraying the Son of Man with a kiss?"

[49]When Jesus' followers saw what was going to happen, they said, "Lord, should we strike with our swords?" [50]And one of them struck the servant of the high priest, cutting off his right ear.

[51]But Jesus answered, "No more of this!" And he touched the man's ear and healed him.

[52]Then Jesus said to the chief priests, the officers of the temple guard, and the elders, who had come for him, "Am I leading a rebellion, that you have come with swords and clubs? [53]Every day I was with you in the temple courts, and you did not lay a hand on me. But this is your hour— when darkness reigns."

Peter Disowns Jesus

[54]Then seizing him, they led him away and took him into the house of the high priest. Peter followed at a distance. [55]But when they had kindled a fire in the middle of the courtyard and had sat down together, Peter sat down with them. [56]A servant girl saw him seated there in the firelight. She looked closely at him and said, "This man was with him."

[57]But he denied it. "Woman, I don't know him," he said.

[58]A little later someone else saw him and said, "You also are one of them."

"Man, I am not!" Peter replied.

[59]About an hour later another asserted, "Certainly this fellow was with him, for he is a Galilean."

[60]Peter replied, "Man, I don't know what you're talking about!" Just as he was speaking, the cock crowed. [61]The Lord turned and looked straight at Peter. Then Peter remembered the word the Lord had spoken to him: "Before the cock crows today, you will disown me three times." [62]And he went outside and wept bitterly.

The Soldiers Mock Jesus

[63]The men who were guarding Jesus began mocking and beating him. [64]They blindfolded him and demanded, "Prophesy! Who hit you?" [65]And they said many other insulting things to him.

[b]37 Isaiah 53:12   [c]44 Some early manuscripts do not have verses 43 and 44.

Jesus Before Pilate and Herod

66At daybreak the council of the elders of the people, both the chief priests and teachers of the law, met together, and Jesus was led before them. 67"If you are the Christ,[d]" they said, "tell us."

Jesus answered, "If I tell you, you will not believe me, 68and if I asked you, you would not answer. 69But from now on, the Son of Man will be seated at the right hand of the mighty God."

70They all asked, "Are you then the Son of God?"

He replied, "You are right in saying I am."

71Then they said, "Why do we need any more testimony? We have heard it from his own lips."

23 Then the whole assembly rose and led him off to Pilate. 2And they began to accuse him, saying, "We have found this man subverting our nation. He opposes payment of taxes to Caesar and claims to be Christ,[a] a king."

3So Pilate asked Jesus, "Are you the king of the Jews?"

"Yes, it is as you say," Jesus replied.

4Then Pilate announced to the chief priests and the crowd, "I find no basis for a charge against this man."

5But they insisted, "He stirs up the people all over Judea[b] by his teaching. He started in Galilee and has come all the way here."

6On hearing this, Pilate asked if the man was a Galilean. 7When he learned that Jesus was under Herod's jurisdiction, he sent him to Herod, who was also in Jerusalem at that time.

8When Herod saw Jesus, he was greatly pleased, because for a long time he had been wanting to see him. From what he had heard about him, he hoped to see him perform some miracle. 9He plied him with many questions, but Jesus gave him no answer. 10The chief priests and the teachers of the law were standing there, vehemently accusing him. 11Then Herod and his soldiers ridiculed and mocked him. Dressing him in an elegant robe, they sent him back to Pilate. 12That day Herod and Pilate became friends—before this they had been enemies.

13Pilate called together the chief priests, the rulers and the people, 14and said to them, "You brought me this man as one who was inciting the people to rebellion. I have examined him in your presence and have found no basis for your charges against him. 15Neither has Herod, for he sent him back to us; as you can see, he has done nothing to deserve death. 16Therefore, I will punish him and then release him."[c]

18With one voice they cried out, "Away with this man! Release Barabbas to us!" (19Barabbas had been thrown into prison for an insurrection in the city, and for murder.)

20Wanting to release Jesus, Pilate appealed to them again. 21But they kept shouting, "Crucify him! Crucify him!"

22For the third time he spoke to them: "Why? What crime has this man committed? I have found in him no grounds for the death penalty. Therefore I will have him punished and then release him."

23But with loud shouts they insistently demanded that he be crucified, and their shouts prevailed. 24So Pilate decided to grant their demand. 25He released the man who had been thrown into prison for insurrection and murder, the one they asked for, and surrendered Jesus to their will.

The Crucifixion

26As they led him away, they seized Simon from Cyrene, who was on his way in from the country, and put the cross on him and made him carry it behind Jesus. 27A large number of people followed him, including women who mourned and wailed for him. 28Jesus turned and said to them,

d67 Or Messiah
a2 Or Messiah; also in verses 35 and 39   b5 Or over the land of the Jews
c16 Some manuscripts him. 17Now he was obliged to release one man to them at the Feast.

"Daughters of Jerusalem, do not weep for me; weep for yourselves and for your children. 29For the time will come when you will say, 'Blessed are the barren women, the wombs that never bore and the breasts that never nursed!' 30Then

> "'they will say to the mountains,
> "Fall on us!"
> and to the hills "Cover us!" '*d*

31For if men do these things when the tree is green, what will happen when it is dry?"

32Two other men, both criminals, were also led out with him to be executed. 33When they came to the place called The Skull, there they crucified him, along with the criminals—one on his right, the other on his left. 34Jesus said, "Father, forgive them, for they do not know what they are doing."*e* And they divided up his clothes by casting lots.

35The people stood watching, and the rulers even sneered at him. They said, "He saved others; let him save himself if he is the Christ of God, the Chosen One."

36The soldiers also came up and mocked him. They offered him wine vinegar 37and said, "If you are the king of the Jews, save yourself."

38There was a written notice above him, which read: THIS IS THE KING OF THE JEWS.

39One of the criminals who hung there hurled insults at him: "Aren't you the Christ? Save yourself and us!"

40But the other criminal rebuked him. "Don't you fear God," he said, "since you are under the same sentence? 41We are punished justly, for we are getting what our deeds deserve. But this man has done nothing wrong."

42Then he said, "Jesus, remember me when you come into your kingdom."

43Jesus answered him, "I tell you the truth, today you will be with me in paradise."

Jesus' Death

44It was now about the sixth hour, and darkness came over the whole land until the ninth hour, 45for the sun stopped shining. And the curtain of the temple was torn in two. 46Jesus called out with a loud voice, "Father, into your hands I commit my spirit." When he had said this, he breathed his last.

47The centurion, seeing what had happened, praised God and said, "Surely this was a righteous man." 48When all the people who had gathered to witness this sight saw what took place, they beat their breasts and went away. 49But all those who knew him, including the women who had followed him from Galilee, stood at a distance, watching these things.

Jesus' Burial

50Now there was a man named Joseph, a member of the Council, a good and upright man, 51who had not consented to their decision and action. He came from the Judean town of Arimathea and he was waiting for the kingdom of God. 52Going to Pilate, he asked for Jesus' body. 53Then he took it down, wrapped it in linen cloth and placed it in a tomb cut in the rock, one in which no-one had yet been laid. 54It was Preparation Day, and the Sabbath was about to begin.

55The women who had come with Jesus from Galilee followed Joseph and saw the tomb and how his body was laid in it. 56Then they went home and prepared spices and perfumes. But they rested on the Sabbath in obedience to the commandment.

The Resurrection

24 On the first day of the week, very early in the morning, the women took the spices they had prepared and went to the tomb. 2They found the stone rolled away from the tomb, 3but when they entered, they did not find the body of the Lord Jesus. 4While they were wondering about this, suddenly two men in

---

*d*30 Hosea 10:8   *e*34 Some early manuscripts do not have this sentence.

clothes that gleamed like lightning stood beside them. [5]In their fright the women bowed down with their faces to the ground, but the men said to them, "Why do you look for the living among the dead? [6]He is not here; he has risen! Remember how he told you, while he was still with you in Galilee: [7]'The Son of Man must be delivered into the hands of sinful men, be crucified and on the third day be raised again.'" [8]Then they remembered his words.

[9]When they came back from the tomb, they told all these things to the Eleven and to all the others. [10]It was Mary Magdalene, Joanna, Mary the mother of James, and the others with them who told this to the apostles. [11]But they did not believe the women, because their words seemed to them like nonsense. [12]Peter, however, got up and ran to the tomb. Bending over, he saw the strips of linen lying by themselves, and he went away, wondering to himself what had happened.

On the Road to Emmaus

[13]Now that same day two of them were going to a village called Emmaus, about seven miles[a] from Jerusalem. [14]They were talking with each other about everything that had happened. [15]As they talked and discussed these things with each other, Jesus himself came up and walked along with them; [16]but they were kept from recognising him.

[17]He asked them, "What are you discussing together as you walk along?"

They stood still, their faces downcast. [18]One of them, named Cleopas, asked him, "Are you the only one living in Jerusalem who doesn't know the things that have happened there in these days?"

[19]"What things?" he asked.

"About Jesus of Nazareth," they replied. "He was a prophet, powerful in word and deed before God and all the people. [20]The chief priests and our rulers handed him over to be sentenced to death, and they crucified him; [21]but we had hoped that he was the one who was going to redeem Israel. And what is more, it is the third day since all this took place. [22]In addition, some of our women amazed us. They went to the tomb early this morning [23]but didn't find his body. They came and told us that they had seen a vision of angels, who said he was alive. [24]Then some of our companions went to the tomb and found it just as the women had said, but him they did not see."

[25]He said to them, "How foolish you are, and how slow of heart to believe all that the prophets have spoken! [26]Did not the Christ[b] have to suffer these things and then enter his glory?" [27]And beginning with Moses and all the Prophets, he explained to them what was said in all the Scriptures concerning himself.

[28]As they approached the village to which they were going, Jesus acted as if he were going further. [29]But they urged him strongly, "Stay with us, for it is nearly evening; the day is almost over." So he went in to stay with them.

[30]When he was at the table with them, he took bread, gave thanks, broke it and began to give it to them. [31]Then their eyes were opened and they recognised him, and he disappeared from their sight. [32]They asked each other, "Were not our hearts burning within us while he talked with us on the road and opened the Scriptures to us?"

[33]They got up and returned at once to Jerusalem. There they found the Eleven and those with them, assembled together [34]and saying, "It is true! The Lord has risen and has appeared to Simon." [35]Then the two told what had happened on the way, and how Jesus was recognised by them when he broke the bread.

Jesus Appears to the Disciples

[36]While they were still talking about this, Jesus himself stood among them and said to them, "Peace be

---

[a]13 Greek sixty stadia (about 11 kilometres)
[b]26 Or Messiah; also in verse 46

with you."

37They were startled and frightened, thinking they saw a ghost. 38He said to them, "Why are you troubled, and why do doubts rise in your minds? 39Look at my hands and my feet. It is I myself! Touch me and see; a ghost does not have flesh and bones, as you see I have."

40When he had said this, he showed them his hands and feet. 41And while they still did not believe it because of joy and amazement, he asked them, "Do you have anything here to eat?" 42They gave him a piece of broiled fish, 43and he took it and ate it in their presence.

44He said to them, "This is what I told you while I was still with you: Everything must be fulfilled that is written about me in the Law of Moses, the Prophets and the Psalms."

45Then he opened their minds so they could understand the Scriptures. 46He told them, "This is what is written: The Christ will suffer and rise from the dead on the third day, 47and repentance and forgiveness of sins will be preached in his name to all nations, beginning at Jerusalem. 48You are witnesses of these things. 49I am going to send you what my Father has promised; but stay in the city until you have been clothed with power from on high."

The Ascension

50When he had led them out to the vicinity of Bethany, he lifted up his hands and blessed them. 51While he was blessing them, he left them and was taken up into heaven. 52Then they worshipped him and returned to Jerusalem with great joy. 53And they stayed continually at the temple, praising God.

John

The Word Became Flesh

1 In the beginning was the Word, and the Word was with God, and the Word was God. ²He was with God in the beginning.

³Through him all things were made; without him nothing was made that has been made. ⁴In him was life, and that life was the light of men. ⁵The light shines in the darkness, but the darkness has not understood[a] it.

⁶There came a man who was sent from God; his name was John. ⁷He came as a witness to testify concerning that light, so that through him all men might believe. ⁸He himself was not the light; he came only as a witness to the light. ⁹The true light that gives light to every man was coming into the world.[b]

¹⁰He was in the world, and though the world was made through him, the world did not recognise him. ¹¹He came to that which was his own, but his own did not receive him. ¹²Yet to all who received him, to those who believed in his name, he gave the right to become children of God— ¹³children born not of natural descent,[c] nor of human decision or a husband's will, but born of God.

¹⁴The Word became flesh and lived for a while among us. We have seen his glory, the glory of the one and only ₍Son₎,[d] who came from the Father, full of grace and truth.

¹⁵John testifies concerning him. He cries out, saying, "This was he of whom I said, 'He who comes after me has surpassed me because he was before me.'" ¹⁶From the fullness of his grace we have all received one blessing after another. ¹⁷For the law was given through Moses; grace and truth came through Jesus Christ. ¹⁸No-one has ever seen God, but God the only ₍Son₎,[f] who is at the Father's side, has made him known.

John the Baptist Denies Being the Christ

¹⁹Now this was John's testimony when the Jews of Jerusalem sent priests and Levites to ask him who he was. ²⁰He did not fail to confess, but confessed freely, "I am not the Christ."[g]

²¹They asked him, "Then who are you? Are you Elijah?"

He said, "I am not."

"Are you the Prophet?"

He answered, "No."

²²Finally they said, "Who are you? Give us an answer to take back to those who sent us. What do you say about yourself?"

²³John replied in the words of Isaiah the prophet, "I am the voice of one calling in the desert, 'Make straight the way for the Lord.'"[h]

²⁴Now some Pharisees who had been sent ²⁵questioned him, "Why then do you baptise if you are not the Christ, nor Elijah, nor the Prophet?"

²⁶"I baptise with[i] water," John replied, "but among you stands one you do not know. ²⁷He is the one who

---

[a]5 Or overcome
[b]9 Or This was the true light that gives light to every man who comes into the world
[c]13 Greek of bloods   [d]14 Or the Only Begotten   [e]18 Or but God the only begotten
[f]18 Some manuscripts but the only Son (or but the only begotten Son)
[g]20 Or Messiah. "The Christ" (Greek) and "the Messiah" (Hebrew) both mean "the Anointed One"; also in verse 25.   [h]23 Isaiah 40:3   [i]26, Or in; also in verses 31 and 33

comes after me, the thongs of whose sandals I am not worthy to untie.''

28This all happened at Bethany on the other side of the Jordan, where John was baptising.

Jesus the Lamb of God

29The next day John saw Jesus coming towards him and said, "Look, the Lamb of God, who takes away the sin of the world! 30This is the one I meant when I said, 'A man who comes after me has surpassed me because he was before me.' 31I myself did not know him, but the reason I came baptising with water was that he might be revealed to Israel.''

32Then John gave this testimony: "I saw the Spirit come down from heaven as a dove and remain on him. 33I would not have known him, except that the one who sent me to baptise with water told me, 'The man on whom you see the Spirit come down and remain is he who will baptise with the Holy Spirit.' 34I have seen and I testify that this is the Son of God.''

Jesus' First Disciples

35The next day John was there again with two of his disciples. 36When he saw Jesus passing by, he said, "Look, the Lamb of God!''

37When the two disciples heard him say this, they followed Jesus. 38Turning round, Jesus saw them following and asked, "What do you want?''

They said, "Rabbi'' (which means Teacher), "where are you staying?''

39"Come,'' he replied, "and you will see.''

So they went and saw where he was staying, and spent that day with him. It was about the tenth hour.

40Andrew, Simon Peter's brother, was one of the two who heard what John had said and who had followed Jesus. 41The first thing Andrew did was to find his brother Simon and tell him, "We have found the Messiah'' (that is, the Christ).

42Then he brought Simon to Jesus, who looked at him and said, "You are

Simon son of John. You will be called Cephas'' (which, when translated, is Peter).

Jesus Calls Philip and Nathanael

43The next day Jesus decided to leave for Galilee. Finding Philip, he said to him, "Follow me.''

44Philip, like Andrew and Peter, was from the town of Bethsaida. 45Philip found Nathanael and told him, "We have found the one Moses wrote about in the Law, and about whom the prophets also wrote—Jesus of Nazareth, the son of Joseph.''

46"Nazareth! Can anything good come from there?'' Nathanael asked.

"Come and see,'' said Philip.

47When Jesus saw Nathanael approaching, he said of him, "Here is a true Israelite, in whom there is nothing false.''

48"How do you know me?'' Nathanael asked.

Jesus answered, "I saw you while you were still under the fig-tree before Philip called you.''

49Then Nathanael declared, "Rabbi, you are the Son of God; you are the King of Israel.''

50Jesus said, "You believe*k* because I told you I saw you under the fig-tree. You shall see greater things than that.'' 51He then added, "I tell you*l* the truth, you*l* shall see heaven open, and the angels of God ascending and descending on the Son of Man.''

Jesus Changes Water to Wine

2 On the third day a wedding took place at Cana in Galilee. Jesus' mother was there, 2and Jesus and his disciples had also been invited to the wedding. 3When the wine was gone, Jesus' mother said to him, "They have no more wine.''

4"Dear woman, why do you involve me?'' Jesus replied, "My time has not yet come.''

5His mother said to the servants, "Do whatever he tells you.''

6Nearby stood six stone water jars, the kind used by the Jews for ceremonial washing, each holding from twenty to thirty gallons.*a*

j42 Both *Cephas* (Aramaic) and *Peter* (Greek) mean *rock.*   *k50* Or *Do you believe . . . ?*
l51 The Greek is plural.   *a6* Greek *two to three metretes* (probably about 75 to 115 litres)

7Jesus said to the servants, "Fill the jars with water"; so they filled them to the brim.

8Then he told them, "Now draw some out and take it to the master of the banquet."

They did so, 9and the master of the banquet tasted the water that had been turned into wine. He did not realise where it had come from, though the servants who had drawn the water knew. Then he called the bridegroom aside 10and said, "Everyone brings out the choice wine first and then the cheaper wine after the guests have had too much to drink; but you have saved the best till now."

11This, the first of his miraculous signs, Jesus performed in Cana of Galilee. He thus revealed his glory, and his disciples put their faith in him.

Jesus Clears the Temple

12After this he went down to Capernaum with his mother and brothers and his disciples. There they stayed for a few days.

13When it was almost time for the Jewish Passover, Jesus went up to Jerusalem. 14In the temple courts he found men selling cattle, sheep and doves, and others sitting at tables exchanging money. 15So he made a whip out of cords, and drove all from the temple area, both sheep and cattle; he scattered the coins of the money changers and overturned their tables. 16To those who sold doves he said, "Get these out of here! How dare you turn my Father's house into a market!"

17His disciples remembered that it is written, "Zeal for your house will consume me."b

18Then the Jews demanded of him, "What miraculous sign can you show us to prove your authority to do all this?"

19Jesus answered them, "Destroy this temple, and I will raise it again in three days."

20The Jews replied, "It has taken forty-six years to build this temple,

and you are going to raise it in three days?" 21But the temple he had spoken of was his body. 22After he was raised from the dead, his disciples recalled what he had said. Then they believed the Scripture and the words that Jesus had spoken.

23Now while he was in Jerusalem at the Passover Feast, many people saw the miraculous signs he was doing and believed in his name.c 24But Jesus would not entrust himself to them, for he knew all men. 25He did not need man's testimony about man, for he knew what was in a man.

Jesus Teaches Nicodemus

3 Now there was a man of the Pharisees named Nicodemus, a member of the Jewish ruling council. 2He came to Jesus at night and said, "Rabbi, we know you are a teacher who has come from God. For no-one could perform the miraculous signs you are doing if God were not with him."

3In reply Jesus declared, "I tell you the truth, unless a man is born again,a he cannot see the kingdom of God."

4"How can a man be born when he is old?" Nicodemus asked. "Surely he cannot enter a second time into his mother's womb to be born!"

5Jesus answered, "I tell you the truth, unless a man is born of water and the Spirit, he cannot enter the kingdom of God. 6Flesh gives birth to flesh, but the Spiritb gives birth to spirit. 7You should not be surprised at my saying, 'Youc must be born again.' 8The wind blows wherever it pleases. You hear its sound, but you cannot tell where it comes from or where it is going. So it is with everyone born of the Spirit."

9"How can this be?" Nicodemus asked.

10"You are Israel's teacher," said Jesus, "and do you not understand these things? 11I tell you the truth, we speak of what we know, and we testify to what we have seen, but still you people do not accept our testimony. 12I have spoken to you of

b17 Psalm 69:9   c23 Or and believed in him
a3 Or born from above; also in verse 7   b6 Or but Spirit

earthly things and you do not believe; how then will you believe if I speak of heavenly things? 13No-one has ever gone into heaven except the one who came from heaven—the Son of Man.d 14Just as Moses lifted up the snake in the desert, so the Son of Man must be lifted up, 15that everyone who believes in him may have eternal life.e

16"For God so loved the world that he gave his one and only Son,f that whoever believes in him shall not perish but have eternal life. 17For God did not send his Son into the world to condemn the world, but to save the world through him. 18Whoever believes in him is not condemned, but whoever does not believe stands condemned already because he has not believed in the name of God's one and only Son.g 19This is the verdict: Light has come into the world, but men loved darkness instead of light because their deeds were evil. 20Everyone who does evil hates the light, and will not come into the light for fear that his deeds will be exposed. 21But whoever lives by the truth comes into the light, so that it may be seen plainly that what he has done has been done through God."h

John the Baptist's Testimony About Jesus

22After this, Jesus and his disciples went out into the Judean countryside, where he spent some time with them, and baptised. 23Now John also was baptising at Aenon near Salim, because there was plenty of water, and people were constantly coming to be baptised. 24(This was before John was put in prison.) 25An argument developed between some of John's disciples and a certain Jew over the matter of ceremonial washing. 26They came to John and said to him, "Rabbi, that man who was with you on the other side of the Jordan—the one you testified about—well, he is baptising, and everyone is going to him."

27To this John replied, "A man can receive only what is given him from heaven. 28You yourselves can testify that I said, 'I am not the Christi but am sent ahead of him.' 29The bride belongs to the bridegroom. The friend who attends the bridegroom waits and listens for him, and is full of joy when he hears the bridegroom's voice. That joy is mine, and it is now complete. 30He must become greater; I must become less.

31"The one who comes from above is above all; the one who is from the earth belongs to the earth, and speaks as one from the earth. The one who comes from heaven is above all. 32He testifies to what he has seen and heard, but no-one accepts his testimony. 33The man who has accepted it has certified that God is truthful. 34For the one whom God has sent speaks the words of God; to him God gives the Spirit without limit. 35The Father loves the Son and has placed everything in his hands. 36Whoever believes in the Son has eternal life, but whoever rejects the Son will not see life, for God's wrath remains on him."j

Jesus Talks With a Samaritan Woman

4 The Pharisees heard that Jesus was gaining and baptising more disciples than John, 2although in fact it was not Jesus who baptised, but his disciples. 3When the Lord learned of this, he left Judea and went back once more to Galilee.

4Now he had to go through Samaria. 5So he came to a town in Samaria called Sychar, near the plot of ground Jacob had given to his son Joseph. 6Jacob's well was there, and Jesus, tired as he was from the journey, sat down by the well. It was about the sixth hour.

7When a Samaritan woman came to draw water, Jesus said to her, "Will

c7 The Greek is plural.   d13 Some manuscripts Man, who is in heaven
e15 Or believes may have eternal life in him   f16 Or his only begotten Son
g18 Or God's only begotten Son   h21 Some interpreters end the quotation after verse 15.
i28 Or Messiah   j36 Some interpreters end the quotation after verse 30.

you give me a drink?" [8](His disciples had gone into the town to buy food.)

[9]The Samaritan woman said to him, "You are a Jew and I am a Samaritan woman. How can you ask me for a drink?" (For Jews do not associate with Samaritans.[a])

[10]Jesus answered her, "If you knew the gift of God and who it is that asks you for a drink, you would have asked him and he would have given you living water."

[11]"Sir," the woman said, "you have nothing to draw with and the well is deep. Where can you get this living water? [12]Are you greater than our father Jacob, who gave us the well and drank from it himself, as did also his sons and his flocks and herds?"

[13]Jesus answered, "Everyone who drinks this water will be thirsty again, [14]but whoever drinks the water I give him will never thirst. Indeed, the water I give him will become in him a spring of water welling up to eternal life."

[15]The woman said to him, "Sir, give me this water so that I won't get thirsty and have to keep coming here to draw water."

[16]He told her, "Go, call your husband and come back."

[17]"I have no husband," she replied.

Jesus said to her, "You are right when you say you have no husband. [18]The fact is, you have had five husbands, and the man you now have is not your husband. What you have just said is quite true."

[19]"Sir," the woman said, "I can see that you are a prophet. [20]Our fathers worshipped on this mountain, but you Jews claim that the place where we must worship is in Jerusalem."

[21]Jesus declared, "Believe me, woman, a time is coming when you will worship the Father neither on this mountain nor in Jerusalem. [22]You Samaritans worship what you do not know; we worship what we do know, for salvation is from the Jews. [23]Yet a time is coming and has now come when the true worshippers will worship the Father in spirit and truth, for they are the kind of worshippers the

Father seeks. [24]God is spirit, and his worshippers must worship in spirit and in truth."

[25]The woman said, "I know that Messiah" (called Christ) "is coming. When he comes, he will explain everything to us."

[26]Then Jesus declared, "I who speak to you am he."

The Disciples Rejoin Jesus

[27]Just then his disciples returned and were surprised to find him talking with a woman. But no-one asked, "What do you want?" or "Why are you talking with her?"

[28]Then, leaving her water jar, the woman went back to the town and said to the people, [29]"Come, see a man who told me everything I ever did. Could this be the Christ?"[b] [30]They came out of the town and made their way towards him.

[31]Meanwhile his disciples urged him, "Rabbi, eat something."

[32]But he said to them, "I have food to eat that you know nothing about."

[33]Then his disciples said to each other, "Could someone have brought him food?"

[34]"My food," said Jesus, "is to do the will of him who sent me and to finish his work. [35]Do you not say, 'Four months more and then the harvest'? I tell you, open your eyes and look at the fields! They are ripe for harvest. [36]Even now the reaper draws his wages, even now he harvests the crop for eternal life, so that the sower and the reaper may be glad together. [37]Thus the saying 'One sows and another reaps' is true. [38]I sent you to reap what you have not worked for. Others have done the hard work, and you have reaped the benefits of their labour."

Many Samaritans Believe

[39]Many of the Samaritans from that town believed in him because of the woman's testimony, "He told me everything I ever did." [40]So when the Samaritans came to him, they urged him to stay with them, and he stayed two days. [41]And because of his words

[a]9 Or do not use dishes Samaritans have used

[b]29 Or Messiah

many more became believers.

⁴²They said to the woman, "We no longer believe just because of what you said; now we have heard for ourselves, and we know that this man really is the Saviour of the world."

Jesus Heals the Official's Son

⁴³After the two days he left for Galilee. ⁴⁴(Now Jesus himself had pointed out that a prophet has no honour in his own country.) ⁴⁵When he arrived in Galilee, the Galileans welcomed him. They had seen all that he had done in Jerusalem at the Passover Feast, for they also had been there.

⁴⁶Once more he visited Cana in Galilee, where he had turned the water into wine. And there was a certain royal official whose son lay sick at Capernaum. ⁴⁷When this man heard that Jesus had arrived in Galilee from Judea, he went to him and begged him to come and heal his son, who was close to death.

⁴⁸"Unless you people see miraculous signs and wonders," Jesus told him, "you will never believe."

⁴⁹The royal official said, "Sir, come down before my child dies."

⁵⁰Jesus replied, "You may go. Your son will live."

The man took Jesus at his word and departed. ⁵¹While he was still on the way, his servants met him with the news that his boy was living. ⁵²When he enquired as to the time when his son got better, they said to him, "The fever left him yesterday at the seventh hour."

⁵³Then the father realised that this was the exact time at which Jesus had said to him, "Your son will live." So he and all his household believed.

⁵⁴This was the second miraculous sign that Jesus performed, having come from Judea to Galilee.

The Healing at the Pool

5 Some time later, Jesus went up to Jerusalem for a feast of the Jews.

²Now there is in Jerusalem near the Sheep Gate a pool, which in Aramaic is called Bethesda*ᵃ* and which is surrounded by five covered colonnades. ³Here a great number of disabled people used to lie—the blind, the lame, the paralysed.*ᵇ* ⁵One who was there had been an invalid for thirty-eight years. ⁶When Jesus saw him lying there and learned that he had been in this condition for a long time, he asked him, "Do you want to get well?"

⁷"Sir," the invalid replied, "I have no-one to help me into the pool when the water is stirred. While I am trying to get in, someone else goes down ahead of me."

⁸Then Jesus said to him, "Get up! Pick up your mat and walk." ⁹At once the man was cured; he picked up his mat and walked.

The day on which this took place was a Sabbath, ¹⁰and so the Jews said to the man who had been healed, "It is the Sabbath; the law forbids you to carry your mat."

¹¹But he replied, "The man who made me well said to me, 'Pick up your mat and walk.'"

¹²So they asked him, "Who is this fellow who told you to pick it up and walk?"

¹³The man who was healed had no idea who it was, for Jesus had slipped away into the crowd that was there.

¹⁴Later Jesus found him at the temple and said to him, "See, you are well again. Stop sinning or something worse may happen to you." ¹⁵The man went away and told the Jews that it was Jesus who had made him well.

Life Through the Son

¹⁶So, because Jesus was doing these things on the Sabbath, the Jews persecuted him. ¹⁷Jesus said to them, "My Father is always at his work to this very day, and I, too, am working." ¹⁸For this reason the Jews tried all the harder to kill him; not only was he

ᵃ2 Some manuscripts *Bethzatha*; other manuscripts *Bethsaida*
ᵇ3 Some manuscripts *paralysed—and they waited for the moving of the waters; some less important manuscripts continue 'From time to time an angel of the Lord would come down and stir up the waters. The first one into the pool after each such disturbance would be cured of whatever disease he had.*

breaking the Sabbath, but he was even calling God his own Father, making himself equal with God.

19Jesus gave them this answer: "I tell you the truth, the Son can do nothing by himself; he can do only what he sees his Father doing, because whatever the Father does the Son also does. 20For the Father loves the Son and shows him all he does. Yes, to your amazement he will show him even greater things than these. 21For just as the Father raises the dead and gives them life, even so the Son gives life to whom he is pleased to give it. 22Moreover, the Father judges no-one, but has entrusted all judgment to the Son, 23that all may honour the Son just as they honour the Father. He who does not honour the Son does not honour the Father, who sent him.

24"I tell you the truth, whoever hears my word and believes him who sent me has eternal life and will not be condemned; he has crossed over from death to life. 25I tell you the truth, a time is coming and has now come when the dead will hear the voice of the Son of God and those who hear will live. 26For as the Father has life in himself, so he has granted the Son to have life in himself. 27And he has given him authority to judge because he is the Son of Man.

28"Do not be amazed at this, for a time is coming when all who are in their graves will hear his voice 29and come out—those who have done good will rise to live, and those who have done evil will rise to be condemned. 30By myself I can do nothing; I judge only as I hear, and my judgment is just, for I seek not to please myself but him who sent me.

Testimonies About Jesus

31"If I testify about myself, my testimony is not valid. 32There is another who testifies in my favour, and I know that his testimony about me is valid.

33"You have sent to John and he has testified to the truth. 34Not that I accept human testimony; but I

mention it that you may be saved. 35John was a lamp that burned and gave light, and you chose for a time to enjoy his light.

36"I have testimony weightier than that of John. For the very work that the Father has given me to finish, and which I am doing, testifies that the Father has sent me. 37And the Father who sent me has himself testified concerning me. You have never heard his voice nor seen his form, 38nor does his word dwell in you, for you do not believe the one he sent. 39You diligently studyc the Scriptures because you think that by them you possess eternal life. These are the Scriptures that testify about me, 40yet you refuse to come to me to have life.

41"I do not accept praise from men, 42but I know you. I know that you do not have the love of God in your hearts. 43I have come in my Father's name, and you do not accept me; but if someone else comes in his own name, you will accept him. 44How can you believe if you accept praise from one another, yet make no effort to obtain the praise that comes from the only God?d

45"But do not think I will accuse you before the Father. Your accuser is Moses, on whom your hopes are set. 46If you believed Moses, you would believe me, for he wrote about me. 47But since you do not believe what he wrote, how are you going to believe what I say?"

Jesus Feeds the Five Thousand

6 Some time after this, Jesus crossed to the far shore of the Sea of Galilee (that is, the Sea of Tiberias), 2and a great crowd of people followed him because they saw the miraculous signs he had performed on the sick. 3Then Jesus went up on the hillside and sat down with his disciples. 4The Jewish Passover Feast was near.

5When Jesus looked up and saw a great crowd coming towards him, he said to Philip, "Where shall we buy bread for these people to eat?" 6He asked this only to test him, for he

c39 Or Study diligently (the imperative)   d44 Some early manuscripts the Only One

already had in mind what he was going to do.

7Philip answered him, "Eight months' wages*a* would not buy enough bread for each one to have a bite!"

8Another of his disciples, Andrew, Simon Peter's brother, spoke up, 9"Here is a boy with five small barley loaves and two small fish, but how far will they go among so many?"

10Jesus said, "Make the people sit down." There was plenty of grass in that place, and the men sat down, about five thousand of them. 11Jesus then took the loaves, gave thanks, and distributed to those who were seated as much as they wanted. He did the same with the fish.

12When they had all had enough to eat, he said to his disciples, "Gather the pieces that are left over. Let nothing be wasted." 13So they gathered them and filled twelve baskets with the pieces of the five barley loaves left over by those who had eaten.

14After the people saw the miraculous sign that Jesus did, they began to say, "Surely this is the Prophet who is to come into the world." 15Jesus, knowing that they intended to come and make him king by force, withdrew again into the hills by himself.

Jesus Walks on the Water

16When evening came, his disciples went down to the lake, 17where they got into a boat and set off across the lake for Capernaum. By now it was dark, and Jesus had not yet joined them. 18A strong wind was blowing and the waters grew rough. 19When they had rowed three or three and a half miles,*b* they saw Jesus approaching the boat, walking on the water; and they were terrified. 20But he said to them, "It is I; don't be afraid." 21Then they were willing to take him into the boat, and immediately the boat reached the shore where they were heading.

22The next day the crowd that had stayed on the opposite shore of the lake realised that only one boat had been there, and that Jesus had not entered it with his disciples, but that they had gone away alone. 23Then some boats from Tiberias landed near the place where the people had eaten the bread after the Lord had given thanks. 24Once the crowd realised that neither Jesus nor his disciples were there, they got into the boats and went to Capernaum in search of Jesus.

Jesus the Bread of Life

25When they found him on the other side of the lake, they asked him, "Rabbi, when did you get here?"

26Jesus answered, "I tell you the truth, you are looking for me, not because you saw miraculous signs but because you ate the loaves and had your fill. 27Do not work for food that spoils, but for food that endures to eternal life, which the Son of Man will give you. On him God the Father has placed his seal of approval."

28Then they asked him, "What must we do to do the works God requires?"

29Jesus answered, "The work of God is this: to believe in the one he has sent."

30So they asked him, "What miraculous sign then will you give that we may see it and believe you? What will you do? 31Our forefathers ate the manna in the desert; as it is written: 'He gave them bread from heaven to eat.'*c*

32Jesus said to them, "I tell you the truth, it is not Moses who has given you the bread from heaven, but it is my Father who gives you the true bread from heaven. 33For the bread of God is he who comes down from heaven and gives life to the world."

34"Sir," they said, "from now on give us this bread."

35Then Jesus declared, "I am the bread of life. He who comes to me will never go hungry, and he who believes in me will never be thirsty. 36But as I told you, you have seen me

---

*a*7 Greek *two hundred denarii*   *b*19 Greek *rowed twenty-five or thirty stadia* (about 5 or 6 kilometres)   *c*31 Exodus 16:4; Psalm 78:24

and still you do not believe. 37All that the Father gives me will come to me, and whoever comes to me I will never drive away. 38For I have come down from heaven not to do my will but to do the will of him who sent me. 39And this is the will of him who sent me, that I shall lose none of all that he has given me, but raise them up at the last day. 40For my Father's will is that everyone who looks to the Son and believes in him shall have eternal life, and I will raise him up at the last day."

41At this the Jews began to grumble about him because he said, "I am the bread that came down from heaven." 42They said, "Is this not Jesus, the son of Joseph, whose father and mother we know? How can he now say, 'I came down from heaven'?"

43"Stop grumbling among yourselves," Jesus answered. 44"No-one can come to me unless the Father who sent me draws him, and I will raise him up at the last day. 45It is written in the Prophets: 'They will all be taught by God.'d Everyone who listens to the Father and learns from him comes to me. 46No-one has seen the Father except the one who is from God; only he has seen the Father. 47I tell you the truth, he who believes has everlasting life. 48I am the bread of life. 49Your forefathers ate the manna in the desert, yet they died. 50But here is the bread that comes down from heaven, which a man may eat and not die. 51I am the living bread that came down from heaven. If a man eats of this bread, he will live for ever. This bread is my flesh, which I will give for the life of the world."

52Then the Jews began to argue sharply among themselves, "How can this man give us his flesh to eat?"

53Jesus said to them, "I tell you the truth, unless you eat the flesh of the Son of Man and drink his blood, you have no life in you. 54Whoever eats my flesh and drinks my blood has eternal life, and I will raise him up at the last day. 55For my flesh is real food and my blood is real drink. 56Whoever eats my flesh and drinks my blood remains in me, and I in him. 57Just as the living Father sent me and I live because of the Father, so the one who feeds on me will live because of me. 58This is the bread that came down from heaven. Our forefathers ate manna, and died, but he who feeds on this bread will live for ever." 59He said this while teaching in the synagogue in Capernaum.

Many Disciples Desert Jesus

60On hearing it, many of his disciples said, "This is a hard teaching. Who can accept it?"

61Aware that his disciples were grumbling about this, Jesus said to them, "Does this offend you? 62What if you see the Son of Man ascend to where he was before! 63The Spirit gives life; the flesh counts for nothing. The words I have spoken to you are spirite and they are life. 64Yet there are some of you who do not believe." For Jesus had known from the beginning which of them did not believe and who would betray him. 65He went on to say, "This is why I told you that no-one can come to me unless the Father has enabled him."

66From this time many of his disciples turned back and no longer followed him.

67"You do not want to leave too, do you?" Jesus asked the Twelve.

68Simon Peter answered him, "Lord, to whom shall we go? You have the words of eternal life. 69We believe and know that you are the Holy One of God."

70Then Jesus replied, "Have I not chosen you, the Twelve? Yet one of you is a devil!" 71(He meant Judas, the son of Simon Iscariot, who, though one of the Twelve, was later to betray him.)

Jesus Goes to the Feast of Tabernacles

7 After this, Jesus went around in Galilee, purposely staying away from Judea because the Jews there

d45 Isaiah 54:13   e63 Or Spirit

were waiting to take his life. [2]But when the Jewish Feast of Tabernacles was near, [3]Jesus' brothers said to him, "You ought to leave here and go to Judea, so that your disciples may see the miracles you do. [4]No-one who wants to become a public figure acts in secret. Since you are doing these things, show yourself to the world." [5]For even his own brothers did not believe in him.

[6]Therefore Jesus told them, "The right time for me has not yet come; for you any time is right. [7]The world cannot hate you, but it hates me because I testify that what it does is evil. [8]You go to the Feast. I am not yet[a] going up to this Feast, because for me the right time has not yet come." [9]Having said this, he stayed in Galilee.

[10]However, after his brothers had left for the Feast, he went also, not publicly, but in secret. [11]Now at the Feast the Jews were watching for him and asking, "Where is that man?"

[12]Among the crowds there was widespread whispering about him. Some said, "He is a good man."

Others replied, "No, he deceives the people." [13]But no-one would say anything publicly about him for fear of the Jews.

Jesus Teaches at the Feast

[14]Not until halfway through the Feast did Jesus go up to the temple courts and begin to teach. [15]The Jews were amazed and asked, "How did this man get such learning without having studied?"

[16]Jesus answered, "My teaching is not my own. It comes from him who sent me. [17]If anyone chooses to do God's will, he will find out whether my teaching comes from God or whether I speak on my own. [18]He who speaks on his own does so to gain honour for himself, but he who works for the honour of the one who sent him is a man of truth; there is nothing false about him. [19]Has not Moses given you the law? Yet not one

of you keeps the law. Why are you trying to kill me?"

[20]"You are demon-possessed," the crowd answered. "Who is trying to kill you?"

[21]Jesus said to them, "I did one miracle, and you are all astonished. [22]Yet, because Moses gave you circumcision (though actually it did not come from Moses, but from the patriarchs), you circumcise a child on the Sabbath. [23]Now if a child can be circumcised on the Sabbath so that the law of Moses may not be broken, why are you angry with me for healing the whole man on the Sabbath? [24]Stop judging by mere appearances, and make a right judgment."

Is Jesus the Christ?

[25]At that point some of the people of Jerusalem began to ask, "Isn't this the man they are trying to kill? [26]Here he is, speaking publicly, and they are not saying a word to him. Have the authorities really concluded that he is the Christ?[b] [27]But we know where this man is from; when the Christ comes, no-one will know where he is from."

[28]Then Jesus, still teaching in the temple courts, cried out, "Yes, you know me, and you know where I am from. I am not here on my own, but he who sent me is true. You do not know him, [29]but I know him because I am from him and he sent me."

[30]At this they tried to seize him, but no-one laid a hand on him, because his time had not yet come. [31]Still, many in the crowd put their faith in him. They said, "When the Christ comes, will he do more miraculous signs than this man?"

[32]The Pharisees heard the crowd whispering such things about him. Then the chief priests and the Pharisees sent temple guards to arrest him.

[33]Jesus said, "I am with you for only a short time, and then I go to the one who sent me. [34]You will look for me, but you will not find me; and where I am, you cannot come."

[a]8 Some early manuscripts do not have yet.
[b]26 Or Messiah; also in verses 27, 31, 41, and 42

35The Jews said to one another, "Where does this man intend to go that we cannot find him? Will he go where our people live scattered among the Greeks, and teach the Greeks? 36What did he mean when he said, 'You will look for me, but you will not find me,' and 'Where I am, you cannot come'?"

37On the last and greatest day of the Feast, Jesus stood and said in a loud voice, "If a man is thirsty, let him come to me and drink. 38Whoever believes in me,c as the Scripture has said, streams of living water will flow from within him." 39By this he meant the Spirit, whom those who believed in him were later to receive. Up to that time the Spirit had not been given, since Jesus had not yet been glorified.

40On hearing his words, some of the people said, "Surely this man is the Prophet."

41Others said, "He is the Christ."

Still others asked, "How can the Christ come from Galilee? 42Does not the Scripture say that the Christ will come from David's familyd and from Bethlehem, the town where David lived?" 43Thus the people were divided because of Jesus. 44Some wanted to seize him, but no-one laid a hand on him.

Unbelief of the Jewish Leaders

45Finally the temple guards went back to the chief priests and Pharisees, who asked them, "Why didn't you bring him in?"

46"No-one ever spoke the way this man does," the guards declared.

47"You mean he has deceived you also?" the Pharisees retorted. 48"Has any of the rulers or of the Pharisees believed in him? 49No! But this mob that knows nothing of the law—there is a curse on them."

50Nicodemus, who had gone to Jesus earlier and who was one of their own number, asked, 51"Does our law condemn a man without first hearing him to find out what he is doing?"

52They replied, "Are you from Galilee, too? Look into it, and you will find that a prophete does not come out of Galilee."

[The earliest and most reliable manuscripts do not have John 7:53–8:11.]

53Then each went to his own home.

8 But Jesus went to the Mount of Olives. 2At dawn he appeared again in the temple courts, where all the people gathered round him, and he sat down to teach them. 3The teachers of the law and the Pharisees brought in a woman caught in adultery. They made her stand before the group 4and said to Jesus, "Teacher, this woman was caught in the act of adultery. 5In the Law Moses commanded us to stone such women. Now what do you say?" 6They were using this question as a trap, in order to have a basis for accusing him.

But Jesus bent down and started to write on the ground with his finger. 7When they kept on questioning him, he straightened up and said to them, "If any one of you is without sin, let him be the first to throw a stone at her." 8Again he stooped down and wrote on the ground.

9At this, those who heard began to go away one at a time, the older ones first, until only Jesus was left, with the woman still standing there. 10Jesus straightened up and asked her, "Woman, where are they? Has no-one condemned you?"

11"No-one, sir," she said.

"Then neither do I condemn you," Jesus declared. "Go now and leave your life of sin."

The Validity of Jesus' Testimony

12When Jesus spoke again to the people, he said, "I am the light of the world. Whoever follows me will never walk in darkness, but will have the light of life."

13The Pharisees challenged him,

---

c38 Or If a man is thirsty, / let him come to me. / And let him drink, / who believes in me   d42 Greek seed   e52 Two early manuscripts the Prophet

"Here you are, appearing as your own witness; your testimony is not valid."

14Jesus answered, "Even if I testify on my own behalf, my testimony is valid, for I know where I came from and where I am going. But you have no idea where I come from or where I am going. 15You judge by human standards; I pass judgment on no-one. 16But if I do judge, my decisions are right, because I am not alone. I stand with the Father who sent me. 17In your own Law it is written that the testimony of two men is valid. 18I am one who testifies for myself; my other witness is the one who sent me—the Father."

19Then they asked him, "Where is your father?"

"You do not know me or my Father," Jesus replied. "If you knew me, you would know my Father also." 20He spoke these words while teaching in the temple area near the place where the offerings were put. Yet no-one seized him, because his time had not yet come.

21Once more Jesus said to them, "I am going away, and you will look for me, and you will die in your sin. Where I go, you cannot come."

22This made the Jews ask, "Will he kill himself? Is that why he says, 'Where I go, you cannot come'?"

23But he continued, "You are from below; I am from above. You are of this world; I am not of this world. 24I told you that you would die in your sins; if you do not believe that I am ‚the one I claim to be,‚ᵃ you will indeed die in your sins."

25"Who are you?" they asked.

"Just what I have been claiming all along," Jesus replied. 26"I have much to say in judgment of you. But he who sent me is reliable, and what I have heard from him I tell the world."

27They did not understand that he was telling them about his Father. 28So Jesus said, "When you have lifted up the Son of Man, then you will know who I amᵇ and that I do

nothing on my own but speak just what the Father has taught me. 29The one who sent me is with me; he has not left me alone, for I always do what pleases him." 30Even as he spoke, many put their faith in him.

The Children of Abraham

31To the Jews who had believed him, Jesus said, "If you hold to my teaching, you are really my disciples. 32Then you will know the truth, and the truth will set you free."

33They answered him, "We are Abraham's descendantsᶜ and have never been slaves of anyone. How can you say that we shall be set free?"

34Jesus replied, "I tell you the truth, everyone who sins is a slave to sin. 35Now a slave has no permanent place in the family, but a son belongs to it for ever. 36So if the Son sets you free, you will be free indeed. 37I know you are Abraham's descendants. Yet you are ready to kill me, because you have no room for my word. 38I am telling you what I have seen in the Father's presence, and you do what you have heard from your Father."ᵈ

39"Abraham is our father," they answered.

"If you were Abraham's children," said Jesus, "then you wouldᵉ do the things Abraham did. 40As it is, you are determined to kill me, a man who has told you the truth that I heard from God. Abraham did not do such things. 41You are doing the things your own father does."

"We are not illegitimate children," they protested. "The only Father we have is God himself."

The Children of the Devil

42Jesus said to them, "If God were your Father, you would love me, for I came from God and now am here. I have not come on my own; but he sent me. 43Why is my language not clear to you? Because you are unable to hear what I say. 44You belong to your father, the devil, and you want

ᵃ24 Or *I am he*   ᵇ28 Or *know that I am he*   ᶜ33 Greek *seed;* also in verse 37
ᵈ38 Or *presence. Therefore do what you have heard from the Father.*
ᵉ39 Some early manuscripts *"If you are Abraham's children," said Jesus, "then"*

to carry out your father's desire. He was a murderer from the beginning, not holding to the truth, for there is no truth in him. When he lies, he speaks his native language, for he is a liar and the father of lies. 45Yet because I tell the truth, you do not believe me! 46Can any of you prove me guilty of sin? If I am telling the truth, why don't you believe me? 47He who belongs to God hears what God says. The reason you do not hear is that you do not belong to God."

The Claims of Jesus About Himself

48The Jews answered him, "Aren't we right in saying that you are a Samaritan and demon-possessed?"

49"I am not possessed by a demon," said Jesus, "but I honour my Father and you dishonour me. 50I am not seeking glory for myself; but there is one who seeks it, and he is the judge. 51I tell you the truth, if a man keeps my word, he will never see death."

52At this the Jews exclaimed, "Now we know that you are demon-possessed! Abraham died and so did the prophets, yet you say that if a man keeps your word, he will never taste death. 53Are you greater than our father Abraham? He died, and so did the prophets. Who do you think you are?"

54Jesus replied, "If I glorify myself, my glory means nothing. My Father, whom you claim as your God, is the one who glorifies me. 55Though you do not know him, I know him. If I said I did not, I would be a liar like you, but I do know him and keep his word. 56Your father Abraham rejoiced at the thought of seeing my day; he saw it and was glad."

57"You are not yet fifty years old," the Jews said to him, "and you have seen Abraham!"

58"I tell you the truth," Jesus answered, "before Abraham was born, I am!" 59At this, they picked up stones to stone him, but Jesus hid himself, slipping away from the temple grounds.

Jesus Heals a Man Born Blind

9 As he went along, he saw a man blind from birth. 2His disciples

asked him, "Rabbi, who sinned, this man or his parents, that he was born blind?"

3"Neither this man nor his parents sinned," said Jesus, "but this happened so that the work of God might be displayed in his life. 4As long as it is day, we must do the work of him who sent me. Night is coming, when no-one can work. 5While I am in the world, I am the light of the world."

6Having said this, he spat on the ground, made some mud with the saliva, and put it on the man's eyes. 7"Go," he told him, "wash in the pool of Siloam" (this word means Sent). So the man went and washed, and came home seeing.

8His neighbours and those who had formerly seen him begging asked, "Isn't this the same man who used to sit and beg?" 9Some claimed that he was.

Others said, "No, he only looks like him."

But he himself insisted, "I am the man."

10"How then were your eyes opened?" they demanded.

11He replied, "The man they call Jesus made some mud and put it on my eyes. He told me to go to Siloam and wash. So I went and washed, and then I could see."

12"Where is this man?" they asked him.

"I don't know," he said.

The Pharisees Investigate the Healing

13They brought to the Pharisees the man who had been blind. 14Now the day on which Jesus had made the mud and opened the man's eyes was a Sabbath. 15Therefore the Pharisees also asked him how he had received his sight. "He put mud on my eyes," the man replied, "and I washed, and now I see."

16Some of the Pharisees said, "This man is not from God, for he does not keep the Sabbath."

But others asked, "How can a sinner do such miraculous signs?" So they were divided.

17Finally they turned again to the

blind man, "What have you to say about him? It was your eyes he opened."

The man replied, "He is a prophet."

¹⁸The Jews still did not believe that he had been blind and had received his sight until they sent for the man's parents. ¹⁹"Is this your son?" they asked. "Is this the one you say was born blind? How is it that now he can see?"

²⁰"We know he is our son," the parents answered, "and we know he was born blind. ²¹But how he can see now, or who opened his eyes, we don't know. Ask him. He is of age; he will speak for himself." ²²His parents said this because they were afraid of the Jews, for already the Jews had decided that anyone who acknowledged that Jesus was the Christ*a* would be put out of the synagogue. ²³That was why his parents said, "He is of age; ask him."

²⁴A second time they summoned the man who had been blind. "Give glory to God,"*b* they said. "We know this man is a sinner."

²⁵He replied, "Whether he is a sinner or not, I don't know. One thing I do know. I was blind but now I see!"

²⁶Then they asked him, "What did he do to you? How did he open your eyes?"

²⁷He answered, "I have told you already and you did not listen. Why do you want to hear it again? Do you want to become his disciples, too?"

²⁸Then they hurled insults at him and said, "You are this fellow's disciple! We are disciples of Moses! ²⁹We know that God spoke to Moses, but as for this fellow, we don't even know where he comes from."

³⁰The man answered, "Now that is remarkable! You don't know where he comes from, yet he opened my eyes. ³¹We know that God does not listen to sinners. He listens to the godly man who does his will. ³²Nobody has ever heard of opening the eyes of a man born blind. ³³If this

man were not from God, he could do nothing."

³⁴To this they replied, "You were steeped in sin at birth; how dare you lecture us!" And they threw him out.

Spiritual Blindness

³⁵Jesus heard that they had thrown him out, and when he found him, he said, "Do you believe in the Son of Man?"

³⁶"Who is he, sir?" the man asked. "Tell me so that I may believe in him."

³⁷Jesus said, "You have now seen him; in fact, he is the one speaking with you."

³⁸Then the man said, "Lord, I believe," and he worshipped him.

³⁹Jesus said, "For judgment I have come into this world, so that the blind will see and those who see will become blind."

⁴⁰Some Pharisees who were with him heard him say this and asked, "What? Are we blind too?"

⁴¹Jesus said, "If you were blind, you would not be guilty of sin; but now that you claim you can see, your guilt remains.

The Shepherd and His Flock

10 "I tell you the truth, the man who does not enter the sheep pen by the gate, but climbs in by some other way, is a thief and a robber. ²The man who enters by the gate is the shepherd of his sheep. ³The watchman opens the gate for him, and the sheep listen to his voice. He calls his own sheep by name and leads them out. ⁴When he has brought out all his own, he goes on ahead of them, and his sheep follow him because they know his voice. ⁵But they will never follow a stranger; in fact, they will run away from him because they do not recognise a stranger's voice." ⁶Jesus used this figure of speech, but they did not understand what he was telling them.

⁷Therefore Jesus said again, "I tell you the truth, I am the gate for the sheep. ⁸All who ever came before me were thieves and robbers, but the

---

*a*22 Or Messiah   *b*24 A solemn charge to tell the truth (see Joshua 7:19)

sheep did not listen to them. ⁹I am the gate; whoever enters through me will be saved.ᵃ He will come in and go out, and find pasture. ¹⁰The thief comes only to steal and kill and destroy; I have come that they may have life, and have it to the full.

¹¹"I am the good shepherd. The good shepherd lays down his life for the sheep. ¹²The hired hand is not the shepherd who owns the sheep. So when he sees the wolf coming, he abandons the sheep and runs away. Then the wolf attacks the flock and scatters it. ¹³The man runs away because he is a hired hand and cares nothing for the sheep.

¹⁴I am the good shepherd; I know my sheep and my sheep know me— ¹⁵just as the Father knows me and I know the Father—and I lay down my life for the sheep. ¹⁶I have other sheep that are not of this sheep pen. I must bring them also. They too will listen to my voice, and there shall be one flock and one shepherd. ¹⁷The reason my Father loves me is that I lay down my life—only to take it up again. ¹⁸No-one takes it from me, but I lay it down of my own accord. I have authority to lay it down and authority to take it up again. This command I received from my Father."

¹⁹At these words the Jews were again divided. ²⁰Many of them said, "He is demon-possessed and raving mad. Why listen to him?"

²¹But others said, "These are not the sayings of a man possessed by a demon. Can a demon open the eyes of the blind?"

The Unbelief of the Jews

²²Then came the Feast of Dedicationᵇ at Jerusalem. It was winter, ²³and Jesus was in the temple area walking in Solomon's Colonnade. ²⁴The Jews gathered round him, saying, "How long will you keep us in suspense? If you are the Christ,ᶜ tell us plainly."

²⁵Jesus answered, "I did tell you, but you do not believe. The miracles I do in my Father's name speak for me, ²⁶but you do not believe because you are not my sheep. ²⁷My sheep listen to my voice; I know them, and they follow me. ²⁸I give them eternal life, and they shall never perish; no-one can snatch them out of my hand. ²⁹My Father, who has given them to me, is greater than all;ᵈ no-one can snatch them out of my Father's hand. ³⁰I and the Father are one."

³¹Again the Jews picked up stones to stone him, ³²but Jesus said to them, "I have shown you many great miracles from the Father. For which of these do you stone me?"

³³"We are not stoning you for any of these," replied the Jews, "but for blasphemy, because you, a mere man, claim to be God."

³⁴Jesus answered them, "Is it not written in your Law, 'I have said you are gods'ᵉ? ³⁵If he called them 'gods', to whom the word of God came—and the Scripture cannot be broken— ³⁶what about the one whom the Father set apart as his very own and sent into the world? Why then do you accuse me of blasphemy because I said, 'I am God's Son'? ³⁷Do not believe me unless I do what my Father does. ³⁸But if I do it, even though you do not believe me, believe the miracles, that you may learn and understand that the Father is in me, and I in the Father." ³⁹Again they tried to seize him, but he escaped their grasp.

⁴⁰Then Jesus went back across the Jordan to the place where John had been baptising in the early days. Here he stayed ⁴¹and many people came to him. They said, "Though John never performed a miraculous sign, all that John said about this man was true." ⁴²And in that place many believed in Jesus.

The Death of Lazarus

11 Now a man named Lazarus was sick. He was from Bethany, the village of Mary and her

---

ᵃ9 Or kept safe   ᵇ22 That is, Hanukkah   ᶜ24 Or Messiah
ᵈ29 Many early manuscripts *What my Father has given me is greater than all*
ᵉ34 Psalm 82:6

sister Martha. 2This Mary, whose brother Lazarus now lay sick, was the same one who poured perfume on the Lord and wiped his feet with her hair. 3So the sisters sent word to Jesus, "Lord, the one you love is sick."

4When he heard this, Jesus said, "This sickness will not end in death. No, it is for God's glory so that God's Son may be glorified through it." 5Jesus loved Martha and her sister and Lazarus. 6Yet when he heard that Lazarus was sick, he stayed where he was two more days.

7Then he said to his disciples, "Let us go back to Judea."

8"But Rabbi," they said, "a short while ago the Jews tried to stone you, and yet you are going back there?"

9Jesus answered, "Are there not twelve hours of daylight? A man who walks by day will not stumble, for he sees by this world's light. 10It is when he walks by night that he stumbles, for he has no light."

11After he had said this, he went on to tell them, "Our friend Lazarus has fallen asleep; but I am going there to wake him up."

12His disciples replied, "Lord, if he sleeps, he will get better." 13Jesus had been speaking of his death, but his disciples thought he meant natural sleep.

14So then he told them plainly, "Lazarus is dead, 15and for your sake I am glad I was not there, so that you may believe. But let us go to him."

16Then Thomas (called Didymus) said to the rest of the disciples, "Let us also go, that we may die with him."

Jesus Comforts the Sisters

17On his arrival, Jesus found that Lazarus had already been in the tomb for four days. 18Bethany was less than two miles*a* from Jerusalem, 19and many Jews had come to Martha and Mary to comfort them in the loss of their brother. 20When Martha heard that Jesus was coming, she went out to meet him, but Mary stayed at home.

21"Lord," Martha said to Jesus, "if you had been here, my brother would

not have died. 22But I know that even now God will give you whatever you ask."

23Jesus said to her, "Your brother will rise again."

24Martha answered, "I know he will rise again in the resurrection at the last day."

25Jesus said to her, "I am the resurrection and the life. He who believes in me will live, even though he dies; 26and whoever lives and believes in me will never die. Do you believe this?"

27"Yes, Lord," she told him, "I believe that you are the Christ,*b* the Son of God, who was to come into the world."

28And after she had said this, she went back and called her sister Mary aside. "The Teacher is here," she said, "and is asking for you." 29When Mary heard this, she got up quickly and went to him. 30Now Jesus had not yet entered the village, but was still at the place where Martha had met him. 31When the Jews who had been with Mary in the house, comforting her, noticed how quickly she got up and went out, they followed her, supposing she was going to the tomb to mourn there.

32When Mary reached the place where Jesus was and saw him, she fell at his feet and said, "Lord, if you had been here, my brother would not have died."

33When Jesus saw her weeping, and the Jews who had come along with her also weeping, he was deeply moved in spirit and troubled. 34"Where have you laid him?" he asked.

"Come and see, Lord," they replied.

35Jesus wept.

36Then the Jews said, "See how he loved him!"

37But some of them said, "Could not he who opened the eyes of the blind man have kept this man from dying?"

Jesus Raises Lazarus From the Dead

38Jesus, once more deeply moved,

a18 Greek fifteen stadia (about 3 kilometres)

b27 Or Messiah

came to the tomb. It was a cave with a stone laid across the entrance. 39"Take away the stone," he said.

"But, Lord," said Martha, the sister of the dead man, "by this time there is a bad odour, for he has been there four days."

40Then Jesus said, "Did I not tell you that if you believed, you would see the glory of God?"

41So they took away the stone. Then Jesus looked up and said, "Father, I thank you that you have heard me. 42I knew that you always hear me, but I said this for the benefit of the people standing here, that they may believe that you sent me."

43When he had said this, Jesus called in a loud voice, "Lazarus, come out!" 44The dead man came out, his hands and feet wrapped with strips of linen, and a cloth around his face.

Jesus said to them, "Take off the grave clothes and let him go."

The Plot to Kill Jesus

45Therefore many of the Jews who had come to visit Mary, and had seen what Jesus did, put their faith in him. 46But some of them went to the Pharisees and told them what Jesus had done. 47Then the chief priests and the Pharisees called a meeting of the Sanhedrin.

"What are we accomplishing?" they asked. "Here is this man performing many miraculous signs. 48If we let him go on like this, everyone will believe in him, and then the Romans will come and take away both our place^c and our nation."

49Then one of them, named Caiaphas, who was high priest that year, spoke up, "You know nothing at all! 50You do not realise that it is better for you that one man die for the people than that the whole nation perish."

51He did not say this on his own, but as high priest that year he prophesied that Jesus would die for the Jewish nation, 52and not only for that nation but also for the scattered children of God, to bring them together

and make them one. 53So from that day on they plotted to take his life.

54Therefore Jesus no longer moved about publicly among the Jews. Instead he withdrew to a region near the desert, to a village called Ephraim, where he stayed with his disciples.

55When it was almost time for the Jewish Passover, many went up from the country to Jerusalem for their ceremonial cleansing before the Passover. 56They kept looking for Jesus, and as they stood in the temple area they asked one another, "What do you think? Isn't he coming to the Feast at all?" 57But the chief priests and Pharisees had given orders that if anyone found out where Jesus was, he should report it so that they might arrest him.

Jesus Anointed at Bethany

12 Six days before the Passover, Jesus arrived at Bethany, where Lazarus lived, whom Jesus had raised from the dead. 2Here a dinner was given in Jesus' honour. Martha served, while Lazarus was among those reclining at the table with him. 3Then Mary took about a pint^a of pure nard, an expensive perfume; she poured it on Jesus' feet and wiped his feet with her hair. And the house was filled with the fragrance of the perfume.

4But one of his disciples, Judas Iscariot, who was later to betray him, objected, 5"Why wasn't this perfume sold and the money given to the poor? It was worth a year's wages."^{b} 6He did not say this because he cared about the poor but because he was a thief; as keeper of the money bag, he used to help himself to what was put into it.

7"Leave her alone," Jesus replied. "It was meant that she should save this perfume for the day of my burial. 8You will always have the poor among you, but you will not always have me."

9Meanwhile a large crowd of Jews found out that Jesus was there and

^{c}48 Or temple ^{a}3 Greek a litra (probably about 0.5 litre)
^{b}5 Greek three hundred denarii

came, not only because of him but also to see Lazarus, whom he had raised from the dead. 10So the chief priests made plans to kill Lazarus as well, 11for on account of him many of the Jews were going over to Jesus and putting their faith in him.

The Triumphal Entry

12The next day the great crowd that had come for the Feast heard that Jesus was on his way to Jerusalem. 13They took palm branches and went out to meet him, shouting,

"Hosanna!"*c*

"Blessed is he who comes in the name of the Lord!"*d*

"Blessed is the King of Israel!"

14Jesus found a young donkey and sat upon it, as it is written,

15"Do not be afraid, O Daughter of Zion;

see, your king is coming,

seated on a donkey's colt."*e*

16At first his disciples did not understand all this. Only after Jesus was glorified did they realise that these things had been written about him and that they had done these things to him.

17Now the crowd that was with him had continued to spread the word that he had called Lazarus from the tomb, raising him from the dead.*f* 18Many people, because they had heard that he had given this miraculous sign, went out to meet him. 19So the Pharisees said to one another, "See, this is getting us nowhere. Look how the whole world has gone after him!"

Jesus Predicts His Death

20Now there were some Greeks among those who went up to worship at the Feast. 21They came to Philip, who was from Bethsaida in Galilee, with a request. "Sir," they said, "we would like to see Jesus." 22Philip went to tell Andrew; Andrew and Philip in turn told Jesus.

23Jesus replied, "The hour has come for the Son of Man to be glorified. 24I tell you the truth, unless an ear of wheat falls to the ground and dies, it remains only a single seed. But if it dies, it produces many seeds. 25The man who loves his life will lose it, while the man who hates his life in this world will keep it for eternal life. 26Whoever serves me must follow me; and where I am, my servant also will be. My Father will honour the one who serves me.

27"Now my heart is troubled, and what shall I say? 'Father, save me from this hour'? No, it was for this very reason I came to this hour. 28Father, glorify your name!"

Then a voice came from heaven, "I have glorified it, and will glorify it again." 29The crowd that was there and heard it said it had thundered; others said an angel had spoken to him.

30Jesus said, "This voice was for your benefit, not mine. 31Now is the time for judgment on this world; now the prince of this world will be driven out. 32But I, when I am lifted up from the earth, will draw all men to myself." 33He said this to show the kind of death he was going to die.

34The crowd spoke up, "We have heard from the Law that the Christ*g* will remain for ever, so how can you say, 'The Son of Man must be lifted up'? Who is this 'Son of Man'?"

35Then Jesus told them, "You are going to have the light just a little while longer. Walk while you have the light, before darkness overtakes you. The man who walks in the dark does not know where he is going. 36Put your trust in the light while you have it, so that you may become sons of light." When he had finished speaking, Jesus left and hid himself from them.

The Jews Continue in Their Unbelief

37Even after Jesus had done all

c13 A Hebrew expression meaning "Save!" which became an exclamation of praise
d13 Psalm 118:25,26   *e15* Zech. 9:9
f17 Or *Now the crowd that had been with him when he called Lazarus from the tomb and raised him from the dead were telling everyone*   *g34* Or *Messiah*

these miraculous signs in their presence, they still would not believe in him. ³⁸This was to fulfil the word of Isaiah the prophet:

"Lord, who has believed our
message
and to whom has the arm of the
Lord been revealed?"ʰ

³⁹For this reason they could not believe, because, as Isaiah says elsewhere:

⁴⁰"He has blinded their eyes
and deadened their hearts,
so they can neither see with their
eyes,
nor understand with their hearts,
nor turn—and I would heal
them."ⁱ

⁴¹Isaiah said this because he saw Jesus' glory and spoke about him.

⁴²Yet at the same time many even among the leaders believed in him. But because of the Pharisees they would not confess their faith for fear they would be put out of the synagogue; ⁴³for they loved praise from men more than praise from God.

⁴⁴Then Jesus cried out, "When a man believes in me, he does not believe in me only, but in the one who sent me. ⁴⁵When he looks at me, he sees the one who sent me. ⁴⁶I have come into the world as a light, so that no-one who believes in me should stay in darkness.

⁴⁷"As for the person who hears my words but does not keep them, I do not judge him. For I did not come to judge the world, but to save it. ⁴⁸There is a judge for the one who rejects me and does not accept my words; that very word which I spoke will condemn him at the last day. ⁴⁹For I did not speak of my own accord, but the Father who sent me commanded me what to say and how to say it. ⁵⁰I know that his command leads to eternal life. So whatever I say is just what the Father has told me to say."

Jesus Washes His Disciples' Feet

13 It was just before the Passover Feast. Jesus knew that the time had come for him to leave this world and go to the Father. Having loved his own who were in the world, he now showed them the full extent of his love.ᵃ

²The evening meal was being served, and the devil had already prompted Judas Iscariot, son of Simon, to betray Jesus. ³Jesus knew that the Father had put all things under his power, and that he had come from God and was returning to God; ⁴so he got up from the meal, took off his outer clothing, and wrapped a towel round his waist. ⁵After that, he poured water into a basin and began to wash his disciples' feet, drying them with the towel that was wrapped round him.

⁶He came to Simon Peter, who said to him, "Lord, are you going to wash my feet?"

⁷Jesus replied, "You do not realise now what I am doing, but later you will understand."

⁸"No," said Peter, "you shall never wash my feet."

Jesus answered, "Unless I wash you, you have no part with me."

⁹"Then, Lord," Simon Peter replied, "not just my feet but my hands and my head as well!"

¹⁰Jesus answered, "A person who has had a bath needs only to wash his feet; his whole body is clean. And you are clean, though not every one of you." ¹¹For he knew who was going to betray him, and that was why he said not every one was clean.

¹²When he had finished washing their feet, he put on his clothes and returned to his place. "Do you understand what I have done for you?" he asked them. ¹³"You call me 'Teacher' and 'Lord', and rightly so, for that is what I am. ¹⁴Now that I, your Lord and Teacher, have washed your feet, you also should wash one another's feet. ¹⁵I have set you an example that you should do as I have done for you. ¹⁶I tell you the truth, no servant is greater than his master, nor is a messenger greater than the one who sent him. ¹⁷Now that you know these

ʰ38 Isaiah 53:1   ⁱ40 Isaiah 6:10   ᵃ1 Or *he loved them to the last*

118

things, you will be blessed if you do them.

Jesus Predicts His Betrayal

[18]"I am not referring to all of you; I know those I have chosen. But this is to fulfil the scripture: 'He who shares my bread has lifted up his heel against me.'[b]

[19]"I am telling you now before it happens, so that when it does happen you will believe that I am He. [20]I tell you the truth, whoever accepts anyone I send accepts me; and whoever accepts me accepts the one who sent me."

[21]After he had said this, Jesus was troubled in spirit and testified, "I tell you the truth, one of you is going to betray me."

[22]His disciples stared at one another, at a loss to know which of them he meant. [23]One of them, the disciple whom Jesus loved, was reclining next to him. [24]Simon Peter motioned to this disciple and said, "Ask him which one he means."

[25]Leaning back against Jesus, he asked him, "Lord, who is it?"

[26]Jesus answered, "It is the one to whom I will give this piece of bread when I have dipped it in the dish." Then, dipping the piece of bread, he gave it to Judas Iscariot, son of Simon. [27]As soon as Judas took the bread, Satan entered into him.

"What you are about to do, do quickly," Jesus told him, [28]but no-one at the meal understood why Jesus said this to him. [29]Since Judas had charge of the money, some thought Jesus was telling him to buy what was needed for the Feast, or to give something to the poor. [30]As soon as Judas had taken the bread, he went out. And it was night.

Jesus Predicts Peter's Denial

[31]When he was gone, Jesus said, "Now is the Son of Man glorified and God is glorified in him. [32]If God is glorified in him,[c] God will glorify the Son in himself, and will glorify him at once.

[33]"My children, I will be with you only a little longer. You will look for me, and just as I told the Jews, so I tell you now: Where I am going, you cannot come.

[34]"A new command I give you: Love one another. As I have loved you, so you must love one another. [35]All men will know that you are my disciples if you love one another."

[36]Simon Peter asked him, "Lord, where are you going?"

Jesus replied, "Where I am going, you cannot follow now, but you will follow later."

[37]Peter asked, "Lord, why can't I follow you now? I will lay down my life for you."

[38]Then Jesus answered, "Will you really lay down your life for me? I tell you the truth, before the cock crows, you will disown me three times!

Jesus Comforts His Disciples

14 "Do not let your hearts be troubled. Trust in God;[a] trust also in me. [2]In my Father's house are many rooms; if it were not so, I would have told you. I am going there to prepare a place for you. [3]And if I go and prepare a place for you, I will come back and take you to be with me that you also may be where I am. [4]You know the way to the place where I am going."

Jesus the Way to the Father

[5]Thomas said to him, "Lord, we don't know where you are going, so how can we know the way?"

[6]Jesus answered, "I am the way and the truth and the life. No-one comes to the Father except through me. [7]If you really knew me, you would know[b] my Father as well. From now on, you do know him and have seen him."

[8]Philip said, "Lord, show us the Father and that will be enough for us."

[9]Jesus answered: "Don't you know me, Philip, even after I have been among you such a long time? Anyone

[b]18 Psalm 41:9   [c]32 Many early manuscripts do not have *If God is glorified in him.*
[a]1 Or *You trust in God*
[b]7 Some early manuscripts *If you really have known me, you will know*

119

who has seen me has seen the Father. How can you say, 'Show us the Father'? 10Don't you believe that I am in the Father, and that the Father is in me? The words I say to you are not just my own. Rather, it is the Father, living in me, who is doing his work. 11Believe me when I say that I am in the Father and the Father is in me; or at least believe on the evidence of the miracles themselves. 12I tell you the truth, anyone who has faith in me will do what I have been doing. He will do even greater things than these, because I am going to the Father. 13And I will do whatever you ask in my name, so that the Son may bring glory to the Father. 14You may ask me for anything in my name, and I will do it.

Jesus Promises the Holy Spirit

15"If you love me, you will obey what I command. 16And I will ask the Father, and he will give you another Counsellor to be with you for ever— 17the Spirit of truth. The world cannot accept him, because it neither sees him nor knows him. But you know him, for he lives with you and will be*c* in you. 18I will not leave you as orphans; I will come to you. 19Before long, the world will not see me any more, but you will see me. Because I live, you also will live. 20On that day you will realise that I am in my Father, and you are in me, and I am in you. 21Whoever has my commands and obeys them, he is the one who loves me. He who loves me will be loved by my Father, and I too will love him and show myself to him."

22Then Judas (not Judas Iscariot) said, "But, Lord, why do you intend to show yourself to us and not to the world?"

23Jesus replied, "If anyone loves me, he will obey my teaching. My Father will love him, and we will come to him and make our home with him. 24He who does not love me will not obey my teaching. These words you hear are not my own; they belong to the Father who sent me.

25"All this I have spoken while still

with you. 26But the Counsellor, the Holy Spirit, whom the Father will send in my name, will teach you all things and will remind you of everything I have said to you. 27Peace I leave with you; my peace I give you. I do not give to you as the world gives. Do not let your hearts be troubled and do not be afraid.

28"You heard me say, 'I am going away and I am coming back to you.' If you loved me, you would be glad that I am going to the Father, for the Father is greater than I. 29I have told you now before it happens, so that when it does happen you will believe. 30I will not speak with you much longer, for the prince of this world is coming. He has no hold on me, 31but the world must learn that I love the Father and that I do exactly what my Father has commanded me.

"Come now; let us leave.

The Vine and the Branches

15 "I am the true vine and my Father is the gardener. 2He cuts off every branch in me that bears no fruit, while every branch that does bear fruit he trims clean so that it will be even more fruitful. 3You are already clean because of the word I have spoken to you. 4Remain in me, and I will remain in you. No branch can bear fruit by itself; it must remain in the vine. Neither can you bear fruit unless you remain in me.

5"I am the vine; you are the branches. If a man remains in me and I in him, he will bear much fruit; apart from me you can do nothing. 6If anyone does not remain in me, he is like a branch that is thrown away and withers; such branches are picked up, thrown into the fire and burned. 7If you remain in me and my words remain in you, ask whatever you wish, and it will be given you. 8This is to my Father's glory, that you bear much fruit, showing yourselves to be my disciples.

9"As the Father has loved me, so have I loved you. Now remain in my love. 10If you obey my commands, you will remain in my love, just as I

*c*17 Some early manuscripts *and is*

120

have obeyed my Father's commands and remain in his love. 11I have told you this so that my joy may be in you and that your joy may be complete. 12My command is this: Love each other as I have loved you. 13Greater love has no-one than this, that one lay down his life for his friends. 14You are my friends if you do what I command. 15I no longer call you servants, because a servant does not know his master's business. Instead, I have called you friends, for everything that I learned from my Father I have made known to you. 16You did not choose me, but I chose you to go and bear fruit—fruit that will last. Then the Father will give you whatever you ask in my name. 17This is my command: Love each other.

The World Hates the Disciples

18"If the world hates you, keep in mind that it hated me first. 19If you belonged to the world, it would love you as its own. As it is, you do not belong to the world, but I have chosen you out of the world. That is why the world hates you. 20Remember the words I spoke to you: 'No servant is greater than his master.'*a* If they persecuted me, they will persecute you also. If they obeyed my teaching, they will obey yours also. 21They will treat you this way because of my name, for they do not know the One who sent me. 22If I had not come and spoken to them, they would not be guilty of sin. Now, however, they have no excuse for their sin. 23He who hates me hates my Father as well. 24If I had not done among them what no-one else did, they would not be guilty of sin. But now they have seen these miracles, and yet they have hated both me and my Father. 25But this is to fulfil what is written in their Law: 'They hated me without reason.'*b*

26"When the Counsellor comes, whom I will send to you from the Father, the Spirit of truth who goes out from the Father, he will testify about me; 27but you also must testify, for you have been with me from the beginning.

16 "All this I have told you so that you will not go astray. 2They will put you out of the synagogue; in fact, a time is coming when anyone who kills you will think he is offering a service to God. 3They will do such things because they have not known the Father or me. 4I have told you this, so that when the time comes you will remember that I warned you. I did not tell you this at first because I was with you.

The Work of the Holy Spirit

5"Now I am going to him who sent me, yet none of you asks me, 'Where are you going?' 6Because I have said these things, you are filled with grief. 7But I tell you the truth: It is for your good that I am going away. Unless I go away, the Counsellor will not come to you; but if I go, I will send him to you. 8When he comes, he will convict the world of guilt in regard to sin and righteousness and judgment: 9in regard to sin, because men do not believe in me; 10in regard to righteousness, because I am going to the Father, where you can see me no longer; 11and in regard to judgment, because the prince of this world now stands condemned.

12"I have much more to say to you, more than you can now bear. 13But when he, the Spirit of truth, comes, he will guide you into all truth. He will not speak on his own; he will speak only what he hears, and he will tell you what is yet to come. 14He will bring glory to me by taking from what is mine and making it known to you. 15All that belongs to the Father is mine. That is why I said the Spirit will take from what is mine and make it known to you.

16"In a little while you will see me no more, and then after a little while you will see me."

The Disciples' Grief Will Turn to Joy

17Some of his disciples said to one another, "What does he mean by saying, 'In a little while you will see me no more, and then after a little while you will see me,' and 'Because

*a*20 John 13:16   *b*25 Psalms 35:19; 69:4

I am going to the Father'?" [18]They kept asking, "What does he mean by 'a little while'? We don't understand what he is saying."

[19]Jesus saw that they wanted to ask him about this, so he said to them, "Are you asking one another what I meant when I said, 'In a little while you will see me no more, and then after a little while you will see me'? [20]I tell you the truth, you will weep and mourn while the world rejoices. You will grieve, but your grief will turn to joy. [21]A woman giving birth to a child has pain because her time has come; but when her baby is born she forgets the anguish because of her joy that a child is born into the world. [22]So with you: Now is your time of grief, but I will see you again and you will rejoice, and no-one will take away your joy. [23]In that day you will no longer ask me anything. I tell you the truth, my Father will give you whatever you ask in my name. [24]Until now you have not asked for anything in my name. Ask and you will receive, and your joy will be complete.

[25]"Though I have been speaking figuratively, a time is coming when I will no longer use this kind of language but will tell you plainly about my Father. [26]In that day you will ask in my name. I am not saying that I will ask the Father on your behalf. [27]No, the Father himself loves you because you have loved me and have believed that I came from God. [28]I came from the Father and entered the world; now I am leaving the world and going back to the Father."

[29]Then Jesus' disciples said, "Now you are speaking clearly and without figures of speech. [30]Now we can see that you know all things and that you do not even need to have anyone ask you questions. This makes us believe that you came from God."

[31]"You believe at last!"[a] Jesus answered. [32]"But a time is coming, and has come, when you will be scattered, each to his own home. You will leave me all alone. Yet I am not alone, for my Father is with me.

[33]"I have told you these things, so that in me you may have peace. In this world you will have trouble. But take heart! I have overcome the world."

Jesus Prays for Himself

17 After Jesus said this, he looked towards heaven and prayed:

"Father, the time has come. Glorify your Son, that your Son may glorify you. [2]For you granted him authority over all people that he might give eternal life to all those you have given him. [3]Now this is eternal life: that they may know you, the only true God, and Jesus Christ, whom you have sent. [4]I have brought you glory on earth by completing the work you gave me to do. [5]And now, Father, glorify me in your presence with the glory I had with you before the world began.

Jesus Prays for His Disciples

[6]"I have revealed you[a] to those whom you gave me out of the world. They were yours; you gave them to me and they have obeyed your word. [7]Now they know that everything you have given me comes from you. [8]For I gave them the words you gave me and they accepted them. They knew with certainty that I came from you, and they believed that you sent me. [9]I pray for them. I am not praying for the world, but for those you have given me, for they are yours. [10]All I have is yours, and all you have is mine. And glory has come to me through them. [11]I will remain in the world no longer, but they are still in the world, and I am coming to you. Holy Father, protect them by the power of your name—the name you gave me—so that they may be one as we are one. [12]While I was with them, I protected them and kept them safe by that name you gave me. None has been lost

---

[a]31 Or "Do you now believe?"   [a]6 Greek your name; also in verse 26

except the one doomed to destruction so that Scripture would be fulfilled.

¹³"I am coming to you now, but I say these things while I am still in the world, so that they may have the full measure of my joy within them. ¹⁴I have given them your word and the world has hated them, for they are not of the world any more than I am of the world. ¹⁵My prayer is not that you take them out of the world but that you protect them from the evil one. ¹⁶They are not of the world, even as I am not of it. ¹⁷Sanctifyᵇ them by the truth; your word is truth. ¹⁸As you sent me into the world, I have sent them into the world. ¹⁹For them I sanctify myself, that they too may be truly sanctified.

Jesus Prays for All Believers

²⁰"My prayer is not for them alone. I pray also for those who will believe in me through their message, ²¹that all of them may be one, Father, just as you are in me and I am in you. May they also be in us so that the world may believe that you have sent me. ²²I have given them the glory that you gave me, that they may be one as we are one: ²³I in them and you in me. May they be brought to complete unity to let the world know that you sent me and have loved them even as you have loved me.

²⁴"Father, I want those you have given me to be with me where I am, and to see my glory, the glory you have given me because you loved me before the creation of the world.

²⁵"Righteous Father, though the world does not know you, I know you, and they know that you have sent me. ²⁶I have made you known to them, and will continue to make you known in order that the love you have for me may be in them and that I myself may be in them."

Jesus Arrested

18 When he had finished praying, Jesus left with his disciples and crossed the Kidron Valley. On the other side there was an olive grove, and he and his disciples went into it.

²Now Judas, who betrayed him, knew the place, because Jesus had often met there with his disciples. ³So Judas came to the grove, guiding a detachment of soldiers and some officials from the chief priests and Pharisees. They were carrying torches, lanterns and weapons.

⁴Jesus, knowing all that was going to happen to him, went out and asked them, "Who is it you want?"

⁵"Jesus of Nazareth," they replied.

"I am he," Jesus said. (And Judas the traitor was standing there with them.) ⁶When Jesus said, "I am he," they drew back and fell to the ground.

⁷Again he asked them, "Who is it you want?"

And they said, "Jesus of Nazareth."

⁸"I told you that I am he," Jesus answered. "If you are looking for me, then let these men go." ⁹This happened so that the words he had spoken would be fulfilled: "I have not lost one of those you gave me."ᵃ

¹⁰Then Simon Peter, who had a sword, drew it and struck the high priest's servant, cutting off his right ear. (The servant's name was Malchus.)

¹¹Jesus commanded Peter, "Put your sword away! Shall I not drink the cup the Father has given me?"

Jesus Taken to Annas

¹²Then the detachment of soldiers with its commander and the Jewish officials arrested Jesus. They bound him ¹³and brought him first to Annas, who was the father-in-law of Caiaphas, the high priest that year. ¹⁴Caiaphas was the one who had advised the Jews that it would be good if one man died for the people.

Peter's First Denial

¹⁵Simon Peter and another disciple

ᵇ17 Greek *hagiazo* (set apart for sacred use or make holy); also in verse 19   ᵃ9 John 6:39

123

were following Jesus. Because this disciple was known to the high priest, he went with Jesus into the high priest's courtyard, [16]but Peter had to wait outside at the door. The other disciple, who was known to the high priest, came back, spoke to the girl on duty there and brought Peter in.

[17]"Surely you are not another of this man's disciples?" the girl at the door asked Peter.

He replied, "I am not."

[18]It was cold, and the servants and officials stood round a fire they had made to keep warm. Peter also was standing with them, warming himself.

The High Priest Questions Jesus

[19]Meanwhile, the high priest questioned Jesus about his disciples and his teaching.

[20]"I have spoken openly to the world," Jesus replied. "I always taught in synagogues or at the temple, where all the Jews come together. I said nothing in secret. [21]Why question me? Ask those who heard me. Surely they know what I said."

[22]When Jesus said this, one of the officials near by struck him in the face. "Is that any way to answer the high priest?" he demanded.

[23]"If I said something wrong," Jesus replied, "testify as to what is wrong. But if I spoke the truth, why did you strike me?" [24]Then Annas sent him, still bound, to Caiaphas the high priest.[b]

Peter's Second and Third Denials

[25]As Simon Peter stood warming himself, he was asked, "Surely you are not another of his disciples?"

He denied it, saying, "I am not."

[26]One of the high priest's servants, a relative of the man whose ear Peter had cut off, challenged him, "Didn't I see you with him in the olive grove?" [27]Again Peter denied it, and at that moment a cock began to crow.

Jesus Before Pilate

[28]Then the Jews led Jesus from Caiaphas to the palace of the Roman governor. By now it was early morning, and to avoid ceremonial unclean-

ness the Jews did not enter the palace; they wanted to be able to eat the Passover. [29]So Pilate came out to them and asked, "What charges are you bringing against this man?"

[30]"If he were not a criminal," they replied, "we would not have handed him over to you."

[31]Pilate said, "Take him yourselves and judge him by your own law."

"But we have no right to execute anyone," the Jews objected. [32]This happened so that the words Jesus had spoken indicating the kind of death he was going to die would be fulfilled.

[33]Pilate then went back inside the palace, summoned Jesus and asked him, "Are you the king of the Jews?"

[34]"Is that your own idea," Jesus asked, "or did others talk to you about me?"

[35]"Do you think I am a Jew?" Pilate replied. "It was your people and your chief priests who handed you over to me. What is it you have done?"

[36]Jesus said, "My kingdom is not of this world. If it were, my servants would fight to prevent my arrest by the Jews. But now my kingdom is from another place."

[37]"You are a king, then!" said Pilate.

Jesus answered, "You are right in saying I am a king. In fact, for this reason I was born, and for this I came into the world, to testify to the truth. Everyone on the side of truth listens to me."

[38]"What is truth?" Pilate asked. With this he went out again to the Jews and said, "I find no basis for a charge against him. [39]But it is your custom for me to release to you one prisoner at the time of the Passover. Do you want me to release 'the king of the Jews'?"

[40]They shouted back, "No, not him! Give us Barabbas!" Now Barabbas had taken part in a rebellion.

Jesus Sentenced to be Crucified

19 Then Pilate took Jesus and had him flogged. [2]The soldiers twisted together a crown of thorns

[b]24 Or (*Now Annas had sent him, still bound, to Caiaphas the high priest.*)

and put it on his head. They clothed him in a purple robe ³and went up to him again and again, saying, "Hail, O king of the Jews!" And they struck him in the face.

⁴Once more Pilate came out and said to the Jews, "Look, I am bringing him out to you to let you know that I find no basis for a charge against him." ⁵When Jesus came out wearing the crown of thorns and the purple robe, Pilate said to them, "Here is the man!"

⁶As soon as the chief priests and their officials saw him, they shouted, "Crucify! Crucify!"

But Pilate answered, "You take him and crucify him. As for me, I find no basis for a charge against him."

⁷The Jews insisted, "We have a law, and according to that law he must die, because he claimed to be the Son of God."

⁸When Pilate heard this, he was even more afraid, ⁹and he went back inside the palace. "Where do you come from?" he asked Jesus, but Jesus gave him no answer. ¹⁰"Do you refuse to speak to me?" Pilate said. "Don't you realise I have power either to free you or to crucify you?"

¹¹Jesus answered, "You would have no power over me if it were not given to you from above. Therefore the one who handed me over to you is guilty of a greater sin."

¹²From then on, Pilate tried to set Jesus free, but the Jews kept shouting, "If you let this man go, you are no friend of Caesar. Anyone who claims to be a king opposes Caesar."

¹³When Pilate heard this, he brought Jesus out and sat down on the judge's seat at a place known as The Stone Pavement (which in Aramaic is Gabbatha). ¹⁴It was the day of Preparation of Passover Week, about the sixth hour.

"Here is your king," Pilate said to the Jews.

¹⁵But they shouted, "Take him away! Take him away! Crucify him!"

"Shall I crucify your king?" Pilate asked.

"We have no king but Caesar," the chief priests answered.

¹⁶Finally Pilate handed him over to them to be crucified.

The Crucifixion

So the soldiers took charge of Jesus. ¹⁷Carrying his own cross, he went out to The Place of the Skull (which in Aramaic is called Golgotha). ¹⁸Here they crucified him, and with him two others—one on each side and Jesus in the middle.

¹⁹Pilate had a notice prepared and fastened to the cross. It read: JESUS OF NAZARETH, THE KING OF THE JEWS. ²⁰Many of the Jews read this sign, for the place where Jesus was crucified was near the city, and the sign was written in Aramaic, Latin and Greek. ²¹The chief priests of the Jews protested to Pilate, "Do not write 'The King of the Jews', but that this man claimed to be king of the Jews."

²²Pilate answered, "What I have written, I have written."

²³When the soldiers crucified Jesus, they took his clothes, dividing them into four shares, one for each of them, with the undergarment remaining. This garment was seamless, woven in one piece from top to bottom.

²⁴"Let's not tear it," they said to one another. "Let's decide by lot who will get it."

This happened that the scripture might be fulfilled which said,

"They divided my garments
    among them
and cast lots for my
    clothing."ᵃ

So this is what the soldiers did.

²⁵Near the cross of Jesus stood his mother, his mother's sister, Mary the wife of Clopas, and Mary of Magdala. ²⁶When Jesus saw his mother there, and the disciple whom he loved standing near by, he said to his mother, "Dear woman, here is your son," ²⁷and to the disciple, "Here is your mother." From that time on, this disciple took her into his home.

The Death of Jesus

²⁸Later, knowing that all was now completed, and so that the Scripture

ᵃ24 Psalm 22:18

125

would be fulfilled, Jesus said, "I am thirsty." 29A jar of wine vinegar was there, so they soaked a sponge in it, put the sponge on a stalk of the hyssop plant, and lifted it to Jesus' lips. 30When he had received the drink, Jesus said, "It is finished." With that, he bowed his head and gave up his spirit.

31Now it was the day of Preparation, and the next day was to be a special Sabbath. Because the Jews did not want the bodies left on the crosses during the Sabbath, they asked Pilate to have the legs broken and the bodies taken down. 32The soldiers therefore came and broke the legs of the first man who had been crucified with Jesus, and then those of the other. 33But when they came to Jesus and found that he was already dead, they did not break his legs. 34Instead, one of the soldiers pierced Jesus' side with a spear, bringing a sudden flow of blood and water. 35The man who saw it has given testimony, and his testimony is true. He knows that he tells the truth, and he testifies so that you also may believe. 36These things happened so that the scripture would be fulfilled: "Not one of his bones will be broken,"b 37and, as another scripture says, "They will look on the one they have pierced."c

The Burial of Jesus

38Later, Joseph of Arimathea asked Pilate for the body of Jesus. Now Joseph was a disciple of Jesus, but secretly because he feared the Jews. With Pilate's permission, he came and took the body. 39He was accompanied by Nicodemus, the man who earlier had visited Jesus at night. Nicodemus brought a mixture of myrrh and aloes, about seventy-five pounds.d 40Taking Jesus' body, the two of them wrapped it, with the spices, in strips of linen. This was in accordance with Jewish burial customs. 41At the place where Jesus was crucified, there was a garden, and in the garden a new tomb, in which

no-one had ever been laid. 42Because it was the Jewish day of Preparation and since the tomb was near by, they laid Jesus there.

The Empty Tomb

20 Early on the first day of the week, while it was still dark, Mary of Magdala went to the tomb and saw that the stone had been removed from the entrance. 2So she came running to Simon Peter and the other disciple, the one Jesus loved, and said, "They have taken the Lord out of the tomb, and we don't know where they have put him!"

3So Peter and the other disciple started for the tomb. 4Both were running, but the other disciple outran Peter and reached the tomb first. 5He bent over and looked in at the strips of linen lying there but did not go in. 6Then Simon Peter, who was behind him, arrived and went into the tomb. He saw the strips of linen lying there, 7as well as the burial cloth that had been around Jesus' head. The cloth was folded up by itself, separate from the linen. 8Finally the other disciple, who had reached the tomb first, also went inside. He saw and believed. 9(They still did not understand from Scripture that Jesus had to rise from the dead.)

Jesus Appears to Mary of Magdala

10Then the disciples went back to their homes, 11but Mary stood outside the tomb crying. As she wept, she bent over to look into the tomb 12and saw two angels in white, seated where Jesus' body had been, one at the head and the other at the foot.

13They asked her, "Woman, why are you crying?"

"They have taken my Lord away," she said, "and I don't know where they have put him." 14At this, she turned round and saw Jesus standing there, but she did not realise that it was Jesus.

15"Woman," he said, "why are you crying? Who is it you are looking for?"

---

b36 Exodus 12:46; Num. 9:12; Psalm 34:20   c37 Zech. 12:10
d39 Greek a hundred litrai (about 34 kilograms)

Thinking he was the gardener, she said, "Sir, if you have carried him away, tell me where you have put him, and I will get him."

16Jesus said to her, "Mary."

She turned towards him and cried out in Aramaic, "Rabboni!" (which means Teacher).

17Jesus said, "Do not hold on to me, for I have not yet returned to the Father. Go instead to my brothers and tell them, 'I am returning to my Father and your Father, to my God and your God.'"

18Mary of Magdala went to the disciples with the news: "I have seen the Lord!" And she told them that he had said these things to her.

Jesus Appears to His Disciples

19On the evening of that first day of the week, when the disciples were together, with the doors locked for fear of the Jews, Jesus came and stood among them and said, "Peace be with you!" 20After he said this, he showed them his hands and side. The disciples were overjoyed when they saw the Lord.

21Again Jesus said, "Peace be with you! As the Father has sent me, I am sending you." 22And with that he breathed on them and said, "Receive the Holy Spirit. 23If you forgive anyone his sins, they are forgiven; if you do not forgive them, they are not forgiven."

Jesus Appears to Thomas

24Now Thomas (called Didymus), one of the Twelve, was not with the disciples when Jesus came. 25When the other disciples told him that they had seen the Lord, he declared, "Unless I see the nail marks in his hands and put my finger where the nails were, and put my hand into his side, I will not believe it."

26A week later his disciples were in the house again, and Thomas was with them. Though the doors were locked, Jesus came and stood among them and said, "Peace be with you!" 27Then he said to Thomas, "Put your finger here; see my hands. Reach out your hand and put it into my side. Stop doubting and believe."

28Thomas said to him, "My Lord and my God!"

29Then Jesus told him, "Because you have seen me, you have believed; blessed are those who have not seen and yet have believed."

30Jesus did many other miraculous signs in the presence of his disciples, which are not recorded in this book. 31But these are written that you maya believe that Jesus is the Christ, the Son of God, and that by believing you may have life in his name.

Jesus and the Miraculous Catch of Fish

21 Afterwards Jesus appeared again to his disciples by the Sea of Tiberias.a It happened this way: 2Simon Peter, Thomas (called Didymus), Nathanael from Cana in Galilee, the sons of Zebedee, and two other disciples were together. 3"I'm going out to fish," Simon Peter told them, and they said, "We'll go with you." So they went out and got into the boat, but that night they caught nothing.

4Early in the morning, Jesus stood on the shore, but the disciples did not realise that it was Jesus.

5He called out to them, "Friends, haven't you any fish?"

"No," they answered.

6He said, "Throw your net on the right side of the boat and you will find some." When they did, they were unable to haul the net in because of the large number of fish.

7Then the disciple whom Jesus loved said to Peter, "It is the Lord!" As soon as Simon Peter heard him say, "It is the Lord," he wrapped his outer garment around him (for he had taken it off) and jumped into the water. 8The other disciples followed in the boat, towing the net full of fish, for they were not far from shore, about a hundred yards.b 9When they landed, they saw a fire of burning

a31 Some manuscripts may continue to
a1 That is, Sea of Galilee   b8 Greek about two hundred cubits (about 90 metres)

coals there with fish on it, and some bread.

[10]Jesus said to them, "Bring some of the fish you have just caught."

[11]Simon Peter climbed aboard and dragged the net ashore. It was full of large fish, 153, but even with so many the net was not torn. [12]Jesus said to them, "Come and have breakfast." None of the disciples dared ask him, "Who are you?" They knew it was the Lord. [13]Jesus came, took the bread and gave it to them, and did the same with the fish. [14]This was now the third time Jesus appeared to his disciples after he was raised from the dead.

Jesus Reinstates Peter

[15]When they had finished eating, Jesus said to Simon Peter, "Simon son of John, do you truly love me more than these?"

"Yes, Lord," he said, "you know that I love you."

Jesus said, "Feed my lambs."

[16]Again Jesus said, "Simon son of John, do you truly love me?"

He answered, "Yes, Lord, you know that I love you."

Jesus said, "Take care of my sheep."

[17]The third time he said to him, "Simon son of John, do you love me?"

Peter was hurt because Jesus asked him the third time, "Do you love me?" He said, "Lord, you know all things; you know that I love you."

Jesus said, "Feed my sheep. [18]I tell you the truth, when you were younger you dressed yourself and went where you wanted; but when you are old you will stretch out your hands, and someone else will dress you and lead you where you do not want to go." [19]Jesus said this to indicate the kind of death by which Peter would glorify God. Then he said to him, "Follow me!"

[20]Peter turned and saw that the disciple whom Jesus loved was following them. (This was the one who had leaned back against Jesus at the supper and had said, "Lord, who is going to betray you?") [21]When Peter saw him, he asked, "Lord, what about him?"

[22]Jesus answered, "If I want him to remain alive until I return, what is that to you? You must follow me."

[23]Because of this, the rumour spread among the brothers that this disciple would not die. But Jesus did not say that he would not die; he only said, "If I want him to remain alive until I return, what is that to you?"

[24]This is the disciple who testifies to these things and who wrote them down. We know that his testimony is true.

[25]Jesus did many other things as well. If every one of them were written down, I suppose that even the whole world would not have room for the books that would be written.

Acts

Jesus Taken Up Into Heaven

1 In my former book, Theophilus, I wrote about all that Jesus began to do and to teach 2until the day he was taken up to heaven, after giving instructions through the Holy Spirit to the apostles he had chosen. 3After his suffering, he showed himself to these men and gave many convincing proofs that he was alive. He appeared to them over a period of forty days and spoke about the kingdom of God. 4On one occasion, while he was eating with them, he gave them this command: "Do not leave Jerusalem, but wait for the gift my Father promised, which you have heard me speak about. 5For John baptised with*a* water, but in a few days you will be baptised with the Holy Spirit."

6So when they met together, they asked him, "Lord, are you at this time going to restore the kingdom to Israel?"

7He said to them: "It is not for you to know the times or dates the Father has set by his own authority. 8But you will receive power when the Holy Spirit comes on you; and you will be my witnesses in Jerusalem, and in all Judea and Samaria, and to the ends of the earth."

9After he said this, he was taken up before their very eyes, and a cloud hid him from their sight.

10They were looking intently up into the sky as he was going, when suddenly two men dressed in white stood beside them. 11"Men of Galilee," they said, "why do you stand here looking into the sky? This same Jesus, who has been taken from you into heaven, will come back in the same way you have seen him go into heaven."

Matthias Chosen to Replace Judas

12Then they returned to Jerusalem from the hill called the Mount of Olives, a Sabbath day's walk*b* from the city. 13When they arrived, they went upstairs to the room where they were staying. Those present were Peter, John, James and Andrew; Philip and Thomas, Bartholomew and Matthew; James son of Alphaeus and Simon the Zealot, and Judas son of James. 14They all joined together constantly in prayer, along with the women and Mary the mother of Jesus, and his brothers.

15In those days Peter stood up among the believers*c* (a group numbering about a hundred and twenty) 16and said, "Brothers, the Scripture had to be fulfilled which the Holy Spirit spoke long ago through the mouth of David concerning Judas, who served as guide for those who arrested Jesus—17he was one of our number and shared in this ministry."

18(With the reward he got for his wickedness, Judas bought a field; there he fell headlong, his body burst open and all his intestines spilled out. 19Everyone in Jerusalem heard about this, so they called that field in their language Akeldama, that is, Field of Blood.)

20"For," said Peter, "it is written in the book of Psalms,

" 'May his place be deserted;
    let there be no-one to dwell in
        it,'*d*

*a*5 Or in   *b*12 That is, about ¾ of a mile (about 1,100 metres)   *c*15 Greek brothers
*d*20 Psalm 69:25

129

and,

" 'May another take his place of
    leadership.'e

21Therefore it is necessary to choose
one of the men who have been with
us the whole time the Lord Jesus
went in and out among us,
22beginning from John's baptism to
the time when Jesus was taken up
from us. For one of these must
become a witness with us of his
resurrection."

23So they proposed two men:
Joseph called Barsabbas (also known
as Justus) and Matthias. 24Then they
prayed, "Lord, you know everyone's
heart. Show us which of these two
you have chosen 25to take over this
apostolic ministry, which Judas left to
go where he belongs." 26Then they
drew lots, and the lot fell to Matthias;
so he was added to the eleven
apostles.

The Holy Spirit Comes at Pentecost

2 When the day of Pentecost came,
they were all together in one
place. 2Suddenly a sound like the
blowing of a violent wind came from
heaven and filled the whole house
where they were sitting. 3They saw
what seemed to be tongues of fire that
separated and came to rest on each
of them. 4All of them were filled with
the Holy Spirit and began to speak in
other tonguesa as the Spirit enabled
them.

5Now there were staying in Jerusalem God-fearing Jews from every
nation under heaven. 6When they
heard this sound, a crowd came
together in bewilderment, because
each one heard them speaking in his
own language. 7Utterly amazed, they
asked: "Are not all these men who
are speaking Galileans? 8Then how is
it that each of us hears them in his
own native language? 9Parthians,
Medes and Elamites; residents of
Mesopotamia, Judea and Cappadocia,
Pontus and Asia, 10Phrygia and Pamphylia, Egypt and the parts of Libya
near Cyrene; visitors from Rome
11(both Jews and converts to Judaism);

Cretans and Arabs—we hear them
declaring the wonders of God in our
own tongues!" 12Amazed and perplexed, they asked one another,
"What does this mean?"

13Some, however, made fun of
them and said, "They have had too
much wine."b

Peter Addresses the Crowd

14Then Peter stood up with the
Eleven, raised his voice and
addressed the crowd: "Fellow Jews
and all of you who are in Jerusalem,
let me explain this to you; listen
carefully to what I say. 15These men
are not drunk, as you suppose. It's
only nine in the morning! 16No, this
is what was spoken by the prophet
Joel:

17" 'In the last days, God says,
    I will pour out my Spirit on all
        people.
Your sons and daughters will
        prophesy,
    your young men will see visions,
    your old men will dream dreams.
18Even on my servants, both men
        and women,
    I will pour out my Spirit in those
        days,
    and they will prophesy.
19I will show wonders in the heaven
        above
    and signs on the earth below,
    blood and fire and billows of
        smoke.
20The sun will be turned to darkness
    and the moon to blood
    before the coming of the great
        and glorious day of the Lord.
21And everyone who calls
    on the name of the Lord will be
        saved.'c

22"Men of Israel, listen to this: Jesus
of Nazareth was a man accredited by
God to you by miracles, wonders and
signs, which God did among you
through him, as you yourselves know.
23This man was handed over to you
by God's set purpose and foreknowledge; and you, with the help of
wicked men, put him to death by
nailing him to the cross. 24But God

e20 Psalm 109:8
a4 Or languages; also in verse 11   b13 Or sweet wine   c21 Joel 2:28-32

raised him from the dead, freeing him from the agony of death, because it was impossible for death to keep its hold on him. 25David said about him:

" 'I saw the Lord always before me.
Because he is at my right hand,
I will not be shaken.
26Therefore my heart is glad and my tongue rejoices;
my body also will live in hope,
27because you will not abandon me to the grave,
nor will you let your Holy One see decay.
28You have made known to me the paths of life;
you will fill me with joy in your presence.'d

29"Brothers, I can tell you confidently that the patriarch David died and was buried, and his tomb is here to this day. 30But he was a prophet and knew that God had promised him on oath that he would place one of his descendants on his throne. 31Seeing what was ahead, he spoke of the resurrection of the Christ,e that he was not abandoned to the grave, nor did his body see decay. 32God has raised this Jesus to life, and we are all witnesses of the fact. 33Exalted to the right hand of God, he has received from the Father the promised Holy Spirit and has poured out what you now see and hear. 34For David did not ascend to heaven, and yet he said,

" 'The Lord said to my Lord:
"Sit at my right hand
35until I make your enemies
a footstool for your feet." 'f

36"Therefore let all Israel be assured of this: God has made this Jesus, whom you crucified, both Lord and Christ."

37When the people heard this, they were cut to the heart and said to Peter and the other apostles, "Brothers, what shall we do?"

38Peter replied, "Repent and be baptised, every one of you, in the name of Jesus Christ so that your sins may be forgiven. And you will receive the gift of the Holy Spirit. 39The promise is for you and your children and for all who are far off—for all whom the Lord our God will call."

40With many other words he warned them; and he pleaded with them, "Save yourselves from this corrupt generation." 41Those who accepted his message were baptised, and about three thousand were added to their number that day.

The Fellowship of the Believers

42They devoted themselves to the apostles' teaching and to the fellowship, to the breaking of bread and to prayer. 43Everyone was filled with awe, and many wonders and miraculous signs were done by the apostles. 44All the believers were together and had everything in common. 45Selling their possessions and goods, they gave to anyone as he had need. 46Every day they continued to meet together in the temple courts. They broke bread in their homes and ate together with glad and sincere hearts, 47praising God and enjoying the favour of all the people. And the Lord added to their number daily those who were being saved.

Peter Heals the Crippled Beggar

3 One day Peter and John were going up to the temple at the time of prayer—at three in the afternoon. 2Now a man crippled from birth was being carried to the temple gate called Beautiful, where he was put every day to beg from those going into the temple courts. 3When he saw Peter and John about to enter, he asked them for money. 4Peter looked straight at him, as did John. Then Peter said, "Look at us!" 5So the man gave them his attention, expecting to get something from them.

6Then Peter said, "Silver or gold I do not have, but what I have I give you. In the name of Jesus Christ of Nazareth, walk." 7Taking him by the right hand, he helped him up, and instantly the man's feet and ankles

d28 Psalm 16:8-11   e31 Or Messiah. "The Christ" (Greek) and "the Messiah" (Hebrew) both mean "the Anointed One"; also in verse 36.   f35 Psalm 110:1

became strong. 8He jumped to his feet and began to walk. Then he went with them into the temple courts, walking and jumping, and praising God. 9When all the people saw him walking and praising God, 10they recognised him as the same man who used to sit begging at the temple gate called Beautiful, and they were filled with wonder and amazement at what had happened to him.

Peter Speaks to the Onlookers

11While the beggar held on to Peter and John, all the people were astonished and came running to them in the place called Solomon's Colonnade. 12When Peter saw this, he said to them: "Men of Israel, why does this surprise you? Why do you stare at us as if by our own power or godliness we had made this man walk? 13The God of Abraham, Isaac and Jacob, the God of our fathers, has glorified his servant Jesus. You handed him over to be killed, and you disowned him before Pilate, though he had decided to let him go. 14You disowned the Holy and Righteous One and asked that a murderer be released to you. 15You killed the author of life, but God raised him from the dead. We are witnesses of this. 16By faith in the name of Jesus, this man whom you see and know was made strong. It is Jesus' name and the faith that comes through him that has given this complete healing to him, as you can all see.

17"Now, brothers, I know that you acted in ignorance, as did your leaders. 18But this is how God fulfilled what he had foretold through all the prophets, saying that his Christ*a* would suffer. 19Repent, then, and turn to God, so that your sins may be wiped out, that times of refreshing may come from the Lord, 20and that he may send the Christ, who has been appointed for you—even Jesus. 21He must remain in heaven until the time comes for God to restore everything, as he promised long ago through his holy prophets. 22For Moses said, 'The Lord your God will

raise up for you a prophet like me from among your own people; you must listen to everything he tells you. 23Anyone who does not listen to him will be completely cut off from among his people.'*b*

24"Indeed, all the prophets from Samuel on, as many as have spoken, have foretold these days. 25And you are heirs of the prophets and of the covenant God made with your fathers. He said to Abraham, 'Through your offspring all peoples on earth will be blessed.'*c* 26When God raised up his servant, he sent him first to you to bless you by turning each of you from your wicked ways."

Peter and John Before the Sanhedrin

4 The priests and the captain of the temple guard and the Sadducees came up to Peter and John while they were speaking to the people. 2They were greatly disturbed because the apostles were teaching the people and proclaiming in Jesus the resurrection of the dead. 3They seized Peter and John, and because it was evening, they put them in jail until the next day. 4But many who heard the message believed, and the number of men grew to about five thousand.

5The next day the rulers, elders and teachers of the law met in Jerusalem. 6Annas the high priest was there, and so were Caiaphas, John, Alexander and the other men of the high priest's family. 7They had Peter and John brought before them and began to question them: "By what power or what name did you do this?"

8Then Peter, filled with the Holy Spirit, said to them: "Rulers and elders of the people! 9If we are being called to account today for an act of kindness shown to a cripple and are asked how he was healed, 10then know this, you and everyone else in Israel: It is by the name of Jesus Christ of Nazareth, whom you crucified but whom God raised from the

*a*18 Or Messiah; also in verse 20   *b*23 Deut. 18:15,18,19   *c*25 Gen. 22:18; 26:4

dead, that this man stands before you completely healed. 11He is

"'the stone you builders rejected,
which has become the capstone.'a,b

12Salvation is found in no-one else, for there is no other name under heaven given to men by which we must be saved."

13When they saw the courage of Peter and John and realised that they were unschooled, ordinary men, they were astonished and they took note that these men had been with Jesus. 14But since they could see the man who had been healed standing there with them, there was nothing they could say. 15So they ordered them to withdraw from the Sanhedrin and then conferred together. 16"What are we going to do with these men?" they asked. "Everybody living in Jerusalem knows they have done an outstanding miracle, and we cannot deny it. 17But to stop this thing from spreading any further among the people, we must warn these men to speak no longer to anyone in this name."

18Then they called them in again and commanded them not to speak or teach at all in the name of Jesus. 19But Peter and John replied, "Judge for yourselves whether it is right in God's sight to obey you rather than God. 20For we cannot help speaking about what we have seen and heard."

21After further threats they let them go. They could not decide how to punish them, because all the people were praising God for what had happened. 22For the man who was miraculously healed was over forty years old.

The Believers' Prayer

23On their release, Peter and John went back to their own people and reported all that the chief priests and elders had said to them. 24When they heard this, they raised their voices together in prayer to God. "Sovereign Lord," they said, "you made the heaven and the earth and the sea,

and everything in them. 25You spoke by the Holy Spirit through the mouth of your servant, our father David:

" 'Why do the nations rage
and the peoples plot in vain?
26The kings of the earth take their
stand
and the rulers gather together
against the Lord
and against his Anointed One.'c,d

27Indeed Herod and Pontius Pilate met together with the Gentiles and the people of Israel in this city to conspire against your holy servant Jesus, whom you anointed. 28They did what your power and will had decided beforehand should happen. 29Now, Lord, consider their threats and enable your servants to speak your word with great boldness. 30Stretch out your hand to heal and perform miraculous signs and wonders through the name of your holy servant Jesus."

31After they prayed, the place where they were meeting was shaken. And they were all filled with the Holy Spirit and spoke the word of God boldly.

The Believers Share Their Possessions

32All the believers were one in heart and mind. No-one claimed that any of his possessions was his own, but they shared everything they had. 33With great power the apostles continued to testify to the resurrection of the Lord Jesus, and much grace was upon them all. 34There were no needy persons among them. For from time to time those who owned lands or houses sold them, brought the money from the sales 35and put it at the apostles' feet, and it was distributed to anyone as he had need.

36Joseph, a Levite from Cyprus, whom the apostles called Barnabas (which means Son of Encouragement), 37sold a field he owned and brought the money and put it at the apostles' feet.

a11 Or cornerstone   b11 Psalm 118:22
c26 That is, Christ or Messiah   d26 Psalm 2:1,2

ACTS 5:1

Ananias and Sapphira

5 Now a man named Ananias, together with his wife Sapphira, also sold a piece of property. 2With his wife's full knowledge he kept back part of the money for himself, but brought the rest and put it at the apostles' feet.

3Then Peter said, "Ananias, how is it that Satan has so filled your heart that you have lied to the Holy Spirit and have kept for yourself some of the money you received for the land? 4Didn't it belong to you before it was sold? And after it was sold, wasn't the money at your disposal? What made you think of doing such a thing? You have not lied to men but to God."

5When Ananias heard this, he fell down and died. And great fear seized all who heard what had happened. 6Then the young men came forward, wrapped up his body, and carried him out and buried him.

7About three hours later his wife came in, not knowing what had happened. 8Peter asked her, "Tell me, is this the price you and Ananias got for the land?"

"Yes," she said, "that is the price."

9Peter said to her, "How could you agree to test the Spirit of the Lord? Look! The feet of the men who buried your husband are at the door, and they will carry you out also."

10At that moment she fell down at his feet and died. Then the young men came in, and, finding her dead, carried her out and buried her beside her husband. 11Great fear seized the whole church and all who heard about these events.

The Apostles Heal Many

12The apostles performed many miraculous signs and wonders among the people. And all the believers used to meet together in Solomon's Colonnade. 13No-one else dared join them, even though they were highly regarded by the people. 14Nevertheless, more and more men and women believed in the Lord and were added to their number. 15As a result, people brought the sick into the streets and laid them on beds and mats so that at least Peter's shadow might fall on some of them as he passed by. 16Crowds gathered also from the towns around Jerusalem, bringing their sick and those tormented by evil*a* spirits, and all of them were healed.

The Apostles Persecuted

17Then the high priest and all his associates, who were members of the party of the Sadducees, were filled with jealousy. 18They arrested the apostles and put them in the public jail. 19But during the night an angel of the Lord opened the doors of the jail and brought them out. 20"Go, stand in the temple courts," he said, "and tell the people the full message of this new life."

21At daybreak they entered the temple courts, as they had been told, and began to teach the people.

When the high priest and his associates arrived, they called together the Sanhedrin—the full assembly of the elders of Israel—and sent to the jail for the apostles. 22But on arriving at the jail, the officers did not find them there. So they went back and reported, 23"We found the jail securely locked, with the guards standing at the doors; but when we opened them, we found no-one inside." 24On hearing this report, the captain of the temple guard and the chief priests were puzzled, wondering what would come of this.

25Then someone came and said, "Look! The men you put in jail are standing in the temple courts teaching the people." 26At that, the captain went with his officers and brought the apostles. They did not use force, because they feared that the people would stone them.

27Having brought the apostles, they made them appear before the Sanhedrin to be questioned by the high priest. 28"We gave you strict orders not to teach in this name," he said. "Yet you have filled Jerusalem with your teaching and are determined to make us guilty of this man's blood."

a16 Greek *unclean*

134

29Peter and the other apostles replied: "We must obey God rather than men! 30The God of our fathers raised Jesus from the dead—whom you had killed by hanging him on a tree. 31God exalted him to his own right hand as Prince and Saviour that he might give repentance and forgiveness of sins to Israel. 32We are witnesses of these things, and so is the Holy Spirit, whom God has given to those who obey him."

33When they heard this, they were furious and wanted to put them to death. 34But a Pharisee named Gamaliel, a teacher of the law, who was honoured by all the people, stood up in the Sanhedrin and ordered that the men be put outside for a little while. 35Then he addressed them: "Men of Israel, consider carefully what you intend to do to these men. 36Some time ago Theudas appeared, claiming to be somebody, and about four hundred men rallied to him. He was killed, all his followers were dispersed, and it all came to nothing. 37After him, Judas the Galilean appeared in the days of the census and led a band of people in revolt. He too was killed, and all his followers were scattered. 38Therefore, in the present case I advise you: Leave these men alone! Let them go! For if their purpose or activity is of human origin, it will fail. 39But if it is from God, you will not be able to stop these men; you will only find yourselves fighting against God."

40His speech persuaded them. They called the apostles in and had them flogged. Then they ordered them not to speak in the name of Jesus, and let them go.

41The apostles left the Sanhedrin, rejoicing because they had been counted worthy of suffering disgrace for the Name. 42Day after day, in the temple courts and from house to house, they never stopped teaching and proclaiming the good news that Jesus is the Christ.b

The Choosing of the Seven

6 In those days when the number of disciples was increasing, the Grecian Jews among them complained against those of the Aramaic-speakinga community because their widows were being overlooked in the daily distribution of food. 2So the Twelve gathered all the disciples together and said, "It would not be right for us to neglect the ministry of the word of God in order to wait on tables. 3Brothers, choose seven men from among you who are known to be full of the Spirit and wisdom. We will turn this responsibility over to them 4and will give our attention to prayer and the ministry of the word."

5This proposal pleased the whole group. They chose Stephen, a man full of faith and of the Holy Spirit; also Philip, Procorus, Nicanor, Timon, Parmenas, and Nicolas from Antioch, a convert to Judaism. 6They presented these men to the apostles, who prayed and laid their hands on them.

7So the word of God spread. The number of disciples in Jerusalem increased rapidly, and a large number of priests became obedient to the faith.

Stephen Seized

8Now Stephen, a man full of God's grace and power, did great wonders and miraculous signs among the people. 9Opposition arose, however, from members of the Synagogue of the Freedmen (as it was called)—Jews of Cyrene and Alexandria as well as the provinces of Cilicia and Asia. These men began to argue with Stephen, 10but they could not stand up against his wisdom or the Spirit by which he spoke.

11Then they secretly persuaded some men to say, "We have heard Stephen speak words of blasphemy against Moses and against God."

12So they stirred up the people and the elders and the teachers of the law. They seized Stephen and brought him before the Sanhedrin. 13They produced false witnesses, who testified, "This fellow never stops speaking against the holy place and against the law. 14For we have heard him say that this Jesus of Nazareth

b42 Or Messiah   a1 Or possibly Hebrew-speaking

will destroy this place and change the customs Moses handed down to us."

15All who were sitting in the Sanhedrin looked intently at Stephen, and they saw that his face was like the face of an angel.

Stephen's Speech to the Sanhedrin

7 Then the high priest asked him, "Are these charges true?"

2To this he replied: "Brothers and fathers, listen to me! The God of glory appeared to our father Abraham while he was still in Mesopotamia, before he lived in Haran. 3'Leave your country and your people,' God said, 'and go to the land I will show you.'*a*

4"So he left the land of the Chaldeans and settled in Haran. After the death of his father, God sent him to this land where you are now living. 5He gave him no inheritance here, not even a foot of ground. But God promised him that he and his descendants after him would possess the land, even though at that time Abraham had no child. 6God spoke to him in this way: 'Your descendants will be strangers in a country not their own, and they will be enslaved and ill-treated for four hundred years. 7But I will punish the nation they serve as slaves,' God said, 'and afterwards they will come out of that country and worship me in this place.'*b* 8Then he gave Abraham the covenant of circumcision. And Abraham became the father of Isaac and circumcised him eight days after his birth. Later Isaac became the father of Jacob, and Jacob became the father of the twelve patriarchs.

9"Because the patriarchs were jealous of Joseph, they sold him as a slave into Egypt. But God was with him 10and rescued him from all his troubles. He gave Joseph wisdom and enabled him to gain the goodwill of Pharaoh king of Egypt; so he made him ruler over Egypt and all his palace.

11"Then a famine struck all Egypt and Canaan, bringing great suffering, and our fathers could not find food. 12When Jacob heard that there was grain in Egypt, he sent our fathers on their first visit. 13On their second visit, Joseph told his brothers who he was, and Pharaoh learned about Joseph's family. 14After this, Joseph sent for his father Jacob and his whole family, seventy-five in all. 15Then Jacob went down to Egypt, where he and our fathers died. 16Their bodies were brought back to Shechem and placed in the tomb that Abraham had bought from the sons of Hamor at Shechem for a certain sum of money.

17"As the time drew near for God to fulfil his promise to Abraham, the number of our people in Egypt greatly increased. 18Then another king, who knew nothing about Joseph, became ruler of Egypt. 19He dealt treacherously with our people and oppressed our forefathers by forcing them to throw out their newborn babies so that they would die.

20"At that time Moses was born, and he was no ordinary child.*c* For three months he was cared for in his father's house. 21When he was placed outside, Pharaoh's daughter took him and brought him up as her own son. 22Moses was educated in all the wisdom of the Egyptians and was powerful in speech and action.

23"When Moses was forty years old, he decided to visit his fellow Israelites. 24He saw one of them being ill-treated by an Egyptian, so he went to his defence and avenged him by killing the Egyptian. 25Moses thought that his own people would realise that God was using him to rescue them, but they did not. 26The next day Moses came upon two Israelites who were fighting. He tried to reconcile them by saying, 'Men, you are brothers; why do you want to hurt each other?'

27"But the man who was ill-treating the other pushed Moses aside and said, 'Who made you ruler and judge over us? 28Do you want to kill me as you killed the Egyptian yesterday?'*d* 29When Moses heard this, he fled to

*a*3 Gen. 12:1   *b*7 Gen. 15:13,14
*c*20 Or *was fair in the sight of God*   *d*28 Exodus 2:14

Midian, where he settled as a foreigner and had two sons.

30"After forty years had passed, an angel appeared to Moses in the flames of a burning bush in the desert near Mount Sinai. 31When he saw this, he was amazed at the sight. As he went over to look more closely, he heard the Lord's voice: 32'I am the God of your fathers, the God of Abraham, Isaac and Jacob.'e Moses trembled with fear and did not dare to look.

33"Then the Lord said to him, 'Take off your sandals; the place where you are standing is holy ground. 34I have indeed seen the oppression of my people in Egypt. I have heard their groaning and have come down to set them free. Now come, I will send you back to Egypt.'f

35"This is the same Moses whom they had rejected with the words, 'Who made you ruler and judge?' He was sent to be their ruler and deliverer by God himself, through the angel who appeared to him in the bush. 36He led them out of Egypt and did wonders and miraculous signs in Egypt, at the Red Seag and for forty years in the desert. 37This is that Moses who told the Israelites, 'God will send you a prophet like me from your own people.'h 38He was in the assembly in the desert, with our fathers and with the angel who spoke to him on Mount Sinai; and he received living words to pass on to us.

39"But our fathers refused to obey him. Instead, they rejected him and in their hearts turned back to Egypt. 40They told Aaron, 'Make us gods who will go before us. As for this fellow Moses who led us out of Egypt—we don't know what has happened to him!'i 41That was the time they made an idol in the form of a calf. They brought sacrifices to it and held a celebration in honour of what their hands had made. 42But God turned away and gave them over to the worship of the heavenly bodies.

This agrees with what is written in the book of the prophets:

" 'Did you bring me sacrifices and offerings
  for forty years in the desert, O house of Israel?
43You have lifted up the shrine of Moloch
  and the star of your god Rephan, the idols you made to worship.
Therefore I will send you into exile'j beyond Babylon.

44"Our forefathers had the tabernacle of Testimony with them in the desert. It had been made as God directed Moses, according to the pattern he had seen. 45Having received the tabernacle, our fathers under Joshua brought it with them when they took the land from the nations God drove out before them. It remained in the land until the time of David, 46who enjoyed God's favour and asked that he might provide a dwelling-place for the God of Jacob.k 47But it was Solomon who built the house for him.

48"However, the Most High does not live in houses made by men. As the prophet says:

49" 'Heaven is my throne,
  and the earth is my footstool.
What kind of house will you build for me?

                    says the Lord.
Or where will my resting place be?
50Has not my hand made all these things?'l

51"You stiff-necked people, with uncircumcised hearts and ears! You are just like your fathers: You always resist the Holy Spirit! 52Was there ever a prophet your fathers did not persecute? They even killed those who predicted the coming of the Righteous One. And now you have betrayed and murdered him—53you who have received the law that was put into effect through angels but have not obeyed it."

---

e32 Exodus 3:6   f34 Exodus 3:5,7,8,10   g36 That is, Sea of Reeds   h37 Deut. 18:15
i40 Exodus 32:1   j43 Amos 5:25-27
l50 Isaiah 66:1,2   k46 Some early manuscripts the house of Jacob

137

The Stoning of Stephen

54When they heard this, they were furious and gnashed their teeth at him. 55But Stephen, full of the Holy Spirit, looked up to heaven and saw the glory of God, and Jesus standing at the right hand of God. 56"Look," he said, "I see heaven open and the Son of Man standing at the right hand of God."

57At this they covered their ears and, yelling at the top of their voices, they all rushed at him, 58dragged him out of the city and began to stone him. Meanwhile, the witnesses laid their clothes at the feet of a young man named Saul.

59While they were stoning him, Stephen prayed, "Lord Jesus, receive my spirit." 60Then he fell on his knees and cried out, "Lord, do not hold this sin against them." When he had said this, he fell asleep.

8 And Saul was there, giving approval to his death.

The Church Persecuted and Scattered

On that day a great persecution broke out against the church at Jerusalem, and all except the apostles were scattered throughout Judea and Samaria. 2Godly men buried Stephen and mourned deeply for him. 3But Saul began to destroy the church. Going from house to house, he dragged off men and women and put them in prison.

Philip in Samaria

4Those who had been scattered preached the word wherever they went. 5Philip went down to a city in Samaria and proclaimed the Christa there. 6When the crowds heard Philip and saw the miraculous signs he did, they all paid close attention to what he said. 7With shrieks, evilb spirits came out of many, and many paralytics and cripples were healed. 8So there was great joy in that city.

Simon the Sorcerer

9Now for some time a man named Simon had practised sorcery in the city and amazed all the people of Samaria. He boasted that he was someone great, 10and all the people, both high and low, gave him their attention and exclaimed, "This man is the divine power known as the Great Power." 11They followed him because he had amazed them for a long time with his magic. 12But when they believed Philip as he preached the good news of the kingdom of God and the name of Jesus Christ, they were baptised, both men and women. 13Simon himself believed and was baptised. And he followed Philip everywhere, astonished by the great signs and miracles he saw.

14When the apostles in Jerusalem heard that Samaria had accepted the word of God, they sent Peter and John to them. 15When they arrived, they prayed for them that they might receive the Holy Spirit, 16because the Holy Spirit had not yet come upon any of them; they had simply been baptised intoc the name of the Lord Jesus. 17Then Peter and John placed their hands on them, and they received the Holy Spirit.

18When Simon saw that the Spirit was given at the laying on of the apostles' hands, he offered them money and said, 19"Give me also this ability so that everyone on whom I lay my hands may receive the Holy Spirit."

20Peter answered: "May your money perish with you, because you thought you could buy the gift of God with money! 21You have no part or share in this ministry, because your heart is not right before God. 22Repent of this wickedness and pray to the Lord. Perhaps he will forgive you for having such a thought in your heart. 23For I see that you are full of bitterness and captive to sin."

24Then Simon answered, "Pray to the Lord for me so that nothing you have said may happen to me."

25When they had testified and proclaimed the word of the Lord, Peter and John returned to Jerusalem, preaching the gospel in many Samaritan villages.

a5 Or Messiah   b7 Greek unclean   c16 Or in

Philip and the Ethiopian

26Now an angel of the Lord said to Philip, "Go south to the road—the desert road—that goes down from Jerusalem to Gaza." 27So he started out, and on his way he met an Ethiopian[d] eunuch, an important official in charge of all the treasury of Candace, queen of all the Ethiopians. This man had gone to Jerusalem to worship, 28and on his way home was sitting in his chariot reading the book of Isaiah the prophet. 29The Spirit told Philip, "Go to that chariot and stay near it."

30Then Philip ran up to the chariot and heard the man reading Isaiah the prophet. "Do you understand what you are reading?" Philip asked.

31"How can I," he said, "unless someone explains it to me?" So he invited Philip to come up and sit with him.

32The eunuch was reading this passage of Scripture:

"He was led like a sheep to the slaughter,
    and as a lamb before the shearer is silent,
    so he did not open his mouth.
33In his humiliation he was deprived of justice.
    Who can speak of his descendants?
    For his life was taken from the earth."[e]

34The eunuch asked Philip, "Tell me, please, who is the prophet talking about, himself or someone else?" 35Then Philip began with that very passage of Scripture and told him the good news about Jesus.

36As they travelled along the road, they came to some water and the eunuch said, "Look, here is water. Why shouldn't I be baptised?"[f] 38And he ordered the chariot to stop. Then both Philip and the eunuch went down into the water and Philip baptised him. 39When they came up out of the water, the Spirit of the Lord suddenly took Philip away, and the eunuch did not see him again, but he

went on his way rejoicing. 40Philip, however, appeared at Azotus and travelled about, preaching the gospel in all the towns until he reached Caesarea.

Saul's Conversion

9 Meanwhile, Saul was still breathing out murderous threats against the Lord's disciples. He went to the high priest 2and asked him for letters to the synagogues in Damascus, so that if he found any there who belonged to the Way, whether men or women, he might take them as prisoners to Jerusalem. 3As he neared Damascus on his journey, suddenly a light from heaven flashed around him. 4He fell to the ground and heard a voice say to him, "Saul, Saul, why do you persecute me?"

5"Who are you, Lord?" Saul asked.

"I am Jesus, whom you are persecuting," he replied. 6"Now get up and go into the city, and you will be told what you must do."

7The men travelling with Saul stood there speechless; they heard the sound but did not see anyone. 8Saul got up from the ground, but when he opened his eyes he could see nothing. So they led him by the hand into Damascus. 9For three days he was blind, and did not eat or drink anything.

10In Damascus there was a disciple named Ananias. The Lord called to him in a vision, "Ananias!"

"Yes, Lord," he answered.

11The Lord told him, "Go to the house of Judas on Straight Street and ask for a man from Tarsus named Saul, for he is praying. 12In a vision he has seen a man named Ananias come and place his hands on him to restore his sight."

13"Lord," Ananias answered, "I have heard many reports about this man and all the harm he has done to your saints in Jerusalem. 14And he has come here with authority from the chief priests to arrest all who call on your name."

d27 That is, from the upper Nile region   e33 Isaiah 53:7,8
f36 Some late manuscripts baptised?" 37Philip said, "If you believe with all your heart, you may." The official answered, "I believe that Jesus Christ is the Son of God."

15But the Lord said to Ananias, "Go! This man is my chosen instrument to carry my name before the Gentiles and their kings and before the people of Israel. 16I will show him how much he must suffer for my name."

17Then Ananias went to the house and entered it. Placing his hands on Saul, he said, "Brother Saul, the Lord—Jesus, who appeared to you on the road as you were coming here—has sent me so that you may see again and be filled with the Holy Spirit." 18Immediately, something like scales fell from Saul's eyes, and he could see again. He got up and was baptised, 19and after taking some food, he regained his strength.

Saul in Damascus and Jerusalem

Saul spent several days with the disciples in Damascus. 20At once he began to preach in the synagogues that Jesus is the Son of God. 21All those who heard him were astonished and asked, "Isn't he the man who caused havoc in Jerusalem among those who call on this name? And hasn't he come here to take them as prisoners to the chief priests?" 22Yet Saul grew more and more powerful and baffled the Jews living in Damascus by proving that Jesus is the Christ.[a]

23After many days had gone by, the Jews conspired to kill him, 24but Saul learned of their plan. Day and night they kept close watch on the city gates in order to kill him. 25But his followers took him by night and lowered him in a basket through an opening in the wall.

26When he came to Jerusalem, he tried to join the disciples, but they were all afraid of him, not believing that he really was a disciple. 27But Barnabas took him and brought him to the apostles. He told them how Saul on his journey had seen the Lord and that the Lord had spoken to him, and how in Damascus he had preached fearlessly in the name of Jesus. 28So Saul stayed with them and moved about freely in Jerusalem,

speaking boldly in the name of the Lord. 29He talked and debated with the Grecian Jews, but they tried to kill him. 30When the brothers learned of this, they took him down to Caesarea and sent him off to Tarsus.

31Then the church throughout Judea, Galilee and Samaria enjoyed a time of peace. It was strengthened; and encouraged by the Holy Spirit, it grew in numbers, living in the fear of the Lord.

Aeneas and Dorcas

32As Peter travelled about the country, he went to visit the saints in Lydda. 33There he found a man named Aeneas, a paralytic who had been bedridden for eight years. 34"Aeneas," Peter said to him, "Jesus Christ heals you. Get up and tidy up your mat." Immediately Aeneas got up. 35All those who lived in Lydda and Sharon saw him and turned to the Lord.

36In Joppa there was a disciple named Tabitha (which, when translated, is Dorcas[b]), who was always doing good and helping the poor. 37After that time she became sick and died, and her body was washed and placed in an upstairs room. 38Lydda was near Joppa; so when the disciples heard that Peter was in Lydda, they sent two men to him and urged him, "Please come at once!"

39Peter went with them, and when he arrived he was taken upstairs to the room. All the widows stood around him, crying and showing him the robes and other clothing that Dorcas had made while she was still with them.

40Peter sent them all out of the room; then he got down on his knees and prayed. Turning towards the dead woman, he said, "Tabitha, get up." She opened her eyes, and seeing Peter she sat up. 41He took her by the hand and helped her to her feet. Then he called the believers and the widows and presented her to them alive. 42This became known all over Joppa, and many people believed in the Lord. 43Peter stayed in Joppa for

a22 Or Messiah   b36 Both Tabitha (Aramaic) and Dorcas (Greek) mean gazelle.

140

some time with a tanner named Simon.

Cornelius Calls for Peter

10 At Caesarea there was a man named Cornelius, a centurion in what was known as the Italian Regiment. 2He and all his family were devout and God-fearing; he gave generously to those in need and prayed to God regularly. 3One day at about three in the afternoon he had a vision. He distinctly saw an angel of God, who came to him and said, "Cornelius!"

4Cornelius stared at him in fear. "What is it, Lord?" he asked.

The angel answered, "Your prayers and gifts to the poor have come up as a remembrance before God. 5Now send men to Joppa to bring back a man named Simon who is called Peter. 6He is staying with Simon the tanner, whose house is by the sea."

7When the angel who spoke to him had gone, Cornelius called two of his servants and one of his soldiers who was a devout man. 8He told them everything that had happened and sent them to Joppa.

Peter's Vision

9About noon the following day as they were approaching the city, Peter went up on the roof to pray. 10He became hungry and wanted something to eat, and while the meal was being prepared, he fell into a trance. 11He saw heaven opened and something like a large sheet being let down to earth by its four corners. 12It contained all kinds of four-footed animals, as well as reptiles of the earth and birds of the air. 13Then a voice told him, "Get up, Peter. Kill and eat."

14"Surely not, Lord!" Peter replied. "I have never eaten anything impure or unclean."

15The voice spoke to him a second time, "Do not call anything impure that God has made clean."

16This happened three times, and immediately the sheet was taken back to heaven.

17While Peter was wondering about the meaning of the vision, the men sent by Cornelius found out where Simon's house was and stopped at the gate. 18They called out, asking if Simon who was known as Peter was staying there.

19While Peter was still thinking about the vision, the Spirit said to him, "Simon, three*a* men are looking for you. 20So get up and go downstairs. Do not hesitate to go with them, for I have sent them."

21Peter went down and said to the men, "I'm the one you're looking for. Why have you come?"

22The men replied, "We have come from Cornelius the centurion. He is a righteous and God-fearing man, who is respected by all the Jewish people. A holy angel told him to have you come to his house so that he could hear what you have to say." 23Then Peter invited the men into the house to be his guests.

Peter at Cornelius' House

The next day Peter started out with them, and some of the brothers from Joppa went along. 24The following day he arrived in Caesarea. Cornelius was expecting them and had called together his relatives and close friends. 25As Peter entered the house, Cornelius met him and fell at his feet in reverence. 26But Peter made him get up. "Stand up," he said, "I am only a man myself."

27Talking with him, Peter went inside and found a large gathering of people. 28He said to them: "You are well aware that it is against our law for a Jew to associate with a Gentile or visit him. But God has shown me that I should not call any man impure or unclean. 29So when I was sent for, I came without raising any objection. May I ask why you sent for me?"

30Cornelius answered: "Four days ago I was in my house praying at this hour, at three in the afternoon. Suddenly a man in shining clothes stood before me 31and said, 'Cornelius, God has heard your prayer and remembered your gifts to the poor. 32Send to

a19 One early manuscript two; other manuscripts do not have the number.

Joppa for Simon who is called Peter. He is a guest in the home of Simon the tanner, who lives by the sea.' ³³So I sent for you immediately, and it was good of you to come. Now we are all here in the presence of God to listen to everything the Lord has commanded you to tell us."

³⁴Then Peter began to speak: "I now realise how true it is that God does not show favouritism ³⁵but accepts men from every nation who fear him and do what is right. ³⁶This is the message God sent to the people of Israel, telling the good news of peace through Jesus Christ, who is Lord of all. ³⁷You know what has happened throughout Judea, beginning in Galilee after the baptism that John preached—³⁸how God anointed Jesus of Nazareth with the Holy Spirit and power, and how he went around doing good and healing all who were under the power of the devil, because God was with him.

³⁹"We are witnesses of everything he did in the country of the Jews and in Jerusalem. They killed him by hanging him on a tree, ⁴⁰but God raised him from the dead on the third day and caused him to be seen. ⁴¹He was not seen by all the people, but by witnesses whom God had already chosen—by us who ate and drank with him after he rose from the dead. ⁴²He commanded us to preach to the people and to testify that he is the one whom God appointed as judge of the living and the dead. ⁴³All the prophets testify about him that everyone who believes in him receives forgiveness of sins through his name."

⁴⁴While Peter was still speaking these words, the Holy Spirit came on all who heard the message. ⁴⁵The circumcised believers who had come with Peter were astonished that the gift of the Holy Spirit had been poured out even on the Gentiles. ⁴⁶For they heard them speaking in tongues[b] and praising God.

Then Peter said, ⁴⁷"Can anyone keep these people from being baptised with water? They have received the Holy Spirit just as we have." ⁴⁸So

he ordered that they be baptised in the name of Jesus Christ. Then they asked Peter to stay with them for a few days.

Peter Explains His Actions

11 The apostles and the brothers throughout Judea heard that the Gentiles also had received the word of God. ²So when Peter went up to Jerusalem, the circumcised believers criticised him ³and said, "You went into the house of uncircumcised men and ate with them."

⁴Peter began and explained everything to them precisely as it had happened: ⁵"I was in the city of Joppa praying, and in a trance I saw a vision. I saw something like a large sheet being let down from heaven by its four corners, and it came down to where I was. ⁶I looked into it and saw four-footed animals of the earth, wild beasts, reptiles, and birds of the air. ⁷Then I heard a voice telling me, 'Get up, Peter. Kill and eat.'

⁸"I replied, 'Surely not, Lord Nothing impure or unclean has ever entered my mouth.'

⁹"The voice spoke from heaven a second time, 'Do not call anything impure that God has made clean.' ¹⁰This happened three times, and then it was pulled up to heaven again.

¹¹"Right then three men who had been sent to me from Caesarea stopped at the house where I was staying. ¹²The Spirit told me to have no hesitation about going with them. These six brothers also went with me, and we entered the man's house. ¹³He told us how he had seen an angel appear in his house and say, 'Send to Joppa for Simon who is called Peter. ¹⁴He will bring you a message through which you and all your household will be saved.'

¹⁵"As I began to speak, the Holy Spirit came on them as he had come on us at the beginning. ¹⁶Then I remembered what the Lord had said, 'John baptised with[a] water, but you will be baptised with the Holy Spirit.' ¹⁷So if God gave them the same gift as he gave us, who believed in the

Lord Jesus Christ, who was I to think that I could oppose God!"

18When they heard this, they had no further objections and praised God, saying, "So then, God has even granted the Gentiles repentance unto life."

The Church in Antioch

19Now those who had been scattered by the persecution in connection with Stephen travelled as far as Phoenicia, Cyprus and Antioch, telling the message only to Jews. 20Some of them, however, men from Cyprus and Cyrene, went to Antioch and began to speak to Greeks also, telling them the good news about the Lord Jesus. 21The Lord's hand was with them, and a great number of people believed and turned to the Lord.

22News of this reached the ears of the church at Jerusalem, and they sent Barnabas to Antioch. 23When he arrived and saw the evidence of the grace of God, he was glad and encouraged them all to remain true to the Lord with all their hearts. 24He was a good man, full of the Holy Spirit and faith, and a great number of people were brought to the Lord.

25Then Barnabas went to Tarsus to look for Saul, 26and when he found him, he brought him to Antioch. So for a whole year Barnabas and Saul met with the church and taught great numbers of people. The disciples were first called Christians at Antioch.

27During this time some prophets came down from Jerusalem to Antioch. 28One of them, named Agabus, stood up and through the Spirit predicted that a severe famine would spread over the entire Roman world. (This happened during the reign of Claudius.) 29The disciples, each according to his ability, decided to provide help for the brothers living in Judea. 30This they did, sending their gift to the elders by Barnabas and Saul.

Peter's Miraculous Escape From Prison

12 It was about this time that King Herod arrested some who belonged to the church, intending to persecute them. 2He had James, the brother of John, put to death with the sword. 3When he saw that this pleased the Jews, he proceeded to seize Peter also. This happened during the Feast of Unleavened Bread. 4After arresting him, he put him in prison, handing him over to be guarded by four squads of four soldiers each. Herod intended to bring him out for public trial after the Passover.

5So Peter was kept in prison, but the church was earnestly praying to God for him.

6The night before Herod was to bring him to trial, Peter was sleeping between two soldiers, bound with two chains, and sentries stood guard at the entrance. 7Suddenly an angel of the Lord appeared and a light shone in the cell. He struck Peter on the side and woke him up. "Quick, get up!" he said, and the chains fell off Peter's wrists.

8Then the angel said to him, "Put on your clothes and sandals." And Peter did so. "Wrap your cloak around you and follow me," the angel told him. 9Peter followed him out of the prison, but he had no idea that what the angel was doing was really happening; he thought he was seeing a vision. 10They passed the first and second guards and came to the iron gate leading to the city. It opened for them by itself, and they went through it. When they had walked the length of one street, suddenly the angel left him.

11Then Peter came to himself and said, "Now I know without a doubt that the Lord sent his angel and rescued me from Herod's clutches and from everything the Jewish people were anticipating."

12When this had dawned on him, he went to the house of Mary the mother of John, also called Mark, where many people had gathered and were praying. 13Peter knocked at the outer entrance, and a servant girl named Rhoda came to answer the door. 14When she recognised Peter's voice, she was so overjoyed she ran back without opening it and exclaimed, "Peter is at the door!"

¹⁵"You're out of your mind," they told her. When she kept insisting that it was so, they said, "It must be his angel."

¹⁶But Peter kept on knocking, and when they opened the door and saw him, they were astonished. ¹⁷Peter motioned with his hand for them to be quiet and described how the Lord had brought him out of prison. "Tell James and the brothers about this," he said, and then he left for another place.

¹⁸In the morning, there was a great commotion among the soldiers. "What could have happened to Peter?" they asked. ¹⁹After Herod had a thorough search made for him and did not find him, he cross-examined the guards and ordered that they be executed.

Herod's Death

Then Herod went from Judea to Caesarea and stayed there a while. ²⁰He had been quarrelling with the people of Tyre and Sidon; they now joined together and sought an audience with him. Having secured the support of Blastus, a trusted personal servant of the king, they asked for peace, because they depended on the king's country for their food supply.

²¹On the appointed day Herod, wearing his royal robes, sat on his throne and delivered a public address to the people. ²²They shouted, "This is the voice of a god, not of a man." ²³Immediately, because Herod did not give praise to God, an angel of the Lord struck him down, and he was eaten by worms and died.

²⁴But the word of God continued to increase and spread.

²⁵When Barnabas and Saul had finished their mission, they returned from*ᵃ* Jerusalem, taking with them John, also called Mark.

Barnabas and Saul Sent Off

13 In the church at Antioch there were prophets and teachers: Barnabas, Simeon called Niger, Lucius of Cyrene, Manaen (who had been brought up with Herod the tetrarch) and Saul. ²While they were worshipping the Lord and fasting, the Holy Spirit said, "Set apart for me Barnabas and Saul for the work to which I have called them." ³So after they had fasted and prayed, they placed their hands on them and sent them off.

On Cyprus

⁴The two of them, sent on their way by the Holy Spirit, went down to Seleucia and sailed from there to Cyprus. ⁵When they arrived at Salamis, they proclaimed the word of God in the Jewish synagogues. John was with them as their helper.

⁶They travelled through the whole island until they came to Paphos. There they met a Jewish sorcerer and false prophet named Bar-Jesus, ⁷who was an attendant of the proconsul, Sergius Paulus. The proconsul, an intelligent man, sent for Barnabas and Saul because he wanted to hear the word of God. ⁸But Elymas the sorcerer (for that is what his name means) opposed them and tried to turn the proconsul from the faith. ⁹Then Saul, who was also called Paul, filled with the Holy Spirit, looked straight at Elymas and said, ¹⁰"You are a child of the devil and an enemy of everything that is right! You are full of all kinds of deceit and trickery. Will you never stop perverting the right ways of the Lord? ¹¹Now the hand of the Lord is against you. You are going to be blind, and for a time you will be unable to see the light of the sun."

Immediately mist and darkness came over him, and he groped about, seeking someone to lead him by the hand. ¹²When the proconsul saw what had happened, he believed, for he was amazed at the teaching about the Lord.

In Pisidian Antioch

¹³From Paphos, Paul and his companions sailed to Perga in Pamphylia.

ᵃ25 Some manuscripts to

where John left them to return to Jerusalem. ¹⁴From Perga they went on to Pisidian Antioch. On the Sabbath they entered the synagogue and sat down. ¹⁵After the reading from the Law and the Prophets, the synagogue rulers sent word to them, saying, "Brothers, if you have a message of encouragement for the people, please speak."

¹⁶Standing up, Paul motioned with his hand and said: "Men of Israel and you Gentiles who worship God, listen to me! ¹⁷The God of the people of Israel chose our fathers and made the people prosper during their stay in Egypt. With mighty power he led them out of that country ¹⁸and endured their conduct*ᵃ* for forty years in the desert. ¹⁹He overthrew seven nations in Canaan and gave their land to his people as their inheritance. ²⁰All this took about 450 years.

"After this, God gave them judges until the time of Samuel the prophet. ²¹Then the people asked for a king, and he gave them Saul son of Kish, of the tribe of Benjamin, who ruled for forty years. ²²After removing Saul, he made David their king. He testified concerning him: 'I have found David son of Jesse a man after my own heart; he will do everything I want him to do.'

²³"From this man's descendants God has brought to Israel the Saviour Jesus, as he promised. ²⁴Before the coming of Jesus, John preached repentance and baptism to all the people of Israel. ²⁵As John was completing his work, he said: 'Who do you think I am? I am not that one. No, but he is coming after me, whose sandals I am not worthy to untie.'

²⁶"Brothers, children of Abraham, and you God-fearing Gentiles, it is to us that this message of salvation has been sent. ²⁷The people of Jerusalem and their rulers did not recognise him and yet in condemning him they fulfilled the words of the prophets that are read every Sabbath. ²⁸Though they found no proper ground for a death sentence, they

asked Pilate to have him executed. ²⁹When they had carried out all that was written about him, they took him down from the tree and laid him in a tomb. ³⁰But God raised him from the dead, ³¹and for many days he was seen by those who had travelled with him from Galilee to Jerusalem. They are now his witnesses to our people.

³²"We tell you the good news: What God promised our fathers ³³he has fulfilled for us, their children, by raising up Jesus. As it is written in the second Psalm:

" 'You are my Son;
    today I have become your
        Father.'*ᵇ,ᶜ*

³⁴The fact that God raised him from the dead, never to decay, is stated in these words:

" 'I will give you the holy and sure
    blessings promised to David.'*ᵈ*

³⁵So it is stated elsewhere:

" 'You will not let your Holy One
    see decay.'*ᵉ*

³⁶"For when David had served God's purpose in his own generation, he fell asleep; he was buried with his fathers and his body decayed. ³⁷But the one whom God raised from the dead did not see decay.

³⁸"Therefore, my brothers, I want you to know that through Jesus the forgiveness of sins is proclaimed to you. ³⁹Through him everyone who believes is justified from everything you could not be justified from by the law of Moses. ⁴⁰Take care that what the prophets have said does not happen to you:

⁴¹" 'Look, you scoffers,
    wonder and perish,
for I am going to do something in
        your days
    that you would never believe,
        even if someone told you.'*f*

⁴²As Paul and Barnabas were leaving the synagogue, the people invited them to speak further about these things on the next Sabbath. ⁴³When the congregation was dismissed,

---

ᵃ18 Some manuscripts and cared for them   *ᵇ33 Or have begotten you*   *ᶜ33 Psalm 2:7*
ᵈ34 Isaiah 55:3   *ᵉ35 Psalm 16:10*   *f41 Hab. 1:5*

many of the Jews and devout converts to Judaism followed Paul and Barnabas, who talked with them and urged them to continue in the grace of God.

44On the next Sabbath almost the whole city gathered to hear the word of the Lord. 45When the Jews saw the crowds, they were filled with jealousy and talked abusively against what Paul was saying.

46Then Paul and Barnabas answered them boldly: "We had to speak the word of God to you first. Since you reject it and do not consider yourselves worthy of eternal life, we now turn to the Gentiles. 47For this is what the Lord has commanded us:

" 'I have made you[g] a light for the Gentiles,
    that you[g] may bring salvation to the ends of the earth.'[h]"

48When the Gentiles heard this, they were glad and honoured the word of the Lord; and all who were appointed for eternal life believed.

49The word of the Lord spread through the whole region. 50But the Jews incited the God-fearing women of high standing and the leading men of the city. They stirred up persecution against Paul and Barnabas, and expelled them from their region. 51So they shook the dust from their feet in protest against them and went to Iconium. 52And the disciples were filled with joy and with the Holy Spirit.

In Iconium

14 At Iconium Paul and Barnabas went as usual into the Jewish synagogue. There they spoke so effectively that a great number of Jews and Gentiles believed. 2But the Jews who refused to believe stirred up the Gentiles and poisoned their minds against the brothers. 3So Paul and Barnabas spent considerable time there, speaking boldly for the Lord, who confirmed the message of his grace by enabling them to do miraculous signs and wonders. 4The people of the city were divided; some sided

with the Jews, others with the apostles. 5There was a plot afoot among the Gentiles and Jews, together with their leaders, to ill-treat them and stone them. 6But they found out about it and fled to the Lycaonian cities of Lystra and Derbe and to the surrounding country, 7where they continued to preach the good news.

In Lystra and Derbe

8In Lystra there sat a man crippled in his feet, who was lame from birth and had never walked. 9He listened to Paul as he was speaking. Paul looked directly at him, saw that he had faith to be healed 10and called out, "Stand up on your feet!" At that, the man jumped up and began to walk.

11When the crowd saw what Paul had done, they shouted in the Lycaonian language, "The gods have come down to us in human form!" 12Barnabas they called Zeus, and Paul they called Hermes because he was the chief speaker. 13The priest of Zeus, whose temple was just outside the city, brought bulls and wreaths to the city gates because he and the crowd wanted to offer sacrifices to them.

14But when the apostles Barnabas and Paul heard of this, they tore their clothes and rushed out into the crowd, shouting: 15"Men, why are you doing this? We too are only men, human like you. We are bringing you good news, telling you to turn from these worthless things to the living God, who made heaven and earth and sea and everything in them. 16In the past, he let all nations go their own way. 17Yet he has not left himself without testimony: He has shown kindness by giving you rain from heaven and crops in their seasons; he provides you with plenty of food and fills your hearts with joy." 18Even with these words, they had difficulty keeping the crowd from sacrificing to them.

19Then some Jews came from Antioch and Iconium and won the crowd over. They stoned Paul and

g47 The Greek is singular.   h47 Isaiah 49:6

146

dragged him outside the city, thinking he was dead. 20But after the disciples had gathered round him, he got up and went back into the city. The next day he and Barnabas left for Derbe.

The Return to Antioch in Syria

21They preached the good news in that city and won a large number of disciples. Then they returned to Lystra, Iconium and Antioch, 22strengthening the disciples and encouraging them to remain true to the faith. "We must go through many hardships to enter the kingdom of God," they said. 23Paul and Barnabas appointed elders*a* for them in each church and, with prayer and fasting, committed them to the Lord in whom they had put their trust. 24After going through Pisidia, they came into Pamphylia, 25and when they had preached the word in Perga, they went down to Attalia.

26From Attalia they sailed back to Antioch, where they had been committed to the grace of God for the work they had now completed. 27On arriving there, they gathered the church together and reported all that God had done through them and how he had opened the door of faith to the Gentiles. 28And they stayed there a long time with the disciples.

The Council at Jerusalem

15 Some men came down from Judea to Antioch and were teaching the brothers: "Unless you are circumcised, according to the custom taught by Moses, you cannot be saved." 2This brought Paul and Barnabas into sharp dispute and debate with them. So Paul and Barnabas were appointed, along with some other believers, to go up to Jerusalem to see the apostles and elders about this question. 3The church sent them on their way, and as they travelled through Phoenicia and Samaria, they told how the Gentiles had been converted. This news made all the brothers very glad. 4When they came

to Jerusalem, they were welcomed by the church and the apostles and elders, to whom they reported everything God had done through them.

5Then some of the believers who belonged to the party of the Pharisees stood up and said, "The Gentiles must be circumcised and required to obey the law of Moses."

6The apostles and elders met to consider this question. 7After much discussion, Peter got up and addressed them: "Brothers, you know that some time ago God made a choice among you that the Gentiles might hear from my lips the message of the gospel and believe. 8God, who knows the heart, showed that he accepted them by giving the Holy Spirit to them, just as he did to us. 9He made no distinction between us and them, for he purified their hearts by faith. 10Now then, why do you try to test God by putting on the necks of the disciples a yoke that neither we nor our fathers have been able to bear? 11No! We believe it is through the grace of our Lord Jesus that we are saved, just as they are."

12The whole assembly became silent as they listened to Barnabas and Paul telling about the miraculous signs and wonders God had done among the Gentiles through them. 13When they finished, James spoke up: "Brothers, listen to me. 14Simon*a* has described to us how God at first showed his concern by taking from the Gentiles a people for himself. 15The words of the prophets are in agreement with this, as it is written:

16" 'After this I will return
    and rebuild David's fallen tent.
  Its ruins I will rebuild,
    and I will restore it,
17that the remnant of men may seek
    the Lord,
  and all the Gentiles who bear my
    name,
  says the Lord, who does these
    things*b*
18 that have been known for ages.*c*

---

*a*23 Or *Barnabas ordained elders; or Barnabas had elders elected*
*a*14 Greek *Simeon*, a variant of *Simon*; that is, *Peter*   *b*17 Amos 9:11,12
*c*17,18 Some manuscripts *things'— / *18*known to the Lord for ages is his work*

¹⁹"It is my judgment, therefore, that we should not make it difficult for the Gentiles who are turning to God. ²⁰Instead we should write to them, telling them to abstain from food polluted by idols, from sexual immorality, from the meat of strangled animals and from blood. ²¹For Moses has been preached in every city from the earliest times and is read in the synagogues on every Sabbath."

The Council's Letter to Gentile Believers

²²Then the apostles and elders, with the whole church, decided to choose some of their own men and send them to Antioch with Paul and Barnabas. They chose Judas (called Barsabbas) and Silas, two men who were leaders among the brothers. ²³With them they sent the following letter:

The apostles and elders, your brothers,

To the Gentile believers in Antioch, Syria and Cilicia:

Greetings.

²⁴We have heard that some went out from us without our authorisation and disturbed you, troubling your minds by what they said. ²⁵So we all agreed to choose some men and send them to you with our dear friends Barnabas and Paul— ²⁶men who have risked their lives for the name of our Lord Jesus Christ. ²⁷Therefore we are sending Judas and Silas to confirm by word of mouth what we are writing. ²⁸It seemed good to the Holy Spirit and to us not to burden you with anything beyond the following requirements: ²⁹You are to abstain from food sacrificed to idols, from blood, from the meat of strangled animals and from sexual immorality. You will do well to avoid these things.

Farewell.

³⁰The men were sent off and went down to Antioch, where they gathered the church together and delivered the letter. ³¹The people read it and were glad for its encouraging message. ³²Judas and Silas, who themselves were prophets, said much to encourage and strengthen the brothers. ³³After spending some time there, they were sent off by the brothers with the blessing of peace to return to those who had sent them.ᵈ ³⁵But Paul and Barnabas remained in Antioch, where they and many others taught and preached the word of the Lord.

Disagreement Between Paul and Barnabas

³⁶Some time later Paul said to Barnabas, "Let us go back and visit the brothers in all the towns where we preached the word of the Lord and see how they are doing." ³⁷Barnabas wanted to take John, also called Mark, with them, ³⁸but Paul did not think it wise to take him, because he had deserted them in Pamphylia and had not continued with them in the work. ³⁹They had such a sharp disagreement that they parted company. Barnabas took Mark and sailed for Cyprus, ⁴⁰but Paul chose Silas and left, commended by the brothers to the grace of the Lord. ⁴¹He went through Syria and Cilicia, strengthening the churches.

Timothy Joins Paul and Silas

16 He came to Derbe and then to Lystra, where a disciple named Timothy lived, whose mother was a Jewess and a believer, but whose father was a Greek. ²The brothers at Lystra and Iconium spoke well of him. ³Paul wanted to take him along on the journey, so he circumcised him because of the Jews who lived in that area, for they all knew that his father was a Greek. ⁴As they travelled from town to town, they delivered the decisions reached by the apostles and elders in Jerusalem for the people to obey. ⁵So the

ᵈ33 Some manuscripts *them,* ³⁴ *but Silas decided to remain there* churches were strengthened in the faith and grew daily in numbers.

Paul's Vision of the Man of Macedonia

6Paul and his companions travelled throughout the region of Phrygia and Galatia, having been kept by the Holy Spirit from preaching the word in the province of Asia. 7When they came to the border of Mysia, they tried to enter Bithynia, but the Spirit of Jesus would not allow them to. 8So they passed by Mysia and went down to Troas. 9During the night Paul had a vision of a man of Macedonia standing and begging him, "Come over to Macedonia and help us." 10After Paul had seen the vision, we got ready at once to leave for Macedonia, concluding that God had called us to preach the gospel to them.

Lydia's Conversion in Philippi

11From Troas we put out to sea and sailed straight for Samothrace, and the next day on to Neapolis. 12From there we travelled to Philippi, a Roman colony and the leading city of that district of Macedonia. And we stayed there several days.

13On the Sabbath we went outside the city gate to the river, where we expected to find a place of prayer. We sat down and began to speak to the women who had gathered there. 14One of those listening was a woman named Lydia, a dealer in purple cloth from the city of Thyatira, who was a worshipper of God. The Lord opened her heart to respond to Paul's message. 15When she and the members of her household were baptised, she invited us to her home. "If you consider me a believer in the Lord," she said, "come and stay at my house." And she persuaded us.

Paul and Silas in Prison

16Once when we were going to the place of prayer, we were met by a slave girl who had a spirit by which she predicted the future. She earned a great deal of money for her owners by fortune-telling. 17This girl followed Paul and the rest of us, shouting,

"These men are servants of the Most High God, who are telling you the way to be saved." 18She kept this up for many days. Finally Paul became so troubled that he turned round and said to the spirit, "In the name of Jesus Christ I command you to come out of her!" At that moment the spirit left her.

19When the owners of the slave girl realised that their hope of making money was gone, they seized Paul and Silas and dragged them into the market-place to face the authorities. 20They brought them before the magistrates and said, "These men are Jews, and are throwing our city into an uproar 21by advocating customs unlawful for us Romans to accept or practise."

22The crowd joined in the attack against Paul and Silas, and the magistrates ordered them to be stripped and beaten. 23After they had been severely flogged, they were thrown into prison, and the jailer was commanded to guard them carefully. 24Upon receiving such orders, he put them in the inner cell and fastened their feet in the stocks.

25About midnight Paul and Silas were praying and singing hymns to God, and the other prisoners were listening to them. 26Suddenly there was such a violent earthquake that the foundations of the prison were shaken. At once all the prison doors flew open, and everybody's chains came loose. 27The jailer woke up, and when he saw the prison doors open, he drew his sword and was about to kill himself because he thought the prisoners had escaped. 28But Paul shouted, "Don't harm yourself! We are all here!"

29The jailer called for lights, rushed in and fell trembling before Paul and Silas. 30He then brought them out and asked, "Sirs, what must I do to be saved?"

31They replied, "Believe in the Lord Jesus, and you will be saved— you and your household." 32Then they spoke the word of the Lord to him and to all the others in his house. 33At that hour of the night the jailer took them and washed their wounds; then immediately he and all his family were baptised. 34The jailer brought them into his house and set a meal before them, and the whole family was filled with joy, because they had come to believe in God.

35When it was daylight, the magistrates sent their officers to the jailer with the order: "Release those men." 36The jailer told Paul, "The magistrates have ordered that you and Silas be released. Now you can leave. Go in peace."

37But Paul said to the officers: "They beat us publicly without a trial, even though we are Roman citizens, and threw us into prison. And now do they want to get rid of us quietly? No! Let them come themselves and escort us out."

38The officers reported this to the magistrates, and when they heard that Paul and Silas were Roman citizens, they were alarmed. 39They came to appease them and escorted them from the prison, requesting them to leave the city. 40After Paul and Silas came out of the prison, they went to Lydia's house, where they met with the brothers and encouraged them. Then they left.

In Thessalonica

17 When they had passed through Amphipolis and Apollonia, they came to Thessalonica, where there was a Jewish synagogue. 2As his custom was, Paul went into the synagogue, and on three Sabbath days he reasoned with them from the Scriptures, 3explaining and proving that the Christ*a* had to suffer and rise from the dead. "This Jesus I am proclaiming to you is the Christ,"*a* he said. 4Some of the Jews were persuaded and joined Paul and Silas, as did a large number of God-fearing Greeks and not a few prominent women.

5But the Jews were jealous; so they rounded up some bad characters from the market-place, formed a mob and started a riot in the city. They rushed to Jason's house in search of Paul and Silas in order to bring them out to the crowd.*b* 6But when they did not find them, they dragged Jason and some other brothers before the city officials, shouting: "These men who have caused trouble all over the world have now come here, 7and Jason has welcomed them into his house. They are all defying Caesar's decrees, saying that there is another king, one called Jesus." 8When they heard this, the crowd and the city officials were thrown into turmoil. 9Then they put Jason and the others on bail and let them go.

In Berea

10As soon as it was night, the brothers sent Paul and Silas away to Berea. On arriving there, they went to the Jewish synagogue. 11Now the Bereans were of more noble character than the Thessalonians, for they received the message with great eagerness and examined the Scriptures every day to see if what Paul said was true. 12Many of the Jews believed, as did also a number of prominent Greek women and many Greek men.

13When the Jews in Thessalonica learned that Paul was preaching the word of God at Berea, they went there too, agitating the crowds and stirring them up. 14The brothers immediately sent Paul to the coast, but Silas and Timothy stayed at Berea. 15The men who accompanied Paul brought him to Athens and then left with instructions for Silas and Timothy to join him as soon as possible.

In Athens

16While Paul was waiting for them in Athens, he was greatly distressed to see that the city was full of idols. 17So he reasoned in the synagogue with the Jews and the God-fearing Greeks, as well as in the market-place day by day with those who happened to be there. 18A group of Epicurean and Stoic philosophers began to dispute with him. Some of them asked, "What is this babbler trying to say?"

*a*3 Or Messiah   *b*5 Or the assembly of the people

Others remarked, "He seems to be advocating foreign gods." They said this because Paul was preaching the good news about Jesus and the resurrection. 19Then they took him and brought him to a meeting of the Areopagus, where they said to him, "May we know what this new teaching is that you are presenting? 20You are bringing some strange ideas to our ears, and we want to know what they mean." 21(All the Athenians and the foreigners who lived there spent their time doing nothing but talking about and listening to the latest ideas.)

22Paul then stood up in the meeting of the Areopagus and said: "Men of Athens! I see that in every way you are very religious. 23For as I walked around and observed your objects of worship, I even found an altar with this inscription: TO AN UNKNOWN GOD. Now what you worship as something unknown I am going to proclaim to you.

24"The God who made the world and everything in it is the Lord of heaven and earth and does not live in temples built by hands. 25And he is not served by human hands, as if he needed anything, because he himself gives all men life and breath and everything else. 26From one man he made every nation of men, that they should inhabit the whole earth; and he determined the times set for them and the exact places where they should live. 27God did this so that men would seek him and perhaps reach out for him and find him, though he is not far from each one of us. 28'For in him we live and move and have our being.' As some of your own poets have said, 'We are his offspring.'

29"Therefore since we are God's offspring, we should not think that the divine being is like gold or silver or stone—an image made by man's design and skill. 30In the past God overlooked such ignorance, but now he commands all people everywhere to repent. 31For he has set a day when he will judge the world with justice by the man he has appointed. He has

given proof of this to all men by raising him from the dead."

32When they heard about the resurrection of the dead, some of them sneered, but others said, "We want to hear you again on this subject." 33At that, Paul left the Council. 34A few men became followers of Paul and believed. Among them was Dionysius, a member of the Areopagus, also a woman named Damaris, and a number of others.

In Corinth

18 After this, Paul left Athens and went to Corinth. 2There he met a Jew named Aquila, a native of Pontus, who had recently come from Italy with his wife Priscilla, because Claudius had ordered all the Jews to leave Rome. Paul went to see them, 3and because he was a tentmaker as they were, he stayed and worked with them. 4Every Sabbath he reasoned in the synagogue, trying to persuade Jews and Greeks.

5When Silas and Timothy came from Macedonia, Paul devoted himself exclusively to preaching, testifying to the Jews that Jesus was the Christ.ᵃ 6But when the Jews opposed Paul and became abusive, he shook out his clothes in protest and said to them, "Your blood be on your own heads! I am clear of my responsibility. From now on I will go to the Gentiles."

7Then Paul left the synagogue and went next door to the house of Titius Justus, a worshipper of God. 8Crispus, the synagogue ruler, and his entire household believed in the Lord; and many of the Corinthians who heard him believed and were baptised.

9One night the Lord spoke to Paul in a vision: "Do not be afraid; keep on speaking, do not be silent. 10For I am with you, and no-one is going to attack and harm you, because I have many people in this city." 11So Paul stayed for a year and a half, teaching them the word of God.

12While Gallio was proconsul of Achaia, the Jews made a united attack on Paul and brought him into court.

ᵃ5 Or Messiah; also in verse 28

151

13"This man," they charged, "is persuading the people to worship God in ways contrary to the law."

14Just as Paul was about to speak, Gallio said to the Jews, "If you Jews were making a complaint about some misdemeanour or serious crime, it would be reasonable for me to listen to you. 15But since it involves questions about words and names and your own law—settle the matter yourselves. I will not be a judge of such things." 16So he had them ejected from the court. 17Then they all turned on Sosthenes the synagogue ruler and beat him in front of the court. But Gallio showed no concern whatever.

Priscilla, Aquila and Apollos

18Paul stayed on in Corinth for some time. Then he left the brothers and sailed for Syria, accompanied by Priscilla and Aquila. Before he sailed, he had his hair cut off at Cenchrea because of a vow he had taken. 19They arrived at Ephesus, where Paul left Priscilla and Aquila. He himself went into the synagogue and reasoned with the Jews. 20When they asked him to spend more time with them, he declined. 21But as he left, he promised, "I will come back if it is God's will." Then he set sail from Ephesus. 22When he landed at Caesarea, he went up and greeted the church and then went down to Antioch.

23After spending some time in Antioch, Paul set out from there and travelled from place to place throughout the region of Galatia and Phrygia, strengthening all the disciples.

24Meanwhile a Jew named Apollos, a native of Alexandria, came to Ephesus. He was a learned man, with a thorough knowledge of the Scriptures. 25He had been instructed in the way of the Lord, and he spoke with great fervour and taught about Jesus accurately, though he knew only the baptism of John. 26He began to speak boldly in the synagogue. When Priscilla and Aquila heard him, they invited him to their home and

explained to him the way of God more adequately.

27When Apollos wanted to go to Achaia, the brothers encouraged him and wrote to the disciples there to welcome him. On arriving, he was a great help to those who by grace had believed. 28For he vigorously refuted the Jews in public debate, proving from the Scriptures that Jesus was the Christ.

Paul in Ephesus

19 While Apollos was at Corinth, Paul took the road through the interior and arrived at Ephesus. There he found some disciples 2and asked them, "Did you receive the Holy Spirit when*a* you believed?"

They answered, "No, we have not even heard that there is a Holy Spirit."

3So Paul asked, "Then what baptism did you receive?"

"John's baptism," they replied.

4Paul said, "John's baptism was a baptism of repentance. He told the people to believe in the one coming after him, that is, in Jesus." 5On hearing this, they were baptised into*b* the name of the Lord Jesus. 6When Paul placed his hands on them, the Holy Spirit came on them, and they spoke in tongues*c* and prophesied. 7There were about twelve men in all.

8Paul entered the synagogue and spoke boldly there for three months, arguing persuasively about the kingdom of God. 9But some of them became obstinate; they refused to believe and publicly maligned the Way. So Paul left them. He took the disciples with him and had discussions daily in the lecture hall of Tyrannus. 10This went on for two years, so that all the Jews and Greeks who lived in the province of Asia heard the word of the Lord.

11God did extraordinary miracles through Paul. 12Handkerchiefs and aprons that had touched him were taken to the sick, and their illnesses were cured and the evil spirits left them.

---

a2 Or after   b5 Or in   c6 Or other languages

¹³Some Jews who went around driving out evil spirits tried to invoke the name of the Lord Jesus over those who were demon-possessed. They would say, "In the name of Jesus, whom Paul preaches, I command you to come out." ¹⁴Seven sons of Sceva, a Jewish chief priest, were doing this. ¹⁵The evil spirit answered them, "Jesus I know and Paul I know about, but who are you?" ¹⁶Then the man who had the evil spirit jumped on them and overpowered them all. He gave them such a beating that they ran out of the house naked and bleeding.

¹⁷When this became known to the Jews and Greeks living in Ephesus, they were all seized with fear, and the name of the Lord Jesus was held in high honour. ¹⁸Many of those who believed now came and openly confessed their evil deeds. ¹⁹A number who had practised sorcery brought their scrolls together and burned them publicly. When they calculated the value of the scrolls, the total came to fifty thousand drachmas.*d* ²⁰In this way the word of the Lord spread widely and grew in power.

²¹After all this had happened, Paul decided to go to Jerusalem, passing through Macedonia and Achaia. "After I have been there," he said, "I must visit Rome also." ²²He sent two of his helpers, Timothy and Erasttus, to Macedonia, while he stayed in the province of Asia a little longer.

The Riot in Ephesus

²³About that time there arose a great disturbance about the Way. ²⁴A silversmith named Demetrius, who made silver shrines of Artemis, brought in no little business for the craftsmen. ²⁵He called them together, along with the workmen in related trades, and said: "Men, you know we receive a good income from this business. ²⁶And you see and hear how this fellow Paul has convinced and led astray large numbers of people here in Ephesus and in practically the whole province of Asia. He says that man-made gods are no gods at all. ²⁷There is danger not only that our trade will lose its good name, but also that the temple of the great goddess Artemis will be discredited, and the goddess herself, who is worshipped throughout the province of Asia and the world, will be robbed of her divine majesty."

²⁸When they heard this, they were furious and began shouting: "Great is Artemis of the Ephesians!" ²⁹Soon the whole city was in an uproar. The people seized Gaius and Aristarchus, Paul's travelling companions from Macedonia, and rushed as one man into the theatre. ³⁰Paul wanted to appear before the crowd, but the disciples would not let him. ³¹Even some of the officials of the province, friends of Paul, sent him a message begging him not to venture into the theatre.

³²The assembly was in confusion: Some were shouting one thing, some another. Most of the people did not even know why they were there. ³³The Jews pushed Alexander to the front, and some of the crowd shouted instructions to him. He motioned for silence in order to make a defence before the people. ³⁴But when they realised he was a Jew, they all shouted in unison for about two hours: "Great is Artemis of the Ephesians!"

³⁵The city clerk quietened the crowd and said: "Men of Ephesus, doesn't all the world know that the city of Ephesus is the guardian of the temple of the great Artemis and of her image, which fell from heaven? ³⁶Therefore, since these facts are undeniable, you ought to be quiet and not do anything rash. ³⁷You have brought these men here, though they have neither robbed temples nor blasphemed our goddess. ³⁸If, then, Demetrius and his fellow craftsmen have a grievance against anybody, the courts are open and there are proconsuls. They can press charges. ³⁹If there is anything further you want to bring up, it must be settled in a legal assembly. ⁴⁰As it is, we are in danger of being charged with rioting

---

*d*19 A drachma was a silver coin worth about a day's wages.

because of today's events. In that case we would not be able to account for this commotion, since there is no reason for it." ⁴¹After he had said this, he dismissed the assembly.

Through Macedonia and Greece

20 When the uproar had ended, Paul sent for the disciples and, after encouraging them, said good-bye and set out for Macedonia. ²He travelled through that area, speaking many words of encouragement to the people, and finally arrived in Greece, ³where he stayed three months. Because the Jews made a plot against him just as he was about to sail for Syria, he decided to go back through Macedonia. ⁴He was accompanied by Sopater son of Pyrrhus from Berea, Aristarchus and Secundus from Thessalonica, Gaius from Derbe, Timothy also, and from the province of Asia Tychicus and Trophimus. ⁵These men went on ahead and waited for us at Troas. ⁶But we sailed from Philippi after the Feast of Unleavened Bread, and five days later joined the others at Troas, where we stayed seven days.

Eutychus Raised From the Dead at Troas

⁷On the first day of the week we came together to break bread. Paul spoke to the people and, because he intended to leave the next day, kept on talking until midnight. ⁸There were many lamps in the upstairs room where we were meeting. ⁹Seated in a window was a young man named Eutychus, who was sinking into a deep sleep as Paul talked on and on. When he was sound asleep, he fell to the ground from the third storey and was picked up dead. ¹⁰Paul went down, threw himself on the young man and put his arms around him. "Don't be alarmed," he said. "He's alive!" ¹¹Then he went upstairs again and broke bread and ate. After talking until daylight, he left. ¹²The people took the young man home alive and were greatly comforted.

Paul's Farewell to the Ephesian Elders

¹³We went on ahead to the ship and sailed for Assos, where we were going to take Paul aboard. He had made this arrangement because he was going there on foot. ¹⁴When he met us at Assos, we took him aboard and went on to Mitylene. ¹⁵The next day we set sail from there and arrived off Kios. The day after that we crossed over to Samos, and on the following day arrived at Miletus. ¹⁶Paul had decided to sail past Ephesus to avoid spending time in the province of Asia, for he was in a hurry to reach Jerusalem, if possible, by the day of Pentecost.

¹⁷From Miletus, Paul sent to Ephesus for the elders of the church. ¹⁸When they arrived, he said to them: "You know how I lived the whole time I was with you, from the first day I came into the province of Asia. ¹⁹I served the Lord with great humility and with tears, although I was severely tested by the plots of the Jews. ²⁰You know that I have not hesitated to preach anything that would be helpful to you but have taught you publicly and from house to house. ²¹I have declared to both Jews and Greeks that they must turn to God in repentance and have faith in our Lord Jesus.

²²"And now, compelled by the Spirit, I am going to Jerusalem, not knowing what will happen to me there. ²³I only know that in every city the Holy Spirit warns me that prison and hardships are facing me. ²⁴However, I consider my life worth nothing to me, if only I may finish the race and complete the task the Lord Jesus has given me—the task of testifying to the gospel of God's grace.

²⁵"Now I know that none of you among whom I have gone about preaching the kingdom will ever see me again. ²⁶Therefore, I declare to you today that I am innocent of the blood of all men. ²⁷For I have not hesitated to proclaim to you the whole will of God. ²⁸Keep watch over yourselves and all the flock of which the

Holy Spirit has made you overseers.[a] Be shepherds of the church of God,[b] which he bought with his own blood. [29]I know that after I leave, savage wolves will come in among you and will not spare the flock. [30]Even from your own number men will arise and distort the truth in order to draw away disciples after them. [31]So be on your guard! Remember that for three years I never stopped warning each of you night and day with tears.

[32]"Now I commit you to God and to the word of his grace, which can build you up and give you an inheritance among all those who are sanctified. [33]I have not coveted anyone's silver or gold or clothing. [34]You yourselves know that these hands of mine have supplied my own needs and the needs of my companions. [35]In everything I did, I showed you that by this kind of hard work we must help the weak, remembering the words the Lord Jesus himself said: 'It is more blessed to give than to receive.' "

[36]When he had said this, he knelt down with all of them and prayed. [37]They all wept as they embraced him and kissed him. [38]What grieved them most was his statement that they would never see his face again. Then they accompanied him to the ship.

On to Jerusalem

21 After we had torn ourselves away from them, we put out to sea and sailed straight to Cos. The next day we went to Rhodes and from there to Patara. [2]We found a ship crossing over to Phoenicia, went on board and set sail. [3]After sighting Cyprus and passing to the south of it, we sailed on to Syria. We landed at Tyre, where our ship was to unload its cargo. [4]Finding the disciples there, we stayed with them seven days. Through the Spirit they urged Paul not to go on to Jerusalem. [5]But when our time was up, we left and continued on our way. All the disciples and their wives and children accompanied us out of the city, and there on the beach we knelt to pray. [6]After saying good-bye to each other, we

went aboard the ship, and they returned home.

[7]We continued our voyage from Tyre and landed at Ptolemais, where we greeted the brothers and stayed with them for a day. [8]Leaving the next day, we reached Caesarea and stayed at the house of Philip the evangelist, one of the Seven. [9]He had four unmarried daughters who prophesied.

[10]After we had been there a number of days, a prophet named Agabus came down from Judea. [11]Coming over to us, he took Paul's belt, tied his own hands and feet with it and said, "The Holy Spirit says, 'In this way the Jews of Jerusalem will bind the owner of this belt and will hand him over to the Gentiles.' "

[12]When we heard this, we and the people there pleaded with Paul not to go up to Jerusalem. [13]Then Paul answered, "Why are you weeping and breaking my heart? I am ready not only to be bound, but also to die in Jerusalem for the name of the Lord Jesus." [14]When he would not be dissuaded, we gave up and said, "The Lord's will be done."

[15]After this, we got ready and went up to Jerusalem. [16]Some of the disciples from Caesarea accompanied us and brought us to the home of Mnason, where we were to stay. He was a man from Cyprus and one of the early disciples.

Paul's Arrival at Jerusalem

[17]When we arrived at Jerusalem, the brothers received us warmly. [18]The next day Paul and the rest of us went to see James, and all the elders were present. [19]Paul greeted them and reported in detail what God had done among the Gentiles through his ministry.

[20]When they heard this, they praised God. Then they said to Paul: "You see, brother, how many thousands of Jews have believed, and all of them are zealous for the law. [21]They have been informed that you teach all the Jews who live among the Gentiles to turn away from Moses,

[a]28 Traditionally bishops   *[b]28 Many manuscripts of* the Lord

telling them not to circumcise their children or live according to our customs. 22What shall we do? They will certainly hear that you have come, 23so do what we tell you. There are four men with us who have made a vow. 24Take these men, join in their purification rites and pay their expenses, so that they can have their heads shaved. Then everybody will know there is no truth in these reports about you, but that you yourself are living in obedience to the law. 25As for the Gentile believers, we have written to them our decision that they should abstain from food sacrificed to idols, from blood, from the meat of strangled animals and from sexual immorality."

26The next day Paul took the men and purified himself along with them. Then he went to the temple to give notice of the date when the days of purification would end and the offering would be made for each of them.

Paul Arrested

27When the seven days were nearly over, some Jews from the province of Asia saw Paul at the temple. They stirred up the whole crowd and seized him, 28shouting, "Men of Israel, help us! This is the man who teaches all men everywhere against our people and our law and this place. And besides, he has brought Greeks into the temple area and defiled this holy place." 29(They had previously seen Trophimus the Ephesian in the city with Paul and assumed that Paul had brought him into the temple area.)

30The whole city was aroused, and the people came running from all directions. Seizing Paul, they dragged him from the temple, and immediately the gates were shut. 31While they were trying to kill him, news reached the commander of the Roman troops that the whole city of Jerusalem was in an uproar. 32He at once took some officers and soldiers and ran down to the crowd. When the rioters saw the commander and

his soldiers, they stopped beating Paul.

33The commander came up and arrested him and ordered him to be bound with two chains. Then he asked who he was and what he had done. 34Some in the crowd shouted one thing and some another, and since the commander could not get at the truth because of the uproar, he ordered that Paul be taken into the barracks. 35When Paul reached the steps, the violence of the mob was so great he had to be carried by the soldiers. 36The crowd that followed kept shouting, "Away with him!"

Paul Speaks to the Crowd

37As the soldiers were about to take Paul into the barracks, he asked the commander, "May I say something to you?"

"Do you speak Greek?" he replied. 38"Aren't you the Egyptian who started a revolt and led four thousand terrorists out into the desert some time ago?"

39Paul answered, "I am a Jew, from Tarsus in Cilicia, a citizen of no ordinary city. Please let me speak to the people."

40Having received the commander's permission, Paul stood on the steps and motioned to the crowd. When they were all silent, he said to them in Aramaic[a]:

22

1"Brothers and fathers, listen now to my defence."

2When they heard him speak to them in Aramaic, they became very quiet.

Then Paul said: 3"I am a Jew, born in Tarsus of Cilicia, but brought up in this city. Under Gamaliel I was thoroughly trained in the law of our fathers and was just as zealous for God as any of you are today. 4I persecuted the followers of this Way to their death, arresting both men and women and throwing them into prison, 5as also the high priest and all the council can testify. I even obtained letters from them to their brothers in Damascus, and went there

---

a40 Or possibly Hebrew; also in verse 2

to bring these people as prisoners to Jerusalem to be punished.

6"About noon as I came near Damascus, suddenly a bright light from heaven flashed around me. 7I fell to the ground and heard a voice say to me, 'Saul! Saul! Why do you persecute me?'

8"'Who are you, Lord?' I asked.

"'I am Jesus of Nazareth, whom you are persecuting,' he replied. 9My companions saw the light, but they did not understand the voice of him who was speaking to me.

10"'What shall I do, Lord?' I asked.

"'Get up,' the Lord said, 'and go into Damascus. There you will be told all that you have been assigned to do.' 11My companions led me by the hand into Damascus, because the brilliance of the light had blinded me.

12"A man named Ananias came to see me. He was a devout observer of the law and highly respected by all the Jews living there. 13He stood beside me and said, 'Brother Saul, receive your sight!' And at that very moment I was able to see him.

14"Then he said: 'The God of our fathers has chosen you to know his will and to see the Righteous One and to hear words from his mouth. 15You will be his witness to all men of what you have seen and heard. 16And now what are you waiting for? Get up, be baptised and wash your sins away, calling on his name.'

17"When I returned to Jerusalem and was praying at the temple, I fell into a trance 18and saw the Lord speaking. 'Quick!' he said to me. 'Leave Jerusalem immediately, because they will not accept your testimony about me.'

19"'Lord,' I replied, 'these men know that I went from one synagogue to another to imprison and beat those who believe in you. 20And when the blood of your martyr*a* Stephen was shed, I stood there giving my approval and guarding the clothes of those who were killing him.'

21"Then the Lord said to me, 'Go; I

will send you far away to the Gentiles.'"

Paul the Roman Citizen

22The crowd listened to Paul until he said this. Then they raised their voices and shouted, "Rid the earth of him! He's not fit to live!"

23As they were shouting and throwing off their cloaks and flinging dust into the air, 24the commander ordered Paul to be taken into the barracks. He directed that he be flogged and questioned in order to find out why the people were shouting at him like this. 25As they stretched him out to flog him, Paul said to the centurion standing there, "Is it legal for you to flog a Roman citizen who hasn't even been found guilty?"

26When the centurion heard this, he went to the commander and reported it. "What are you going to do?" he asked. "This man is a Roman citizen."

27The commander went to Paul and asked, "Tell me, are you a Roman citizen?"

"Yes, I am," he answered.

28Then the commander said, "I had to pay a big price for my citizenship."

"But I was born a citizen," Paul replied.

29Those who were about to question him withdrew immediately. The commander himself was alarmed when he realised that he had put Paul, a Roman citizen, in chains.

Before the Sanhedrin

30The next day, since the commander wanted to find out exactly why Paul was being accused by the Jews, he released him and ordered the chief priests and all the Sanhedrin to assemble. Then he brought Paul and had him stand before them.

23 Paul looked straight at the Sanhedrin and said, "My brothers, I have fulfilled my duty to God in all good conscience to this day." 2At this the high priest Ananias ordered those standing near Paul to strike him on the mouth. 3Then Paul said to him, "God will strike you, you

a20 Or witness

whitewashed wall! You sit there to judge me according to the law, yet you yourself violate the law by commanding that I be struck!"

4Those who were standing near Paul said, "You dare to insult God's high priest?"

5Paul replied, "Brothers, I did not realise that he was the high priest; for it is written: 'Do not speak evil about the ruler of your people.'*a*"

6Then Paul, knowing that some of them were Sadducees and the others Pharisees, called out in the Sanhedrin, "My brothers, I am a Pharisee, the son of a Pharisee. I stand on trial because of my hope in the resurrection of the dead." 7When he said this, a dispute broke out between the Pharisees and the Sadducees, and the assembly was divided. 8(The Sadducees say that there is no resurrection, and that there are neither angels nor spirits, but the Pharisees acknowledge them all.)

9There was a great uproar, and some of the teachers of the law who were Pharisees stood up and argued vigorously. "We find nothing wrong with this man," they said. "What if a spirit or an angel has spoken to him?" 10The dispute became so violent that the commander was afraid Paul would be torn to pieces by them. He ordered the troops to go down and take him away from them by force and bring him into the barracks.

11The following night the Lord stood near Paul and said, "Take courage! As you have testified about me in Jerusalem, so you must also testify in Rome."

The Plot to Kill Paul

12The next morning the Jews formed a conspiracy and bound themselves with an oath not to eat or drink until they had killed Paul. 13More than forty men were involved in this plot. 14They went to the chief priests and elders and said, "We have taken a solemn oath not to eat anything until we have killed Paul. 15Now then, you and the Sanhedrin petition the commander to bring him

before you on the pretext of wanting more accurate information about his case. We are ready to kill him before he gets here."

16But when the son of Paul's sister heard of this plot, he went into the barracks and told Paul.

17Then Paul called one of the centurions and said, "Take this young man to the commander; he has something to tell him." 18So he took him to the commander.

The centurion said, "Paul, the prisoner, sent for me and asked me to bring this young man to you because he has something to tell you."

19The commander took the young man by the hand, drew him aside and asked, "What is it you want to tell me?"

20He said: "The Jews have agreed to ask you to bring Paul before the Sanhedrin tomorrow on the pretext of wanting more accurate information about him. 21Don't give in to them, because more than forty of them are waiting in ambush for him. They have taken an oath not to eat or drink until they have killed him. They are ready now, waiting for your consent to their request."

22The commander dismissed the young man and cautioned him, "Don't tell anyone that you have reported this to me."

Paul Transferred to Caesarea

23Then he called two of his centurions and ordered them, "Get ready a detachment of two hundred soldiers, seventy horsemen and two hundred spearmen to go to Caesarea at nine tonight. 24Provide mounts for Paul so that he may be taken safely to Governor Felix."

25He wrote a letter as follows:

26Claudius Lysias,

To His Excellency, Governor Felix:

Greetings.

27This man was seized by the Jews and they were about to kill him, but I came with my troops

*a*5 Exodus 22:28

158

and rescued him, for I had learned that he is a Roman citizen. [28]I wanted to know why they were accusing him, so I brought him to their Sanhedrin. [29]I found that the accusation had to do with questions about their law, but there was no charge against him that deserved death or imprisonment. [30]When I was informed of a plot to be carried out against the man, I sent him to you at once. I also ordered his accusers to present to you their case against him.

[31]So the soldiers, carrying out their orders, took Paul with them during the night and brought him as far as Antipatris. [32]The next day they let the cavalry go on with him, while they returned to the barracks. [33]When the cavalry arrived in Caesarea, they delivered the letter to the governor and handed Paul over to him. [34]The governor read the letter and asked what province he was from. Learning that he was from Cilicia, [35]he said, "I will hear your case when your accusers get here." Then he ordered that Paul be kept under guard in Herod's palace.

The Trial Before Felix

24 Five days later the high priest Ananias went down to Caesarea with some of the elders and a lawyer named Tertullus, and they brought their charges against Paul before the governor. [2]When Paul was called in, Tertullus presented his case before Felix: "We have enjoyed a long period of peace under you, and your foresight has brought about reforms in this nation. [3]Everywhere and in every way, most excellent Felix, we acknowledge this with profound gratitude. [4]But in order not to weary you further, I would request that you be kind enough to hear us briefly.

[5]"We have found this man to be a troublemaker, stirring up riots among the Jews all over the world. He is a ring-leader of the Nazarene sect [6]and even tried to desecrate the temple; so we seized him. [8]By*a* examining him yourself you will be able to learn the truth about all these charges we are bringing against him."

[9]The Jews joined in the accusation, asserting that these things were true.

[10]When the governor motioned for him to speak, Paul replied: "I know that for a number of years you have been a judge over this nation; so I gladly make my defence. [11]You can easily verify that no more than twelve days ago I went up to Jerusalem to worship. [12]My accusers did not find me arguing with anyone at the temple, or stirring up a crowd in the synagogues or anywhere else in the city. [13]And they cannot prove to you the charges they are now making against me. [14]However, I admit that I worship the God of our fathers, as a follower of the Way, which they call a sect. I believe everything that agrees with the Law and that is written in the Prophets, [15]and I have the same hope in God as these men, that there will be a resurrection of both the righteous and the wicked. [16]So I strive always to keep my conscience clear before God and man.

[17]"After an absence of several years, I came to Jerusalem to bring my people gifts for the poor and to present offerings. [18]I was ceremonially clean when they found me in the temple courts doing this. There was no crowd with me, nor was I involved in any disturbance. [19]But there are some Jews from the province of Asia, who ought to be here before you and bring charges if they have anything against me. [20]Or these who are here should state what crime they found in me when I stood before the Sanhedrin—[21]unless it was this one thing I shouted as I stood in their presence: 'It is concerning the resurrection of the dead that I am on trial before you today.' "

[22]Then Felix, who was well

---

*a*6-8 Some manuscripts *him and wanted to judge him according to our law.* [7]*But the commander, Lysias, came and with the use of much force snatched him from our hands* [8]*and ordered his accusers to come before you. By*

acquainted with the Way, adjourned the proceedings. "When Lysias the commander comes," he said, "I will decide your case." 23He ordered the centurion to keep Paul under guard but to give him some freedom and permit his friends to take care of his needs.

24Several days later Felix came with his wife Drusilla, who was a Jewess. He sent for Paul and listened to him as he spoke about faith in Christ Jesus. 25As Paul discoursed on righteousness, self-control and the judgment to come, Felix was afraid and said, "That's enough for now! You may leave. When I find it convenient, I will send for you." 26At the same time he was hoping that Paul would offer him a bribe, so he sent for him frequently and talked with him.

27When two years had passed, Felix was succeeded by Porcius Festus, but because Felix wanted to grant a favour to the Jews, he left Paul in prison.

The Trial Before Festus

25 Three days after arriving in the province, Festus went up from Caesarea to Jerusalem, 2where the chief priests and Jewish leaders appeared before him and presented the charges against Paul. 3They urgently requested Festus, as a favour to them, to have Paul transferred to Jerusalem, for they were preparing an ambush to kill him along the way. 4Festus answered, "Paul is being held at Caesarea, and I myself am going there soon. 5Let some of your leaders come with me and press charges against the man there, if he has done anything wrong."

6After spending eight or ten days with them, he went down to Caesarea, and the next day he convened the court and ordered that Paul be brought before him. 7When Paul appeared, the Jews who had come down from Jerusalem stood around him, bringing many serious charges against him, which they could not prove.

8Then Paul made his defence: "I have done nothing wrong against the law of the Jews or against the temple or against Caesar."

9Festus, wishing to do the Jews a favour, said to Paul, "Are you willing to go up to Jerusalem and stand trial before me there on these charges?"

10Paul answered: "I am now standing before Caesar's court, where I ought to be tried. I have not done any wrong to the Jews, as you yourself know very well. 11If, however, I am guilty of doing anything deserving death, I do not refuse to die. But if the charges brought against me by these Jews are not true, no-one has the right to hand me over to them. I appeal to Caesar!"

12After Festus had conferred with his council, he declared: "You have appealed to Caesar. To Caesar you will go!"

Festus Consults King Agrippa

13A few days later King Agrippa and Bernice arrived at Caesarea to pay their respects to Festus. 14Since they were spending many days there, Festus discussed Paul's case with the king. He said: "There is a man here whom Felix left as a prisoner. 15When I went to Jerusalem, the chief priests and elders of the Jews brought charges against him and asked that he be condemned.

16"I told them that it is not the Roman custom to hand over any man before he has faced his accusers and has had an opportunity to defend himself against their charges. 17When they came here with me, I did not delay the case, but convened the court the next day and ordered the man to be brought in. 18When his accusers got up to speak, they did not charge him with any of the crimes I had expected. 19Instead, they had some points of dispute with him about their own religion and about a dead man named Jesus whom Paul claimed was alive. 20I was at a loss how to investigate such matters; so I asked if he would be willing to go to Jerusalem and stand trial there on these charges. 21When Paul made his appeal to be held over for the

Emperor's decision, I ordered him to be held until I could send him to Caesar."

22Then Agrippa said to Festus, "I would like to hear this man myself."

He replied, "Tomorrow you will hear him."

Paul Before Agrippa

23The next day Agrippa and Bernice came with great pomp and entered the audience room with the high ranking officers and the leading men of the city. At the command of Festus, Paul was brought in. 24Festus said: "King Agrippa, and all who are present with us, you see this man! The whole Jewish community has petitioned me about him in Jerusalem and here in Caesarea, shouting that he ought not to live any longer. 25I found he had done nothing deserving of death, but because he made his appeal to the Emperor I decided to send him to Rome. 26But I have nothing definite to write to His Majesty about him. Therefore I have brought him before all of you, and especially before you, King Agrippa, so that as a result of this investigation I may have something to write. 27For I think it is unreasonable to send on a prisoner without specifying the charges against him."

26 Then Agrippa said to Paul, "You have permission to speak for yourself."

So Paul motioned with his hand and began his defence: 2"King Agrippa, I consider myself fortunate to stand before you today as I make my defence against all the accusations of the Jews, 3and especially so because you are well acquainted with all the Jewish customs and controversies. Therefore, I beg you to listen to me patiently.

4"The Jews all know the way I have lived ever since I was a child, from the beginning of my life in my own country, and also in Jerusalem. 5They have known me for a long time and can testify, if they are willing, that according to the strictest sect of our religion, I lived as a Pharisee.

6And now it is because of my hope in what God has promised our fathers that I am on trial today. 7This is the promise our twelve tribes are hoping to see fulfilled as they earnestly serve God day and night. O King, it is because of this hope that the Jews are accusing me. 8Why should any of you consider it incredible that God raises the dead?

9"I too was convinced that I ought to do all that was possible to oppose the name of Jesus of Nazareth. 10And that is just what I did in Jerusalem. On the authority of the chief priests I put many of the saints in prison, and when they were put to death, I cast my vote against them. 11Many a time I went from one synagogue to another to have them punished, and I tried to force them to blaspheme. In my obsession against them, I even went to foreign cities to persecute them.

12"On one of these journeys I was going to Damascus with the authority and commission of the chief priests. 13About noon, O King, as I was on the road, I saw a light from heaven, brighter than the sun, blazing around me and my companions. 14We all fell to the ground, and I heard a voice saying to me in Aramaic,a 'Saul, Saul, why do you persecute me? It is hard for you to kick against the goads.'

15"Then I asked, 'Who are you, Lord?'

" 'I am Jesus, whom you are persecuting,' the Lord replied. 16'Now get up and stand on your feet. I have appeared to you to appoint you as a servant and as a witness of what you have seen of me and what I will show you. 17I will rescue you from your own people and from the Gentiles. I am sending you 18to open their eyes and turn them from darkness to light, and from the power of Satan to God, so that they may receive forgiveness of sins and a place among those who are sanctified by faith in me.'

19"So then, King Agrippa, I was not disobedient to the vision from heaven. 20First to those in Damascus, then to those in Jerusalem and in all Judea, and to the Gentiles also, I

a14 Or Hebrew

preached that they should repent and turn to God and prove their repentance by their deeds. 21That is why the Jews seized me in the temple courts and tried to kill me. 22But I have had God's help to this very day, and so I stand here and testify to small and great alike. I am saying nothing beyond what the prophets and Moses said would happen—23that the Christ[b] would suffer and, as the first to rise from the dead, would proclaim light to his own people and to the Gentiles."

24At this point Festus interrupted Paul's defence. "You are out of your mind, Paul!" he shouted. "Your great learning is driving you insane."

25"I am not insane, most excellent Festus," Paul replied. "What I am saying is true and reasonable. 26The king is familiar with these things, and I can speak freely to him. I am convinced that none of this has escaped his notice, because it was not done in a corner. 27King Agrippa, do you believe the prophets? I know you do."

28Then Agrippa said to Paul, "Do you think that in such a short time you can persuade me to be a Christian?"

29Paul replied, "Short time or long—I pray God that not only you but all who are listening to me today may become what I am, except for these chains."

30The king rose, and with him the governor and Bernice and those sitting with them. 31They left the room, and while talking with one another, they said, "This man is not doing anything that deserves death or imprisonment."

32Agrippa said to Festus, "This man could have been set free, if he had not appealed to Caesar."

Paul Sails for Rome

27 When it was decided that we would sail for Italy, Paul and some other prisoners were handed over to a centurion named Julius, who belonged to the Imperial Regiment. 2We boarded a ship from Adramyttium about to sail for ports along the coast of the province of Asia, and we put out to sea. Aristarchus, a Macedonian from Thessalonica, was with us.

3The next day we landed at Sidon; and Julius, in kindness to Paul, allowed him to go to his friends so they might provide for his needs. 4From there we put out to sea again and passed to the lee of Cyprus because the winds were against us. 5When we had sailed across the open sea off the coast of Cilicia and Pamphylia, we landed at Myra in Lycia. 6There the centurion found an Alexandrian ship sailing for Italy and put us on board. 7We made slow headway for many days and had difficulty arriving off Cnidus. When the wind did not allow us to hold our course, we sailed to the lee of Crete, opposite Salmone. 8We moved along the coast with difficulty and came to a place called Fair Havens, near the town of Lasea.

9Much time had been lost, and sailing had already become dangerous because by now it was after the Fast.[a] So Paul warned them, 10"Men, I can see that our voyage is going to be disastrous and bring great loss to ship and cargo, and to our own lives also." 11But the centurion, instead of listening to what Paul said, followed the advice of the pilot and of the owner of the ship. 12Since the harbour was unsuitable to winter in, the majority decided that we should sail on, hoping to reach Phoenix and winter there. This was a harbour in Crete, facing both south-west and north-west.

The Storm

13When a gentle south wind began to blow, they thought they had obtained what they wanted; so they weighed anchor and sailed along the shore of Crete. 14Before very long, a wind of hurricane force, called the "North-easter", swept down from the island. 15The ship was caught by the storm and could not head into the wind; so we gave way to it and were

b23 Or Messiah   a9 That is, the Day of Atonement (Yom Kippur)

driven along. ¹⁶As we passed to the lee of a small island called Cauda, we were hardly able to make the lifeboat secure. ¹⁷When the men had hoisted it aboard, they passed ropes under the ship itself to hold it together. Fearing that they would run aground on the sand-bars of Syrtis, they lowered the sea anchor and let the ship be driven along. ¹⁸We took such a violent battering from the storm that the next day they began to throw the cargo overboard. ¹⁹On the third day, they threw the ship's tackle overboard with their own hands. ²⁰When neither sun nor stars appeared for many days and the storm continued raging, we finally gave up all hope of being saved.

²¹After the men had gone a long time without food, Paul stood up before them and said: "Men, you should have taken my advice not to sail from Crete; then you would have spared yourselves this damage and loss. ²²But now I urge you to keep up your courage, because not one of you will be lost; only the ship will be destroyed. ²³Last night an angel of the God whose I am and whom I serve stood beside me ²⁴and said, 'Do not be afraid, Paul. You must stand trial before Caesar; and God has graciously given you the lives of all who sail with you.' ²⁵So keep up your courage, men, for I have faith in God that it will happen just as he told me. ²⁶Nevertheless, we must run aground on some island."

The Shipwreck

²⁷On the fourteenth night we were still being driven across the Adriatic^b Sea, when about midnight the sailors sensed they were approaching land. ²⁸They took soundings and found that the water was one hundred and twenty feet^c deep. A short time later they took soundings again and found it was ninety feet^d deep. ²⁹Fearing that we would be dashed against the rocks, they dropped four anchors from the stern and prayed for daylight. ³⁰In an attempt to escape from the ship, the sailors let the lifeboat down into the sea, pretending they were going to lower some anchors from the bow. ³¹Then Paul said to the centurion and the soldiers, "Unless these men stay with the ship, you cannot be saved." ³²So the soldiers cut the ropes that held the lifeboat and let it fall away.

³³Just before dawn Paul urged them all to eat. "For the last fourteen days," he said, "you have been in constant suspense and have gone without food—you haven't eaten anything. ³⁴Now I urge you to take some food. You need it to survive. Not one of you will lose a single hair from his head." ³⁵After he said this, he took some bread and gave thanks to God in front of them all. Then he broke it and began to eat. ³⁶They were all encouraged and ate some food themselves. ³⁷Altogether there were 276 of us on board. ³⁸When they had eaten as much as they wanted, they lightened the ship by throwing the grain into the sea.

³⁹When daylight came, they did not recognise the land, but they saw a bay with a sandy beach, where they decided to run the ship aground if they could. ⁴⁰Cutting loose the anchors, they left them in the sea and at the same time untied the ropes that held the rudders. Then they hoisted the foresail to the wind and made for the beach. ⁴¹But the ship struck a sand-bar and ran aground. The bow stuck fast and would not move, and the stern was broken to pieces by the pounding of the surf.

⁴²The soldiers planned to kill the prisoners to prevent any of them from swimming away and escaping. ⁴³But the centurion wanted to spare Paul's life and kept them from carrying out their plan. He ordered those who could swim to jump overboard first and get to land. ⁴⁴The rest were to get there on planks or on pieces of the ship. In this way everyone reached land in safety.

---

^b27 In ancient times the name referred to an area extending well south of Italy.
^c28 Greek *twenty orguias* (about 37 metres) ^d28 Greek *fifteen orguias* (about 27 metres)

Ashore on Malta

28 Once safely on shore, we found out that the island was called Malta. ²The islanders showed us unusual kindness. They built a fire and welcomed us all because it was raining and cold. ³Paul gathered a pile of brushwood and, as he put it on the fire, a viper, driven out by the heat, fastened itself on his hand. ⁴When the islanders saw the snake hanging from his hand, they said to each other, "This man must be a murderer; for though he escaped from the sea, Justice has not allowed him to live." ⁵But Paul shook the snake off into the fire and suffered no ill effects. ⁶The people expected him to swell up or suddenly fall over dead, but after waiting a long time and seeing nothing unusual happen to him, they changed their minds and said he was a god.

⁷There was an estate near by that belonged to Publius, the chief official of the island. He welcomed us to his home and for three days entertained us hospitably. ⁸His father was sick in bed, suffering from fever and dysentery. Paul went in to see him and, after prayer, placed his hands on him and healed him. ⁹When this had happened, the rest of the sick on the island came and were cured. ¹⁰They honoured us in many ways and when we were ready to sail, they furnished us with the supplies we needed.

Arrival at Rome

¹¹After three months we put out to sea in a ship that had wintered in the island. It was an Alexandrian ship with the figurehead of the twin gods Castor and Pollux. ¹²We put in at Syracuse and stayed there three days. ¹³From there we set sail and arrived at Rhegium. The next day the south wind came up, and on the following day we reached Puteoli. ¹⁴There we found some brothers who invited us to spend a week with them. And so we went to Rome. ¹⁵The brothers there had heard that we were coming, and they travelled as far as the Forum of Appius and the Three Taverns to meet us. At the sight of these men

Paul thanked God and was encouraged. ¹⁶When we got to Rome, Paul was allowed to live by himself, with a soldier to guard him.

Paul Preaches at Rome Under Guard

¹⁷Three days later he called together the leaders of the Jews. When they had assembled, Paul said to them: "My brothers, although I have done nothing against our people or against the customs of our ancestors, I was arrested in Jerusalem and handed over to the Romans. ¹⁸They examined me and wanted to release me, because I was not guilty of any crime deserving death. ¹⁹But when the Jews objected, I was compelled to appeal to Caesar—not that I had any charge to bring against my own people. ²⁰For this reason I have asked to see you and talk with you. It is because of the hope of Israel that I am bound with this chain."

²¹They replied, "We have not received any letters from Judea concerning you, and none of the brothers who has come from there has reported or said anything bad about you. ²²But we want to hear what your views are, for we know that people everywhere are talking against this sect."

²³They arranged to meet Paul on a certain day, and came in even larger numbers to the place where he was staying. From morning till evening he explained and declared to them the kingdom of God and tried to convince them about Jesus from the Law of Moses and from the Prophets. ²⁴Some were convinced by what he said, but others would not believe. ²⁵They disagreed among themselves and began to leave after Paul had made this final statement: "The Holy Spirit spoke the truth to your forefathers when he said through Isaiah the prophet:

²⁶" 'Go to this people and say,
   "You will be ever hearing but
      never understanding;
   you will be ever seeing but never
      perceiving."

27For this people's heart has become
  calloused;
    they hardly hear with their ears,
    and they have closed their eyes.
  Otherwise they might see with their
    eyes,
    hear with their ears,
    understand with their hearts
  and turn and I would heal them.'*a*

28"Therefore I want you to know that God's salvation has been sent to the Gentiles, and they will listen!"*b*

30For two whole years Paul stayed there in his own rented house and welcomed all who came to see him. 31Boldly and without hindrance he preached the kingdom of God and taught about the Lord Jesus Christ.

---

*a*27 Isaiah 6:9,10
*b*28 Some manuscripts *listen!" 29After he said this, the Jews left, arguing vigorously among themselves.*

Romans

1 Paul, a servant of Christ Jesus, called to be an apostle and set apart for the gospel of God—²the gospel he promised beforehand through his prophets in the Holy Scriptures ³regarding his Son, who as to his human nature was a descendant of David, ⁴and who through the Spirit*a* of holiness was declared with power to be the Son of God,*b* by his resurrection from the dead: Jesus Christ our Lord. ⁵Through him and for his name's sake, we received grace and apostleship to call people from among all the Gentiles to the obedience that comes from faith. ⁶And you also are among those who are called to belong to Jesus Christ.

⁷To all in Rome who are loved by God and called to be saints:

Grace and peace to you from God our Father and from the Lord Jesus Christ.

Paul's Longing to Visit Rome

⁸First, I thank my God through Jesus Christ for all of you, because your faith is being reported all over the world. ⁹God, whom I serve with my whole heart in preaching the gospel of his Son, is my witness how constantly I remember you ¹⁰in my prayers at all times; and I pray that now at last by God's will the way may be opened for me to come to you.

¹¹I long to see you so that I may impart to you some spiritual gift to make you strong—¹²that is, that you and I may be mutually encouraged by each other's faith. ¹³I do not want you to be unaware, brothers, that I planned many times to come to you (but have been prevented from doing so until now) in order that I might have a harvest among you, just as I have had among the other Gentiles.

¹⁴I am bound both to Greeks and non-Greeks, both to the wise and the foolish. ¹⁵That is why I am so eager to preach the gospel also to you who are at Rome.

¹⁶I am not ashamed of the gospel, because it is the power of God for the salvation of everyone who believes: first for the Jew, then for the Gentile. ¹⁷For in the gospel a righteousness from God is revealed, a righteousness that is by faith from first to last,*c* just as it is written: "The righteous will live by faith."*d*

God's Wrath Against Mankind

¹⁸The wrath of God is being revealed from heaven against all the godlessness and wickedness of men who suppress the truth by their wickedness, ¹⁹since what may be known about God is plain to them, because God has made it plain to them. ²⁰For since the creation of the world God's invisible qualities—his eternal power and divine nature—have been clearly seen, being understood from what has been made, so that men are without excuse. ²¹For although they knew God, they neither glorified him as God nor gave thanks to him, but their thinking became futile and their foolish hearts were darkened. ²²Although they claimed to be wise, they became fools

---

a4 Or *who as to his spirit* *b4* Or *was appointed to be the Son of God with power*
c17 Or *is from faith to faith* *d17* Hab. 2:4

166

²³and exchanged the glory of the immortal God for images made to look like mortal man and birds and animals and reptiles.

²⁴Therefore God gave them over in the sinful desires of their hearts to sexual impurity for the degrading of their bodies with one another. ²⁵They exchanged the truth of God for a lie, and worshipped and served created things rather than the Creator—who is forever praised. Amen.

²⁶Because of this, God gave them over to shameful lusts. Even their women exchanged natural relations for unnatural ones. ²⁷In the same way the men also abandoned natural relations with women and were inflamed with lust for one another. Men committed indecent acts with other men, and received in themselves the due penalty for their perversion.

²⁸Furthermore, since they did not think it worth while to retain the knowledge of God, he gave them over to a depraved mind, to do what ought not to be done. ²⁹They have become filled with every kind of wickedness, evil, greed and depravity. They are full of envy, murder, strife, deceit and malice. They are gossips, ³⁰slanderers, God-haters, insolent, arrogant and boastful; they invent ways of doing evil; they disobey their parents; ³¹they are senseless, faithless, heartless, ruthless. ³²Although they know God's righteous decree that those who do such things deserve death, they not only continue to do these very things but also approve of those who practise them.

God's Righteous Judgment

2 You, therefore, have no excuse, you who pass judgment on someone else, for at whatever point you judge the other, you are condemning yourself, because you who pass judgment do the same things. ²Now we know that God's judgment against those who do such things is based on truth. ³So when you, a mere man, pass judgment on them and yet do the same things, do you think you will escape God's judgment? ⁴Or do you

⁰⁶ Psalm 62:12; Prov. 24:12

show contempt for the riches of his kindness, tolerance and patience, not realising that God's kindness leads you towards repentance?

⁵But because of your stubbornness and your unrepentant heart, you are storing up wrath against yourself for the day of God's wrath, when his righteous judgment will be revealed. ⁶God "will give to each person according to what he has done".ᵃ ⁷To those who by persistence in doing good seek glory, honour and immortality, he will give eternal life. ⁸But for those who are self-seeking and who reject the truth and follow evil, there will be wrath and anger. ⁹There will be trouble and distress for every human being who does evil: first for the Jew, then for the Gentile; ¹⁰but glory, honour and peace for everyone who does good: first for the Jew, then for the Gentile. ¹¹For God does not show favouritism.

¹²All who sin apart from the law will also perish apart from the law, and all who sin under the law will be judged by the law. ¹³For it is not those who hear the law who are righteous in God's sight, but it is those who obey the law who will be declared righteous. ¹⁴(Indeed, when Gentiles, who do not have the law, do by nature things required by the law, they are a law for themselves, even though they do not have the law, ¹⁵since they show that the requirements of the law are written on their hearts, their consciences also bearing witness, and their thoughts now accusing, now even defending them.) ¹⁶This will take place on the day when God will judge men's secrets through Jesus Christ, as my gospel declares.

The Jews and the Law

¹⁷Now you, if you call yourself a Jew; if you rely on the law and brag about your relationship to God; ¹⁸if you know his will and approve of what is superior because you are instructed by the law; ¹⁹if you are convinced that you are a guide for the blind, a light for those who are in

167

the dark, 20an instructor of the foolish, a teacher of infants, because you have in the law the embodiment of knowledge and truth—21you, then, who teach others, do you not teach yourself? You who preach against stealing, do you steal? 22You who say that people should not commit adultery, do you commit adultery? You who abhor idols, do you rob temples? 23You who brag about the law, do you dishonour God by breaking the law? 24As it is written: "God's name is blasphemed among the Gentiles because of you."b

25Circumcision has value if you observe the law, but if you break the law, you have become as though you had not been circumcised. 26If those who are not circumcised keep the law's requirements, will they not be regarded as though they were circumcised? 27The one who is not circumcised physically and yet obeys the law will condemn you who, even though you have thec written code and circumcision, are a law-breaker.

28A man is not a Jew if he is only one outwardly, nor is circumcision merely outward and physical. 29No, a man is a Jew if he is one inwardly; and circumcision is circumcision of the heart, by the Spirit, not by the written code. Such a man's praise is not from men, but from God.

God's Faithfulness

3 What advantage, then, is there in being a Jew, or what value is there in circumcision? 2Much in every way! First of all, they have been entrusted with the very words of God.

3What if some did not have faith? Will their lack of faith nullify God's faithfulness? 4Not at all! Let God be true, and every man a liar. As it is written:

"So that you may be proved right in your words
and prevail in your judging."a

5But if our unrighteousness brings out God's righteousness more clearly, what shall we say? That God is unjust in bringing his wrath on us? (I am using a human argument.) 6Certainly not! If that were so, how could God judge the world? 7Someone might argue, "If my falsehood enhances God's truthfulness and so increases his glory, why am I still condemned as a sinner?" 8Why not say—as we are being slanderously reported as saying and as some claim that we say—"Let us do evil that good may result"? Their condemnation is deserved.

No-one Is Righteous

9What shall we conclude then? Are we any better?b Not at all! We have already made the charge that Jews and Gentiles alike are all under sin. 10As it is written:

"There is no-one righteous, not even one;
11 there is no-one who understands,
    no-one who seeks God.
12All have turned away,
    they have together become worthless;
  there is no-one who does good,
    not even one."c
13"Their throats are open graves;
    their tongues practise deceit."d
  "The poison of vipers is on their lips."e
14 "Their mouths are full of cursing and bitterness."f
15"Their feet are swift to shed blood;
16 ruin and misery mark their ways;
17and the way of peace they do not know."g
18 "There is no fear of God before their eyes."h

19Now we know that whatever the law says, it says to those who are under the law, so that every mouth may be silenced and the whole world held accountable to God. 20Therefore no-one will be declared righteous in his sight by observing the law; rather,

---

b24 Isaiah 52:5; Ezek. 36:22   c27 Or who, by means of a
b9 Or worse   c12 Psalms 14:1-3; 53:1-3; Eccles. 7:20
e13 Psalm 140:3   f14 Psalm 10:7   g17 Isaiah 59:7,8
d13 Psalm 5:9   a4 Psalm 51:4   h18 Psalm 36:1

through the law we become conscious of sin.

Righteousness Through Faith

21But now a righteousness from God, apart from law, has been made known, to which the Law and the Prophets testify. 22This righteousness from God comes through faith in Jesus Christ to all who believe. There is no difference, 23for all have sinned and fall short of the glory of God, 24and are justified freely by his grace through the redemption that came by Christ Jesus. 25God presented him as a sacrifice of atonement,*i* through faith in his blood. He did this to demonstrate his justice, because in his forbearance he had left the sins committed beforehand unpunished 26—he did it to demonstrate his justice at the present time, so as to be just and the one who justifies the man who has faith in Jesus.

27Where, then, is boasting? It is excluded. On what principle? On that of observing the law? No, but on that of faith. 28For we maintain that a man is justified by faith apart from observing the law. 29Is God the God of Jews only? Is he not the God of Gentiles too? Yes, of Gentiles too, 30since there is only one God, who will justify the circumcised by faith and the uncircumcised through that same faith. 31Do we, then, nullify the law by this faith? Not at all! Rather, we uphold the law.

Abraham Justified by Faith

4 What then shall we say that Abraham, our forefather, discovered in this matter? 2If, in fact, Abraham was justified by works, he had something to boast about—but not before God. 3What does the Scripture say? "Abraham believed God, and it was credited to him as righteousness."*a*

4Now when a man works, his wages are not credited to him as a gift, but as an obligation. 5However, to the man who does not work but trusts God who justifies the wicked,

his faith is credited as righteousness. 6David says the same thing when he speaks of the blessedness of the man to whom God credits righteousness apart from works:

7"Blessed are they
  whose transgressions are
    forgiven,
  whose sins are covered.
8Blessed is the man
  whose sin the Lord will never
    count against him."*b*

9Is this blessedness only for the circumcised, or also for the uncircumcised? We have been saying that Abraham's faith was credited to him as righteousness. 10Under what circumstances was it credited? Was it after he was circumcised, or before? It was not after, but before! 11And he received the sign of circumcision, a seal of the righteousness that he had by faith while he was still uncircumcised. So then, he is the father of all who believe but have not been circumcised, in order that righteousness might be credited to them. 12And he is also the father of the circumcised who not only are circumcised but who also walk in the footsteps of the faith that our father Abraham had before he was circumcised.

13It was not through law that Abraham and his offspring received the promise that he would be heir of the world, but through the righteousness that comes by faith. 14For if those who live by law are heirs, faith has no value and the promise is worthless, 15because law brings wrath. And where there is no law there is no transgression.

16Therefore, the promise comes by faith, so that it may be by grace and may be guaranteed to all Abraham's offspring—not only to those who are of the law but also to those who are of the faith of Abraham. He is the father of us all. 17As it is written: "I have made you a father of many nations."*c* He is our father in the sight of God, in whom he believed—the God who gives life to the dead and

*i*25 Or *as the one who would turn aside his wrath, taking away sin*
*a*3 Gen. 15:6; also in verse 22   *b*8 Psalm 32:1,2   *c*17 Gen. 17:5

169

calls things that are not as though they were.

[18]Against all hope, Abraham in hope believed and so became the father of many nations, just as it had been said to him, "So shall your offspring be."[d] [19]Without weakening in his faith, he faced the fact that his body was as good as dead—since he was about a hundred years old—and that Sarah's womb was also dead. [20]Yet he did not waver through unbelief regarding the promise of God, but was strengthened in his faith and gave glory to God, [21]being fully persuaded that God had power to do what he had promised. [22]This is why "it was credited to him as righteousness." [23]The words "it was credited to him" were written not for him alone, [24]but also for us, to whom God will credit righteousness—for us who believe in him who raised Jesus our Lord from the dead. [25]He was delivered over to death for our sins and was raised to life for our justification.

Peace and Joy

5 Therefore, since we have been justified through faith, we[a] have peace with God through our Lord Jesus Christ, [2]through whom we have gained access by faith into this grace in which we now stand. And we[a] rejoice in the hope of the glory of God. [3]Not only so, but we[a] also rejoice in our sufferings, because we know that suffering produces perseverance; [4]perseverance, character; and character, hope. [5]And hope does not disappoint us, because God has poured out his love into our hearts by the Holy Spirit, whom he has given us.

[6]You see, at just the right time, when we were still powerless, Christ died for the ungodly. [7]Very rarely will anyone die for a righteous man, though for a good man someone might possibly dare to die. [8]But God demonstrates his own love for us in this: While we were still sinners, Christ died for us.

[9]Since we have now been justified

by his blood, how much more shall we be saved from God's wrath through him! [10]For if, when we were God's enemies, we were reconciled to him through the death of his Son, how much more, having been reconciled, shall we be saved through his life! [11]Not only is this so, but we also rejoice in God through our Lord Jesus Christ, through whom we have now received reconciliation.

Death Through Adam, Life Through Christ

[12]Therefore, just as sin entered the world through one man, and death through sin, and in this way death came to all men, because all sinned— [13]for before the law was given, sin was in the world. But sin is not taken into account when there is no law. [14]Nevertheless, death reigned from the time of Adam to the time of Moses, even over those who did not sin by breaking a command, as did Adam, who was a pattern of the one to come.

[15]But the gift is not like the trespass. For if the many died by the trespass of the one man, how much more did God's grace and the gift that came by the grace of the one man, Jesus Christ, overflow to the many! [16]Again, the gift of God is not like the result of the one man's sin: The judgment followed one sin and brought condemnation, but the gift followed many trespasses and brought justification. [17]For if, by the trespass of the one man, death reigned through that one man, how much more will those who receive God's abundant provision of grace and of the gift of righteousness reign in life through the one man, Jesus Christ.

[18]Consequently, just as the result of one trespass was condemnation for all men, so also the result of one act of righteousness was justification that brings life for all men. [19]For just as through the disobedience of the one man the many were made sinners, so also through the obedience of the one man the many will be made righteous.

[d]18 Gen. 15:5   [a]1,2,3 Or *let us*

[20]The law was added so that the trespass might increase. But where sin increased, grace increased all the more, [21]so that, just as sin reigned in death, so also grace might reign through righteousness to bring eternal life through Jesus Christ our Lord.

Dead to Sin, Alive in Christ

6 What shall we say, then? Shall we go on sinning, so that grace may increase? [2]By no means! We died to sin; how can we live in it any longer? [3]Or don't you know that all of us who were baptised into Christ Jesus were baptised into his death? [4]We were therefore buried with him through baptism into death in order that, just as Christ was raised from the dead through the glory of the Father, we too may live a new life.

[5]If we have been united with him in his death, we will certainly also be united with him in his resurrection. [6]For we know that our old self was crucified with him so that the body of sin might be rendered powerless, that we should no longer be slaves to sin—[7]because anyone who has died has been freed from sin.

[8]Now if we died with Christ, we believe that we will also live with him. [9]For we know that since Christ was raised from the dead, he cannot die again; death no longer has mastery over him. [10]The death he died, he died to sin once for all; but the life he lives, he lives to God.

[11]In the same way, count yourselves dead to sin but alive to God in Christ Jesus. [12]Therefore do not let sin reign in your mortal body so that you obey its evil desires. [13]Do not offer the parts of your body to sin, as instruments of wickedness, but rather offer yourselves to God, as those who have been brought from death to life; and offer the parts of your body to him as instruments of righteousness. [14]For sin shall not be your master, because you are not under law, but under grace.

Slaves to Righteousness

[15]What then? Shall we sin because

we are not under law but under grace? By no means! [16]Don't you know that when you offer yourselves to someone to obey him as slaves, you are slaves to the one whom you obey—whether you are slaves to sin, which leads to death, or to obedience, which leads to righteousness? [17]But thanks be to God that, though you used to be slaves to sin, you wholeheartedly obeyed the form of teaching to which you were entrusted. [18]You have been set free from sin and have become slaves to righteousness.

[19]I put this in human terms because you are weak in your natural selves. Just as you used to offer the parts of your body in slavery to impurity and to ever-increasing wickedness, so now offer them in slavery to righteousness leading to holiness. [20]When you were slaves to sin, you were free from the control of righteousness. [21]What benefit did you reap at that time from the things you are now ashamed of? Those things result in death! [22]But now that you have been set free from sin and have become slaves to God, the benefit you reap leads to holiness, and the result is eternal life. [23]For the wages of sin is death, but the gift of God is eternal life in[a] Christ Jesus our Lord.

An Illustration From Marriage

7 Do you not know, brothers—for I am speaking to men who know the law—that the law has authority over a man only as long as he lives? [2]For example, by law a married woman is bound to her husband as long as he is alive, but if her husband dies, she is released from the law of marriage. [3]So then, if she marries another man while her husband is still alive, she is called an adulteress. But if her husband dies, she is released from that law and is not an adulteress, even though she marries another man.

[4]So, my brothers, you also died to the law through the body of Christ, that you might belong to another, to

[a]23 Or through

171

him who was raised from the dead, in order that we might bear fruit to God. [5]For when we were controlled by the sinful nature,[a] the sinful passions aroused by the law were at work in our bodies, so that we bore fruit for death. [6]But now, by dying to what once bound us, we have been released from the law so that we serve in the new way of the Spirit, and not in the old way of the written code.

Struggling With Sin

[7]What shall we say, then? Is the law sin? Certainly not! Indeed I would not have known what sin was except through the law. For I would not have known what it was to covet if the law had not said, "Do not covet."[b] [8]But sin, seizing the opportunity afforded by the commandment, produced in me every kind of covetous desire. For apart from law, sin is dead. [9]Once I was alive apart from law; but·when the commandment came, sin sprang to life and I died. [10]I found that the very commandment that was intended to bring life actually brought death. [11]For sin, seizing the opportunity afforded by the commandment, deceived me, and through the commandment put me to death. [12]So then, the law is holy, and the commandment is holy, righteous and good.

[13]Did that which is good, then, become death to me? By no·means! But in order that sin might be recognised as sin, it produced death in me through what was good, so that through the commandment sin might become utterly sinful.

[14]We know that the law is spiritual; but I am unspiritual, sold as a slave to sin. [15]I do not understand what I do. For what I want to do I do not do, but what I hate I do. [16]And if I do what I do not want to do, I agree that the law is good. [17]As it is, it is no longer I myself who do it, but it is sin

living in me. [18]I know that nothing good lives in me, that is, in my sinful nature.[c] For I have the desire to do what is good, but I cannot carry it out. [19]For what I do is not the good I want to do; no, the evil I do not want to do—this I keep on doing. [20]Now if I do what I do not want to do, it is no longer I who do it, but it is sin living in me that does it.

[21]So I find this law at work: When I want to do good, evil is right there with me. [22]For in my inner being I delight in God's law; [23]but I see another law at work in the members of my body, waging war against the law of my mind and making me a prisoner of the law of sin at work within my members. [24]What a wretched man I am! Who will rescue me from this body of death? [25]Thanks be to God—through Jesus Christ our Lord!

So then, I myself in my mind am a slave to God's law, but in the sinful nature a slave to the law of sin.

Life Through the Spirit

8 Therefore, there is now no condemnation for those who are in Christ Jesus,[a] [2]because through Christ Jesus the law of the Spirit of life set me free from the law of sin and death. [3]For what the law was powerless to do in that it was weakened by the sinful nature,[b] God did by sending his own Son in the likeness of sinful man to be a sin offering.[c] And so he condemned sin in sinful man, [4]in order that the righteous requirements of the law might be fully met in us, who do not live according to the sinful nature but according to the Spirit.

[5]Those who live according to the sinful nature have their minds set on what that nature desires; but those who live in accordance with the Spirit have their minds set on what the Spirit desires. [6]The mind of sinful

---

[a]5 Or *the flesh; also in verse 25*   [b]7 Exodus 20:17; Deut. 5:21   [c]18 Or *my flesh*

[a]1 Some later manuscripts *Jesus, who do not live according to the sinful nature but according to the Spirit.*

[b]3 Or *the flesh; also in verses 4, 5, 8, 9, 12 and 13*   [c]3 Or *man, for sin*

man is death, but the mind controlled by the Spirit is life and peace; 7the sinful mind is hostile to God; it does not submit to God's law, nor can it do so. 8Those controlled by the sinful nature cannot please God.

9You, however, are controlled not by the sinful nature but by the Spirit, if the Spirit of God lives in you. And if anyone does not have the Spirit of Christ, he does not belong to Christ. 10But if Christ is in you, your body is dead because of sin, yet your spirit is alive because of righteousness. 11And if the Spirit of him who raised Jesus from the dead is living in you, he who raised Christ from the dead will also give life to your mortal bodies through his Spirit, who lives in you.

12Therefore, brothers, we have an obligation—but it is not to the sinful nature, to live according to it. 13For if you live according to the sinful nature, you will die; but if by the Spirit you put to death the misdeeds of the body, you will live, 14because those who are led by the Spirit of God are sons of God. 15For you did not receive a spirit that makes you a slave again to fear, but you received the Spirit of sonship.d And by him we cry, "Abba,e Father." 16The Spirit himself testifies with our spirit that we are God's children. 17Now if we are children, then we are heirs—heirs of God and co-heirs with Christ, if indeed we share in his sufferings in order that we may also share in his glory.

Future Glory

18I consider that our present sufferings are not worth comparing with the glory that will be revealed in us. 19The creation waits in eager expectation for the sons of God to be revealed. 20For the creation was subjected to frustration, not by its own choice, but by the will of the one who subjected it, in hope 21that the creation itself will be liberated from its bondage to decay and brought into the glorious freedom of the children of God.

22We know that the whole creation has been groaning as in the pains of childbirth right up to the present time. 23Not only so, but we ourselves, who have the firstfruits of the Spirit, groan inwardly as we wait eagerly for our adoption as sons, the redemption of our bodies. 24For in this hope we were saved. But hope that is seen is no hope at all. Who hopes for what he already has? 25But if we hope for what we do not yet have, we wait for it patiently.

26In the same way, the Spirit helps us in our weakness. We do not know whatf we ought to pray, but the Spirit himself intercedes for us with groans that words cannot express. 27And he who searches our hearts knows the mind of the Spirit, because the Spirit intercedes for the saints in accordance with God's will.

More Than Conquerors

28And we know that in all things God works for the good of those who love him,g who have been called according to his purpose. 29For those God foreknew he also predestined to be conformed to the likeness of his Son, that he might be the firstborn among many brothers. 30And those he predestined, he also called; those he called, he also justified; those he justified, he also glorified.

31What, then, shall we say in response to this? If God is for us, who can be against us? 32He who did not spare his own Son, but gave him up for us all—how will he not also, along with him, graciously give us all things? 33Who will bring any charge against those whom God has chosen? It is God who justifies. 34Who is he that condemns? Christ Jesus, who died—more than that, who was raised to life—is at the right hand of God and is also interceding for us. 35Who shall separate us from the love of Christ? Shall trouble or hardship or

d15 Or adoption   e15 Aramaic for Father   f26 Or how
g28 Some manuscripts And we know that all things work together for good to those who love God

persecution or famine or nakedness or danger or sword? 36As it is written:

"For your sake we face death all day
    long;
we are considered as sheep to be
    slaughtered."h

37No, in all these things we are more than conquerors through him who loved us. 38For I am convinced that neither death nor life, neither angels nor demons,i neither the present nor the future, nor any powers, 39neither height nor depth, nor anything else in all creation, will be able to separate us from the love of God that is in Christ Jesus our Lord.

God's Sovereign Choice

9 I speak the truth in Christ—I am not lying, my conscience confirms it in the Holy Spirit—2I have great sorrow and unceasing anguish in my heart. 3For I could wish that I myself were cursed and cut off from Christ for the sake of my brothers, those of my own race, 4the people of Israel. Theirs is the adoption as sons; theirs the divine glory, the covenants, the receiving of the law, the temple worship and the promises. 5Theirs are the patriarchs, and from them is traced the human ancestry of Christ, who is God over all, for ever praised!a Amen.

6It is not as though God's word had failed. For not all who are descended from Israel are Israel. 7Nor because they are his descendants are they all Abraham's children. On the contrary, "It is through Isaac that your offspring will be reckoned."b 8In other words, it is not the natural children who are God's children, but it is the children of the promise who are regarded as Abraham's offspring. 9For this was how the promise was stated: "At the appointed time I will return, and Sarah will have a son."c

10Not only that, but Rebecca's children had one and the same father, our father Isaac. 11Yet, before the twins were born or had done anything good or bad—in order that God's purpose in election might stand: 12not by works but by him who calls—she was told, "The older will serve the younger."d 13Just as it is written: "Jacob I loved, but Esau I hated."e

14What then shall we say? Is God unjust? Not at all! 15For he says to Moses,

"I will have mercy on whom I have
    mercy,
and I will have compassion on
    whom I have compassion."f

16It does not, therefore, depend on man's desire or effort, but on God's mercy. 17For the Scripture says to Pharaoh: "I raised you up for this very purpose, that I might display my power in you and that my name might be proclaimed in all the earth."g 18Therefore God has mercy on whom he wants to have mercy, and he hardens whom he wants to harden.

19One of you will say to me: "Then why does God still blame us? For who resists his will?" 20But who are you, O man, to talk back to God? "Shall what is formed say to him who formed it, 'Why did you make me like this?' "h 21Does not the potter have the right to make out of the same lump of clay some pottery for noble purposes and some for common use?

22What if God, choosing to show his wrath and make his power known, bore with great patience the objects of his wrath—prepared for destruction? 23What if he did this to make the riches of his glory known to the objects of his mercy, whom he prepared in advance for glory —24even us, whom he also called, not only from the Jews but also from the Gentiles? 25As he says in Hosea:

"I will call them 'my people' who
    are not my people;
and I will call her 'my loved one'
    who is not my loved one,"i

---

h36 Psalm 44:22   i38 Or not heavenly rulers
a5 Or Christ, who is over all. God be for ever praised! Or Christ. God who is over all be for ever praised!
b7 Gen. 21:12   c9 Gen. 18:10,14   d12 Gen. 25:23   e13 Mal. 1:2,3
f15 Exodus 33:19   g17 Exodus 9:16   h20 Isaiah 29:16; 45:9   i25 Hosea 2:23

26and,

"It will happen that in the very
place where it was said to them,
'You are not my people,'
they will be called 'sons of the
living God'."*i*

27Isaiah cries out concerning
Israel:

"Though the number of the
Israelites be like the sand by the
sea,
only the remnant will be saved.
28For the Lord will carry out
his sentence on earth with speed
and finality."*k*

29It is just as Isaiah said
previously:

"Unless the Lord Almighty
had left us descendants,
we would have become like Sodom,
and we would have been like
Gomorrah."*l*

Israel's Unbelief

30What then shall we say? That the
Gentiles, who did not pursue righteousness, have obtained it, a righteousness that is by faith; 31but Israel,
who pursued a law of righteousness,
has not attained it. 32Why not?
Because they pursued it not by faith
but as if it were by works. They
stumbled over the "stumbling-stone".
33As it is written:

"See, I lay in Zion a stone that
causes men to stumble
and a rock that makes them fall,
and the one who trusts in him will
never be put to shame."*m*

10 Brothers, my heart's desire
and prayer to God for the
Israelites is that they may be saved.
2For I can testify about them that they
are zealous for God, but their zeal is
not based on knowledge. 3Since they
did not know the righteousness that
comes from God and sought to establish their own, they did not submit to
God's righteousness. 4Christ is the
end of the law so that there may be
righteousness for everyone who
believes.

5Moses describes in this way the
righteousness that is by the law: "The
man who does these things will live
by them."*a* 6But the righteousness that
is by faith says: "Do not say in your
heart, 'Who will ascend into
heaven?'*b* (that is, to bring Christ
down) 7or 'Who will descend into
the deep?'*c* (that is, to bring Christ
up from the dead). 8But what does it
say? "The word is near you; it is in
your mouth and in your heart,"*d* that
is, the word of faith we are proclaiming; 9That if you confess with your
mouth, "Jesus is Lord," and believe
in your heart that God raised him
from the dead, you will be saved.
10For it is with your heart that you
believe and are justified, and it is
with your mouth that you confess and
are saved. 11As the Scripture says,
"Everyone who trusts in him will
never be put to shame."*e* 12For there
is no difference between Jew and
Gentile—the same Lord is Lord of all
and richly blesses all who call on
him, 13for, "Everyone who calls on
the name of the Lord will be saved."*f*

14How, then, can they call on the
one they have not believed in? And
how can they believe in the one of
whom they have not heard? And how
can they hear without someone
preaching to them? 15And how can
they preach unless they are sent? As
it is written, "How beautiful are the
feet of those who bring good news!"*g*

16But not all the Israelites accepted
the good news. For Isaiah says, "Lord,
who has believed our message?"*h*
17Consequently, faith comes from
hearing the message, and the message
is heard through the word of Christ.
18But I ask, Did they not hear? Of
course they did:

"Their voice has gone out into all
the earth,

---

*i*26 Hosea 1:10   *k*28 Isaiah 10:22,23   *l*29 Isaiah 1:9   *m*33 Isaiah 8:14; 28:16
*a*5 Lev. 18:5   *b*6 Deut. 30:12   *c*7 Deut. 30:13   *d*8 Deut. 30:14
*e*11 Isaiah 28:16   *f*13 Joel 2:32   *g*15 Isaiah 52:7   *h*16 Isaiah 53:1

their words to the ends of the world.''[i]

[19]Again I ask, did Israel not understand? First, Moses says,

"I will make you envious by those
    who are not a nation;
I will make you angry by a
    nation that has no
    understanding.''[j]

[20]And Isaiah boldly says,

"I was found by those who did not
    seek me;
I revealed myself to those who
    did not ask for me.''[k]

[21]But concerning Israel he says,

"All day long I have held out my
    hands
to a disobedient and obstinate
    people.''[l]

The Remnant of Israel

11 I ask then, Did God reject his
    people? By no means! I am an
Israelite myself, a descendant of
Abraham, from the tribe of Benjamin.
[2]God did not reject his people, whom
he foreknew. Don't you know what
the Scripture says in the passage
about Elijah—how he appealed to
God against Israel: [3]"Lord, they have
killed your prophets and torn down
your altars; I am the only one left,
and they are trying to kill me''[a]? [4]And
what was God's answer to him? "I
have reserved for myself seven thousand who have not bowed the knee
to Baal.''[b] [5]So too, at the present time
there is a remnant chosen by grace.
[6]And if by grace, then it is no longer
by works; if it were, grace would no
longer be grace.[c]

[7]What then? What Israel sought so
earnestly it did not obtain, but the
elect did. The others were hardened,
[8]as it is written:

"God gave them a spirit of stupor,
    eyes so that they could not see

and ears so that they could not
    hear,
to this very day.''[d]

[9]And David says:

"May their table become a snare
    and a trap,
a stumbling block and a
    retribution for them.
[10]May their eyes be darkened so
    they cannot see,
and their backs be bent for ever.''[e]

Ingrafted Branches

[11]Again I ask, Did they stumble so
as to fall beyond recovery? Not at all!
Rather, because of their transgression, salvation has come to the Gentiles to make Israel envious. [12]But if
their transgression means riches for
the world, and their loss means riches
for the Gentiles, how much greater
riches will their fulness bring!

[13]I am talking to you Gentiles. Inas-
much as I am the apostle to the
Gentiles, I make much of my ministry
[14]in the hope that I may somehow
arouse my own people to envy and
save some of them. [15]For if their
rejection is the reconciliation of the
world, what will their acceptance be
but life from the dead? [16]If the part
of the dough offered as firstfruits is
holy, then the whole batch is holy; if
the root is holy, so are the branches.

[17]If some of the branches have
been broken off, and you, though a
wild olive shoot, have been grafted in
among the others and now share in
the nourishing sap from the olive
root, [18]do not boast over those
branches. If you do, consider this:
You do not support the root, but the
root supports you. [19]You will say then,
"Branches were broken off so that I
could be grafted in." [20]Granted. But
they were broken off because of
unbelief, and you stand by faith. Do
not be arrogant, but be afraid. [21]For
if God did not spare the natural

---

[i]18 Psalm 19:4   [i]19 Deut. 32:21   [k]20 Isaiah 65:1   [l]21 Isaiah 65:2
[a]3 1 Kings 19:10,14   [b]4 1 Kings 19:18
[c]6 Some manuscripts by grace. But if by works, then it is no longer grace; if it were, work
would no longer be work.
[d]8 Deut. 29:4; Isaiah 29:10   [e]10 Psalm 69:22,23

branches, he will not spare you either.

22Consider therefore the kindness and sternness of God: sternness to those who fell, but kindness to you, provided that you continue in his kindness. Otherwise, you also will be cut off. 23And if they do not persist in unbelief, they will be grafted in, for God is able to graft them in again. 24After all, if you were cut out of an olive tree that is wild by nature, and contrary to nature were grafted into a cultivated olive tree, how much more readily will these, the natural branches, be grafted into their own olive tree!

All Israel Will Be Saved

25I do not want you to be ignorant of this mystery, brothers, so that you may not be conceited: Israel has experienced a hardening in part until the full number of the Gentiles has come in. 26And so all Israel will be saved, as it is written:

"The deliverer will come from
    Zion;
  he will turn godlessness away
    from Jacob.
27And this isf my covenant with them
  when I take away their sins."g

28As far as the gospel is concerned, they are enemies on your account; but as far as election is concerned, they are loved on account of the patriarchs, 29for God's gifts and his call are irrevocable. 30Just as you who were at one time disobedient to God have now received mercy as a result of their disobedience, 31so they too have now become disobedient in order that they too may nowh receive mercy as a result of God's mercy to you. 32For God has bound all men over to disobedience so that he may have mercy on them all.

Doxology

33Oh, the depth of the riches of the wisdom andi knowledge of God! How unsearchable his judgments,

and his paths beyond tracing out!
34"Who has known the mind of the
    Lord?
  Or who has been his
    counsellor?"j
35"Who has ever given to God,
    that God should repay him?"k
36For from him and through him and
    to him are all things.
  To him be the glory for ever!
    Amen.

Living Sacrifices

12 Therefore, I urge you, brothers, in view of God's mercy, to offer your bodies as living sacrifices, holy and pleasing to God—which is your spiritual worship. 2Do not conform any longer to the pattern of this world, but be transformed by the renewing of your mind. Then you will be able to test and approve what God's will is—his good, pleasing and perfect will.

3For by the grace given me I say to every one of you: Do not think of yourself more highly than you ought, but rather think of yourself with sober judgment, in accordance with the measure of faith God has given you. 4Just as each of us has one body with many members, and these members do not all have the same function, 5so in Christ we who are many form one body, and each member belongs to all the others. 6We have different gifts, according to the grace given us. If a man's gift is prophesying, let him use it in proportion to his faith. 7If it is serving, let him serve; if it is teaching, let him teach; 8if it is encouraging, let him encourage; if it is contributing to the needs of others, let him give generously; if it is leadership, let him govern diligently; if it is showing mercy, let him do it cheerfully.

Love

9Love must be sincere. Hate what is evil; cling to what is good. 10Be devoted to one another in brotherly

---

f27 Or will be   g27 Isaiah 59:20,21; 27:9
i33 Or riches and the wisdom and the   h31 Some manuscripts do not have now.
j34 Isaiah 40:13   k35 Job 41:11

love. Honour one another above yourselves. 11Never be lacking in zeal, but keep your spiritual fervour, serving the Lord. 12Be joyful in hope, patient in affliction, faithful in prayer. 13Share with God's people who are in need. Practise hospitality.

14Bless those who persecute you; bless and do not curse. 15Rejoice with those who rejoice; mourn with those who mourn. 16Live in harmony with one another. Do not be proud, but be willing to associate with people of low position.*a* Do not be conceited.

17Do not repay anyone evil for evil. Be careful to do what is right in the eyes of everybody. 18If it is possible, as far as it depends on you, live at peace with everyone. 19Do not take revenge, my friends, but leave room for God's wrath, for it is written: "It is mine to avenge; I will repay,"*b* says the Lord. 20On the contrary:

"If your enemy is hungry, feed
    him;
  if he is thirsty, give him
    something to drink.
In doing this, you will heap
    burning coals on his head."*c*

21Do not be overcome by evil, but overcome evil with good.

Submission to the Authorities

13 Everyone must submit himself to the governing authorities, for there is no authority except that which God has established. The authorities that exist have been established by God. 2Consequently, he who rebels against the authority is rebelling against what God has instituted, and those who do so will bring judgment on themselves. 3For rulers hold no terror for those who do right, but for those who do wrong. Do you want to be free from fear of the one in authority? Then do what is right and he will commend you. 4For he is God's servant to do you good. But if you do wrong, be afraid, for he does not bear the sword for nothing. He is God's servant, an agent of wrath to bring punishment on the wrongdoer.

5Therefore, it is necessary to submit to the authorities, not only because of possible punishment but also because of conscience.

6This is also why you pay taxes, for the authorities are God's servants, who give their full time to governing. 7Give everyone what you owe him: If you owe taxes, pay taxes; if revenue, then revenue; if respect, then respect; if honour, then honour.

Love, for the Day Is Near

8Let no debt remain outstanding, except the continuing debt to love one another, for he who loves his fellow-man has fulfilled the law. 9The commandments, "Do not commit adultery," "Do not murder," "Do not steal," "Do not covet,"*a* and whatever other commandment there may be, are summed up in this one rule: "Love your neighbour as yourself."*b* 10Love does no harm to its neighbour. Therefore love is the fulfilment of the law.

11And do this, understanding the present time. The hour has come for you to wake up from your slumber, because our salvation is nearer now than when we first believed. 12The night is nearly over; the day is almost here. So let us put aside the deeds of darkness and put on the armour of light. 13Let us behave decently, as in the daytime, not in orgies and drunkenness, not in sexual immorality and debauchery, not in dissension and jealousy. 14Rather, clothe yourselves with the Lord Jesus Christ, and do not think about how to gratify the desires of the sinful nature.*c*

The Weak and the Strong

14 Accept him whose faith is weak, without passing judgment on disputable matters. 2One man's faith allows him to eat everything, but another man, whose faith is weak, eats only vegetables. 3The man who eats everything must not look down on him who does not, and the man who does not eat everything must not condemn the man who does,

---

*a*16 Or *willing to do menial work*   *b*19 Deut. 32:35   *c*20 Prov. 25:21,22
*a*9 Exodus 20:13–15,17; Deut. 5:17–19,21   *b*9 Lev. 19:18   *c*14 Or *the flesh*

for God has accepted him. 4Who are you to judge someone else's servant? To his own master he stands or falls. And he will stand, for the Lord is able to make him stand.

5One man considers one day more sacred than another; another man considers every day alike. Each one should be fully convinced in his own mind. 6He who regards one day as special, does so to the Lord. He who eats meat, eats to the Lord, for he gives thanks to God; and he who abstains, does so to the Lord and gives thanks to God. 7For none of us lives to himself alone and none of us dies to himself alone. 8If we live, we live to the Lord; and if we die, we die to the Lord. So, whether we live or die, we belong to the Lord.

9For this very reason, Christ died and returned to life so that he might be the Lord of both the dead and the living. 10You, then, why do you judge your brother? Or why do you look down on your brother? For we will all stand before God's judgment seat. 11It is written:

" 'As surely as I live,' says the Lord,
'Every knee will bow before me;
    every tongue will confess to
        God.' "a

12So then, each of us will give an account of himself to God.

13Therefore let us stop passing judgment on one another. Instead, make up your mind not to put any stumbling-block or obstacle in your brother's way. 14As one who is in the Lord Jesus, I am fully convinced that no food is unclean in itself. But if anyone regards something as unclean, then for him it is unclean. 15If your brother is distressed because of what you eat, you are no longer acting in love. Do not by your eating destroy your brother for whom Christ died. 16Do not allow what you consider good to be spoken of as evil. 17For the kingdom of God is not a matter of eating and drinking, but of righteousness, peace and joy in the

Holy Spirit, 18because anyone who serves Christ in this way is pleasing to God and approved by men.

19Let us therefore make every effort to do what leads to peace and to mutual edification. 20Do not destroy the work of God for the sake of food. All food is clean, but it is wrong for a man to eat anything that causes someone else to stumble. 21It is better not to eat meat or drink wine or to do anything else that will cause your brother to fall.

22So whatever you believe about these things keep between yourself and God. Blessed is the man who does not condemn himself by what he approves. 23But the man who has doubts is condemned if he eats, because his eating is not from faith; and everything that does not come from faith is sin.

15 We who are strong ought to bear with the failings of the weak and not to please ourselves. 2Each of us should please his neighbour for his good, to build him up. 3For even Christ did not please himself but, as it is written: "The insults of those who insult you have fallen on me."a 4For everything that was written in the past was written to teach us, so that through endurance and the encouragement of the Scriptures we might have hope.

5May the God who gives endurance and encouragement give you a spirit of unity among yourselves as you follow Christ Jesus, 6so that with one heart and mouth you may glorify the God and Father of our Lord Jesus Christ.

7Accept one another, then, just as Christ accepted you, in order to bring praise to God. 8For I tell you that Christ has become a servant of the Jewsb on behalf of God's truth, to confirm the promises made to the patriarchs 9so that the Gentiles may glorify God for his mercy, as it is written:

"Therefore I will praise you among
    the Gentiles;

---

a11 Isaiah 49:18; 45:23   a3 Psalm 69:9   b8 Greek circumcision

I will sing hymns to your name."*c*

[10]Again, it says,

"Rejoice, O Gentiles, with his
people."*d*

[11]And again,

"Praise the Lord, all you Gentiles,
and sing praises to him, all you
peoples."*e*

[12]And again, Isaiah says,

"The root of Jesse will spring up,
one who will arise to rule over
the nations;
the Gentiles will hope in him."*f*

[13]May the God of hope fill you with
all joy and peace as you trust in him,
so that you may overflow with hope
by the power of the Holy Spirit.

Paul the Minister to the Gentiles

[14]I myself am convinced, my
brothers, that you yourselves are full
of goodness, complete in knowledge
and competent to instruct one
another. [15]I have written to you quite
boldly on some points, as if to remind
you of them again, because of the
grace God gave me [16]to be a minister
of Christ Jesus to the Gentiles with
the priestly duty of proclaiming the
gospel of God, so that the Gentiles
might become an offering acceptable
to God, sanctified by the Holy Spirit.

[17]Therefore I glory in Christ Jesus
in my service to God. [18]I will not
venture to speak of anything except
what Christ has accomplished
through me in leading the Gentiles to
obey God by what I have said and
done—[19]by the power of signs and
miracles, through the power of the
Spirit. So from Jerusalem all the way
around to Illyricum, I have fully proclaimed the gospel of Christ. [20]It has
always been my ambition to preach
the gospel where Christ was not
known, so that I would not be building on someone else's foundation.
[21]Rather, as it is written:

"Those who were not told about
him will see,

and those who have not heard
will understand."*g*

[22]This is why I have often been
hindered from coming to you.

Paul's Plan to Visit Rome

[23]But now that there is no more
place for me to work in these regions,
and since I have been longing for
many years to see you, [24]I plan to do
so when I go to Spain. I hope to visit
you while passing through and to
have you assist me on my journey
there, after I have enjoyed your company for a while. [25]Now, however, I
am on my way to Jerusalem in the
service of the saints there. [26]For
Macedonia and Achaia were pleased
to make a contribution for the poor
among the saints in Jerusalem. [27]They
were pleased to do it, and indeed
they owe it to them. For if the Gentiles have shared in the Jews' spiritual
blessings, they owe it to the Jews to
share with them their material blessings. [28]So after I have completed this
task and have made sure that they
have received this fruit, I will go to
Spain and visit you on the way. [29]I
know that when I come to you, I will
come in the full measure of the blessing of Christ.

[30]I urge you, brothers, by our Lord
Jesus Christ and by the love of the
Spirit, to join me in my struggle by
praying to God for me. [31]Pray that I
may be rescued from the unbelievers
in Judea and that my service in Jerusalem may be acceptable to the saints
there, [32]so that by God's will I may
come to you with joy and together
with you be refreshed. [33]The God of
peace be with you all. Amen.

Personal Greetings

16 I commend to you our sister
Phoebe, a servant*a* of the
church in Cenchrea. [2]I ask you to
receive her in the Lord in a way
worthy of the saints and to give her
any help she may need from you, for
she has been a great help to many
people, including me.

c9 2 Samuel 22:50; Psalm 18:49   *d10* Deut. 32:43   *e11* Psalm 117:1
f12 Isaiah 11:10   *g21* Isaiah 52:15   *a1* Or *deaconess*

³Greet Priscilla[b] and Aquila, my fellow-workers in Christ Jesus. ⁴They risked their lives for me. Not only I but all the churches of the Gentiles are grateful to them.

⁵Greet also the church that meets at their house.

Greet my dear friend Epenetus, who was the first convert to Christ in the province of Asia. ⁶Greet Mary, who worked very hard for you. ⁷Greet Andronicus and Junias, my relatives who have been in prison with me. They are outstanding among the apostles, and they were in Christ before I was.

⁸Greet Ampliatus, whom I love in the Lord. ⁹Greet Urbanus, our fellow-worker in Christ, and my dear friend Stachys. ¹⁰Greet Apelles, tested and approved in Christ.

Greet those who belong to the household of Aristobulus. ¹¹Greet Herodion, my relative.

Greet those in the household of Narcissus who are in the Lord. ¹²Greet Tryphena and Tryphosa, those women who work hard in the Lord.

Greet my dear friend Persis, another woman who has worked very hard in the Lord. ¹³Greet Rufus, chosen in the Lord, and his mother, who has been a mother to me, too. ¹⁴Greet Asyncritus, Phlegon, Hermes, Patrobas, Hermas and the brothers with them. ¹⁵Greet Philologus, Julia, Nereus and his sister, and Olympas and all the saints with them.

¹⁶Greet one another with a holy kiss.

All the churches of Christ send greetings.

¹⁷I urge you, brothers, to watch out for those who cause divisions and put obstacles in your way that are contrary to the teaching you have learned. Keep away from them. ¹⁸For such people are not serving our Lord Christ, but their own appetites. By smooth talk and flattery they deceive the minds of naïve people. ¹⁹Everyone has heard about your obedience, so I am full of joy over you; but I want you to be wise about what is good, and innocent about what is evil.

²⁰The God of peace will soon crush Satan under your feet.

The grace of our Lord Jesus be with you.

²¹Timothy, my fellow-worker, sends his greetings to you, as do Lucius, Jason and Sosipater, my relatives.

²²I, Tertius, who wrote down this letter, greet you in the Lord.

²³Gaius, whose hospitality I and the whole church here enjoy, sends you his greetings.

Erastus, who is the city's director of public works, and our brother Quartus send you their greetings.[c]

²⁵Now to him who is able to establish you by my gospel and the proclamation of Jesus Christ, according to the revelation of the mystery hidden for long ages past, ²⁶but now revealed and made known through the prophetic writings by the command of the eternal God, so that all nations might believe and obey him—²⁷to the only wise God be glory for ever through Jesus Christ! Amen.

b3 Greek Prisca, a variant of Priscilla
c23 Some manuscripts their greetings. ²⁴May the grace of our Lord Jesus Christ be with all of you. Amen.

1 Corinthians

1 Paul, called to be an apostle of Christ Jesus by the will of God, and our brother Sosthenes,

2To the church of God in Corinth, to those sanctified in Christ Jesus and called to be holy, together with all those everywhere who call on the name of our Lord Jesus Christ—their Lord and ours:

3Grace and peace to you from God our Father and the Lord Jesus Christ.

Thanksgiving

4I always thank God for you because of his grace given you in Christ Jesus. 5For in him you have been enriched in every way—in all your speaking and in all your knowledge—6because our testimony about Christ was confirmed in you. 7Therefore you do not lack any spiritual gift as you eagerly wait for our Lord Jesus Christ to be revealed. 8He will keep you strong to the end, so that you will be blameless on the day of our Lord Jesus Christ. 9God, who has called you into fellowship with his Son Jesus Christ our Lord, is faithful.

Divisions in the Church

10I appeal to you, brothers, in the name of our Lord Jesus Christ, that all of you agree with one another so that there may be no divisions among you and that you may be perfectly united in mind and thought. 11My brothers, some from Chloe's household have informed me that there are quarrels among you. 12What I mean is this: One of you says, "I follow Paul"; another, "I follow Apollos";

another, "I follow Cephas";a still another, "I follow Christ."

13Is Christ divided? Was Paul crucified for you? Were you baptised intob the name of Paul? 14I am thankful that I did not baptise any of you except Crispus and Gaius, 15so no-one can say that you were baptised into my name. (16Yes, I also baptised the household of Stephanas; beyond that, I don't remember if I baptised anyone else.) 17For Christ did not send me to baptise, but to preach the gospel—not with words of human wisdom, lest the cross of Christ be emptied of its power.

Christ the Wisdom and Power of God

18For the message of the cross is foolishness to those who are perishing, but to us who are being saved it is the power of God. 19For it is written:

"I will destroy the wisdom of the wise;
the intelligence of the intelligent I will frustrate."c

20Where is the wise man? Where is the scholar? Where is the philosopher of this age? Has not God made foolish the wisdom of the world? 21For since in the wisdom of God the world through its wisdom did not know him, God was pleased through the foolishness of what was preached to save those who believe. 22Jews demand miraculous signs and Greeks look for wisdom, 23but we preach Christ crucified: a stumbling block to Jews and

---

a12 That is, Peter   b13 Or in; also in verse 15   c19 Isaiah 29:14

foolishness to Gentiles, 24but to those whom God has called, both Jews and Greeks, Christ the power of God and the wisdom of God. 25For the foolishness of God is wiser than man's wisdom, and the weakness of God is stronger than man's strength.

26Brothers, think of what you were when you were called. Not many of you were wise by human standards; not many were influential; not many were of noble birth. 27But God chose the foolish things of the world to shame the wise; God chose the weak things of the world to shame the strong. 28He chose the lowly things of this world and the despised things—and the things that are not—to nullify the things that are, 29so that no-one may boast before him. 30It is because of him that you are in Christ Jesus, who has become for us wisdom from God—that is, our righteousness, holiness and redemption. 31Therefore, as it is written: "Let him who boasts boast in the Lord."d

2 When I came to you, brothers, I did not come with eloquence or superior wisdom as I proclaimed to you the testimony about God.a 2For I resolved to know nothing while I was with you except Jesus Christ and him crucified. 3I came to you in weakness and fear, and with much trembling. 4My message and my preaching were not with wise and persuasive words, but with a demonstration of the Spirit's power, 5so that your faith might not rest on men's wisdom, but on God's power.

Wisdom From the Spirit

6We do, however, speak a message of wisdom among the mature, but not the wisdom of this age or of the rulers of this age, who are coming to nothing. 7No, we speak of God's secret wisdom, a wisdom that has been hidden and that God destined for our glory before time began. 8None of the rulers of this age understood it, for if they had, they would not have crucified the Lord of glory. 9However, as it is written:

"No eye has seen,
    no ear has heard,
no mind has conceived
    what God has prepared for
        those who love him"b—

10but God has revealed it to us by his Spirit.

The Spirit searches all things, even the deep things of God. 11For who among men knows the thoughts of a man except the man's spirit within him? In the same way no-one knows the thoughts of God except the Spirit of God. 12We have not received the spirit of the world but the Spirit who is from God, that we may understand what God has freely given us. 13This is what we speak, not in words taught us by human wisdom but in words taught by the Spirit, expressing spiritual truths in spiritual words.c 14The man without the Spirit does not accept the things that come from the Spirit of God, for they are foolishness to him, and he cannot understand them, because they are spiritually discerned. 15The spiritual man makes judgments about all things, but he himself is not subject to any man's judgment:

16"For who has known the mind of
    the Lord
    that he may instruct him?"d

But we have the mind of Christ.

On Divisions in the Church

3 Brothers, I could not address you as spiritual but as worldly—mere infants in Christ. 2I gave you milk, not solid food, for you were not yet ready for it. Indeed, you are still not ready. 3You are still worldly. For since there is jealousy and quarrelling among you, are you not worldly? Are you not acting like mere men? 4For when one says, "I follow Paul," and another, "I follow Apollos," are you not mere men?

5What, after all, is Apollos? And what is Paul? Only servants, through whom you came to believe—as the Lord has assigned to each his task. 6I

---

d31 Jer. 9:24   a1 Some manuscripts as I proclaimed to you God's mystery
b 9 Isaiah 64:4
c13 Or Spirit, interpreting spiritual truths to spiritual men   d16 Isaiah 40:13

183

planted the seed, Apollos watered it, but God made it grow. [7]So neither he who plants nor he who waters is anything, but only God, who makes things grow. [8]The man who plants and the man who waters have one purpose, and each will be rewarded according to his own labour. [9]For we are God's fellow-workers; you are God's field, God's building.

[10]By the grace God has given me, I laid a foundation as an expert builder, and someone else is building on it. But each one should be careful how he builds. [11]For no-one can lay any foundation other than the one already laid, which is Jesus Christ. [12]If any man builds on this foundation using gold, silver, costly stones, wood, hay or straw, [13]his work will be shown for what it is, because the Day will bring it to light. It will be revealed with fire, and the fire will test the quality of each man's work. [14]If what he has built survives, he will receive his reward. [15]If it is burned up, he will suffer loss; he himself will be saved, but only as one escaping through the flames.

[16]Don't you know that you yourselves are God's temple and that God's Spirit lives in you? [17]If anyone destroys God's temple, God will destroy him; for God's temple is sacred, and you are that temple.

[18]Do not deceive yourselves. If any one of you thinks he is wise by the standards of this age, he should become a "fool" so that he may become wise. [19]For the wisdom of this world is foolishness in God's sight. As it is written: "He catches the wise in their craftiness";[a] [20]and again, "The Lord knows that the thoughts of the wise are futile."[b] [21]So then, no more boasting about men! All things are yours, [22]whether Paul or Apollos or Cephas[c] or the world or life or death or the present or the future—all are yours, [23]and you are of Christ, and Christ is of God.

Apostles of Christ

4 So then, men ought to regard us as servants of Christ and as those entrusted with the secret things of God. [2]Now it is required that those who have been given a trust must prove faithful. [3]I care very little if I am judged by you or by any human court; indeed, I do not even judge myself. [4]My conscience is clear, but that does not make me innocent. It is the Lord who judges me. [5]Therefore judge nothing before the appointed time; wait till the Lord comes. He will bring to light what is hidden in darkness and will expose the motives of men's hearts. At that time each will receive his praise from God.

[6]Now, brothers, I have applied these things to myself and Apollos for your benefit, so that you may learn from us the meaning of the saying, "Do not go beyond what is written." Then you will not take pride in one man over against another. [7]For who makes you different from anyone else? What do you have that you did not receive? And if you did receive it, why do you boast as though you did not?

[8]Already you have all you want! Already you have become rich! You have become kings—and that without us! How I wish that you really had become kings so that we might be kings with you! [9]For it seems to me that God has put us apostles on display at the end of the procession, like men condemned to die in the arena. We have been made a spectacle to the whole universe, to angels as well as to men. [10]We are fools for Christ, but you are so wise in Christ! We are weak, but you are strong! You are honoured, we are dishonoured! [11]To this very hour we go hungry and thirsty, we are in rags, we are brutally treated, we are homeless. [12]We work hard with our own hands. When we are cursed, we bless; when we are persecuted, we endure it; [13]when we are slandered, we answer kindly. Up to this moment we have become the scum of the earth, the refuse of the world.

[14]I am not writing this to shame you, but to warn you, as my dear children. [15]Even though you have ten

[a]19 Job 5:13   [b]20 Psalm 94:11   [c]22 That is, Peter

184

thousand guardians in Christ, you do not have many fathers, for in Christ Jesus I became your father through the gospel. [16]Therefore I urge you to imitate me. [17]For this reason I am sending to you Timothy, my son whom I love, who is faithful in the Lord. He will remind you of my way of life in Christ Jesus, which agrees with what I teach everywhere in every church.

[18]Some of you have become arrogant, as if I were not coming to you. [19]But I will come to you very soon, if the Lord is willing, and then I will find out not only how these arrogant people are talking, but what power they have. [20]For the kingdom of God is not a matter of talk but of power. [21]What do you prefer? Shall I come to you with a whip, or in love and with a gentle spirit?

Expel the Immoral Brother!

5 It is actually reported that there is sexual immorality among you, and of a kind that does not occur even among pagans: A man has his father's wife. [2]And you are proud! Shouldn't you rather have been filled with grief and have put out of your fellowship the man who did this? [3]Even though I am not physically present, I am with you in spirit. And I have already passed judgment on the one who did this, just as if I were present. [4]When you are assembled in the name of our Lord Jesus and I am with you in spirit, and the power of our Lord Jesus is present, [5]hand this man over to Satan, so that the sinful nature[a] may be destroyed and his spirit saved on the day of the Lord.

[6]Your boasting is not good. Don't you know that a little yeast works through the whole batch of dough? [7]Get rid of the old yeast that you may be a new batch without yeast—as you really are. For Christ, our Passover lamb, has been sacrificed. [8]Therefore let us keep the Festival, not with the old yeast, the yeast of malice and wickedness, but with bread without yeast, the bread of sincerity and truth.

[9]I have written to you in my letter not to associate with sexually immoral people—[10]not at all meaning the people of this world who are immoral, or the greedy and swindlers, or idolaters. In that case you would have to leave this world. [11]But now I am writing to you that you must not associate with anyone who calls himself a brother but is sexually immoral or greedy, an idolater or a slanderer, a drunkard or a swindler. With such a man do not even eat.

[12]What business is it of mine to judge those outside the church? Are you not to judge those inside? [13]God will judge those outside. "Expel the wicked man from among you."[b]

Lawsuits Among Believers

6 If any of you has a dispute with another, dare he take it before the ungodly for judgment instead of before the saints? [2]Do you not know that the saints will judge the world? And if you are to judge the world, are you not competent to judge trivial cases? [3]Do you not know that we will judge angels? How much more the things of this life! [4]Therefore, if you have disputes about such matters, appoint as judges even men of little account in the church![c] [5]I say this to shame you. Is it possible that there is nobody among you wise enough to judge a dispute between believers? [6]But instead, one brother goes to law against another—and this in front of unbelievers!

[7]The very fact that you have lawsuits among you means you have been completely defeated already. Why not rather be wronged? Why not rather be cheated? [8]Instead, you yourselves cheat and do wrong, and you do this to your brothers.

[9]Do you not know that the wicked will not inherit the kingdom of God? Do not be deceived: Neither the sexually immoral nor idolaters nor adulterers nor male prostitutes nor homosexual offenders [10]nor thieves nor the greedy nor drunkards nor slanderers nor swindlers will inherit

[a]5 Or that his body; or that the flesh [b]13 Deut. 17:7; 19:19; 22:21,24; 24:7
[c]4 Or matters, do you appoint as judges men of little account in the church?

the kingdom of God. 11And that is what some of you were. But you were washed, you were sanctified, you were justified in the name of the Lord Jesus Christ and by the Spirit of our God.

Sexual Immorality

12"Everything is permissible for me"—but not everything is beneficial. "Everything is permissible for me"—but I will not be mastered by anything. 13"Food for the stomach and the stomach for food"—but God will destroy them both. The body is not meant for sexual immorality, but for the Lord, and the Lord for the body. 14By his power God raised the Lord from the dead, and he will raise us also. 15Do you not know that your bodies are members of Christ himself? Shall I then take the members of Christ and unite them with a prostitute? Never! 16Do you not know that he who unites himself with a prostitute is one with her in body? For it is said, "The two will become one flesh."b 17But he who unites himself with the Lord is one with him in spirit.

18Flee from sexual immorality. All other sins a man commits are outside his body, but he who sins sexually sins against his own body. 19Do you not know that your body is a temple of the Holy Spirit, who is in you, whom you have received from God? You are not your own; 20you were bought at a price. Therefore honour God with your body.

Marriage

7 Now for the matters you wrote about: It is good for a man not to marry. 2But since there is so much immorality, each man should have his own wife, and each woman her own husband. 3The husband should fulfil his marital duty to his wife, and likewise the wife to her husband. 4The wife's body does not belong to her alone but also to her husband. In the same way, the husband's body does not belong to him alone but also to his wife. 5Do not deprive each

b16 Gen. 2:24

other except by mutual consent and for a time, so that you may devote yourselves to prayer. Then come together again so that Satan will not tempt you because of your lack of self-control. 6I say this as a concession, not as a command. 7I wish that all men were as I am. But each man has his own gift from God; one has this gift, another has that.

8Now to the unmarried and the widows I say: It is good for them to stay unmarried, as I am. 9But if they cannot control themselves, they should marry, for it is better to marry than to burn with passion.

10To the married I give this command (not I, but the Lord): A wife must not separate from her husband. 11But if she does, she must remain unmarried or else be reconciled to her husband. And a husband must not divorce his wife.

12To the rest I say this (I, not the Lord): If any brother has a wife who is not a believer and she is willing to live with him, he must not divorce her. 13And if a woman has a husband who is not a believer and he is willing to live with her, she must not divorce him. 14For the unbelieving husband has been sanctified through his wife, and the unbelieving wife has been sanctified through her believing husband. Otherwise your children would be unclean, but as it is, they are holy.

15But if the unbeliever leaves, let him do so. A believing man or woman is not bound in such circumstances; God has called us to live in peace. 16How do you know, wife, whether you will save your husband? Or, how do you know, husband, whether you will save your wife?

17Nevertheless, each one should retain the place in life that the Lord assigned to him and to which God has called him. This is the rule I lay down in all the churches. 18Was a man already circumcised when he was called? He should not become uncircumcised. Was a man uncircumcised when he was called? He should not be circumcised. 19Circumcision is nothing and uncircumcision is nothing. Keeping God's commands is what counts. [20]Each one should remain in the situation which he was in when God called him. [21]Were you a slave when you were called? Don't let it trouble you—although if you can gain your freedom, do so. [22]For he who was a slave when he was called by the Lord is the Lord's freedman; similarly, he who was a free man when he was called is Christ's slave. [23]You were bought at a price; do not become slaves of men. [24]Brothers, each man, as responsible to God, should remain in the situation God called him to.

[25]Now about virgins: I have no command from the Lord, but I give a judgment as one who by the Lord's mercy is trustworthy. [26]Because of the present crisis, I think that it is good for you to remain as you are. [27]Are you married? Do not seek a divorce. Are you unmarried? Do not look for a wife. [28]But if you do marry, you have not sinned; and if a virgin marries, she has not sinned. But those who marry will face many troubles in this life, and I want to spare you this.

[29]What I mean, brothers, is that the time is short. From now on those who have wives should live as if they had none; [30]those who mourn, as if they did not; those who are happy, as if they were not; those who buy something, as if it were not theirs to keep; [31]those who use the things of the world, as if not engrossed in them. For this world in its present form is passing away.

[32]I would like you to be free from concern. An unmarried man is concerned about the Lord's affairs—how he can please the Lord. [33]But a married man is concerned about the affairs of this world—how he can please his wife—[34]and his interests are divided. An unmarried woman or virgin is concerned about the Lord's affairs: Her aim is to be devoted to the Lord in both body and spirit. But a married woman is concerned about the affairs of this world—how she can please her husband. [35]I am saying this for your own good, not to restrict you, but that you may live in a right way in undivided devotion to the Lord.

[36]If anyone thinks he is acting improperly towards the virgin he is engaged to, and if she is getting on in years and he feels he ought to marry, he should do as he wants. He is not sinning. They should get married. [37]But the man who has settled the matter in his own mind, who is under no compulsion but has control over his own will, and who has made up his mind not to marry the virgin—this man also does the right thing. [38]So then, he who marries the virgin does right, but he who does not marry her does even better.[a]

[39]A woman is bound to her husband as long as he lives. But if her husband dies, she is free to marry anyone she wishes, but he must belong to the Lord. [40]In my judgment, she is happier if she stays as she is—and I think that I too have the Spirit of God.

Food Sacrificed to Idols

8 Now about food sacrificed to idols: We know that we all possess knowledge.[a] Knowledge puffs up, but love builds up. [2]The man who thinks he knows something does not yet know as he ought to know. [3]But the man who loves God is known by God.

[4]So then, about eating food sacrificed to idols: We know that an idol is nothing at all in the world and that there is no God but one. [5]For even if there are so-called gods, whether in heaven or on earth (as indeed there are many "gods" and many "lords"), [6]yet for us there is but one God, the

---

[a]36-38 Or [37]If anyone thinks he is not treating his daughter properly, and if she is getting on in years, and he feels she ought to marry, he should do as he wants. He is not sinning. They should get married. [37]But the man who has settled the matter in his own mind, who is under no compulsion but has control over his own will, and who has made up his mind to keep the virgin unmarried—this man also does the right thing. [38]So then, he who gives his virgin in marriage does right, but he who does not give her in marriage does even better.
[a]1 Or "We all possess knowledge," as you say

Father, from whom all things came and for whom we live; and there is but one Lord, Jesus Christ, through whom all things came and through whom we live.

[7]But not everyone knows this. Some people are still so accustomed to idols that when they eat such food they think of it as having been sacrificed to an idol, and since their conscience is weak, it is defiled. [8]But food does not bring us near to God; we are no worse if we do not eat, and no better if we do.

[9]Be careful, however, that the exercise of your freedom does not become a stumbling-block to the weak. [10]For if anyone with a weak conscience sees you who have this knowledge eating in an idol's temple, won't he be emboldened to eat what has been sacrificed to idols? [11]So this weak brother, for whom Christ died, is destroyed by your knowledge. [12]When you sin against your brothers in this way and wound their weak conscience, you sin against Christ. [13]Therefore, if what I eat causes my brother to fall into sin, I will never eat meat again, so that I will not cause him to fall.

The Rights of an Apostle

9 Am I not free? Am I not an apostle? Have I not seen Jesus our Lord? Are you not the result of my work in the Lord? [2]Even though I may not be an apostle to others, surely I am to you! For you are the seal of my apostleship in the Lord.

[3]This is my defence to those who sit in judgment on me. [4]Don't we have the right to food and drink? [5]Don't we have the right to take a believing wife along with us, as do the other apostles and the Lord's brothers and Cephas[a]? [6]Or is it only I and Barnabas who must work for a living?

[7]Who serves as a soldier at his own expense? Who plants a vineyard and does not eat of its grapes? Who tends a flock and does not drink of the milk? [8]Do I say this merely from a human point of view? Doesn't the

Law say the same thing? [9]For it is written in the Law of Moses: "Do not muzzle an ox while it is treading out the grain."[b] Is it about oxen that God is concerned? [10]Surely he says this for us, doesn't he? Yes, this was written for us, because when the ploughman ploughs and the thresher threshes, they ought to do so in the hope of sharing in the harvest. [11]If we have sown spiritual seed among you, is it too much if we reap a material harvest from you? [12]If others have this right of support from you, shouldn't we have it all the more?

But we did not use this right. On the contrary, we put up with anything rather than hinder the gospel of Christ. [13]Don't you know that those who work in the temple get their food from the temple, and those who serve at the altar share in what is offered on the altar? [14]In the same way, the Lord has commanded that those who preach the gospel should receive their living from the gospel.

[15]But I have not used any of these rights. And I am not writing this in the hope that you will do such things for me. I would rather die than have anyone deprive me of this boast. [16]Yet when I preach the gospel, I cannot boast, for I am compelled to preach. Woe to me if I do not preach the gospel! [17]If I preach voluntarily, I have a reward; if not voluntarily, I am simply discharging the trust committed to me. [18]What then is my reward? Just this: that in preaching the gospel I may offer it free of charge, and so not make use of my rights in preaching it.

[19]Though I am free and belong to no man, I make myself a slave to everyone, to win as many as possible. [20]To the Jews I became like a Jew, to win the Jews. To those under the law I became like one under the law (though I myself am not under the law), so as to win those under the law. [21]To those not having the law I became like one not having the law (though I am not free from God's law but am under Christ's law), so as to win those not having the law. [22]To

[a]5 That is, Peter   [b]9 Deut. 25:4

the weak I became weak, to win the weak. I have become all things to all men so that by all possible means I might save some. 23I do all this for the sake of the gospel, that I may share in its blessings.

24Do you not know that in a race all the runners run, but only one gets the prize? Run in such a way as to get the prize. 25Everyone who competes in the games goes into strict training. They do it to get a crown that will not last; but we do it to get a crown that will last for ever. 26Therefore I do not run like a man running aimlessly; I do not fight like a man beating the air. 27No, I beat my body and make it my slave so that after I have preached to others, I myself will not be disqualified for the prize.

Warnings From Israel's History

10 For I do not want you to be ignorant of the fact, brothers, that our forefathers were all under the cloud and that they all passed through the sea. 2They were all baptised into Moses in the cloud and in the sea. 3They all ate the same spiritual food 4and drank the same spiritual drink; for they drank from the spiritual rock that accompanied them, and that rock was Christ. 5Nevertheless, God was not pleased with most of them; their bodies were scattered over the desert.

6Now these things occurred as examples,a to keep us from setting our hearts on evil things as they did. 7Do not be idolaters, as some of them were; as it is written: "The people sat down to eat and drink and got up to indulge in pagan revelry."b 8We should not commit sexual immorality, as some of them did—and in one day twenty-three thousand of them died. 9We should not test the Lord, as some of them did—and were killed by snakes. 10And do not grumble, as some of them did—and were killed by the destroying angel.

11These things happened to them as examples and were written down as warnings for us, on whom the

fulfilment of the ages has come. 12So, if you think you are standing firm, be careful that you don't fall! 13No temptation has seized you except what is common to man. And God is faithful; he will not let you be tempted beyond what you can bear. But when you are tempted, he will also provide a way out so that you can stand up under it.

Idol Feasts and the Lord's Supper

14Therefore, my dear friends, flee from idolatry. 15I speak to sensible people; judge for yourselves what I say. 16Is not the cup of thanksgiving for which we give thanks a participation in the blood of Christ? And is not the bread that we break a participation in the body of Christ? 17Because there is one loaf, we, who are many, are one body, for we all partake of the one loaf.

18Consider the people of Israel: Do not those who eat the sacrifices participate in the altar? 19Do I mean then that a sacrifice offered to an idol is anything, or that an idol is anything? 20No, but the sacrifices of pagans are offered to demons, not to God, and I do not want you to be participants with demons. 21You cannot drink the cup of the Lord and the cup of demons too; you cannot have a part in both the Lord's table and the table of demons. 22Are we trying to arouse the Lord's jealousy? Are we stronger than he?

The Believer's Freedom

23"Everything is permissible"—but not everything is beneficial. "Everything is permissible"—but not everything is constructive. 24Nobody should seek his own good, but the good of others.

25Eat anything sold in the meat market without raising questions of conscience, 26for, "The earth is the Lord's, and everything in it."c

27If some unbeliever invites you to a meal and you want to go, eat whatever is put before you without raising questions of conscience. 28But if anyone says to you, "This has been offered in sacrifice," then do not eat

---

a6 Or types; also in verse 11   b7 Exodus 32:6   c26 Psalm 24:1

it, both for the sake of the man who told you and for conscience' sake[d]—29the other man's conscience, I mean, not yours. For why should my freedom be judged by another's conscience? 30If I take part in the meal with thankfulness, why am I denounced because of something I thank God for?

31So whether you eat or drink or whatever you do, do it all for the glory of God. 32Do not cause anyone to stumble, whether Jews, Greeks or the church of God—33even as I try to please everybody in every way. For I am not seeking my own good but the good of many, so that they may be saved.

11

1Follow my example, as I follow the example of Christ.

Propriety in Worship

2I praise you for remembering me in everything and for holding to the teachings,[a] just as I passed them on to you.

3Now I want you to realise that the head of every man is Christ, and the head of the woman is man, and the head of Christ is God. 4Every man who prays or prophesies with his head covered dishonours his head. 5And every woman who prays or prophesies with her head uncovered dishonours her head—it is just as though her head were shaved. 6If a woman does not cover her head, she should have her hair cut off; and if it is a disgrace for a woman to have her hair cut or shaved off, she should cover her head. 7A man ought not to cover his head,[b] since he is the image and glory of God; but the woman is the glory of man. 8For man did not come from woman, but woman from man; 9neither was man created for woman, but woman for man. 10For this reason, and because of the angels, the woman ought to have a sign of authority on her head.

11In the Lord, however, woman is not independent of man, nor is man independent of woman. 12For as woman came from man, so also man is born of woman. But everything comes from God. 13Judge for yourselves: Is it proper for a woman to pray to God with her head uncovered? 14Does not the very nature of things teach you that if a man has long hair, it is a disgrace to him, 15but that if a woman has long hair, it is her glory? For long hair is given to her as a covering. 16If anyone wants to be contentious about this, we have no other practice—nor do the churches of God.

The Lord's Supper

17In the following directives I have no praise for you, for your meetings do more harm than good. 18In the first place, I hear that when you come together as a church, there are divisions among you, and to some extent I believe it.19No doubt there have to be differences among you to show which of you have God's approval. 20When you come together, it is not the Lord's Supper you eat, 21for as you eat, each of you goes ahead without waiting for anybody else. One remains hungry, another gets drunk. 22Don't you have homes to eat and drink in? Or do you despise the church of God and humiliate those who have nothing? What shall I say to you? Shall I praise you for this? Certainly not!

23For I received from the Lord what I also passed on to you: The Lord Jesus, on the night he was betrayed, took bread, 24and when he had given thanks, he broke it and said, "This is my body, which is for you; do this in remembrance of me." 25In the same way, after supper he took the cup, saying, "This cup is the new covenant in my blood; do this, whenever you drink it, in remembrance of me." 26For whenever you eat this bread

[d]28 Some manuscripts conscience' sake, for "the earth is the Lord's and everything in it"
[a]2 Or traditions
[b]4-7 Or 'Every man who prays or prophesies with long hair dishonours his head. 5And every woman who prays or prophesies with no covering of hair, on her head dishonours her head—she is just like one of the "shorn women". 6If a woman has no covering, let her be for now with short hair, but since it is a disgrace for a woman to have her hair shorn or shaved, she should grow it again. 7A man ought not to have long hair

and drink this cup, you proclaim the Lord's death until he comes.

27Therefore, whoever eats the bread or drinks the cup of the Lord in an unworthy manner will be guilty of sinning against the body and blood of the Lord. 28A man ought to examine himself before he eats of the bread and drinks of the cup. 29For anyone who eats and drinks without recognising the body of the Lord eats and drinks judgment on himself. 30That is why many among you are weak and sick, and a number of you have fallen asleep. 31But if we judged ourselves, we would not come under judgment. 32When we are judged by the Lord, we are being disciplined so that we will not be condemned with the world.

33So then, my brothers, when you come together to eat, wait for each other. 34If anyone is hungry, he should eat at home, so that when you meet together it may not result in judgment.

And when I come I will give further directions.

Spiritual Gifts

12 Now about spiritual gifts, brothers, I do not want you to be ignorant. 2You know that when you were pagans, somehow or other you were influenced and led astray to dumb idols. 3Therefore I tell you that no-one who is speaking by the Spirit of God says, "Jesus be cursed," and no-one can say, "Jesus is Lord," except by the Holy Spirit.

4There are different kinds of gifts, but the same Spirit. 5There are different kinds of service, but the same Lord. 6There are different kinds of working, but the same God works all of them in all men.

7Now to each one the manifestation of the Spirit is given for the common good. 8To one there is given through the Spirit the message of wisdom, to another the message of knowledge by means of the same Spirit, 9to another faith by the same Spirit, to another gifts of healing by that one Spirit, 10to another miraculous powers, to

another prophecy, to another the ability to distinguish between spirits, to another the ability to speak in different kinds of tongues,a and to still another the interpretation of tongues.a 11All these are the work of one and the same Spirit, and he gives them to each one, just as he determines.

One Body, Many Parts

12The body is a unit, though it is made up of many parts; and though all its parts are many, they form one body. So it is with Christ. 13For we were all baptised byb one Spirit into one body—whether Jews or Greeks, slave or free—and we were all given the one Spirit to drink.

14Now the body is not made up of one part but of many. 15If the foot should say, "Because I am not a hand, I do not belong to the body," it would not for that reason cease to be part of the body. 16And if the ear should say, "Because I am not an eye, I do not belong to the body," it would not for that reason cease to be part of the body. 17If the whole body were an eye, where would the sense of hearing be? If the whole body were an ear, where would the sense of smell be? 18But in fact God has arranged the parts in the body, every one of them, just as he wanted them to be. 19If they were all one part, where would the body be? 20As it is, there are many parts, but one body.

21The eye cannot say to the hand, "I don't need you!" And the head cannot say to the feet, "I don't need you!" 22On the contrary, those parts of the body that seem to be weaker are indispensable, 23and the parts that we think are less honourable we treat with special honour. And the parts that are unpresentable are treated with special modesty, 24while our presentable parts need no special treatment. But God has combined the members of the body and has given greater honour to the parts that lacked it, 25so that there should be no division in the body, but that its parts should have equal concern for each other. 26If one part suffers, every part

---

a10 Or languages; also in verse 28   b13 Or with; or in

suffers with it; if one part is honoured, every part rejoices with it.

27Now you are the body of Christ, and each one of you is a part of it. 28And in the church God has appointed first of all apostles, second prophets, third teachers, then workers of miracles, also those having gifts of healing, those able to help others, those with gifts of administration, and those speaking in different kinds of tongues. 29Are all apostles? Are all prophets? Are all teachers? Do all work miracles? 30Do all have gifts of healing? Do all speak in tongues?c Do all interpret? 31But eagerly desired the greater gifts.

Love

And now I will show you the most excellent way.

13 If I speak in the tonguesa of men and of angels, but have not love, I am only a resounding gong or a clanging cymbal. 2If I have the gift of prophecy and can fathom all mysteries and all knowledge, and if I have a faith that can move mountains, but have not love, I am nothing. 3If I give all I possess to the poor and surrender my body to the flames,b but have not love, I gain nothing.

4Love is patient, love is kind. It does not envy, it does not boast, it is not proud. 5It is not rude, it is not self-seeking, it is not easily angered, it keeps no record of wrongs. 6Love does not delight in evil but rejoices with the truth. 7It always protects, always trusts, always hopes, always perseveres.

8Love never fails. But where there are prophecies, they will cease; where there are tongues, they will be stilled; where there is knowledge, it will pass away. 9For we know in part and we prophesy in part, 10but when perfection comes, the imperfect disappears. 11When I was a child, I talked like a child, I thought like a child, I reasoned like a child. When I became a man, I put childish ways

behind me. 12Now we see but a poor reflection; then we shall see face to face. Now I know in part; then I shall know fully, even as I am fully known.

13And now these three remain: faith, hope and love. But the greatest of these is love.

Gifts of Prophecy and Tongues

14 Follow the way of love and eagerly desire spiritual gifts, especially the gift of prophecy. 2For anyone who speaks in a tonguea does not speak to men but to God. Indeed, no-one understands him; he utters mysteries with his spirit.b 3But everyone who prophesies speaks to men for their strengthening, encouragement and comfort. 4He who speaks in a tongue edifies himself, but he who prophesies edifies the church. 5I would like every one of you to speak in tongues,c but I would rather have you prophesy. He who prophesies is greater than one who speaks in tongues,c unless he interprets, so that the church may be edified.

6Now, brothers, if I come to you and speak in tongues, what good will I be to you, unless I bring you some revelation or knowledge or prophecy or word of instruction? 7Even in the case of lifeless things that make sounds, such as the flute or harp, how will anyone know what tune is being played unless there is a distinction in the notes? 8Again, if the trumpet does not sound a clear call, who will get ready for battle? 9So it is with you. Unless you speak intelligible words with your tongue, how will anyone know what you are saying? You will just be speaking into the air. 10Undoubtedly there are all sorts of languages in the world, yet none of them is without meaning. 11If then I do not grasp the meaning of what someone is saying, I am a foreigner to the speaker, and he is a foreigner to me. 12So it is with you. Since you are eager to have spiritual gifts, try to excel in gifts that build up the church.

c30 Or other languages   d31 Or But you are eagerly desiring   a1 Or languages
b3 Some early manuscripts body that I may boast
a2 Or another language; also in verses 4, 13, 14, 19, 26 and 27
b2 Or by the Spirit   c5 Or other languages; also in verses 6, 18, 22, 23 and 39

13For this reason the man who speaks in a tongue should pray that he may interpret what he says. 14For if I pray in a tongue, my spirit prays, but my mind is unfruitful. 15So what shall I do? I will pray with my spirit, but I will also pray with my mind; I will sing with my spirit, but I will also sing with my mind. 16If you are praising God with your spirit, how can one who finds himself among those who do not understandd say "Amen" to your thanksgiving, since he does not know what you are saying? 17You may be giving thanks well enough, but the other man is not edified.

18I thank God that I speak in tongues more than all of you. 19But in the church I would rather speak five intelligible words to instruct others than ten thousand words in a tongue.

20Brothers, stop thinking like children. In regard to evil be infants, but in your thinking be adults. 21In the Law it is written:

"Through men of strange tongues
    and through the lips of
        foreigners
I will speak to this people,
    but even then they will not listen
        to me,"e

says the Lord.

22Tongues, then, are a sign, not for believers but for unbelievers; prophecy, however, is for believers, not for unbelievers. 23So if the whole church comes together and everyone speaks in tongues, and some who do not understandf or some unbelievers come in, will they not say that you are out of your mind? 24But if an unbeliever or someone who does not understandg comes in while everybody is prophesying, he will be convinced by all that he is a sinner and will be judged by all, 25and the secrets of his heart will be laid bare. So he will fall down and worship God, exclaiming, "God is really among you!"

Orderly Worship

26What then shall we say, brothers?

When you come together, everyone has a hymn, or a word of instruction, a revelation, a tongue or an interpretation. All of these must be done for the strengthening of the church. 27If anyone speaks in a tongue, two—or at the most three—should speak, one at a time, and someone must interpret. 28If there is no interpreter, the speaker should keep quiet in the church and speak to himself and God.

29Two or three prophets should speak, and the others should weigh carefully what is said. 30And if a revelation comes to someone who is sitting down, the first speaker should stop. 31For you can all prophesy in turn so that everyone may be instructed and encouraged. 32The spirits of prophets are subject to the control of prophets. 33For God is not a God of disorder but of peace.

As in all the congregations of the saints, 34women should remain silent in the churches. They are not allowed to speak, but must be in submission, as the Law says. 35If they want to enquire about something, they should ask their own husbands at home; for it is disgraceful for a woman to speak in the church. 36Did the word of God originate with you? Or are you the only people it has reached?h

37If anybody thinks he is a prophet or spiritually gifted, let him acknowledge that what I am writing to you is the Lord's command. 38If he ignores this, he himself will be ignored.h

39Therefore, my brothers, be eager to prophesy, and do not forbid speaking in tongues. 40But everything should be done in a fitting and orderly way.

The Resurrection of Christ

15 Now, brothers, I want to remind you of the gospel I preached to you, which you received and on which you have taken your stand. 2By this gospel you are saved, if you hold firmly to the word I preached to you. Otherwise, you have believed in vain.

3For what I received I passed on to

---

d16 Or among the enquirers   e21 Isaiah 28:11,12; Deut. 28:49   f23 Or some enquirers
g24 Or or some enquirer   h38 Some manuscripts this, let him ignore this

193

you as of first importance:[a] that Christ died for our sins according to the Scriptures, [4]that he was buried, that he was raised on the third day according to the Scriptures, [5]and that he appeared to Peter,[b] and then to the Twelve. [6]After that, he appeared to more than five hundred of the brothers at the same time, most of whom are still living, though some have fallen asleep. [7]Then he appeared to James, then to all the apostles, [8]and last of all he appeared to me also, as to one abnormally born.

[9]For I am the least of the apostles and do not even deserve to be called an apostle, because I persecuted the church of God. [10]But by the grace of God I am what I am, and his grace to me was not without effect. No, I worked harder than all of them—yet not I, but the grace of God that was with me. [11]Whether, then, it was I or they, this is what we preach, and this is what you believed.

The Resurrection of the Dead

[12]But if it is preached that Christ has been raised from the dead, how can some of you say that there is no resurrection of the dead? [13]If there is no resurrection of the dead, then not even Christ has been raised. [14]And if Christ has not been raised, our preaching is useless and so is your faith. [15]More than that, we are then found to be false witnesses about God, for we have testified about God that he raised Christ from the dead. But he did not raise him if in fact the dead are not raised. [16]For if the dead are not raised, then Christ has not been raised either. [17]And if Christ has not been raised, your faith is futile; you are still in your sins. [18]Then those also who have fallen asleep in Christ are lost. [19]If only for this life we have hope in Christ, we are to be pitied more than all men.

[20]But Christ has indeed been raised from the dead, the firstfruits of those who have fallen asleep. [21]For since death came through a man, the resurrection of the dead comes also through a man. [22]For as in Adam all

die, so in Christ all will be made alive. [23]But each in his own turn: Christ, the firstfruits; then, when he comes, those who belong to him. [24]Then the end will come, when he hands over the kingdom to God the Father after he has destroyed all dominion, authority and power. [25]For he must reign until he has put all his enemies under his feet. [26]The last enemy to be destroyed is death. [27]For he "has put everything under his feet".[c] Now when it says that "everything" has been put under him, it is clear that this does not include God himself, who put everything under Christ. [28]When he has done this, then the Son himself will be made subject to him who put everything under him, so that God may be all in all.

[29]Now if there is no resurrection, what will those do who are baptised for the dead? If the dead are not raised at all, why are people baptised for them? [30]And as for us, why do we endanger ourselves every hour? [31]I die every day—I mean that, brothers—just as surely as I glory over you in Christ Jesus our Lord. [32]If I fought wild beasts in Ephesus for merely human reasons, what have I gained? If the dead are not raised,

"Let us eat and drink,
for tomorrow we die."[d]

[33]Do not be misled: "Bad company corrupts good character." [34]Come back to your senses as you ought, and stop sinning; for there are some who are ignorant of God—I say this to your shame.

The Resurrection Body

[35]But someone may ask, "How are the dead raised? With what kind of body will they come?" [36]How foolish! What you sow does not come to life unless it dies. [37]When you sow, you do not plant the body that will be, but just a seed, perhaps of wheat or of something else. [38]But God gives it a body as he has determined, and to each kind of seed he gives its own body. [39]All flesh is not the same: Men have one kind of flesh, animals have

a3 Or you at the first   *b5* Greek Cephas   *c27* Psalm 8:6   *d32* Isaiah 22:13

another, birds another and fish another. [40]There are also heavenly bodies and there are earthly bodies; but the splendour of the heavenly bodies is one kind, and the splendour of the earthly bodies is another. [41]The sun has one kind of splendour, the moon another and the stars another; and star differs from star in splendour.

[42]So will it be with the resurrection of the dead. The body that is sown is perishable, it is raised imperishable; [43]it is sown in dishonour, it is raised in glory; it is sown in weakness, it is raised in power; [44]it is sown a natural body, it is raised a spiritual body.

If there is a natural body, there is also a spiritual body. [45]So it is written: "The first man Adam became a living being";[e] the last Adam, a life-giving spirit. [46]The spiritual did not come first, but the natural, and after that the spiritual. [47]The first man was of the dust of the earth, the second man from heaven. [48]As was the earthly man, so are those who are of the earth; and as is the man from heaven, so also are those who are of heaven. [49]And just as we have borne the likeness of the earthly man, so shall we[f] bear the likeness of the man from heaven.

[50]I declare to you, brothers, that flesh and blood cannot inherit the kingdom of God, nor does the perishable inherit the imperishable. [51]Listen, I tell you a mystery: We will not all sleep, but we will all be changed—[52]in a flash, in the twinkling of an eye, at the last trumpet. For the trumpet will sound, the dead will be raised imperishable, and we will be changed. [53]For the perishable must clothe itself with the imperishable, and the mortal with immortality. [54]When the perishable has been clothed with the imperishable, and the mortal with immortality, then the saying that is written will come true: "Death has been swallowed up in victory."[g]

[55]"Where, O death, is your victory?
Where, O death, is your sting?"[h]

[56]The sting of death is sin, and the power of sin is the law. [57]But thanks be to God! He gives us the victory through our Lord Jesus Christ.

[58]Therefore, my dear brothers, stand firm. Let nothing move you. Always give yourselves fully to the work of the Lord, because you know that your labour in the Lord is not in vain.

The Collection for God's People

16 Now about the collection for God's people: Do what I told the Galatian churches to do. [2]On the first day of every week, each one of you should set aside a sum of money in keeping with his income, saving it up, so that when I come no collections will have to be made. [3]Then, when I arrive, I will give letters of introduction to the men you approve and send them with your gift to Jerusalem. [4]If it seems advisable for me to go also, they will accompany me.

Personal Requests

[5]After I go through Macedonia, I will come to you—for I will be going through Macedonia. [6]Perhaps I will stay with you awhile, or even spend the winter, so that you can help me on my journey, wherever I go. [7]I do not want to see you now and make only a passing visit; I hope to spend some time with you, if the Lord permits. [8]But I will stay on at Ephesus until Pentecost, [9]because a great door for effective work has opened to me, and there are many who oppose me.

[10]If Timothy comes, see to it that he has nothing to fear while he is with you, for he is carrying on the work of the Lord, just as I am. [11]No-one, then, should refuse to accept him. Send him on his way in peace so that he may return to me. I am expecting him along with the brothers.

[12]Now about our brother Apollos: I strongly urged him to go to you with the brothers. He was quite unwilling

---

[e]45 Gen. 2:7
[f]49 Some early manuscripts *so let us*   [g]54 Isaiah 25:8   [h]55 Hosea 13:14

to go now, but he will go when he has the opportunity.

[13]Be on your guard; stand firm in the faith; be men of courage; be strong. [14]Do everything in love.

[15]You know that the household of Stephanas were the first converts in Achaia, and they have devoted themselves to the service of the saints. I urge you, brothers, [16]to submit to such as these and to everyone who joins in the work, and labours at it. [17]I was glad when Stephanas, Fortunatus and Achaicus arrived, because they have supplied what was lacking from you. [18]For they refreshed my spirit and yours also. Such men deserve recognition.

Final Greetings

[19]The churches in the province of Asia send you greetings. Aquila and Priscilla[a] greet you warmly in the Lord, and so does the church that meets at their house. [20]All the brothers here send you greetings. Greet one another with a holy kiss.

[21]I, Paul, write this greeting in my own hand.

[22]If anyone does not love the Lord—a curse be on him. Come, O Lord![b]

[23]The grace of the Lord Jesus be with you.

[24]My love to all of you in Christ Jesus. Amen.[c]

---

[a]19 Greek *Prisca*, a variant of *Priscilla*
[b]22 In Aramaic the expression *Come, O Lord* is *Marana tha*.
[c]24 Some manuscripts do not have *Amen*.

2 Corinthians

1 Paul, an apostle of Christ Jesus by the will of God, and Timothy our brother,

To the church of God in Corinth, together with all the saints throughout Achaia:

2Grace and peace to you from God our Father and the Lord Jesus Christ.

The God of All Comfort

3Praise be to the God and Father of our Lord Jesus Christ, the Father of compassion and the God of all comfort, 4who comforts us in all our troubles, so that we can comfort those in any trouble with the comfort we ourselves have received from God. 5For just as the sufferings of Christ flow over into our lives, so also through Christ our comfort overflows. 6If we are distressed, it is for your comfort and salvation; if we are comforted, it is for your comfort, which produces in you patient endurance of the same sufferings we suffer. 7And our hope for you is firm, because we know that just as you share in our sufferings, so also you share in our comfort.

8We do not want you to be uninformed, brothers, about the hardships we suffered in the province of Asia. We were under great pressure, far beyond our ability to endure, so that we despaired even of life. 9Indeed, in our hearts we felt the sentence of death. But this happened that we might not rely on ourselves but on God, who raises the dead. 10He has delivered us from such a deadly peril, and he will deliver us. On him we have set our hope that he will continue to deliver us, 11as you help us by your prayers. Then many will give

thanks on our[a] behalf for the gracious favour granted us in answer to the prayers of many.

Paul's Change of Plans

12Now this is our boast: Our conscience testifies that we have conducted ourselves in the world, and especially in our relations with you, in the holiness and sincerity that are from God. We have done so not according to worldly wisdom but according to God's grace. 13For we do not write to you anything you cannot read or understand. And I hope that, 14as you have understood us in part, you will come to understand fully that you can boast of us just as we will boast of you in the day of the Lord Jesus.

15Because I was confident of this, I planned to visit you first so that you might benefit twice. 16I planned to visit you on my way to Macedonia and to come back to you from Macedonia, and then to have you send me on my way to Judea. 17When I planned this, did I do it lightly? Or do I make my plans in a worldly manner so that in the same breath I say, "Yes, yes" and "No, no"?

18But as surely as God is faithful, our message to you is not "Yes" and "No". 19For the Son of God, Jesus Christ, who was preached among you by me and Silas[b] and Timothy, was not "Yes" and "No", but in him it has always been "Yes". 20For no matter how many promises God has made, they are "Yes" in Christ. And so through him the "Amen" is spoken by us to the glory of God. 21Now it is God who makes both us and you stand firm in Christ. He anointed us, 22set his seal of ownership on us, and put his Spirit in our hearts as a

---

a11 Many manuscripts your   b19 Greek Silvanus, a variant of Silas

deposit, guaranteeing what is to come. 23I call God as my witness that it was in order to spare you that I did not return to Corinth. 24Not that we lord it over your faith, but we work with you for your joy, because it is by faith you stand firm. 2 1So I made up my mind that I would not make another painful visit to you. 2For if I grieve you, who is left to make me glad but you whom I have grieved? 3I wrote as I did so that when I came I should not be distressed by those who ought to make me rejoice. I had confidence in all of you, that you would all share my joy. 4For I wrote to you out of great distress and anguish of heart and with many tears, not to grieve you but to let you know the depth of my love for you.

Forgiveness for the Sinner

5If anyone has caused grief, he has not so much grieved me as he has grieved all of you, to some extent—not to put it too severely. 6The punishment inflicted on him by the majority is sufficient for him. 7Now instead, you ought to forgive and comfort him, so that he will not be overwhelmed by excessive sorrow. 8I urge you, therefore, to reaffirm your love for him. 9The reason I wrote to you was to see if you would stand the test and be obedient in everything. 10If you forgive anyone, I also forgive him. And what I have forgiven—if there was anything to forgive—I have forgiven in the sight of Christ for your sake, 11in order that Satan might not outwit us. For we are not unaware of his schemes.

Ministers of the New Covenant

12Now when I went to Troas to preach the gospel of Christ and found that the Lord had opened a door for me, 13I still had no peace of mind, because I did not find my brother Titus there. So I said good-bye to them and went on to Macedonia.

14But thanks be to God, who always leads us in triumphal procession in Christ and through us spreads everywhere the fragrance of the knowledge of him. 15For we are to God the aroma of Christ among those who are being saved and those who are perishing. 16To the one we are the smell of death; to the other, the fragrance of life. And who is equal to such a task? 17Unlike so many, we do not peddle the word of God for profit. On the contrary, in Christ we speak before God with sincerity, like men sent from God.

3 Are we beginning to commend ourselves again? Or do we need, like some people, letters of recommendation to you or from you? 2You yourselves are our letter, written on our hearts, known and read by everybody. 3You show that you are a letter from Christ, the result of our ministry, written not with ink but with the Spirit of the living God, not on tablets of stone but on tablets of human hearts.

4Such confidence as this is ours through Christ before God. 5Not that we are competent to claim anything for ourselves, but our competence comes from God. 6He has made us competent as ministers of a new covenant—not of the letter but of the Spirit; for the letter kills, but the Spirit gives life.

The Glory of the New Covenant

7Now if the ministry that brought death, which was engraved in letters on stone, came with glory, so that the Israelites could not look steadily at the face of Moses because of its glory, fading though it was, 8will not the ministry of the Spirit be even more glorious? 9If the ministry that condemns men is glorious, how much more glorious is the ministry that brings righteousness! 10For what was glorious has no glory now in comparison with the surpassing glory. 11And if what was fading away came with glory, how much greater is the glory of that which lasts!

12Therefore, since we have such a hope, we are very bold. 13We are not like Moses, who would put a veil over his face to keep the Israelites from gazing at it while the radiance was fading away. 14But their minds were made dull, for to this day the same veil remains when the old covenant is read. It has not been removed, because only in Christ is it taken away. 15Even to this day when Moses is read, a veil covers their hearts. 16But whenever anyone turns to the Lord, the veil is taken away. 17Now the Lord is the Spirit, and where the Spirit of the Lord is, there is freedom. 18And we, who with unveiled faces all reflect*a* the Lord's glory, are being transformed into his likeness with ever-increasing glory, which comes from the Lord, who is the Spirit.

Treasures in Jars of Clay

4 Therefore, since through God's mercy we have this ministry, we do not lose heart. 2Rather, we have renounced secret and shameful ways; we do not use deception, nor do we distort the word of God. On the contrary, by setting forth the truth plainly we commend ourselves to every man's conscience in the sight of God. 3And even if our gospel is veiled, it is veiled to those who are perishing. 4The god of this age has blinded the minds of unbelievers, so that they cannot see the light of the gospel of the glory of Christ, who is the image of God. 5For we do not preach ourselves, but Jesus Christ as Lord, and ourselves as your servants for Jesus' sake. 6For God, who said, "Let light shine out of darkness,"*a* made his light shine in our hearts to give us the light of the knowledge of the glory of God in the face of Christ.

7But we have this treasure in jars of clay to show that this all-surpassing power is from God and not from us. 8We are hard pressed on every side, but not crushed; perplexed, but not in despair; 9persecuted, but not abandoned; struck down, but not destroyed. 10We always carry around in our body the death of Jesus, so that the life of Jesus may also be revealed in our body. 11For we who are alive are always being given over to death for Jesus' sake, so that his life may be

revealed in our mortal body. 12So then, death is at work in us, but life is at work in you.

13It is written: "I believed; therefore I have spoken."*b* With that same spirit of faith we also believe and therefore speak, 14because we know that the one who raised the Lord Jesus from the dead will also raise us with Jesus and present us with you in his presence. 15All this is for your benefit, so that the grace that is reaching more and more people may cause thanksgiving to overflow to the glory of God.

16Therefore we do not lose heart. Though outwardly we are wasting away, yet inwardly we are being renewed day by day. 17For our light and momentary troubles are achieving for us an eternal glory that far outweighs them all. 18So we fix our eyes not on what is seen, but on what is unseen. For what is seen is temporary, but what is unseen is eternal.

Our Heavenly Dwelling

5 Now we know that if the earthly tent we live in is destroyed, we have a building from God, an eternal house in heaven, not built by human hands. 2Meanwhile we groan, longing to be clothed with our heavenly dwelling, 3because when we are clothed, we will not be found naked. 4For while we are in this tent, we groan and are burdened, because we do not wish to be unclothed but to be clothed with our heavenly dwelling, so that what is mortal may be swallowed up by life. 5Now it is God who has made us for this very purpose and has given us the Spirit as a deposit, guaranteeing what is to come.

6Therefore we are always confident and know that as long as we are at home in the body we are away from the Lord. 7We live by faith, not by sight. 8We are confident, I say, and would prefer to be away from the body and at home with the Lord. 9So we make it our goal to please him, whether we are at home in the body

*a18 Or contemplate   *a6 Gen. 1:3   *b13 Psalm 116:10

or away from it. [10]For we must all appear before the judgment seat of Christ, that each one may receive what is due to him for the things done while in the body, whether good or bad.

The Ministry of Reconciliation

[11]Since, then, we know what it is to fear the Lord, we try to persuade men. What we are is plain to God, and I hope it is also plain to your conscience. [12]We are not trying to commend ourselves to you again, but are giving you an opportunity to take pride in us, so that you can answer those who take pride in what is seen rather than in what is in the heart. [13]If we are out of our mind, it is for the sake of God; if we are in our right mind, it is for you. [14]For Christ's love compels us, because we are convinced that one died for all, and therefore all died. [15]And he died for all, that those who live should no longer live for themselves but for him who died for them and was raised again.

[16]So from now on we regard no-one from a worldly point of view. Though we once regarded Christ in this way, we do so no longer. [17]Therefore, if anyone is in Christ, he is a new creation; the old has gone, the new has come! [18]All this is from God, who reconciled us to himself through Christ and gave us the ministry of reconciliation: [19]that God was reconciling the world to himself in Christ, not counting men's sins against them. And he has committed to us the message of reconciliation. [20]We are therefore Christ's ambassadors, as though God were making his appeal through us. We implore you on Christ's behalf: Be reconciled to God. [21]God made him who had no sin to be sin[a] for us, so that in him we might become the righteousness of God.

6 As God's fellow workers we urge you not to receive God's grace in vain. [2]For he says,

"In the time of my favour I heard you,
and in the day of salvation I helped you."[a]

I tell you, now is the time of God's favour, now is the day of salvation.

Paul's Hardships

[3]We put no stumbling-block in anyone's path, so that our ministry will not be discredited. [4]Rather, as servants of God we commend ourselves in every way: in great endurance; in troubles, hardships and distresses; [5]in beatings, imprisonments and riots; in hard work, sleepless nights and hunger; [6]in purity, understanding, patience and kindness; in the Holy Spirit and in sincere love; [7]in truthful speech and in the power of God; with weapons of righteousness in the right hand and in the left; [8]through glory and dishonour, bad report and good report; genuine, yet regarded as impostors; [9]known, yet regarded as unknown; dying, and yet we live on; beaten, and yet not killed; [10]sorrowful, yet always rejoicing; poor, yet making many rich; having nothing, and yet possessing everything.

[11]We have spoken freely to you, Corinthians, and opened wide our hearts to you. [12]We are not withholding our affection from you, but you are withholding yours from us. [13]As a fair exchange—I speak as to my children—open wide your hearts also.

Do Not Be Yoked With Unbelievers

[14]Do not be yoked together with unbelievers. For what do righteousness and wickedness have in common? Or what fellowship can light have with darkness? [15]What harmony is there between Christ and Belial?[b] What does a believer have in common with an unbeliever? [16]What agreement is there between the temple of God and idols? For we are the temple of the living God. As God has said: "I will live with them and walk among them, and I will be their God, and they will be my people."[c]

---

[a]21 Or be a sin offering   [a]2 Isaiah 49:8
[c]16 Lev. 26:12; Jer. 32:38; Ezek. 37:27
[b]15 Greek Beliar, a variant of Belial

17"Therefore come out from them
and be separate,
says the Lord.
Touch no unclean thing,
and I will receive you."d
18"I will be a Father to you,
and you will be my sons and
daughters,
says the Lord Almighty."e

7 Since we have these promises,
dear friends, let us purify ourselves from everything that contami-
nates body and spirit, perfecting holiness out of reverence for God.

Paul's Joy

2Make room for us in your hearts.
We have wronged no-one, we have
corrupted no-one, we have exploited
no-one. 3I do not say this to condemn
you; I have said before that you have
such a place in our hearts that we
would live or die with you. 4I have
great confidence in you; I take great
pride in you. I am greatly encouraged;
in all our troubles my joy knows no
bounds.

5For when we came into Macedonia, this body of ours had no rest,
but we were harassed at every turn—
conflicts on the outside, fears within.
6But God, who comforts the downcast,
comforted us by the coming of Titus,
7and not only by his coming but also
by the comfort they had given him.
He told us about your longing for me,
your deep sorrow, your ardent concern for me, so that my joy was
greater than ever.

8Even if I caused you sorrow by my
letter, I do not regret it. Though I did
regret it—I see that my letter hurt
you, but only for a little while—9yet
now I am happy, not because you
were made sorry, but because your
sorrow led you to repentance. For
you became sorrowful as God
intended and so were not harmed in
any way by us. 10Godly sorrow brings
repentance that leads to salvation and
leaves no regret, but worldly sorrow
brings death. 11See what this godly
sorrow has produced in you: what

earnestness, what eagerness to clear
yourselves, what indignation, what
alarm, what longing, what concern,
what readiness to see justice done. At
every point you have proved yourselves to be innocent in this matter.
12So even though I wrote to you, it
was not on account of the one who
did the wrong or of the injured party,
but rather that before God you could
see for yourselves how devoted to us
you are. 13By all this we are
encouraged.

In addition to our own encouragement, we were especially delighted to
see how happy Titus was, because his
spirit has been refreshed by all of
you. 14I had boasted to him about
you, and you have not embarrassed
me. But just as everything we said to
you was true, so our boasting about
you to Titus has proved to be true as
well. 15And his affection for you is all
the greater when he remembers that
you were all obedient, receiving him
with fear and trembling. 16I am glad
I can have complete confidence in
you.

Generosity Encouraged

8 And now, brothers, we want you
to know about the grace that God
has given the Macedonian churches.
2Out of the most severe trial, their
overflowing joy and their extreme
poverty welled up in rich generosity.
3For I testify that they gave as much
as they are able, and even beyond
their ability. Entirely on their own,
4they urgently pleaded with us for the
privilege of sharing in this service to
the saints. 5And they did not do as we
expected, but they gave themselves
first to the Lord and then to us in
keeping with God's will. 6So we urged
Titus, since he had earlier made a
beginning, to bring also to completion
this act of grace on your part. 7But
just as you excel in everything—in
faith, in speech, in knowledge, in
complete earnestness and in your
love for usg—see that you also excel
in this grace of giving.

d17 Isaiah 52:11; Ezek. 20:34,41   e18 2 Samuel 7:14; 7:8
g7 Some manuscripts in our love for you

[8]I am not commanding you, but I want to test the sincerity of your love by comparing it with the earnestness of others. [9]For you know the grace of our Lord Jesus Christ, that though he was rich, yet for your sakes he became poor, so that you through his poverty might become rich.

[10]And here is my advice about what is best for you in this matter: Last year you were the first not only to give but also to have the desire to do so. [11]Now finish the work, so that your eager willingness to do it may be matched by your completion of it, according to your means. [12]For if the willingness is there, the gift is acceptable according to what one has, not according to what he does not have.

[13]Our desire is not that others might be relieved while you are hard pressed, but that there might be equality. [14]At the present time your plenty will supply what they need, so that in turn their plenty will supply what you need. Then there will be equality, [15]as it is written: "He that gathered much did not have too much, and he that gathered little did not have too little."[b]

Titus Sent to Corinth

[16]I thank God, who put into the heart of Titus the same concern I have for you. [17]For Titus not only welcomed our appeal, but he is coming to you with much enthusiasm and on his own initiative. [18]And we are sending along with him the brother who is praised by all the churches for his service to the gospel. [19]What is more, he was chosen by the churches to accompany us as we carry the offering, which we administer in order to honour the Lord himself and to show our eagerness to help. [20]We want to avoid any criticism of the way we administer this liberal gift. [21]For we are taking pains to do what is right, not only in the eyes of the Lord but also in the eyes of men.

[22]In addition, we are sending with them our brother who has often proved to us in many ways that he is zealous, and now even more so because of his great confidence in you. [23]As for Titus, he is my partner and fellow-worker among you; as for our brothers, they are representatives of the churches and an honour to Christ. [24]Therefore show these men the proof of your love and the reason for our pride in you, so that the churches can see it.

9

There is no need for me to write to you about this service to the saints. [2]For I know your eagerness to help, and I have been boasting about it to the Macedonians, telling them that since last year you in Achaia were ready to give; and your enthusiasm has stirred most of them to action. [3]But I am sending the brothers in order that our boasting about you in this matter should not prove hollow, but that you may be ready, as I said you would be. [4]For if any Macedonians come with me and find you unprepared, we—not to say anything about you—would be ashamed of having been so confident. [5]So I thought it necessary to urge the brothers to visit you in advance and finish the arrangements for the generous gift you had promised. Then it will be ready as a generous gift, not as one grudgingly given.

Sowing Generously

[6]Remember this: Whoever sows sparingly will also reap sparingly, and whoever sows generously will also reap generously. [7]Each man should give what he has decided in his heart to give, not reluctantly or under compulsion, for God loves a cheerful giver. [8]And God is able to make all grace abound to you, so that in all things at all times, having all that you need, you will abound in every good work. [9]As it is written:

"He has scattered abroad his gifts
    to the poor;
his righteousness endures for
    ever."[a]

[10]Now he who supplies seed to the sower and bread for food will also supply and increase your store of

[b]15 Exodus 16:18   [a]9 Psalm 112:9

seed and will enlarge the harvest of your righteousness. [11]You will be made rich in every way so that you can be generous on every occasion, and through us your generosity will result in thanksgiving to God.

[12]This service that you perform is not only supplying the needs of God's people but is also overflowing in many expressions of thanks to God. [13]Because of the service by which you have proved yourselves, men will praise God for the obedience that accompanies your confession of the gospel of Christ, and for your generosity in sharing with them and with everyone else. [14]And in their prayers for you their hearts will go out to you, because of the surpassing grace God has given you. [15]Thanks be to God for his indescribable gift!

Paul's Defence of His Ministry

10 By the meekness and gentleness of Christ, I appeal to you—I, Paul, who am "timid" when face to face with you, but "bold" when away! [2]I beg you that when I come I may not have to be as bold as I expect to be towards some people who think that we live by the standards of this world. [3]For though we live in the world, we do not wage war as the world does. [4]The weapons we fight with are not the weapons of the world. On the contrary, they have divine power to demolish strongholds. [5]We demolish arguments and every pretension that sets itself up against the knowledge of God, and we take captive every thought to make it obedient to Christ. [6]And we will be ready to punish every act of disobedience, once your obedience is complete.

[7]You are looking only on the surface of things.[a] If anyone is confident that he belongs to Christ, he should consider again that we belong to Christ just as much as he. [8]For even

if I boast somewhat freely about the authority the Lord gave us for building you up rather than pulling you down, I will not be ashamed of it. [9]I do not want to seem to be trying to frighten you with my letters. [10]For some say, "His letters are weighty and forceful, but in person he is unimpressive and his speaking amounts to nothing." [11]Such people should realise that what we are in our letters when we are absent, we will be in our actions when we are present.

[12]We do not dare to classify or compare ourselves with some who commend themselves. When they measure themselves by themselves and compare themselves with themselves, they are not wise. [13]We, however, will not boast beyond proper limits, but will confine our boasting to the field God has assigned to us, a field that reaches even to you. [14]We are not going too far in our boasting, as would be the case if we had not come to you, for we did get as far as you with the gospel of Christ. [15]Neither do we go beyond our limits by boasting of work done by others.[b] Our hope is that, as your faith continues to grow, our area of activity among you will greatly expand, [16]so that we can preach the gospel in the regions beyond you. For we do not want to boast about work already done in another man's territory. [17]But, "Let him who boasts boast in the Lord."[c] [18]For it is not the one who commends himself who is approved, but the one whom the Lord commends.

Paul and the False Apostles

11 I hope you will put up with a little of my foolishness; but you are already doing that. [2]I am jealous for you with a godly jealousy. I promised you to one husband, to Christ, so that I might present you as

---

[a]7 Or Look at the obvious facts
[b]13-15 Or [15]We, however, will not boast about things that cannot be measured, but we will boast according to the standard of measurement that the God of measure has assigned us—a measurement that relates even to you. [14]. . . [15]Neither do we boast about things that cannot be measured in regard to the work done by others.
[c]17 Jer. 9:24

a pure virgin to him. ³But I am afraid that just as Eve was deceived by the serpent's cunning, your minds may somehow be led astray from your sincere and pure devotion to Christ. ⁴For if someone comes to you and preaches a Jesus other than the Jesus we preached, or if you receive a different spirit from the one you received, or a different gospel from the one you accepted, you put up with it easily enough. ⁵But I do not think I am in the least inferior to those "super-apostles". ⁶I may not be a trained speaker, but I do have knowledge. We have made this perfectly clear to you in every way.

⁷Was it a sin for me to lower myself in order to elevate you by preaching the gospel of God to you free of charge? ⁸I robbed other churches by receiving support from them so as to serve you. ⁹And when I was with you and needed something, I was not a burden to anyone, for the brothers who came from Macedonia supplied what I needed. I have kept myself from being a burden to you in any way, and will continue to do so. ¹⁰As surely as the truth of Christ is in me, nobody in the regions of Achaia will stop this boasting of mine. ¹¹Why? Because I do not love you? God knows I do! ¹²And I will keep on doing what I am doing in order to cut the ground from under those who want an opportunity to be considered equal with us in the things they boast about.

¹³For such men are false apostles, deceitful workmen, masquerading as apostles of Christ. ¹⁴And no wonder, for Satan himself masquerades as an angel of light. ¹⁵It is not surprising, then, if his servants masquerade as servants of righteousness. Their end will be what their actions deserve.

Paul Boasts About His Sufferings

¹⁶I repeat: Let no-one take me for a fool. But if you do, then receive me just as you would a fool, so that I may do a little boasting. ¹⁷In this self-confident boasting I am not talking as the Lord would, but as a fool. ¹⁸Since many are boasting in the way the world does, I too will boast. ¹⁹You gladly put up with fools since you are so wise! ²⁰In fact, you even put up with anyone who enslaves you or exploits you or takes advantage of you or pushes himself forward or slaps you in the face. ²¹To my shame I admit that we were too weak for that!

What anyone else dares to boast about—I am speaking as a fool—I also dare to boast about. ²²Are they Hebrews? So am I. Are they Israelites? So am I. Are they Abraham's descendants? So am I. ²³Are they servants of Christ? (I am out of my mind to talk like this.) I am more. I have worked much harder, been in prison more frequently, been flogged more severely, and been exposed to death again and again. ²⁴Five times I received from the Jews the forty lashes minus one. ²⁵Three times I was beaten with rods, once I was stoned, three times I was shipwrecked, I spent a night and a day in the open sea, ²⁶I have been constantly on the move. I have been in danger from rivers, in danger from bandits, in danger from my own countrymen, in danger from Gentiles; in danger in the city, in danger in the country, in danger at sea; and in danger from false brothers. ²⁷I have laboured and toiled and have often gone without sleep; I have known hunger and thirst and have often gone without food; I have been cold and naked. ²⁸Besides everything else, I face daily the pressure of my concern for all the churches. ²⁹Who is weak, and I do not feel weak? Who is led into sin, and I do not inwardly burn?

³⁰If I must boast, I will boast of the things that show my weakness. ³¹The God and Father of the Lord Jesus, who is to be praised for ever, knows that I am not lying. ³²In Damascus the governor under King Aretas had the city of the Damascenes guarded in order to arrest me. ³³But I was lowered in a basket from a window in the wall and slipped through his hands.

Paul's Vision and His Thorn

12 I must go on boasting. Although there is nothing to be gained, I will go on to visions and revelations from the Lord. [2]I know a man in Christ who fourteen years ago was caught up to the third heaven. Whether it was in the body or out of the body I do not know—God knows. [3]And I know that this man—whether in the body or apart from the body I do not know, but God knows—[4]was caught up to Paradise. He heard inexpressible things, things that man is not permitted to tell. [5]I will boast about a man like that, but I will not boast about myself, except about my weaknesses. [6]Even if I should choose to boast, I would not be a fool, because I would be speaking the truth. But I refrain, so no-one will think more of me than is warranted by what I do or say.

[7]To keep me from becoming conceited because of these surpassingly great revelations, there was given me a thorn in my flesh, a messenger of Satan, to torment me. [8]Three times I pleaded with the Lord to take it away from me. [9]But he said to me, "My grace is sufficient for you, for my power is made perfect in weakness." Therefore I will boast all the more gladly about my weaknesses, so that Christ's power may rest on me. [10]That is why, for Christ's sake, I delight in weaknesses, in insults, in hardships, in persecutions, in difficulties. For when I am weak, then I am strong.

Paul's Concern for the Corinthians

[11]I have made a fool of myself, but you drove me to it. I ought to have been commended by you, for I am not in the least inferior to the "super-apostles", even though I am nothing. [12]The things that mark an apostle—signs, wonders and miracles—were done among you with great perseverance. [13]How were you inferior to the other churches, except that I was never a burden to you? Forgive me this wrong!

[14]Now I am ready to visit you for the third time, and I will not be a burden to you, because what I want is not your possessions but you. After all, children should not have to save up for their parents, but parents for their children. [15]So I will very gladly spend for you everything I have and expend myself as well. If I love you more, will you love me less? [16]Be that as it may, I have not been a burden to you. Yet, crafty fellow that I am, I caught you by trickery! [17]Did I exploit you through any of the men I sent you? [18]I urged Titus to go to you and I sent our brother with him. Titus did not exploit you, did he? Did we not act in the same spirit and follow the same course?

[19]Have you been thinking all along that we have been defending ourselves to you? We have been speaking in the sight of God as those in Christ; and everything we do, dear friends, is for your strengthening. [20]For I am afraid that when I come I may not find you as I want you to be, and you may not find me as you want me to be. I fear that there may be quarrelling, jealousy, outbursts of anger, factions, slander, gossip, arrogance and disorder. [21]I am afraid that when I come again my God will humble me before you, and I will be grieved over many who have sinned earlier and have not repented of the impurity, sexual sin and debauchery in which they have indulged.

Final Warnings

13 This will be my third visit to you. "Every matter must be established by the testimony of two or three witnesses."[a] [2]I already gave you a warning when I was with you the second time. I now repeat it while absent: On my return I will not spare those who sinned earlier or any of the others, [3]since you are demanding proof that Christ is speaking through me. He is not weak in dealing with you, but is powerful among you. [4]For to be sure, he was crucified in weakness, yet he lives by God's power. Likewise, we are

[a]1 Deut. 19:15

205

weak in him, yet by God's power we will live with him to serve you.

⁵Examine yourselves to see whether you are in the faith; test yourselves. Do you not realise that Christ Jesus is in you—unless, of course, you fail the test? ⁶And I trust that you will discover that we have not failed the test. ⁷Now we pray to God that you will not do anything wrong. Not that people will see that we have stood the test but that you will do what is right even though we may seem to have failed. ⁸For we cannot do anything against the truth, but only for the truth. ⁹We are glad whenever we are weak but you are strong; and our prayer is for your perfection. ¹⁰This is why I write these things when I am absent, that when I come I may not have to be harsh in my use of authority—the authority the Lord gave me for building you up, not for tearing you down.

Final Greetings

¹¹Finally, brothers, good-bye. Aim for perfection, listen to my appeal, be of one mind, live in peace. And the God of love and peace will be with you.

¹²Greet one another with a holy kiss. ¹³All the saints send their greetings.

¹⁴May the grace of the Lord Jesus Christ, and the love of God, and the fellowship of the Holy Spirit be with you all.

Galatians

1 Paul, an apostle—sent not from men nor by man, but by Jesus Christ and God the Father, who raised him from the dead—2and all the brothers with me,

To the churches in Galatia:

3Grace and peace to you from God our Father and the Lord Jesus Christ, 4who gave himself for our sins to rescue us from the present evil age, according to the will of our God and Father, 5to whom be glory for ever and ever. Amen.

No Other Gospel

6I am astonished that you are so quickly deserting the one who called you by the grace of Christ and are turning to a different gospel 7—which is really no gospel at all. Evidently some people are throwing you into confusion and are trying to pervert the gospel of Christ. 8But even if we or an angel from heaven should preach a gospel other than the one we preached to you, let him be eternally condemned! 9As we have already said, so now I say again: If anybody is preaching to you a gospel other than what you accepted, let him be eternally condemned!

10Am I now trying to win the approval of men, or of God? Or am I trying to please men? If I were still trying to please men, I would not be a servant of Christ.

Paul Called by God

11I want you to know, brothers, that the gospel I preached is not something that man made up. 12I did not receive it from any man, nor was I taught it; rather, I received it by revelation from Jesus Christ.

13For you have heard of my previous way of life in Judaism, how intensely I persecuted the church of God and tried to destroy it. 14I was advancing in Judaism beyond many Jews of my own age and was extremely zealous for the traditions of my fathers. 15But when God, who set me apart from birth*a* and called me by his grace, was pleased 16to reveal his Son in me so that I might preach him among the Gentiles, I did not consult any man, 17nor did I go up to Jerusalem to see those who were apostles before I was, but I went immediately into Arabia and later returned to Damascus.

18Then after three years, I went up to Jerusalem to get acquainted with Peter*b* and stayed with him fifteen days. 19I saw none of the other apostles—only James, the Lord's brother. 20I assure you before God that what I am writing to you is no lie. 21Later I went to Syria and Cilicia. 22I was personally unknown to the churches of Judea that are in Christ. 23They only heard the report: "The man who formerly persecuted us is now preaching the faith he once tried to destroy." 24And they praised God because of me.

Paul Accepted by the Apostles

2 Fourteen years later I went up again to Jerusalem, this time with Barnabas. I took Titus along also. 2I went in response to a revelation and set before them the gospel that I preach among the Gentiles. But I did this privately to those who seemed to

*a*15 Or from my mother's womb   *b*18 Greek Cephas

be leaders, for fear that I was running or had run my race in vain. ³Yet not even Titus, who was with me, was compelled to be circumcised, even though he was a Greek. ⁴ ₜThis matter arose, because some false brothers had infiltrated our ranks to spy on the freedom we have in Christ Jesus and to make us slaves. ⁵We did not give in to them for a moment, so that the truth of the gospel might remain with you.

⁶As for those who seemed to be important—whatever they were makes no difference to me; God does not judge by external appearance—those men added nothing to my message. ⁷On the contrary, they saw that I had been given the task of preaching the gospel to the Gentiles,ᵃ just as Peter had been given the task of preaching the gospel to the Jews.ᵇ ⁸For God, who was at work in the ministry of Peter as an apostle to the Jews, was also at work in my ministry as an apostle to the Gentiles. ⁹James, Peterᶜ and John, those reputed to be pillars, gave me and Barnabas the right hand of fellowship when they recognised the grace given to me. They agreed that we should go to the Gentiles, and they to the Jews. ¹⁰All they asked was that we should continue to remember the poor, the very thing I was eager to do.

Paul Opposes Peter

¹¹When Peter came to Antioch, I opposed him to his face, because he was in the wrong. ¹²Before certain men came from James, he used to eat with the Gentiles. But when they arrived, he began to draw back and separate himself from the Gentiles because he was afraid of those who belonged to the circumcision group. ¹³The other Jews joined him in his hypocrisy, so that by their hypocrisy even Barnabas was led astray.

¹⁴When I saw that they were not acting in line with the truth of the gospel, I said to Peter in front of them all, "You are a Jew, yet you live like a Gentile and not like a Jew. How is it, then, that you force Gentiles to follow Jewish customs?

¹⁵"We who are Jews by birth and not 'Gentile sinners' ¹⁶know that a man is not justified by observing the law, but by faith in Jesus Christ. So we, too, have put our faith in Christ Jesus that we may be justified by faith in Christ and not by observing the law, because by observing the law no-one will be justified.

¹⁷"If, while we seek to be justified in Christ, it becomes evident that we ourselves are sinners, does that mean that Christ promotes sin? Absolutely not! ¹⁸If I rebuild what I destroyed, I prove that I am a law-breaker. ¹⁹For through the law I died to the law so that I might live for God. ²⁰I have been crucified with Christ and I no longer live, but Christ lives in me. The life I live in the body, I live by faith in the Son of God, who loved me and gave himself for me. ²¹I do not set aside the grace of God, for if righteousness could be gained through the law, Christ died for nothing!"ᵈ

Faith or Observance of the Law

3 You foolish Galatians! Who has bewitched you? Before your very eyes Jesus Christ was clearly portrayed as crucified. ²I would like to learn just one thing from you: Did you receive the Spirit by observing the law, or by believing what you heard? ³Are you so foolish? After beginning with the Spirit, are you now trying to attain your goal by human effort? ⁴Have you suffered so much for nothing—if it really was for nothing? ⁵Does God give you his Spirit and work miracles among you because you observe the law, or because you believe what you heard?

⁶Consider Abraham: "He believed God, and it was credited to him as righteousness."ᵃ ⁷Understand, then, that those who believe are children of Abraham. ⁸The Scripture foresaw that God would justify the Gentiles

---

ᵃ7 Greek *uncircumcised*   ᵇ7 Greek *circumcised*; also in verses 8 and 9
ᶜ9 Greek *Cephas*; also in verses 11 and 14
verse 14.   ᵈ6 Gen. 15:6
ᵈ21 Some interpreters end the quotation after

by faith, and announced the gospel in advance to Abraham: "All nations will be blessed through you."[b] [9]So those who have faith are blessed along with Abraham, the man of faith.

[10]All who rely on observing the law are under a curse, for it is written: "Cursed is everyone who does not continue to do everything written in the Book of the Law."[c] [11]Clearly no-one is justified before God by the law, because, "The righteous will live by faith."[d] [12]The law is not based on faith; on the contrary, "The man who does these things will live by them."[e] [13]Christ redeemed us from the curse of the law by becoming a curse for us, for it is written: "Cursed is everyone who is hung on a tree."[f] [14]He redeemed us in order that the blessing given to Abraham might come to the Gentiles through Christ Jesus, so that by faith we might receive the promise of the Spirit.

The Law and the Promise

[15]Brothers, let me take an example from everyday life. Just as no-one can set aside or add to a human covenant that has been duly established, so it is in this case. [16]The promises were spoken to Abraham and to his seed. The Scripture does not say "and to seeds," meaning many people, but "and to your seed",[g] meaning one person, who is Christ. [17]What I mean is this: The law, introduced 430 years later, does not set aside the covenant previously established by God and thus do away with the promise. [18]For if the inheritance depends on the law, then it no longer depends on a promise; but God in his grace gave it to Abraham through a promise.

[19]What, then, was the purpose of the law? It was added because of transgressions until the Seed to whom the promise referred had come. The law was put into effect through angels by a mediator. [20]A mediator, however, does not represent just one party; but God is one.

[21]Is the law, therefore, opposed to the promises of God? Absolutely not! For if a law had been given that could impart life, then righteousness would certainly have come by the law. [22]But the Scripture declares that the whole world is a prisoner of sin, so that what was promised, being given through faith in Jesus Christ, might be given to those who believe.

[23]Before this faith came, we were held prisoners by the law, locked up until faith should be revealed. [24]So the law was put in charge to lead us to Christ[h] that we might be justified by faith. [25]Now that faith has come, we are no longer under the supervision of the law.

Sons of God

[26]You are all sons of God through faith in Christ Jesus, [27]for all of you who were baptised into Christ have clothed yourselves with Christ. [28]There is neither Jew nor Greek, slave nor free, male nor female, for you are all one in Christ Jesus. [29]If you belong to Christ, then you are Abraham's seed, and heirs according to the promise.

4 What I am saying is that as long as the heir is a child, he is no different from a slave, although he owns the whole estate. [2]He is subject to guardians and trustees until the time set by his father. [3]So also, when we were children, we were in slavery under the basic principles of the world. [4]But when the time had fully come, God sent his Son, born of a woman, born under law, [5]to redeem those under law, that we might receive the full rights of sons. [6]Because you are sons, God sent the Spirit of his Son into our hearts, the Spirit who calls out, "Abba,[a] Father." [7]So you are no longer a slave, but a son; and since you are a son, God has made you also an heir.

Paul's Concern for the Galatians

[8]Formerly, when you did not know God, you were slaves to those who by nature are not gods. [9]But now that you know God—or rather are known by God—how is it that you are turn-

[b]9 Gen. 12:3; 18:18; 22:18   [c]10 Deut. 27:26   [d]11 Hab. 2:4   [e]12 Lev. 18:5   [f]13 Deut. 21:23
[g]16 Gen. 12:7; 13:15; 24:7   [h]24 Or charge until Christ came   [a]6 Aramaic for Father

ing back to those weak and miserable principles? Do you wish to be enslaved by them all over again? 10You are observing special days and months and seasons and years! 11I fear for you, that somehow I have wasted my efforts on you.

12I plead with you, brothers, become like me, for I became like you. You have done me no wrong. 13As you know, it was because of an illness that I first preached the gospel to you. 14Even though my illness was a trial to you, you did not treat me with contempt or scorn. Instead, you welcomed me as if I were an angel of God, as if I were Christ Jesus himself. 15What has happened to all your joy? I can testify that, if you could have done so, you would have torn out your eyes and given them to me. 16Have I now become your enemy by telling you the truth?

17Those people are zealous to win you over, but for no good. What they want is to alienate you ,from us, so that you may be zealous for them. 18It is fine to be zealous, provided the purpose is good, and to be so always and not just when I am with you. 19My dear children, for whom I am again in the pains of childbirth until Christ is formed in you, 20how I wish I could be with you now and change my tone, because I am perplexed about you!

Hagar and Sarah

21Tell me, you who want to be under the law, are you not aware of what the law says? 22For it is written that Abraham had two sons, one by the slave woman and the other by the free woman. 23His son by the slave woman was born in the ordinary way; but his son by the free woman was born as the result of a promise.

24These things may be taken figuratively, for the women represent two covenants. One covenant is from Mount Sinai and bears children who are to be slaves: This is Hagar. 25Now Hagar stands for Mount Sinai in Arabia and corresponds to the present city of Jerusalem, because she is in slavery with her children. 26But the Jerusalem that is above is free, and she is our mother. 27For it is written:

"Be glad, O barren woman,
  who bears no children;
break forth and cry aloud,
  you who have no labour pains;
because more are the children of
  the desolate woman
  than of her who has a
  husband."[b]

28Now you, brothers, like Isaac, are children of promise. 29At that time the son born in the ordinary way persecuted the son born by the power of the Spirit. It is the same now. 30But what does the Scripture say? "Get rid of the slave woman and her son, for the slave woman's son will never share in the inheritance with the free woman's son."[c] 31Therefore, brothers, we are not children of the slave woman, but of the free woman.

Freedom in Christ

5 It is for freedom that Christ has set us free. Stand firm, then, and do not let yourselves be burdened again by a yoke of slavery.

2Mark my words! I, Paul, tell you that if you let yourselves be circumcised, Christ will be of no value to you at all. 3Again I declare to every man who lets himself be circumcised that he is required to obey the whole law. 4You who are trying to be justified by law have been alienated from Christ; you have fallen away from grace. 5But by faith we eagerly await through the Spirit the righteousness for which we hope. 6For in Christ Jesus neither circumcision nor uncircumcision has any value. The only thing that counts is faith expressing itself through love.

7You were running a good race. Who cut in on you and kept you from obeying the truth? 8That kind of persuasion does not come from the one who calls you. 9"A little yeast works through the whole batch of dough." 10I am confident in the Lord that you will take no other view. The one who is throwing you into confusion will

b27 Isaiah 54:1   c30 Gen. 21:10

pay the penalty, whoever he may be.
¹¹Brothers, if I am still preaching circumcision, why am I still being persecuted? In that case the offence of the cross has been abolished. ¹²As for those agitators, I wish they would go the whole way and emasculate themselves!

Life by the Spirit

¹³You, my brothers, were called to be free. But do not use your freedom to indulge the sinful nature;ᵃ rather, serve one another in love. ¹⁴The entire law is summed up in a single command: "Love your neighbour as yourself."ᵇ ¹⁵If you keep on biting and devouring each other, watch out or you will be destroyed by each other.

¹⁶So I say, live by the Spirit, and you will not gratify the desires of the sinful nature. ¹⁷For the sinful nature desires what is contrary to the Spirit, and the Spirit what is contrary to the sinful nature. They are in conflict with each other, so that you do not do what you want. ¹⁸But if you are led by the Spirit, you are not under law.

¹⁹The acts of the sinful nature are obvious: sexual immorality, impurity and debauchery; ²⁰idolatry and witchcraft; hatred, discord, jealousy, fits of rage, selfish ambition, dissensions, factions ²¹and envy; drunkenness, orgies, and the like. I warn you, as I did before, that those who live like this will not inherit the kingdom of God.

²²But the fruit of the Spirit is love, joy, peace, patience, kindness, goodness, faithfulness, ²³gentleness and self-control. Against such things there is no law. ²⁴Those who belong to Christ Jesus have crucified the sinful nature with its passions and desires. ²⁵Since we live by the Spirit, let us keep in step with the Spirit. ²⁶Let us not become conceited, provoking and envying each other.

Doing Good to All

6 Brothers, if someone is caught in a sin, you who are spiritual should restore him gently. But watch yourself, or you also may be tempted. ²Carry each other's burdens, and in this way you will fulfil the law of Christ. ³If anyone thinks he is something when he is nothing, he deceives himself. ⁴Each one should test his own actions. Then he can take pride in himself, without comparing himself to somebody else, ⁵for each one should carry his own load.

⁶Anyone who receives instruction in the word must share all good things with his instructor.

⁷Do not be deceived: God cannot be mocked. A man reaps what he sows. ⁸The one who sows to please his sinful nature, from that natureᵃ will reap destruction; the one who sows to please the Spirit, from the Spirit will reap eternal life. ⁹Let us not become weary in doing good, for at the proper time we will reap a harvest if we do not give up. ¹⁰Therefore, as we have opportunity, let us do good to all people, especially to those who belong to the family of believers.

Not Circumcision but a New Creation

¹¹See what large letters I use as I write to you with my own hand!

¹²Those who want to make a good impression outwardly are trying to compel you to be circumcised. The only reason they do this is to avoid being persecuted for the cross of Christ. ¹³Not even those who are circumcised obey the law, yet they want you to be circumcised that they may boast about your flesh. ¹⁴May I never boast except in the cross of our Lord Jesus Christ, through which the world has been crucified to me, and I to the world. ¹⁵Neither circumcision nor uncircumcision means anything; what counts is a new creation. ¹⁶Peace and mercy to all who follow this rule, even to the Israel of God.

¹⁷Finally, let no-one cause me trouble, for I bear on my body the marks of Jesus.

¹⁸The grace of our Lord Jesus Christ be with your spirit, brothers. Amen.

ᵃ13 Or the flesh; also in verses 16, 17, 19 and 24   ᵇ14 Lev. 19:18
ᵃ8 Or his flesh, from the flesh

Ephesians

1 Paul, an apostle of Christ Jesus
by the will of God,

To the saints in Ephesus,*a* the faithful*b* in Christ Jesus:

2Grace and peace to you from God
our Father and the Lord Jesus Christ.

Spiritual Blessings in Christ

3Praise be to the God and Father of
our Lord Jesus Christ, who has
blessed us in the heavenly realms
with every spiritual blessing in Christ.
4For he chose us in him before the
creation of the world to be holy and
blameless in his sight. In love 5he*c*
predestined us to be adopted as his
sons through Jesus Christ, in accordance with his pleasure and will—6to
the praise of his glorious grace, which
he has freely given us in the One he
loves. 7In him we have redemption
through his blood, the forgiveness of
sins, in accordance with the riches of
God's grace 8that he lavished on us
with all wisdom and understanding.
9And he*d* made known to us the
mystery of his will according to his
good pleasure, which he purposed in
Christ, 10to be put into effect when
the times will have reached their
fulfilment—to bring all things in
heaven and on earth together under
one head, even Christ.

11In him we were also chosen,*e*
having been predestined according to
the plan of him who works out everything in conformity with the purpose
of his will, 12in order that we, who
were the first to hope in Christ, might
be for the praise of his glory. 13And

you also were included in Christ
when you heard the word of truth,
the gospel of your salvation. Having
believed, you were marked in him
with a seal, the promised Holy Spirit,
14who is a deposit guaranteeing our
inheritance until the redemption of
those who are God's possession—to
the praise of his glory.

Thanksgiving and Prayer

15For this reason, ever since I heard
about your faith in the Lord Jesus and
your love for all the saints, 16I have
not stopped giving thanks for you,
remembering you in my prayers. 17I
keep asking that the God of our Lord
Jesus Christ, the glorious Father, may
give you the Spirit*f* of wisdom and
revelation, so that you may know him
better. 18I pray also that the eyes of
your heart may be enlightened in
order that you may know the hope to
which he has called you, the riches
of his glorious inheritance in the
saints, 19and his incomparably great
power for us who believe. That power
is like the working of his mighty
strength, 20which he exerted in Christ
when he raised him from the dead
and seated him at his right hand in
the heavenly realms, 21far above all
rule and authority, power and dominion, and every title that can be given,
not only in the present age but also in
the one to come. 22And God placed
all things under his feet and
appointed him to be head over everything for the church, 23which is his
body, the fulness of him who fills
everything in every way.

---

a1 Some early manuscripts do not have in Ephesus.   *b1 Or* believers who are
c4, 5 Or sight in love. *1He   *d8, 9 Or* us. With all wisdom and understanding, *4he
e11 Or were made heirs   *f17 Or* a spirit

Made Alive in Christ

2 As for you, you were dead in your transgressions and sins, ²in which you used to live when you followed the ways of this world and of the ruler of the kingdom of the air, the spirit who is now at work in those who are disobedient. ³All of us also lived among them at one time, gratifying the cravings of our sinful nature*a* and following its desires and thoughts. Like the rest, we were by nature objects of wrath. ⁴But because of his great love for us, God, who is rich in mercy, ⁵made us alive with Christ even when we were dead in transgressions—it is by grace you have been saved. ⁶And God raised us up with Christ and seated us with him in the heavenly realms in Christ Jesus, ⁷in order that in the coming ages he might show the incomparable riches of his grace, expressed in his kindness to us in Christ Jesus. ⁸For it is by grace you have been saved, through faith—and this not from yourselves, it is the gift of God—⁹not by works, so that no-one can boast. ¹⁰For we are God's workmanship, created in Christ Jesus to do good works, which God prepared in advance for us to do.

One in Christ

¹¹Therefore, remember that formerly you who are Gentiles by birth and called "uncircumcised" by those who call themselves "the circumcision" (that done in the body by the hands of men)—¹²remember that at that time you were separate from Christ, excluded from citizenship in Israel and foreigners to the covenants of the promise, without hope and without God in the world. ¹³But now in Christ Jesus you who once were far away have been brought near through the blood of Christ.

¹⁴For he himself is our peace, who has made the two one and has destroyed the barrier, the dividing wall of hostility, ¹⁵by abolishing in his flesh the law with its commandments and regulations. His purpose was to create in himself one new man out of

*a*3 Or *our flesh*

the two, thus making peace, ¹⁶and in this one body to reconcile both of them to God through the cross, by which he put to death their hostility. ¹⁷He came and preached peace to you who were far away and peace to those who were near. ¹⁸For through him we both have access to the Father by one Spirit.

¹⁹Consequently, you are no longer foreigners and aliens, but fellow-citizens with God's people and members of God's household, ²⁰built on the foundation of the apostles and prophets, with Christ Jesus himself as the chief cornerstone. ²¹In him the whole building is joined together and rises to become a holy temple in the Lord. ²²And in him you too are being built together to become a dwelling in which God lives by his Spirit.

Paul the Preacher to the Gentiles

3 For this reason I, Paul, the prisoner of Christ Jesus for the sake of you Gentiles—

²Surely you have heard about the administration of God's grace that was given to me for you, ³that is, the mystery made known to me by revelation, as I have already written briefly. ⁴In reading this, then, you will be able to understand my insight into the mystery of Christ, ⁵which was not made known to men in other generations as it has now been revealed by the Spirit to God's holy apostles and prophets. ⁶This mystery is that through the gospel the Gentiles are heirs together with Israel, members together of one body, and sharers together in the promise in Christ Jesus.

⁷I became a servant of this gospel by the gift of God's grace given me through the working of his power. ⁸Although I am less than the least of all God's people, this grace was given me: to preach to the Gentiles the unsearchable riches of Christ, ⁹and to make plain to everyone the administration of this mystery, which for ages past was kept hidden in God, who created all things. ¹⁰His intent was that now, through the church, the

manifold wisdom of God should be made known to the rulers and authorities in the heavenly realms, 11according to his eternal purpose which he accomplished in Christ Jesus our Lord. 12In him and through faith in him we may approach God with freedom and confidence. 13I ask you, therefore, not to be discouraged because of my sufferings for you, which are your glory.

A Prayer for the Ephesians

14For this reason I kneel before the Father, 15from whom his whole family*a* in heaven and on earth derives its name. 16I pray that out of his glorious riches he may strengthen you with power through his Spirit in your inner being, 17so that Christ may dwell in your hearts through faith. And I pray that you, being rooted and established in love, 18may have power, together with all the saints, to grasp how wide and long and high and deep is the love of Christ, 19and to know this love that surpasses knowledge—that you may be filled to the measure of all the fulness of God.

20Now to him who is able to do immeasurably more than all we ask or imagine, according to his power that is at work within us, 21to him be glory in the church and in Christ Jesus throughout all generations, for ever and ever! Amen.

Unity in the Body of Christ

4 As a prisoner for the Lord, then, I urge you to live a life worthy of the calling you have received. 2Be completely humble and gentle; be patient, bearing with one another in love. 3Make every effort to keep the unity of the Spirit through the bond of peace. 4There is one body and one Spirit—just as you were called to one hope when you were called—5one Lord, one faith, one baptism; 6one God and Father of all, who is over all and through all and in all.

7But to each one of us grace has been given as Christ apportioned it. 8This is why it*a* says:

"When he ascended on high, he led captives in his train and gave gifts to men."*b*

9(What does "he ascended" mean except that he also descended to the lower, earthly regions? 10He who descended is the very one who ascended higher than all the heavens, in order to fill the whole universe.) 11It was he who gave some to be apostles, some to be prophets, some to be evangelists, and some to be pastors and teachers, 12to prepare God's people for works of service, so that the body of Christ may be built up 13until we all reach unity in the faith and in the knowledge of the Son of God and become mature, attaining to the whole measure of the fulness of Christ.

14Then we will no longer be infants, tossed back and forth by the waves, and blown here and there by every wind of teaching and by the cunning and craftiness of men in their deceitful scheming. 15Instead, speaking the truth in love, we will in all things grow up into him who is the Head, that is, Christ. 16From him the whole body, joined and held together by every supporting ligament, grows and builds itself up in love, as each part does its work.

Living as Children of Light

17So I tell you this, and insist on it in the Lord, that you must no longer live as the Gentiles do, in the futility of their thinking. 18They are darkened in their understanding and separated from the life of God because of the ignorance that is in them due to the hardening of their hearts. 19Having lost all sensitivity, they have given themselves over to sensuality so as to indulge in every kind of impurity, with a continual lust for more.

20You, however, did not come to know Christ that way. 21Surely you heard of him and were taught in him in accordance with the truth that is in Jesus. 22You were taught, with regard to your former way of life, to put off your old self, which is being cor-

*a*15 Or *whom all fatherhood*   *a*8 Or *God*   *b*8 Psalm 68:18

214

rupted by its deceitful desires; 23to be made new in the attitude of your minds; 24and to put on the new self, created to be like God in true righteousness and holiness.

25Therefore each of you must put off falsehood and speak truthfully to his neighbour, for we are all members of one body. 26"In your anger do not sin"c: Do not let the sun go down while you are still angry, 27and do not give the devil a foothold. 28He who has been stealing must steal no longer, but must work, doing something useful with his own hands, that he may have something to share with those in need.

29Do not let any unwholesome talk come out of your mouths, but only what is helpful for building others up according to their needs, that it may benefit those who listen. 30And do not grieve the Holy Spirit of God, with whom you were sealed for the day of redemption. 31Get rid of all bitterness, rage and anger, brawling and slander, along with every form of malice. 32Be kind and compassionate to one another, forgiving each other, just as in Christ God forgave you.

5 Be imitators of God, therefore, as dearly loved children 2and live a life of love, just as Christ loved us and gave himself up for us as a fragrant offering and sacrifice to God.

3But among you there must not be even a hint of sexual immorality, or of any kind of impurity, or of greed, because these are improper for God's holy people. 4Nor should there be obscenity, foolish talk or coarse joking, which are out of place, but rather thanksgiving. 5For of this you can be sure: No immoral, impure or greedy person—such a man is an idolater—has any inheritance in the kingdom of Christ and of God.a 6Let no-one deceive you with empty words, for because of such things God's wrath comes on those who are disobedient. 7Therefore do not be partners with them.

8For you were once darkness, but now you are light in the Lord. Live as children of light 9(for the fruit of the

light consists in all goodness, righteousness and truth) 10and find out what pleases the Lord. 11Have nothing to do with the fruitless deeds of darkness, but rather expose them. 12For it is shameful even to mention what the disobedient do in secret. 13But everything exposed by the light becomes visible, 14for it is light that makes everything visible. This is why it is said:

"Wake up, O sleeper,
rise from the dead,
and Christ will shine on you."

15Be very careful, then, how you live—not as unwise but as wise, 16making the most of every opportunity, because the days are evil. 17Therefore do not be foolish, but understand what the Lord's will is. 18Do not get drunk on wine, which leads to debauchery. Instead, be filled with the Spirit. 19Speak to one another with psalms, hymns and spiritual songs. Sing and make music in your heart to the Lord, 20always giving thanks to God the Father for everything, in the name of our Lord Jesus Christ.

21Submit to one another out of reverence for Christ.

Wives and Husbands

22Wives, submit to your husbands as to the Lord. 23For the husband is the head of the wife as Christ is the head of the church, his body, of which he is the Saviour. 24Now as the church submits to Christ, so also wives should submit to their husbands in everything.

25Husbands, love your wives, just as Christ loved the church and gave himself up for her 26to make her holy, cleansingb her by the washing with water through the word, 27and to present her to himself as a radiant church, without stain or wrinkle or any other blemish, but holy and blameless. 28In this same way, husbands ought to love their wives as their own bodies. He who loves his wife loves himself. 29After all, no-one ever hated his own body, but he feeds

c26 *Psalm 4:4*   a5 *Or kingdom of the Christ and God*   b26 *Or having cleansed*

215

and cares for it, just as Christ does the church—30for we are members of his body. 31"For this reason a man will leave his father and mother and be united to his wife, and the two will become one flesh."c 32This is a profound mystery—but I am talking about Christ and the church. 33However, each one of you also must love his wife as he loves himself, and the wife must respect her husband.

Children and Parents

6 Children, obey your parents in the Lord, for this is right. 2"Honour your father and mother"—which is the first commandment with a promise—3"that it may go well with you and that you may enjoy long life on the earth."d

4Fathers, do not exasperate your children; instead, bring them up in the training and instruction of the Lord.

Slaves and Masters

5Slaves, obey your earthly masters with respect and fear, and with sincerity of heart, just as you would obey Christ. 6Obey them not only to win their favour when their eye is on you, but like slaves of Christ, doing the will of God from your heart. 7Serve wholeheartedly, as if you were serving the Lord, not men, 8because you know that the Lord will reward everyone for whatever good he does, whether he is slave or free.

9And masters, treat your slaves in the same way. Do not threaten them, since you know that he who is both their Master and yours is in heaven, and there is no favouritism with him.

The Armour of God

10Finally, be strong in the Lord and in his mighty power. 11Put on the full armour of God so that you can take your stand against the devil's schemes. 12For our struggle is not against flesh and blood, but against the rulers, against the authorities, against the powers of this dark world and against the spiritual forces of evil in the heavenly realms. 13Therefore put on the full armour of God, so that when the day of evil comes, you may be able to stand your ground, and after you have done everything, to stand. 14Stand firm then, with the belt of truth buckled round your waist, with the breastplate of righteousness in place, 15and with your feet fitted with the readiness that comes from the gospel of peace. 16In addition to all this, take up the shield of faith, with which you can extinguish all the flaming arrows of the evil one. 17Take the helmet of salvation and the sword of the Spirit, which is the word of God. 18And pray in the Spirit on all occasions with all kinds of prayers and requests. With this in mind, be alert and always keep on praying for all the saints.

19Pray also for me, that whenever I open my mouth, words may be given me so that I will fearlessly make known the mystery of the gospel, 20for which I am an ambassador in chains. Pray that I may declare it fearlessly, as I should.

Final Greetings

21Tychicus, the dear brother and faithful servant in the Lord, will tell you everything, so that you also may know how I am and what I am doing. 22I am sending him to you for this very purpose, that you may know how we are, and that he may encourage you.

23Peace to the brothers, and love with faith from God the Father and the Lord Jesus Christ. 24Grace to all who love our Lord Jesus Christ with an undying love.

c31 Gen. 2:24   d3 Deut. 5:16

Philippians

1 Paul and Timothy, servants of Christ Jesus,

To all the saints in Christ Jesus at Philippi, together with the overseers[a] and deacons:

2Grace and peace to you from God our Father and the Lord Jesus Christ.

Thanksgiving and Prayer

3I thank my God every time I remember you. 4In all my prayers for all of you, I always pray with joy 5because of your partnership in the gospel from the first day until now, 6being confident of this, that he who began a good work in you will carry it on to completion until the day of Christ Jesus.

7It is right for me to feel this way about all of you, since I have you in my heart; for whether I am in chains or defending and confirming the gospel, all of you share in God's grace with me. 8God can testify how I long for all of you with the affection of Christ Jesus.

9And this is my prayer: that your love may abound more and more in knowledge and depth of insight, 10so that you may be able to discern what is best and may be pure and blameless until the day of Christ, 11filled with the fruit of righteousness that comes through Jesus Christ—to the glory and praise of God.

Paul's Chains Advance the Gospel

12Now I want you to know, brothers, that what has happened to me has really served to advance the gospel. 13As a result, it has become clear throughout the whole palace guard[b] and to everyone else that I am in chains for Christ. 14Because of my chains, most of the brothers in the Lord have been encouraged to speak the word of God more courageously and fearlessly.

15It is true that some preach Christ out of envy and rivalry, but others out of good will. 16The latter do so in love, knowing that I am put here for the defence of the gospel. 17The former preach Christ out of selfish ambition, not sincerely, supposing that they can stir up trouble for me while I am in chains. 18But what does it matter? The important thing is that in every way, whether from false motives or true, Christ is preached. And because of this I rejoice.

Yes, and I will continue to rejoice, 19for I know that through your prayers and the help given by the Spirit of Jesus Christ, what has happened to me will turn out for my deliverance.[c] 20I eagerly expect and hope that I will in no way be ashamed, but will have sufficient courage so that now as always Christ will be exalted in my body, whether by life or by death. 21For to me, to live is Christ and to die is gain. 22If I am to go on living in the body, this will mean fruitful labour for me. Yet what shall I choose? I do not know! 23I am torn between the two: I desire to depart and be with Christ, which is better by far; 24but it is more necessary for you that I remain in the body. 25Convinced of this, I know that I will remain, and I will continue with all of you for your progress and joy in the faith, 26so that through my being with you again your joy in Christ Jesus will overflow on account of me.

a1 Traditionally bishops   b13 Or whole palace   c19 Or salvation

217

27Whatever happens, conduct yourselves in a manner worthy of the gospel of Christ. Then, whether I come and see you or only hear about you in my absence, I will know that you stand firm in one spirit, contending as one man for the faith of the gospel 28without being frightened in any way by those who oppose you. This is a sign to them that they will be destroyed, but that you will be saved—and that by God. 29For it has been granted to you on behalf of Christ not only to believe on him, but also to suffer for him, 30since you are going through the same struggle you saw I had, and now hear that I still have.

Imitating Christ's Humility

2 If you have any encouragement from being united with Christ, if any comfort from his love, if any fellowship with the Spirit, if any tenderness and compassion, 2then make my joy complete by being like-minded, having the same love, being one in spirit and purpose. 3Do nothing out of selfish ambition or vain conceit, but in humility consider others better than yourselves. 4Each of you should look not only to your own interests, but also to the interests of others.
5Your attitude should be the same as that of Christ Jesus:

6Who, being in very nature*a* God,
   did not consider equality with
      God something to be
      grasped,
7but made himself nothing,
   taking the very nature*b* of a
      servant,
   being made in human likeness.
8And being found in appearance as a
      man,
   he humbled himself
   and became obedient to death—
      even death on a cross!
9Therefore God exalted him to the
      highest place
   and gave him the name that is
      above every name,
10that at the name of Jesus every knee
      should bow,

in heaven and on earth and under
      the earth,
11and every tongue confess that Jesus
   Christ is Lord,
   to the glory of God the Father.

Shining as Stars

12Therefore, my dear friends, as you have always obeyed—not only in my presence, but now much more in my absence—continue to work out your salvation with fear and trembling, 13for it is God who works in you to will and to act according to his good purpose.
14Do everything without complaining or arguing, 15so that you may become blameless and pure, children of God without fault in a crooked and depraved generation, in which you shine like stars in the universe 16as you hold out*c* the word of life—in order that I may boast on the day of Christ that I did not run or labour for nothing. 17But even if I am being poured out like a drink offering on the sacrifice and service coming from your faith, I am glad and rejoice with all of you. 18So you too should be glad and rejoice with me.

Timothy and Epaphroditus

19I hope in the Lord Jesus to send Timothy to you soon, that I also may be cheered when I receive news about you. 20I have no-one else like him, who takes a genuine interest in your welfare. 21For everyone looks out for his own interests, not those of Jesus Christ. 22But you know that Timothy has proved himself, because as a son with his father he has served with me in the work of the gospel. 23I hope, therefore, to send him as soon as I see how things go with me. 24And I am confident in the Lord that I myself will come soon.
25But I think it is necessary to send back to you Epaphroditus, my brother, fellow-worker and fellow-soldier, who is also your messenger, whom you sent to take care of my needs. 26For he longs for all of you and is distressed because you heard he was ill. 27Indeed he was ill, and

a6 Or in the form of   *b7 Or the form*   *c16 Or hold on to*

218

almost died. But God had mercy on him, and not on him only but also on me, to spare me sorrow upon sorrow. [28]Therefore . am all the more eager to send him, so that when you see him again you may be glad and I may have less anxiety. [29]Welcome him in the Lord with great joy, and honour men like him, [30]because he almost died for the work of Christ, risking his life to make up for the help you could not give me.

No Confidence in the Flesh

3 Finally, my brothers, rejoice in the Lord! It is no trouble for me to write the same things to you again, and it is a safeguard for you.

[2]Watch out for those dogs, those men who do evil, those mutilators of the flesh. [3]For it is we who are the circumcision, we who worship by the Spirit of God, who glory in Christ Jesus, and who put no confidence in the flesh—[4]though I myself have reasons for such confidence.

If anyone else thinks he has reasons to put confidence in the flesh, I have more: [5]circumcised on the eighth day, of the people of Israel, of the tribe of Benjamin, a Hebrew of Hebrews; in regard to the law, a Pharisee; [6]as for zeal, persecuting the church; as for legalistic righteousness, faultless.

[7]But whatever was to my profit I now consider loss for the sake of Christ. [8]What is more, I consider everything a loss compared to the surpassing greatness of knowing Christ Jesus my Lord, for whose sake I have lost all things. I consider them rubbish, that I may gain Christ [9]and be found in him, not having a righteousness of my own that comes from the law, but that which is through faith in Christ—the righteousness that comes from God and is by faith. [10]I want to know Christ and the power of his resurrection and the fellowship of sharing in his sufferings, becoming like him in his death, [11]and so, somehow, to attain to the resurrection from the dead.

[a]3 Or loyal Syzygus

Pressing on Towards the Goal

[12]Not that I have already obtained all this, or have already been made perfect, but I press on to take hold of that for which Christ Jesus took hold of me.[13]Brothers, I do not consider myself yet to have taken hold of it. But one thing I do: Forgetting what is behind and straining towards what is ahead, [14]I press on towards the goal to win the prize for which God has called me heavenwards in Christ Jesus.

[15]All of us who are mature should take such a view of things. And if on some point you think differently, that too God will make clear to you. [16]Only let us live up to what we have already attained.

[17]Join with others in following my example, brothers, and take note of those who live according to the pattern we gave you. [18]For, as I have often told you before and now say again even with tears, many live as enemies of the cross of Christ. [19]Their destiny is destruction, their god is their stomach, and their glory is in their shame. Their mind is on earthly things. [20]But our citizenship is in heaven. And we eagerly await a Saviour from there, the Lord Jesus Christ, [21]who, by the power that enables him to bring everything under his control, will transform our lowly bodies so that they will be like his glorious body.

4 Therefore, my brothers, you whom I love and long for, my joy and crown, that is how you should stand firm in the Lord, dear friends!

Exhortations

[2]I plead with Euodia and I plead with Syntyche to agree with each other in the Lord. [3]Yes, and I ask you, loyal yoke-fellow,[a] help these women who have contended at my side in the cause of the gospel, along with Clement and the rest of my fellow-workers, whose names are in the book of life.

[4]Rejoice in the Lord always. I will

say it again: Rejoice! [5]Let your gentleness be evident to all. The Lord is near. [6]Do not be anxious about anything, but in everything, by prayer and petition, with thanksgiving, present your requests to God. [7]And the peace of God, which transcends all understanding, will guard your hearts and your minds in Christ Jesus.

[8]Finally, brothers, whatever is true, whatever is noble, whatever is right, whatever is pure, whatever is lovely, whatever is admirable—if anything is excellent or praiseworthy—think about such things. [9]Whatever you have learned or received or heard from me, or seen in me—put it into practice. And the God of peace will be with you.

Thanks for Their Gifts

[10]I rejoice greatly in the Lord that at last you have renewed your concern for me. Indeed, you have been concerned, but you had no opportunity to show it. [11]I am not saying this because I am in need, for I have learned to be content whatever the circumstances. [12]I know what it is to be in need, and I know what it is to have plenty. I have learned the secret of being content in any and every situation, whether well fed or hungry, whether living in plenty or in want.

[13]I can do everything through him who gives me strength.

[14]Yet it was good of you to share in my troubles. [15]Moreover, as you Philippians know, in the early days of your acquaintance with the gospel, when I set out from Macedonia, not one church shared with me in the matter of giving and receiving, except you only; [16]for even when I was in Thessalonica, you sent me aid again and again when I was in need. [17]Not that I am looking for a gift, but I am looking for what may be credited to your account. [18]I have received full payment and even more; I am amply supplied, now that I have received from Epaphroditus the gifts you sent. They are a fragrant offering, an acceptable sacrifice, pleasing to God. [19]And my God will meet all your needs according to his glorious riches in Christ Jesus.

[20]To our God and Father be glory for ever and ever. Amen.

Final Greetings

[21]Greet all the saints in Christ Jesus. The brothers who are with me send greetings. [22]All the saints send you greetings, especially those who belong to Caesar's household.

[23]The grace of the Lord Jesus Christ be with your spirit. Amen.[b]

---

[b]23 Some manuscripts do not have *Amen*.

Colossians

1 Paul, an apostle of Christ Jesus by the will of God, and Timothy our brother,

²To the holy and faithful[a] brothers in Christ at Colosse:

Grace and peace to you from God our Father.[b]

Thanksgiving and Prayer

³We always thank God, the Father of our Lord Jesus Christ, when we pray for you, ⁴because we have heard of your faith in Christ Jesus and of the love you have for all the saints— ⁵the faith and love that spring from the hope that is stored up for you in heaven and that you have already heard about in the word of truth, the gospel ⁶that has come to you. All over the world this gospel is producing fruit and growing, just as it has been doing among you since the day you heard it and understood God's grace in all its truth. ⁷You learned it from Epaphras, our dear fellow-servant, who is a faithful minister of Christ on our[c] behalf, ⁸and who also told us of your love in the Spirit.

⁹For this reason, since the day we heard about you, we have not stopped praying for you and asking God to fill you with the knowledge of his will through all spiritual wisdom and understanding. ¹⁰And we pray this in order that you may live a life worthy of the Lord and may please him in every way: bearing fruit in every good work, growing in the knowledge of God, ¹¹being strengthened with all

power according to his glorious might so that you may have great endurance and patience, and joyfully ¹²giving thanks to the Father, who has qualified you[d] to share in the inheritance of the saints in the kingdom of light. ¹³For he has rescued us from the dominion of darkness and brought us into the kingdom of the Son he loves, ¹⁴in whom we have redemption,[e] the forgiveness of sins.

The Supremacy of Christ

¹⁵He is the image of the invisible God, the firstborn over all creation. ¹⁶For by him all things were created: things in heaven and on earth, visible and invisible, whether thrones or powers or rulers or authorities; all things were created by him and for him. ¹⁷He is before all things, and in him all things hold together. ¹⁸And he is the head of the body, the church; he is the beginning and the firstborn from among the dead, so that in everything he might have the supremacy. ¹⁹For God was pleased to have all his fulness dwell in him, ²⁰and through him to reconcile to himself all things, whether things on earth or things in heaven, by making peace through his blood, shed on the cross.

²¹Once you were alienated from God and were enemies in your minds because of your evil behaviour. ²²But now he has reconciled you by Christ's physical body through death to present you holy in his sight, without blemish and free from accusation— ²³if you continue in your faith, established and firm, not moved from the

---

a2 Or believing   b2 Some manuscripts Father and the Lord Jesus Christ
c7 Some manuscripts your   d12 Some manuscripts us
e14 A few late manuscripts redemption through his blood

221

hope held out in the gospel. This is the gospel that you heard and that has been proclaimed to every creature under heaven, and of which I, Paul, have become a servant.

Paul's Labour for the Church

24Now I rejoice in what was suffered for you, and I fill up in my flesh what is still lacking in regard to Christ's afflictions, for the sake of his body, which is the church. 25I have become its servant by the commission God gave me to present to you the word of God in its fulness—26the mystery that has been kept hidden for ages and generations, but is now disclosed to the saints. 27To them God has chosen to make known among the Gentiles the glorious riches of this mystery, which is Christ in you, the hope of glory.

28We proclaim him, admonishing and teaching everyone with all wisdom, so that we may present everyone perfect in Christ. 29To this end I labour, struggling with all his energy, which so powerfully works in me.

2 I want you to know how much I am struggling for you and for those at Laodicea, and for all who have not met me personally. 2My purpose is that they may be encouraged in heart and united in love, so that they may have the full riches of complete understanding, in order that they may know the mystery of God, namely, Christ,a 3in whom are hidden all the treasures of wisdom and knowledge. 4I tell you this so that no-one may deceive you by finesounding arguments. 5For though I am absent from you in body, I am present with you in spirit and delight to see how orderly you are and how firm your faith in Christ is.

Freedom From Human Regulations Through Life With Christ

6So then, just as you received Christ Jesus as Lord, continue to live in him, 7rooted and built up in him, strengthened in the faith as you were

taught, and overflowing with thankfulness.

8See to it that no-one takes you captive through hollow and deceptive philosophy, which depends on human tradition and the basic principles of this world rather than on Christ.

9For in Christ all the fulness of the Deity lives in bodily form, 10and you have been given fulness in Christ, who is the head over every power and authority. 11In him you were also circumcised, in the putting off of the sinful nature,b not with a circumcision done by the hands of men but with the circumcision done by Christ, 12having been buried with him in baptism and raised with him through your faith in the power of God, who raised him from the dead.

13When you were dead in your sins and in the uncircumcision of your sinful nature,c God made youd alive with Christ. He forgave us all our sins, 14having cancelled the written code, with its regulations, that was against us and that stood opposed to us; he took it away, nailing it to the cross. 15And having disarmed the powers and authorities, he made a public spectacle of them, triumphing over them by the cross.e

16Therefore do not let anyone judge you by what you eat or drink, or with regard to a religious festival, a New Moon celebration or a Sabbath day. 17These are a shadow of the things that were to come; the reality, however, is found in Christ. 18Do not let anyone who delights in false humility and the worship of angels disqualify you for the prize. Such a person goes into great detail about what he has seen, and his unspiritual mind puffs him up with idle notions. 19He has lost connection with the Head, from whom the whole body, supported and held together by its ligaments and sinews, grows as God causes it to grow.

20Since you died with Christ to the basic principles of this world, why, as though you still belonged to it, do you

---

a2 Some manuscripts God, even the Father, and of Christ   b11 Or the flesh   c13 Or your flesh   d13 Some manuscripts us   e15 Or them in him

submit to its rules: 21"Do not handle! Do not taste! Do not touch!"? 22These are all destined to perish with use, because they are based on human commands and teachings. 23Such regulations indeed have an appearance of wisdom, with their self-imposed worship, their false humility and their harsh treatment of the body, but they lack any value in restraining sensual indulgence.

Rules for Holy Living

3 Since, then, you have been raised with Christ, set your hearts on things above, where Christ is seated at the right hand of God. 2Set your minds on things above, not on earthly things. 3For you died, and your life is now hidden with Christ in God. 4When Christ, who is your*d* life, appears, then you also will appear with him in glory.

5Put to death, therefore, whatever belongs to your earthly nature: sexual immorality, impurity, lust, evil desires and greed, which is idolatry. 6Because of these, the wrath of God is coming.*b* 7You used to walk in these ways, in the life you once lived. 8But now you must rid yourselves of all such things as these: anger, rage, malice, slander and filthy language from your lips. 9Do not lie to each other, since you have taken off your old self with its practices 10and have put on the new self, which is being renewed in knowledge in the image of its Creator. 11Here there is no Greek or Jew, circumcised or uncircumcised, barbarian, Scythian, slave or free, but Christ is all, and is in all.

12Therefore, as God's chosen people, holy and dearly loved, clothe yourselves with compassion, kindness, humility, gentleness and patience. 13Bear with each other and forgive whatever grievances you may have against one another. Forgive as the Lord forgave you. 14And over all these virtues put on love, which binds them all together in perfect unity.

15Let the peace of Christ rule in your hearts, since as members of one body you were called to peace. And be thankful. 16Let the word of Christ dwell in you richly as you teach and admonish one another with all wisdom, and as you sing psalms, hymns and spiritual songs with gratitude in your hearts to God. 17And whatever you do, whether in word or deed, do it all in the name of the Lord Jesus, giving thanks to God the Father through him.

Rules for Christian Households

18Wives, submit to your husbands, as is fitting in the Lord.

19Husbands, love your wives and do not be harsh with them.

20Children, obey your parents in everything, for this pleases the Lord.

21Fathers, do not embitter your children, or they will become discouraged.

22Slaves, obey your earthly masters in everything; and do it, not only when their eye is on you and to win their favour, but with sincerity of heart and reverence for the Lord. 23Whatever you do, work at it with all your heart, as working for the Lord, not for men, 24since you know that you will receive an inheritance from the Lord as a reward. It is the Lord Christ you are serving. 25Anyone who does wrong will be repaid for his wrong, and there is no favouritism.

4 Masters, provide your slaves with what is right and fair, because you know that you also have a Master in heaven.

Further Instructions

2Devote yourselves to prayer, being watchful and thankful. 3And pray for us, too, that God may open a door for our message, so that we may proclaim the mystery of Christ, for which I am in chains. 4Pray that I may proclaim it clearly, as I should. 5Be wise in the way you act towards outsiders; make the most of every opportunity. 6Let your conversation be always full of grace, seasoned with salt, so that you may know how to answer everyone.

*a*4 Some manuscripts our
*b*6 Some early manuscripts coming on those who are disobedient

Final Greetings

7Tychicus will tell you all the news about me. He is a dear brother, a faithful minister and fellow-servant in the Lord. 8I am sending him to you for the express purpose that you may know about our*a* circumstances and that he may encourage your hearts. 9He is coming with Onesimus, our faithful and dear brother, who is one of you. They will tell you everything that is happening here.

10My fellow-prisoner Aristarchus sends you his greetings, as does Mark, the cousin of Barnabas. (You have received instructions about him; if he comes to you, welcome him.) 11Jesus, who is called Justus, also sends greetings. These are the only Jews among my fellow-workers for the kingdom of God, and they have proved a comfort to me. 12Epaphras, who is one of you and a servant of Christ Jesus, sends greetings. He is always wrestling in prayer for you, that you may stand firm in all the will of God, mature and fully assured. 13I vouch for him that he is working hard for you and for those at Laodicea and Hierapolis. 14Our dear friend Luke, the doctor, and Demas send greetings. 15Give my greetings to the brothers at Laodicea, and to Nympha and the church in her house.

16After this letter has been read to you, see that it is also read in the church of the Laodiceans and that you in turn read the letter from Laodicea.

17Tell Archippus: "See to it that you complete the work you have received in the Lord."

18I, Paul, write this greeting in my own hand. Remember my chains. Grace be with you.

a8 Some manuscripts that he may know about your

1 Thessalonians

1 Paul, Silas[a] and Timothy,

To the church of the Thessalonians in God the Father and the Lord Jesus Christ:

Grace and peace to you.[b]

Thanksgiving for the Thessalonians' Faith

2We always thank God for all of you, mentioning you in our prayers. 3We continually remember before our God and Father your work produced by faith, your labour prompted by love, and your endurance inspired by hope in our Lord Jesus Christ.

4Brothers loved by God, we know that he has chosen you, 5because our gospel came to you not simply with words, but also with power, with the Holy Spirit and with deep conviction. You know how we lived among you for your sake. 6You became imitators of us and of the Lord; in spite of severe suffering, you welcomed the message with the joy given by the Holy Spirit. 7And so you became a model to all the believers in Macedonia and Achaia. 8The Lord's message rang out from you not only in Macedonia and Achaia—your faith in God has become known everywhere. Therefore we do not need to say anything about it, 9for they themselves report what kind of reception you gave us. They tell how you turned to God from idols to serve the living and true God, 10and to wait for his Son from heaven, whom he raised from the dead—Jesus, who rescues us from the coming wrath.

Paul's Ministry in Thessalonica

2 You know, brothers, that our visit to you was not a failure. 2We had previously suffered and been insulted in Philippi, as you know, but with the help of our God we dared to tell you his gospel in spite of strong opposition. 3For the appeal we make does not spring from error or impure motives, nor are we trying to trick you. 4On the contrary, we speak as men approved by God to be entrusted with the gospel. We are not trying to please men but God, who tests our hearts. 5You know we never used flattery, nor did we put on a mask to cover up greed—God is our witness. 6We were not looking for praise from men, not from you or anyone else.

7As apostles of Christ we could have been a burden to you, but we were gentle among you, like a mother caring for her little children. 8We loved you so much that we were delighted to share with you not only the gospel of God but our lives as well, because you had become so dear to us. 9Surely you remember, brothers, our toil and hardship; we worked night and day in order not to be a burden to anyone while we preached the gospel of God to you.

10You are witnesses, and so is God, of how holy, righteous and blameless we were among you who believed. 11For you know that we dealt with each of you as a father deals with his own children, 12encouraging, comforting and urging you to live lives worthy of God, who calls you into his kingdom and glory.

a1 Greek *Silvanus*, a variant of Silas
b1 Some early manuscripts *you from God our Father and the Lord Jesus Christ*

[13]And we also thank God continually because, when you received the word of God, which you heard from us, you accepted it not as the word of men, but as it actually is, the word of God, which is at work in you who believe. [14]For you, brothers, became imitators of God's churches in Judea, which are in Christ Jesus: You suffered from your own countrymen the same things those churches suffered from the Jews, [15]who killed the Lord Jesus and the prophets and also drove us out. They displease God and are hostile to all men [16]in their effort to keep us from speaking to the Gentiles so that they may be saved. In this way they always heap up their sins to the limit. The wrath of God has come upon them at last.[a]

Paul's Longing to See the Thessalonians

[17]But, brothers, when we were torn away from you for a short time (in person, not in thought), out of our intense longing we made every effort to see you. [18]For we wanted to come to you—certainly I, Paul, did, again and again—but Satan stopped us. [19]For what is our hope, our joy, or the crown in which we will glory in the presence of our Lord Jesus Christ when he comes? Is it not you? [20]Indeed, you are our glory and joy.

3 So when we could stand it no longer, we thought it best to be left by ourselves in Athens. [2]We sent Timothy, who is our brother and God's fellow-worker[a] in spreading the gospel of Christ, to strengthen and encourage you in your faith, [3]so that no-one would be unsettled by these trials. You know quite well that we were destined for them. [4]In fact, when we were with you, we kept telling you that we would be persecuted. And it turned out that way, as you well know. [5]For this reason, when I could stand it no longer, I sent to find out about your faith. I was afraid that in some way the tempter might have tempted you and our efforts might have been useless.

Timothy's Encouraging Report

[6]But Timothy has just now come to us from you and has brought good news about your faith and love. He has told us that you always have pleasant memories of us and that you long to see us, just as we also long to see you. [7]Therefore, brothers, in all our distress and persecution we were encouraged about you because of your faith. [8]For now we really live, since you are standing firm in the Lord. [9]How can we thank God enough for you in return for all the joy we have in the presence of our God because of you? [10]Night and day we pray most earnestly that we may see you again and supply what is lacking in your faith.

[11]Now may our God and Father himself and our Lord Jesus clear the way for us to come to you. [12]May the Lord make your love increase and overflow for each other and for everyone else, just as ours does for you. [13]May he strengthen your hearts so that you will be blameless and holy in the presence of our God and Father when our Lord Jesus comes with all his holy ones.

Living to Please God

4 Finally, brothers, we instructed you how to live in order to please God, as in fact you are living. Now we ask you and urge you in the Lord Jesus to do this more and more. [2]You know what instructions we gave you by the authority of the Lord Jesus.

[3]It is God's will that you should be holy; that you should avoid sexual immorality; [4]that each of you should learn to control his own body[a] in a way that is holy and honourable, [5]not in passionate lust like the heathen, who do not know God; [6]and that in this matter no-one should wrong his brother or take advantage of him. The Lord will punish men for all such sins, as we have already told you and warned you. [7]For God did not call us

---

[a]16 Or them fully
[a]2 Some manuscripts brother and fellow worker; other manuscripts brother and God's servant
[a]4 Or learn to live with his own wife; or learn to acquire a wife

to be impure, but to live a holy life. 8Therefore, he who rejects this instruction does not reject man but God, who gives you his Holy Spirit.

9Now about brotherly love we do not need to write to you, for you yourselves have been taught by God to love each other. 10And in fact, you do love all the brothers throughout Macedonia. Yet we urge you, brothers, to do so more and more.

11Make it your ambition to lead a quiet life, to mind your own business and to work with your hands, just as we told you, 12so that your daily life may win the respect of outsiders and so that you will not be dependent on anybody.

The Coming of the Lord

13Brothers, we do not want you to be ignorant about those who fall asleep, or to grieve like the rest of men, who have no hope. 14We believe that Jesus died and rose again and so we believe that God will bring with Jesus those who have fallen asleep in him. 15According to the Lord's own word, we tell you that we who are still alive, who are left till the coming of the Lord, will certainly not precede those who have fallen asleep. 16For the Lord himself will come down from heaven, with a loud command, with the voice of the archangel and with the trumpet call of God, and the dead in Christ will rise first. 17After that, we who are still alive and are left will be caught up with them in the clouds to meet the Lord in the air. And so we will be with the Lord for ever. 18Therefore encourage each other with these words.

5 Now, brothers, about times and dates we do not need to write to you, 2for you know very well that the day of the Lord will come like a thief in the night. 3While people are saying, "Peace and safety", destruction will come on them suddenly, as labour pains on a pregnant woman, and they will not escape.

4But you, brothers, are not in darkness so that this day should surprise you like a thief. 5You are all sons of the light and sons of the day. We do not belong to the night or to the darkness. 6So then, let us not be like others, who are asleep, but let us be alert and self-controlled. 7For those who sleep, sleep at night, and those who get drunk, get drunk at night. 8But since we belong to the day, let us be self-controlled, putting on faith and love as a breastplate, and the hope of salvation as a helmet. 9For God did not appoint us to suffer wrath but to receive salvation through our Lord Jesus Christ. 10He died for us so that, whether we are awake or asleep, we may live together with him. 11Therefore encourage one another and build each other up, just as in fact you are doing.

Final Instructions

12Now we ask you, brothers, to respect those who work hard among you, who are over you in the Lord and who admonish you. 13Hold them in the highest regard in love because of their work. Live in peace with each other. 14And we urge you, brothers, warn those who are idle, encourage the timid, help the weak, be patient with everyone. 15Make sure that nobody pays back wrong for wrong, but always try to be kind to each other and to everyone else.

16Be joyful always; 17pray continually; 18give thanks in all circumstances, for this is God's will for you in Christ Jesus.

19Do not put out the Spirit's fire; 20do not treat prophecies with contempt. 21Test everything. Hold on to the good. 22Avoid every kind of evil.

23May God himself, the God of peace, sanctify you through and through. May your whole spirit, soul and body be kept blameless at the coming of our Lord Jesus Christ. 24The one who calls you is faithful and he will do it.

25Brothers, pray for us. 26Greet all the brothers with a holy kiss. 27I charge you before the Lord to have this letter read to all the brothers.

28The grace of our Lord Jesus Christ be with you.

227

2 Thessalonians

1

Paul, Silas[a] and Timothy,

To the church of the Thessalonians in God our Father and the Lord Jesus Christ:

[2]Grace and peace to you from God the Father and the Lord Jesus Christ.

Thanksgiving and Prayer

[3]We ought always to thank God for you, brothers, and rightly so, because your faith is growing more and more, and the love every one of you has for each other is increasing. [4]Therefore, among God's churches we boast about your perseverance and faith in all the persecutions and trials you are enduring.

[5]All this is evidence that God's judgment is right, and as a result you will be counted worthy of the kingdom of God, for which you are suffering. [6]God is just: He will pay back trouble to those who trouble you [7]and give relief to you who are troubled, and to us as well. This will happen when the Lord Jesus is revealed from heaven in blazing fire with his powerful angels. [8]He will punish those who do not know God and do not obey the gospel of our Lord Jesus. [9]They will be punished with everlasting destruction and shut out from the presence of the Lord and from the majesty of his power [10]on the day he comes to be glorified in his holy people and to be marvelled at among all those who have believed. This includes you, because you believed our testimony to you.

[11]With this in mind, we constantly pray for you, that our God may count you worthy of his calling, and that by his power he may fulfil every good purpose of yours and every act prompted by your faith. [12]We pray this so that the name of our Lord Jesus may be glorified in you, and you in him, according to the grace of our God and the Lord Jesus Christ.[b]

The Man of Lawlessness

2

Concerning the coming of our Lord Jesus Christ and our being gathered to him, we ask you, brothers, [2]not to become easily unsettled or alarmed by some prophecy, report or letter supposed to have come from us, saying that the day of the Lord has already come. [3]Don't let anyone deceive you in any way, for ,that day will not come, until the rebellion occurs and the man of lawlessness[a] is revealed, the man doomed to destruction. [4]He opposes and exalts himself over everything that is called God or is worshipped, and even sets himself up in God's temple, proclaiming himself to be God.

[5]Don't you remember that when I was with you I used to tell you these things? [6]And now you know what is holding him back, so that he may be revealed at the proper time. [7]For the secret power of lawlessness is already at work; but the one who now holds it back will continue to do so till he is taken out of the way. [8]And then the lawless one will be revealed, whom the Lord Jesus will overthrow with the breath of his mouth and destroy by the splendour of his coming. [9]The coming of the lawless one will be in accordance with the work of Satan

---

[a]1 Greek *Silvanus*, a variant of *Silas*
[a]3 Some manuscripts *sin*
[b]12 Or *God and Lord, Jesus Christ*

228

displayed in all kinds of counterfeit miracles, signs and wonders, 10and in every sort of evil that deceives those who are perishing. They perish because they refused to love the truth and so be saved. 11For this reason God sends them a powerful delusion so that they will believe the lie 12and so that all will be condemned who have not believed the truth but have delighted in wickedness.

Stand Firm

13But we ought always to thank God for you, brothers loved by the Lord, because from the beginning God chose youb to be saved through the sanctifying work of the Spirit and through belief in the truth. 14He called you to this through our gospel, that you might share in the glory of our Lord Jesus Christ. 15So then, brothers, stand firm and hold to the teachingsc we passed on to you, whether by word of mouth or by letter.

16May our Lord Jesus Christ himself and God our Father, who loved us and by his grace gave us eternal encouragement and good hope, 17encourage your hearts and strengthen you in every good deed and word.

Request for Prayer

3 Finally, brothers, pray for us that the message of the Lord may spread rapidly and be honoured, just as it was with you. 2And pray that we may be delivered from wicked and evil men, for not everyone has faith. 3But the Lord is faithful, and he will strengthen and protect you from the evil one. 4We have confidence in the Lord that you are doing and will continue to do the things we command. 5May the Lord direct your

hearts into God's love and Christ's perseverance.

Warning Against Idleness

6In the name of the Lord Jesus Christ, we command you, brothers, to keep away from every brother who is idle and does not live according to the teachingd you received from us. 7For you yourselves know how you ought to follow our example. We were not idle when we were with you, 8nor did we eat anyone's food without paying for it. On the contrary, we worked night and day, labouring and toiling so that we would not be a burden to any of you. 9We did this, not because we do not have the right to such help, but in order to make ourselves a model for you to follow. 10For even when we were with you, we gave you this rule: "If a man will not work, he shall not eat."

11We hear that some among you are idle. They are not busy; they are busybodies. 12Such people we command and urge in the Lord Jesus Christ to settle down and earn the bread they eat. 13And as for you, brothers, never tire of doing what is right.

14If anyone does not obey our instruction in this letter, take special note of him. Do not associate with him, in order that he may feel ashamed. 15Yet do not regard him as an enemy, but warn him as a brother.

Final Greetings

16Now may the Lord of peace himself give you peace at all times and in every way. The Lord be with all of you.

17I, Paul, write this greeting in my own hand, which is the distinguishing mark in all my letters. This is how I write.

18The grace of our Lord Jesus Christ be with you all.

---

b13 Some manuscripts because God chose you as his firstfruits
c15 Or traditions   d6 Or tradition

1 Timothy

1 Paul, an apostle of Christ Jesus by the command of God our Saviour and of Christ Jesus our hope,

²To Timothy my true son in the faith:

Grace, mercy and peace from God the Father and Christ Jesus our Lord.

Warning Against False Teachers of the Law

³As I urged you when I went into Macedonia, stay there in Ephesus so that you may command certain men not to teach false doctrines any longer ⁴nor to devote themselves to myths and endless genealogies. These promote controversies rather than God's work—which is by faith. ⁵The goal of this command is love, which comes from a pure heart and a good conscience and a sincere faith. ⁶Some have wandered away from these and turned to meaningless talk. ⁷They want to be teachers of the law, but they do not know what they are talking about or what they so confidently affirm.

⁸We know that the law is good if a man uses it properly. ⁹We also know that law is made not for good men but for lawbreakers and rebels, the ungodly and sinful, the unholy and irreligious; for those who kill their fathers or mothers, for murderers, ¹⁰for adulterers and perverts, for slave traders and liars and perjurers—and for whatever else is contrary to the sound doctrine ¹¹that conforms to the glorious gospel of the blessed God, which he entrusted to me.

The Lord's Grace to Paul

¹²I thank Christ Jesus our Lord, who has given me strength, that he considered me faithful, appointing me to his service. ¹³Even though I was once a blasphemer and a persecutor and a violent man, I was shown mercy because I acted in ignorance and unbelief. ¹⁴The grace of our Lord was poured out on me abundantly, along with the faith and love that are in Christ Jesus.

¹⁵Here is a trustworthy saying that deserves full acceptance: Christ Jesus came into the world to save sinners—of whom I am the worst. ¹⁶But for that very reason I was shown mercy so that in me, the worst of sinners, Christ Jesus might display his unlimited patience as an example for those who would believe on him and receive eternal life. ¹⁷Now to the King eternal, immortal, invisible, the only God, be honour and glory for ever and ever. Amen.

¹⁸Timothy, my son, I give you this instruction in keeping with the prophecies once made about you, so that by following them you may fight the good fight, ¹⁹holding on to faith and a good conscience. Some have rejected these and so have shipwrecked their faith. ²⁰Among them are Hymenaeus and Alexander, whom I have handed over to Satan to be taught not to blaspheme.

Instructions on Worship

2 I urge, then, first of all, that requests, prayers, intercession and thanksgiving be made for everyone—²for kings and all those in authority, that we may live peaceful and quiet lives in all godliness and holiness. ³This is good, and pleases God our Saviour, ⁴who wants all men

1 TIMOTHY 4:4

to be saved and to come to a knowledge of the truth. ⁵For there is one God and one mediator between God and men, the man Christ Jesus, ⁶who gave himself as a ransom for all men—the testimony given in its proper time. ⁷And for this purpose I was appointed a herald and an apostle—I am telling the truth, I am not lying—and a teacher of the true faith to the Gentiles.

⁸I want men everywhere to lift up holy hands in prayer, without anger or disputing.

⁹I also want women to dress modestly, with decency and propriety, not with braided hair or gold or pearls or expensive clothes, ¹⁰but with good deeds, appropriate for women who profess to worship God.

¹¹A woman should learn in quietness and full submission. ¹²I do not permit a woman to teach or to have authority over a man; she must be silent. ¹³For Adam was formed first, then Eve. ¹⁴And Adam was not the one deceived; it was the woman who was deceived and became a sinner. ¹⁵But women will be kept safe⁰ through childbirth, if they continue in faith, love and holiness with propriety.

Overseers and Deacons

3 Here is a trustworthy saying: If anyone sets his heart on being an overseer,ᵃ he desires a noble task. ²Now the overseer must be above reproach, the husband of but one wife, temperate, self-controlled, respectable, hospitable, able to teach, ³not given to much wine, not violent but gentle, not quarrelsome, not a lover of money. ⁴He must manage his own family well and see that his children obey him with proper respect. ⁵(If anyone does not know how to manage his own family, how can he take care of God's church?) ⁶He must not be a recent convert, or he may become conceited and fall under the same judgment as the devil. ⁷He must also have a good reputation with outsiders, so that he

will not fall into disgrace and into the devil's trap.

⁸Deacons, likewise, are to be men worthy of respect, sincere, not indulging in much wine, and not pursuing dishonest gain. ⁹They must keep hold of the deep truths of the faith with a clear conscience. ¹⁰They must first be tested; and then if there is nothing against them, let them serve as deacons.

¹¹In the same way, their wivesᵇ are to be women worthy of respect, not malicious talkers but temperate and trustworthy in everything.

¹²A deacon must be the husband of but one wife and must manage his children and his household well. ¹³Those who have served well gain an excellent standing and great assurance in their faith in Christ Jesus.

¹⁴Although I hope to come to you soon, I am writing you these instructions so that, ¹⁵if I am delayed, you will know how people ought to conduct themselves in God's household, which is the church of the living God, the pillar and foundation of the truth. ¹⁶Beyond all question, the mystery of godliness is great:

Heᶜ appeared in a body,
    was vindicated by the Spirit,
    was seen by angels,
        was preached among the
        nations,
was believed on in the world,
    was taken up in glory.

Instructions to Timothy

4 The Spirit clearly says that in later times some will abandon the faith and follow deceiving spirits and things taught by demons. ²Such teachings come through hypocritical liars, whose consciences have been seared as with a hot iron. ³They forbid people to marry and order them to abstain from certain foods, which God created to be received with thanksgiving by those who believe and who know the truth. ⁴For everything God created is good, and nothing is to be rejected if it is

---

ᵃ15 Or be saved   ᵃ1 Traditionally *bishop*; also in verse 2   ᵇ11 Or *way, deaconesses*
ᶜ16 Some manuscripts *God*

231

received with thanksgiving, 5because it is consecrated by the word of God and prayer.

6If you point these things out to the brothers, you will be a good minister of Christ Jesus, brought up in the truths of the faith and of the good teaching that you have followed. 7Have nothing to do with godless myths and old wives' tales; rather, train yourself to be godly. 8For physical training is of some value, but godliness has value for all things, holding promise for both the present life and the life to come.

9This is a trustworthy saying that deserves full acceptance 10(and for this we labour and strive), that we have put our hope in the living God, who is the Saviour of all men, and especially of those who believe.

11Command and teach these things. 12Don't let anyone look down on you because you are young, but set an example for the believers in speech, in life, in love, in faith and in purity. 13Until I come, devote yourself to the public reading of Scripture, to preaching and to teaching. 14Do not neglect your gift, which was given you through a prophetic message when the body of elders laid their hands on you.

15Be diligent in these matters; give yourself wholly to them, so that everyone may see your progress. 16Watch your life and doctrine closely. Persevere in them, because if you do, you will save both yourself and your hearers.

Advice About Widows, Elders and Slaves

5 Do not rebuke an older man harshly, but exhort him as if he were your father. Treat younger men as brothers, 2older women as mothers, and younger women as sisters, with absolute purity.

3Give proper recognition to those widows who are really in need. 4But if a widow has children or grand-children, these should learn first of all to put their religion into practice by caring for their own family and so

repaying their parents and grand-parents, for this is pleasing to God. 5The widow who is really in need and left all alone puts her hope in God and continues night and day to pray and to ask God for help. 6But the widow who lives for pleasure is dead even while she lives. 7Give the people these instructions, too, so that no-one may be open to blame. 8If anyone does not provide for his relatives, and especially for his immediate family, he has denied the faith and is worse than an unbeliever.

9No widow may be put on the list of widows unless she is over sixty, has been faithful to her husband,a 10and is well known for her good deeds, such as bringing up children, showing hospitality, washing the feet of the saints, helping those in trouble and devoting herself to all kinds of good deeds.

11As for younger widows, do not put them on such a list. For when their sensual desires overcome their dedication to Christ, they want to marry. 12Thus they bring judgment on themselves, because they have broken their first pledge. 13Besides, they get into the habit of being idle and going about from house to house. And not only do they become idlers, but also gossips and busybodies, saying things they ought not to. 14So I counsel younger widows to marry, to have children, to manage their homes and to give the enemy no opportunity for slander. 15Some have in fact already turned away to follow Satan.

16If any woman who is a believer has widows in her family, she should help them and not let the church be burdened with them, so that the church can help those widows who are really in need.

17The elders who direct the affairs of the church well are worthy of double honour, especially those whose work is preaching and teaching. 18For the Scripture says, "Do not muzzle the ox while it is treading out the grain,"b and "The worker deserves his wages."c 19Do not entertain an accusation against an elder

a9 Or *has had but one husband*   *b18* Deut. 25:4   *c18* Luke 10:7

unless it is brought by two or three witnesses. [20]Those who sin are to be rebuked publicly, so that the others may take warning.

[21]I charge you, in the sight of God and Christ Jesus and the elect angels, to keep these instructions without partiality, and to do nothing out of favouritism.

[22]Do not be hasty in the laying on of hands, and do not share in the sins of others. Keep yourself pure.

[23]Stop drinking only water, and use a little wine because of your stomach and your frequent illnesses.

[24]The sins of some men are obvious, reaching the place of judgment ahead of them; the sins of others trail behind them. [25]In the same way, good deeds are obvious, and even those that are not cannot be hidden.

6 All who are under the yoke of slavery should consider their masters worthy of full respect, so that God's name and our teaching may not be slandered. [2]Those who have believing masters are not to show less respect for them because they are brothers. Instead, they are to serve them even better, because those who benefit from their service are believers, and dear to them. These are the things you are to teach and urge on them.

Love of Money

[3]If anyone teaches false doctrines and does not agree to the sound instruction of our Lord Jesus Christ and to godly teaching, [4]he is conceited and understands nothing. He has an unhealthy interest in controversies and arguments that result in envy, quarrelling, malicious talk, evil suspicions [5]and constant friction between men of corrupt mind, who have been robbed of the truth and who think that godliness is a means to financial gain.

[6]But godliness with contentment is great gain. [7]For we brought nothing into the world, and we can take nothing out of it. [8]But if we have food and clothing, we will be content with that. [9]People who want to get rich fall into temptation and a trap and into many foolish and harmful desires that plunge men into ruin and destruction. [10]For the love of money is a root of all kinds of evil. Some people, eager for money, have wandered from the faith and pierced themselves with many griefs.

Paul's Charge to Timothy

[11]But you, man of God, flee from all this, and pursue righteousness, godliness, faith, love, endurance and gentleness. [12]Fight the good fight of the faith. Take hold of the eternal life to which you were called when you made your good confession in the presence of many witnesses. [13]In the sight of God, who gives life to everything, and of Christ Jesus, who while testifying before Pontius Pilate made the good confession, I charge you [14]to keep this commandment without spot or blame until the appearing of our Lord Jesus Christ, [15]which God will bring about in his own time—God, the blessed and only Ruler, the King of kings and Lord of lords, [16]who alone is immortal and who lives in unapproachable light, whom no-one has seen or can see. To him be honour and might for ever. Amen.

[17]Command those who are rich in this present world not to be arrogant nor to put their hope in wealth, which is so uncertain, but to put their hope in God, who richly provides us with everything for our enjoyment. [18]Command them to do good, to be rich in good deeds, and to be generous and willing to share. [19]In this way they will lay up treasure for themselves as a firm foundation for the coming age, so that they may take hold of the life that is truly life.

[20]Timothy, guard what has been entrusted to your care. Turn away from godless chatter and the opposing ideas of what is falsely called knowledge, [21]which some have professed and in so doing have wandered from the faith.

Grace be with you.

2 Timothy

1 Paul, an apostle of Christ Jesus by the will of God, according to the promise of life that is in Christ Jesus,

²To Timothy, my dear son:

Grace, mercy and peace from God the Father and Christ Jesus our Lord.

Encouragement to Be Faithful

³I thank God, whom I serve, as my forefathers did, with a clear conscience, as night and day I constantly remember you in my prayers. ⁴Recalling your tears, I long to see you, so that I may be filled with joy. ⁵I have been reminded of your sincere faith, which first lived in your grandmother Lois and in your mother Eunice and, I am persuaded, now lives in you also. ⁶For this reason I remind you to fan into flame the gift of God, which is in you through the laying on of my hands. ⁷For God did not give us a spirit of timidity, but a spirit of power, of love and of self-discipline.

⁸So do not be ashamed to testify about our Lord, or ashamed of me his prisoner. But join with me in suffering for the gospel, by the power of God, ⁹who has saved us and called us to a holy life—not because of anything we have done but because of his own purpose and grace. This grace was given us in Christ Jesus before the beginning of time, ¹⁰but it has now been revealed through the appearing of our Saviour, Christ Jesus, who has destroyed death and has brought life and immortality to light through the gospel. ¹¹And of this gospel I was appointed a herald and an apostle and a teacher. ¹²That is why I am suffering as I am. Yet I am not ashamed, because I know whom I have believed, and am convinced that he is able to guard what I have entrusted to him for that day.

¹³What you heard from me, keep as the pattern of sound teaching, with faith and love in Christ Jesus. ¹⁴Guard the good deposit that was entrusted to you—guard it with the help of the Holy Spirit who lives in us.

¹⁵You know that everyone in the province of Asia has deserted me, including Phygelus and Hermogenes.

¹⁶May the Lord show mercy to the household of Onesiphorus, because he often refreshed me and was not ashamed of my chains. ¹⁷On the contrary, when he was in Rome, he searched hard for me until he found me. ¹⁸May the Lord grant that he will find mercy from the Lord on that day! You know very well in how many ways he helped me in Ephesus.

2 You then, my son, be strong in the grace that is in Christ Jesus. ²And the things you have heard me say in the presence of many witnesses entrust to reliable men who will also be qualified to teach others. ³Endure hardship with us like a good soldier of Christ Jesus. ⁴No-one serving as a soldier gets involved in civilian affairs—he wants to please his commanding officer. ⁵Similarly, if anyone competes as an athlete, he does not receive the victor's crown unless he competes according to the rules. ⁶The hardworking farmer should be the first to receive a share of the crops. ⁷Reflect on what I am saying, for the Lord will give you insight into all this.

⁸Remember Jesus Christ, raised from the dead, descended from David. This is my gospel, ⁹for which

I am suffering even to the point of being chained like a criminal. But God's word is not chained. [10]Therefore I endure everything for the sake of the elect, that they too may obtain the salvation that is in Christ Jesus, with eternal glory.

[11]Here is a trustworthy saying:

If we died with him,
  we will also live with him;
[12]if we endure,
  we will also reign with him.
If we disown him,
  he will also disown us;
[13]if we are faithless,
  he will remain faithful,
  for he cannot disown himself.

A Workman Approved by God

[14]Keep reminding them of these things. Warn them before God against quarrelling about words; it is of no value, and only ruins those who listen. [15]Do your best to present yourself to God as one approved, a workman who does not need to be ashamed and who correctly handles the word of truth. [16]Avoid godless chatter, because those who indulge in it will become more and more ungodly. [17]Their teaching will spread like gangrene. Among them are Hymenaeus and Philetus, [18]who have wandered away from the truth. They say that the resurrection has already taken place, and they destroy the faith of some. [19]Nevertheless, God's solid foundation stands firm, sealed with this inscription: "The Lord knows those who are his,"[a] and, "Everyone who confesses the name of the Lord must turn away from wickedness."

[20]In a large house there are articles not only of gold and silver, but also of wood and clay; some are for noble purposes and some for ignoble. [21]If a man cleanses himself from the latter, he will be an instrument for noble purposes, made holy, useful to the Master and prepared to do any good work.

[22]Flee the evil desires of youth, and pursue righteousness, faith, love and peace, along with those who call on the Lord out of a pure heart. [23]Don't have anything to do with foolish and stupid arguments, because you know they produce quarrels. [24]And the Lord's servant must not quarrel; instead, he must be kind to everyone, able to teach, not resentful. [25]Those who oppose him he must gently instruct, in the hope that God will grant them repentance leading them to a knowledge of the truth, [26]and that they will come to their senses and escape from the trap of the devil, who has taken them captive to do his will.

Godlessness in the Last Days

3 But mark this: There will be terrible times in the last days. [2]People will be lovers of themselves, lovers of money, boastful, proud, abusive, disobedient to their parents, ungrateful, unholy, [3]without love, unforgiving, slanderous, without self-control, brutal, not lovers of the good, [4]treacherous, rash, conceited, lovers of pleasure rather than lovers of God—[5]having a form of godliness but denying its power. Have nothing to do with them.

[6]They are the kind who worm their way into homes and gain control over weak-willed women, who are loaded down with sins and are swayed by all kinds of evil desires, [7]always learning but never able to acknowledge the truth. [8]Just as Jannes and Jambres opposed Moses, so also these men oppose the truth—men of depraved minds, who, as far as the faith is concerned, are rejected. [9]But they will not get very far because, as in the case of those men, their folly will be clear to everyone.

Paul's Charge to Timothy

[10]You, however, know all about my teaching, my way of life, my purpose, faith, patience, love, endurance, [11]persecutions, sufferings—what kinds of things happened to me in Antioch, Iconium and Lystra, the persecutions I endured. Yet the Lord rescued me from all of them. [12]In fact, everyone

---

[a]19 Num. 16:5 (see Septuagint)

235

who wants to live a godly life in Christ Jesus will be persecuted, 13while evil men and impostors will go from bad to worse, deceiving and being deceived. 14But as for you, continue in what you have learned and have become convinced of, because you know those from whom you learned it, 15and how from infancy you have known the holy Scriptures, which are able to make you wise for salvation through faith in Christ Jesus. 16All Scripture is God-breathed and is useful for teaching, rebuking, correcting and training in righteousness, 17so that the man of God may be thoroughly equipped for every good work.

4 In the presence of God and of Christ Jesus, who will judge the living and the dead, and in view of his appearing and his kingdom, I give you this charge: 2Preach the Word; be prepared in season and out of season; correct, rebuke and encourage—with great patience and careful instruction. 3For the time will come when men will not put up with sound doctrine. Instead, to suit their own desires, they will gather around them a great number of teachers to say what their itching ears want to hear. 4They will turn their ears away from the truth and turn aside to myths. 5But you, keep your head in all situations, endure hardship, do the work of an evangelist, discharge all the duties of your ministry.

6For I am already being poured out like a drink offering, and the time has come for my departure. 7I have fought the good fight, I have finished the race, I have kept the faith. 8Now there is in store for me the crown of righteousness, which the Lord, the righteous Judge, will award to me on that day—and not only to me, but also to all who have longed for his appearing.

Personal Remarks

9Do your best to come to me quickly, 10for Demas, because he loved this world, has deserted me and has gone to Thessalonica. Crescens has gone to Galatia, and Titus to Dalmatia. 11Only Luke is with me. Get Mark and bring him with you, because he is helpful to me in my ministry. 12I sent Tychicus to Ephesus. 13When you come, bring the cloak that I left with Carpus at Troas, and my scrolls, especially the parchments.

14Alexander the metalworker did me a great deal of harm. The Lord will repay him for what he has done. 15You too should be on your guard against him, because he strongly opposed our message.

16At my first defence, no-one came to my support, but everyone deserted me. May it not be held against them. 17But the Lord stood at my side and gave me strength, so that through me the message might be fully proclaimed and all the Gentiles might hear it. And I was delivered from the lion's mouth. 18The Lord will rescue me from every evil attack and will bring me safely to his heavenly kingdom. To him be glory for ever and ever. Amen.

Final Greetings

19Greet Priscilla*a* and Aquila and the household of Onesiphorus. 20Erastus stayed in Corinth, and I left Trophimus sick in Miletus. 21Do your best to get here before winter. Eubulus greets you, and so do Pudens, Linus, Claudia and all your brothers. 22The Lord be with your spirit. Grace be with you.

a19 Greek *Prisca,* a variant of *Priscilla*

Titus

1 Paul, a servant of God and an apostle of Jesus Christ for the faith of God's elect and the knowledge of the truth that leads to godliness—[2]a faith and knowledge resting on the hope of eternal life, which God, who does not lie, promised before the beginning of time, [3]and at his appointed season he brought his word to light through the preaching entrusted to me by the command of God our Saviour.

[4]To Titus, my true son in our common faith:

Grace and peace from God the Father and Christ Jesus our Saviour.

Titus' Task on Crete

[5]The reason I left you in Crete was that you might straighten out what was left unfinished and appoint[e] elders in every town, as I directed you. [6]An elder must be blameless, the husband of but one wife, a man whose children believe and are not open to the charge of being wild and disobedient. [7]Since an overseer[b] is entrusted with God's work, he must be blameless—not overbearing, not quick-tempered, not given to much wine, not violent, not pursuing dishonest gain. [8]Rather he must be hospitable, one who loves what is good, who is self-controlled, upright, holy and disciplined. [9]He must hold firmly to the trustworthy message as it has been taught, so that he can encourage others by sound doctrine and refute those who oppose it.

[10]For there are many rebellious people, mere talkers and deceivers, especially those of the circumcision group. [11]They must be silenced, because they are ruining whole households by teaching things they ought not to teach—and that for the sake of dishonest gain. [12]Even one of their own prophets has said, "Cretans are always liars, evil brutes, lazy gluttons." [13]This testimony is true. Therefore, rebuke them sharply, so that they will be sound in the faith [14]and will pay no attention to Jewish myths or to the commands of those who reject the truth. [15]To the pure, all things are pure, but to those who are corrupted and do not believe, nothing is pure. In fact, both their minds and consciences are corrupted. [16]They claim to know God, but by their actions they deny him. They are detestable, disobedient and unfit for doing anything good.

What Must Be Taught to Various Groups

2 You must teach what is in accord with sound doctrine. [2]Teach the older men to be temperate, worthy of respect, self-controlled, and sound in faith, in love and in endurance.

[3]Likewise, teach the older women to be reverent in the way they live, not to be slanderers or addicted to much wine, but to teach what is good. [4]Then they can train the younger women to love their husbands and children, [5]to be self-controlled and pure, to be busy at home, to be kind, and to be subject to their husbands, so that no-one will malign the word of God.

[6]Similarly, encourage the young men to be self-controlled. [7]In everything set them an example by doing

[e]5 Or *ordain*   [b]7 Traditionally *bishop*

237

what is good. In your teaching show integrity, seriousness 8and soundness of speech that cannot be condemned, so that those who oppose you may be ashamed because they have nothing bad to say about us.

9Teach slaves to be subject to their masters in everything, to try to please them, not to talk back to them, 10and not to steal from them, but to show that they can be fully trusted, so that in every way they will make the teaching about God our Saviour attractive.

11For the grace of God that brings salvation has appeared to all men. 12It teaches us to say "No" to ungodliness and worldly passions, and to live self-controlled, upright and godly lives in this present age, 13while we wait for the blessed hope—the glorious appearing of our great God and Saviour, Jesus Christ, 14who gave himself for us to redeem us from all wickedness and to purify for himself a people that are his very own, eager to do what is good.

15These, then, are the things you should teach. Encourage and rebuke with all authority. Do not let anyone despise you.

Doing What Is Good

3 Remind the people to be subject to rulers and authorities, to be obedient, to be ready to do whatever is good, 2to slander no-one, to be peaceable and considerate, and to show true humility towards all men.

3At one time we too were foolish, disobedient, deceived and enslaved by all kinds of passions and pleasures. We lived in malice and envy, being hated and hating one another.

4But when the kindness and love of God our Saviour appeared, 5he saved us, not because of righteous things we had done, but because of his mercy. He saved us through the washing of rebirth and renewal by the Holy Spirit, 6whom he poured out on us generously through Jesus Christ our Saviour, 7so that, having been justified by his grace, we might become heirs having the hope of eternal life. 8This is a trustworthy saying. And I want you to stress these things, so that those who have trusted in God may be careful to devote themselves to doing what is good. These things are excellent and profitable for everyone.

9But avoid foolish controversies and genealogies and arguments and quarrels about the law, because these are unprofitable and useless. 10Warn a divisive person once, and then warn him a second time. After that, have nothing to do with him. 11You may be sure that such a man is warped and sinful; he is self-condemned.

Final Remarks

12As soon as I send Artemas or Tychicus to you, do your best to come to me at Nicopolis, because I have decided to winter there. 13Do everything you can to help Zenas the lawyer and Apollos on their way and see that they have everything they need. 14Our people must learn to devote themselves to doing what is good, in order that they may provide for daily necessities and not live unproductive lives.

15Everyone with me sends you greetings. Greet those who love us in the faith.

Grace be with you all.

Philemon

[1]Paul, a prisoner of Christ Jesus, and Timothy our brother,

To Philemon our dear friend and fellow-worker, [2]to Apphia our sister, to Archippus our fellow-soldier and to the church that meets in your home:

[3]Grace to you and peace from God our Father and the Lord Jesus Christ.

Thanksgiving and Prayer

[4]I always thank my God as I remember you in my prayers, [5]because I hear about your faith in the Lord Jesus and your love for all the saints. [6]I pray that you may be active in sharing your faith, so that you will have a full understanding of every good thing we have in Christ. [7]Your love has given me great joy and encouragement, because you, brother, have refreshed the hearts of the saints.

Paul's Plea for Onesimus

[8]Therefore, although in Christ I could be bold and order you to do what you ought to do, [9]yet I appeal to you on the basis of love. I then, as Paul—an old man and now also a prisoner of Christ Jesus—[10]I appeal to you for my son Onesimus,ᵃ who became my son while I was in chains. [11]Formerly he was useless to you, but now he has become useful both to you and to me.

[12]I am sending him—who is my very heart—back to you. [13]I would have liked to keep him with me so that he could take your place in helping me while I am in chains for the gospel. [14]But I did not want to do anything without your consent, so that any favour you do will be spontaneous and not forced. [15]Perhaps the reason he was separated from you for a little while was that you might have him back for good—[16]no longer as a slave, but better than a slave, as a dear brother. He is very dear to me but even dearer to you, both as a man and as a brother in the Lord.

[17]So if you consider me a partner, welcome him as you would welcome me. [18]If he has done you any wrong or owes you anything, charge it to me. [19]I, Paul, am writing this with my own hand. I will pay it back—not to mention that you owe me your very self. [20]I do wish, brother, that I may have some benefit from you in the Lord; refresh my heart in Christ. [21]Confident of your obedience, I write to you, knowing that you will do even more than I ask.

[22]And one thing more: Prepare a guest room for me, because I hope to be restored to you in answer to your prayers.

[23]Epaphras, my fellow-prisoner for Christ Jesus, sends you greetings. [24]And so do Mark, Aristarchus, Demas and Luke, my fellow-workers.

[25]The grace of the Lord Jesus Christ be with your spirit.

ᵃ10 Onesimus means useful.

Hebrews

The Son Superior to Angels

1 In the past God spoke to our forefathers through the prophets at many times and in various ways, [2]but in these last days he has spoken to us by his Son, whom he appointed heir of all things, and through whom he made the universe. [3]The Son is the radiance of God's glory and the exact representation of his being, sustaining all things by his powerful word. After he had provided purification for sins, he sat down at the right hand of the Majesty in heaven. [4]So he became as much superior to the angels as the name he has inherited is superior to theirs.

[5]For to which of the angels did God ever say,

> "You are my Son;
> today I have become your
> Father"[a,b]?

Or again,

> "I will be his Father,
> and he will be my Son"[c]?

[6]And again, when God brings his firstborn into the world, he says,

> "Let all God's angels worship
> him."[d]

[7]In speaking of the angels he says,

> "He makes his angels winds,
> his servants flames of fire."[e]

[8]But about the Son he says,

> "Your throne, O God, will last for
> ever and ever,
> and righteousness will be the
> sceptre of your kingdom.

[9]You have loved righteousness and
> hated wickedness;
> therefore God, your God, has set
> you above your companions
> by anointing you with the oil of
> joy."[f]

[10]He also says,

> "In the beginning, O Lord, you laid
> the foundations of the earth,
> and the heavens are the work of
> your hands.
[11]They will perish, but you remain;
> they will all wear out like a
> garment.
[12]You will roll them up like a robe;
> like a garment they will be
> changed.
> But you remain the same,
> and your years will never end."[g]

[13]To which of the angels did God ever say,

> "Sit at my right hand
> until I make your enemies
> a footstool for your feet"[h]?

[14]Are not all angels ministering spirits sent to serve those who will inherit salvation?

Warning to Pay Attention

2 We must pay more careful attention, therefore, to what we have heard, so that we do not drift away. [2]For if the message spoken by angels was binding, and every violation and disobedience received its just punishment, [3]how shall we escape if we ignore such a great salvation? This salvation, which was first announced by the Lord, was confirmed to us by those who heard him. [4]God also testified to it by signs, wonders and

---

[a]5 Or *have begotten you*   [b]5 Psalm 2:7   [c]5 2 Samuel 7:14
[d]6 Deut. 32:43 (see Dead Sea Scrolls and Septuagint)   [e]7 Psalm 104:4
[f]9 Psalm 45:6,7   [g]12 Psalm 102:25–27   [h]13 Psalm 110:1

240

various miracles, and gifts of the Holy Spirit distributed according to his will.

Jesus Made Like His Brothers

[5]It is not to angels that he has subjected the world to come, about which we are speaking. [6]But there is a place where someone has testified:

"What is man that you are mindful of him,
   the son of man that you care for him?
[7]You made him a little[a] lower than the angels;
   you crowned him with glory and honour
[8]   and put everything under his feet."[b]

In putting everything under him, God left nothing that is not subject to him. Yet at present we do not see everything subject to him. [9]But we see Jesus, who was made a little lower than the angels, now crowned with glory and honour because he suffered death, so that by the grace of God he might taste death for everyone.

[10]In bringing many sons to glory, it was fitting that God, for whom and through whom everything exists, should make the author of their salvation perfect through suffering. [11]Both the one who makes men holy and those who are made holy are of the same family. So Jesus is not ashamed to call them brothers. [12]He says,

"I will declare your name to my brothers;
   in the presence of the congregation I will sing your praises."[c]

[13]And again,

"I will put my trust in him."[d]

And again he says,

"Here am I, and the children God has given me."[e]

[14]Since the children have flesh and blood, he too shared in their humanity so that by his death he might destroy him who holds the power of death—that is, the devil—[15]and free those who all their lives were held in slavery by their fear of death. [16]For surely it is not angels he helps, but Abraham's descendants. [17]For this reason he had to be made like his brothers in every way, in order that he might become a merciful and faithful high priest in service to God, and that he might make atonement for[f] the sins of the people. [18]Because he himself suffered when he was tempted, he is able to help those who are being tempted.

Jesus Greater Than Moses

3 Therefore, holy brothers, who share in the heavenly calling, fix your thoughts on Jesus, the apostle and high priest whom we confess. [2]He was faithful to the one who appointed him, just as Moses was faithful in all God's house. [3]Jesus has been found worthy of greater honour than Moses, just as the builder of a house has greater honour than the house itself. [4]For every house is built by someone, but God is the builder of everything. [5]Moses was faithful as a servant in all God's house, testifying to what would be said in the future. [6]But Christ is faithful as a son over God's house. And we are his house, if we hold on to our courage and the hope of which we boast.

Warning Against Unbelief

[7]So, as the Holy Spirit says:

"Today, if you hear his voice,
[8]   do not harden your hearts
   as you did in the rebellion,
   during the time of testing in the desert,
[9]where your fathers tested and tried me
   and for forty years saw what I did.
[10]That is why I was angry with that

---

a7 Or him for a little while; also in verse 9
c12 Psalm 22:22   d13 Isaiah 8:17
e13 Isaiah 8:18   f17 Or and that he might turn aside God's wrath, taking away

b8 Psalm 8:4-6

generation,
and I said, 'Their hearts are
always going astray,
and they have not known my
ways.'

[11]So I declared on oath in my anger,
'They shall never enter my
rest.' "[a]

[12]See to it, brothers, that none of
you has a sinful, unbelieving heart
that turns away from the living God.
[13]But encourage one another daily, as
long as it is called Today, so that
none of you may be hardened by
sin's deceitfulness. [14]We have come
to share in Christ if we hold firmly
till the end the confidence we had at
first. [15]As has just been said:

"Today, if you hear his voice,
do not harden your hearts
as you did in the rebellion."[b]

[16]Who were they who heard and
rebelled? Were they not all those
Moses led out of Egypt? [17]And with
whom was he angry for forty years?
Was it not with those who sinned,
whose bodies fell in the desert? [18]And
to whom did God swear that they
would never enter his rest if not to
those who disobeyed?[c] [19]So we see
that they were not able to enter,
because of their unbelief.

A Sabbath-Rest for the People of God

4 Therefore, since the promise of
entering his rest still stands, let
us be careful that none of you be
found to have fallen short of it. [2]For
we also have had the gospel preached
to us, just as they did; but the message
they heard was of no value to them,
because those who heard did not
combine it with faith.[a] [3]Now we who
have believed enter that rest, just as
God has said,

"So I declared on oath in my anger,
'They shall never enter my
rest.' "[b]

And yet his work has been finished
since the creation of the world. [4]For

somewhere he has spoken about the
seventh day in these words: "And on
the seventh day God rested from all
his work."[c] [5]And again in the passage
above he says, "They shall never
enter my rest."

[6]It still remains that some will enter
that rest, and those who formerly had
the gospel preached to them did not
go in, because of their disobedience.
[7]Therefore God again set a certain
day, calling it Today, when a long
time later he spoke through David, as
was said before:

"Today, if you hear his voice,
do not harden your hearts."[d]

[8]For if Joshua had given them rest,
God would not have spoken later
about another day. [9]There remains,
then, a Sabbath-rest for the people of
God; [10]for anyone who enters God's
rest also rests from his own work, just
as God did from his. [11]Let us, therefore, make every effort to enter that
rest, so that no-one will fall by following their example of disobedience.

[12]For the word of God is living and
active. Sharper than any double-
edged sword, it penetrates even to
dividing soul and spirit, joints and
marrow; it judges the thoughts and
attitudes of the heart. [13]Nothing in all
creation is hidden from God's sight.
Everything is uncovered and laid
bare before the eyes of him to whom
we must give account.

Jesus the Great High Priest

[14]Therefore, since we have a great
high priest who has gone through the
heavens,[e] Jesus the Son of God, let us
hold firmly to the faith we profess.
[15]For we do not have a high priest
who is unable to sympathise with our
weaknesses, but we have one who
has been tempted in every way, just
as we are—yet was without sin. [16]Let
us then approach the throne of grace
with confidence, so that we may
receive mercy and find grace to help
us in our time of need.

---

[a]11 Psalm 95:7-11   [b]15 Psalm 95:7,8   [c]18 Or *disbelieved*
[a]2 Many manuscripts *because they did not share in the faith of those who obeyed*
[b]3 Psalm 95:11; also in verse 5   [c]4 Gen. 2:2   [d]7 Psalm 95:7,8
[e]14 Or *gone into heaven*

5 Every high priest is selected from among men and is appointed to represent them in matters related to God, to offer gifts and sacrifices for sins. [2]He is able to deal gently with those who are ignorant and are going astray, since he himself is subject to weakness. [3]This is why he has to offer sacrifices for his own sins, as well as for the sins of the people.

[4]No-one takes this honour upon himself; he must be called by God, just as Aaron was. [5]So Christ also did not take upon himself the glory of becoming a high priest. But God said to him,

"You are my Son;
    today I have become your
        Father." [a,b]

[6]And he says in another place,

"You are a priest for ever,
    in the order of Melchizedek." [c]

[7]During the days of Jesus' life on earth, he offered up prayers and petitions with loud cries and tears to the one who could save him from death, and he was heard because of his reverent submission. [8]Although he was a son, he learned obedience from what he suffered [9]and, once made perfect, he became the source of eternal salvation for all who obey him [10]and was designated by God to be high priest in the order of Melchizedek.

Warning Against Falling Away

[11]We have much to say about this, but it is hard to explain because you are slow to learn. [12]In fact, though by this time you ought to be teachers, you need someone to teach you the elementary truths of God's word all over again. You need milk, not solid food! [13]Anyone who lives on milk, being still an infant, is not acquainted with the teaching about righteousness. [14]But solid food is for the mature, who by constant use have trained themselves to distinguish good from evil.

6 Therefore let us leave the elementary teachings about Christ and go on to maturity, not laying again the foundation of repentance from acts that lead to death, and of faith in God, [2]instruction about baptisms, the laying on of hands, the resurrection of the dead, and eternal judgment. [3]And God permitting, we will do so.

[4]It is impossible for those who have once been enlightened, who have tasted the heavenly gift, who have shared in the Holy Spirit, [5]who have tasted the goodness of the word of God and the powers of the coming age, [6]if they fall away, to be brought back to repentance, because [a] to their loss they are crucifying the Son of God all over again and subjecting him to public disgrace.

[7]Land that drinks in the rain often falling on it and that produces a crop useful to those for whom it is farmed receives the blessing of God. [8]But land that produces thorns and thistles is worthless and is in danger of being cursed. In the end it will be burned.

[9]Even though we speak like this, dear friends, we are confident of better things in your case—things that accompany salvation. [10]God is not unjust; he will not forget your work and the love you have shown him as you have helped his people and continue to help them. [11]We want each of you to show this same diligence to the very end, in order to make your hope sure. [12]We do not want you to become lazy, but to imitate those who through faith and patience inherit what has been promised.

The Certainty of God's Promise

[13]When God made his promise to Abraham, since there was no-one greater for him to swear by, he swore by himself, [14]saying, "I will surely bless you and give you many descendants." [b] [15]And so after waiting patiently, Abraham received what was promised.

[16]Men swear by someone greater

[a]5 Or *have begotten you*   [b]5 Psalm 2:7
[a]6 Or *repentance while*   [b]14 Gen. 22:17   [c]6 Psalm 110:4

than themselves, and the oath confirms what is said and puts an end to all argument. [17]Because God wanted to make the unchanging nature of his purpose very clear to the heirs of what was promised, he confirmed it with an oath. [18]God did this so that, by two unchangeable things in which it is impossible for God to lie, we who have fled to take hold of the hope offered to us may be greatly encouraged. [19]We have this hope as an anchor for the soul, firm and secure. It enters the inner sanctuary behind the curtain, [20]where Jesus, who went before us, has entered on our behalf. He has become a high priest for ever, in the order of Melchizedek.

Melchizedek the Priest

7 This Melchizedek was king of Salem and priest of God Most High. He met Abraham returning from the defeat of the kings and blessed him, [2]and Abraham gave him a tenth of everything. First, his name means "king of righteousness"; then also, "king of Salem" means "king of peace". [3]Without father or mother, without genealogy, without beginning of days or end of life, like the Son of God he remains a priest for ever.

[4]Just think how great he was: Even the patriarch Abraham gave him a tenth of the plunder! [5]Now the law requires the descendants of Levi who become priests to collect a tenth from the people—that is, their brothers—even though their brothers are descended from Abraham. [6]This man, however, did not trace his descent from Levi, yet he collected a tenth from Abraham and blessed him who had the promises. [7]And without doubt the lesser person is blessed by the greater. [8]In the one case, the tenth is collected by men who die; but in the other case, by him who is declared to be living. [9]One might even say that Levi, who collects the tenth, paid the tenth through Abraham, [10]because when Melchizedek met Abraham, Levi was still in the body of his ancestor.

Jesus Like Melchizedek

[11]If perfection could have been attained through the Levitical priesthood (for on the basis of it the law was given to the people), why was there still need for another priest to come—one in the order of Melchizedek, not in the order of Aaron? [12]For when there is a change of the priesthood, there must also be a change of the law. [13]He of whom these things are said belonged to a different tribe, and no-one from that tribe has ever served at the altar. [14]For it is clear that our Lord descended from Judah, and in regard to that tribe Moses said nothing about priests. [15]And what we have said is even more clear if another priest like Melchizedek appears, [16]one who has become a priest not on the basis of a regulation as to his ancestry but on the basis of the power of an indestructible life. [17]For it is declared:

"You are a priest for ever,
    in the order of Melchizedek."[a]

[18]The former regulation is set aside because it was weak and useless [19](for the law made nothing perfect), and a better hope is introduced, by which we draw near to God.

[20]And it was not without an oath! Others became priests without any oath, [21]but he became a priest with an oath when God said to him:

"The Lord has sworn
    and will not change his mind:
    'You are a priest for ever.' "[b]

[22]Because of this oath, Jesus has become the guarantee of a better covenant.

[23]Now there were many of those priests, since death prevented them from continuing in office; [24]but because Jesus lives for ever, he has a permanent priesthood. [25]Therefore he is able to save completely[c] those who come to God through him, because he always lives to intercede for them.

[26]Such a high priest meets our need—one who is holy, blameless,

[a]17 Psalm 110:4   [b]21 Psalm 110:4   [c]25 Or *for ever*

pure, set apart from sinners, exalted above the heavens. [27]Unlike the other high priests, he does not need to offer sacrifices day after day, first for his own sins, and then for the sins of the people. He sacrificed for their sins once for all when he offered himself. [28]For the law appoints as high priests men who are weak; but the oath, which came after the law, appointed the Son, who has been made perfect for ever.

The High Priest of a New Covenant

8 The point of what we are saying is this: We do have such a high priest, who sat down at the right hand of the throne of the Majesty in heaven, [2]and who serves in the sanctuary, the true tabernacle set up by the Lord, not by man.

[3]Every high priest is appointed to offer both gifts and sacrifices, and so it was necessary for this one also to have something to offer. [4]If he were on earth, he would not be a priest, for there are already men who offer the gifts prescribed by the law. [5]They serve at a sanctuary that is a copy and shadow of what is in heaven. This is why Moses was warned when he was about to build the tabernacle: "See to it that you make everything according to the pattern shown you on the mountain."[a] [6]But the ministry Jesus has received is as superior to theirs as the covenant of which he is mediator is superior to the old one, and it is founded on better promises.

[7]For if there had been nothing wrong with that first covenant, no place would have been sought for another. [8]But God found fault with the people and said:[b]

"The time is coming, declares the Lord,
  when I will make a new covenant
  with the house of Israel
  and with the house of Judah.
[9]It will not be like the covenant
  I made with their forefathers
  when I took them by the hand
  to lead them out of Egypt,

because they did not remain
    faithful to my covenant,
  and I turned away from them,
      declares the Lord.
[10]This is the covenant I will make
  with the house of Israel
  after that time, declares the Lord.
I will put my laws in their minds
  and write them on their hearts.
I will be their God,
  and they will be my people.
[11]No longer will a man teach his
    neighbour,
  or a man his brother, saying,
  'Know the Lord,'
because they will all know me,
  from the least of them to the
      greatest.
[12]For I will forgive their wickedness
  and will remember their sins no
      more."[c]

[13]By calling this covenant "new", he has made the first one obsolete; and what is obsolete and ageing will soon disappear.

Worship in the Earthly Tabernacle

9 Now the first covenant had regulations for worship and also an earthly sanctuary. [2]A tabernacle was set up. In its first room were the lampstand, the table and the consecrated bread; this was called the Holy Place. [3]Behind the second curtain was a room called the Most Holy Place, [4]which had the golden altar of incense and the gold-covered ark of the covenant. This ark contained the gold jar of manna, Aaron's rod that had budded, and the stone tablets of the covenant. [5]Above the ark were the cherubim of the Glory, overshadowing the place of atonement. But we cannot discuss these things in detail now.

[6]When everything had been arranged like this, the priests entered regularly into the outer room to carry on their ministry. [7]But only the high priest entered the inner room, and that only once a year, and never without blood, which he offered for

[a]5 Exodus 25:40   [b]8 Some manuscripts may be translated *fault and said to the people.*
[c]12 Jer. 31:31-34

himself and for the sins the people had committed in ignorance. [8]The Holy Spirit was showing by this that the way into the Most Holy Place had not yet been disclosed as long as the first tabernacle was still standing. [9]This is an illustration for the present time, indicating that the gifts and sacrifices being offered were not able to clear the conscience of the worshipper. [10]They are only a matter of food and drink and various ceremonial washings—external regulations applying until the time of the new order.

The Blood of Christ

[11]When Christ came as high priest of the good things that are already here,[a] he went through the greater and more perfect tabernacle that is not man-made, that is to say, not a part of this creation. [12]He did not enter by means of the blood of goats and calves; but he entered the Most Holy Place once for all by his own blood, having obtained eternal redemption. [13]The blood of goats and bulls and the ashes of a heifer sprinkled on those who are ceremonially unclean sanctify them so that they are outwardly clean. [14]How much more, then, will the blood of Christ, who through the eternal Spirit offered himself unblemished to God, cleanse our consciences from acts that lead to death, so that we may serve the living God!

[15]For this reason Christ is the mediator of a new covenant, that those who are called may receive the promised eternal inheritance—now that he has died as a ransom to set them free from the sins committed under the first covenant.

[16]In the case of a will,[b] it is necessary to prove the death of the one who made it, [17]because a will is in force only when somebody has died; it never takes effect while the one who made it is living. [18]This is why even the first covenant was not put into effect without blood. [19]When

Moses had proclaimed every commandment of the law to all the people, he took the blood of calves, together with water, scarlet wool and branches of hyssop, and sprinkled the scroll and all the people. [20]He said, "This is the blood of the covenant, which God has commanded you to keep."[c] [21]In the same way, he sprinkled with the blood both the tabernacle and everything used in its ceremonies. [22]In fact, the law requires that nearly everything be cleansed with blood, and without the shedding of blood there is no forgiveness.

[23]It was necessary, then, for the copies of the heavenly things to be purified with these sacrifices, but the heavenly things themselves to be purified with better sacrifices than these. [24]For Christ did not enter a man-made sanctuary that was only a copy of the true one; he entered heaven itself, now to appear for us in God's presence. [25]Nor did he enter heaven to offer himself again and again, the way the high priest enters the Most Holy Place every year with blood that is not his own. [26]Then Christ would have had to suffer many times since the creation of the world. But now he has appeared once for all at the end of the ages to do away with sin by the sacrifice of himself. [27]Just as man is destined to die once, and after that to face judgment, [28]so Christ was sacrificed once to take away the sins of many people; and he will appear a second time, not to bear sin, but to bring salvation to those who are waiting for him.

Christ's Sacrifice Once for All

10 The law is only a shadow of the good things that are coming—not the realities themselves. For this reason it can never, by the same sacrifices repeated endlessly year after year, make perfect those who draw near to worship. [2]If it could, would they not have stopped being offered? For the worshippers

---

[a]11 Some early manuscripts *are to come*
[b]16 Same Greek word as *covenant*; also in verse 17
[c]20 Exodus 24:8

would have been cleansed once for all, and would no longer have felt guilty for their sins. [3]But those sacrifices are an annual reminder of sins, [4]because it is impossible for the blood of bulls and goats to take away sins.

[5]Therefore, when Christ came into the world, he said:

> "Sacrifice and offering you did not
>   desire,
>   but a body you prepared for me;
> [6] with burnt offerings and sin
>   offerings
>   you were not pleased.
> [7] Then I said, 'Here I am—it is
>   written about me in the scroll—
>   I have come to do your will, O
>   God.' "[a]

[8]First he said, "Sacrifices and offerings, burnt offerings and sin offerings you did not desire, nor were you pleased with them" (although the law required them to be made). [9]Then he said, "Here I am, I have come to do your will." He sets aside the first to establish the second. [10]And by that will, we have been made holy through the sacrifice of the body of Jesus Christ once for all.

[11]Day after day every priest stands and performs his religious duties; again and again he offers the same sacrifices, which can never take away sins. [12]But when this priest had offered for all time one sacrifice for sins, he sat down at the right hand of God. [13]Since that time he waits for his enemies to be made his footstool, [14]because by one sacrifice he has made perfect for ever those who are being made holy.

[15]The Holy Spirit also testifies to us about this. First he says:

> [16]"This is the covenant I will make
>   with them
>   after that time, says the Lord.
> I will put my laws in their hearts,
>   and I will write them on their
>   minds."[b]

[17]Then he adds:

> "Their sins and lawless acts
>   I will remember no more."[c]

[18]And where these have been forgiven, there is no longer any sacrifice for sin.

A Call to Persevere

[19]Therefore, brothers, since we have confidence to enter the Most Holy Place by the blood of Jesus, [20]by a new and living way opened for us through the curtain, that is, his body, [21]and since we have a great priest over the house of God, [22]let us draw near to God with a sincere heart in full assurance of faith, having our hearts sprinkled to cleanse us from a guilty conscience and having our bodies washed with pure water. [23]Let us hold unswervingly to the hope we profess, for he who promised is faithful. [24]And let us consider how we may spur one another on towards love and good deeds. [25]Let us not give up meeting together, as some are in the habit of doing, but let us encourage one another—and all the more as you see the Day approaching.

[26]If we deliberately keep on sinning after we have received the knowledge of the truth, no sacrifice for sins is left, [27]but only a fearful expectation of judgment and of raging fire that will consume the enemies of God. [28]Anyone who rejected the law of Moses died without mercy on the testimony of two or three witnesses. [29]How much more severely do you think a man deserves to be punished who has trampled the Son of God under foot, who has treated as an unholy thing the blood of the covenant that sanctified him, and who has insulted the Spirit of grace? [30]For we know him who said, "It is mine to avenge; I will repay,"[d] and again, "The Lord will judge his people."[e] [31]It is a dreadful thing to fall into the hands of the living God.

[32]Remember those earlier days

---

[a]7 Psalm 40:6-8 (see Septuagint)   [b]16 Jer. 31:33   [c]17 Jer. 31:34
[d]30 Deut. 32:35   [e]30 Deut. 32:36; Psalm 135:14

after you had received the light, when you stood your ground in a great contest in the face of suffering. 33Sometimes you were publicly exposed to insult and persecution; at other times you stood side by side with those who were so treated. 34You sympathised with those in prison and joyfully accepted the confiscation of your property, because you knew that you yourselves had better and lasting possessions.

35So do not throw away your confidence; it will be richly rewarded. 36You need to persevere so that when you have done the will of God, you will receive what he has promised. 37For in just a very little while,

"He who is coming will come and will not delay.
38   But my righteous one*f* will live by faith.
And if he shrinks back,
   I will not be pleased with him."*g*

39But we are not of those who shrink back and are destroyed, but of those who believe and are saved.

By Faith

11 Now faith is being sure of what we hope for and certain of what we do not see. 2This is what the ancients were commended for.

3By faith we understand that the universe was formed at God's command, so that what is seen was not made out of what was visible.

4By faith Abel offered God a better sacrifice than Cain did. By faith he was commended as a righteous man, when God spoke well of his offerings. And by faith he still speaks, even though he is dead.

5By faith Enoch was taken from this life, so that he did not experience death; he could not be found, because God had taken him away. For before he was taken, he was commended as one who pleased God. 6And without faith it is impossible to please God, because anyone who comes to him

must believe that he exists and that he rewards those who earnestly seek him.

7By faith Noah, when warned about things not yet seen, in holy fear built an ark to save his family. By his faith he condemned the world and became heir of the righteousness that comes by faith.

8By faith Abraham, when called to go to a place he would later receive as his inheritance, obeyed and went, even though he did not know where he was going. 9By faith he made his home in the promised land like a stranger in a foreign country; he lived in tents, as did Isaac and Jacob, who were heirs with him of the same promise. 10For he was looking forward to the city with foundations, whose architect and builder is God.

11By faith Abraham, even though he was past age—and Sarah herself was barren—was enabled to become a father because he*a* considered him faithful who had made the promise. 12And so from this one man, and he as good as dead, came descendants as numerous as the stars in the sky and as countless as the sand on the seashore.

13All these people were still living by faith when they died. They did not receive the things promised; they only saw them and welcomed them from a distance. And they admitted that they were aliens and strangers on earth. 14People who say such things show that they are looking for a country of their own. 15If they had been thinking of the country they had left, they would have had opportunity to return. 16Instead, they were longing for a better country—a heavenly one. Therefore God is not ashamed to be called their God, for he has prepared a city for them.

17By faith Abraham, when God tested him, offered Isaac as a sacrifice. He who had received the promises was about to sacrifice his one and only son, 18even though God had said to him, "It is through Isaac that your

*f*38 One early manuscript But the righteous   *g*38 Hab. 2:3,4
*a*11 Or By faith even Sarah, who was past age, was enabled to bear children because she

offspring[b] will be reckoned."[c]
[19]Abraham reasoned that God could raise the dead, and figuratively speaking, he did receive Isaac back from death.

[20]By faith Isaac blessed Jacob and Esau in regard to their future.

[21]By faith Jacob, when he was dying, blessed each of Joseph's sons, and worshipped as he leaned on the top of his staff.

[22]By faith Joseph, when his end was near, spoke about the exodus of the Israelites from Egypt and gave instructions about his bones.

[23]By faith Moses' parents hid him for three months after he was born, because they saw he was no ordinary child, and they were not afraid of the king's edict.

[24]By faith Moses, when he had grown up, refused to be known as the son of Pharaoh's daughter. [25]He chose to be il'·treated along with the people of God rather than to enjoy the pleasures of sin for a short time. [26]He regarded disgrace for the sake of Christ as of greater value than the treasures of Egypt, because he was looking ahead to his reward. [27]By faith he left Egypt, not fearing the king's anger; he persevered because he saw him who is invisible. [28]By faith he kept the Passover and the sprinkling of blood, so that the destroyer of the firstborn would not touch the firstborn of Israel.

[29]By faith the people passed through the Red Sea[d] as on dry land; but when the Egyptians tried to do so, they were drowned.

[30]By faith the walls of Jericho fell, after the people had marched around them for seven days.

[31]By faith the prostitute Rahab, because she welcomed the spies, was not killed with those who were disobedient.[e]

[32]And what more shall I say? I do not have time to tell about Gideon, Barak, Samson, Jephthah, David, Samuel and the prophets, [33]who through faith conquered kingdoms,

administered justice, and gained what was promised; who shut the mouths of lions, [34]quenched the fury of the flames, and escaped the edge of the sword; whose weakness was turned to strength; and who became powerful in battle and routed foreign armies. [35]Women received back their dead, raised to life again. Others were tortured and refused to be released, so that they might gain a better resurrection. [36]Some faced jeers and flogging, while still others were chained and put in prison. [37]They were stoned;[f] they were sawn in two; they were put to death by the sword. They went about in sheepskins and goatskins, destitute, persecuted and ill-treated—[38]the world was not worthy of them. They wandered in deserts and mountains, and in caves and holes in the ground.

[39]These were all commended for their faith, yet none of them received what had been promised. [40]God had planned something better for us so that only together with us would they be made perfect.

God Disciplines His Sons

12 Therefore, since we are surrounded by such a great cloud of witnesses, let us throw off everything that hinders and the sin that so easily entangles, and let us run with perseverance the race marked out for us. [2]Let us fix our eyes on Jesus, the author and perfecter of our faith, who for the joy set before him endured the cross, scorning its shame, and sat down at the right hand of the throne of God. [3]Consider him who endured such opposition from sinful men, so that you will not grow weary and lose heart.

[4]In your struggle against sin, you have not yet resisted to the point of shedding your blood. [5]And you have forgotten that word of encouragement that addresses you as sons:

"My son, do not make light of the Lord's discipline,

[b]18 Greek *seed*   [c]18 Gen. 21:12   [d]29 That is, Sea of Reeds   [e]31 Or *unbelieving*
[f]37 Some early manuscripts *stoned; they were put to the test;*

249

and do not lose heart when he
rebukes you,
[6]because the Lord disciplines those
he loves,
and he punishes everyone he
accepts as a son."[a]

[7]Endure hardship as discipline;
God is treating you as sons. For what
son is not disciplined by his father?
[8]If you are not disciplined (and everyone undergoes discipline), then you
are illegitimate children and not true
sons. [9]Moreover, we have all had
human fathers who disciplined us
and we respected them for it. How
much more should we submit to the
Father of our spirits and live! [10]Our
fathers disciplined us for a little while
as they thought best; but God disciplines us for our good, that we may
share in his holiness. [11]No discipline
seems pleasant at the time, but painful. Later on, however, it produces a
harvest of righteousness and peace
for those who have been trained by
it.

[12]Therefore, strengthen your feeble
arms and weak knees! [13]"Make level
paths for your feet,"[b] so that the lame
may not be disabled, but rather
healed.

Warning Against Refusing God

[14]Make every effort to live in peace
with all men and to be holy; without
holiness no-one will see the Lord.
[15]See to it that no-one misses the
grace of God and that no bitter root
grows up to cause trouble and defile
many. [16]See that no-one is sexually
immoral, or is godless like Esau, who
for a single meal sold his inheritance
rights as the oldest son. [17]Afterwards,
as you know, when he wanted to
inherit this blessing, he was rejected.
He could bring about no change of
mind, though he sought the blessing
with tears.

[18]You have not come to a mountain
that can be touched and that is burning with fire; to darkness, gloom and
storm; [19]to a trumpet blast or to such
a voice speaking words, so that those

who heard it begged that no further
word be spoken to them, [20]because
they could not bear what was commanded: "If even an animal touches
the mountain, it must be stoned."[c]
[21]The sight was so terrifying that
Moses said, "I am trembling with
fear."[d]

[22]But you have come to Mount
Zion, to the heavenly Jerusalem, the
city of the living God. You have come
to thousands upon thousands of
angels in joyful assembly, [23]to the
church of the first-born, whose names
are written in heaven. You have come
to God, the judge of all men, to the
spirits of righteous men made perfect,
[24]to Jesus the mediator of a new
covenant, and to the sprinkled blood
that speaks a better word than the
blood of Abel.

[25]See to it that you do not refuse
him who speaks. If they did not
escape when they refused him who
warned them on earth, how much
less will we, if we turn away from
him who warns us from heaven? [26]At
that time his voice shook the earth,
but now he has promised, "Once
more I will shake not only the earth
but also the heavens."[e] [27]The words
"once more" indicate the removing of
what can be shaken—that is, created
things—so that what cannot be
shaken may remain.

[28]Therefore, since we are receiving
a kingdom that cannot be shaken, let
us be thankful, and so worship God
acceptably with reverence and awe,
[29]for our God is a consuming fire.

Concluding Exhortations

13 Keep on loving each other as
brothers. [2]Do not forget to
entertain strangers, for by so doing
some people have entertained angels
without knowing it. [3]Remember those
in prison as if you were their fellow
prisoners, and those who are ill-
treated as if you yourselves were
suffering.

[4]Marriage should be honoured by
all, and the marriage bed kept pure,

[a]6 Prov. 3:11,12   [b]13 Prov. 4:26   [c]20 Exodus 19:12,13
[d]21 Deut. 9:19   [e]26 Haggai 2:6

for God will judge the adulterer and all the sexually immoral. 5Keep your lives free from the love of money and be content with what you have, because God has said,

"Never will I leave you;
    never will I forsake you."*a*

6So we say with confidence,

"The Lord is my helper; I will not be afraid.
    What can man do to me?"*b*

7Remember your leaders, who spoke the word of God to you. Consider the outcome of their way of life and imitate their faith. 8Jesus Christ is the same yesterday and today and for ever.

9Do not be carried away by all kinds of strange teachings. It is good for our hearts to be strengthened by grace, not by ceremonial foods, which are of no value to those who eat them. 10We have an altar from which those who minister at the tabernacle have no right to eat.

11The high priest carries the blood of animals into the Most Holy Place as a sin offering, but the bodies are burned outside the camp. 12And so Jesus also suffered outside the city gate to make the people holy through his own blood. 13Let us, then, go to him outside the camp, bearing the disgrace he bore. 14For here we do not have an enduring city, but we are looking for the city that is to come.

15Through Jesus, therefore, let us continually offer to God a sacrifice of praise—the fruit of lips that confess his name. 16And do not forget to do good and to share with others, for with such sacrifices God is pleased.

17Obey your leaders and submit to their authority. They keep watch over you as men who must give an account. Obey them so that their work will be a joy, not a burden, for that would be of no advantage to you.

18Pray for us. We are sure that we have a clear conscience and desire to live honourably in every way. 19I particularly urge you to pray so that I may be restored to you soon.

20May the God of peace, who through the blood of the eternal covenant brought back from the dead our Lord Jesus, that great Shepherd of the sheep, 21equip you with everything good for doing his will, and may he work in us what is pleasing to him, through Jesus Christ, to whom be glory for ever and ever. Amen.

22Brothers, I urge you to bear with my word of exhortation, for I have written you only a short letter.

23I want you to know that our brother Timothy has been released. If he arrives soon, I will come with him to see you.

24Greet all your leaders and all God's people. Those from Italy send you their greetings.

25Grace be with you all.

*a*5 Deut. 31:6   *b*6 Psalm 118:6,7

James

1 James, a servant of God and of the Lord Jesus Christ,

To the twelve tribes scattered among the nations:

Greetings:

Trials and Temptations

2Consider it pure joy, my brothers, whenever you face trials of many kinds, 3because you know that the testing of your faith develops perseverance. 4Perseverance must finish its work so that you may be mature and complete, not lacking anything. 5If any of you lacks wisdom, he should ask God, who gives generously to all without finding fault, and it will be given to him. 6But when he asks, he must believe and not doubt, because he who doubts is like a wave of the sea, blown and tossed by the wind. 7That man should not think he will receive anything from the Lord; 8he is a double-minded man, unstable in all he does.

9The brother in humble circumstances ought to take pride in his high position. 10But the one who is rich should take pride in his low position, because he will pass away like a wild flower. 11For the sun rises with scorching heat and withers the plant; its blossom falls and its beauty is destroyed. In the same way, the rich man will fade away even while he goes about his business.

12Blessed is the man who perseveres under trial, because when he has stood the test, he will receive the crown of life that God has promised to those who love him.

13When tempted, no-one should say, "God is tempting me." For God cannot be tempted by evil, nor does he tempt anyone; 14but each one is tempted when, by his own evil desire, he is dragged away and enticed. 15Then, after desire has conceived, it gives birth to sin; and sin, when it is full-grown, gives birth to death.

16Don't be deceived, my dear brothers. 17Every good and perfect gift is from above, coming down from the Father of the heavenly lights, who does not change like shifting shadows. 18He chose to give us birth through the word of truth, that we might be a kind of firstfruits of all he created.

Listening and Doing

19My dear brothers, take note of this: Everyone should be quick to listen, slow to speak and slow to become angry, 20for man's anger does not bring about the righteous life that God desires. 21Therefore, get rid of all moral filth and the evil that is so prevalent, and humbly accept the word planted in you, which can save you.

22Do not merely listen to the word, and so deceive yourselves. Do what it says. 23Anyone who listens to the word but does not do what it says is like a man who looks at his face in a mirror 24and, after looking at himself, goes away and immediately forgets what he looks like. 25But the man who looks intently into the perfect law that gives freedom, and continues to do this, not forgetting what he has heard, but doing it—he will be blessed in what he does.

26If anyone considers himself religious and yet does not keep a tight rein on his tongue, he deceives him-

self and his religion is worthless.
27Religion that God our Father accepts as pure and faultless is this: to look after orphans and widows in their distress and to keep oneself from being polluted by the world.

Favouritism Forbidden

2 My brothers, as believers in our glorious Lord Jesus Christ, don't show favouritism. 2Suppose a man comes into your meeting wearing a gold ring and fine clothes, and a poor man in shabby clothes also comes in. 3If you show special attention to the man wearing fine clothes and say, "Here's a good seat for you," but say to the poor man, "You stand there" or "Sit on the floor by my feet," 4have you not discriminated among yourselves and become judges with evil thoughts?

5Listen, my dear brothers: Has not God chosen those who are poor in the eyes of the world to be rich in faith and to inherit the kingdom he promised those who love him? 6But you have insulted the poor. Is it not the rich who are exploiting you? Are they not the ones who are dragging you into court? 7Are they not the ones who are slandering the noble name of him to whom you belong?

8If you really keep the royal law found in Scripture, "Love your neighbour as yourself,"a you are doing right. 9But if you show favouritism, you sin and are convicted by the law as law-breakers. 10For whoever keeps the whole law and yet stumbles at just one point is guilty of breaking all of it. 11For he who said, "Do not commit adultery,"b also said, "Do not murder."c If you do not commit adultery but do commit murder, you have become a law-breaker.

12Speak and act as those who are going to be judged by the law that gives freedom, 13because judgment without mercy will be shown to anyone who has not been merciful. Mercy triumphs over judgment!

Faith and Deeds

14What good is it, my brothers, if a man claims to have faith but has no deeds? Can such faith save him? 15Suppose a brother or sister is without clothes and daily food. 16If one of you says to him, "Go, I wish you well; keep warm and well fed," but does nothing about his physical needs, what good is it? 17In the same way, faith by itself, if it is not accompanied by action, is dead.

18But someone will say, "You have faith; I have deeds."

Show me your faith without deeds, and I will show you my faith by what I do. 19You believe that there is one God. Good! Even the demons believe that—and shudder.

20You foolish man, do you want evidence that faith without deeds is useless?d 21Was not our ancestor Abraham considered righteous for what he did when he offered his son Isaac on the altar? 22You see that his faith and his actions were working together, and his faith was made complete by what he did. 23And the scripture was fulfilled that says, "Abraham believed God, and it was credited to him as righteousness,"e and he was called God's friend. 24You see that a person is justified by what he does and not by faith alone.

25In the same way, was not even Rahab the prostitute considered righteous for what she did when she gave lodging to the spies and sent them off in a different direction? 26As the body without the spirit is dead, so faith without deeds is dead.

Taming the Tongue

3 Not many of you should presume to be teachers, my brothers, because you know that we who teach will be judged more strictly. 2We all stumble in many ways. If anyone is never at fault in what he says, he is a perfect man, able to keep his whole body in check.

3When we put bits into the mouths

a8 Lev. 19:18   b11 Exodus 20:14; Deut. 5:18   c11 Exodus 20:13; Deut. 5:17
d20 Some early manuscripts *dead*   e23 Gen. 15:6

of horses to make them obey us, we can turn the whole animal. 4Or take ships as an example. Although they are so large and are driven by strong winds, they are steered by a very small rudder wherever the pilot wants to go. 5Likewise the tongue is a small part of the body, but it makes great boasts. Consider what a great forest is set on fire by a small spark. 6The tongue also is a fire, a world of evil among the parts of the body. It corrupts the whole person, sets the whole course of his life on fire, and is itself set on fire by hell.

7All kinds of animals, birds, reptiles and creatures of the sea are being tamed and have been tamed by man, 8but no man can tame the tongue. It is a restless evil, full of deadly poison.

9With the tongue we praise our Lord and Father, and with it we curse men, who have been made in God's likeness. 10Out of the same mouth come praise and cursing. My brothers, this should not be. 11Can both fresh water and salt water flow from the same spring? 12My brothers, can a fig-tree bear olives, or a grape-vine bear figs? Neither can a salt spring produce fresh water.

Two Kinds of Wisdom

13Who is wise and understanding among you? Let him show it by his good life, by deeds done in the humility that comes from wisdom. 14But if you harbour bitter envy and selfish ambition in your hearts, do not boast about it or deny the truth. 15Such "wisdom" does not come down from heaven but is earthly, unspiritual, of the devil. 16For where you have envy and selfish ambition, there you find disorder and every evil practice.

17But the wisdom that comes from heaven is first of all pure; then peaceloving, considerate, submissive, full of mercy and good fruit, impartial and sincere. 18Peacemakers who sow in peace raise a harvest of righteousness.

Submit Yourselves to God

4 What causes fights and quarrels among you? Don't they come from your desires that battle within you? 2You want something but don't get it. You kill and covet, but you cannot have what you want. You quarrel and fight. You do not have, because you do not ask God. 3When you ask, you do not receive, because you ask with wrong motives, that you may spend what you get on your pleasures.

4You adulterous people, don't you know that friendship with the world is hatred towards God? Anyone who chooses to be a friend of the world becomes an enemy of God. 5Or do you think Scripture says without reason that the spirit he caused to live in us tends towards envy,ᵃ 6but he gives us more grace? That is why Scripture says:

"God opposes the proud
but gives grace to the humble."ᵇ

7Submit yourselves, then, to God. Resist the devil, and he will flee from you. 8Come near to God and he will come near to you. Wash your hands, you sinners, and purify your hearts, you double-minded. 9Grieve, mourn and wail. Change your laughter to mourning and your joy to gloom. 10Humble yourselves before the Lord, and he will lift you up.

11Brothers, do not slander one another. Anyone who speaks against his brother or judges him speaks against the law and judges it. When you judge the law, you are not keeping it, but sitting in judgment on it. 12There is only one Lawgiver and Judge, the one who is able to save and destroy. But you—who are you to judge your neighbour?

Boasting About Tomorrow

13Now listen, you who say, "Today or tomorrow we will go to this or that city, spend a year there, carry on business and make money." 14Why,

ᵃ5 Or that God jealously longs for the spirit that he made to live in us; or that the Spirit he caused to live in us longs jealously
ᵇ6 Prov. 3:34

you do not even know what will happen tomorrow. What is your life? You are a mist that appears for a little while and then vanishes. [15]Instead, you ought to say, "If it is the Lord's will, we will live and do this or that." [16]As it is, you boast and brag. All such boasting is evil. [17]Anyone, then, who knows the good he ought to do and doesn't do it, sins.

Warning to Rich Oppressors

5 Now listen, you rich people, weep and wail because of the misery that is coming upon you. [2]Your wealth has rotted, and moths have eaten your clothes. [3]Your gold and silver are corroded. Their corrosion will testify against you and eat your flesh like fire. You have hoarded wealth in the last days. [4]Look! The wages you failed to pay the workmen who mowed your fields are crying out against you. The cries of the harvesters have reached the ears of the Lord Almighty. [5]You have lived on earth in luxury and self-indulgence. You have fattened yourselves in the day of slaughter. [6]You have condemned and murdered innocent men, who were not opposing you.

Patience in Suffering

[7]Be patient, then, brothers, until the Lord's coming. See how the farmer waits for the land to yield its valuable crop and how patient he is for the autumn and spring rains. [8]You too, be patient and stand firm, because the Lord's coming is near. [9]Don't grumble against each other, brothers, or you will be judged. The Judge is standing at the door!

[10]Brothers, as an example of patience in the face of suffering, take the prophets who spoke in the name of the Lord. [11]As you know, we consider blessed those who have persevered. You have heard of Job's perseverance and have seen what the Lord finally brought about. The Lord is full of compassion and mercy.

[12]Above all, my brothers, do not swear—not by heaven or by earth or by anything else. Let your "Yes" be yes, and your "No", no, or you will be condemned.

The Prayer of Faith

[13]Is any one of you in trouble? He should pray. Is anyone happy? Let him sing songs of praise. [14]Is any one of you sick? He should call the elders of the church to pray over him and anoint him with oil in the name of the Lord. [15]And the prayer offered in faith will make the sick person well; the Lord will raise him up. If he has sinned, he will be forgiven. [16]Therefore confess your sins to each other and pray for each other so that you may be healed. The prayer of a righteous man is powerful and effective.

[17]Elijah was a man just like us. He prayed earnestly that it would not rain, and it did not rain on the land for three and a half years. [18]Again he prayed, and the heavens gave rain, and the earth produced its crops.

[19]My brothers, if one of you should wander from the truth and someone should bring him back, [20]remember this: Whoever turns a sinner from the error of his way will save him from death and cover over a multitude of sins.

1 Peter

1 Peter, an apostle of Jesus Christ,

To God's elect, strangers in the world, scattered throughout Pontus, Galatia, Cappadocia, Asia and Bithynia, 2who have been chosen according to the foreknowledge of God the Father, through the sanctifying work of the Spirit, for obedience to Jesus Christ and sprinkling by his blood:

Grace and peace be yours in abundance.

Praise to God for a Living Hope

3Praise be to the God and Father of our Lord Jesus Christ! In his great mercy he has given us new birth into a living hope through the resurrection of Jesus Christ from the dead, 4and into an inheritance that can never perish, spoil or fade—kept in heaven for you, 5who through faith are shielded by God's power until the coming of the salvation that is ready to be revealed in the last time. 6In this you greatly rejoice, though now for a little while you may have had to suffer grief in all kinds of trials. 7These have come so that your faith—of greater worth than gold, which perishes even though refined by fire—may be proved genuine and may result in praise, glory and honour when Jesus Christ is revealed. 8Though you have not seen him, you love him; and even though you do not see him now, you believe in him and are filled with an inexpressible and glorious joy, 9for you are receiving the goal of your faith, the salvation of your souls.

10Concerning this salvation, the prophets, who spoke of the grace that was to come to you, searched intently and with the greatest care, 11trying to find out the time and circumstances to which the Spirit of Christ in them was pointing when he predicted the sufferings of Christ and the glories that would follow. 12It was revealed to them that they were not serving themselves but you, when they spoke of the things that have now been told you by those who have preached the gospel to you by the Holy Spirit sent from heaven. Even angels long to look into these things.

Be Holy

13Therefore, prepare your minds for action; be self-controlled; set your hope fully on the grace to be given you when Jesus Christ is revealed. 14As obedient children, do not conform to the evil desires you had when you lived in ignorance. 15But just as he who called you is holy, so be holy in all you do; 16for it is written: "Be holy, because I am holy."ᵃ

17Since you call on a Father who judges each man's work impartially, live your lives as strangers here in reverent fear. 18For you know that it was not with perishable things such as silver or gold that you were redeemed from the empty way of life handed down to you from your forefathers, 19but with the precious blood of Christ, a lamb without blemish or defect. 20He was chosen before the creation of the world, but was revealed in these last times for your sake. 21Through him you believe in God, who raised him from the dead and glorified him, and so your faith and hope are in God.

ᵃ16 Lev. 11:44,45; 19:2; 20:7

22Now that you have purified yourselves by obeying the truth so that you have sincere love for your brothers, love one another deeply, from the heart.b 23For you have been born again, not of perishable seed, but of imperishable, through the living and enduring word of God. 24For,

"All men are like grass,
and all their glory is like the
flowers of the field;
the grass withers and the flowers
fall,
25 but the word of the Lord stands
for ever."c

And this is the word that was preached to you.

2 Therefore, rid yourselves of all malice and all deceit, hypocrisy, envy, and slander of every kind. 2Like newborn babies, crave pure spiritual milk, so that by it you may grow up in your salvation, 3now that you have tasted that the Lord is good.

The Living Stone and a Chosen People

4As you come to him, the living Stone—rejected by men but chosen by God and precious to him—5you also, like living stones, are being built into a spiritual house to be a holy priesthood, offering spiritual sacrifices acceptable to God through Jesus Christ. 6For in Scripture it says:

"See, I lay a stone in Zion,
a chosen and precious
cornerstone,
and the one who trusts in him
will never be put to shame."a

7Now to you who believe, this stone is precious. But to those who do not believe,

"The stone the builders rejected
has become the capstone,"b,c

8and,

"A stone that causes men to
stumble
and a rock that makes them
fall."d

They stumble because they disobey the message—which is also what they were destined for.

9But you are a chosen people, a royal priesthood, a holy nation, a people belonging to God, that you may declare the praises of him who called you out of darkness into his wonderful light. 10Once you were not a people, but now you are the people of God; once you had not received mercy, but now you have received mercy.

11Dear friends, I urge you, as aliens and strangers in the world, to abstain from sinful desires, which war against your soul. 12Live such good lives among the pagans that, though they accuse you of doing wrong, they may see your good deeds and glorify God on the day he visits us.

Submission to Rulers and Masters

13Submit yourselves for the Lord's sake to every authority instituted among men: whether to the king, as the supreme authority, 14or to governors, who are sent by him to punish those who do wrong and to commend those who do right. 15For it is God's will that by doing good you should silence the ignorant talk of foolish men. 16Live as free men, but do not use your freedom as a cover-up for evil; live as servants of God. 17Show proper respect to everyone: Love the brotherhood of believers, fear God, honour the king.

18Slaves, submit yourselves to your masters with all respect, not only to those who are good and considerate, but also to those who are harsh. 19For it is commendable if a man bears up under the pain of unjust suffering because he is conscious of God. 20But how is it to your credit if you receive a beating for doing wrong and endure it? But if you suffer for doing good and you endure it, this is commendable before God. 21To this you were called, because Christ suffered for you, leaving you an example, that you should follow in his steps.

b22 Some early manuscripts *from a pure heart*
c25 Isaiah 40:6–8   a6 Isaiah 28:16   b7 Or *cornerstone*   c7 Psalm 118:22
d8 Isaiah 8:14

257

[22]"He committed no sin,
and no deceit was found in his
mouth."[e]

[23]When they hurled their insults at
him, he did not retaliate; when he
suffered, he made no threats. Instead,
he entrusted himself to him who
judges justly. [24]He himself bore our
sins in his body on the tree, so that
we might die to sins and live for
righteousness; by his wounds you
have been healed. [25]For you were
like sheep going astray, but now you
have returned to the Shepherd and
Overseer of your souls.

Wives and Husbands

3 Wives, in the same way be submissive to your husbands so that,
if any of them do not believe the
word, they may be won over without
talk by the behaviour of their wives,
[2]when they see the purity and reverence of your lives. [3]Your beauty
should not come from outward adorn-
ment, such as braided hair and the
wearing of gold jewellery and fine
clothes. [4]Instead, it should be that of
your inner self, the unfading beauty
of a gentle and quiet spirit, which is
of great worth in God's sight. [5]For this
is the way the holy women of the past
who put their hope in God used to
make themselves beautiful. They
were submissive to their own husbands, [6]like Sarah, who obeyed Abraham and called him her master. You
are her daughters if you do what is
right and do not give way to fear.

[7]Husbands, in the same way be
considerate as you live with your
wives, and treat them with respect as
the weaker partner and as heirs with
you of the gracious gift of life, so that
nothing will hinder your prayers.

Suffering for Doing Good

[8]Finally, all of you, live in harmony
with one another; be sympathetic,
love as brothers, be compassionate
and humble. [9]Do not repay evil with
evil or insult with insult, but with
blessing, because to this you were
called so that you may inherit a
blessing. [10]For,

"Whoever would love life
and see good days
must keep his tongue from evil
and his lips from deceitful
speech.
[11]He must turn from evil and do
good;
he must seek peace and pursue it.
[12]For the eyes of the Lord are on the
righteous
and his ears are attentive to their
prayer,
but the face of the Lord is against
those who do evil."[a]

[13]Who is going to harm you if you
are eager to do good? [14]But even if
you should suffer for what is right,
you are blessed. "Do not fear what
they fear;[b] do not be frightened."[c]
[15]But in your hearts set apart Christ
as Lord. Always be prepared to give
an answer to everyone who asks you
to give the reason for the hope that
you have. But do this with gentleness
and respect, [16]keeping a clear conscience, so that those who speak maliciously against your good behaviour
in Christ may be ashamed of their
slander. [17]It is better, if it is God's
will, to suffer for doing good than for
doing evil. [18]For Christ died for sins
once for all, the righteous for the
unrighteous, to bring you to God. He
was put to death in the body but
made alive by the Spirit, [19]through
whom[d] also he went and preached to
the spirits in prison [20]who disobeyed
long ago when God waited patiently
in the days of Noah while the ark
was being built. In it only a few
people, eight in all, were saved
through water, [21]and this water symbolises baptism that now saves you
also—not the removal of dirt from the
body but the pledge of a good conscience towards God. It saves you by
the resurrection of Jesus Christ, [22]who
has gone into heaven and is at God's
right hand—with angels, authorities
and powers in submission to him.

[e]22 Isaiah 53:9
[a]12 Psalm 34:12-16   [b]14 Or not fear their threats   [c]14 Isaiah 8:12
[d]18,19 Or the spirit [19]through which

Living for God

4 Therefore, since Christ suffered in his body, arm yourselves also with the same attitude, because he who has suffered in his body is done with sin. [2]As a result, he does not live the rest of his earthly life for evil human desires, but rather for the will of God. [3]For you have spent enough time in the past doing what pagans choose to do—living in debauchery, lust, drunkenness, orgies, carousing and detestable idolatry. [4]They think it strange that you do not plunge with them into the same flood of dissipation, and they heap abuse on you. [5]But they will have to give account to him who is ready to judge the living and the dead. [6]For this is the reason the gospel was preached even to those who are now dead, so that they might be judged according to men in regard to the body, but live according to God in regard to the spirit.

[7]The end of all things is near. Therefore be clear minded and self-controlled so that you can pray. [8]Above all, love each other deeply, because love covers over a multitude of sins. [9]Offer hospitality to one another without grumbling. [10]Each one should use whatever gift he has received to serve others, faithfully administering God's grace in its various forms. [11]If anyone speaks, he should do it as one speaking the very words of God. If anyone serves, he should do it with the strength God provides, so that in all things God may be praised through Jesus Christ. To him be the glory and the power for ever and ever. Amen.

Suffering for Being a Christian

[12]Dear friends, do not be surprised at the painful trial you are suffering, as though something strange were happening to you. [13]But rejoice that you participate in the sufferings of Christ, so that you may be overjoyed when his glory is revealed. [14]If you are insulted because of the name of Christ, you are blessed, for the Spirit of glory and of God rests on you. [15]If you suffer, it should not be as a murderer or thief or any other kind of criminal, or even as a meddler. [16]However, if you suffer as a Christian, do not be ashamed, but praise God that you bear that name. [17]For it is time for judgment to begin with the family of God; and if it begins with us, what will the outcome be for those who do not obey the gospel of God? [18]And,

> "If it is hard for the righteous to be saved,
> what will become of the ungodly and the sinner?"[a]

[19]So then, those who suffer according to God's will should commit themselves to their faithful Creator and continue to do good.

To Elders and Young Men

5 To the elders among you, I appeal as a fellow-elder, a witness of Christ's sufferings and one who also will share in the glory to be revealed: [2]Be shepherds of God's flock that is under your care, serving as overseers—not because you must, but because you are willing, as God wants you to be; not greedy for money, but eager to serve; [3]not lording it over those entrusted to you, but being examples to the flock. [4]And when the Chief Shepherd appears, you will receive the crown of glory that will never fade away.

[5]Young men, in the same way be submissive to those who are older. Clothe yourselves with humility towards one another, because,

> "God opposes the proud
> but gives grace to the humble."[a]

[6]Humble yourselves, therefore, under God's mighty hand, that he may lift you up in due time. [7]Cast all your anxiety on him because he cares for you.

[8]Be self-controlled and alert. Your enemy the devil prowls around like a

---

[a]18 Prov. 11:31   [a]5 Prov. 3:34

259

roaring lion looking for someone to devour. ⁹Resist him, standing firm in the faith, because you know that your brothers throughout the world are undergoing the same kind of sufferings.

¹⁰And the God of all grace, who called you to his eternal glory in Christ, after you have suffered a little while, will himself restore you and make you strong, firm and steadfast. ¹¹To him be the power for ever and ever. Amen.

Final Greetings

¹²With the help of Silas,ᵇ whom I regard as a faithful brother, I have written to you briefly, encouraging you and testifying that this is the true grace of God. Stand fast in it.

¹³She who is in Babylon, chosen together with you, sends you her greetings, and so does my son Mark. ¹⁴Greet one another with a kiss of love.

Peace to all of you who are in Christ.

ᵇ12 Greek *Silvanus*, a variant of *Silas*

2 Peter

1 Simon Peter, a servant and apostle of Jesus Christ,

To those who through the righteousness of our God and Saviour Jesus Christ have received a faith as precious as ours:

2Grace and peace be yours in abundance through the knowledge of God and of Jesus our Lord.

Making One's Calling and Election Sure

3His divine power has given us everything we need for life and godliness through our knowledge of him who called us by his own glory and goodness. 4Through these he has given us his very great and precious promises, so that through them you may participate in the divine nature and escape the corruption in the world caused by evil desires.

5For this very reason, make every effort to add to your faith goodness; and to goodness, knowledge; 6and to knowledge, self-control; and to self-control, perseverance; and to perseverance, godliness; 7and to godliness, brotherly kindness; and to brotherly kindness, love. 8For if you possess these qualities in increasing measure, they will keep you from being ineffective and unproductive in your knowledge of our Lord Jesus Christ. 9But if anyone does not have them, he is near-sighted and blind, and has forgotten that he has been cleansed from his past sins.

10Therefore, my brothers, be all the more eager to make your calling and election sure. For if you do these things, you will never fall, 11and you will receive a rich welcome into the eternal kingdom of our Lord and Saviour Jesus Christ.

a17 Matt. 17:5; Mark 9:7; Luke 9:35

Prophecy of Scripture

12So I will always remind you of these things, even though you know them and are firmly established in the truth you now have. 13I think it is right to refresh your memory as long as I live in the tent of this body, 14because I know that I will soon put it aside, as our Lord Jesus Christ has made clear to me. 15And I will make every effort to see that after my departure you will always be able to remember these things.

16We did not follow cleverly invented stories when we told you about the power and coming of our Lord Jesus Christ, but we were eye-witnesses of his majesty. 17For he received honour and glory from God the Father when the voice came to him from the Majestic Glory, saying, "This is my Son, whom I love; with him I am well pleased."a 18We ourselves heard this voice that came from heaven when we were with him on the sacred mountain.

19And we have the word of the prophets made more certain, and you will do well to pay attention to it, as to a light shining in a dark place, until the day dawns and the morning star rises in your hearts. 20Above all, you must understand that no prophecy of Scripture came about by the prophet's own interpretation. 21For prophecy never had its origin in the will of man, but men spoke from God as they were carried along by the Holy Spirit.

False Teachers and Their Destruction

2 But there were also false prophets among the people, just as there will be false teachers among you. They will secretly introduce destructive heresies, even denying the sovereign Lord who bought them—bringing swift destruction on themselves. 2Many will follow their shameful ways and will bring the way of truth into disrepute. 3In their greed these teachers will exploit you with stories they have made up. Their condemnation has long been hanging over them, and their destruction has not been sleeping.

4For if God did not spare angels when they sinned, but sent them to hell,a putting them into gloomy dungeonsb to be held for judgment; 5if he did not spare the ancient world when he brought the flood on its ungodly people, but protected Noah, a preacher of righteousness, and seven others; 6if he condemned the cities of Sodom and Gomorrah by burning them to ashes, and made them an example of what is going to happen to the ungodly; 7and if he rescued Lot, a righteous man, who was distressed by the filthy lives of lawless men 8(for that righteous man, living among them day after day, was tormented in his righteous soul by the lawless deeds he saw and heard)—9if this is so, then the Lord knows how to rescue godly men from trials and to hold the unrighteous for the day of judgment, while continuing their punishment.c 10This is especially true of those who follow the corrupt desire of the sinful natured and despise authority.

Bold and arrogant, these men are not afraid to slander celestial beings; 11yet even angels, although they are stronger and more powerful, do not bring slanderous accusations against such beings in the presence of the Lord. 12But these men blaspheme in matters they do not understand. They are like brute beasts, creatures of instinct, born only to be caught and destroyed, and like beasts they too will perish.

13They will be paid back with harm for the harm they have done. Their idea of pleasure is to carouse in broad daylight. They are blots and blemishes, revelling in their pleasures while they feast with you.e 14With eyes full of adultery, they never stop sinning; they seduce the unstable; they are experts in greed—an accursed brood! 15They have left the straight way and wandered off to follow the way of Balaam son of Beor, who loved the wages of wickedness. 16But he was rebuked for his wrongdoing by a donkey—a beast without speech—who spoke with a man's voice and restrained the prophet's madness.

17These men are springs without water and mists driven by a storm. Blackest darkness is reserved for them. 18For they mouth empty, boastful words and, by appealing to the lustful desires of sinful human nature, they entice people who are just escaping from those who live in error. 19They promise them freedom, while they themselves are slaves of depravity—for a man is a slave to whatever has mastered him. 20If they have escaped the corruption of the world by knowing our Lord and Saviour Jesus Christ and are again entangled in it and overcome, they are worse off at the end than they were at the beginning. 21It would have been better for them not to have known the way of righteousness, than to have known it and then to turn their backs on the sacred commandment that was passed on to them. 22Of them the proverbs are true: "A dog returns to its vomit,"f and, "A sow that is washed goes back to her wallowing in the mud."

The Day of the Lord

3 Dear friends, this is now my second letter to you. I have written both of them as reminders to stimulate you to wholesome thinking. 2I want you to recall the words spoken in the past by the holy prophets and the command given by

---

a4 Greek Tartarus   b4 Some manuscripts into chains of darkness
c9 Or unrighteous for punishment until the day of judgment   d10 Or the flesh
e13 Some manuscripts in their love feasts   f22 Prov. 26:11

our Lord and Saviour through your apostles.

³First of all, you must understand that in the last days scoffers will come, scoffing and following their own evil desires. ⁴They will say, "Where is this 'coming' he promised? Ever since our fathers died, everything goes on as it has since the beginning of creation." ⁵But they deliberately forget that long ago by God's word the heavens existed and the earth was formed out of water and with water. ⁶By water also the world of that time was deluged and destroyed. ⁷By the same word the present heavens and earth are reserved for fire, being kept for the day of judgment and destruction of ungodly men.

⁸But do not forget this one thing, dear friends: With the Lord a day is like a thousand years, and a thousand years are like a day. ⁹The Lord is not slow in keeping his promise, as some understand slowness. He is patient with you, not wanting anyone to perish, but everyone to come to repentance.

¹⁰But the day of the Lord will come like a thief. The heavens will disappear with a roar; the elements will be destroyed by fire, and the earth and everything in it will be laid bare.ᵃ

¹¹Since everything will be destroyed in this way, what kind of people ought you to be? You ought to live holy and godly lives ¹²as you look forward to the day of God and speed its coming.ᵇ That day will bring about the destruction of the heavens by fire, and the elements will melt in the heat. ¹³But in keeping with his promise we are looking forward to a new heaven and a new earth, the home of righteousness.

¹⁴So then, dear friends, since you are looking forward to this, make every effort to be found spotless, blameless and at peace with him. ¹⁵Bear in mind that our Lord's patience means salvation, just as our dear brother Paul also wrote to you with the wisdom that God gave him. ¹⁶He writes the same way in all his letters, speaking in them of these matters. His letters contain some things that are hard to understand, which ignorant and unstable people distort, as they do the other Scriptures, to their own destruction.

¹⁷Therefore, dear friends, since you already know this, be on your guard so that you may not be carried away by the error of lawless men and fall from your secure position. ¹⁸But grow in the grace and knowledge of our Lord and Saviour Jesus Christ. To him be glory both now and for ever! Amen.

ᵃ10 Some manuscripts *be burned up*
ᵇ12 Or *as you wait eagerly for the day of God to come*

1 John

The Word of Life

1 That which was from the beginning, which we have heard, which we have seen with our eyes, which we have looked at and our hands have touched—this we proclaim concerning the Word of life. ²The life appeared; we have seen it and testify to it, and we proclaim to you the eternal life, which was with the Father and has appeared to us. ³We proclaim to you what we have seen and heard, so that you also may have fellowship with us. And our fellowship is with the Father and with his Son, Jesus Christ. ⁴We write this to make our*ᵃ* joy complete.

Walking in the Light

⁵This is the message we have heard from him and declare to you: God is light; in him there is no darkness at all. ⁶If we claim to have fellowship with him yet walk in the darkness, we lie and do not live by the truth. ⁷But if we walk in the light, as he is in the light, we have fellowship with one another, and the blood of Jesus, his Son, purifies us from all*ᵇ* sin.

⁸If we claim to be without sin, we deceive ourselves and the truth is not in us. ⁹If we confess our sins, he is faithful and just and will forgive us our sins and purify us from all unrighteousness. ¹⁰If we claim we have not sinned, we make him out to be a liar and his word has no place in our lives.

2 My dear children, I write this to you so that you will not sin. But if anybody does sin, we have one who speaks to the Father in our defence—Jesus Christ, the Righteous One. ²He is the atoning sacrifice for our sins, and not only for ours but also for*ᵃ* the sins of the whole world.

³We know that we have come to know him if we obey his commands. ⁴The man who says, "I know him," but does not do what he commands is a liar, and the truth is not in him. ⁵But if anyone obeys his word, God's love is truly made complete in him. This is how we know we are in him: ⁶Whoever claims to live in him must walk as Jesus did.

⁷Dear friends, I am not writing you a new command but an old one, which you have had since the beginning. This old command is the message you have heard. ⁸Yet I am writing you a new command; its truth is seen in him and you, because the darkness is passing and the true light is already shining.

⁹Anyone who claims to be in the light but hates his brother is still in the darkness. ¹⁰Whoever loves his brother lives in the light, and there is nothing in him*ᵇ* to make him stumble. ¹¹But whoever hates his brother is in the darkness and walks around in the darkness; he does not know where he is going, because the darkness has blinded him.

¹²I write to you, dear children,
   because your sins have been
      forgiven on account of his
      name.
¹³I write to you, fathers,
   because you have known him
      who is from the beginning.
I write to you, young men,
   because you have overcome the
      evil one.
I write to you, dear children,

ᵃ4 Some manuscripts *your*   *ᵇ7* Or *every*
ᵃ2 Or *He is the one who turns aside God's wrath, taking away our sins, and not only ours but also*   *ᵇ10* Or *it*

because you have known the
Father.
14I write to you, fathers,
because you have known him
who is from the beginning.
I write to you, young men,
because you are strong,
and the word of God lives in
you,
and you have overcome the evil
one.

Do Not Love the World

15Do not love the world or anything in the world. If anyone loves the world, the love of the Father is not in him. 16For everything in the world—the cravings of sinful man, the lust of his eyes and the boasting of what he has and does—comes not from the Father but from the world. 17The world and its desires pass away, but the man who does the will of God lives for ever.

Warning Against Antichrists

18Dear children, this is the last hour; and as you have heard that the antichrist is coming, even now many antichrists have come. This is how we know it is the last hour. 19They went out from us, but they did not really belong to us. For if they had belonged to us, they would have remained with us; but their going showed that none of them belonged to us.

20But you have an anointing from the Holy One, and all of you know the truth.c 21I do not write to you because you do not know the truth, but because you do know it and because no lie comes from the truth. 22Who is the liar? It is the man who denies that Jesus is the Christ. Such a man is the antichrist—he denies the Father and the Son. 23No-one who denies the Son has the Father; whoever acknowledges the Son has the Father also.

24See that what you have heard from the beginning remains in you. If it does, you also will remain in the Son and in the Father. 25And this is what he promised us—even eternal life.

26I am writing these things to you about those who are trying to lead you astray. 27As for you, the anointing you received from him remains in you, and you do not need anyone to teach you. But as his anointing teaches you about all things and as that anointing is real, not counterfeit—just as it has taught you, remain in him.

Children of God

28And now, dear children, continue in him, so that when he appears we may be confident and unashamed before him at his coming.

29If you know that he is righteous, you know that everyone who does what is right has been born of him.

3 How great is the love the Father has lavished on us, that we should be called children of God! And that is what we are! The reason the world does not know us is that it did not know him. 2Dear friends, now we are children of God, and what we will be has not yet been made known. But we know that when he appears,a we shall be like him, for we shall see him as he is. 3Everyone who has this hope in him purifies himself, just as he is pure.

4Everyone who sins breaks the law; in fact, sin is lawlessness. 5But you know that he appeared so that he might take away our sins. And in him is no sin. 6No-one who lives in him keeps on sinning. No-one who continues to sin has either seen him or known him.

7Dear children, do not let anyone lead you astray. He who does what is right is righteous, just as he is righteous. 8He who does what is sinful is of the devil, because the devil has been sinning from the beginning. The reason the Son of God appeared was to destroy the devil's work. 9No-one who is born of God will continue to sin, because God's seed remains in him; he cannot go on sinning, because he has been born of God. 10This is how we know who the children of God are and who the children of the devil are: Anyone who does not do

---

c20 Some manuscripts and you know all things

a2 Or when it is made known

what is right is not a child of God; neither is anyone who does not love his brother.

Love One Another

[11]This is the message you heard from the beginning: We should love one another. [12]Do not be like Cain, who belonged to the evil one and murdered his brother. And why did he murder him? Because his own actions were evil and his brother's were righteous. [13]Do not be surprised, my brothers, if the world hates you. [14]We know that we have passed from death to life, because we love our brothers. Anyone who does not love remains in death. [15]Anyone who hates his brother is a murderer, and you know that no murderer has eternal life in him.

[16]This is how we know what love is: Jesus Christ laid down his life for us. And we ought to lay down our lives for our brothers. [17]If anyone has material possessions and sees his brother in need but has no pity on him, how can the love of God be in him? [18]Dear children, let us not love with words or tongue but with actions and in truth. [19]This then is how we know that we belong to the truth, and how we set our hearts at rest in his presence [20]whenever our hearts condemn us. For God is greater than our hearts, and he knows everything.

[21]Dear friends, if our hearts do not condemn us, we have confidence before God [22]and receive from him anything we ask, because we obey his commands and do what pleases him. [23]And this is his command: to believe in the name of his Son, Jesus Christ, and to love one another as he commanded us. [24]Those who obey his commands live in him, and he in them. And this is how we know that he lives in us: We know it by the Spirit he gave us.

Test the Spirits

4 Dear friends, do not believe every spirit, but test the spirits to see whether they are from God, because many false prophets have gone out into the world. [2]This is how you can recognise the Spirit of God: Every spirit that acknowledges that Jesus Christ has come in the flesh is from God, [3]but every spirit that does not acknowledge Jesus is not from God. This is the spirit of the antichrist, which you have heard is coming and even now is already in the world.

[4]You, dear children, are from God and have overcome them, because the one who is in you is greater than the one who is in the world. [5]They are from the world and therefore speak from the viewpoint of the world, and the world listens to them. [6]We are from God, and whoever knows God listens to us; but whoever is not from God does not listen to us. This is how we recognise the Spirit[a] of truth and the spirit of falsehood.

God's Love and Ours

[7]Dear friends, let us love one another, for love comes from God. Everyone who loves has been born of God and knows God. [8]Whoever does not love does not know God, because God is love. [9]This is how God showed his love among us: He sent his one and only Son[b] into the world that we might live through him. [10]This is love: not that we loved God, but that he loved us and sent his Son as an atoning sacrifice for[c] our sins. [11]Dear friends, since God so loved us, we also ought to love one another. [12]No-one has ever seen God; but if we love each other, God lives in us and his love is made complete in us.

[13]We know that we live in him and he in us, because he has given us of his Spirit. [14]And we have seen and testify that the Father has sent his Son to be the Saviour of the world. [15]If anyone acknowledges that Jesus is the Son of God, God lives in him and he in God. [16]And so we know and rely on the love God has for us.

God is love. Whoever lives in love lives in God, and God in him. [17]Love

*6 Or spirit
b Or his only begotten Son   *c10 Or as the one who would turn aside his wrath, taking away*

is made complete among us so that we will have confidence on the day of judgment, because in this world we are like him. 18There is no fear in love. But perfect love drives out fear, because fear has to do with punishment. The man who fears is not made perfect in love.

19We love because he first loved us. 20If anyone says, "I love God," yet hates his brother, he is a liar. For anyone who does not love his brother, whom he has seen, cannot love God, whom he has not seen. 21And he has given us this command: Whoever loves God must also love his brother.

Faith in the Son of God

5 Everyone who believes that Jesus is the Christ is born of God, and everyone who loves the father loves his child as well. 2This is how we know that we love the children of God: by loving God and carrying out his commands. 3This is love for God: to obey his commands. And his commands are not burdensome, 4for everyone born of God overcomes the world. This is the victory that has overcome the world, even our faith. 5Who is it that overcomes the world? Only he who believes that Jesus is the Son of God.

6This is the one who came by water and blood—Jesus Christ. He did not come by water only, but by water and blood. And it is the Spirit who testifies, because the Spirit is the truth. 7For there are three that testify: 8thea Spirit, the water and the blood; and the three are in agreement. 9We accept man's testimony, but God's testimony is greater because it is the testimony of God, which he has given about his Son. 10Anyone who believes

in the Son of God has this testimony in his heart. Anyone who does not believe God has made him out to be a liar, because he has not believed the testimony God has given about his Son. 11And this is the testimony: God has given us eternal life, and this life is in his Son. 12He who has the Son has life; he who does not have the Son of God does not have life.

Concluding Remarks

13I write these things to you who believe in the name of the Son of God so that you may know that you have eternal life. 14This is the assurance we have in approaching God: that if we ask anything according to his will, he hears us. 15And if we know that he hears us—whatever we ask—we know that we have what we asked of him.

16If anyone sees his brother commit a sin that does not lead to death, he should pray and God will give him life. I refer to those whose sin does not lead to death. There is a sin that leads to death. I am not saying that he should pray about that. 17All wrong-doing is sin, and there is sin that does not lead to death.

18We know that anyone born of God does not continue to sin; the one who was born of God keeps him safe, and the evil one does not touch him. 19We know that we are children of God, and that the whole world is under the control of the evil one. 20We know also that the Son of God has come and has given us understanding, so that we may know him who is true. And we are in him who is true—even in his Son Jesus Christ. He is the true God and eternal life.

21Dear children, keep yourselves from idols.

---

a7,8 Late manuscripts of the Vulgate testify in heaven: the Father, the Word and the Holy Spirit, and these three are one. 8And there are three that testify on earth: the

2 John

¹The elder,

To the chosen lady and her children, whom I love in the truth—and not I only, but also all who know the truth—²because of the truth, which lives in us and will be with us for ever:

³Grace, mercy and peace from God the Father and from Jesus Christ, the Father's Son, will be with us in truth and love.

⁴It has given me great joy to find some of your children walking in the truth, just as the Father commanded us. ⁵And now, dear lady, I am not writing you a new command but one we have had from the beginning. I ask that we love one another. ⁶And this is love: that we walk in obedience to his commands. As you have heard from the beginning, his command is that you walk in love.

⁷Many deceivers, who do not acknowledge Jesus Christ as coming in the flesh, have gone out into the world. Any such person is the deceiver and the antichrist. ⁸Watch out that you do not lose what you have worked for, but that you may be rewarded fully. ⁹Anyone who runs ahead and does not continue in the teaching of Christ does not have God; whoever continues in the teaching has both the Father and the Son. ¹⁰If anyone comes to you and does not bring this teaching, do not take him into your house or welcome him. ¹¹Anyone who welcomes him shares in his wicked work.

¹²I have much to write to you, but I do not want to use paper and ink. Instead, I hope to visit you and talk with you face to face, so that our joy may be complete.

¹³The children of your chosen sister send their greetings.

3 John

¹The elder,

To my dear friend Gaius, whom I love in the truth.

²Dear friend, I pray that you may enjoy good health and that all may go well with you, even as your soul is getting along well. ³It gave me great joy to have some brothers come and tell about your faithfulness to the truth and how you continue to walk in the truth. ⁴I have no greater joy than to hear that my children are walking in the truth.

⁵Dear friend, you are faithful in what you are doing for the brothers, even though they are strangers to you. ⁶They have told the church about your love. You will do well to send them on their way in a manner worthy of God. ⁷It was for the sake of the Name that they went out, receiving no help from the pagans. ⁸We ought therefore to show hospitality to such men so that we may work together for the truth.

⁹I wrote to the church, but Diotrephes, who loves to be first, will have nothing to do with us. ¹⁰So if I come, I will call attention to what he is doing, gossiping maliciously about us. Not satisfied with that, he refuses to welcome the brothers. He also stops those who want to do so and puts them out of the church.

¹¹Dear friend, do not imitate what is evil but what is good. Anyone who does what is good is from God. Anyone who does what is evil has not seen God. ¹²Demetrius is well spoken of by everyone—and even by the truth itself. We also speak well of him, and you know that our testimony is true.

¹³I have much to write to you, but I do not want to do so with pen and ink. ¹⁴I hope to see you soon, and we will talk face to face.

Peace to you. The friends here send their greetings. Greet the friends there by name.

Jude

¹Jude, a servant of Jesus Christ and a brother of James,

To those who have been called, who are loved by God the Father and kept by[a] Jesus Christ:

²Mercy, peace and love be yours in abundance.

The Sin and Doom of Godless Men

³Dear friends, although I was very eager to write to you about the salvation we share, I felt I had to write and urge you to contend for the faith that was once for all entrusted to the saints. ⁴For certain men whose condemnation was written about[b] long ago have secretly slipped in among you. They are godless men, who change the grace of our God into a licence for immorality and deny Jesus Christ our only Sovereign and Lord.

⁵Though you already know all this, I want to remind you that the Lord[c] delivered his people out of Egypt, but later destroyed those who did not believe. ⁶And the angels who did not keep their positions of authority but abandoned their own home—these he has kept in darkness, bound with everlasting chains for judgment on the great Day. ⁷In a similar way, Sodom and Gomorrah and the surrounding towns gave themselves up to sexual immorality and perversion. They serve as an example of those who suffer the punishment of eternal fire.

⁸In the very same way, these dreamers pollute their own bodies, reject authority and slander celestial beings. ⁹But even the archangel Michael, when he was disputing with the devil about the body of Moses, did not dare to bring a slanderous accusation against him, but said, "The Lord rebuke you!" ¹⁰Yet these men speak abusively against whatever they do not understand; and what things they do understand by instinct, like unreasoning animals—these are the very things that destroy them.

¹¹Woe to them! They have taken the way of Cain; they have rushed for profit into Balaam's error; they have been destroyed in Korah's rebellion. ¹²These men are blemishes at your love feasts, eating with you without the slightest qualm—shepherds who feed only themselves. They are clouds without rain, blown along by the wind; autumn trees, without fruit and uprooted—twice dead. ¹³They are wild waves of the sea, foaming up their shame; wandering stars, for whom blackest darkness has been reserved for ever.

¹⁴Enoch, the seventh from Adam, prophesied about these men: "See, the Lord is coming with thousands upon thousands of his holy ones ¹⁵to judge everyone, and to convict all the ungodly of all the ungodly acts they have done in the ungodly way, and of all the harsh words ungodly sinners have spoken against him." ¹⁶These men are grumblers and faultfinders; they follow their own evil desires; they boast about themselves and flatter others for their own advantage.

A Call to Persevere

¹⁷But, dear friends, remember what the apostles of our Lord Jesus Christ foretold. ¹⁸They said to you, "In the last times there will be scoffers who will follow their own ungodly

---

*a*1 Or for; or in   *b*4 Or men who were marked out for condemnation
*c*5 Some early manuscripts Jesus

desires." [19]These are the men who divide you, who follow mere natural instincts and do not have the Spirit.

[20]But you, dear friends, build yourselves up in your most holy faith and pray in the Holy Spirit. [21]Keep yourselves in God's love as you wait for the mercy of our Lord Jesus Christ to bring you to eternal life. [22]Be merciful to those who doubt; [23]snatch others from the fire and save them; to others show mercy, mixed with fear—hating even the clothing stained by corrupted flesh.

Doxology

[24]To him who is able to keep you from falling and to present you before his glorious presence without fault and with great joy—[25]to the only God our Saviour be glory, majesty, power and authority, through Jesus Christ our Lord, before all ages, now and for evermore! Amen.

Revelation

1 The revelation of Jesus Christ, which God gave him to show his servants what must soon take place. He made it known by sending his angel to his servant John, 2who testifies to everything he saw—that is, the word of God and the testimony of Jesus Christ. 3Blessed is the one who reads the words of this prophecy, and blessed are those who hear it and take to heart what is written in it, because the time is near.

Greetings and Doxology

4John,

To the seven churches in the province of Asia:

Grace and peace to you from him who is, and who was, and who is to come, and from the seven spirits[a] before his throne, 5and from Jesus Christ, who is the faithful witness, the firstborn from the dead, and the ruler of the kings of the earth.

To him who loves us and has freed us from our sins by his blood, 6and has made us to be a kingdom and priests to serve his God and Father—to him be glory and power for ever and ever! Amen.

7Look, he is coming with the clouds,
   and every eye will see him,
   even those who pierced him;
and all the peoples of the earth
   will mourn because of him.
      So shall it be! Amen.

8"I am the Alpha and the Omega," says the Lord God, "who is, and who was, and who is to come, the Almighty."

One Like a Son of Man

9I, John, your brother and companion in the suffering and kingdom and patient endurance that are ours in Jesus, was on the island of Patmos because of the word of God and the testimony of Jesus. 10On the Lord's Day I was in the Spirit, and I heard behind me a loud voice like a trumpet, 11which said: "Write on a scroll what you see and send it to the seven churches: to Ephesus, Smyrna, Pergamum, Thyatira, Sardis, Philadelphia and Laodicea."

12I turned round to see the voice that was speaking to me. And when I turned I saw seven golden lampstands, 13and among the lampstands was someone "like a son of man",[b] dressed in a robe reaching down to his feet and with a golden sash round his chest. 14His head and hair were white like wool, as white as snow, and his eyes were like blazing fire. 15His feet were like bronze glowing in a furnace, and his voice was like the sound of rushing waters. 16In his right hand he held seven stars, and out of his mouth came a sharp double-edged sword. His face was like the sun shining in all its brilliance.

17When I saw him, I fell at his feet as though dead. Then he placed his right hand on me and said: "Do not be afraid. I am the First and the Last. 18I am the Living One; I was dead, and behold I am alive for ever and ever! And I hold the keys of death and Hades. 19Write, therefore, what you have seen, what is now and what will take place later. 20The mystery of the

---

*a*4 Or *the sevenfold Spirit*   *b*13 Daniel 7:13

272

seven stars that you saw in my right hand and of the seven golden lampstands is this: The seven stars are the angels[c] of the seven churches, and the seven lampstands are the seven churches.

To the Church in Ephesus

2 "To the angel[a] of the church in Ephesus write:

These are the words of him who holds the seven stars in his right hand and walks among the seven golden lampstands: 2I know your deeds, your hard work and your perseverance. I know that you cannot tolerate wicked men, that you have tested those who claim to be apostles but are not, and have found them false. 3You have persevered and have endured hardships for my name, and have not grown weary.

4Yet I hold this against you: You have forsaken your first love. 5Remember the height from which you have fallen! Repent and do the things you did at first. If you do not repent, I will come to you and remove your lampstand from its place. 6But you have this in your favour: You hate the practices of the Nicolaitans, which I also hate.

7He who has an ear, let him hear what the Spirit says to the churches. To him who overcomes, I will give the right to eat from the tree of life, which is in the paradise of God.

To the Church in Smyrna

8"To the angel of the church in Smyrna write:

These are the words of him who is the First and the Last, who died and came to life again. 9I know your afflictions and your poverty—yet you are rich! I know the slander of those who say they are Jews and are not, but are a synagogue of Satan. 10Do not be afraid of what you are about to suffer. I tell you, the devil will put some of you in prison to test you, and you will suffer persecution for ten days. Be faithful, even to the point of death, and I will give you the crown of life.

11He who has an ear, let him hear what the Spirit says to the churches. He who overcomes will not be hurt at all by the second death.

To the Church in Pergamum

12"To the angel of the church in Pergamum write:

These are the words of him who has the sharp, double-edged sword. 13I know where you live—where Satan has his throne. Yet you remain true to my name. You did not renounce your faith in me, even in the days of Antipas, my faithful witness, who was put to death in your city—where Satan lives.

14Nevertheless, I have a few things against you: You have people there who hold to the teaching of Balaam, who taught Balak to entice the Israelites to sin by eating food sacrificed to idols and by committing sexual immorality. 15Likewise you also have those who hold to the teaching of the Nicolaitans. 16Repent therefore! Otherwise, I will soon come to you and will fight against them with the sword of my mouth.

17He who has an ear, let him hear what the Spirit says to the churches. To him who overcomes, I will give some of the hidden manna. I will also give him a white stone with a new name written on it, known only to him who receives it.

To the Church in Thyatira

18"To the angel of the church in Thyatira write:

These are the words of the Son of God, whose eyes are like blazing fire and whose feet are like burnished bronze. 19I know your

c20 Or messengers   a1 Or messenger; also in verses 8, 12 and 18

deeds, your love and faith, your service and perseverance, and that you are now doing more than you did at first.

20Nevertheless, I have this against you: You tolerate that woman Jezebel, who calls herself a prophetess. By her teaching she misleads my servants into sexual immorality and the eating of food sacrificed to idols. 21I have given her time to repent of her immorality, but she is unwilling. 22So I will cast her on a bed of suffering, and I will make those who commit adultery with her suffer intensely, unless they repent of her ways. 23I will strike her children dead. Then all the churches will know that I am he who searches hearts and minds, and I will repay each of you according to your deeds. 24Now I say to the rest of you in Thyatira, to you who do not hold to her teaching and have not learned Satan's so-called deep secrets (I will not impose any other burden on you): 25Only hold on to what you have until I come.

26To him who overcomes and does my will to the end, I will give authority over the nations—

27He will rule them with an iron sceptre;
    he will dash them to pieces like pottery[b]—

just as I have received authority from my Father. 28I will also give him the morning star. 29He who has an ear, let him hear what the Spirit says to the churches.

To the Church in Sardis

3 "To the angel[a] of the church in Sardis write:

These are the words of him who holds the seven spirits[b] of God and the seven stars. I know your deeds; you have a reputation of being alive, but you are dead. 2Wake up! Strengthen what remains and is about to die, for I have not found your deeds complete in the sight of my God. 3Remember, therefore, what you have received and heard; obey it, and repent. But if you do not wake up, I will come like a thief, and you will not know at what time I will come to you.

4Yet you have a few people in Sardis who have not soiled their clothes. They will walk with me, dressed in white, for they are worthy. 5He who overcomes will, like them, be dressed in white. I will never erase his name from the book of life, but will acknowledge his name before my Father and his angels. 6He who has an ear, let him hear what the Spirit says to the churches.

To the Church in Philadelphia

7"To the angel of the church in Philadelphia write:

These are the words of him who is holy and true, who holds the key of David. What he opens, no-one can shut; and what he shuts, no-one can open. 8I know your deeds. See, I have placed before you an open door that no-one can shut. I know that you have little strength, yet you have kept my word and have not denied my name. 9I will make those who are of the synagogue of Satan, who claim to be Jews though they are not, but are liars—I will make them come and fall down at your feet and acknowledge that I have loved you. 10Since you have kept my command to endure patiently, I will also keep you from the hour of trial that is going to come upon the whole world to test those who live on the earth.

11I am coming soon. Hold on to what you have, so that no-one will take your crown. 12Him who overcomes I will make a pillar in the temple of my God. Never again will he leave it. I will write on him the name of my God and the name of the city of my God,

---

b27 Psalm 2:9   a1 Or messenger; also in verses 7 and 14   b1 Or the sevenfold Spirit

the new Jerusalem, which is coming down out of heaven from my God; and I will also write on him my new name. 13He who has an ear, let him hear what the Spirit says to the churches.

To the Church in Laodicea

14"To the angel of the church in Laodicea write:

These are the words of the Amen, the faithful and true witness, the ruler of God's creation. 15I know your deeds, that you are neither cold nor hot. I wish you were either one or the other! 16So, because you are lukewarm—neither hot nor cold—I am about to spit you out of my mouth. 17You say, 'I am rich; I have acquired wealth and do not need a thing.' But you do not realise that you are wretched, pitiful, poor, blind and naked. 18I counsel you to buy from me gold refined in the fire, so that you can become rich; and white clothes to wear, so that you can cover your shameful nakedness; and salve to put on your eyes, so that you can see.

19Those whom I love I rebuke and discipline. So be earnest, and repent. 20Here I am! I stand at the door and knock. If anyone hears my voice and opens the door, I will come in and eat with him, and he with me.

21To him who overcomes, I will give the right to sit with me on my throne, just as I overcame and sat down with my Father on his throne. 22He who has an ear, let him hear what the Spirit says to the churches.

The Throne in Heaven

4 After this I looked, and there before me was a door standing open in heaven. And the voice I had first heard speaking to me like a trumpet said, "Come up here, and I will show you what must take place after this." 2At once I was in the Spirit, and there before me was a

throne in heaven with someone sitting on it. 3And the one who sat there had the appearance of jasper and carnelian. A rainbow, resembling an emerald, encircled the throne. 4Surrounding the throne were twenty-four other thrones, and seated on them were twenty-four elders. They were dressed in white and had crowns of gold on their heads. 5From the throne came flashes of lightning, rumblings and peals of thunder. Before the throne, seven lamps were blazing. These are the seven spirits[o] of God. 6Also before the throne there was what looked like a sea of glass, clear as crystal.

In the centre, around the throne, were four living creatures, and they were covered with eyes, in front and behind. 7The first living creature was like a lion, the second was like an ox, the third had a face like a man, the fourth was like a flying eagle. 8Each of the four living creatures had six wings and was covered with eyes all around, even under his wings. Day and night they never stop saying:

"Holy, holy, holy
is the Lord God Almighty,
who was, and is, and is to come."

9Whenever the living creatures give glory, honour and thanks to him who sits on the throne and who lives for ever and ever, 10the twenty-four elders fall down before him who sits on the throne, and worship him who lives for ever and ever. They lay their crowns before the throne and say:

11"You are worthy, our Lord and God,
to receive glory and honour and power,
for you created all things,
and by your will they were created
and have their being."

The Scroll and the Lamb

5 Then I saw in the right hand of him who sat on the throne a scroll with writing on both sides and sealed with seven seals. 2And I saw a

05 Or the sevenfold Spirit

mighty angel proclaiming in a loud voice, "Who is worthy to break the seals and open the scroll?" ³But no-one in heaven or on earth or under the earth could open the scroll or even look inside it. ⁴I wept and wept because no-one was found who was worthy to open the scroll or look inside. ⁵Then one of the elders said to me, "Do not weep! See, the Lion of the tribe of Judah, the Root of David, has triumphed. He is able to open the scroll and its seven seals."

⁶Then I saw a Lamb, looking as if it had been slain, standing in the centre of the throne, encircled by the four living creatures and the elders. He had seven horns and seven eyes, which are the seven spirits*a* of God sent out into all the earth. ⁷He came and took the scroll from the right hand of him who sat on the throne. ⁸And when he had taken it, the four living creatures and the twenty-four elders fell down before the Lamb. Each one had a harp and they were holding golden bowls full of incense, which are the prayers of the saints. ⁹And they sang a new song:

"You are worthy to take the scroll
    and to open its seals,
because you were slain,
    and with your blood you
    purchased men for God
from every tribe and language
    and people and nation.
¹⁰You have made them to be a
    kingdom and priests to serve
    our God,
    and they will reign on the
    earth."

¹¹Then I looked and heard the voice of many angels, numbering thousands upon thousands, and ten thousand times ten thousand. They encircled the throne and the living creatures and the elders. ¹²In a loud voice they sang:

"Worthy is the Lamb, who was
    slain,
to receive power and wealth and
    wisdom and strength
and honour and glory and praise!"

¹³Then I heard every creature in heaven and on earth and under the earth and on the sea, and all that is in them, singing:

"To him who sits on the throne
    and to the Lamb
be praise and honour and glory
    and power,
    for ever and ever!"

¹⁴The four living creatures said, "Amen", and the elders fell down and worshipped.

The Seals

6 I watched as the Lamb opened the first of the seven seals. Then I heard one of the four living creatures say in a voice like thunder, "Come!" ²I looked, and there before me was a white horse! Its rider held a bow, and he was given a crown, and he rode out as a conqueror bent on conquest.

³When the Lamb opened the second seal, I heard the second living creature say, "Come!" ⁴Then another horse came out, a fiery red one. Its rider was given power to take peace from the earth and to make men slay each other. To him was given a large sword.

⁵When the Lamb opened the third seal, I heard the third living creature say, "Come!" I looked, and there before me was a black horse! Its rider was holding a pair of scales in his hand. ⁶Then I heard what sounded like a voice among the four living creatures, saying, "A quart*a* of wheat for a day's wages,*b* and three quarts of barley for a day's wages,*b* and do not damage the oil and the wine!"

⁷When the Lamb opened the fourth seal, I heard the voice of the fourth living creature say, "Come!" ⁸I looked, and there before me was a pale horse! Its rider was named Death, and Hades was following close behind him. They were given power over a fourth of the earth to kill by sword, famine and plague, and by the wild beasts of the earth.

---

*a*6 Or *the sevenfold Spirit*   *a*6 Greek *a choinix* (probably about a litre)
*b*6 Greek *a denarius*

⁹When he opened the fifth seal, I saw under the altar the souls of those who had been slain because of the word of God and the testimony they had maintained. ¹⁰They called out in a loud voice, "How long, Sovereign Lord, holy and true, until you judge the inhabitants of the earth and avenge our blood?" ¹¹Then each of them was given a white robe, and they were told to wait a little longer, until the number of their fellow-servants and brothers who were to be killed as they had been was completed.

¹²I watched as he opened the sixth seal. There was a great earthquake. The sun turned black like sackcloth made of goat hair, the whole moon turned blood red, ¹³and the stars in the sky fell to earth, as late figs drop from a fig-tree when shaken by a strong wind. ¹⁴The sky receded like a scroll, rolling up, and every mountain and island was removed from its place.

¹⁵Then the kings of the earth, the princes, the generals, the rich, the mighty, and every slave and every free man hid in caves and among the rocks of the mountains. ¹⁶They called to the mountains and the rocks, "Fall on us and hide us from the face of him who sits on the throne and from the wrath of the Lamb! ¹⁷For the great day of their wrath has come, and who can stand?"

144,000 Sealed

7 After this I saw four angels standing at the four corners of the earth, holding back the four winds of the earth to prevent any wind from blowing on the land or on the sea or on any tree. ²Then I saw another angel coming up from the east, having the seal of the living God. He called out in a loud voice to the four angels who had been given power to harm the land and the sea: ³"Do not harm the land or the sea or the trees until we put a seal on the foreheads of the servants of our God." ⁴Then I heard the number of those who were sealed: 144,000 from all the tribes of Israel.

⁵From the tribe of Judah 12,000 were sealed,

from the tribe of Reuben 12,000,

⁶from the tribe of Gad 12,000,

from the tribe of Asher 12,000,

from the tribe of Naphtali 12,000,

from the tribe of Manasseh 12,000,

⁷from the tribe of Simeon 12,000,

from the tribe of Levi 12,000,

from the tribe of Issachar 12,000,

⁸from the tribe of Zebulun 12,000,

from the tribe of Joseph 12,000,

from the tribe of Benjamin 12,000.

The Great Multitude in White Robes

⁹After this I looked and there before me was a great multitude that no-one could count, from every nation, tribe, people and language, standing before the throne and in front of the Lamb. They were wearing white robes and were holding palm branches in their hands. ¹⁰And they cried out in a loud voice:

"Salvation belongs to our God,
who sits on the throne,
and to the Lamb."

¹¹All the angels were standing round the throne and around the elders and the four living creatures. They fell down on their faces before the throne and worshipped God, ¹²saying:

"Amen!
Praise and glory
and wisdom and thanks and honour
and power and strength
be to our God for ever and ever.
Amen!"

¹³Then one of the elders asked me, "These in white robes—who are they, and where did they come from?"

¹⁴I answered, "Sir, you know."

And he said, "These are they who have come out of the great tribulation; they have washed their robes and made them white in the blood of the Lamb. ¹⁵Therefore,

"they are before the throne of God
and serve him day and night in his temple;
and he who sits on the throne will spread his tent over them.
¹⁶Never again will they hunger;
never again will they thirst.

The sun will not beat upon them,
nor any scorching heat.
17For the Lamb at the centre of the
throne will be their shepherd;
he will lead them to springs of
living water.
And God will wipe away every tear
from their eyes.''

The Seventh Seal and the Golden Censer

8 When he opened the seventh
seal, there was silence in heaven
for about half an hour.

2And I saw the seven angels who
stand before God, and to them were
given seven trumpets.

3Another angel, who had a golden
censer, came and stood at the altar.
He was given much incense to offer,
with the prayers of all the saints, on
the golden altar before the throne.
4The smoke of the incense, together
with the prayers of the saints, went
up before God from the angel's hand.
5Then the angel took the censer, filled
it with fire from the altar, and hurled
it on the earth; and there came peals
of thunder, rumblings, flashes of
lightning and an earthquake.

The Trumpets

6Then the seven angels who had
the seven trumpets prepared to sound
them.

7The first angel sounded his trumpet, and there came hail and fire
mixed with blood, and it was hurled
down upon the earth. A third of the
earth was burned up, a third of the
trees were burned up, and all the
green grass was burned up.

8The second angel sounded his
trumpet, and something like a huge
mountain, all ablaze, was thrown into
the sea. A third of the sea turned into
blood, 9a third of the living creatures
in the sea died, and a third of the
ships were destroyed.

10The third angel sounded his
trumpet, and a great star, blazing like
a torch, fell from the sky on a third of
the rivers and on the springs of
water—11the name of the star is
Wormwood.a A third of the waters

a11 That is, Bitterness.

turned bitter, and many people died
from the waters that had become
bitter.

12The fourth angel sounded his
trumpet, and a third of the sun was
struck, a third of the moon, and a
third of the stars, so that a third of
them turned dark. A third of the day
was without light, and also a third of
the night.

13As I watched, I heard an eagle
that was flying in mid-air call out in
a loud voice: "Woe! Woe! Woe to the
inhabitants of the earth, because of
the trumpet blasts about to be
sounded by the other three angels!''

9 The fifth angel sounded his trumpet, and I saw a star that had
fallen from the sky to the earth. The
star was given the key to the shaft of
the Abyss. 2When he opened the
Abyss, smoke rose from it like the
smoke from a gigantic furnace. The
sun and sky were darkened by the
smoke from the Abyss. 3And out of
the smoke locusts came down upon
the earth and were given power like
that of scorpions of the earth. 4They
were told not to harm the grass of the
earth or any plant or tree, but only
those people who did not have the
seal of God on their foreheads. 5They
were not given power to kill them,
but only to torture them for five
months. And the agony they suffered
was like that of the sting of a scorpion
when it strikes a man. 6During those
days men will seek death, but will
not find it; they will long to die, but
death will elude them.

7The locusts looked like horses prepared for battle. On their heads they
wore something like crowns of gold,
and their faces resembled human
faces. 8Their hair was like women's
hair, and their teeth were like lions'
teeth. 9They had breastplates like
breastplates of iron, and the sound of
their wings was like the thundering
of many horses and chariots rushing
into battle. 10They had tails and stings
like scorpions, and in their tails they
had power to torment people for five
months. 11They had as king over them
the angel of the Abyss, whose name

in Hebrew is Abaddon, and in Greek, Apollyon.ᵃ

¹²The first woe is past; two other woes are yet to come.

¹³The sixth angel blew his trumpet, and I heard a voice coming from the hornsᵇ of the golden altar that is before God. ¹⁴It said to the sixth angel who had the trumpet, "Release the four angels who are bound at the great river Euphrates." ¹⁵And the four angels who had been kept ready for this very hour and day and month and year were released to kill a third of mankind. ¹⁶The number of the mounted troops was two hundred million. I heard their number.

¹⁷The horses and riders I saw in my vision looked like this: Their breastplates were fiery red, dark blue, and yellow as sulphur. The heads of the horses resembled the heads of lions, and out of their mouths came fire, smoke and sulphur. ¹⁸A third of mankind was killed by the three plagues of fire, smoke and sulphur that came out of their mouths. ¹⁹The power of the horses was in their mouths and in their tails; for their tails were like snakes, having heads with which they inflict injury.

²⁰The rest of mankind that were not killed by these plagues still did not repent of the work of their hands; they did not stop worshipping demons, and idols of gold, silver, bronze, stone and wood—idols that cannot see or hear or walk. ²¹Nor did they repent of their murders, their magic arts, their sexual immorality or their thefts.

The Angel and the Little Scroll

10 Then I saw another mighty angel coming down from heaven. He was robed in a cloud, with a rainbow above his head; his face was like the sun, and his legs were like fiery pillars. ²He was holding a little scroll, which lay open in his hand. He planted his right foot on the sea and his left foot on the land, ³and he gave a loud shout like the roar of a lion. When he shouted, the voices of the seven thunders spoke.

⁴And when the seven thunders spoke, I was about to write; but I heard a voice from heaven say, "Seal up what the seven thunders have said and do not write it down."

⁵Then the angel I had seen standing on the sea and on the land raised his right hand to heaven. ⁶And he swore by him who lives for ever and ever, who created the heavens and all that is in them, the earth and all that is in it, and the sea and all that is in it, and said, "There will be no more delay! ⁷But in the days when the seventh angel is about to sound his trumpet, the mystery of God will be accomplished, just as he announced to his servants the prophets."

⁸Then the voice that I had heard from heaven spoke to me once more: "Go, take the scroll that lies open in the hand of the angel who is standing on the sea and on the land."

⁹So I went to the angel and asked him to give me the little scroll. He said to me, "Take it and eat it. It will turn your stomach sour, but in your mouth it will be as sweet as honey." ¹⁰I took the little scroll from the angel's hand and ate it. It tasted as sweet as honey in my mouth, but when I had eaten it, my stomach turned sour. ¹¹Then I was told, "You must prophesy again about many peoples, nations, languages and kings."

The Two Witnesses

11 I was given a reed like a measuring rod and was told, "Go and measure the temple of God and the altar, and count the worshippers there. ²But exclude the outer court; do not measure it, because it has been given to the Gentiles. They will trample on the holy city for 42 months. ³And I will give power to my two witnesses, and they will prophesy for 1,260 days, clothed in sackcloth." ⁴These are the two olive trees and the two lampstands that stand before the Lord of the earth. ⁵If anyone tries to harm them, fire comes from their mouths and devours their enemies.

ᵃ11 *Abaddon* and *Apollyon* mean *Destroyer.*   ᵇ13 That is, projections

This is how anyone who wants to harm them must die. [6]These men have power to shut up the sky so that it will not rain during the time they are prophesying; and they have power to turn the waters into blood and to strike the earth with every kind of plague as often as they want.

[7]Now when they have finished their testimony, the beast that comes up from the Abyss will attack them, and overpower and kill them. [8]Their bodies will lie in the street of the great city, which is figuratively called Sodom and Egypt, where also their Lord was crucified. [9]For three and a half days men from every people, tribe, language and nation will gaze on their bodies and refuse them burial. [10]The inhabitants of the earth will gloat over them and will celebrate by sending each other gifts, because these two prophets had tormented those who live on earth.

[11]But after the three and a half days a breath of life from God entered them, and they stood on their feet, and terror struck those who saw them. [12]Then they heard a loud voice from heaven saying to them, "Come up here." And they went up to heaven in a cloud, while their enemies looked on.

[13]At that very hour there was a severe earthquake and a tenth of the city collapsed. Seven thousand people were killed in the earthquake, and the survivors were terrified and gave glory to the God of heaven.

[14]The second woe has passed; the third woe is coming soon.

The Seventh Trumpet

[15]The seventh angel sounded his trumpet, and there were loud voices in heaven, which said:

"The kingdom of the world has
   become the kingdom of our
   Lord and of his Christ,
   and he will reign for ever and
   ever."

[16]And the twenty-four elders, who were seated on their thrones before God, fell on their faces and worshipped God, [17]saying:

"We give thanks to you, Lord God
   Almighty,
   who is and who was,
because you have taken your great
   power
   and have begun to reign.
[18]The nations were angry;
   and your wrath has come.
The time has come for judging the
   dead,
   and for rewarding your servants
   the prophets
and your saints and those who
   reverence your name,
   both small and great—
and for destroying those who
   destroy the earth."

[19]Then God's temple in heaven was opened, and within his temple was seen the ark of his covenant. And there came flashes of lightning, rumblings, peals of thunder, an earthquake and a great hailstorm.

The Woman and the Dragon

12 A great and wondrous sign appeared in heaven: a woman clothed with the sun, with the moon under her feet and a crown of twelve stars on her head. [2]She was pregnant and cried out in pain as she was about to give birth. [3]Then another sign appeared in heaven: an enormous red dragon with seven heads and ten horns and seven crowns on his heads. [4]His tail swept a third of the stars out of the sky and flung them to the earth. The dragon stood in front of the woman who was about to give birth, so that he might devour her child the moment it was born. [5]She gave birth to a son, a male child, who will rule all the nations with an iron sceptre. And her child was snatched up to God and to his throne. [6]The woman fled into the desert to a place prepared for her by God, where she might be taken care of for 1,260 days.

[7]And there was war in heaven. Michael and his angels fought against the dragon, and the dragon and his angels fought back. [8]But he was not strong enough, and they lost their place in heaven. [9]The great dragon was hurled down—that ancient

serpent called the devil or Satan, who leads the whole world astray. He was hurled to the earth, and his angels with him.

¹⁰Then I heard a loud voice in heaven say:

"Now have come the salvation and
  the power and the kingdom
  of our God,
and the authority of his Christ.
For the accuser of our brothers,
  who accuses them before our
    God day and night,
  has been hurled down.
¹¹They overcame him
  by the blood of the Lamb
  and by the word of their
    testimony;
they did not love their lives so
    much
  as to shrink from death.
¹²Therefore rejoice, you heavens
  and you who dwell in them!
But woe to the earth and the sea,
  because the devil has gone down
    to you!
He is filled with fury,
  because he knows that his time is
    short."

¹³When the dragon saw that he had been hurled to the earth, he pursued the woman who had given birth to the male child. ¹⁴The woman was given the two wings of a great eagle, so that she might fly to the place prepared for her in the desert, where she would be taken care of for a time, times and half a time, out of the serpent's reach. ¹⁵Then from his mouth the serpent spewed water like a river, to overtake the woman and sweep her away with the torrent. ¹⁶But the earth helped the woman by opening its mouth and swallowing the river that the dragon had spewed out of his mouth. ¹⁷Then the dragon was enraged at the woman and went off to make war against the rest of her offspring—those who obey God's commandments and hold to the testimony

13 of Jesus. ¹And the dragon*ᵃ* stood on the shore of the sea.

The Beast out of the Sea

And I saw a beast coming out of the sea. He had ten horns and seven heads, with ten crowns on his horns, and on each head a blasphemous name. ²The beast I saw resembled a leopard, but had feet like those of a bear and a mouth like that of a lion. The dragon gave the beast his power and his throne and great authority. ³One of the heads of the beast seemed to have had a fatal wound, but the fatal wound had been healed. The whole world was astonished and followed the beast. ⁴Men worshipped the dragon because he had given authority to the beast, and they also worshipped the beast and asked, "Who is like the beast? Who can make war against him?"

⁵The beast was given a mouth to utter proud words and blasphemies and to exercise his authority for forty-two months. ⁶He opened his mouth to blaspheme God, and to slander his name and his dwelling-place and those who live in heaven. ⁷He was given power to make war against the saints and to conquer them. And he was given authority over every tribe, people, language and nation. ⁸All inhabitants of the earth will worship the beast—all whose names have not been written in the book of life belonging to the Lamb that was slain from the creation of the world.*ᵇ*

⁹He who has an ear, let him hear.

¹⁰If anyone is to go into captivity,
  into captivity he will go.
If anyone is to be killed with the
    sword,
  with the sword he will be killed.

This calls for patient endurance and faithfulness on the part of the saints.

The Beast out of the Earth

¹¹Then I saw another beast, coming out of the earth. He had two horns like a lamb, but he spoke like a dragon. ¹²He exercised all the authority of the first beast on his behalf, and made the earth and its inhabitants

ᵃ1 Some late manuscripts And I
ᵇ8 Or written from the creation of the world in the book of life belonging to the Lamb that was slain

worship the first beast, whose fatal wound had been healed. 13And he performed great and miraculous signs, even causing fire to come down from heaven to earth in full view of men. 14Because of the signs he was given power to do on behalf of the first beast, he deceived the inhabitants of the earth. He ordered them to set up an image in honour of the beast who was wounded by the sword and yet lived. 15He was given power to give breath to the image of the first beast, so that it could speak and cause all who refused to worship the image to be killed. 16He also forced everyone, small and great, rich and poor, free and slave, to receive a mark on his right hand or on his forehead, 17so that no-one could buy or sell unless he had the mark, which is the name of the beast or the number of his name.

18This calls for wisdom. If anyone has insight, let him calculate the number of the beast, for it is man's number. His number is 666.

The Lamb and the 144,000

14 Then I looked, and there before me was the Lamb, standing on Mount Zion, and with him 144,000 who had his name and his Father's name written on their foreheads. 2And I heard a sound from heaven like the roar of rushing waters and like a loud peal of thunder. The sound I heard was like that of harpists playing their harps. 3And they sang a new song before the throne and before the four living creatures and the elders. No-one could learn the song except the 144,000 who had been redeemed from the earth. 4These are those who did not defile themselves with women, for they kept themselves pure. They follow the Lamb wherever he goes. They were purchased from among men and offered as firstfruits to God and the Lamb. 5No lie was found in their mouths; they are blameless.

The Three Angels

6Then I saw another angel flying in mid-air, and he had the eternal gospel to proclaim to those who live on the earth—to every nation, tribe, language and people. 7He said in a loud voice, "Fear God and give him glory, because the hour of his judgment has come. Worship him who made the heavens, the earth, the sea and the springs of water."

8A second angel followed and said, "Fallen! Fallen is Babylon the Great, which made all the nations drink the maddening wine of her adulteries."

9A third angel followed them and said in a loud voice: "If anyone worships the beast and his image and receives his mark on the forehead or on the hand, 10he, too, will drink of the wine of God's fury, which has been poured full strength into the cup of his wrath. He will be tormented with burning sulphur in the presence of the holy angels and of the Lamb. 11And the smoke of their torment rises for ever and ever. There is no rest day or night for those who worship the beast and his image, or for anyone who receives the mark of his name." 12This calls for patient endurance on the part of the saints who obey God's commandments and remain faithful to Jesus.

13Then I heard a voice from heaven say, "Write: Blessed are the dead who die in the Lord from now on."

"Yes," says the Spirit, "they will rest from their labour, for their deeds will follow them."

The Harvest of the Earth

14I looked, and there before me was a white cloud, and seated on the cloud was one "like a son of man"[a] with a crown of gold on his head and a sharp sickle in his hand. 15Then another angel came out of the temple and called in a loud voice to him who was sitting on the cloud, "Take your sickle and reap, because the time to reap has come, for the harvest of the earth is ripe." 16So he that was seated on the cloud swung his sickle over the earth, and the earth was harvested.

17Another angel came out of the

[a]14 Daniel 7:13

temple in heaven, and he too had a sharp sickle. [18]Still another angel, who had charge of the fire, came from the altar and called in a loud voice to him who had the sharp sickle, "Take your sharp sickle and gather the clusters of grapes from the earth's vine, because its grapes are ripe." [19]The angel swung his sickle on the earth, gathered its grapes and threw them into the great winepress of God's wrath. [20]They were trampled in the winepress outside the city, and blood flowed out of the press, rising as high as the horses' bridles for a distance of 1,600 stadia.[b]

Seven Angels With Seven Plagues

15 I saw in heaven another great and marvellous sign: seven angels with the seven last plagues—last, because with them God's wrath is completed. [2]And I saw what looked like a sea of glass mixed with fire and, standing beside the sea, those who had been victorious over the beast and his image and over the number of his name. They held harps given them by God [3]and sang the song of Moses the servant of God and the song of the Lamb:

"Great and marvellous are your
        deeds,
    Lord God Almighty.
Just and true are your ways,
    King of the ages.
[4]Who will not fear you, O Lord,
    and bring glory to your name?
For you alone are holy.
All nations will come
    and worship before you,
for your righteous acts have been
    revealed."

[5]After this I looked and in heaven the temple, that is, the tabernacle of Testimony, was opened. [6]Out of the temple came the seven angels with the seven plagues. They were dressed in clean, shining linen and wore golden sashes round their chests. [7]Then one of the four living creatures gave to the seven angels seven golden bowls filled with the wrath of God, who lives for ever and ever. [8]And the

temple was filled with smoke from the glory of God and from his power, and no-one could enter the temple until the seven plagues of the seven angels were completed.

The Seven Bowls of God's Wrath

16 Then I heard a loud voice from the temple saying to the seven angels, "Go, pour out the seven bowls of God's wrath on the earth." [2]The first angel went and poured out his bowl on the land, and ugly and painful sores broke out on the people who had the mark of the beast and worshipped his image.

[3]The second angel poured out his bowl on the sea, and it turned into blood like that of a dead man, and every living thing in the sea died.

[4]The third angel poured out his bowl on the rivers and springs of water, and they became blood. [5]Then I heard the angel in charge of the waters say:

"You are just in these judgments,
    you who are and who were, the
        Holy One,
    because you have so judged;
[6]for they have shed the blood of
        your saints and prophets,
    and you have given them blood
        to drink as they deserve."

[7]And I heard the altar respond:

"Yes, Lord God Almighty,
    true and just are your
        judgments."

[8]The fourth angel poured out his bowl on the sun, and the sun was given power to scorch people with fire. [9]They were seared by the intense heat and they cursed the name of God, who had control over these plagues, but they refused to repent and glorify him.

[10]The fifth angel poured out his bowl on the throne of the beast, and his kingdom was plunged into darkness. Men gnawed their tongues in agony [11]and cursed the God of heaven because of their pains and

[b]20 That is, about 180 miles (about 300 kilometres)

their sores, but they refused to repent of what they had done.

12Then the sixth angel poured out his bowl on the great river Euphrates, and its water was dried up to prepare the way for the kings from the East. 13Then I saw three evila spirits that looked like frogs; they came out of the mouth of the dragon, out of the mouth of the beast and out of the mouth of the false prophet. 14They are spirits of demons performing miraculous signs, and they go out to the kings of the whole world, to gather them for the battle on the great day of God Almighty.

15"Behold, I come like a thief! Blessed is he who stays awake and keeps his clothes with him, so that he may not go naked and be shamefully exposed."

16Then they gathered the kings together to the place that in Hebrew is called Armageddon.

17The seventh angel poured out his bowl into the air, and out of the temple came a loud voice from the throne, saying, "It is done!" 18Then there came flashes of lightning, rumblings, peals of thunder and a severe earthquake. No earthquake like it has ever occurred since man has been on earth, so tremendous was the quake. 19The great city split into three parts, and the cities of the nations collapsed. God remembered Babylon the Great and gave her the cup filled with the wine of the fury of his wrath. 20Every island fled away and the mountains could not be found. 21From the sky huge hailstones of about a hundred pounds each fell upon men. And they cursed God on account of the plague of hail, because the plague was so terrible.

The Woman on the Beast

17 One of the seven angels who had the seven bowls came and said to me, "Come, I will show you the punishment of the great prostitute, who sits on many waters. 2With her the kings of the earth committed adultery and the inhabitants of the earth were intoxicated with the wine of her adulteries."

3Then the angel carried me away in the Spirit into a desert. There I saw a woman sitting on a scarlet beast that was covered with blasphemous names and had seven heads and ten horns. 4The woman was dressed in purple and scarlet, and was glittering with gold, precious stones and pearls. She held a golden cup in her hand, filled with abominable things and the filth of her adulteries. 5This title was written on her forehead:

MYSTERY
BABYLON THE GREAT
THE MOTHER OF PROSTITUTES
AND OF THE ABOMINATIONS OF THE
EARTH.

6I saw that the woman was drunk with the blood of the saints, the blood of those who bore testimony to Jesus.

When I saw her, I was greatly astonished. 7Then the angel said to me: "Why are you astonished? I will explain to you the mystery of the woman and of the beast she rides, which has the seven heads and ten horns. 8The beast, which you saw, once was, now is not, and will come up out of the Abyss and go to his destruction. The inhabitants of the earth whose names have not been written in the book of life from the creation of the world will be astonished when they see the beast, because he once was, now is not, and yet will come.

9"This calls for a mind with wisdom. The seven heads are seven hills on which the woman sits. They are also seven kings. 10Five have fallen, one is, the other has not yet come; but when he does come, he must remain for a little while. 11The beast who once was, and now is not, is an eighth king. He belongs to the seven and is going to his destruction.

12"The ten horns you saw are ten kings who have not yet received a kingdom, but who for one hour will receive authority as kings along with the beast. 13They have one purpose and will give their power and

a13 Greek unclean

284

authority to the beast. ¹⁴They will make war against the Lamb, but the Lamb will overcome them because he is Lord of lords and King of kings —and with him will be his called, chosen and faithful followers."

¹⁵Then the angel said to me, "The waters you saw, where the prostitute sits, are peoples, multitudes, nations and languages. ¹⁶The beast and the ten horns you saw will hate the prostitute. They will bring her to ruin and leave her naked; they will eat her flesh and burn her with fire. ¹⁷For God has put it into their hearts to accomplish his purpose by agreeing to give the beast their power to rule, until God's words are fulfilled. ¹⁸The woman you saw is the great city that rules over the kings of the earth."

The Fall of Babylon

18 After this I saw another angel coming down from heaven. He had great authority, and the earth was illuminated by his splendour. ²With a mighty voice he shouted:

"Fallen! Fallen is Babylon the Great!
  She has become a home for
    demons
and a haunt for every evil*a* spirit,
  a haunt for every unclean and
    detestable bird.
³For all the nations have drunk
  the maddening wine of her
    adulteries.
The kings of the earth committed
  adultery with her,
and the merchants of the earth
  grew rich from her excessive
    luxuries."

⁴Then I heard another voice from heaven say:

"Come out of her, my people,
  so that you will not share in her
    sins,
  so that you will not receive any
    of her plagues;
⁵for her sins are piled up to heaven,
  and God has remembered her
    crimes.
⁶Give back to her as she has given;
  pay her back double for what
    she has done.

a2 Greek unclean

Mix her a double portion from
  her own cup.
⁷Give her as much torture and grief
  as the glory and luxury she gave
    herself.
In her heart she boasts,
  'I sit as queen; I am not a widow,
  and I will never mourn.'
⁸Therefore in one day her plagues
    will overtake her:
  death, mourning and famine.
She will be consumed by fire,
  for mighty is the Lord God who
    judges her.

⁹"When the kings of the earth who committed adultery with her and shared her luxury see the smoke of her burning, they will weep and mourn over her. ¹⁰Terrified at her torment, they will stand far off and cry:

" 'Woe! Woe, O great city,
  O Babylon, city of power!
In one hour your doom has come!'

¹¹"The merchants of the earth will weep and mourn over her because no-one buys their cargoes any more—¹²cargoes of gold, silver, precious stones and pearls; fine linen, purple, silk and scarlet cloth; every sort of citron wood, and articles of every kind made of ivory, costly wood, bronze, iron and marble; ¹³cargoes of cinnamon and spice, of incense, myrrh and frankincense, of wine and olive oil, of fine flour and wheat; cattle and sheep; horses and carriages; and bodies and souls of men.

¹⁴"They will say, 'The fruit you longed for is gone from you. All your riches and splendour have vanished, never to be recovered.' ¹⁵The merchants who sold these things and gained their wealth from her will stand far off, terrified at her torment. They will weep and mourn ¹⁶and cry out:

" 'Woe! Woe, O great city,
  dressed in fine linen, purple and
    scarlet,
  and glittering with gold, precious
    stones and pearls!

285

17In one hour such great wealth has
    been brought to ruin!'

"Every sea captain, and all who
travel by ship, the sailors, and all who
earn their living from the sea, will
stand far off. 18When they see the
smoke of her burning, they will
exclaim, 'Was there ever a city like
this great city?' 19They will throw dust
on their heads, and with weeping and
mourning cry out:

" 'Woe! Woe, O great city,
    where all who had ships on the
        sea
    became rich through her
        wealth!
In one hour she has been brought
    to ruin!'
20Rejoice over her, O heaven!
    Rejoice, saints and apostles and
        prophets!
God has judged her for the way
    she treated you.' "

21Then a mighty angel picked up a
boulder the size of a large millstone
and threw it into the sea, and said:

"With such violence
    the great city of Babylon will be
        thrown down,
    never to be found again.
22The music of harpists and
        musicians, flute players and
        trumpeters,
    will never be heard in you
        again.
No workman of any trade
    will ever be found in you again.
The sound of a millstone
    will never be heard in you
        again.
23The light of a lamp
    will never shine in you again.
The voice of bridegroom and bride
    will never be heard in you
        again.
Your merchants were the world's
    great men.
    By your magic spell all the
        nations were led astray.
24In her was found the blood of
    prophets and of the saints,
    and of all who have been killed
        on the earth."

286

Hallelujah!

19 After this I heard what
    sounded like the roar of a
great multitude in heaven shouting:

"Hallelujah!
Salvation and glory and power
    belong to our God,
2   for true and just are his
        judgments.
He has condemned the great
    prostitute
    who corrupted the earth by her
        adulteries.
He has avenged on her the blood
    of his servants."

3And again they shouted:

"Hallelujah!
The smoke from her goes up for
    ever and ever."

4The twenty-four elders and the
four living creatures fell down and
worshipped God, who was seated on
the throne. And they cried:

"Amen, Hallelujah!"

5Then a voice came from the
throne, saying:

"Praise our God,
    all you his servants,
you who fear him,
    both small and great!"

6Then I heard what sounded like a
great multitude, like the roar of rushing waters and like loud peals of
thunder, shouting:

"Hallelujah!
    For our Lord God Almighty
        reigns.
7Let us rejoice and be glad
    and give him glory!
For the wedding of the Lamb has
    come,
    and his bride has made herself
        ready.
8Fine linen, bright and clean,
    was given her to wear."
(Fine linen stands for the righteous
acts of the saints.)

9Then the angel said to me, "Write:
'Blessed are those who are invited to
the wedding supper of the Lamb!' "
And he added, "These are the true

words of God."

10At this I fell at his feet to worship him. But he said to me, "Do not do it! I am a fellow-servant with you and with your brothers who hold to the testimony of Jesus. Worship God! For the testimony of Jesus is the spirit of prophecy."

The Rider on the White Horse

11I saw heaven standing open and there before me was a white horse, whose rider is called Faithful and True. With justice he judges and makes war. 12His eyes are like blazing fire, and on his head are many crowns. He has a name written on him that no-one but he himself knows. 13He is dressed in a robe dipped in blood, and his name is the Word of God. 14The armies of heaven were following him, riding on white horses and dressed in fine linen, white and clean. 15Out of his mouth comes a sharp sword with which to strike down the nations. "He will rule them with an iron sceptre."*a* He treads the winepress of the fury of the wrath of God Almighty. 16On his robe and on his thigh he has this name written:

KING OF KINGS AND LORD OF LORDS.

17And I saw an angel standing in the sun, who cried in a loud voice to all the birds flying in mid-air, "Come, gather together for the great supper of God, 18so that you may eat the flesh of kings, generals, and mighty men, of horses and their riders, and the flesh of all people, free and slave, small and great."

19Then I saw the beast and the kings of the earth and their armies gathered together to make war against the rider on the horse and his army. 20But the beast was captured, and with him the false prophet who had performed the miraculous signs on his behalf. With these signs he had deluded those who had received the mark of the beast and worshipped his image. The two of them were thrown alive into the fiery lake of burning sulphur. 21The rest of them were

*a*15 Psalm 2:9

killed with the sword that came out of the mouth of the rider on the horse, and all the birds gorged themselves on their flesh.

The Thousand Years

20 And I saw an angel coming down out of heaven, having the key to the Abyss and holding in his hand a great chain. 2He seized the dragon, that ancient serpent, who is the devil, or Satan, and bound him for a thousand years. 3He threw him into the Abyss, and locked and sealed it over him, to keep him from deceiving the nations any more until the thousand years were ended. After that, he must be set free for a short time.

4I saw thrones on which were seated those who had been given authority to judge. And I saw the souls of those who had been beheaded because of their testimony for Jesus and because of the word of God. They had not worshipped the beast or his image and had not received his mark on their foreheads or their hands. They came to life and reigned with Christ for a thousand years. 5(The rest of the dead did not come to life until the thousand years were ended.) This is the first resurrection. 6Blessed and holy are those who have part in the first resurrection. The second death has no power over them, but they will be priests of God and of Christ and will reign with him for a thousand years.

Satan's Doom

7When the thousand years are over, Satan will be released from his prison 8and will go out to deceive the nations in the four corners of the earth—Gog and Magog—to gather them for battle. In number they are like the sand on the sea-shore. 9They marched across the breadth of the earth and surrounded the camp of God's people, the city he loves. But fire came down from heaven and devoured them. 10And the devil, who deceived them, was thrown into the lake of burning sulphur, where the beast and the false prophet had been thrown. They will be tormented day and night for ever and ever.

The Dead Are Judged

11Then I saw a great white throne and him who was seated on it. Earth and sky fled from his presence, and there was no place for them. 12And I saw the dead, great and small, standing before the throne, and books were opened. Another book was opened, which is the book of life. The dead were judged according to what they had done as recorded in the books. 13The sea gave up the dead that were in it, and death and Hades gave up the dead that were in them, and each person was judged according to what he had done. 14Then death and Hades were thrown into the lake of fire. The lake of fire is the second death. 15If anyone's name was not found written in the book of life, he was thrown into the lake of fire.

The New Jerusalem

21 Then I saw a new heaven and a new earth, for the first heaven and the first earth had passed away, and there was no longer any sea. 2I saw the Holy City, the new Jerusalem, coming down out of heaven from God, prepared as a bride beautifully dressed for her husband. 3And I heard a loud voice from the throne saying, "Now the dwelling of God is with men, and he will live with them. They will be his people, and God himself will be with them and be their God. 4He will wipe every tear from their eyes. There will be no more death or mourning or crying or pain, for the old order of things has passed away."

5He who was seated on the throne said, "I am making everything new!" Then he said, "Write this down, for these words are trustworthy and true."

6He said to me: "It is done. I am the Alpha and the Omega, the Beginning and the End. To him who is thirsty I will give to drink without

cost from the spring of the water of life. 7He who overcomes will inherit all this, and I will be his God and he will be my son. 8But the cowardly, the unbelieving, the vile, the murderers, the sexually immoral, those who practise magic arts, the idolaters and all liars—their place will be in the fiery lake of burning sulphur. This is the second death."

9One of the seven angels who had the seven bowls full of the seven last plagues came and said to me, "Come, I will show you the bride, the wife of the Lamb." 10And he carried me away in the Spirit to a mountain great and high, and showed me the Holy City, Jerusalem, coming down out of heaven from God. 11It shone with the glory of God, and its brilliance was like that of a very precious jewel, like a jasper, clear as crystal. 12It had a great, high wall with twelve gates, and with twelve angels at the gates. On the gates were written the names of the twelve tribes of Israel. 13There were three gates on the east, three on the north, three on the south and three on the west. 14The wall of the city had twelve foundations, and on them were the names of the twelve apostles of the Lamb.

15The angel who talked with me had a measuring rod of gold to measure the city, its gates and its wall. 16The city was laid out like a square, as long as it was wide. He measured the city with the rod and found it to be 12,000 stadia[a] in length, and as wide and high as it is long. 17He measured its wall and it was 144 cubits[b] thick,[c] by man's measurement, which the angel was using. 18The wall was made of jasper, and the city of pure gold, as pure as glass. 19The foundations of the city walls were decorated with every kind of precious stone. The first foundation was jasper, the second sapphire, the third chalcedony, the fourth emerald, 20the fifth sardonyx, the sixth carnelian, the seventh chrysolite, the eighth beryl, the ninth topaz, the tenth chrysoprase, the eleventh jacinth, and the twelfth

a16 That is, about 1,400 miles (about 2,200 kilometres)
b17 That is, about 200 feet (about 65 metres)
c17 Or high

amethyst.*d* 21The twelve gates were twelve pearls, each gate made of a single pearl. The street of the city is of pure gold, like transparent glass.

22I did not see a temple in the city, because the Lord God Almighty and the Lamb are its temple. 23The city does not need the sun or the moon to shine on it, for the glory of God gives it light, and the Lamb is its lamp. 24The nations will walk by its light, and the kings of the earth will bring their splendour into it. 25On no day will its gates ever be shut, for there will be no night there. 26The glory and honour of the nations will be brought into it. 27Nothing impure will ever enter it, nor will anyone who does what is shameful or deceitful, but only those whose names are written in the Lamb's book of life.

The River of Life

22 Then the angel showed me the river of the water of life, as clear as crystal, flowing from the throne of God and of the Lamb 2down the middle of the great street of the city. On each side of the river stood the tree of life, bearing twelve crops of fruit, yielding its fruit every month. And the leaves of the tree are for the healing of the nations. 3No longer will there be any curse. The throne of God and of the Lamb will be in the city, and his servants will serve him. 4They will see his face, and his name will be on their foreheads. 5There will be no more night. They will not need the light of a lamp or the light of the sun, for the Lord God will give them light. And they will reign for ever and ever.

6The angel said to me, "These words are trustworthy and true. The Lord, the God of the spirits of the prophets, sent his angel to show his servants the things that must soon take place."

Jesus Is Coming

7"Behold, I am coming soon! Blessed is he who keeps the words of the prophecy in this book."

8I, John, am the one who heard and saw these things. And when I had heard and seen them, I fell down to worship at the feet of the angel who had been showing them to me. 9But he said to me, "Do not do it! I am a fellow-servant with you and with your brothers the prophets and of all who keep the words of this book. Worship God!"

10Then he told me, "Do not seal up the words of the prophecy of this book, because the time is near. 11Let him who does wrong continue to do wrong; let him who is vile continue to be vile; let him who does right continue to do right; and let him who is holy continue to be holy."

12"Behold, I am coming soon! My reward is with me, and I will give to everyone according to what he has done. 13I am the Alpha and the Omega, the First and the Last, the Beginning and the End.

14"Blessed are those who wash their robes, that they may have the right to the tree of life and may go through the gates into the city. 15Outside are the dogs, those who practise magic arts, the sexually immoral, the murderers, the idolaters and everyone who loves and practises falsehood.

16"I, Jesus, have sent my angel to give you*a* this testimony for the churches. I am the Root and the Offspring of David, and the bright Morning Star."

17The Spirit and the bride say, "Come!" And let him who hears say, "Come!" Whoever is thirsty, let him come; and whoever wishes, let him take the free gift of the water of life.

18I warn everyone who hears the words of the prophecy of this book: If anyone adds anything to them, God will add to him the plagues described in this book. 19And if anyone takes

d20 The precise identification of some of these precious stones is uncertain.
a16 The Greek is plural.

words away from this book of prophecy, God will take away from him his share in the tree of life and in the holy city, which are described in this book.

20 He who testifies to these things says, "Yes, I am coming soon."

Amen. Come, Lord Jesus.

21 The grace of the Lord Jesus be with God's people. Amen.

THE
BOOK OF PSALMS

Psalms

BOOK I
Psalms 1–41

Psalm 1

¹Blessed is the man
    who does not walk in the counsel
        of the wicked
or stand in the way of sinners
    or sit in the seat of mockers.
²But his delight is in the law of the
        LORD,
    and on his law he meditates day
        and night.
³He is like a tree planted by streams
        of water,
    which yields its fruit in season
and whose leaf does not wither.
    Whatever he does prospers.

⁴Not so the wicked!
    They are like chaff
        that the wind blows away.
⁵Therefore the wicked will not stand
        in the judgment,
    nor sinners in the assembly of the
        righteous.

⁶For the LORD watches over the way
        of the righteous,
    but the way of the wicked will
        perish.

Psalm 2

¹Why do the nations rage
    and the peoples plot in vain?
²The kings of the earth take their
        stand
    and the rulers gather together
        against the LORD
    and against his Anointed One.ᵃ
³"Let us break their chains," they
        say,
    "and throw off their fetters."

⁴The One enthroned in heaven
        laughs;
    the LORD scoffs at them.
⁵Then he rebukes them in his anger
    and terrifies them in his wrath,
        saying,
⁶"I have installed my Kingᵇ
    on Zion, my holy hill."

⁷I will proclaim the decree of the
        LORD:

He said to me, "You are my Son;ᶜ
    today I have become your
        Father.ᵈ
⁸Ask of me,
    and I will make the nations your
        inheritance,
    the ends of the earth your
        possession.
⁹You will rule them with an iron
        sceptre;ᵉ
    you will dash them to pieces like
        pottery."

¹⁰Therefore, you kings, be wise;
    be warned, you rulers of the
        earth.
¹¹Serve the LORD with fear
    and rejoice with trembling.
¹²Kiss the Son, lest he be angry
    and you be destroyed in your
        way,
    for his wrath can flare up in a
        moment.
    Blessed are all who take refuge
        in him.

ᵃ2 Or *anointed one*   ᵇ6 Or *king*   ᶜ7 Or *son*; also in verse 12
ᵈ7 Or *have begotten you*   ᵉ9 Or *will break them with a rod of iron*

293

Psalm 3

A psalm of David. When he fled from his son Absalom.

[1]O LORD, how many are my foes!
How many rise up against me!
[2]Many are saying of me,
"God will not deliver him."
Selah[a]

[3]But you are a shield around me, O LORD,
my Glorious One, who lifts up my head.
[4]To the LORD I cry aloud,
and he answers me from his holy hill.
Selah

[5]I lie down and sleep;
I wake again, because the LORD sustains me.
[6]I will not fear the tens of thousands drawn up against me on every side.

[7]Arise, O LORD!
Deliver me, O my God!
For you have struck all my enemies on the jaw;
you have broken the teeth of the wicked.

[8]From the LORD comes deliverance.
May your blessing be on your people.
Selah

Psalm 4

For the director of music. With stringed instruments. A psalm of David.

[1]Answer me when I call to you,
O my righteous God.
Give me relief from my distress;
be merciful to me and hear my prayer.

[2]How long, O men, will you turn my glory into shame?[a]
How long will you love delusions and seek false gods?[b]
Selah
[3]Know that the LORD has set apart the godly for himself;
the LORD will hear when I call to him.

[4]In your anger do not sin;
when you are on your beds,
search your hearts and be silent.
Selah

[5]Offer right sacrifices
and trust in the LORD.

[6]Many are asking, "Who can show us any good?"
Let the light of your face shine upon us, O LORD.
[7]You have filled my heart with greater joy
than when their grain and new wine abound.
[8]I will lie down and sleep in peace,
for you alone, O LORD,
make me dwell in safety.

Psalm 5

For the director of music. For flutes. A psalm of David.

[1]Give ear to my words, O LORD,
consider my sighing.
[2]Listen to my cry for help,
my King and my God,
for to you I pray.
[3]Morning by morning, O LORD, you hear my voice;
morning by morning I lay my requests before you
and wait in expectation.

[4]You are not a God who takes pleasure in evil;
with you the wicked cannot dwell.
[5]The arrogant cannot stand in your presence;
you hate all who do wrong.
[6]You destroy those who tell lies;
bloodthirsty and deceitful men the LORD abhors.

[7]But I, by your great mercy,
will come into your house;
in reverence will I bow down towards your holy temple.
[8]Lead me, O LORD, in your righteousness
because of my enemies—
make straight your way before me.

*a*2 A word of uncertain meaning, occurring frequently in the Psalms; possibly a musical term
*a*2 Or you *dishonour my Glorious One*   *b*2 Hebrew *seek lies*

⁹Not a word from their mouth can be
trusted;
their heart is filled with
destruction.
Their throat is an open grave;
with their tongue they speak
deceit.
¹⁰Declare them guilty, O God!
Let their intrigues be their
downfall.
Banish them for their many sins,
for they have rebelled against
you.
¹¹But let all who take refuge in you
be glad;
let them ever sing for joy.
Spread your protection over them,
that those who love your name
may rejoice in you.
¹²For surely, O LORD, you bless the
righteous;
you surround them with your
favour as with a shield.

Psalm 6

For the director of music. With stringed
instruments. According to *sheminith.ᵃ* A
psalm of David.

¹O LORD, do not rebuke me in your
anger
or discipline me in your wrath.
²Be merciful to me, LORD, for I am
faint;
O LORD, heal me, for my bones
are in agony.
³My soul is in anguish.
How long, O LORD, how long?
⁴Turn, O LORD, and deliver me;
save me because of your
unfailing love.
⁵No-one remembers you when he is
dead.
Who praises you from his grave?ᵇ
⁶I am worn out from groaning;
all night long I flood my bed with
weeping
and drench my couch with tears.
⁷My eyes grow weak with sorrow;
they fail because of all my foes.

⁸Away from me, all you who do evil,

for the LORD has heard my
weeping.
⁹The LORD has heard my cry for
mercy;
the LORD accepts my prayer.
¹⁰May all my enemies be ashamed
and dismayed;
may they turn back in sudden
disgrace.

Psalm 7

A *shiggaionᵃ* of David, which he sang to
the LORD concerning Cush, a Benjamite.

¹O LORD my God, I take refuge in
you;
save and deliver me from all who
pursue me,
²or they will tear me like a lion
and rip me to pieces with no-one
to rescue me.

³O LORD my God, if I have done this
and there is guilt on my hands—
⁴if I have done evil to him who is at
peace with me
or without cause have robbed my
foe—
⁵then let my enemy pursue and
overtake me;
let him trample my life to the
ground
and make me sleep in the dust.
Selah

⁶Arise, O LORD, in your anger;
rise up against the rage of my
enemies.
Awake, my God; decree justice.
⁷Let the assembled peoples gather
round you.
Rule over them from on high;
⁸ let the LORD judge the peoples.
Judge me, O LORD, according to my
righteousness,
according to my integrity, O Most
High.
⁹O righteous God,
who searches minds and hearts,
bring to an end the violence of the
wicked
and make the righteous secure.

¹⁰My shieldᵇ is God Most High,
who saves the upright in heart.

ᵃTitle: Probably a musical term   ᵇ5 Hebrew *Sheol*
ᵃTitle: Probably a literary or musical term   ᵇ10 Or *sovereign*

11God is a righteous judge,
  a God who expresses his wrath
    every day.
12If he does not relent,
  he*c* will sharpen his sword;
  he will bend and string his bow.
13He has prepared his deadly
    weapons;
  he makes ready his flaming
    arrows.
14He who is pregnant with evil
  and conceives trouble gives birth
    to disillusionment.
15He who digs a hole and scoops it
    out
  falls into the pit he has made.
16The trouble he causes recoils on
    himself;
  his violence comes down on his
    own head.

17I will give thanks to the LORD
    because of his righteousness
  and will sing praise to the name
    of the LORD Most High.

Psalm 8

For the director of music. According to
gittith.a A psalm of David.

1O LORD, our Lord,
  how majestic is your name in all
    the earth!

You have set your glory
    above the heavens.
2From the lips of children and
    infants
  you have ordained praise*b*
  because of your enemies,
    to silence the foe and the
      avenger.
3When I consider your heavens,
    the work of your fingers,
  the moon and the stars,
    which you have set in place,
4what is man that you are mindful of
    him,
  the son of man that you care for
    him?
5You made him a little lower than
    the heavenly beings*c*

and crowned him with glory and
    honour.
6You made him ruler over the works
    of your hands;
  you put everything under his feet:
7all flocks and herds,
    and the beasts of the field,
8the birds of the air,
    and the fish of the sea,
  all that swim the paths of the
    seas.

9O LORD, our Lord,
  how majestic is your name in all
    the earth!

Psalm 9*a*

For the director of music. To ,the tune
of "The Death of the Son". A psalm of
David.

1I will praise you, O LORD, with all
    my heart;
  I will tell of all your wonders.
2I will be glad and rejoice in you;
  I will sing praise to your name, O
    Most High.

3My enemies turn back;
  they stumble and perish before
    you.
4For you have upheld my right and
    my cause;
  you have sat on your throne,
    judging righteously.
5You have rebuked the nations and
    destroyed the wicked;
  you have blotted out their name
    for ever and ever.
6Endless ruin has overtaken the
    enemy,
  you have uprooted their cities;
    even the memory of them has
      perished.

7The LORD reigns for ever;
  he has established his throne for
    judgment.
8He will judge the world in
    righteousness;
  he will govern the peoples with
    justice.
9The LORD is a refuge for the
    oppressed,

---

*c*12 Or *If a man does not repent. / God*
*b*2 Or *strength*   *c*5 Or *than God*
*a*Psalms 9 and 10 may have been originally a single acrostic poem, the stanzas of which begin
with the successive letters of the Hebrew alphabet. In the Septuagint they constitute one psalm.

*a*Title: Probably a musical term

a stronghold in times of trouble.
¹⁰Those who know your name will
trust in you,
for you, LORD, have never
forsaken those who seek you.

¹¹Sing praises to the LORD, enthroned
in Zion;
proclaim among the nations what
he has done.
¹²For he who avenges blood
remembers;
he does not ignore the cry of the
afflicted.
¹³O LORD, see how my enemies
persecute me!
Have mercy and lift me up from
the gates of death,
¹⁴that I may declare your praises
in the gates of the Daughter of
Zion
and there rejoice in your
salvation.
¹⁵The nations have fallen into the pit
they have dug;
their feet are caught in the net
they have hidden.
¹⁶The LORD is known by his justice;
the wicked are ensnared by the
work of their hands.
*Higgaion.*ᵇ *Selah*

¹⁷The wicked return to the grave,ᶜ
all the nations that forget God.
¹⁸But the needy will not always be
forgotten,
nor the hope of the afflicted ever
perish.

¹⁹Arise, O LORD, let not man
triumph;
let the nations be judged in your
presence.
²⁰Strike them with terror, O LORD;
let the nations know they are but
men. *Selah*

Psalm 10ᵃ

¹Why, O LORD, do you stand far off?
Why do you hide yourself in
times of trouble?

²In his arrogance the wicked man
hunts down the weak,

who are caught in the schemes he
devises.
³He boasts of the cravings of his
heart;
he blesses the greedy and reviles
the LORD.
⁴In his pride the wicked does not
seek him;
in all his thoughts there is no
room for God.
⁵His ways are always prosperous;
he is haughty and your laws are
far from him;
he sneers at all his enemies.
⁶He says to himself, "Nothing will
shake me;
I'll always be happy and never
have trouble."
⁷His mouth is full of curses and lies
and threats;
trouble and evil are under his
tongue.
⁸He lies in wait near the villages;
from ambush he murders the
innocent,
watching in secret for his victims.
⁹He lies in wait like a lion in cover;
he lies in wait to catch the
helpless;
he catches the helpless and drags
them off in his net.
¹⁰His victims are crushed, they
collapse;
they fall under his strength.
¹¹He says to himself, "God has
forgotten;
he covers his face and never
sees."

¹²Arise, LORD! Lift up your hand, O
God.
Do not forget the helpless.
¹³Why does the wicked man revile
God?
Why does he say to himself,
"He won't call me to account"?
¹⁴But you, O God, do see trouble and
grief;
you consider it to take it in hand.
The victim commits himself to you;
you are the helper of the
fatherless.
¹⁵Break the arm of the wicked and
evil man;

ᵇ16 Or *Meditation*; possibly a musical notation   ᶜ17 Hebrew *Sheol*
ᵃPsalms 9 and 10 may have been originally a single acrostic poem, the stanzas of which begin
with the successive letters of the Hebrew alphabet. In the Septuagint they constitute one psalm.

call him to account for his
wickedness
that would not be found out.
16The LORD is King for ever and
ever;
the nations will perish from his
land.
17You hear, O LORD, the desire of the
afflicted;
you encourage them, and you
listen to their cry,
18defending the fatherless and the
oppressed,
in order that man, who is of the
earth, may terrify no more.

Psalm 11

For the director of music. Of David.

1In the LORD I take refuge.
How then can you say to me:
"Flee like a bird to your
mountain.
2For look, the wicked bend their
bows;
they set their arrows against the
strings
to shoot from the shadows
at the upright in heart.
3When the foundations are being
destroyed,
what can the righteous do?"a

4The LORD is in his holy temple;
the LORD is on his heavenly
throne.
He observes the sons of men;
his eyes examine them.
5The LORD examines the righteous,
but the wickedb and those who
love violence
his soul hates.
6On the wicked he will rain
fiery coals and burning sulphur;
a scorching wind will be their lot.
7For the LORD is righteous,
he loves justice;
upright men will see his face.

Psalm 12

For the director of music. According to
sheminith.a A psalm of David.

1Help, LORD, for the godly are no
more;

the faithful have vanished from
among men.
2Everyone lies to his neighbour;
their flattering lips speak with
deception.
3May the LORD cut off all flattering
lips
and every boastful tongue
4that says, "We will triumph with
our tongues;
we own our lipsb—who is our
master?"
5"Because of the oppression of the
weak
and the groaning of the needy,
I will now arise," says the LORD.
"I will protect them from those
who malign them."
6And the words of the LORD are
flawless,
like silver refined in a furnace of
clay,
purified seven times.

7O LORD, you will keep us safe
and protect us from such people
for ever.
8The wicked freely strut about
when what is vile is honoured
among men.

Psalm 13

For the director of music. A psalm of
David.

1How long, O LORD? Will you forget
me for ever?
How long will you hide your face
from me?
2How long must I wrestle with my
thoughts
and every day have sorrow in my
heart?
How long will my enemy triumph
over me?
3Look on me and answer, O LORD my
God.
Give light to my eyes, or I will
sleep in death;
4my enemy will say, "I have
overcome him,"

a3 Or what is the Righteous One doing
b5 Or The LORD, the Righteous One, examines the wicked,/
aTitle: Probably a musical term
b4 Or / our lips are our ploughshares

and my foes will rejoice when I
fall.
⁵But I trust in your unfailing love;
my heart rejoices in your
salvation.
⁶I will sing to the LORD,
for he has been good to me.

Psalm 14

For the director of music. Of David.

¹The fool*a* says in his heart,
"There is no God."
They are corrupt, their deeds are
vile;
there is no-one who does good.
²The LORD looks down from heaven
on the sons of men
to see if there are any who
understand,
any who seek God.
³All have turned aside,
they have together become
corrupt;
there is no-one who does good,
not even one.
⁴Will evildoers never learn—
those who devour my people as
men eat bread
and who do not call on the LORD?
⁵There they are, overwhelmed with
dread,
for God is present in the
company of the righteous.
⁶You evildoers frustrate the plans of
the poor,
but the LORD is their refuge.
⁷Oh, that salvation for Israel would
come out of Zion!
When the LORD restores the
fortunes of his people,
let Jacob rejoice and Israel be
glad!

Psalm 15

A psalm of David.

¹LORD, who may dwell in your
sanctuary?
Who may live on your holy hill?

²He whose walk is blameless
and who does what is righteous,
who speaks the truth from his heart
3 and has no slander on his tongue,
who does his neighbour no wrong
and casts no slur on his fellow-
man,
⁴who despises a vile man
but honours those who fear the
LORD,
who keeps his oath
even when it hurts,
⁵who lends his money without usury
and does not accept a bribe
against the innocent.

He who does these things
will never be shaken.

Psalm 16

A miktam*a* of David.

¹Keep me safe, O God,
for in you I take refuge.

²I said to the LORD, "You are my
Lord;
apart from you I have no good
thing."
³As for the saints who are in the
land,
they are the glorious ones in
whom is all my delight.*b*
⁴The sorrows of those will increase
who run after other gods.
I will not pour out their libations of
blood
or take up their names on my
lips.

⁵LORD, you have assigned me my
portion and my cup;
you have made my lot secure.
⁶The boundary lines have fallen for
me in pleasant places;
surely I have a delightful
inheritance.

⁷I will praise the LORD, who counsels
me;
even at night my heart instructs
me.
⁸I have set the LORD always before
me.
Because he is at my right hand,
I shall not be shaken.

a1 The Hebrew words rendered fool in Psalms denote one who is morally deficient.
aTitle: Probably a literary or musical term
b3 Or As for the pagan priests who are in the land / and the nobles in whom all delight, I said:

9Therefore my heart is glad and my
tongue rejoices;
my body also will rest secure,
10because you will not abandon me
to the grave,c
nor will you let your Holy Oned
see decay.
11You have made knowne to me the
path of life;
you will fill me with joy in your
presence,
with eternal pleasures at your
right hand.

Psalm 17

A prayer of David.

1Hear, O LORD, my righteous plea;
listen to my cry.
Give ear to my prayer—
it does not rise from deceitful
lips.
2May my vindication come from you;
may your eyes see what is right.

3Though you probe my heart and
examine me at night,
though you test me, you will find
nothing;
I have resolved that my mouth
will not sin.
4As for the deeds of men—
by the word of your lips
I have kept myself
from the ways of the violent.
5My steps have held to your paths;
my feet have not slipped.

6I call on you, O God, for you will
answer me;
give ear to me and hear my
prayer.
7Show the wonder of your great
love,
you who save by your right hand
those who take refuge in you
from their foes.
8Keep me as the apple of your eye;
hide me in the shadow of your
wings
9from the wicked who assail me,
from my mortal enemies who
surround me.
10They close up their callous hearts,

and their mouths speak with
arrogance.
11They have tracked me down, they
now surround me,
with eyes alert, to throw me to
the ground.
12They are like a lion hungry for
prey,
like a great lion crouching in
cover.
13Rise up, O LORD, confront them,
bring them down;
rescue me from the wicked by
your sword.
14O LORD, by your hand save me
from such men,
from men of this world whose
reward is in this life.

You still the hunger of those you
cherish;
their sons have plenty,
and they store up wealth for their
children.
15And I—in righteousness I shall see
your face;
when I awake, I shall be satisfied
with seeing your likeness.

Psalm 18

For the director of music. Of David the
servant of the LORD. He sang to the LORD
the words of this song when the LORD
delivered him from the hand of all his
enemies and from the hand of Saul.
He said:

1I love you, O LORD, my strength.

2The LORD is my rock, my fortress
and my deliverer;
my God is my rock, in whom I
take refuge.
He is my shield and the horna of
my salvation, my stronghold.
3I call to the LORD, who is worthy of
praise,
and I am saved from my
enemies.
4The cords of death entangled me;
the torrents of
destruction
overwhelmed me.
5The cords of the graveb coiled
around me;

c10 Hebrew *Sheol*   d10 Or *your faithful one*   e11 Or *You will make known*
a2 *Horn* here symbolises strength.   b5 Hebrew *Sheol*

the snares of death confronted
   me.
⁶In my distress I called to the LORD;
   I cried to my God for help.
From his temple he heard my voice;
   my cry came before him, into his
   ears.

⁷The earth trembled and quaked,
   and the foundations of the
    mountains shook;
they trembled because he was
   angry.
⁸Smoke rose from his nostrils;
   consuming fire came from his
    mouth,
burning coals blazed out of it.
⁹He parted the heavens and came
   down;
dark clouds were under his feet.
¹⁰He mounted the cherubim and
   flew;
he soared on the wings of the
   wind.
¹¹He made darkness his covering, his
   canopy around him—
the dark rain clouds of the sky.
¹²Out of the brightness of his
   presence clouds advanced,
with hailstones and bolts of
   lightning.
¹³The LORD thundered from heaven;
   the voice of the Most High
    resounded.^c
¹⁴He shot his arrows and scattered
   the enemies,
great bolts of lightning and routed
   them.
¹⁵The valleys of the sea were
   exposed
and the foundations of the earth
   laid bare
at your rebuke, O LORD,
   at the blast of breath from your
    nostrils.

¹⁶He reached down from on high
   and took hold of me;
he drew me out of deep waters.
¹⁷He rescued me from my powerful
   enemy,
from my foes, who were too
   strong for me.

¹⁸They confronted me in the day of
   my disaster,
but the LORD was my support.
¹⁹He brought me out into a spacious
   place;
he rescued me because he
   delighted in me.

²⁰The LORD has dealt with me
   according to my righteousness;
according to the cleanness of my
   hands he has rewarded me.
²¹For I have kept the ways of the
   LORD;
I have not done evil by turning
   from my God.
²²All his laws are before me;
   I have not turned away from his
   decrees.
²³I have been blameless before him
   and have kept myself from sin.
²⁴The LORD has rewarded me
   according to my righteousness,
according to the cleanness of my
   hands in his sight.

²⁵To the faithful you show yourself
   faithful,
to the blameless you show
   yourself blameless,
²⁶to the pure you show yourself pure,
   but to the crooked you show
   yourself shrewd.
²⁷You save the humble
   but bring low those whose eyes
   are haughty.
²⁸You, O LORD, keep my lamp
   burning;
my God turns my darkness into
   light.
²⁹With your help I can advance
   against a troop;^d
with my God I can scale a wall.

³⁰As for God, his way is perfect;
   the word of the LORD is flawless.
He is a shield
   for all who take refuge in him.
³¹For who is God besides the LORD?
   And who is the Rock except our
   God?
³²It is God who arms me with
   strength
and makes my way perfect.

^c13 Some Hebrew manuscripts and Septuagint (see also 2 Samuel 22:14); most Hebrew
manuscripts resounded, / amid hailstones and bolts of lightning
^d29 Or can run through a barricade

³³He makes my feet like the feet of a
deer;
he enables me to stand on the
heights.
³⁴He trains my hands for battle;
my arms can bend a bow of
bronze.
³⁵You give me your shield of victory,
and your right hand sustains me;
you stoop down to make me
great.
³⁶You broaden the path beneath me,
so that my ankles do not turn
over.
³⁷I pursued my enemies and
overtook them;
I did not turn back till they were
destroyed.
³⁸I crushed them so that they could
not rise;
they fell beneath my feet.
³⁹You armed me with strength for
battle;
you made my adversaries bow at
my feet.
⁴⁰You made my enemies turn their
backs in flight,
and I destroyed my foes.
⁴¹They cried for help, but there was
no-one to save them—
to the LORD, but he did not
answer.
⁴²I beat them as fine as dust borne
on the wind;
I poured them out like mud in
the streets.
⁴³You have delivered me from the
attacks of the people;
you have made me the head of
nations;
people I did not know are subject
to me.
⁴⁴As soon as they hear me, they obey
me;
foreigners cringe before me.
⁴⁵They all lose heart;
they come trembling from their
strongholds.
⁴⁶The LORD lives! Praise be to my
Rock!
Exalted be God my Saviour!
⁴⁷He is the God who avenges me,

who subdues nations under me,
⁴⁸ who saves me from my enemies.
You exalted me above my foes;
from violent men you rescued
me.
⁴⁹Therefore I will praise you among
the nations, O LORD;
I will sing praises to your name.
⁵⁰He gives his king great victories;
he shows unfailing kindness to
his anointed,
to David and his descendants for
ever.

Psalm 19

For the director of music. A psalm of
David.

¹The heavens declare the glory of
God;
the skies proclaim the work of his
hands.
²Day after day they pour forth
speech;
night after night they display
knowledge.
³There is no speech or language
where their voice is not heard.^a
⁴Their voice^b goes out into all the
earth,
their words to the ends of the
world.

In the heavens he has pitched a
tent for the sun,
⁵ which is like a bridegroom
coming forth from his pavilion,
like a champion rejoicing to run
his course.
⁶It rises at one end of the heavens
and makes its circuit to the other;
nothing is hidden from its heat.

⁷The law of the LORD is perfect,
reviving the soul.
The statutes of the LORD are
trustworthy,
making wise the simple.
⁸The precepts of the LORD are right,
giving joy to the heart.
The commands of the LORD are
radiant,
giving light to the eyes.
⁹The fear of the LORD is pure,
enduring for ever.

^a3 Or They have no speech, there are no words; / no sound is heard from them
^b4 Septuagint, Jerome and Syriac; Hebrew line

The ordinances of the LORD are
sure
and altogether righteous.
10They are more precious than gold,
than much pure gold;
they are sweeter than honey,
than honey from the comb.
11By them is your servant warned;
in keeping them there is great
reward.

12Who can discern his errors?
Forgive my hidden faults.
13Keep your servant also from wilful
sins;
may they not rule over me.
Then will I be blameless,
innocent of great transgression.

14May the words of my mouth and
the meditation of my heart
be pleasing in your sight,
O LORD, my Rock and my
Redeemer.

Psalm 20

For the director of music. A psalm of
David.

1May the LORD answer you when
you are in distress;
may the name of the God of
Jacob protect you.
2May he send you help from the
sanctuary
and grant you support from Zion.
3May he remember all your
sacrifices
and accept your burnt
offerings.   Selah
4May he give you the desire of your
heart
and make all your plans succeed.
5We will shout for joy when you are
victorious
and will lift up our banners in
the name of our God.
May the LORD grant all your
requests.

6Now I know that the LORD saves his
anointed;
he answers him from his holy
heaven
with the saving power of his right
hand.

7Some trust in chariots and some in
horses,
but we trust in the name of the
LORD our God.
8They are brought to their knees and
fall,
but we rise up and stand firm.
9O LORD, save the king!
Answera us when we call!

Psalm 21

For the director of music. A psalm of
David.

1O LORD, the king rejoices in your
strength.
How great is his joy in the
victories you give!
2You have granted him the desire of
his heart
and have not withheld the
request of his lips.   Selah
3You welcomed him with rich
blessings
and placed a crown of pure gold
on his head.
4He asked you for life, and you gave
it to him—
length of days, for ever and ever.
5Through the victories you gave, his
glory is great;
you have bestowed on him
splendour and majesty.
6Surely you have granted him
eternal blessings
and made him glad with the joy
of your presence.
7For the king trusts in the LORD;
through the unfailing love of the
Most High
he will not be shaken.
8Your hand will lay hold on all your
enemies;
your right hand will seize your
foes.
9At the time of your appearing
you will make them like a fiery
furnace.
In his wrath the LORD will swallow
them up,
and his fire will consume them.
10You will destroy their descendants
from the earth,

a9 Or save! / O King, answer

their posterity from mankind.
11Though they plot evil against you
and devise wicked schemes, they
cannot succeed;
12for you will make them turn their
backs
when you aim at them with
drawn bow.

13Be exalted, O LORD, in your
strength;
we will sing and praise your
might.

Psalm 22

*For the director of music. To ,the tune
of, "The Doe of the Morning". A psalm
of David.*

1My God, my God, why have you
forsaken me?
Why are you so far from saving
me,
so far from the words of my
groaning?
2O my God, I cry out by day, but you
do not answer,
by night, and am not silent.

3Yet you are enthroned as the Holy
One;
you are the praise of Israel.ᵃ
4In you our fathers put their trust;
they trusted and you delivered
them.
5They cried to you and were saved;
in you they trusted and were not
disappointed.

6But I am a worm and not a man,
scorned by men and despised by
the people.
7All who see me mock me;
they hurl insults, shaking their
heads:
8"He trusts in the LORD;
let the LORD rescue him.
Let him deliver him,
since he delights in him."

9Yet you brought me out of the
womb;
you made me trust in you
even at my mother's breast.

10From birth I was cast upon you;
from my mother's womb you
have been my God.
11Do not be far from me,
for trouble is near
and there is no-one to help.

12Many bulls surround me;
strong bulls of Bashan encircle
me.
13Roaring lions tearing their prey
open their mouths wide against
me.
14I am poured out like water,
and all my bones are out of joint.
My heart has turned to wax;
it has melted away within me.
15My strength is dried up like a
potsherd,
and my tongue sticks to the roof
of my mouth;
you lay meᵇ in the dust of death.
16Dogs have surrounded me;
a band of evil men has encircled
me,
they have piercedᶜ my hands and
my feet.
17I can count all my bones;
people stare and gloat over me.
18They divide my garments among
them
and cast lots for my clothing.

19But you, O LORD, be not far off;
O my Strength, come quickly to
help me.
20Deliver my life from the sword,
my precious life from the power
of the dogs.
21Rescue me from the mouth of the
lions;
savedᵈ me from the horns of the
wild oxen.

22I will declare your name to my
brothers;
in the congregation I will praise
you.
23You who fear the LORD, praise him!
All you descendants of Jacob,
honour him!
Revere him, all you descendants
of Israel!

²⁴For he has not despised or
disdained
the suffering of the afflicted one;
he has not hidden his face from
him
but has listened to his cry for
help.

²⁵From you comes my praise in the
great assembly;
before those who fear you[e] will I
fulfil my vows.
²⁶The poor will eat and be satisfied;
they who seek the LORD will
praise him—
may your hearts live for ever!
²⁷All the ends of the earth
will remember and turn to the
LORD,
and all the families of the nations
will bow down before him,
²⁸for dominion belongs to the LORD
and he rules over the nations.

²⁹All the rich of the earth will feast
and worship;
all who go down to the dust will
kneel before him—
those who cannot keep
themselves alive.
³⁰Posterity will serve him;
future generations will be told
about the LORD.
³¹They will proclaim his
righteousness
to a people yet unborn—
for he has done it.

Psalm 23

A psalm of David.

¹The LORD is my shepherd, I shall
lack nothing.
2 He makes me lie down in green
pastures,
he leads me beside quiet waters,
3 he restores my soul.
He guides me in paths of
righteousness
for his name's sake.
⁴Even though I walk
through the valley of the shadow
of death,[a]
I will fear no evil,
for you are with me;

your rod and your staff,
they comfort me.
⁵You prepare a table before me
in the presence of my enemies.
You anoint my head with oil;
my cup overflows.
⁶Surely goodness and love will
follow me
all the days of my life,
and I will dwell in the house of the
LORD
for ever.

Psalm 24

Of David. A psalm.

¹The earth is the LORD's, and
everything in it,
the world, and all who live in it;
²for he founded it upon the seas
and established it upon the
waters.

³Who may ascend the hill of the
LORD?
Who may stand in his holy place?
⁴He who has clean hands and a pure
heart,
who does not lift up his soul to
an idol
or swear by what is false.
⁵He will receive blessing from the
LORD
and vindication from God his
Saviour.
⁶Such is the generation of those who
seek him,
who seek your face, O God of
Jacob.[a]   Selah

⁷Lift up your heads, O you gates;
be lifted up, you ancient doors,
that the King of glory may come
in.
⁸Who is this King of glory?
The LORD strong and mighty,
the LORD mighty in battle.
⁹Lift up your heads, O you gates;
lift them up, you ancient doors,
that the King of glory may come
in.
¹⁰Who is he, this King of glory?
The LORD Almighty—
he is the King of glory.   Selah

---

e25 Hebrew him   a4 Or through the darkest valley
a6 Two Hebrew manuscripts and Syriac (see also Septuagint); most Hebrew manuscripts face,
Jacob

Psalm 25[a]
Of David.

[1]To you, O LORD, I lift up my soul;
[2] in you I trust, O my God.
Do not let me be put to shame,
nor let my enemies triumph over
me.

[3]No-one whose hope is in you
will ever be put to shame,
but they will be put to shame
who are treacherous without
excuse.

[4]Show me your ways, O LORD,
teach me your paths;
[5]guide me in your truth and teach
me,
for you are God my Saviour,
and my hope is in you all day
long.

[6]Remember, O LORD, your great
mercy and love,
for they are from of old.
[7]Remember not the sins of my youth
and my rebellious ways;
according to your love remember
me,
for you are good, O LORD.

[8]Good and upright is the LORD;
therefore he instructs sinners in
his ways.
[9]He guides the humble in what is
right
and teaches them his way.
[10]All the ways of the LORD are loving
and faithful
for those who keep the demands
of his covenant.
[11]For the sake of your name, O LORD,
forgive my iniquity, though it is
great.
[12]Who, then, is the man that fears
the LORD?
He will instruct him in the way
chosen for him.
[13]He will spend his days in
prosperity,
and his descendants will inherit
the land.
[14]The LORD confides in those who
fear him;
he makes his covenant known to
them.

[15]My eyes are ever on the LORD,
for only he will release my feet
from the snare.
[16]Turn to me and be gracious to me,
for I am lonely and afflicted.
[17]The troubles of my heart have
multiplied;
free me from my anguish.
[18]Look upon my affliction and my
distress
and take away all my sins.
[19]See how my enemies have
increased
and how fiercely they hate me!
[20]Guard my life and rescue me;
let me not be put to shame,
for I take refuge in you.
[21]May integrity and uprightness
protect me,
because my hope is in you.
[22]Redeem Israel, O God,
from all their troubles!

Psalm 26
Of David.

[1]Vindicate me, O LORD,
for I have led a blameless life;
I have trusted in the LORD
without wavering.
[2]Test me, O LORD, and try me,
examine my heart and my mind;
[3]for your love is ever before me,
and I walk continually in your
truth.
[4]I do not sit with deceitful men,
nor do I consort with hypocrites;
[5]I abhor the assembly of evildoers
and refuse to sit with the wicked.
[6]I wash my hands in innocence,
and go about your altar, O LORD,
[7]proclaiming aloud your praise
and telling of all your wonderful
deeds.
[8]I love the house where you live, O
LORD,
the place where your glory
dwells.
[9]Do not take away my soul along
with sinners
or my life with bloodthirsty men,
[10]in whose hands are wicked
schemes,

---

[a]This psalm is an acrostic poem, the verses of which begin with the successive letters of the
Hebrew alphabet.

whose right hands are full of
bribes.
11But I lead a blameless life;
redeem me and be merciful to
me.

12My feet stand on level ground;
in the great assembly I will praise
the LORD.

Psalm 27
Of David.

1The LORD is my light and my
salvation—
whom shall I fear?
The LORD is the stronghold of my
life—
of whom shall I be afraid?
2When evil men advance against me
to devour my flesh,[a]
when my enemies and my foes
attack me,
they will stumble and fall.
3Though an army besiege me,
my heart will not fear;
though war break out against me,
even then will I be confident.

4One thing I ask of the LORD,
this is what I seek:
that I may dwell in the house of the
LORD
all the days of my life,
to gaze upon the beauty of the LORD
and to seek him in his temple.
5For in the day of trouble
he will keep me safe in his
dwelling;
he will hide me in the shelter of his
tabernacle
and set me high upon a rock.
6Then my head will be exalted
above the enemies who surround
me;
at his tabernacle will I sacrifice
with shouts of joy;
I will sing and make music to the
LORD.

7Hear my voice when I call, O LORD;
be merciful to me and answer
me.
8My heart says of you, "Seek his[b]
face!"
Your face, LORD, I will seek.

9Do not hide your face from me,
do not turn your servant away in
anger;
you have been my helper.
Do not reject me or forsake me,
O God my Saviour.
10Though my father and mother
forsake me,
the LORD will receive me.
11Teach me your way, O LORD;
lead me in a straight path
because of my oppressors.
12Do not hand me over to the desire
of my foes,
for false witnesses rise up against
me,
breathing out violence.
13I am still confident of this:
I will see the goodness of the
LORD
in the land of the living.
14Wait for the LORD;
be strong and take heart
and wait for the LORD.

Psalm 28
Of David.

1To you I call, O LORD my Rock;
do not turn a deaf ear to me.
For if you remain silent,
I shall be like those who have
gone down to the pit.
2Hear my cry for mercy
as I call to you for help,
as I lift up my hands
towards your Most Holy Place.

3Do not drag me away with the
wicked,
with those who do evil,
who speak cordially with their
neighbours
but harbour malice in their
hearts.
4Repay them for their deeds
and for their evil work;
repay them for what their hands
have done
and bring back upon them what
they deserve.
5Since they show no regard for the
works of the LORD
and what his hands have done,
he will tear them down
and never build them up again.

---

a2 Or to slander me   *b8 Or To you, O my heart, he has said, "Seek my*

⁶Praise be to the LORD,
for he has heard my cry for
mercy.
⁷The LORD is my strength and my
shield;
my heart trusts in him, and I am
helped.
My heart leaps for joy
and I will give thanks to him in
song.
⁸The LORD is the strength of his
people,
a fortress of salvation for his
anointed one.
⁹Save your people and bless your
inheritance;
be their shepherd and carry them
for ever.

Psalm 29

A psalm of David.

¹Ascribe to the LORD, O mighty ones,
ascribe to the LORD glory and
strength.
²Ascribe to the LORD the glory due to
his name;
worship the LORD in the
splendour of his[a] holiness.
³The voice of the LORD is over the
waters;
the God of glory thunders,
the LORD thunders over the
mighty waters.
⁴The voice of the LORD is powerful;
the voice of the LORD is majestic.
⁵The voice of the LORD breaks the
cedars;
the LORD breaks in pieces the
cedars of Lebanon.
⁶He makes Lebanon skip like a calf,
Sirion[b] like a young wild ox.
⁷The voice of the LORD strikes
with flashes of lightning.
⁸The voice of the LORD shakes the
desert;
the LORD shakes the Desert of
Kadesh.
⁹The voice of the LORD twists the
oaks[c]
and strips the forests bare.

And in his temple all cry, "Glory!"
¹⁰The LORD sits[d] enthroned over the
flood;
the LORD is enthroned as King for
ever.
¹¹The LORD gives strength to his
people;
the LORD blesses his people with
peace.

Psalm 30

A psalm. A song. For the dedication of
the temple.[a] Of David.

¹I will exalt you, O LORD,
for you lifted me out of the
depths
and did not let my enemies gloat
over me.
²O LORD my God, I called to you for
help
and you healed me.
³O LORD, you brought me up from
the grave;[b]
you spared me from going down
into the pit.
⁴Sing to the LORD, you saints of his;
praise his holy name.
⁵For his anger lasts only a moment,
but his favour lasts a lifetime;
weeping may remain for a night,
but rejoicing comes in the
morning.
⁶When I felt secure, I said,
"I shall never be shaken."
⁷O LORD, when you favoured me,
you made my mountain[c] stand
firm;
but when you hid your face,
I was dismayed.
⁸To you, O LORD, I called;
to the Lord I cried for mercy:
⁹"What gain is there in my
destruction,[d]
in my going down into the pit?
Will the dust praise you?
Will it proclaim your
faithfulness?
¹⁰Hear, O LORD, and be merciful to
me;
O LORD, be my help."

---

*a*2 Or LORD with the splendour of   *b*6 That is, Mount Hermon
*c*9 Or LORD makes the deer give birth
*d*10 Or sat   *e*Title: Or palace   *b*3 Hebrew Sheol   *c*7 Or hill country
*d*9 Or there if I am silenced

11You turned my wailing into
dancing;
you removed my sackcloth and
clothed me with joy,
12that my heart may sing to you and
not be silent.
O LORD my God, I will give you
thanks for ever.

Psalm 31

For the director of music. A psalm of
David.

1In you, O LORD, I have taken
refuge;
let me never be put to shame;
deliver me in your righteousness.
2Turn your ear to me,
come quickly to my rescue;
be my rock of refuge,
a strong fortress to save me.
3Since you are my rock and my
fortress,
for the sake of your name lead
and guide me.
4Free me from the trap that is set for
me,
for you are my refuge.
5Into your hands I commit my spirit;
redeem me, O LORD, the God of
truth.

6I hate those who cling to worthless
idols;
I trust in the LORD.
7I will be glad and rejoice in your
love,
for you saw my affliction
and knew the anguish of my soul.
8You have not handed me over to the
enemy
but have set my feet in a spacious
place.

9Be merciful to me, O LORD, for I am
in distress;
my eyes grow weak with sorrow,
my soul and my body with grief.
10My life is consumed by anguish
and my years by groaning;
my strength fails because of my
affliction,a
and my bones grow weak.
11Because of all my enemies,
I am the utter contempt of my
neighbours;
I am a dread to my friends—

those who see me on the street
flee from me.
12I am forgotten by them as though I
were dead;
I have become like broken
pottery.
13For I hear the slander of many;
there is terror on every side;
they conspire against me
and plot to take my life.

14But I trust in you, O LORD;
I say, "You are my God."
15My times are in your hands;
deliver me from my enemies
and from those who pursue me.
16Let your face shine on your
servant;
save me in your unfailing love.
17Let me not be put to shame, O
LORD,
for I have cried out to you;
but let the wicked be put to shame
and lie silent in the grave.b
18Let their lying lips be silenced,
for with pride and contempt
they speak arrogantly against the
righteous.

19How great is your goodness,
which you have stored up for
those who fear you,
which you bestow in the sight of
men
on those who take refuge in you.
20In the shelter of your presence you
hide them
from the intrigues of men;
in your dwelling you keep them
safe
from the strife of tongues.

21Praise be to the LORD,
for he showed his wonderful love
to me
when I was in a besieged city.
22In my alarm I said,
"I am cut off from your sight!"
Yet you heard my cry for mercy
when I called to you for help.
23Love the LORD, all his saints!
The LORD preserves the faithful,
but the proud he pays back in
full.
24Be strong and take heart,
all you who hope in the LORD.

a10 Or guilt   b17 Hebrew Sheol

Psalm 32

Of David. A *maskil.[a]*

[1]Blessed is he
whose transgressions are
forgiven,
whose sins are covered.
[2]Blessed is the man
whose sin the LORD does not
count against him
and in whose spirit is no deceit.

[3]When I kept silent,
my bones wasted away
through my groaning all day long.
[4]For day and night
your hand was heavy upon me;
my strength was sapped
as in the heat of summer.   Selah
[5]Then I acknowledged my sin to you
and did not cover up my iniquity.
I said, "I will confess
my transgressions to the LORD"—
and you forgave
the guilt of my sin.   Selah

[6]Therefore let everyone who is godly
pray to you
while you may be found;
surely when the mighty waters rise,
they will not reach him.
[7]You are my hiding place;
you will protect me from trouble
and surround me with songs of
deliverance.   Selah

[8]I will instruct you and teach you in
the way you should go;
I will counsel you and watch
over you.
[9]Do not be like the horse or the
mule,
which have no understanding
but must be controlled by bit and
bridle
or they will not come to you.
[10]Many are the woes of the wicked,
but the LORD's unfailing love
surrounds the man who trusts in
him.
[11]Rejoice in the LORD and be glad,
you righteous;
sing, all you who are upright in
heart!

Psalm 33

[1]Sing joyfully to the LORD, you
righteous;
it is fitting for the upright to
praise him.
[2]Praise the LORD with the harp;
make music to him on the ten-
stringed lyre.
[3]Sing to him a new song;
play skilfully, and shout for joy.

[4]For the word of the LORD is right
and true;
he is faithful in all he does.
[5]The LORD loves righteousness and
justice;
the earth is full of his unfailing
love.

[6]By the word of the LORD were the
heavens made,
their starry host by the breath of
his mouth.
[7]He gathers the waters of the sea
into jars;[a]
he puts the deep into storehouses.
[8]Let all the earth fear the LORD;
let all the people of the world
revere him.
[9]For he spoke, and it came to be;
he commanded, and it stood firm.
[10]The LORD foils the plans of the
nations;
he thwarts the purposes of the
peoples.
[11]But the plans of the LORD stand
firm for ever,
the purposes of his heart through
all generations.

[12]Blessed is the nation whose God is
the LORD,
the people he chose for his
inheritance.
[13]From heaven the LORD looks down
and sees all mankind;
[14]from his dwelling-place he watches
all who live on earth—
[15]he who forms the hearts of all,
who considers everything they
do.
[16]No king is saved by the size of his
army;

---

[a]Title: Probably a literary or musical term

[a]7 Or *sea as into a heap*

no warrior escapes by his great
strength.
17A horse is a vain hope for
deliverance;
despite all its great strength it
cannot save.
18But the eyes of the LORD are on
those who fear him,
on those whose hope is in his
unfailing love,
19to deliver them from death
and keep them alive in famine.
20We wait in hope for the LORD;
he is our help and our shield.
21In him our hearts rejoice,
for we trust in his holy name.
22May your unfailing love rest upon
us, O LORD,
even as we put our hope in you.

Psalm 34*a*

Of David. When he feigned insanity
before Abimelech, who drove him away,
and he left.

1I will extol the LORD at all times;
his praise will always be on my
lips.
2My soul will boast in the LORD;
let the afflicted hear and rejoice.
3Glorify the LORD with me;
let us exalt his name together.
4I sought the LORD, and he answered
me;
he delivered me from all my
fears.
5Those who look to him are radiant;
their faces are never covered
with shame.
6This poor man called, and the LORD
heard him;
he saved him out of all his
troubles.
7The angel of the LORD encamps
around those who fear him,
and he delivers them.
8Taste and see that the LORD is good;
blessed is the man who takes
refuge in him.
9Fear the LORD, you his saints,
for those who fear him lack
nothing.

10The lions may grow weak and
hungry,
but those who seek the LORD lack
no good thing.
11Come, my children, listen to me;
I will teach you the fear of the
LORD.
12Whoever of you loves life
and desires to see many good
days,
13keep your tongue from evil
and your lips from speaking lies.
14Turn from evil and do good;
seek peace and pursue it.
15The eyes of the LORD are on the
righteous
and his ears are attentive to their
cry;
16the face of the LORD is against
those who do evil,
to cut off the memory of them
from the earth.
17The righteous cry out, and the
LORD hears them;
he delivers them from all their
troubles.
18The LORD is close to the broken-
hearted
and saves those who are crushed
in spirit.
19A righteous man may have many
troubles,
but the LORD delivers him from
them all;
20he protects all his bones,
not one of them will be broken.
21Evil will slay the wicked;
the foes of the righteous will be
condemned.
22The LORD redeems his servants;
no-one who takes refuge in him
will be condemned.

Psalm 35

Of David.

1Contend, O LORD, with those who
contend with me;
fight against those who fight
against me.
2Take up shield and buckler;
arise and come to my aid.
3Brandish spear and javelin*a*

*a*This psalm is an acrostic poem, the verses of which begin with the successive letters of the
Hebrew alphabet.   *a*3 Or *and block the way*

against those who pursue me.
Say to my soul,
"I am your salvation."

4May those who seek my life
be disgraced and put to shame;
may those who plot my ruin
be turned back in dismay;
5May they be like chaff before the
wind,
with the angel of the LORD
driving them away;
6may their path be dark and
slippery,
with the angel of the LORD
pursuing them.
7Since they hid their net for me
without cause
and without cause dug a pit for
me,
8may ruin overtake them by
surprise—
may the net they hid entangle
them,
may they fall into the pit, to their
ruin.
9Then my soul will rejoice in the
LORD
and delight in his salvation.
10My whole being will exclaim,
"Who is like you, O LORD?
You rescue the poor from those too
strong for them,
the poor and needy from those
who rob them."

11Ruthless witnesses come forward;
they question me on things I
know nothing about.
12They repay me evil for good
and leave my soul forlorn.
13Yet when they were ill, I put on
sackcloth
and humbled myself with fasting.
When my prayers returned to me
unanswered,
14 I went about mourning
as though for my friend or
brother.
I bowed my head in grief
as though weeping for my
mother.
15But when I stumbled, they
gathered in glee;
attackers gathered against me

when I was unaware.
They slandered me without
ceasing.
16Like the ungodly they maliciously
mocked;[b]
they gnashed their teeth at me.

17O LORD, how long will you look
on?
Rescue my life from their
ravages,
my precious life from these lions.
18I will give you thanks in the great
assembly;
among throngs of people I will
praise you.
19Let not those gloat over me
who are my enemies without
cause;
let not those who hate me without
reason
maliciously wink the eye.
20They do not speak peaceably,
but devise false accusations
against those who live quietly in
the land.
21They gape at me and say, "Aha!
Aha!
With our own eyes we have seen
it."

22O LORD, you have seen this; be not
silent.
Do not be far from me, O LORD.
23Awake, and rise to my defence!
Contend for me, my God and
LORD.
24Vindicate me in your
righteousness, O LORD my God;
do not let them gloat over me.
25Do not let them think, "Aha, just
what we wanted!"
or say, "We have swallowed him
up."
26May all who gloat over my distress
be put to shame and confusion;
may all who exalt themselves over
me
be clothed with shame and
disgrace.
27May those who delight in my
vindication
shout for joy and gladness;
may they always say, "The LORD be
exalted,

_b16_ Septuagint; Hebrew may mean _ungodly circle of mockers._

who delights in the well-being of
his servant."
28My tongue will speak of your
righteousness
and of your praises all day long.

Psalm 36

For the director of music. Of David the
servant of the LORD.

1An oracle is within my heart
concerning the sinfulness of the
wicked:[a]
There is no fear of God
before his eyes.
2For in his own eyes he flatters
himself
too much to detect or hate his sin.
3The words of his mouth are wicked
and deceitful;
he has ceased to be wise and to
do good.
4Even on his bed he plots evil;
he commits himself to a sinful
course
and does not reject what is
wrong.
5Your love, O LORD, reaches to the
heavens,
your faithfulness to the skies.
6Your righteousness is like the
mighty mountains,
your justice like the great deep.
O LORD, you preserve both man
and beast.
7 How priceless is your unfailing
love!
Both high and low among men
find[b] refuge in the shadow of
your wings.
8They feast in the abundance of your
house;
you give them drink from your
river of delights.
9For with you is the fountain of life;
in your light we see light.
10Continue your love to those who
know you,
your righteousness to the upright
in heart.
11May the foot of the proud not come
against me,

nor the hand of the wicked drive
me away.
12See how the evildoers lie fallen—
thrown down, not able to rise!

Psalm 37[a]
Of David.

1Do not fret because of evil men
or be envious of those who do
wrong;
2for like the grass they will soon
wither,
like green plants they will soon
die away.

3Trust in the LORD and do good;
dwell in the land and enjoy safe
pasture.
4Delight yourself in the LORD
and he will give you the desires
of your heart.

5Commit your way to the LORD;
trust in him and he will do this:
6He will make your righteousness
shine like the dawn,
the justice of your cause like the
noonday sun.

7Be still before the LORD and wait
patiently for him;
do not fret when men succeed in
their ways,
when they carry out their wicked
schemes.

8Refrain from anger and turn from
wrath;
do not fret—it leads only to evil.
9For evil men will be cut off,
but those who hope in the LORD
will inherit the land.

10A little while, and the wicked will
be no more;
though you look for them, they
will not be found.
11But the meek will inherit the land
and enjoy great peace.

12The wicked plot against the
righteous
and gnash their teeth at them;
13but the Lord laughs at the wicked,
for he knows their day is coming.

a1 Or heart: / Sin proceeds from the wicked.
b7 Or love, O God! / Men find; or love! / Both heavenly beings and men / find
aThis psalm is an acrostic poem, the stanzas of which begin with the successive letters of the
Hebrew alphabet.

¹⁴The wicked draw the sword
and bend the bow
to bring down the poor and needy,
to slay those whose ways are
upright.
¹⁵But their swords will pierce their
own hearts,
and their bows will be broken.
¹⁶Better the little that the righteous
have
than the wealth of many wicked;
¹⁷for the power of the wicked will be
broken,
but the LORD upholds the
righteous.
¹⁸The days of the blameless are
known to the LORD,
and their inheritance will endure
for ever.
¹⁹In times of disaster they will not
wither;
in days of famine they will enjoy
plenty.
²⁰But the wicked will perish:
The LORD's enemies will be like
the beauty of the fields,
they will vanish—vanish like
smoke.
²¹The wicked borrow and do not
repay,
but the righteous give generously;
²²those the LORD blesses will inherit
the land,
but those he curses will be cut
off.
²³The LORD delights in the way of the
man
whose steps he has made firm;
²⁴though he stumble, he will not fall,
for the LORD upholds him with
his hand.
²⁵I was young and now I am old,
yet I have never seen the
righteous forsaken
or their children begging bread.
²⁶They are always generous and lend
freely;
their children will be blessed.
²⁷Turn from evil and do good;
then you will always live
securely.

²⁸For the LORD loves the just
and will not forsake his faithful
ones.

They will be protected for ever,
but the offspring of the wicked
will be cut off;
²⁹the righteous will inherit the land
and dwell in it for ever.
³⁰The mouth of the righteous man
utters wisdom,
and his tongue speaks what is
just.
³¹The law of his God is in his heart;
his feet do not slip.
³²The wicked lie in wait for the
righteous,
seeking their very lives;
³³but the LORD will not leave them in
their power
or let them be condemned when
brought to trial.
³⁴Wait for the LORD
and keep his way.
He will exalt you to possess the
land;
when the wicked are cut off, you
will see it.
³⁵I have seen a wicked and ruthless
man
flourishing like a green tree in its
native soil,
³⁶but he soon passed away and was
no more;
though I looked for him, he could
not be found.
³⁷Consider the blameless, observe
the upright;
there is a future[b] for the man of
peace.
³⁸But all sinners will be destroyed;
the future[c] of the wicked will be
cut off.
³⁹The salvation of the righteous
comes from the LORD;
he is their stronghold in time of
trouble.
⁴⁰The LORD helps them and delivers
them;
he delivers them from the wicked
and saves them,
because they take refuge in him.

b37 Or there will be posterity   c38 Or posterity

Psalm 38

A psalm of David. A petition.

1O LORD, do not rebuke me in your
anger
    or discipline me in your wrath.
2For your arrows have pierced me,
    and your hand has come down
        upon me.
3Because of your wrath there is no
    health in my body;
    my bones have no soundness
        because of my sin.
4My guilt has overwhelmed me
    like a burden too heavy to bear.

5My wounds fester and are
    loathsome
    because of my sinful folly.
6I am bowed down and brought very
    low;
    all day long I go about mourning.
7My back is filled with searing pain;
    there is no health in my body.
8I am feeble and utterly crushed;
    I groan in anguish of heart.

9All my longings lie open before you,
    O LORD;
    my sighing is not hidden from
        you.
10My heart pounds, my strength fails
    me;
    even the light has gone from my
        eyes.
11My friends and companions avoid
    me because of my wounds;
    my neighbours stay far away.
12Those who seek my life set their
    traps,
    those who would harm me talk of
        my ruin;
    all day long they plot deception.

13I am like a deaf man, who cannot
    hear,
    like a mute, who cannot open his
        mouth;
14I have become like a man who
    does not hear,
    whose mouth can offer no reply.
15I wait for you, O LORD;
    you will answer, O Lord my God.
16For I said, "Do not let them gloat
    or exalt themselves over me
        when my foot slips."

17For I am about to fall,
    and my pain is ever with me.

18I confess my iniquity;
    I am troubled by my sin.
19Many are those who are my
    vigorous enemies;
    those who hate me without
        reason are numerous.
20Those who repay my good with
    evil
    slander me when I seek what is
        good.

21O LORD, do not forsake me;
    be not far from me, O my God.
22Come quickly to help me,
    O LORD my Saviour.

Psalm 39

For the director of music. For Jeduthun.
A psalm of David.

1I said, "I will watch my ways
    and keep my tongue from sin;
    I will put a muzzle on my mouth
        as long as the wicked are in my
            presence."
2But when I was silent and still,
    not even saying anything good,
    my anguish increased.
3My heart grew hot within me,
    and as I meditated, the fire
        burned;
    then I spoke with my tongue:

4"Show me, O LORD, my life's end
    and the number of my days;
    let me know how fleeting is my
        life.
5You have made my days a mere
    handbreadth;
    the span of my years is as nothing
        before you.
    Each man's life is but a breath.
                                    Selah
6Man is a mere phantom as he goes
    to and fro:
    He bustles about, but only in
        vain;
    he heaps up wealth, not knowing
        who will get it.

7"But now, Lord, what do I look for?
    My hope is in you.
8Save me from all my transgressions;
    do not make me the scorn of
        fools.
9I was silent; I would not open my
    mouth,

315

for you are the one who has done
this.
¹⁰Remove your scourge from me;
I am overcome by the blow of
your hand.
¹¹You rebuke and discipline men for
their sin;
you consume their wealth like a
moth—
each man is but a breath.   *Selah*

¹²"Hear my prayer, O LORD,
listen to my cry for help;
be not deaf to my weeping.
For I dwell with you as an alien,
a stranger, as all my fathers were.
¹³Look away from me, that I may
rejoice again
before I depart and am no more."

Psalm 40

For the director of music. Of David.
A psalm.

¹I waited patiently for the LORD;
he turned to me and heard my
cry.
²He lifted me out of the slimy pit,
out of the mud and mire;
he set my feet on a rock
and gave me a firm place to
stand.
³He put a new song in my mouth,
a hymn of praise to our God.
Many will see and fear
and put their trust in the LORD.

⁴Blessed is the man
who makes the LORD his trust,
who does not look to the proud,
to those who turn aside to false
gods.ᵃ
⁵Many, O LORD my God,
are the wonders you have done.
The things you planned for us
no-one can recount to you;
were I to speak and tell of them,
they would be too many to
declare.

⁶Sacrifice and offering you did not
desire,
but my ears you have pierced;ᵇ·ᶜ
burnt offerings and sin offerings
you did not require.

⁷Then I said, "Here I am, I have
come—
it is written about me in the
scroll.ᵈ
⁸I desire to do your will, O my God;
your law is within my heart."
⁹I proclaim righteousness in the great
assembly;
I do not seal my lips,
as you know, O LORD.
¹⁰I do not hide your righteousness in
my heart;
I speak of your faithfulness and
salvation.
I do not conceal your love and your
truth
from the great assembly.

¹¹Do not withhold your mercy from
me, O LORD;
may your love and your truth
always protect me.
¹²For troubles without number
surround me;
my sins have overtaken me, and I
cannot see.
They are more than the hairs of my
head,
and my heart fails within me.

¹³Be pleased, O LORD, to save me;
O LORD, come quickly to help me.
¹⁴May all who seek to take my life
be put to shame and confusion;
may all who desire my ruin
be turned back in disgrace.
¹⁵May those who say to me, "Aha!
Aha!"
be appalled at their own shame.
¹⁶But may all who seek you
rejoice and be glad in you;
may those who love your salvation
always say,
"The LORD be exalted!"

¹⁷Yet I am poor and needy;
may the Lord think of me.
You are my help and my deliverer;
O my God, do not delay.

Psalm 41

For the director of music. A psalm of
David.

¹Blessed is he who has regard for the
weak;

ᵃ4 Or to falsehood
ᵇ6 Hebrew; Septuagint but a body you have prepared for me (see also Symmachus and
Theodotion)
ᶜ6 Or opened   ᵈ7 Or come / with the scroll written for me

the LORD delivers him in times of
trouble.
²The LORD will protect him and
preserve his life;
he will bless him in the land
and not surrender him to the
desire of his foes.
³The LORD will sustain him on his
sick-bed
and restore him from his bed of
illness.

⁴I said, "O LORD, have mercy on me;
heal me, for I have sinned
against you."
⁵My enemies say of me in malice,
"When will he die and his name
perish?"
⁶Whenever one comes to see me,
he speaks falsely, while his heart
gathers slander;
then he goes out and spreads it
abroad.
⁷All my enemies whisper together
against me;
they imagine the worst for me,
saying,
⁸"A vile disease has beset him;
he will never get up from the
place where he lies."
⁹Even my close friend, whom I
trusted,
he who shared my bread,
has lifted up his heel against me.

¹⁰But you, O LORD, have mercy on
me;
raise me up, that I may repay
them.
¹¹I know that you are pleased with
me,
for my enemy does not triumph
over me.
¹²In my integrity you uphold me
and set me in your presence for
ever.

¹³Praise be to the LORD, the God of
Israel,
from everlasting to everlasting.
Amen and Amen.

BOOK II

Psalms 42–72

Psalm 42ᵃ

For the director of music. A *maskil* ᵇ of
the Sons of Korah.

¹As the deer pants for streams of
water,
so my soul pants for you, O God.
²My soul thirsts for God, for the
living God.
When can I go and meet with
God?
³My tears have been my food
day and night,
while men say to me all day long,
"Where is your God?"
⁴These things I remember
as I pour out my soul:
how I used to go with the
multitude,
leading the procession to the
house of God,
with shouts of joy and thanksgiving
among the festive throng.
⁵Why are you downcast, O my soul?
Why so disturbed within me?
Put your hope in God,
for I will yet praise him,
my Saviour and ⁶my God.

Myᶜ soul is downcast within me;
therefore I will remember you
from the land of the Jordan,
the heights of Hermon—from
Mount Mizar.
⁷Deep calls to deep
in the roar of your waterfalls;
all your waves and breakers
have swept over me.
⁸By day the LORD directs his love,
at night his song is with me—
a prayer to the God of my life.
⁹I say to God my Rock,
"Why have you forgotten me?
Why must I go about mourning,
oppressed by the enemy?"
¹⁰My bones suffer mortal agony
as my foes taunt me,

ᵃIn many Hebrew manuscripts Psalms 42 and 43 constitute one psalm.
ᵇTitle: Probably a literary or musical term
ᶜ5, 6 A few Hebrew manuscripts, Septuagint and Syriac; most Hebrew manuscripts *praise him
for his saving help.* / *O my God, my*

saying to me all day long,
"Where is your God?"

11Why are you downcast, O my soul?
Why so disturbed within me?
Put your hope in God,
for I will yet praise him,
my Saviour and my God.

Psalm 43[a]

1Vindicate me, O God,
and plead my cause against an
ungodly nation;
rescue me from deceitful and
wicked men.
2You are God my stronghold.
Why have you rejected me?
Why must I go about mourning,
oppressed by the enemy?
3Send forth your light and your truth,
let them guide me;
let them bring me to your holy
mountain,
to the place where you dwell.
4Then will I go to the altar of God,
to God, my joy and my delight.
I will praise you with the harp,
O God, my God.

5Why are you downcast, O my soul?
Why so disturbed within me?
Put your hope in God,
for I will yet praise him,
my Saviour and my God.

Psalm 44

For the director of music. Of the Sons of
Korah. A maskil.[a]

1We have heard with our ears, O
God;
our fathers have told us
what you did in their days,
in days long ago.
2With your hand you drove out the
nations
and planted our fathers;
you crushed the peoples
and made our fathers flourish.
3It was not by their sword that they
won the land,
nor did their arm bring them
victory;
it was your right hand, your arm,

and the light of your face, for you
loved them.

4You are my King and my God,
who decrees[b] victories for Jacob.
5Through you we push back our
enemies;
through your name we trample
our foes.
6I do not trust in my bow,
my sword does not bring me
victory;
7but you give us victory over our
enemies,
you put our adversaries to shame.
8In God we make our boast all day
long,
and we will praise your name for
ever.   Selah

9But now you have rejected and
humbled us;
you no longer go out with our
armies.
10You made us retreat before the
enemy,
and our adversaries have
plundered us.
11You gave us up to be devoured like
sheep
and have scattered us among the
nations.
12You sold your people for a
pittance,
gaining nothing from their sale.

13You have made us a reproach to
our neighbours,
the scorn and derision of those
around us.
14You have made us a byword
among the nations;
the peoples shake their heads at
us.
15My disgrace is before me all day
long,
and my face is covered with
shame
16at the taunts of those who reproach
and revile me,
because of the enemy, who is
bent on revenge.
17All this happened to us,
though we had not forgotten you
or been false to your covenant.

_a_Title: Probably a literary or musical term
_b_4 Septuagint, Aquila and Syriac; Hebrew _King, O God; / command_

18Our hearts had not turned back;
  our feet had not strayed from
  your path.
19But you crushed us and made us a
  haunt for jackals
  and covered us over with deep
  darkness.
20If we had forgotten the name of
  our God
  or spread out our hands to a
  foreign god,
21would not God have discovered it,
  since he knows the secrets of the
  heart?
22Yet for your sake we face death all
  day long;
  we are considered as sheep to be
  slaughtered.
23Awake, O Lord! Why do you sleep?
  Rouse yourself! Do not reject us
  for ever.
24Why do you hide your face
  and forget our misery and
  oppression?
25We are brought down to the dust;
  our bodies cling to the ground.
26Rise up and help us;
  redeem us because of your
  unfailing love.

Psalm 45

For the director of music. To the tune
of, "Lilies". Of the Sons of Korah. A
maskil.a A wedding song.

1My heart is stirred by a noble
  theme
  as I recite my verses for the king;
  my tongue is the pen of a skilful
  writer.
2You are the most excellent of men
  and your lips have been anointed
  with grace,
  since God has blessed you for
  ever.
3Gird your sword upon your side, O
  mighty one;
  clothe yourself with splendour
  and majesty.
4In your majesty ride forth
  victoriously
  on behalf of truth, humility and
  righteousness;

*a*Title: Probably a literary or musical term
*b*12 Or *A Tyrian robe is among the gifts*

let your right hand display
  awesome deeds.
5Let your sharp arrows pierce the
  hearts of the king's enemies;
  let the nations fall beneath your
  feet.
6Your throne, O God, will last for
  ever and ever;
  a sceptre of justice will be the
  sceptre of your kingdom.
7You love righteousness and hate
  wickedness;
  therefore God, your God, has set
  you above your companions
  by anointing you with the oil of
  joy.
8All your robes are fragrant with
  myrrh and aloes and cassia;
  from palaces adorned with ivory
  the music of the strings makes
  you glad.
9Daughters of kings are among your
  honoured women;
  at your right hand is the royal
  bride in gold of Ophir.
10Listen, O daughter, consider and
  give ear:
  Forget your people and your
  father's house.
11The king is enthralled by your
  beauty;
  honour him, for he is your lord.
12The Daughter of Tyre will come
  with a gift,b
  men of wealth will seek your
  favour.
13All glorious is the princess within
  her chamber,:
  her gown is interwoven with
  gold.
14In embroidered garments she is led
  to the king;
  her virgin companions follow her
  and are brought to you.
15They are led in with joy and
  gladness;
  they enter the palace of the king.
16Your sons will take the place of
  your fathers;
  you will make them princes
  throughout the land.
17I will perpetuate your memory
  through all generations;

therefore the nations will praise
you for ever and ever.

Psalm 46

For the director of music. Of the Sons of
Korah. According to *alamoth.*[a] A song.

[1]God is our refuge and strength,
an ever present help in trouble.
[2]Therefore we will not fear, though
the earth give way
and the mountains fall into the
heart of the sea,
[3]though its waters roar and foam
and the mountains quake with
their surging. *Selah*

[4]There is a river whose streams
make glad the city of God,
the holy place where the Most
High dwells.
[5]God is within her, she will not fall;
God will help her at break of
day.
[6]Nations are in uproar, kingdoms
fall;
he lifts his voice, the earth melts.

[7]The LORD Almighty is with us;
the God of Jacob is our fortress.
Selah

[8]Come and see the works of the
LORD,
the desolations he has brought on
the earth.
[9]He makes wars cease to the ends of
the earth;
he breaks the bow and shatters
the spear,
he burns the shields[b] with fire.
[10]"Be still, and know that I am God;
I will be exalted among the
nations,
I will be exalted in the earth."
[11]The LORD Almighty is with us;
the God of Jacob is our fortress.
Selah

Psalm 47

For the director of music. Of the Sons of
Korah. A psalm.

[1]Clap your hands, all you nations;
shout to God with cries of joy.

[2]How awesome is the LORD Most
High,
the great King over all the earth!
[3]He subdued nations under us,
peoples under our feet.
[4]He chose our inheritance for us,
the pride of Jacob, whom he
loved. *Selah*

[5]God has ascended amid shouts of
joy,
the LORD amid the sounding of
trumpets.
[6]Sing praises to God, sing praises;
sing praises to our King, sing
praises.
[7]For God is the King of all the earth;
sing to him a psalm[a] of praise.
[8]God reigns over the nations;
God is seated on his holy throne.
[9]The nobles of the nations assemble
as the people of the God of
Abraham,
for the kings[b] of the earth belong to
God;
he is greatly exalted.

Psalm 48

A song. A psalm of the Sons of Korah.

[1]Great is the LORD, and most worthy
of praise,
in the city of our God, his holy
mountain.
[2]It is beautiful in its loftiness,
the joy of the whole earth.
Like the utmost heights of Zaphon[a]
is Mount Zion,
the[b] city of the Great King.
[3]God is in her citadels;
he has shown himself to be her
fortress.

[4]When the kings joined forces,
when they advanced together,
[5]they saw her, and were astounded;
they fled in terror.
[6]Trembling seized them there,
pain like that of a woman in
labour.

---

[a]Title: Probably a musical term   [b]Or *chariots*
[a]7 Or *a maskil* (probably a literary or musical term)   [b]9 Or *shields*
[a]2 *Zaphon* can refer to a sacred mountain or the direction north.
[b]2 Or *earth,* / *Mount Zion, on the northern side* / *of the*

⁷You destroyed them like ships of
    Tarshish
    shattered by an east wind.
⁸As we have heard,
    so have we seen
  in the city of the LORD Almighty,
  in the city of our God:
    God makes her secure for
    ever.   *Selah*

⁹Within your temple, O God,
    we meditate on your unfailing
    love.
¹⁰Like your name, O God,
    your praise reaches to the ends of
    the earth;
    your right hand is filled with
    righteousness.
¹¹Mount Zion rejoices,
    the villages of Judah are glad
    because of your judgments.

¹²Walk about Zion, go round her,
    count her towers,
¹³consider well her ramparts,
    view her citadels,
    that you may tell of them to the
    next generation.
¹⁴For this God is our God for ever
    and ever;
    he will be our guide even to the
    end.

Psalm 49

For the director of music. Of the Sons of
    Korah. A psalm.

¹Hear this, all you peoples;
    listen, all who live in this world,
²both low and high,
    rich and poor alike:
³My mouth will speak words of
    wisdom;
    the utterance from my heart will
    give understanding.
⁴I will turn my ear to a proverb;
    with the harp I will expound my
    riddle:
⁵Why should I fear when evil days
    come,
    when wicked deceivers surround
    me—

⁶those who trust in their wealth
    and boast of their great riches?
⁷No man can redeem the life of
    another
    or give to God a ransom for
    him—
⁸the ransom for a life is costly,
    no payment is ever enough—
⁹that he should live on for ever
    and not see decay.

¹⁰For all can see that wise men die;
    the foolish and the senseless alike
    perish
    and leave their wealth to others.
¹¹Their tombs will remain their
    houses*a* for ever,
    their dwellings for endless
    generations,
    though they had*b* named lands
    after themselves.

¹²But man, despite his riches, does
    not endure;
    he is*c* like the beasts that perish.

¹³This is the fate of those who trust
    in themselves,
    and of their followers, who
    approve their sayings.   *Selah*
¹⁴Like sheep they are destined for
    the grave,*d*
    and death will feed on them.
  The upright will rule over them in
    the morning;
    their forms will decay in the
    grave,*d*
    far from their princely mansions.
¹⁵But God will redeem my soul*e* from
    the grave;
    he will surely take me to himself.
                                Selah

¹⁶Do not be overawed when a man
    grows rich,
    when the splendour of his house
    increases;
¹⁷for he will take nothing with him
    when he dies,
    his splendour will not descend
    with him.
¹⁸Though while he lived he counted
    himself blessed—

---

*a*11 Septuagint and Syriac; Hebrew *In their thoughts their houses will remain*
*b*11 Or */ for they have*
*c*12 Hebrew; Septuagint and Syriac *But a man who has riches without understanding / is*
*d*14 Hebrew *Sheol*; also in verse 15
*e*15 Or *redeem me*

and men praise you when you
prosper—
19he will join the generation of his
fathers,
who will never see the light of
life,.
20A man who has riches without
understanding
is like the beasts that perish.

Psalm 50

A psalm of Asaph.

1The Mighty One, God, the LORD,
speaks and summons the earth
from the rising of the sun to the
place where it sets.
2From Zion, perfect in beauty,
God shines forth.
3Our God comes and will not be
silent;
a fire devours before him,
and around him a tempest rages.
4He summons the heavens above,
and the earth, that he may judge
his people:
5"Gather to me my consecrated ones,
who made a covenant with me by
sacrifice."
6And the heavens proclaim his
righteousness,
for God himself is judge.   *Selah*

7"Hear, O my people, and I will
speak,
O Israel, and I will testify against
you:
I am God, your God.
8I do not rebuke you for your
sacrifices
or your burnt offerings, which are
ever before me.
9I have no need of a bull from your
stall
or of goats from your pens,
10for every animal of the forest is
mine,
and the cattle on a thousand hills.
11I know every bird in the
mountains,
and the creatures of the field are
mine.
12If I were hungry I would not tell
you,

for the world is mine, and all that
is in it.
13Do I eat the flesh of bulls
or drink the blood of goats?
14Sacrifice thank-offerings to God,
fulfil your vows to the Most High,
15and call upon me in the day of
trouble;
I will deliver you, and you will
honour me."

16But to the wicked, God says:

"What right have you to recite my
laws
or take my covenant on your lips?
17You hate my instruction
and cast my words behind you.
18When you see a thief, you join
with him;
you throw in your lot with
adulterers.
19You use your mouth for evil
and harness your tongue to
deceit.
20You speak continually against your
brother
and slander your own mother's
son.
21These things you have done and I
kept silent;
you thought I was altogether*a* like
you.
But I will rebuke you
and accuse you to your face.
22"Consider this, you who forget
God,
or I will tear you to pieces, with
none to rescue:
23He who sacrifices thank-offerings
honours me,
and he prepares the way
so that I may show him*b* the
salvation of God."

Psalm 51

For the director of music. A psalm of
David. When the prophet Nathan came
to him after David had committed
adultery with Bathsheba.

1Have mercy on me, O God,
according to your unfailing love;
according to your great compassion
blot out my transgressions.

a21 Or thought the 'I AM' was
b23 Or and to him who considers his way / I will show

²Wash away all my iniquity
　and cleanse me from my sin.

³For I know my transgressions,
　and my sin is always before me.
⁴Against you, you only, have I sinned
　and done what is evil in your
　　sight,
so that you are proved right when
　you speak
　and justified when you judge.
⁵Surely I have been a sinner from
　birth,
　sinful from the time my mother
　　conceived me.
⁶Surely you desire truth in the inner
　parts;ᵃ
　you teachᵇ me wisdom in the
　　inmost place.

⁷Cleanse me with hyssop, and I shall
　be clean;
　wash me, and I shall be whiter
　　than snow.
⁸Let me hear joy and gladness;
　let the bones you have crushed
　　rejoice.
⁹Hide your face from my sins
　and blot out all my iniquity.

¹⁰Create in me a pure heart, O God,
　and renew a steadfast spirit
　　within me.
¹¹Do not cast me from your presence
　or take your Holy Spirit from me.
¹²Restore to me the joy of your
　salvation
　and grant me a willing spirit, to
　　sustain me.

¹³Then I will teach transgressors
　your ways,
　and sinners will turn back to you.
¹⁴Save me from bloodguilt, O God,
　the God who saves me,
　and my tongue will sing of your
　　righteousness.
¹⁵O Lord, open my lips,
　and my mouth will declare your
　　praise.
¹⁶You do not delight in sacrifice, or I
　would bring it;
　you do not take pleasure in burnt
　　offerings.

¹⁷The sacrifices of God areᶜ a broken
　spirit;
　a broken and contrite heart,
　O God, you will not despise.
¹⁸In your good pleasure make Zion
　prosper;
　build up the walls of Jerusalem.
¹⁹Then there will be righteous
　sacrifices,
　whole burnt offerings to delight
　　you;
　then bulls will be offered on your
　　altar.

Psalm 52

For the director of music. A maskilᵈ of
David. When Doeg the Edomite had
gone to Saul and told him: "David has
gone to the house of Ahimelech."

¹Why do you boast of evil, you
　mighty man?
　Why do you boast all day long,
　you who are a disgrace in the
　　eyes of God?
²Your tongue plots destruction;
　it is like a sharpened razor,
　you who practise deceit.
³You love evil rather than good,
　falsehood rather than speaking
　　the truth.　　　　　　Selah
⁴You love every harmful word,
　O you deceitful tongue!

⁵Surely God will bring you down to
　everlasting ruin:
　He will snatch you up and tear
　you from your tent;
　he will uproot you from the land
　　of the living.　　　　Selah
⁶The righteous will see and fear;
　they will laugh at him, saying,
⁷"Here now is the man
　who did not make God his
　　stronghold
　but trusted in his great wealth
　and grew strong by destroying
　　others!"

⁸But I am like an olive tree
　flourishing in the house of God;
I trust in God's unfailing love
　for ever and ever.

ᵃ6 The meaning of the Hebrew for this phrase is uncertain.　ᵇ6 Or you desired ... ; / you taught　ᶜ17 Or My sacrifice, O God, is　ᵈTitle: Probably a literary or musical term

⁹I will praise you for ever for what
  you have done;
  in your name I will hope, for
  your name is good.
I will praise you in the presence
  of your saints.

Psalm 53

For the director of music. According to
mahalath.[a] A *maskil*[b] of David.

¹The fool says in his heart,
  "There is no God."
They are corrupt, and their ways
  are vile;
  there is no-one who does good.

²God looks down from heaven
  on the sons of men
to see if there are any who
  understand,
  any who seek God.

³Everyone has turned away,
  they have together become
  corrupt;
there is no-one who does good,
  not even one.

⁴Will the evildoers never learn—
  those who devour my people as
  men eat bread
  and who do not call on God?

⁵There they were, overwhelmed with
  dread,
  where there was nothing to
  dread.
God scattered the bones of those
  who attacked you;
  you put them to shame, for God
  despised them.

⁶Oh, that salvation for Israel would
  come out of Zion!
When God restores the fortunes
  of his people,
  let Jacob rejoice and Israel be
  glad!

Psalm 54

For the director of music. With stringed
instruments. A *maskil*[a] of David. When
the Ziphites had gone to Saul and said,
"Is not David hiding among us?"

¹Save me, O God, by your name;
  vindicate me by your might.

²Hear my prayer, O God;
  listen to the words of my mouth.

³Strangers are attacking me;
  ruthless men seek my life—
  men without regard for
  God.   *Selah*

⁴Surely God is my help;
  the Lord is the one who sustains
  me.

⁵Let evil recoil on those who slander
  me;
  in your faithfulness destroy them.

⁶I will sacrifice a freewill offering to
  you;
  I will praise your name, O LORD,
  for it is good.

⁷For he has delivered me from all
  my troubles,
  and my eyes have looked in
  triumph on my foes.

Psalm 55

For the director of music. With stringed
instruments. A *maskil*[a] of David.

¹Listen to my prayer, O God,
  do not ignore my plea;
² hear me and answer me.
  My thoughts trouble me and I am
  distraught
³   at the voice of the enemy,
  at the stares of the wicked;
for they bring down suffering upon
  me
  and revile me in their anger.

⁴My heart is in anguish within me;
  the terrors of death assail me.

⁵Fear and trembling have beset me;
  horror has overwhelmed me.

⁶I said, "Oh, that I had the wings of
  a dove!
  I would fly away and be at rest—
⁷I would flee far away
  and stay in the desert;   *Selah*
⁸I would hurry to my place of
  shelter,
  far from the tempest and storm."

---

*a*Title: Probably a musical term
*b*Title: Probably a literary or musical term
*c*Title: Probably a literary or musical term

⁹Confuse the wicked, O Lord,
        confound their speech,
    for I see violence and strife in
        the city.
¹⁰Day and night they prowl about on
        its walls;
    malice and abuse are within it.
¹¹Destructive forces are at work in
        the city;
    threats and lies never leave its
        streets.

¹²If an enemy were insulting me,
        I could endure it;
    if a foe were raising himself against
        me,
    I could hide from him.
¹³But it is you, a man like myself,
    my companion, my close friend,
¹⁴with whom I once enjoyed sweet
        fellowship
    as we walked with the throng at
        the house of God.

¹⁵Let death take my enemies by
        surprise;
    let them go down alive to the
        grave,[b]
    for evil finds lodging among
        them.

¹⁶But I call to God,
    and the LORD saves me.
¹⁷Evening, morning and noon
    I cry out in distress,
    and he hears my voice.
¹⁸He ransoms me unharmed
    from the battle waged against me,
    even though many oppose me.
¹⁹God, who is enthroned for ever,
    will hear them and afflict
        them—   Selah
    men who never change their ways
    and have no fear of God.

²⁰My companion attacks his friends;
    he violates his covenant.
²¹His speech is smooth as butter,
    yet war is in his heart;
    his words are more soothing than
        oil,
    yet they are drawn swords.

²²Cast your cares on the LORD
    and he will sustain you;
    he will never let the righteous
        fall.

²³But you, O God, will bring down
        the wicked
    into the pit of corruption;
    bloodthirsty and deceitful men
    will not live out half their days.

But as for me, I trust in you.

Psalm 56

For the director of music. To ,the tune
of, "A Dove on Distant Oaks". Of David.
A *miktam.*[a] When the Philistines had
seized him in Gath.

¹Be merciful to me, O God, for men
        hotly pursue me;
    all day long they press their
        attack.
²My slanderers pursue me all day
        long;
    many are attacking me in their
        pride.

³When I am afraid,
    I will trust in you.
⁴In God, whose word I praise,
    in God I trust; I will not be
        afraid.
    What can mortal man do to me?

⁵All day long they twist my words;
    they are always plotting to harm
        me.
⁶They conspire, they lurk,
    they watch my steps,
    eager to take my life.
⁷On no account let them escape;
    in your anger, O God, bring down
        the nations.
⁸Record my lament;
    list my tears on your scroll[b]—
    are they not in your record?

⁹Then my enemies will turn back
    when I call for help.
    By this I will know that God is
        for me.
¹⁰In God, whose word I praise,
    in the LORD, whose word I
        praise—
¹¹in God I trust; I will not be afraid.
    What can man do to me?

¹²I am under vows to you, O God;
    I will present my thank-offerings
        to you.

b15 Hebrew *Sheol*   a Title: Probably a literary or musical term
b8 Or / put my tears in your wineskin

325

13For you have delivered my soul
    from death
  and my feet from stumbling,
  that I may walk before God
    in the light of life.c

Psalm 57

For the director of music. ˌTo the tune
of, "Do Not Destroy". Of David. A
miktam.a When he had fled from Saul
into the cave.

1Have mercy on me, O God, have
    mercy on me,
  for in you my soul takes refuge.
  I will take refuge in the shadow of
    your wings
  until the disaster has passed.

2I cry out to God Most High,
  to God, who fulfils ˌhis purposeˌ
    for me.
3He sends from heaven and saves
    me,
  rebuking those who hotly pursue
    me;   Selah
  God sends his love and his
    faithfulness.

4I am in the midst of lions;
  I lie among ravenous beasts—
  men whose teeth are spears and
    arrows,
  whose tongues are sharp swords.

5Be exalted, O God, above the
    heavens;
  let your glory be over all the
    earth.

6They spread a net for my feet—
  I was bowed down in distress.
  They dug a pit in my path—
  but they have fallen into it
    themselves.   Selah

7My heart is steadfast, O God,
  my heart is steadfast;
  I will sing and make music.
8Awake, my soul!
  Awake, harp and lyre!
  I will awaken the dawn.

9I will praise you, O Lord, among the
    nations;

  I will sing of you among the
    peoples.
10For great is your love, reaching to
    the heavens;
  your faithfulness reaches to the
    skies.

11Be exalted, O God, above the
    heavens;
  let your glory be over all the
    earth.

Psalm 58

For the director of music. ˌTo the tune
of, "Do Not Destroy". Of David. A
miktam.a

1Do you rulers indeed speak justly?
  Do you judge uprightly among
    men?
2No, in your heart you devise
    injustice,
  and your hands mete out violence
    on the earth.
3Even from birth the wicked go
    astray;
  from the womb they are
    wayward and speak lies.
4Their venom is like the venom of a
    snake,
  like that of a cobra that has
    stopped its ears,
5that will not heed the tune of the
    charmer,
  however skilful the enchanter
    may be.

6Break the teeth in their mouths, O
    God;
  tear out, O LORD, the fangs of the
    lions!
7Let them vanish like water that
    flows away;
  when they draw the bow, let
    their arrows be blunted.
8Like a slug melting away as it
    moves along,
  like a stillborn child, may they
    not see the sun.
9Before your pots can feel ˌthe heat
    ofˌ the thorns—
  whether they be green or dry—
  the wicked will be swept away.b

---

c13 Or the land of the living   aTitle: Probably a literary or musical term
aTitle: Probably a literary or musical term
b9 The meaning of the Hebrew for this verse is uncertain.

[10]The righteous will be glad when
  they are avenged,
  when they bathe their feet in the
    blood of the wicked.
[11]Then men will say,
  "Surely the righteous still are
    rewarded;
  surely there is a God who judges
    the earth."

Psalm 59

For the director of music. ˌTo the tune
of, "Do Not Destroy". Of David. A
miktam.ᵃ When Saul had sent men to
watch David's house in order to kill
him.

[1]Deliver me from my enemies, O
    God;
  protect me from those who rise
    up against me.
[2]Deliver me from evildoers
  and save me from bloodthirsty
    men.

[3]See how they lie in wait for me!
  Fierce men conspire against me
  for no offence or sin of mine, O
    LORD.
[4]I have done no wrong, yet they are
    ready to attack me.
  Arise to help me; look on my
    plight!
[5]O LORD God Almighty, the God of
    Israel,
  rouse yourself to punish all the
    nations;
  show no mercy to wicked traitors.
                              Selah

[6]They return at evening,
  snarling like dogs,
  and prowl about the city.
[7]See what they spew from their
    mouths—
  they spew out swords from their
    lips,
  and they say, "Who can hear us?"
[8]But you, O LORD, laugh at them;
  you scoff at all those nations.

[9]O my Strength, I watch for you;
  you, O God, are my fortress, [10]my
    loving God.

God will go before me
  and will let me gloat over those
    who slander me.
[11]But do not kill them, O Lord our
    shield,ᵇ
  or my people will forget.
In your might make them wander
    about,
  and bring them down.
[12]For the sins of their mouths,
  for the words of their lips,
  let them be caught in their pride.
For the curses and lies they utter,
[13] consume them in wrath,
  consume them till they are no
    more.
Then it will be known to the ends
    of the earth
  that God rules over Jacob.   *Selah*

[14]They return at evening,
  snarling like dogs,
  and prowl about the city.
[15]They wander about for food
  and howl if not satisfied.
[16]But I will sing of your strength,
  in the morning I will sing of your
    love;
for you are my fortress,
  my refuge in times of trouble.

[17]O my Strength, I sing praise to you;
  you, O God, are my fortress, my
    loving God.

Psalm 60

For the director of music. To ˌthe tune
of, "The Lily of the Covenant". A
miktamᵃ of David. For teaching. When
he fought Aram Naharaimᵇ and Aram
Zobah.ᶜ and when Joab returned and
struck down twelve thousand Edomites
in the Valley of Salt.

[1]You have rejected us, O God, and
    burst forth upon us;
  you have been angry—now
    restore us!
[2]You have shaken the land and torn
    it open;
  mend its fractures, for it is
    quaking.

ᵃTitle: Probably a literary or musical term
ᵇ11 Or *sovereign*   ᵃTitle: Probably a literary or musical term
ᵇTitle: That is, Arameans of north-west Mesopotamia
ᶜTitle: That is, Arameans of central Syria

327

3You have shown your people
desperate times;
you have given us wine that
makes us stagger.
4But for those who fear you, you
have raised a banner
to be unfurled against the
bow.   Selah

5Save us and help us with your right
hand,
that those you love may be
delivered.
6God has spoken from his sanctuary:
"In triumph I will parcel out
Shechem
and measure off the Valley of
Succoth.
7Gilead is mine, and Manasseh is
mine;
Ephraim is my helmet,
Judah my sceptre.
8Moab is my washbasin,
upon Edom I toss my sandal;
over Philistia I shout in triumph."

9Who will bring me to the fortified
city?
Who will lead me to Edom?
10Is it not you, O God, you who have
rejected us
and no longer go out with our
armies?
11Give us aid against the enemy,
for the help of man is worthless.
12With God we shall gain the victory,
and he will trample down our
enemies.

Psalm 61

For the director of music. With stringed
instruments. Of David.

1Hear my cry, O God;
listen to my prayer.
2From the ends of the earth I call to
you,
I call as my heart grows faint;
lead me to the rock that is higher
than I.
3For you have been my refuge,
a strong tower against the foe.
4I long to dwell in your tent for ever
and take refuge in the shelter of
your wings.   Selah

5For you have heard my vows, O
God;
you have given me the heritage
of those who fear your name.
6Increase the days of the king's life,
his years for many generations.
7May he be enthroned in God's
presence for ever;
appoint your love and
faithfulness to protect him.
8Then will I ever sing praise to your
name
and fulfil my vows day after day.

Psalm 62

For the director of music. To Jeduthun.
A psalm of David.

1My soul finds rest in God alone;
my salvation comes from him.
2He alone is my rock and my
salvation;
he is my fortress, I shall never be
shaken.

3How long will you assault a man?
Would all of you throw him
down—
this leaning wall, this tottering
fence?
4They fully intend to topple him
from his lofty place;
they take delight in lies.
With their mouths they bless,
but in their hearts they
curse.   Selah

5Find rest, O my soul, in God alone;
my hope comes from him.
6He alone is my rock and my
salvation;
he is my fortress, I shall not be
shaken.
7My salvation and my honour
depend on God;a
he is my mighty rock, my refuge.
8Trust in him at all times, O people;
pour out your hearts to him,
for God is our refuge.   Selah

9Lowborn men are but a breath,
the highborn are but a lie;
if weighed on a balance, they are
nothing;
together they are only a breath.

a7 Or / God Most High is my salvation and my honour

¹⁰Do not trust in extortion
or take pride in stolen goods;
though your riches increase,
do not set your heart on them.

¹¹One thing God has spoken,
two things have I heard:
that you, O God, are strong,
¹² and that you, O Lord, are loving.
Surely you will reward each person
according to what he has done.

Psalm 63

A psalm of David. When he was in the
desert of Judah.

¹O God, you are my God,
earnestly I seek you;
my soul thirsts for you,
my body longs for you,
in a dry and weary land
where there is no water.

²I have seen you in the sanctuary
and beheld your power and your
glory.
³Because your love is better than
life,
my lips will glorify you.
⁴I will praise you as long as I live,
and in your name I will lift up
my hands.
⁵My soul will be satisfied as with the
richest of foods;
with singing lips my mouth will
praise you.

⁶On my bed I remember you;
I think of you through the
watches of the night.
⁷Because you are my help,
I sing in the shadow of your
wings.
⁸I stay close to you;
your right hand upholds me.

⁹They who seek my life will be
destroyed;
they will go down to the depths
of the earth.
¹⁰They will be given over to the
sword
and become food for jackals.
¹¹But the king will rejoice in God;

a5 Or us

all who swear by God's name
will praise him,
while the mouths of liars will be
silenced.

Psalm 64

For the director of music. A psalm of
David.

¹Hear me, O God, as I voice my
complaint;
protect my life from the threat of
the enemy.
²Hide me from the conspiracy of the
wicked,
from that noisy crowd of
evildoers,
³who sharpen their tongues like
swords
and aim their words like deadly
arrows.
⁴They shoot from ambush at the
innocent man;
they shoot at him suddenly,
without fear.

⁵They encourage each other in evil
plans,
they talk about hiding their
snares;
they say, "Who will see them?"*a*
⁶They plot injustice and say,
"We have devised a perfect
plan!"
Surely the mind and heart of
man are cunning.

⁷But God will shoot them with
arrows;
suddenly they will be struck
down.
⁸He will turn their own tongues
against them
and bring them to ruin;
all who see them will shake their
heads in scorn.
⁹All mankind will fear;
they will proclaim the works of
God
and ponder what he has done.

¹⁰Let the righteous rejoice in the
LORD
and take refuge in him;
let all the upright in heart praise
him!

Psalm 65

For the director of music. A psalm of
David. A song.

[1]Praise awaits[a] you, O God, in Zion;
to you our vows will be fulfilled.
[2]O you who hear prayer,
to you all men will come.
[3]When we were overwhelmed by
sins,
you atoned for our transgressions.
[4]Blessed is the man you choose
and bring near to live in your
courts!
We are filled with the good things
of your house,
of your holy temple.
[5]You answer us with awesome deeds
of righteousness,
O God our Saviour,
the hope of all the ends of the earth
and of the farthest seas,
[6]who formed the mountains by your
power,
having armed yourself with
strength,
[7]who stilled the roaring of the seas,
the roaring of their waves,
and the turmoil of the nations.
[8]Those living far away fear your
wonders;
where morning dawns and
evening fades
you call forth songs of joy.
[9]You care for the land and water it;
you enrich it abundantly.
The streams of God are filled with
water
to provide the people with corn,
for so you have ordained it.[b]
[10]You drench its furrows
and level its ridges;
you soften it with showers
and bless its crops.
[11]You crown the year with your
bounty,
and your carts overflow with
abundance.
[12]The grasslands of the desert
overflow;
the hills are clothed with
gladness.
[13]The meadows are covered with
flocks

and the valleys are mantled with
corn;
they shout for joy and sing.

Psalm 66

For the director of music. A song. A
psalm.

[1]Shout with joy to God, all the earth!
[2] Sing to the glory of his name;
offer him glory and praise!
[3]Say to God, "How awesome are
your deeds!
So great is your power
that your enemies cringe before
you.
[4]All the earth bows down to you;
they sing praise to you,
they sing praise to your name."
Selah

[5]Come and see what God has done,
how awesome his works on man's
behalf!
[6]He turned the sea into dry land,
they passed through the river on
foot—
come, let us rejoice in him.
[7]He rules for ever by his power,
his eyes watch the nations—
let not the rebellious rise up
against him. *Selah*

[8]Praise our God, O peoples,
let the sound of his praise be
heard;
[9]he has preserved our lives
and kept our feet from slipping.
[10]For you, O God, tested us;
you refined us like silver.
[11]You brought us into prison
and laid burdens on our backs.
[12]You let men ride over our heads;
we went through fire and water,
but you brought us to a place of
abundance.
[13]I will come to your temple with
burnt offerings
and fulfil my vows to you—
[14]vows my lips promised and my
mouth spoke
when I was in trouble.
[15]I will sacrifice fat animals to you
and an offering of rams;
I will offer bulls and goats. *Selah*

[a]1 Or *befits;* the meaning of the Hebrew for this word is uncertain.
[b]9 Or *for that is how you prepare the land*

¹⁶Come and listen, all you who fear
God;
let me tell you what he has done
for me.
¹⁷I cried out to him with my mouth;
his praise was on my tongue.
¹⁸If I had cherished sin in my heart,
the Lord would not have listened;
¹⁹but God has surely listened
and heard my voice in prayer.
²⁰Praise be to God,
who has not rejected my prayer
or withheld his love from me!

Psalm 67

For the director of music. With stringed
instruments. A psalm. A song.

¹May God be gracious to us and
bless us
and make his face shine upon
us;   *Selah*
²may your ways be known on earth,
your salvation among all nations.

³May the peoples praise you, O God;
may all the peoples praise you.
⁴May the nations be glad and sing
for joy,
for you rule the peoples justly
and guide the nations of the
earth.   *Selah*
⁵May the peoples praise you, O God;
may all the peoples praise you.

⁶Then the land will yield its harvest,
and God, our God, will bless us.
⁷God will bless us,
and all the ends of the earth will
fear him.

Psalm 68

For the director of music. Of David. A
psalm. A song.

¹May God arise, may his enemies be
scattered;
may his foes flee before him.
²As smoke is blown away by the
wind,
may you blow them away;
as wax melts before the fire,
may the wicked perish before
God.

³But may the righteous be glad
and rejoice before God;
may they be happy and joyful.

⁴Sing to God, sing praise to his
name,
extol him who rides on the
clouds^a—
his name is the LORD—
and rejoice before him.
⁵A father to the fatherless, a
defender of widows,
is God in his holy dwelling.
⁶God sets the lonely in families,^b
he leads forth the prisoners with
singing;
but the rebellious live in a sun-
scorched land.

⁷When you went out before your
people, O God,
when you marched through the
wasteland,   *Selah*
⁸the earth shook,
the heavens poured down rain,
before God, the One of Sinai,
before God, the God of Israel.
⁹You gave abundant showers, O
God;
you refreshed your weary
inheritance.
¹⁰Your people settled in it,
and from your bounty, O God,
you provided for the poor.

¹¹The Lord announced the word,
and great was the company of
those who proclaimed it:
¹²"Kings and armies flee in haste;
in the camps men divide the
plunder.
¹³Even while you sleep among the
campfires,^c
the wings of ˎmy˒ dove are
sheathed with silver,
its feathers with shining gold."
¹⁴When the Almighty^d scattered the
kings in the land,
it was like snow fallen on
Zalmon.

¹⁵The mountains of Bashan are
majestic mountains;
rugged are the mountains of
Bashan.

---

^a4 Or / prepare the way for him who rides through the deserts
^b6 Or the desolate in a homeland
^c13 Or saddlebags   ^d14 Hebrew Shaddai

16Why gaze in envy, O rugged
mountains,
at the mountain where God
chooses to reign,
where the LORD himself will
dwell for ever?

17The chariots of God are tens of
thousands
and thousands of thousands:
the Lord ₍has come₎ from Sinai
into his sanctuary.

18When you ascended on high,
you led captives in your train;
you received gifts from men,
even from*e* the rebellious—
that you,*f* O LORD God, might
dwell there.

19Praise be to the Lord, to God our
Saviour,
who daily bears our
burdens.   *Selah*

20Our God is a God who saves;
from the Sovereign LORD comes
escape from death.

21Surely God will crush the heads of
his enemies,
the hairy crowns of those who go
on in their sins.

22The Lord says, "I will bring you
from Bashan;
I will bring you from the depths
of the sea,

23that you may plunge your feet in
the blood of your foes,
while the tongues of your dogs
have their share."

24Your procession has come into
view, O God,
the procession of my God and
King into the sanctuary.

25In front are the singers, after them
the musicians;
with them are the maidens
playing tambourines.

26Praise God in the great
congregation;
praise the LORD in the assembly
of Israel.

27There is the little tribe of
Benjamin, leading them,

there the great throng of Judah's
princes,
and there the princes of Zebulun
and of Naphtali.

28Summon your power, O God;*g*
show us your strength, O God, as
you have done before.

29Because of your temple at
Jerusalem
kings will bring you gifts.

30Rebuke the beast among the reeds,
the herd of bulls among the
calves of the nations.
Humbled, may it bring bars of
silver.
Scatter the nations who delight in
war.

31Envoys will come from Egypt;
Cush*h* will submit herself to God.

32Sing to God, O kingdoms of the
earth,
sing praise to the Lord,   *Selah*

33to him who rides the ancient skies
above,
who thunders with mighty voice.

34Proclaim the power of God,
whose majesty is over Israel,
whose power is in the skies.

35You are awesome, O God, in your
sanctuary;
the God of Israel gives power and
strength to his people.

Praise be to God!

Psalm 69

For the director of music. To ₍the tune
of₎ "Lilies". Of David.

1Save me, O God,
for the waters have come up to
my neck.

2I sink in the miry depths,
where there is no foothold.
I have come into the deep waters;
the floods engulf me.

3I am worn out calling for help;
my throat is parched.
My eyes fail,
looking for my God.

4Those who hate me without reason
outnumber the hairs of my head;
many are my enemies without
cause,

e18 Or gifts for men, / even   f18 Or they
*g28 Many Hebrew manuscripts, Septuagint and Syriac; most Hebrew manuscripts Your God
has summoned power for you*
h31 That is, the upper Nile region

those who seek to destroy me.
I am forced to restore
what I did not steal.
⁵You know my folly, O God;
my guilt is not hidden from you.

⁶May those who hope in you
not be disgraced because of me,
O Lord, the LORD Almighty;
may those who seek you
not be put to shame because of
me,
O God of Israel.
⁷For I endure scorn for your sake,
and shame covers my face.
⁸I am a stranger to my brothers,
an alien to my own mother's
sons;
⁹for zeal for your house consumes
me,
and the insults of those who
insult you fall on me.
¹⁰When I weep and fast,
I must endure scorn;
¹¹when I put on sackcloth,
people make sport of me.
¹²Those who sit at the gate mock me,
and I am the song of the
drunkards.
¹³But I pray to you, O LORD,
in the time of your favour;
in your great love, O God,
answer me with your sure
salvation.
¹⁴Rescue me from the mire,
do not let me sink;
deliver me from those who hate me,
from the deep waters.
¹⁵Do not let the floodwaters engulf
me
or the depths swallow me up
or the pit close its mouth over
me.
¹⁶Answer me, O LORD, out of the
goodness of your love;
in your great mercy turn to me.
¹⁷Do not hide your face from your
servant;
answer me quickly, for I am in
trouble.
¹⁸Come near and rescue me;
redeem me because of my foes.
¹⁹You know how I am scorned,
disgraced and shamed;
all my enemies are before you.

⁰22 Or snare / and their fellowship become

²⁰Scorn has broken my heart
and has left me helpless;
I looked for sympathy, but there
was none,
for comforters, but I found none.
²¹They put gall in my food
and gave me vinegar for my
thirst.

²²May the table set before them
become a snare;
may it become retribution and*ᵃ* a
trap.
²³May their eyes be darkened so that
they cannot see,
and their backs be bent for ever.
²⁴Pour out your wrath on them;
let your fierce anger overtake
them.
²⁵May their place be deserted;
let there be no-one to dwell in
their tents.
²⁶For they persecute those you
wound
and talk about the pain of those
you hurt.
²⁷Charge them with crime upon
crime;
do not let them share in your
salvation.
²⁸May they be blotted out of the
book of life
and not be listed with the
righteous.

²⁹I am in pain and distress;
may your salvation, O God,
protect me.

³⁰I will praise God's name in song
and glorify him with
thanksgiving.
³¹This will please the LORD more
than an ox,
more than a bull with its horns
and hoofs.
³²The poor will see and be glad—
you who seek God, may your
hearts live!
³³The LORD hears the needy
and does not despise his captive
people.

³⁴Let heaven and earth praise him,
the seas and all that move in
them,
³⁵for God will save Zion

333

and rebuild the cities of Judah.
Then people will settle there and
possess it;
36 the children of his servants will
inherit it,
and those who love his name will
dwell there.

Psalm 70

For the director of music. Of David.
A petition.

1Hasten, O God, to save me;
O LORD, come quickly to help me.
2May those who seek my life
be put to shame and confusion;
may all who desire my ruin
be turned back in disgrace.
3May those who say to me, "Aha!
Aha!"
turn back because of their shame.
4But may all who seek you
rejoice and be glad in you;
may those who love your salvation
always say,
"Let God be exalted!"

5Yet I am poor and needy;
come quickly to me, O God.
You are my help and my deliverer;
O LORD, do not delay.

Psalm 71

1In you, O LORD, I have taken
refuge;
let me never be put to disgrace.
2Rescue me and deliver me in your
righteousness;
turn your ear to me and save me.
3Be my rock of refuge,
to which I can always go;
give the command to save me,
for you are my rock and my
fortress.
4Deliver me, O my God, from the
hand of the wicked,
from the grasp of evil and cruel
men.
5For you have been my hope, O
Sovereign LORD,
my confidence since my youth.
6From my birth I have relied on you;
you brought me forth from my
mother's womb.
I will ever praise you.
7I have become like a portent to
many,

but you are my strong refuge.
8My mouth is filled with your praise,
declaring your splendour all day
long.

9Do not cast me away when I am
old;
do not forsake me when my
strength is gone.
10For my enemies speak against me;
those who wait to kill me
conspire together.
11They say, "God has forsaken him;
pursue him and seize him,
for no-one will rescue him."
12Be not far from me, O God;
come quickly, O my God, to help
me.
13May my accusers perish in shame;
may those who want to harm me
be covered with scorn and
disgrace.

14But as for me, I shall always have
hope;
I will praise you more and more.
15My mouth will tell of your
righteousness,
of your salvation all day long,
though I know not its measure.
16I will come and proclaim your
mighty acts, O Sovereign LORD;
I will proclaim your
righteousness, yours alone.
17Since my youth, O God, you have
taught me,
and to this day I declare your
marvellous deeds.
18Even when I am old and grey,
do not forsake me, O God,
till I declare your power to the next
generation,
your might to all who are to
come.

19Your righteousness reaches to the
skies, O God,
you who have done great things.
Who, O God, is like you?
20Though you have made me see
troubles, many and bitter,
you will restore my life again;
from the depths of the earth
you will again bring me up.
21You will increase my honour
and comfort me once again.

22I will praise you with the harp

for your faithfulness, O my God;
I will sing praise to you with the
lyre,
O Holy One of Israel.
²³My lips will shout for joy
when I sing praise to you—
I, whom you have redeemed.
²⁴My tongue will tell of your
righteous acts
all day long,
for those who wanted to harm me
have been put to shame and
confusion.

Psalm 72

Of Solomon.

¹Endow the king with your justice, O
God,
the royal son with your
righteousness.
²He will*a* judge your people in
righteousness,
your afflicted ones with justice.
³The mountains will bring prosperity
to the people,
the hills the fruit of righteousness.
⁴He will defend the afflicted among
the people
and save the children of the
needy;
he will crush the oppressor.

⁵He will endure*b* as long as the sun,
as long as the moon, through all
generations.
⁶He will be like rain falling on a
mown field,
like showers watering the earth.
⁷In his days the righteous will
flourish;
prosperity will abound till the
moon is no more.

⁸He will rule from sea to sea
and from the River*c* to the ends
of the earth.*d*
⁹The desert tribes will bow before
him
and his enemies will lick the
dust.
¹⁰The kings of Tarshish and of
distant shores
will bring tribute to him;
the kings of Sheba and Seba

will present him gifts.
¹¹All kings will bow down to him
and all nations will serve him.

¹²For he will deliver the needy who
cry out,
the afflicted who have no-one to
help.
¹³He will take pity on the weak and
the needy
and save the needy from death.
¹⁴He will rescue them from
oppression and violence,
for precious is their blood in his
sight.

¹⁵Long may he live!
May gold from Sheba be given to
him.
May people ever pray for him
and bless him all day long.
¹⁶Let corn abound throughout the
land;
on the tops of the hills may it
sway.
Let its fruit flourish like Lebanon;
let it thrive like the grass of the
field.
¹⁷May his name endure for ever;
may it continue as long as the
sun.

All nations will be blessed through
him,
and they will call him blessed.

¹⁸Praise be to the LORD God, the God
of Israel,
who alone does marvellous
deeds.
¹⁹Praise be to his glorious name
for ever;
may the whole earth be filled
with his glory.
Amen and Amen.

²⁰This concludes the prayers of David
son of Jesse.

BOOK III

Psalms 73–89

Psalm 73

A psalm of Asaph.

¹Surely God is good to Israel,
to those who are pure in heart.

*a*2 Or *May he; similarly in verses 3–11 and 17*   *b*5 Septuagint; Hebrew / *You will be feared*
*c*8 That is, the Euphrates   *d*8 Or *the end of the land*

335

²But as for me, my feet had almost
  slipped;
  I had nearly lost my foothold.
³For I envied the arrogant
  when I saw the prosperity of the
  wicked.

⁴They have no struggles;
  their bodies are healthy and
  strong.ᵃ
⁵They are free from the burdens
  common to man;
  they are not plagued by human
  ills.
⁶Therefore pride is their necklace;
  they clothe themselves with
  violence.
⁷From their callous hearts comes
  iniquity;ᵇ
  the evil conceits of their minds
  know no limits.
⁸They scoff, and speak with malice;
  in their arrogance they threaten
  oppression.
⁹Their mouths lay claim to heaven,
  and their tongues take possession
  of the earth.
¹⁰Therefore their people turn to
  them
  and drink up waters in
  abundance.ᶜ
¹¹They say, "How can God know?
  Does the Most High have
  knowledge?"

¹²This is what the wicked are like—
  always carefree, they increase in
  wealth.

¹³Surely in vain have I kept my
  heart pure;
  in vain have I washed my hands
  in innocence.
¹⁴All day long I have been plagued;
  I have been punished every
  morning.

¹⁵If I had said, "I will speak thus,"
  I would have betrayed this
  generation of your children.
¹⁶When I tried to understand all this,
  it was oppressive to me
¹⁷till I entered the sanctuary of God;
  then I understood their final
  destiny.

¹⁸Surely you place them on slippery
  ground;
  you cast them down to ruin.
¹⁹How suddenly are they destroyed,
  completely swept away by
  terrors!
²⁰As a dream when one awakes,
  so when you arise, O Lord,
  you will despise them as
  fantasies.

²¹When my heart was grieved
  and my spirit embittered,
²²I was senseless and ignorant;
  I was a brute beast before you.

²³Yet I am always with you;
  you hold me by my right hand.
²⁴You guide me with your counsel,
  and afterwards you will take me
  into glory.
²⁵Whom have I in heaven but you?
  And being with you, I desire
  nothing on earth.
²⁶My flesh and my heart may fail,
  but God is the strength of my
  heart
  and my portion for ever.

²⁷Those who are far from you will
  perish;
  you destroy all who are
  unfaithful to you.
²⁸But as for me, it is good to be near
  God.
  I have made the Sovereign LORD
  my refuge;
  I will tell of all your deeds.

Psalm 74

A maskilᵈ of Asaph.

¹Why have you rejected us for ever,
  O God?
  Why does your anger smoulder
  against the sheep of your
  pasture?
²Remember the people you
  purchased of old,

ᵃ4 With a different word division of the Hebrew; Masoretic Text *struggles at their death; /
their bodies are healthy*
ᵇ7 Syriac (see also Septuagint); Hebrew *Their eyes bulge with fat*
ᶜ10 The meaning of the Hebrew for this verse is uncertain.
ᵈTitle: Probably a literary or musical term

the tribe you redeemed as your
        inheritance—
    Mount Zion, where you dwelt.

³Pick your way through these
        everlasting ruins,
    all this destruction the enemy has
        brought on the sanctuary.

⁴Your foes roared in the place where
        you met with us;
    they set up their standards as
        signs.

⁵They behaved like men wielding
        axes
    to cut through a thicket of trees.

⁶They smashed all the carved
        panelling
    with their axes and hatchets.

⁷They burned your sanctuary to the
        ground;
    they defiled the dwelling-place of
        your Name.

⁸They said in their hearts, "We will
        crush them completely!"
    They burned every place where
        God was worshipped in the
        land.

⁹We are given no miraculous signs;
    no prophets are left,
    and none of us knows how long
        this will be.

¹⁰How long will the enemy mock
        you, O God?
    Will the foe revile your name for
        ever?

¹¹Why do you hold back your hand,
        your right hand?
    Take it from the folds of your
        garment and destroy them!

¹²But you, O God, are my king from
        of old;
    you bring salvation upon the
        earth.

¹³It was you who split open the sea
        by your power;
    you broke the heads of the
        monster in the waters.

¹⁴It was you who crushed the heads
        of Leviathan
    and gave him as food to the
        creatures of the desert.

¹⁵It was you who opened up springs
        and streams;
    you dried up the ever-flowing
        rivers.

¹⁶The day is yours, and yours also
        the night;
    you established the sun and
        moon.

¹⁷It was you who set all the
        boundaries of the earth;
    you made both summer and
        winter.

¹⁸Remember how the enemy has
        mocked you, O LORD,
    how foolish people have reviled
        your name.

¹⁹Do not hand over the life of your
        dove to wild beasts;
    do not forget the lives of your
        afflicted people for ever.

²⁰Have regard for your covenant,
    because haunts of violence fill
        the dark places of the land.

²¹Do not let the oppressed retreat in
        disgrace;
    may the poor and needy praise
        your name.

²²Rise up, O God, and defend your
        cause;
    remember how fools mock you
        all day long.

²³Do not ignore the clamour of your
        adversaries,
    the uproar of your enemies,
        which rises continually.

Psalm 75

For the director of music. ⟨To the tune
of⟩ "Do Not Destroy". A psalm of Asaph.
A song.

¹We give thanks to you, O God,
    we give thanks, for your Name is
        near;
    men tell of your wonderful
        deeds.

²You say, "I choose the appointed
        time;
    it is I who judge uprightly.

³When the earth and all its people
        quake,
    it is I who hold its pillars
        firm.   *Selah*

⁴To the arrogant I say, 'Boast no
        more,'
    and to the wicked, 'Do not lift up
        your horns.

⁵Do not lift your horns against
        heaven;

do not speak with outstretched
neck.' "

⁶No-one from the east or the west
or from the desert can exalt a
man.
⁷But it is God who judges:
He brings one down, he exalts
another.
⁸In the hand of the LORD is a cup
full of foaming wine mixed with
spices;
he pours it out, and all the wicked
of the earth
drink it down to its very dregs.
⁹As for me, I will declare this for
ever;
I will sing praise to the God of
Jacob.
¹⁰I will cut off the horns of all the
wicked,
but the horns of the righteous
shall be lifted up.

Psalm 76

For the director of music. With stringed
instruments. A psalm of Asaph. A song.

¹In Judah God is known;
his name is great in Israel.
²His tent is in Salem,
his dwelling-place in Zion.
³There he broke the flashing arrows,
the shields and the swords, the
weapons of war.   Selah

⁴You are resplendent with light,
more majestic than mountains
rich with game.
⁵Valiant men lie plundered,
they sleep their last sleep;
not one of the warriors
can lift his hands.
⁶At your rebuke, O God of Jacob,
both horse and chariot lie still.
⁷You alone are to be feared.
Who can stand before you when
you are angry?
⁸From heaven you pronounced
judgment,
and the land feared and was
quiet—
⁹when you, O God, rose up to judge,

to save all the afflicted of the
land.   Selah
¹⁰Surely your wrath against men
brings you praise,
and the survivors of your wrath
are restrained.ᵃ

¹¹Make vows to the LORD your God
and fulfil them;
let all the neighbouring lands
bring gifts to the One to be
feared.
¹²He breaks the spirit of rulers;
he is feared by the kings of the
earth.

Psalm 77

For the director of music. To Jeduthun.
Of Asaph. A psalm.

¹I cried out to God for help;
I cried out to God to hear me.
²When I was in distress, I sought the
Lord;
at night I stretched out untiring
hands
and my soul refused to be
comforted.

³I remembered you, O God, and I
groaned;
I mused, and my spirit grew faint.
        Selah
⁴You kept my eyes from closing;
I was too troubled to speak.
⁵I thought about the former days,
the years of long ago;
⁶I remembered my songs in the
night.
My heart mused and my spirit
enquired:

⁷"Will the LORD reject us for ever?
Will he never show his favour
again?
⁸Has his unfailing love vanished for
ever?
Has his promise failed for all
time?
⁹Has God forgotten to be merciful?
Has he in anger withheld his
compassion?"   Selah

¹⁰Then I thought, "To this I will
appeal:

ᵃ10 Or Surely the wrath of men brings you praise, / and with the remainder of wrath you arm
yourself

the years of the right hand of the
Most High.''
11I will remember the deeds of the
LORD;
yes, I will remember your
miracles of long ago.
12I will meditate on all your works
and consider all your mighty
deeds.
13Your ways, O God, are holy.
What god is so great as our God?
14You are the God who performs
miracles;
you display your power among
the peoples.
15With your mighty arm you
redeemed your people,
the descendants of Jacob and
Joseph. *Selah*

16The waters saw you, O God,
the waters saw you and writhed;
the very depths were convulsed.
17The clouds poured down water,
the skies resounded with thunder;
your arrows flashed back and
forth.
18Your thunder was heard in the
whirlwind,
your lightning lit up the world;
the earth trembled and quaked.
19Your path led through the sea,
your way through the mighty
waters,
though your footprints were not
seen.
20You led your people like a flock
by the hand of Moses and Aaron.

Psalm 78

A *maskil*ᵃ of Asaph.

1O my people, hear my teaching;
listen to the words of my mouth.
2I will open my mouth in parables,
I will utter things hidden from of
old—
3things we have heard and known,
things our fathers have told us.
4We will not hide them from their
children;
we will tell the next generation
the praiseworthy deeds of the LORD,
his power, and the wonders he
has done.

ᵃTitle: Probably a literary or musical term

5He decreed statutes for Jacob
and established the law in Israel,
which he commanded our
forefathers
to teach their children,
6so that the next generation would
know them,
even the children yet to be born,
and they in turn would tell their
children.
7Then they would put their trust in
God
and would not forget his deeds
but would keep his commands.
8They would not be like their
forefathers—
a stubborn and rebellious
generation,
whose hearts were not loyal to God,
whose spirits were not faithful to
him.

9The men of Ephraim, though armed
with bows,
turned back on the day of battle;
10they did not keep God's covenant
and refused to live by his law.
11They forgot what he had done,
the wonders he had shown them.
12He did miracles in the sight of
their fathers
in the land of Egypt, in the region
of Zoan.
13He divided the sea and led them
through;
he made the water stand firm like
a wall.
14He guided them with the cloud by
day
and with light from the fire all
night.
15He split the rocks in the desert
and gave them water as abundant
as the seas;
16he brought streams out of a rocky
crag
and made water flow down like
rivers.
17But they continued to sin against
him,
rebelling in the desert against the
Most High.
18They wilfully put God to the test

339

by demanding the food they
craved.
¹⁹They spoke against God, saying,
"Can God spread a table in the
desert?
²⁰When he struck the rock, water
gushed out,
and streams flowed abundantly.
But can he also give us food?
Can he supply meat for his
people?"
²¹When the LORD heard them, he
was very angry;
his fire broke out against Jacob,
and his wrath rose against Israel,
²²for they did not believe in God
or trust in his deliverance.
²³Yet he gave a command to the
skies above
and opened the doors of the
heavens;
²⁴he rained down manna for the
people to eat,
he gave them the grain of
heaven.
²⁵Men ate the bread of angels;
he sent them all the food they
could eat.
²⁶He let loose the east wind from the
heavens
and led forth the south wind by
his power.
²⁷He rained meat down on them like
dust,
flying birds like sand on the
seashore.
²⁸He made them come down inside
their camp,
all around their tents.
²⁹They ate till they had more than
enough,
for he had given them what they
craved.
³⁰But before they turned from the
food they craved,
even while it was still in their
mouths;
³¹God's anger rose against them;
he put to death the sturdiest
among them,
cutting down the young men of
Israel.
³²In spite of all this, they kept on
sinning;

in spite of his wonders, they did
not believe.
³³So he ended their days in futility
and their years in terror.
³⁴Whenever God slew them, they
would seek him;
they eagerly turned to him again.
³⁵They remembered that God was
their Rock,
that God Most High was their
Redeemer.
³⁶But then they would flatter him
with their mouths,
lying to him with their tongues;
³⁷their hearts were not loyal to him,
they were not faithful to his
covenant.
³⁸Yet he was merciful;
he atoned for their iniquities
and did not destroy them.
Time after time he restrained his
anger
and did not stir up his full wrath.
³⁹He remembered that they were but
flesh,
a passing breeze that does not
return.
⁴⁰How often they rebelled against
him in the desert
and grieved him in the
wasteland!
⁴¹Again and again they put God to
the test;
they vexed the Holy One of
Israel.
⁴²They did not remember his
power—
the day he redeemed them from
the oppressor,
⁴³the day he displayed his
miraculous signs in Egypt,
his wonders in the region of
Zoan.
⁴⁴He turned their rivers to blood;
they could not drink from their
streams.
⁴⁵He sent swarms of flies that
devoured them
and frogs that devastated them.
⁴⁶He gave their crops to the
grasshopper,
their produce to the locust.
⁴⁷He destroyed their vines with hail
and their sycamore-figs with
sleet.

48He gave over their cattle to the
hail,
their livestock to bolts of
lightning.
49He unleashed against them his hot
anger,
his wrath, indignation and
hostility—
a band of destroying angels.
50He prepared a path for his anger;
he did not spare them from death
but gave them over to the plague.
51He struck down all the firstborn of
Egypt,
the firstfruits of manhood in the
tents of Ham.
52But he brought his people out like
a flock;
he led them like sheep through
the desert.
53He guided them safely, so they
were unafraid;
but the sea engulfed their
enemies.
54Thus he brought them to the
border of his holy land,
to the hill country his right hand
had taken.
55He drove out nations before them
and allotted their lands to them
as an inheritance;
he settled the tribes of Israel in
their homes.

56But they put God to the test
and rebelled against the Most
High;
they did not keep his statutes.
57Like their fathers they were
disloyal and faithless,
as unreliable as a faulty bow.
58They angered him with their high
places;
they aroused his jealousy with
their idols.
59When God heard them, he was
very angry;
he rejected Israel completely.
60He abandoned the tabernacle of
Shiloh,
the tent he had set up among
men.
61He sent the ark of his might into
captivity,
his splendour into the hands of
the enemy.

62He gave his people over to the
sword;
he was very angry with his
inheritance.
63Fire consumed their young men,
and their maidens had no
wedding songs;
64their priests were put to the sword,
and their widows could not weep.

65Then the Lord awoke as from
sleep,
as a man wakes from the stupor
of wine.
66He beat back his enemies;
he put them to everlasting shame.
67Then he rejected the tents of
Joseph,
he did not choose the tribe of
Ephraim;
68but he chose the tribe of Judah,
Mount Zion, which he loved.
69He built his sanctuary like the high
mountains,
like the earth that he established
for ever.
70He chose David his servant
and took him from the sheep
pens;
71from tending the sheep he brought
him
to be the shepherd of his people
Jacob,
of Israel his inheritance.
72And David shepherded them with
integrity of heart;
with skilful hands he led them.

Psalm 79
A psalm of Asaph.

1O God, the nations have invaded
your inheritance;
they have defiled your holy
temple,
they have reduced Jerusalem to
rubble.
2They have given the dead bodies of
your servants
as food to the birds of the air,
the flesh of your saints to the
beasts of the earth.
3They have poured out blood like
water
all around Jerusalem,
and there is no-one to bury the
dead.

⁴We are objects of reproach to our
  neighbours,
    of scorn and derision to those
    around us.

⁵How long, O LORD? Will you be
  angry for ever?
    How long will your jealousy burn
    like fire?

⁶Pour out your wrath on the nations
    that do not acknowledge you,
  on the kingdoms
    that do not call on your name;

⁷for they have devoured Jacob
    and destroyed his homeland.

⁸Do not hold against us the sins of
    the fathers;
  may your mercy come quickly to
    meet us,
    for we are in desperate need.

⁹Help us, O God our Saviour,
    for the glory of your name;
  deliver us and atone for our sins
    for your name's sake.

¹⁰Why should the nations say,
    "Where is their God?"
  Before our eyes, make known
    among the nations
    that you avenge the outpoured
    blood of your servants.

¹¹May the groans of the prisoners
    come before you;
  by the strength of your arm
    preserve those condemned to die.

¹²Pay back into the laps of our
    neighbours seven times
  the reproach they have hurled at
    you, O Lord.

¹³Then we your people, the sheep of
    your pasture,
    will praise you for ever;
  from generation to generation
    we will recount your praise.

Psalm 80

For the director of music. To the tune of,
"The Lilies of the Covenant". Of Asaph.
A psalm.

¹Hear us, O Shepherd of Israel,
    you who lead Joseph like a flock;
  you who sit enthroned between the
    cherubim, shine forth

² before Ephraim, Benjamin and
    Manasseh.
  Awaken your might;
    come and save us.

³Restore us, O God;
    make your face shine upon us,
    that we may be saved.

⁴O LORD God Almighty,
    how long will your anger
    smoulder
    against the prayers of your
    people?

⁵You have fed them with the bread
    of tears;
  you have made them drink tears
    by the bowlful.

⁶You have made us a source of
    contention to our neighbours,
    and our enemies mock us.

⁷Restore us, O God Almighty;
    make your face shine upon us,
    that we may be saved.

⁸You brought a vine out of Egypt;
    you drove out the nations and
    planted it.

⁹You cleared the ground for it,
    and it took root and filled the
    land.

¹⁰The mountains were covered with
    its shade,
  the mighty cedars with its
    branches.

¹¹It sent out its boughs to the Sea,ᵃ
    its shoots as far as the River.ᵇ

¹²Why have you broken down its
    walls
  so that all who pass by pick its
    grapes?

¹³Boars from the forest ravage it
    and the creatures of the field
    feed on it.

¹⁴Return to us, O God Almighty!
    Look down from heaven and see!
  Watch over this vine,

¹⁵ the root your right hand has
    planted,
  the sonᶜ you have raised up for
    yourself.

¹⁶Your vine is cut down, it is burned
    with fire;

ᵃ11 Probably the Mediterranean
ᵇ11 That is, the Euphrates
ᶜ15 Or branch

at your rebuke your people
perish.
¹⁷Let your hand rest on the man at
your right hand,
the son of man you have raised
up for yourself.
¹⁸Then we will not turn away from
you;
revive us, and we will call on
your name.

¹⁹Restore us, O LORD God Almighty;
make your face shine upon us,
that we may be saved.

Psalm 81

For the director of music. According to
gittith.ᵃ Of Asaph.

¹Sing for joy to God our strength;
shout aloud to the God of Jacob!
²Begin the music, strike the
tambourine,
play the melodious harp and lyre.

³Sound the ram's horn at the New
Moon,
and when the moon is full, on the
day of our Feast;
⁴this is a decree for Israel,
an ordinance of the God of Jacob.
⁵He established it as a statute for
Joseph
when he went out against Egypt,
where we heard a language we
did not understand.ᵇ

⁶He says, "I removed the burden
from their shoulders;
their hands were set free from
the basket.
⁷In your distress you called and I
rescued you,
I answered you out of a
thundercloud;
I tested you at the waters of
Meribah.   Selah

⁸"Hear, O my people, and I will
warn you—
if you would but listen to me, O
Israel!
⁹You shall have no foreign god
among you;
you shall not bow down to an
alien god.
¹⁰I am the LORD your God,

who brought you up out of Egypt.
Open wide your mouth and I will
fill it.

¹¹"But my people would not listen to
me;
Israel would not submit to me.
¹²So I gave them over to their
stubborn hearts
to follow their own devices.

¹³"If my people would but listen to
me,
if Israel would follow my ways,
¹⁴how quickly would I subdue their
enemies
and turn my hand against their
foes!
¹⁵Those who hate the LORD would
cringe before him,
and their punishment would last
for ever.
¹⁶But you would be fed with the
finest of wheat;
with honey from the rock I would
satisfy you."

Psalm 82

A psalm of Asaph.

¹God presides in the great assembly;
he gives judgment among the
"gods":

²"How long will youᵃ defend the
unjust
and show partiality to the
wicked?   Selah
³Defend the cause of the weak and
fatherless;
maintain the rights of the poor
and oppressed.
⁴Rescue the weak and needy;
deliver them from the hand of
the wicked.

⁵"They know nothing, they
understand nothing.
They walk about in darkness;
all the foundations of the earth
are shaken.

⁶"I said, 'You are "gods";
;you are all sons of the Most
High.'
⁷But you will die like mere men;

ᵃTitle: Probably a musical term   ᵇ5 Or / and we heard a voice we had not known
ᵃ2 The Hebrew is plural.

you will fall like every other
ruler."

8Rise up, O God, judge the earth,
for all the nations are your
inheritance.

Psalm 83

A song. A psalm of Asaph.

1O God, do not keep silent;
be not quiet, O God, be not still.
2See how your enemies are astir,
how your foes rear their heads.
3With cunning they conspire against
your people;
they plot against those you
cherish.
4"Come," they say, "let us destroy
them as a nation,
that the name of Israel be
remembered no more."
5With one mind they plot together;
they form an alliance against
you—
6the tents of Edom and the
Ishmaelites,
of Moab and the descendants of
Hagar,
7Gebal,[a] Ammon and Amalek,
Philistia, with the people of Tyre.
8Even Assyria has joined them
to lend strength to the
descendants of Lot.   *Selah*

9Do to them as you did to Midian,
as you did to Sisera and Jabin at
the river Kishon,
10who perished at Endor
and became like refuse on the
ground.
11Make their nobles like Oreb and
Zeeb,
all their princes like Zebah and
Zalmunna,
12who said, "Let us take possession
of the pasture-lands of God."
13Make them like tumbleweed, O my
God,
like chaff before the wind.
14As fire consumes the forest
or a flame sets the mountains
ablaze,
15so pursue them with your tempest
and terrify them with your storm.

16Cover their faces with shame
so that men will seek your name,
O LORD.
17May they ever be ashamed and
dismayed;
may they perish in disgrace.
18Let them know that you, whose
name is the LORD—
that you alone are the Most High
over all the earth.

Psalm 84

For the director of music. According to
gittith.[a] Of the Sons of Korah. A psalm.

1How lovely is your dwelling-place,
O LORD Almighty!
2My soul yearns, even faints
for the courts of the LORD;
my heart and my flesh cry out
for the living God.

3Even the sparrow has found a
home,
and the swallow a nest for
herself,
where she may have her young—
a place near your altar,
O LORD Almighty, my King and
my God.
4Blessed are those who dwell in your
house;
they are ever praising
you.   *Selah*

5Blessed are those whose strength is
in you,
who have set their hearts on
pilgrimage.
6As they pass through the Valley of
Baca,
they make it a place of springs;
the autumn rains also cover it
with pools.[b]
7They go from strength to strength
till each appears before God in
Zion.

8Hear my prayer, O LORD God
Almighty;
listen to me, O God of
Jacob.   *Selah*
9Look upon our shield,[c] O God;
look with favour on your
anointed one.

---

*a7 That is, Byblos   *aTitle: Probably a musical term   *b6 Or blessings*
c9 Or sovereign

¹⁰Better is one day in your courts
    than a thousand elsewhere;
  I would rather be a doorkeeper in
    the house of my God
      than dwell in the tents of the
        wicked.
¹¹For the LORD God is a sun and
    shield;
  the LORD bestows favour and
    honour;
  no good thing does he withhold
    from those whose walk is
      blameless.
¹²O LORD Almighty,
  blessed is the man who trusts in
    you.

Psalm 85

For the director of music. Of the Sons of
Korah. A psalm.

¹You showed favour to your land, O
    LORD;
  you restored the fortunes of
    Jacob.
²You forgave the iniquity of your
    people
  and covered all their sins.   *Selah*
³You set aside all your wrath
  and turned from your fierce
    anger.

⁴Restore us again, O God our
    Saviour,
  and put away your displeasure
    towards us.
⁵Will you be angry with us for ever?
  Will you prolong your anger
    through all generations?
⁶Will you not revive us again,
  that your people may rejoice in
    you?
⁷Show us your unfailing love, O
    LORD,
  and grant us your salvation.

⁸I will listen to what God the LORD
    will say;
  he promises peace to his people,
    his saints—
  but let them not return to folly.
⁹Surely his salvation is near those
    who fear him,
  that his glory may dwell in our
    land.

¹⁰Love and faithfulness meet
    together;
  righteousness and peace kiss each
    other.
¹¹Faithfulness springs forth from the
    earth,
  and righteousness looks down
    from heaven.
¹²The LORD will indeed give what is
    good,
  and our land will yield its
    harvest.
¹³Righteousness goes before him
  and prepares the way for his
    steps.

Psalm 86

A prayer of David.

¹Hear, O LORD, and answer me,
  for I am poor and needy.
²Guard my life, for I am devoted to
    you.
  You are my God; save your
    servant
    who trusts in you.
³Have mercy on me, O Lord,
  for I call to you all day long.
⁴Bring joy to your servant,
  for to you, O Lord,
  I lift up my soul.

⁵You are kind and forgiving, O Lord,
  abounding in love to all who call
    to you.
⁶Hear my prayer, O LORD;
  listen to my cry for mercy.
⁷In the day of my trouble I will call
    to you,
  for you will answer me.

⁸Among the gods there is none like
    you, O Lord;
  no deeds can compare with
    yours.
⁹All the nations you have made
  will come and worship before
    you, O Lord;
  they will bring glory to your
    name.
¹⁰For you are great and do
    marvellous deeds;
  you alone are God.

¹¹Teach me your way, O LORD,
  and I will walk in your truth;
  give me an undivided heart,
    that I may fear your name.

¹²I will praise you, O Lord my God,
  with all my heart;
  I will glorify your name for ever.
¹³For great is your love towards me;
  you have delivered my soul from
  the depths of the grave.*ᵃ*

¹⁴The arrogant are attacking me, O
  God;
  a band of ruthless men seeks my
  life—
  men without regard for you.
¹⁵But you, O Lord, are a
  compassionate and gracious
  God,
  slow to anger, abounding in love
  and faithfulness.
¹⁶Turn to me and have mercy on me;
  grant your strength to your
  servant
  and save the son of your
  maidservant.*ᵇ*
¹⁷Give me a sign of your goodness,
  that my enemies may see it and
  be put to shame,
  for you, O LORD, have helped me
  and comforted me.

Psalm 87

Of the Sons of Korah. A psalm. A song.

¹He has set his foundation on the
  holy mountain;
² the LORD loves the gates of Zion
  more than all the dwellings of
  Jacob.
³Glorious things are said of you,
  O city of God: *Selah*
⁴"I will record Rahab*ᵃ* and Babylon
  among those who acknowledge
  me—
  Philistia too, and Tyre, along with
  Cush*ᵇ*—
  and will say, 'This*ᶜ* one was born
  in Zion.' "
⁵Indeed, of Zion it will be said,
  "This one and that one were born
  in her,
  and the Most High himself will
  establish her."

⁶The LORD will write in the register
  of the peoples:
  "This one was born in Zion."
          Selah
⁷As they make music they will sing,
  "All my fountains are in you."

Psalm 88

A song. A psalm of the Sons of Korah.
For the director of music. According to
mahalath leannoth.ᵃ A *maskilᵇ* of Heman
  the Ezrahite.

¹O LORD, the God who saves me,
  day and night I cry out before
  you.
²May my prayer come before you;
  turn your ear to my cry.

³For my soul is full of trouble
  and my life draws near the
  grave.*ᶜ*
⁴I am counted among those who go
  down to the pit;
  I am like a man without strength.
⁵I am set apart with the dead,
  like the slain who lie in the
  grave,
  whom you remember no more,
  who are cut off from your care.

⁶You have put me in the lowest pit,
  in the darkest depths.
⁷Your wrath lies heavily upon me;
  you have overwhelmed me with
  all your waves.   *Selah*
⁸You have taken from me my closest
  friends
  and have made me repulsive to
  them.
  I am confined and cannot escape;
⁹ my eyes are dim with grief.

  I call to you, O LORD, every day;
  I spread out my hands to you.
¹⁰Do you show your wonders to the
  dead?
  Do those who are dead rise up
  and praise you?   *Selah*

---

*ᵃ*13 Hebrew *Sheol*   *ᵇ*16 Or *save your faithful son*
*ᵃ*4 A poetic name for Egypt   *ᵇ*4 That is, the upper Nile region
*ᶜ*4 Or *"O Rahab and Babylon, / Philistia, Tyre and Cush, / I will record concerning those who
  acknowledge me: / 'This*
*ᵃ*Title: Possibly a tune, "The Suffering of Affliction"
*ᵇ*Title: Probably a literary or musical term
*ᶜ*3 Hebrew *Sheol*

[11]Is your love declared in the grave,
your faithfulness in Destruction?[d]
[12]Are your wonders known in the
place of darkness,
or your righteous deeds in the
land of oblivion?
[13]But I cry to you for help, O LORD;
in the morning my prayer comes
before you.
[14]Why, O LORD, do you reject me
and hide your face from me?
[15]From my youth I have been
afflicted and close to death;
I have suffered your terrors and
am in despair.
[16]Your wrath has swept over me;
your terrors have destroyed me.
[17]All day long they surround me like
a flood;
they have completely engulfed
me.
[18]You have taken my companions
and loved ones from me;
the darkness is my closest friend.

Psalm 89

A *maskil*[a] of Ethan the Ezrahite.

[1]I will sing of the LORD's great love
for ever;
with my mouth I will make your
faithfulness known through all
generations.
[2]I will declare that your love stands
firm for ever,
that you established your
faithfulness in heaven itself.
[3]You said, "I have made a covenant
with my chosen one,
I have sworn to David my
servant,
[4]'I will establish your line for ever
and make your throne firm
through all generations.' " *Selah*
[5]The heavens praise your wonders,
O LORD,
your faithfulness too, in the
assembly of the holy ones.
[6]For who in the skies above can
compare with the LORD?
Who is like the LORD among the
heavenly beings?
[7]In the council of the holy ones God
is greatly feared;

he is more awesome than all who
surround him.
[8]O LORD God Almighty, who is like
you?
You are mighty, O LORD, and
your faithfulness surrounds you.
[9]You rule over the surging sea;
when its waves mount up, you
still them.
[10]You crushed Rahab like one of the
slain;
with your strong arm you
scattered your enemies.
[11]The heavens are yours, and yours
also the earth;
you founded the world and all
that is in it.
[12]You created the north and the
south;
Tabor and Hermon sing for joy at
your name.
[13]Your arm is endued with power;
your hand is strong, your right
hand exalted.
[14]Righteousness and justice are the
foundation of your throne;
love and faithfulness go before
you.
[15]Blessed are those who have
learned to acclaim you,
who walk in the light of your
presence, O LORD.
[16]They rejoice in your name all day
long;
they exult in your righteousness.
[17]For you are their glory and
strength,
and by your favour you exalt our
horn.[b]
[18]Indeed, our shield[c] belongs to the
LORD,
our king to the Holy One of
Israel.
[19]Once you spoke in a vision,
to your faithful people you said:
"I have bestowed strength on a
warrior;
I have exalted a young man from
among the people.
[20]I have found David my servant;
with my sacred oil I have
anointed him.

[d]11 Hebrew *Abaddon*   [a]Title: Probably a literary or musical term
[b]17 *Horn* here symbolises strong one.   [c]18 Or *sovereign*

347

21My hand will sustain him;
surely my arm will strengthen
him.
22No enemy will subject him to
tribute;
no wicked man will oppress him.
23I will crush his foes before him
and strike down his adversaries.
24My faithful love will be with him,
and through my name his horn[d]
will be exalted.
25I will set his hand over the sea,
his right hand over the rivers.
26He will call out to me, 'You are my
Father,
my God, the Rock my Saviour.'
27I will also appoint him my
firstborn,
the most exalted of the kings of
the earth.
28I will maintain my love to him for
ever,
and my covenant with him will
never fail.
29I will establish his line for ever,
his throne as long as the heavens
endure.
30"If his sons forsake my law
and do not follow my statutes,
31if they violate my decrees
and fail to keep my commands,
32I will punish their sin with the rod,
their iniquity with flogging;
33but I will not take my love from
him,
nor will I ever betray my
faithfulness.
34I will not violate my covenant
or alter what my lips have
uttered.
35Once for all, I have sworn by my
holiness—
and I will not lie to David—
36that his line will continue for ever
and his throne endure before me
like the sun;
37it will be established for ever like
the moon,
the faithful witness in the sky."
Selah
38But you have rejected, you have
spurned,
you have been very angry with
your anointed one.

39You have renounced the covenant
with your servant
and have defiled his crown in the
dust.
40You have broken through all his
walls
and reduced his strongholds to
ruins.
41All who pass by have plundered
him;
he has become the scorn of his
neighbours.
42You have exalted the right hand of
his foes;
you have made all his enemies
rejoice.
43You have turned back the edge of
his sword
and have not supported him in
battle.
44You have put an end to his
splendour
and cast his throne to the ground.
45You have cut short the days of his
youth;
you have covered him with a
mantle of shame.
Selah

46How long, O LORD? Will you hide
yourself for ever?
How long will your wrath burn
like fire?
47Remember how fleeting is my life.
For what futility you have created
all men!
48What man can live and not see
death,
or save himself from the power of
the grave?[e]
Selah
49O Lord, where is your former great
love,
which in your faithfulness you
swore to David?
50Remember, Lord, how your servant
has[f] been mocked,
how I bear in my heart the taunts
of all the nations,
51the taunts with which your
enemies have mocked, O LORD,
with which they have mocked
every step of your anointed one.
52Praise be to the LORD for ever!
Amen and Amen.

d24 *Horn* here symbolises strength.   e48 Hebrew *Sheol*   f50 Or *your servants have*

348

BOOK IV

Psalms 90-106

Psalm 90

A prayer of Moses the man of God.

¹Lord, you have been our dwelling-
place
throughout all generations.
²Before the mountains were born
or you brought forth the earth
and the world,
from everlasting to everlasting
you are God.

³You turn men back to dust,
saying, "Return to dust, O sons of
men."
⁴For a thousand years in your sight
are like a day that has just gone
by,
or like a watch in the night.
⁵You sweep men away in the sleep
of death;
they are like the new grass of the
morning—
⁶though in the morning it springs up
new,
by evening it is dry and withered.

⁷We are consumed by your anger
and terrified by your indignation.
⁸You have set our iniquities before
you,
our secret sins in the light of your
presence.
⁹All our days pass away under your
wrath;
we finish our years with a moan.
¹⁰The length of our days is seventy
years—
or eighty, if we have the strength;
yet their span*ᵃ* is but trouble and
sorrow,
for they quickly pass, and we fly
away.
¹¹Who knows the power of your
anger?
For your wrath is as great as the
fear that is due to you.
¹²Teach us to number our days
aright,
that we may gain a heart of
wisdom.

¹³Relent, O LORD! How long will it
be?
Have compassion on your
servants.
¹⁴Satisfy us in the morning with your
unfailing love,
that we may sing for joy and be
glad all our days.
¹⁵Make us glad for as many days as
you have afflicted us,
for as many years as we have
seen trouble.
¹⁶May your deeds be shown to your
servants,
your splendour to their children.

¹⁷May the favour*ᵇ* of the Lord our
God rest upon us;
establish the work of our hands
for us—
yes, establish the work of our
hands.

Psalm 91

¹He who dwells in the shelter of the
Most High
will rest in the shadow of the
Almighty.*ᵃ*
²I will say of the LORD, "He is my
refuge and my fortress,
my God, in whom I trust."

³Surely he will save you from the
fowler's snare
and from the deadly pestilence.
⁴He will cover you with his feathers,
and under his wings you will find
refuge;
his faithfulness will be your
shield and rampart.
⁵You will not fear the terror of night,
nor the arrow that flies by day,
⁶nor the pestilence that stalks in the
darkness,
nor the plague that destroys at
midday.
⁷A thousand may fall at your side,
ten thousand at your right hand,
but it will not come near you.
⁸You will only observe with your
eyes
and see the punishment of the
wicked.

⁹If you make the Most High your
dwelling—

ᵃ10 Or yet the best of them *ᵇ17 Or beauty* *ᵃ1 Hebrew Shaddai*

even the LORD, who is my
refuge—
[10]then no harm will befall you,
no disaster will come near your
tent.
[11]For he will command his angels
concerning you
to guard you in all your ways;
[12]they will lift you up in their hands,
so that you will not strike your
foot against a stone.
[13]You will tread upon the lion and
the cobra;
you will trample the great lion
and the serpent.
[14]"Because he loves me," says the
LORD, "I will rescue him;
I will protect him, for he
acknowledges my name.
[15]He will call upon me, and I will
answer him;
I will be with him in trouble,
I will deliver him and honour
him.
[16]With long life will I satisfy him
and show him my salvation."

Psalm 92

A psalm. A song. For the Sabbath day.

[1]It is good to praise the LORD
and make music to your name, O
Most High,
[2]to proclaim your love in the
morning
and your faithfulness at night,
[3]to the music of the ten-stringed lyre
and the melody of the harp.

[4]For you make me glad by your
deeds, O LORD;
I sing for joy at the work of your
hands.
[5]How great are your works, O LORD,
how profound your thoughts!
[6]The senseless man does not know,
fools do not understand,
[7]that though the wicked spring up
like grass
and all evildoers flourish,
they will be for ever destroyed.

[8]But you, O LORD, are exalted for
ever.

[9]For surely your enemies, O LORD,
surely your enemies will perish
all evildoers will be scattered.
[10]You have exalted my horn[a] like
that of a wild ox;
fine oils have been poured upon
me.
[11]My eyes have seen the defeat of
my adversaries;
my ears have heard the rout of
my wicked foes.

[12]The righteous will flourish like a
palm tree,
they will grow like a cedar of
Lebanon;
[13]planted in the house of the LORD,
they will flourish in the courts of
our God.
[14]They will still bear fruit in old age,
they will stay fresh and green,
[15]proclaiming, "The LORD is upright;
he is my Rock, and there is no
wickedness in him."

Psalm 93

[1]The LORD reigns, he is robed in
majesty;
the LORD is robed in majesty
and is armed with strength.
The world is firmly established;
it cannot be moved.
[2]Your throne was established long
ago;
you are from all eternity.

[3]The seas have lifted up, O LORD,
the seas have lifted up their
voice;
the seas have lifted up their
pounding waves.
[4]Mightier than the thunder of the
great waters,
mightier than the breakers of the
sea—
the LORD on high is mighty.

[5]Your statutes stand firm;
holiness adorns your house
for endless days, O LORD.

Psalm 94

[1]O LORD, the God who avenges,
O God who avenges, shine forth.

---

[a]10 Horn here symbolises strength.

²Rise up, O Judge of the earth;
   pay back to the proud what they
      deserve.
³How long will the wicked, O LORD,
   how long will the wicked be
      jubilant?

⁴They pour out arrogant words;
   all the evildoers are full of
      boasting.
⁵They crush your people, O LORD;
   they oppress your inheritance.
⁶They slay the widow and the alien;
   they murder the fatherless.
⁷They say, "The LORD does not see;
   the God of Jacob pays no heed."

⁸Take heed, you senseless ones
      among the people;
   you fools, when will you become
      wise?
⁹Does he who implanted the ear not
      hear?
   Does he who formed the eye not
      see?
¹⁰Does he who disciplines nations
      not punish?
   Does he who teaches man lack
      knowledge?
¹¹The LORD knows the thoughts of
      man;
   he knows that they are futile.

¹²Blessed is the man you discipline,
      O LORD,
   the man you teach from your law;
¹³you grant him relief from days of
      trouble,
   till a pit is dug for the wicked.
¹⁴For the LORD will not reject his
      people;
   he will never forsake his
      inheritance.
¹⁵Judgment will again be founded on
      righteousness,
   and all the upright in heart will
      follow it.

¹⁶Who will rise up for me against the
      wicked?
   Who will take a stand for me
      against evildoers?
¹⁷Unless the LORD had given me
      help,
   I would soon have dwelt in the
      silence of death.
¹⁸When I said, "My foot is slipping,"

your love, O LORD, supported me.
¹⁹When anxiety was great within me,
   your consolation brought joy to
      my soul.

²⁰Can a corrupt throne be allied with
      you—
   one that brings on misery by its
      decrees?
²¹They band together against the
      righteous
   and condemn the innocent to
      death.
²²But the LORD has become my
      fortress,
   and my God the rock in whom I
      take refuge.
²³He will repay them for their sins
   and destroy them for their
      wickedness;
   the LORD our God will destroy
      them.

Psalm 95

¹Come, let us sing for joy to the
      LORD;
   let us shout aloud to the Rock of
      our salvation.
²Let us come before him with
      thanksgiving
   and extol him with music and
      song.

³For the LORD is the great God,
   the great King above all gods.
⁴In his hand are the depths of the
      earth,
   and the mountain peaks belong to
      him.
⁵The sea is his, for he made it,
   and his hands formed the dry
      land.

⁶Come, let us bow down in worship,
   let us kneel before the LORD our
      Maker;
⁷for he is our God
   and we are the people of his
      pasture,
   the flock under his care.

Today, if you hear his voice,
⁸   do not harden your hearts as you
      did at Meribah,ᵃ
   as you did that day at Massahᵇ in
      the desert,

ᵃ8 Meribah means quarrelling.   ᵇ8 Massah means testing.

⁹where your fathers tested and tried
me,
though they had seen what I did.
¹⁰For forty years I was angry with
that generation;
I said, "They are a people whose
hearts go astray,
and they have not known my
ways."
¹¹So I declared on oath in my anger,
"They shall never enter my rest."

Psalm 96

¹Sing to the LORD a new song;
sing to the LORD, all the earth.
²Sing to the LORD, praise his name;
proclaim his salvation day after
day.
³Declare his glory among the nations,
his marvellous deeds among all
peoples.

⁴For great is the LORD and most
worthy of praise;
he is to be feared above all gods.
⁵For all the gods of the nations are
idols,
but the LORD made the heavens.
⁶Splendour and majesty are before
him;
strength and glory are in his
sanctuary.

⁷Ascribe to the LORD, O families of
nations,
ascribe to the LORD glory and
strength.
⁸Ascribe to the LORD the glory due to
his name;
bring an offering and come into
his courts.
⁹Worship the LORD in the splendour
of hisᵍ holiness;
tremble before him, all the earth.

¹⁰Say among the nations, "The LORD
reigns."
The world is firmly established, it
cannot be moved;
he will judge the peoples with
equity.
¹¹Let the heavens rejoice, let the
earth be glad;
let the sea resound, and all that is
in it;

---

¹² let the fields be jubilant, and
everything in them.
Then all the trees of the forest will
sing for joy;
¹³ they will sing before the LORD,
for he comes,
he comes to judge the earth.
He will judge the world in
righteousness
and the peoples in his truth.

Psalm 97

¹The LORD reigns, let the earth be
glad;
let the distant shores rejoice.

²Clouds and thick darkness surround
him;
righteousness and justice are the
foundation of his throne.
³Fire goes before him
and consumes his foes on every
side.
⁴His lightning lights up the world;
the earth sees and trembles.
⁵The mountains melt like wax before
the LORD,
before the Lord of all the earth.
⁶The heavens proclaim his
righteousness,
and all the peoples see his glory.

⁷All who worship images are put to
shame,
those who boast in idols—
worship him, all you gods!

⁸Zion hears and rejoices
and the villages of Judah are glad
because of your judgments, O
LORD.
⁹For you, O LORD, are the Most High
over all the earth;
you are exalted far above all
gods.

¹⁰Let those who love the LORD hate
evil,
for he guards the lives of his
faithful ones
and delivers them from the hand
of the wicked.
¹¹Light is shed upon the righteous
and joy on the upright in heart.
¹²Rejoice in the LORD, you who are
righteous,
and praise his holy name.

ᵍ9 Or LORD with the splendour of

Psalm 98
A psalm.

[1] Sing to the LORD a new song,
  for he has done marvellous
    things;
  his right hand and his holy arm
  have worked salvation for him.
[2] The LORD has made his salvation
    known
  and revealed his righteousness to
    the nations.
[3] He has remembered his love
  and his faithfulness to the house
    of Israel;
  all the ends of the earth have seen
    the salvation of our God.

[4] Shout for joy to the LORD, all the
    earth,
  burst into jubilant song with
    music;
[5] make music to the LORD with the
    harp,
  with the harp and the sound of
    singing,
[6] with trumpets and the blast of the
    ram's horn—
  shout for joy before the LORD, the
    King.

[7] Let the sea resound, and everything
    in it,
  the world, and all who live in it.
[8] Let the rivers clap their hands,
  let the mountains sing together
    for joy;
[9] let them sing before the LORD,
  for he comes to judge the earth.
He will judge the world in
    righteousness
  and the peoples with equity.

Psalm 99

[1] The LORD reigns,
  let the nations tremble;
he sits enthroned between the
    cherubim,
  let the earth shake.
[2] Great is the LORD in Zion;
  he is exalted over all the nations.
[3] Let them praise your great and
    awesome name—
  he is holy.

[4] The King is mighty, he loves
    justice—
  you have established equity;
in Jacob you have done
  what is just and right.
[5] Exalt the LORD our God
  and worship at his footstool;
  he is holy.

[6] Moses and Aaron were among his
    priests,
  Samuel was among those who
    called on his name;
they called on the LORD
  and he answered them.
[7] He spoke to them from the pillar of
    cloud;
  they kept his statutes and the
    decrees he gave them.

[8] O LORD our God,
  you answered them;
you were to Israel[a] a forgiving God,
  though you punished their
    misdeeds.[b]
[9] Exalt the LORD our God
  and worship at his holy
    mountain,
  for the LORD our God is holy.

Psalm 100
A psalm. For giving thanks.

[1] Shout for joy to the LORD, all the
    earth.
[2] Serve the LORD with gladness;
  come before him with joyful
    songs.
[3] Know that the LORD is God.
  It is he who made us, and we are
    his;[a]
we are his people, the sheep of
  his pasture.
[4] Enter his gates with thanksgiving
  and his courts with praise;
  give thanks to him and praise his
    name.
[5] For the LORD is good and his love
    endures for ever;
  his faithfulness continues through
    all generations.

Psalm 101
Of David. A psalm.

[1] I will sing of your love and justice;

---

a8 Hebrew them   b8 Or / an avenger of the wrongs done to them
a3 Or and not we ourselves

to you, O LORD, I will sing praise.
²I will be careful to lead a blameless
life—
when will you come to me?

I will walk in my house
with blameless heart.
³I will set before my eyes
no vile thing.

The deeds of faithless men I hate;
they shall not cling to me.
⁴Men of perverse heart shall be far
from me;
I will have nothing to do with
evil.

⁵Whoever slanders his neighbour in
secret,
him will I put to silence;
whoever has haughty eyes and a
proud heart,
him will I not endure.

⁶My eyes will be on the faithful in
the land,
that they may dwell with me;
he whose walk is blameless
will minister to me.

⁷No-one who practises deceit
will dwell in my house;
no-one who speaks falsely
will stand in my presence.

⁸Every morning I will put to silence
all the wicked in the land;
I will cut off every evildoer
from the city of the LORD.

Psalm 102

A prayer of an afflicted man. When he
is faint and pours out his lament before
the LORD.

¹Hear my prayer, O LORD;
let my cry for help come to you.
²Do not hide your face from me
when I am in distress.
Turn your ear to me;
when I call, answer me quickly.

³For my days vanish like smoke;
my bones burn like glowing
embers.
⁴My heart is blighted and withered
like grass;
I forget to eat my food.

⁵Because of my loud groaning
I am reduced to skin and bones.
⁶I am like a desert owl,
like an owl among the ruins.
⁷I lie awake; I have become
like a bird alone on a housetop.
⁸All day long my enemies taunt me;
those who rail against me use my
name as a curse.
⁹For I eat ashes as my food
and mingle my drink with tears
¹⁰because of your great wrath,
for you have taken me up and
thrown me aside.
¹¹My days are like the evening
shadow;
I wither away like grass.

¹²But you, O LORD, sit enthroned for
ever;
your renown endures through all
generations.
¹³You will arise and have
compassion on Zion,
for it is time to show favour to
her;
the appointed time has come.
¹⁴For her stones are dear to your
servants;
her very dust moves them to pity.
¹⁵The nations will fear the name of
the LORD,
all the kings of the earth will
revere your glory.
¹⁶For the LORD will rebuild Zion
and appear in his glory.
¹⁷He will respond to the prayer of
the destitute;
he will not despise their plea.
¹⁸Let this be written for a future
generation,
that a people not yet created may
praise the LORD:
¹⁹"The LORD looked down from his
sanctuary on high,
from heaven he viewed the earth,
²⁰to hear the groans of the prisoners
and release those condemned to
death."
²¹So the name of the LORD will be
declared in Zion
and his praise in Jerusalem
²²when the peoples and the
kingdoms

ᵃ23 Or By his power

assemble to worship the LORD.

²³In the course of my life[a] he broke
my strength;
he cut short my days.
²⁴So I said:
"Do not take me away, O my
God, in the midst of my days;
your years go on through all
generations.
²⁵In the beginning you laid the
foundations of the earth,
and the heavens are the work of
your hands.
²⁶They will perish, but you remain;
they will all wear out like a
garment.
Like clothing you will change them
and they will be discarded.
²⁷But you remain the same,
and your years will never end.
²⁸The children of your servants will
live in your presence;
their descendants will be
established before you."

Psalm 103
Of David.

¹Praise the LORD, O my soul;
all my inmost being, praise his
holy name.
²Praise the LORD, O my soul,
and forget not all his benefits.

³He forgives all my[a] sins
and heals all my diseases;
⁴he redeems my life from the pit
and crowns me with love and
compassion.
⁵He satisfies my desires with good
things,
so that my youth is renewed like
the eagle's.

⁶The LORD works righteousness
and justice for all the oppressed.
⁷He made known his ways to Moses,
his deeds to the people of Israel:
⁸The LORD is compassionate and
gracious,
slow to anger, abounding in love.
⁹He will not always accuse,
nor will he harbour his anger for
ever;
¹⁰he does not treat us as our sins
deserve

or repay us according to our
iniquities.
¹¹For as high as the heavens are
above the earth,
so great is his love for those who
fear him;
¹²as far as the east is from the west,
so far has he removed our
transgressions from us.
¹³As a father has compassion on his
children,
so the LORD has compassion on
those who fear him;
¹⁴for he knows how we are formed,
he remembers that we are dust.
¹⁵As for man, his days are like grass,
he flourishes like a flower of the
field;
¹⁶the wind blows over it and it is
gone,
and its place remembers it no
more.
¹⁷But from everlasting to everlasting
the LORD's love is with those who
fear him,
and his righteousness with their
children's children—
¹⁸with those who keep his covenant
and remember to obey his
precepts.

¹⁹The LORD has established his
throne in heaven,
and his kingdom rules over all.

²⁰Praise the LORD, you his angels,
you mighty ones who do his
bidding,
who obey his word.
²¹Praise the LORD, all his heavenly
hosts,
you his servants who do his will.
²²Praise the LORD, all his works
everywhere in his dominion.

Praise the LORD, O my soul.

Psalm 104

¹Praise the LORD, O my soul.

O LORD my God, you are very great;
you are clothed with splendour
and majesty.
²He wraps himself in light as with a
garment;
he stretches out the heavens like
a tent

a3 Hebrew your (referring to my soul); also in verses 3b–5

³ and lays the beams of his upper
   chambers on their waters.
   He makes the clouds his chariot
   and rides on the wings of the
   wind.
⁴He makes winds his messengers,ᵃ
   flames of fire his servants.
⁵He set the earth on its foundations;
   it can never be moved.
⁶You covered it with the deep as
   with a garment;
   the waters stood above the
   mountains.
⁷But at your rebuke the waters fled,
   at the sound of your thunder they
   took to flight;
⁸they flowed over the mountains,
   they went down into the valleys,
   to the place you assigned for
   them.
⁹You set a boundary they cannot
   cross;
   never again will they cover the
   earth.

¹⁰He makes springs pour water into
   the ravines;
   it flows between the mountains.
¹¹They give water to all the beasts of
   the field;
   the wild donkeys quench their
   thirst.
¹²The birds of the air nest by the
   waters;
   they sing among the branches.
¹³He waters the mountains from his
   upper chambers;
   the earth is satisfied by the fruit
   of his work.
¹⁴He makes grass grow for the cattle,
   and plants for man to cultivate—
   bringing forth food from the
   earth:
¹⁵wine that gladdens the heart of
   man,
   oil to make his face shine,
   and bread that sustains his heart.
¹⁶The trees of the LORD are well
   watered,
   the cedars of Lebanon that he
   planted.
¹⁷There the birds make their nests;
   the stork has its home in the pine
   trees.

¹⁸The high mountains belong to the
   wild goats;
   the crags are a refuge for the
   coneys.ᵇ
¹⁹The moon marks off the seasons,
   and the sun knows when to go
   down.
²⁰You bring darkness, it becomes
   night,
   and all the beasts of the forest
   prowl.
²¹The lions roar for their prey
   and seek their food from God.
²²The sun rises, and they steal away;
   they return and lie down in their
   dens.
²³Then man goes out to his work,
   to his labour until evening.

²⁴How many are your works, O
   LORD!
   In wisdom you made them all;
   the earth is full of your creatures.
²⁵There is the sea, vast and spacious,
   teeming with creatures beyond
   number—
   living things both large and small.
²⁶There the ships go to and fro,
   and the leviathan, which you
   formed to frolic there.

²⁷These all look to you
   to give them their food at the
   proper time.
²⁸When you give it to them,
   they gather it up;
   when you open your hand,
   they are satisfied with good
   things.
²⁹When you hide your face,
   they are terrified;
   when you take away their breath,
   they die and return to the dust.
³⁰When you send your Spirit,
   they are created,
   and you renew the face of the
   earth.

³¹May the glory of the LORD endure
   for ever;
   may the LORD rejoice in his
   works.
³²He looks at the earth, and it
   trembles;
   he touches the mountains, and
   they smoke.

ᵃ4 Or angels   ᵇ18 That is, the hyrax or rock badger

356

³³I will sing to the LORD all my life;
  I will sing praise to my God as
    long as I live.
³⁴May my meditation be pleasing to
    him,
  as I rejoice in the LORD.
³⁵But may sinners vanish from the
    earth
  and the wicked be no more.

Praise the LORD, O my soul.

Praise the LORD.^c

Psalm 105

¹Give thanks to the LORD, call on his
    name;
  make known among the nations
    what he has done.
²Sing to him, sing praise to him;
  tell of all his wonderful acts.
³Glory in his holy name;
  let the hearts of those who seek
    the LORD rejoice.
⁴Look to the LORD and his strength;
  seek his face always.
⁵Remember the wonders he has
    done,
  his miracles, and the judgments
    he pronounced,
⁶O descendants of Abraham his
    servant,
  O sons of Jacob, his chosen ones.

⁷He is the LORD our God;
  his judgments are in all the earth.
⁸He remembers his covenant for
    ever,
  the word he commanded, for a
    thousand generations,
⁹the covenant he made with
    Abraham,
  the oath he swore to Isaac.
¹⁰He confirmed it to Jacob as a
    decree,
  to Israel as an everlasting
    covenant:
¹¹"To you I will give the land of
    Canaan
  as the portion you will inherit."

¹²When they were but few in
    number,
  few indeed, and strangers in it,
¹³they wandered from nation to
    nation,

from one kingdom to another.
¹⁴He allowed no-one to oppress
    them;
  for their sake he rebuked kings:
¹⁵"Do not touch my anointed ones;
  do my prophets no harm."

¹⁶He called down famine on the
    land
  and destroyed all their supplies
    of food;
¹⁷and he sent a man before them—
  Joseph, sold as a slave.
¹⁸They bruised his feet with
    shackles,
  his neck was put in irons,
¹⁹till what he foretold came to pass,
  till the word of the LORD proved
    him true.
²⁰The king sent and released him,
  the ruler of peoples set him free.
²¹He made him master of his
    household,
  ruler over all he possessed,
²²to discipline his princes as he
    pleased
  and teach his elders wisdom.

²³Then Israel entered Egypt;
  Jacob lived as an alien in the
    land of Ham.
²⁴The LORD made his people very
    fruitful;
  he made them too numerous for
    their foes,
²⁵whose hearts he turned to hate his
    people,
  to conspire against his servants.
²⁶He sent Moses his servant,
  and Aaron, whom he had chosen.
²⁷They performed his miraculous
    signs among them,
  his wonders in the land of Ham.
²⁸He sent darkness and made the
    land dark—
  for had they not rebelled against
    his words?
²⁹He turned their waters into blood,
  causing their fish to die.
³⁰Their land teemed with frogs,
  which went up into the bedrooms
    of their rulers.
³¹He spoke, and there came swarms
    of flies,
  and gnats throughout their
    country.

^c35 Hebrew *Hallelu Yah*

32He turned their rain into hail,
   with lightning throughout their
   land;
33he struck down their vines and fig-
   trees
   and shattered the trees of their
   country.
34He spoke, and the locusts came,
   grasshoppers without number;
35they ate up every green thing in
   their land,
   ate up the produce of their soil.
36Then he struck down all the
   firstborn in their land,
   the firstfruits of all their
   manhood.
37He brought out Israel, laden with
   silver and gold,
   and from among their tribes no-
   one faltered.
38Egypt was glad when they left,
   because dread of Israel had
   fallen on them.
39He spread out a cloud as a
   covering,
   and a fire to give light at night.
40They asked, and he brought them
   quail
   and satisfied them with the bread
   of heaven.
41He opened the rock and water
   gushed out;
   like a river it flowed in the
   desert.
42For he remembered his holy
   promise
   given to his servant Abraham.
43He brought out his people with
   rejoicing,
   his chosen ones with shouts of
   joy;
44he gave them the lands of the
   nations,
   and they fell heir to what others
   had toiled for—
45that they might keep his precepts
   and observe his laws.

Praise the LORD.a

Psalm 106

1Praise the LORD.a

Give thanks to the LORD, for he is
   good;

his love endures for ever.
2Who can proclaim the mighty acts
   of the LORD
   or fully declare his praise?
3Blessed are they who maintain
   justice,
   who constantly do what is right.
4Remember me, O LORD, when you
   show favour to your people,
   come to my aid when you save
   them,
5that I may enjoy the prosperity of
   your chosen ones,
   that I may share in the joy of
   your nation
   and join your inheritance in
   giving praise.

6We have sinned, even as our
   fathers did;
   we have done wrong and acted
   wickedly.
7When our fathers were in Egypt,
   they gave no thought to your
   miracles;
   they did not remember your many
   kindnesses,
   and they rebelled by the sea, the
   Red Sea.b
8Yet he saved them for his name's
   sake,
   to make his mighty power known.
9He rebuked the Red Sea, and it
   dried up;
   he led them through the depths
   as through a desert.
10He saved them from the hand of
   the foe;
   from the hand of the enemy he
   redeemed them.
11The waters covered their
   adversaries;
   not one of them survived.
12Then they believed his promises
   and sang his praise.
13But they soon forgot what he had
   done
   and did not wait for his counsel.
14In the desert they gave in to their
   craving;
   in the wasteland they put God to
   the test.
15So he gave them what they asked
   for,

a45 Hebrew *Hallelu Yah*   a1 Hebrew *Hallelu Yah*; also in verse 48
b7 Hebrew *Yam Suph*; that is, Sea of Reeds; also in verses 9 and 22

but sent a wasting disease upon them.

[16]In the camp they grew envious of Moses
and of Aaron, who was consecrated to the LORD.

[17]The earth opened up and swallowed Dathan;
it buried the company of Abiram.

[18]Fire blazed among their followers;
a flame consumed the wicked.

[19]At Horeb they made a calf
and worshipped an idol cast from metal.

[20]They exchanged their Glory
for an image of a bull, which eats grass.

[21]They forgot the God who saved them,
who had done great things in Egypt,

[22]miracles in the land of Ham
and awesome deeds by the Red Sea.

[23]So he said he would destroy them—
had not Moses, his chosen one,
stood in the breach before him
to keep his wrath from destroying them.

[24]Then they despised the pleasant land;
they did not believe his promise.

[25]They grumbled in their tents
and did not obey the LORD.

[26]So he swore to them with uplifted hand
that he would make them fall in the desert,

[27]make their descendants fall among the nations
and scatter them throughout the lands.

[28]They yoked themselves to the Baal of Peor
and ate sacrifices offered to lifeless gods;

[29]they provoked the LORD to anger by their wicked deeds,
and a plague broke out among them.

[30]But Phinehas stood up and intervened,

and the plague was checked.

[31]This was credited to him as righteousness
for endless generations to come.

[32]By the waters of Meribah they angered the LORD,
and trouble came to Moses because of them;

[33]for they rebelled against the Spirit of God,
and rash words came from Moses' lips.[c]

[34]They did not destroy the peoples as the LORD had commanded them,

[35]but they mingled with the nations and adopted their customs.

[36]They worshipped their idols,
which became a snare to them.

[37]They sacrificed their sons
and their daughters to demons.

[38]They shed innocent blood,
the blood of their sons and daughters,
whom they sacrificed to the idols of Canaan,
and the land was desecrated by their blood.

[39]They defiled themselves by what they did;
by their deeds they prostituted themselves.

[40]Therefore the LORD was angry with his people
and abhorred his inheritance.

[41]He handed them over to the nations,
and their foes ruled over them.

[42]Their enemies oppressed them
and subjected them to their power.

[43]Many times he delivered them,
but they were bent on rebellion
and they wasted away in their sin.

[44]But he took note of their distress
when he heard their cry;

[45]for their sake he remembered his covenant
and out of his great love he relented.

[c]33 Or against his spirit, / and rash words came from his lips

46He caused them to be pitied
by all who held them captive.

47Save us, O LORD our God,
and gather us from the nations,
that we may give thanks to your
holy name
and glory in your praise.

48Praise be to the LORD, the God of
Israel,
from everlasting to everlasting.
Let all the people say, "Amen!"

Praise the LORD.

BOOK V

Psalms 107–150

Psalm 107

1Give thanks to the LORD, for he is
good;
his love endures for ever.

2Let the redeemed of the LORD say
this—
those he redeemed from the hand
of the foe,

3those he gathered from the lands,
from east and west, from north
and south.*ᵃ*

4Some wandered in desert
wastelands,
finding no way to a city where
they could settle.

5They were hungry and thirsty,
and their lives ebbed away.

6Then they cried out to the LORD in
their trouble,
and he delivered them from their
distress.

7He led them by a straight way
to a city where they could settle.

8Let them give thanks to the LORD for
his unfailing love
and his wonderful deeds for men,

9for he satisfies the thirsty
and fills the hungry with good
things.

10Some sat in darkness and the
deepest gloom,
prisoners suffering in iron chains,

11for they had rebelled against the
words of God

and despised the counsel of the
Most High.

12So he subjected them to bitter
labour;
they stumbled, and there was no-
one to help.

13Then they cried to the LORD in
their trouble,
and he saved them from their
distress.

14He brought them out of darkness
and the deepest gloom
and broke away their chains.

15Let them give thanks to the LORD
for his unfailing love
and his wonderful deeds for men,

16for he breaks down gates of bronze
and cuts through bars of iron.

17Some became fools through their
rebellious ways
and suffered affliction because of
their iniquities.

18They loathed all food
and drew near the gates of death.

19Then they cried to the LORD in
their trouble,
and he saved them from their
distress.

20He sent forth his word and healed
them;
he rescued them from the grave.

21Let them give thanks to the LORD
for his unfailing love
and his wonderful deeds for men.

22Let them sacrifice thank-offerings
and tell of his works with songs
of joy.

23Others went out on the sea in
ships;
they were merchants on the
mighty waters.

24They saw the works of the LORD,
his wonderful deeds in the deep.

25For he spoke and stirred up a
tempest
that lifted high the waves.

26They mounted up to the heavens
and went down to the depths;
in their peril their courage melted
away.

27They reeled and staggered like
drunken men;
they were at their wits' end.

ᵃ3 Hebrew north and the sea

²⁸Then they cried out to the LORD in
their trouble,
and he brought them out of their
distress.
²⁹He stilled the storm to a whisper;
the waves of the sea were
hushed.
³⁰They were glad when it grew calm,
and he guided them to their
desired haven.
³¹Let them give thanks to the LORD
for his unfailing love
and his wonderful deeds for men.
³²Let them exalt him in the assembly
of the people
and praise him in the council of
the elders.

³³He turned rivers into a desert,
flowing springs into thirsty
ground,
³⁴and fruitful land into a salt waste,
because of the wickedness of
those who lived there.
³⁵He turned the desert into pools of
water
and the parched ground into
flowing springs;
³⁶there he brought the hungry to live,
and they founded a city where
they could settle.
³⁷They sowed fields and planted
vineyards
that yielded a fruitful harvest;
³⁸he blessed them, and their
numbers greatly increased,
and he did not let their herds
diminish.

³⁹Then their numbers decreased, and
they were humbled
by oppression, calamity and
sorrow;
⁴⁰he who pours contempt on nobles
made them wander in a trackless
waste.
⁴¹But he lifted the needy out of their
affliction
and increased their families like
flocks.
⁴²The upright see and rejoice,
but all the wicked shut their
mouths.

⁴³Whoever is wise, let him heed
these things
and consider the great love of the
LORD.

Psalm 108
A song. A psalm of David.

¹My heart is steadfast, O God;
I will sing and make music with
all my soul.
²Awake, harp and lyre!
I will awaken the dawn.
³I will praise you, O LORD, among
the nations;
I will sing of you among the
peoples.
⁴For great is your love, higher than
the heavens;
your faithfulness reaches to the
skies.
⁵Be exalted, O God, above the
heavens,
and let your glory be over all the
earth.

⁶Save us and help us with your right
hand,
that those you love may be
delivered.
⁷God has spoken from his sanctuary:
"In triumph I will parcel out
Shechem
and measure off the Valley of
Succoth.
⁸Gilead is mine, Manasseh is mine;
Ephraim is my helmet,
Judah my sceptre.
⁹Moab is my washbasin,
upon Edom I toss my sandal;
over Philistia I shout in triumph."
¹⁰Who will bring me to the fortified
city?
Who will lead me to Edom?
¹¹Is it not you, O God, you who have
rejected us
and no longer go out with our
armies?
¹²Give us aid against the enemy,
for the help of man is worthless.
¹³With God we shall gain the victory,
and he will trample down our
enemies.

Psalm 109
For the director of music. Of David. A
psalm.

¹O God, whom I praise,
do not remain silent,
²for wicked and deceitful men

361

have opened their mouths against
me;
  they have spoken against me with
lying tongues.
3With words of hatred they surround
me;
  they attack me without cause.
4In return for my friendship they
accuse me,
  but I am a man of prayer.
5They repay me evil for good,
  and hatred for my friendship.
6Appoint*a* an evil man*b* to oppose
him;
  let an accuser*c* stand at his right
hand.
7When he is tried, let him be found
guilty,
  and may his prayers condemn
him.
8May his days be few;
  may another take his place of
leadership.
9May his children be fatherless
  and his wife a widow.
10May his children be wandering
beggars;
  may they be driven*d* from their
ruined homes.
11May a creditor seize all he has;
  may strangers plunder the fruits
of his labour.
12May no-one extend kindness to
him
  or take pity on his fatherless
children.
13May his descendants be cut off,
  their names blotted out from the
next generation.
14May the iniquity of his fathers be
remembered before the LORD;
  may the sin of his mother never
be blotted out.
15May their sins always remain
before the LORD,
  that he may cut off the memory
of them from the earth.
16For he never thought of doing a
kindness,
  but hounded to death the poor
and the needy and the broken-
hearted.
17He loved to pronounce a curse—

may it*e* come on him;
  he found no pleasure in blessing—
  may it be*f* far from him.
18He wore cursing as his garment;
  it entered into his body like
water,
  into his bones like oil.
19May it be like a cloak wrapped
about him,
  like a belt tied for ever round
him.
20May this be the LORD's payment to
my accusers,
  to those who speak evil of me.
21But you, O Sovereign LORD,
  deal well with me for your
name's sake;
  out of the goodness of your love,
deliver me.
22For I am poor and needy,
  and my heart is wounded within
me.
23I fade away like an evening
shadow;
  I am shaken off like a locust.
24My knees give way from fasting;
  my body is thin and gaunt.
25I am an object of scorn to my
accusers;
  when they see me, they shake
their heads.
26Help me, O LORD my God;
  save me in accordance with your
love.
27Let them know that it is your hand,
  that you, O LORD, have done it.
28They may curse, but you will bless;
  when they attack they will be put
to shame,
  but your servant will rejoice.
29My accusers will be clothed with
disgrace
  and wrapped in shame as in a
cloak.
30With my mouth I will greatly extol
the LORD;
  in the great throng I will praise
him.
31For he stands at the right hand of
the needy one,
  to save his life from those who
condemn him.

*a*6 Or ,They say, "Appoint (with quotation marks at the end of verse 19)
*b*6 Or the Evil One   *c*6 Or let Satan   *d*10 Septuagint; Hebrew sought
*e*17 Or curse, / and it has   *f*17 Or blessing, / and it is

Psalm 110

Of David. A psalm.

¹The LORD says to my Lord:
"Sit at my right hand
until I make your enemies
a footstool for your feet."

²The LORD will extend your mighty
sceptre from Zion;
you will rule in the midst of your
enemies.

³Your troops will be willing
on your day of battle.
Arrayed in holy majesty,
from the womb of the dawn
you will receive the dew of your
youth.ᵃ

⁴The LORD has sworn
and will not change his mind:
"You are a priest for ever,
in the order of Melchizedek."

⁵The Lord is at your right hand;
he will crush kings on the day of
his wrath.

⁶He will judge nations, heaping up
the dead
and crushing the rulers of the
whole earth.

⁷He will drink from a brook beside
the way;ᵇ
therefore he will lift up his head.

Psalm 111ᵃ

¹Praise the LORD.ᵇ

I will extol the LORD with all my
heart
in the council of the upright and
in the assembly.

²Great are the works of the LORD;
they are pondered by all who
delight in them.

³Glorious and majestic are his deeds,
and his righteousness endures for
ever.

⁴He has caused his wonders to be
remembered;
the LORD is gracious and
compassionate.

⁵He provides food for those who fear
him;
he remembers his covenant for
ever.

⁶He has shown his people the power
of his works,
giving them the lands of other
nations.

⁷The works of his hands are faithful
and just;
all his precepts are trustworthy.

⁸They are steadfast for ever and
ever,
done in faithfulness and
uprightness.

⁹He provided redemption for his
people;
he ordained his covenant for
ever—
holy and awesome is his name.

¹⁰The fear of the LORD is the
beginning of wisdom;
all who follow his precepts have
good understanding.
To him belongs eternal praise.

Psalm 112ᵃ

¹Praise the LORD.ᵇ

Blessed is the man who fears the
LORD,
who finds great delight in his
commands.

²His children will be mighty in the
land;
each generation of the upright
will be blessed.

³Wealth and riches are in his house,
and his righteousness endures for
ever.

⁴Even in darkness light dawns for
the upright,
for the gracious and
compassionate and
righteous man.ᶜ

⁵Good will come to him who is
generous and lends freely,
who conducts his affairs with
justice.

ᵃ3 Or / your young men will come to you like the dew.
ᵇ7 Or / The One who grants succession will set him in authority
ᵃThis psalm is an acrostic poem, the lines of which begin with the successive letters of the
Hebrew alphabet.
ᵇ1 Hebrew Hallelu Yah
ᶜ4 Or / for the LORD, is gracious and compassionate and righteous

⁶Surely he will never be shaken;
   a righteous man will be
     remembered for ever.
⁷He will have no fear of bad news;
   his heart is steadfast, trusting in
     the LORD.
⁸His heart is secure, he will have no
   fear;
   in the end he will look in
     triumph on his foes.
⁹He has scattered abroad his gifts to
   the poor,
   his righteousness endures for
     ever;
   his horn^d will be lifted high in
     honour.

¹⁰The wicked man will see and be
   vexed,
   he will gnash his teeth and waste
     away;
   the longings of the wicked will
     come to nothing.

Psalm 113

¹Praise the LORD.^a

Praise, O servants of the LORD,
   praise the name of the LORD.
²Let the name of the LORD be
   praised,
   both now and for evermore.
³From the rising of the sun to the
   place where it sets
   the name of the LORD is to be
     praised.

⁴The LORD is exalted over all the
   nations,
   his glory above the heavens.
⁵Who is like the LORD our God,
   the One who sits enthroned on
     high,
⁶who stoops down to look
   on the heavens and the earth?

⁷He raises the poor from the dust
   and lifts the needy from the ash
     heap;
⁸he seats them with princes,
   with the princes of their people.
⁹He settles the barren woman in her
   home
   as a happy mother of children.

Praise the LORD.

Psalm 114

¹When Israel came out of Egypt,
   the house of Jacob from a people
     of foreign tongue,
²Judah became God's sanctuary,
   Israel his dominion.
³The sea looked and fled,
   the Jordan turned back;
⁴the mountains skipped like rams,
   the hills like lambs.

⁵Why was it, O sea, that you fled,
   O Jordan, that you turned back,
⁶you mountains, that you skipped
    like rams,
   you hills, like lambs?

⁷Tremble, O earth, at the presence of
   the Lord,
   at the presence of the God of
     Jacob,
⁸who turned the rock into a pool,
   the hard rock into springs of
     water.

Psalm 115

¹Not to us, O LORD, not to us
   but to your name be the glory,
   because of your love and
     faithfulness.

²Why do the nations say,
   "Where is their God?"
³Our God is in heaven;
   he does whatever pleases him.
⁴But their idols are silver and gold,
   made by the hands of men.
⁵They have mouths, but cannot
   speak,
   eyes, but they cannot see;
⁶they have ears, but cannot hear,
   noses, but they cannot smell;
⁷they have hands, but cannot feel,
   feet, but they cannot walk;
   nor can they utter a sound with
     their throats.
⁸Those who make them will be like
   them,
   and so will all who trust in them.

⁹O house of Israel, trust in the
   LORD—
   he is their help and shield.
¹⁰O house of Aaron, trust in the
   LORD—
   he is their help and shield:

^d9 Horn here symbolises dignity.   ^a1 Hebrew Hallelu Yah; also in verse 9

[11]You who fear him, trust in the
LORD—
he is their help and shield.
[12]The LORD remembers us and will
bless us:
He will bless the house of Israel,
he will bless the house of Aaron,
[13]he will bless those who fear the
LORD—
small and great alike.

[14]May the LORD make you increase,
both you and your children.
[15]May you be blessed by the LORD,
the Maker of heaven and earth.

[16]The highest heavens belong to the
LORD,
but the earth he has given to
man.
[17]It is not the dead who praise the
LORD,
those who go down to silence;
[18]it is we who extol the LORD,
both now and for evermore.

Praise the LORD.[a]

Psalm 116

[1]I love the LORD, for he heard my
voice;
he heard my cry for mercy.
[2]Because he turned his ear to me,
I will call on him as long as I
live.

[3]The cords of death entangled me,
the anguish of the grave[a] came
upon me;
I was overcome by trouble and
sorrow.
[4]Then I called on the name of the
LORD:
"O LORD, save me!"

[5]The LORD is gracious and righteous;
our God is full of compassion.
[6]The LORD protects the simple-
hearted;
when I was in great need, he
saved me.

[7]Be at rest once more, O my soul,
for the LORD has been good to
you.

[8]For you, O LORD, have delivered my
soul from death,
my eyes from tears,
my feet from stumbling,
[9]that I may walk before the LORD
in the land of the living.
[10]I believed; therefore[b] I said,
"I am greatly afflicted."
[11]And in my dismay I said,
"All men are liars."

[12]How can I repay the LORD
for all his goodness to me?
[13]I will lift up the cup of salvation
and call on the name of the LORD.
[14]I will fulfil my vows to the LORD
in the presence of all his people.

[15]Precious in the sight of the LORD
is the death of his saints.
[16]O LORD, truly I am your servant;
I am your servant, the son of your
maidservant;[c]
you have freed me from my
chains.
[17]I will sacrifice a thank-offering to
you
and call on the name of the LORD.
[18]I will fulfil my vows to the LORD
in the presence of all his people,
[19]in the courts of the house of the
LORD—
in your midst, O Jerusalem.

Praise the LORD.[d]

Psalm 117

[1]Praise the LORD, all you nations;
extol him, all you peoples.
[2]For great is his love towards us,
and the faithfulness of the LORD
endures for ever.

Praise the LORD.[d]

Psalm 118

[1]Give thanks to the LORD, for he is
good;
his love endures for ever.

[2]Let Israel say:
"His love endures for ever."
[3]Let the house of Aaron say:
"His love endures for ever."

---

[a]18 Hebrew *Hallelu Yah* [a]3 Hebrew *Sheol* [b]10 Or *believed even when*
[c]16 Or *servant, your faithful son* [d]19, 2 Hebrew *Hallelu Yah*

⁴Let those who fear the LORD say:
  "His love endures for ever."

⁵In my anguish I cried to the LORD,
  and he answered by setting me
  free.
⁶The LORD is with me; I will not be
  afraid.
  What can man do to me?
⁷The LORD is with me; he is my
  helper.
  I will look in triumph on my
  enemies.

⁸It is better to take refuge in the
  LORD
  than to trust in man.
⁹It is better to take refuge in the
  LORD
  than to trust in princes.
¹⁰All the nations surrounded me,
  but in the name of the LORD I cut
  them off.
¹¹They surrounded me on every side,
  but in the name of the LORD I cut
  them off.
¹²They swarmed around me like
  bees,
  but they died out as quickly as
  burning thorns;
  in the name of the LORD I cut
  them off.
¹³I was pushed back and about to
  fall,
  but the LORD helped me.
¹⁴The LORD is my strength and my
  song;
  he has become my salvation.

¹⁵Shouts of joy and victory
  resound in the tents of the
  righteous:
  "The LORD's right hand has done
  mighty things!
¹⁶The LORD's right hand is lifted
  high;
  the LORD's right hand has done
  mighty things!"
¹⁷I will not die but live,
  and will proclaim what the LORD
  has done.
¹⁸The LORD has chastened me
  severely,

but he has not given me over to
  death.
¹⁹Open for me the gates of
  righteousness;
  I will enter and give thanks to the
  LORD.
²⁰This is the gate of the LORD
  through which the righteous may
  enter.
²¹I will give you thanks, for you
  answered me;
  you have become my salvation.

²²The stone the builders rejected
  has become the capstone;
²³the LORD has done this,
  and it is marvellous in our eyes.
²⁴This is the day the LORD has made;
  let us rejoice and be glad in it.

²⁵O LORD, save us;
  O LORD, grant us success.
²⁶Blessed is he who comes in the
  name of the LORD.
  From the house of the LORD we
  bless you.ᵃ
²⁷The LORD is God,
  and he has made his light shine
  upon us.
  With boughs in hand, join in the
  festal procession
  upᵇ to the horns of the altar.

²⁸You are my God, and I will give
  thanks;
  you are my God, and I will exalt
  you.

²⁹Give thanks to the LORD, for he is
  good;
  his love endures for ever.

Psalm 119ᵃ

א Aleph

¹Blessed are they whose ways are
  blameless,
  who walk according to the law of
  the LORD.
²Blessed are they who keep his
  statutes
  and seek him with all their heart.
³They do nothing wrong;
  they walk in his ways.

ᵃ26 The Hebrew is plural.   ᵇ27 Or Bind the festal sacrifice with ropes / and take it
ᵃThis psalm is an acrostic poem; the verses of each stanza begin with the same letter of the
Hebrew alphabet.

4You have laid down precepts
  that are to be fully obeyed.
5Oh, that my ways were steadfast
  in obeying your decrees!
6Then I would not be put to shame
  when I consider all your
  commands.
7I will praise you with an upright
  heart
  as I learn your righteous laws.
8I will obey your decrees;
  do not utterly forsake me.

ב Beth

9How can a young man keep his way
  pure?
  By living according to your word.
10I seek you with all my heart;
  do not let me stray from your
  commands.
11I have hidden your word in my
  heart
  that I might not sin against you.
12Praise be to you, O LORD;
  teach me your decrees.
13With my lips I recount
  all the laws that come from your
  mouth.
14I rejoice in following your statutes
  as one rejoices in great riches.
15I meditate on your precepts
  and consider your ways.
16I delight in your decrees;
  I will not neglect your word.

ג Gimel

17Do good to your servant, and I will
  live;
  I will obey your word.
18Open my eyes that I may see
  wonderful things in your law.
19I am a stranger on earth;
  do not hide your commands from
  me.
20My soul is consumed with longing
  for your laws at all times.
21You rebuke the arrogant, who are
  cursed
  and who stray from your
  commands.
22Remove from me scorn and
  contempt,
  for I keep your statutes.

23Though princes sit together and
  slander me,
  your servant will meditate on
  your decrees.
24Your statutes are my delight;
  they are my counsellors.

ד Daleth

25I am laid low in the dust;
  renew my life according to your
  word.
26I recounted my ways and you
  answered me;
  teach me your decrees.
27Let me understand the teaching of
  your precepts;
  then I will meditate on your
  wonders.
28My soul is weary with sorrow;
  strengthen me according to your
  word.
29Keep me from deceitful ways;
  be gracious to me through your
  law.
30I have chosen the way of truth;
  I have set my heart on your laws.
31I hold fast to your statutes, O LORD;
  do not let me be put to shame.
32I run in the path of your
  commands,
  for you have set my heart free.

ה He

33Teach me, O LORD, to follow your
  decrees;
  then I will keep them to the end.
34Give me understanding, and I will
  keep your law
  and obey it with all my heart.
35Direct me in the path of your
  commands,
  for there I find delight.
36Turn my heart towards your
  statutes
  and not towards selfish gain.
37Turn my eyes away from worthless
  things;
  renew my life according to your
  word.b
38Fulfil your promise to your servant,
  so that you may be feared.
39Take away the disgrace I dread,
  for your laws are good.

b37 Two manuscripts of the Masoretic Text and Dead Sea Scrolls; most manuscripts of the
Masoretic Text *life in your way*

40How I long for your precepts!
  Renew my life in your
    righteousness.

ו Waw

41May your unfailing love come to
    me, O LORD,
  your salvation according to your
    promise;
42then I will answer the one who
    taunts me,
  for I trust in your word.
43Do not snatch the word of truth
    from my mouth,
  for I have put my hope in your
    laws.
44I will always obey your law,
  for ever and ever.
45I will walk about in freedom,
  for I have sought out your
    precepts.
46I will speak of your statutes before
    kings
  and will not be put to shame,
47for I delight in your
    commandments
  because I love them.
48I reach out my hands for your
    commandments, which I love,
  and I meditate on your decrees.

ז Zayin

49Remember your word to your
    servant,
  for you have given me hope.
50My comfort in my suffering is this:
  Your promise renews my life.
51The arrogant mock me without
    restraint,
  but I do not turn from your law.
52I remember your ancient laws, O
    LORD,
  and I find comfort in them.
53Indignation grips me because of
    the wicked,
  who have forsaken your law.
54Your decrees are the theme of my
    song
  wherever I lodge.
55In the night I remember your
    name, O LORD,
  and I will keep your law.
56This has been my practice:
  I obey your precepts.

ח Heth

57You are my portion, O LORD;

I have promised to obey your
    words.
58I have sought your face with all my
    heart;
  be gracious to me according to
    your promise.
59I have considered my ways
  and have turned my steps to your
    statutes.
60I will hasten and not delay
  to obey your commands.
61Though the wicked bind me with
    ropes,
  I will not forget your law.
62At midnight I rise to give you
    thanks
  for your righteous laws.
63I am a friend to all who fear you,
  to all who follow your precepts.
64The earth is filled with your love,
    O LORD;
  teach me your decrees.

ט Teth

65Do good to your servant
  according to your word, O LORD.
66Teach me knowledge and good
    judgment,
  for I believe in your commands.
67Before I was afflicted I went astray,
  but now I obey your word.
68You are good, and what you do is
    good;
  teach me your decrees.
69Though the arrogant have smeared
    me with lies,
  I keep your precepts with all my
    heart.
70Their hearts are callous and
    unfeeling,
  but I delight in your law.
71It was good for me to be afflicted
  so that I might learn your
    decrees.
72The law from your mouth is more
    precious to me
  than thousands of pieces of silver
    and gold.

י Yodh

73Your hands made me and formed
    me;
  give me understanding to learn
    your commands.
74May they who fear you rejoice
  when they see me,

for I have put my hope in your
word.

75I know, O LORD, that your laws are
righteous,
and in faithfulness you have
afflicted me.

76May your unfailing love be my
comfort,
according to your promise to your
servant.

77Let your compassion come to me
that I may live,
for your law is my delight.

78May the arrogant be put to shame
for wronging me without cause;
but I will meditate on your
precepts.

79May those who fear you turn to
me,
those who understand your
statutes.

80May my heart be blameless
towards your decrees,
that I may not be put to shame.

 כ Kaph

81My soul faints with longing for
your salvation,
but I have put my hope in your
word.

82My eyes fail, looking for your
promise;
I say, "When will you comfort
me?"

83Though I am like a wineskin in the
smoke,
I do not forget your decrees.

84How long must your servant wait?
When will you punish my
persecutors?

85The arrogant dig pitfalls for me,
contrary to your law.

86All your commands are
trustworthy;
help me, for men persecute me
without cause.

87They almost wiped me from the
earth,
but I have not forsaken your
precepts.

88Preserve my life according to your
love,
and I will obey the statutes of
your mouth.

ל Lamedh

89Your word, O LORD, is eternal;

it stands firm in the heavens.

90Your faithfulness continues through
all generations;
you established the earth, and it
endures.

91Your laws endure to this day,
for all things serve you.

92If your law had not been my
delight,
I would have perished in my
affliction.

93I will never forget your precepts,
for by them you have renewed
my life.

94Save me, for I am yours;
I have sought out your precepts.

95The wicked are waiting to destroy
me,
but I will ponder your statutes.

96To all perfection I see a limit;
but your commands are
boundless.

מ Mem

97Oh, how I love your law!
I meditate on it all day long.

98Your commands make me wiser
than my enemies,
for they are ever with me.

99I have more insight than all my
teachers,
for I meditate on your statutes.

100I have more understanding than
the elders,
for I obey your precepts.

101I have kept my feet from every
evil path
so that I might obey your word.

102I have not departed from your
laws,
for you yourself have taught me.

103How sweet are your promises to
my taste,
sweeter than honey to my mouth!

104I gain understanding from your
precepts;
therefore I hate every wrong
path.

נ Nun

105Your word is a lamp to my feet
and a light for my path.

106I have taken an oath and
confirmed it,
that I will follow your righteous
laws.

107I have suffered much;
  renew my life, O LORD,
  according to your word.
108Accept, O LORD, the willing praise
    of my mouth,
  and teach me your laws.
109Though I constantly take my life
    in my hands,
  I will not forget your law.
110The wicked have set a snare for
    me,
  but I have not strayed from your
    precepts.
111Your statutes are my heritage for
    ever;
  they are the joy of my heart.
112My heart is set on keeping your
    decrees
  to the very end.

ס Samekh

113I hate double-minded men,
  but I love your law.
114You are my refuge and my shield;
  I have put my hope in your
    word.
115Away from me, you evildoers,
  that I may keep the commands of
    my God!
116Sustain me according to your
    promise, and I shall live;
  do not let my hopes be dashed.
117Uphold me, and I shall be
    delivered;
  I shall always have regard for
    your decrees.
118You reject all who stray from your
    decrees,
  for their deceitfulness is in vain.
119All the wicked of the earth you
    discard like dross;
  therefore I love your statutes.
120My flesh trembles in fear of you;
  I stand in awe of your laws.

ע Ayin

121I have done what is righteous and
    just;
  do not leave me to my
    oppressors.
122Ensure your servant's well-being;
  let not the arrogant oppress me.
123My eyes fail, looking for your
    salvation,
  looking for your righteous
    promise.

124Deal with your servant according
    to your love
  and teach me your decrees.
125I am your servant; give me
    discernment
  that I may understand your
    statutes.
126It is time for you to act, O LORD;
  your law is being broken.
127Because I love your commands
    more than gold, more than pure
    gold,
128and because I consider all your
    precepts right,
  I hate every wrong path.

פ Pe

129Your statutes are wonderful;
  therefore I obey them.
130The entrance of your words gives
    light;
  it gives understanding to the
    simple.
131I open my mouth and pant,
  longing for your commands.
132Turn to me and have mercy on
    me,
  as you always do to those who
    love your name.
133Direct my footsteps according to
    your word;
  let no sin rule over me.
134Redeem me from the oppression
    of men,
  that I may obey your precepts.
135Make your face shine upon your
    servant
  and teach me your decrees.
136Streams of tears flow from my
    eyes,
  for your law is not obeyed.

צ Tsadhe

137Righteous are you, O LORD,
  and your laws are right.
138The statutes you have laid down
    are righteous;
  they are fully trustworthy.
139My zeal wears me out,
  for my enemies ignore your
    words.
140Your promises have been
    thoroughly tested,
  and your servant loves them.
141Though I am lowly and despised,
  I do not forget your precepts.

¹⁴²Your righteousness is everlasting
and your law is true.
¹⁴³Trouble and distress have come
upon me,
but your commands are my
delight.
¹⁴⁴Your statutes are for ever right;
give me understanding that I
may live.

ק Qoph

¹⁴⁵I call with all my heart; answer
me, O LORD,
and I will obey your decrees.
¹⁴⁶I call out to you; save me
and I will keep your statutes.
¹⁴⁷I rise before dawn and cry for
help;
I have put my hope in your
word.
¹⁴⁸My eyes stay open through the
watches of the night,
that I may meditate on your
promises.
¹⁴⁹Hear my voice in accordance with
your love;
renew my life, O LORD,
according to your laws.
¹⁵⁰Those who devise wicked schemes
are near,
but they are far from your law.
¹⁵¹Yet you are near, O LORD,
and all your commands are true.
¹⁵²Long ago I learned from your
statutes
that you established them to last
for ever.

ר Resh

¹⁵³Look upon my suffering and
deliver me,
for I have not forgotten your law.
¹⁵⁴Defend my cause and redeem me;
renew my life according to your
promise.
¹⁵⁵Salvation is far from the wicked,
for they do not seek out your
decrees.
¹⁵⁶Your compassion is great, O LORD;
renew my life according to your
laws.
¹⁵⁷Many are the foes who persecute
me,
but I have not turned from your
statutes.
¹⁵⁸I look on the faithless with
loathing,

for they do not obey your word.
¹⁵⁹See how I love your precepts;
preserve my life, O LORD,
according to your love.
¹⁶⁰All your words are true;
all your righteous laws are
eternal.

שׂ Sin and Shin

¹⁶¹Rulers persecute me without
cause,
but my heart trembles at your
word.
¹⁶²I rejoice in your promise
like one who finds great spoil.
¹⁶³I hate and abhor falsehood
but I love your law.
¹⁶⁴Seven times a day I praise you
for your righteous laws.
¹⁶⁵Great peace have they who love
your law,
and nothing can make them
stumble.
¹⁶⁶I wait for your salvation, O LORD,
and I follow your commands.
¹⁶⁷I obey your statutes,
for I love them greatly.
¹⁶⁸I obey your precepts and your
statutes,
for all my ways are known to
you.

ת Taw

¹⁶⁹May my cry come before you, O
LORD;
give me understanding according
to your word.
¹⁷⁰May my supplication come before
you;
deliver me according to your
promise.
¹⁷¹May my lips overflow with praise,
for you teach me your decrees.
¹⁷²May my tongue sing of your word,
for all your commands are
righteous.
¹⁷³May your hand be ready to help
me,
for I have chosen your precepts.
¹⁷⁴I long for your salvation, O LORD,
and your law is my delight.
¹⁷⁵Let me live that I may praise you,
and may your laws sustain me.
¹⁷⁶I have strayed like a lost sheep.
Seek your servant,
for I have not forgotten your
commandments.

Psalm 120

A song of ascents.

¹I call on the LORD in my distress,
and he answers me.
²Save me, O LORD, from lying lips
and from deceitful tongues.

³What will he do to you,
and what more besides, O
deceitful tongue?
⁴He will punish you with a warrior's
sharp arrows,
with burning coals of the broom
tree.

⁵Woe to me that I dwell in Meshech,
that I live among the tents of
Kedar!
⁶Too long have I lived
among those who hate peace.
⁷I am a man of peace;
but when I speak, they are for
war.

Psalm 121

A song of ascents.

¹I lift up my eyes to the hills—
where does my help come from?
²My help comes from the LORD,
the Maker of heaven and earth.

³He will not let your foot slip—
he who watches over you will not
slumber;
⁴indeed, he who watches over Israel
will neither slumber nor sleep.

⁵The LORD watches over you—
the LORD is your shade at your
right hand;
⁶the sun will not harm you by day,
nor the moon by night.

⁷The LORD will keep you from all
harm—
he will watch over your life;
⁸the LORD will watch over your
coming and going
both now and for evermore.

Psalm 122

A song of ascents. Of David.

¹I rejoiced with those who said to
me,
"Let us go to the house of the
LORD."
²Our feet are standing
in your gates, O Jerusalem.

³Jerusalem is built like a city
that is closely compacted
together.
⁴That is where the tribes go up,
the tribes of the LORD,
to praise the name of the LORD
according to the statute given to
Israel.
⁵There the thrones for judgment
stand,
the thrones of the house of David.

⁶Pray for the peace of Jerusalem:
"May those who love you be
secure.
⁷May there be peace within your
walls
and security within your
citadels."
⁸For the sake of my brothers and
friends,
I will say, "Peace be within you."
⁹For the sake of the house of the
LORD our God,
I will seek your prosperity.

Psalm 123

A song of ascents.

¹I lift up my eyes to you,
to you whose throne is in heaven.
²As the eyes of slaves look to the
hand of their master,
as the eyes of a maid look to the
hand of her mistress,
so our eyes look to the LORD our
God,
till he shows us his mercy.

³Have mercy on us, O LORD, have
mercy on us,
for we have endured much
contempt.
⁴We have endured much ridicule
from the proud,
much contempt from the
arrogant.

Psalm 124

A song of ascents. Of David.

¹If the LORD had not been on our
side—
let Israel say—
²if the LORD had not been on our
side
when men attacked us,
³when their anger flared against us,

they would have swallowed us
  alive;
[4]the flood would have engulfed us,
  the torrent would have swept
    over us,
[5] the raging waters would have
    swept us away.

[6]Praise be to the LORD,
  who has not let us be torn by
    their teeth.
[7]We have escaped like a bird
  out of the fowler's snare;
the snare has been broken,
  and we have escaped.
[8]Our help is in the name of the
  LORD,
  the Maker of heaven and earth.

Psalm 125
A song of ascents.

[1]Those who trust in the LORD are like
  Mount Zion,
  which cannot be shaken but
    endures for ever.
[2]As the mountains surround
  Jerusalem,
so the LORD surrounds his people
  both now and for evermore.

[3]The sceptre of the wicked will not
  remain
  over the land allotted to the
    righteous,
for then the righteous might use
  their hands to do evil.

[4]Do good, O LORD, to those who are
  good,
  to those who are upright in heart.
[5]But those who turn to crooked ways
  the LORD will banish with the
    evildoers.

Peace be upon Israel.

Psalm 126
A song of ascents.

[1]When the LORD brought back the
  captives to[a] Zion,
  we were like men who dreamed.[b]
[2]Our mouths were filled with
  laughter,
  our tongues with songs of joy.
Then it was said among the nations,

"The LORD has done great things
  for them."
[3]The LORD has done great things for
  us,
  and we are filled with joy.

[4]Restore our fortunes,[c] O LORD,
  like streams in the Negev.
[5]Those who sow in tears
  will reap with songs of joy.
[6]He who goes out weeping,
  carrying seed to sow,
will return with songs of joy,
  carrying sheaves with him.

Psalm 127
A song of ascents. Of Solomon.

[1]Unless the LORD builds the house,
  its builders labour in vain.
Unless the LORD watches over the
  city,
  the watchmen stand guard in
    vain.
[2]In vain you rise early
  and stay up late,
toiling for food to eat—
  for he grants sleep to[a] those he
    loves.

[3]Sons are a heritage from the LORD,
  children a reward from him.
[4]Like arrows in the hands of a
  warrior
  are sons born in one's youth.
[5]Blessed is the man
  whose quiver is full of them.
They will not be put to shame
  when they contend with their
    enemies in the gate.

Psalm 128
A song of ascents.

[1]Blessed are all who fear the LORD,
  who walk in his ways.
[2]You will eat the fruit of your labour;
  blessings and prosperity will be
    yours.
[3]Your wife will be like a fruitful
  vine
  within your house;
your sons will be like olive shoots
  round your table.
[4]Thus is the man blessed
  who fears the LORD.

a1 Or LORD restored the fortunes of   b1 Or men restored to health
c4 Or Bring back our captives   a2 Or eat— / for while they sleep he provides for

⁵May the LORD bless you from Zion
    all the days of your life;
may you see the prosperity of
    Jerusalem,
⁶ and may you live to see your
    children's children.

Peace be upon Israel.

Psalm 129

A song of ascents.

¹They have greatly oppressed me
    from my youth—
let Israel say—
²they have greatly oppressed me
    from my youth,
    but they have not gained the
        victory over me.
³Ploughmen have ploughed my back
    and made their furrows long.
⁴But the LORD is righteous;
    he has cut me free from the cords
        of the wicked.

⁵May all who hate Zion
    be turned back in shame.
⁶May they be like grass on the
    housetops,
    which withers before it can grow;
⁷with it the reaper cannot fill his
    hands,
    nor the one who gathers fill his
        arms.
⁸May those who pass by not say,
    "The blessing of the LORD be
        upon you;
    we bless you in the name of the
        LORD."

Psalm 130

A song of ascents.

¹Out of the depths I cry to you, O
    LORD;
² O Lord, hear my voice.
Let your ears be attentive
    to my cry for mercy.

³If you, O LORD, kept a record of sins,
    O Lord, who could stand?
⁴But with you there is forgiveness;
    therefore you are feared.

⁵I wait for the LORD, my soul waits,
    and in his word I put my hope.
⁶My soul waits for the Lord

more than watchmen wait for the
    morning,
more than watchmen wait for the
    morning.

⁷O Israel, put your hope in the LORD,
    for with the LORD is unfailing
        love
    and with him is full redemption.
⁸He himself will redeem Israel
    from all their sins.

Psalm 131

A song of ascents. Of David.

¹My heart is not proud, O LORD,
    my eyes are not haughty;
I do not concern myself with great
    matters
    or things too wonderful for me.
²But I have stilled and quieted my
    soul;
    like a weaned child with its
        mother,
    like a weaned child is my soul
        within me.

³O Israel, put your hope in the LORD
    both now and for evermore.

Psalm 132

A song of ascents.

¹O LORD, remember David
    and all the hardships he endured.

²He swore an oath to the LORD
    and made a vow to the Mighty
        One of Jacob:
³"I will not enter my house
    or go to my bed—
⁴I will allow no sleep to my eyes,
    no slumber to my eyelids,
⁵till I find a place for the LORD,
    a dwelling for the Mighty One of
        Jacob."

⁶We heard it in Ephrathah,
    we came upon it in the fields of
        Jaar:ᵃ·ᵇ
⁷"Let us go to his dwelling-place;
    let us worship at his footstool—
⁸arise, O LORD, and come to your
    resting place,
    you and the ark of your might.

ᵃ6 That is, Kiriath Jearim
ᵇ6 Or *heard of it in Ephrathah, / we found it in the fields of Jaar.* (and no quotation marks
around verses 7-9)

[9]May your priests be clothed with
   righteousness;
   may your saints sing for joy."

[10]For the sake of David your servant,
   do not reject your anointed one.

[11]The LORD swore an oath to David,
   a sure oath that he will not
   revoke:
   "One of your own descendants
   I will place on your throne—

[12]if your sons keep my covenant
   and the statutes I teach them,
then their sons shall sit
   on your throne for ever and
   ever."

[13]For the LORD has chosen Zion,
   he has desired it for his dwelling:

[14]"This is my resting place for ever
   and ever;
   here I will sit enthroned, for I
   have desired it—

[15]I will bless her with abundant
   provisions;
   her poor will I satisfy with food.

[16]I will clothe her priests with
   salvation,
   and her saints shall ever sing for
   joy.

[17]"Here I will make a horn[c] grow for
   David
   and set up a lamp for my
   anointed one.

[18]I will clothe his enemies with
   shame,
   but the crown on his head shall
   be resplendent."

Psalm 133

A song of ascents. Of David.

[1]How good and pleasant it is
   when brothers live together in
   unity!

[2]It is like precious oil poured on the
   head,
   running down on the beard,
running down on Aaron's beard,
   down upon the collar of his
   robes.

[3]It is as if the dew of Hermon
   were falling on Mount Zion.
For there the LORD bestows his
   blessing,
   even life for evermore.

Psalm 134

A song of ascents.

[1]Praise the LORD, all you servants of
   the LORD
   who minister by night in the
   house of the LORD.

[2]Lift up your hands in the sanctuary
   and praise the LORD.

[3]May the LORD, the Maker of heaven
   and earth,
   bless you from Zion.

Psalm 135

[1]Praise the LORD.[a]

   Praise the name of the LORD;
   Praise him, you servants of the
   LORD,

[2]you who minister in the house of
   the LORD,
   in the courts of the house of our
   God.

[3]Praise the LORD, for the LORD is
   good;
   sing praise to his name, for that is
   pleasant.

[4]For the LORD has chosen Jacob to be
   his own,
   Israel to be his treasured
   possession.

[5]I know that the LORD is great,
   that our Lord is greater than all
   gods.

[6]The LORD does whatever pleases
   him,
   in the heavens and on the earth,
   in the seas and all their depths.

[7]He makes clouds rise from the ends
   of the earth;
   he sends lightning with the rain
   and brings out the wind from his
   storehouses.

[8]He struck down the firstborn of
   Egypt,
   the firstborn of men and animals.

[9]He sent his signs and wonders into
   your midst, O Egypt,
   against Pharaoh and all his
   servants.

[10]He struck down many nations

---

[c]17 *Horn here symbolises strong one, that is,* **king.**
[a]1 Hebrew *Hallelu Yah; also in verses 3 and 21*

and killed mighty kings—
¹¹Sihon king of the Amorites,
 Og king of Bashan
 and all the kings of Canaan—
¹²and he gave their land as an
 inheritance,
 an inheritance to his people
 Israel.

¹³Your name, O LORD, endures for
 ever,
 your renown, O LORD, through all
 generations.
¹⁴For the LORD will vindicate his
 people
 and have compassion on his
 servants.

¹⁵The idols of the nations are silver
 and gold,
 made by the hands of men.
¹⁶They have mouths, but cannot
 speak,
 eyes, but they cannot see;
¹⁷they have ears, but cannot hear,
 nor is there breath in their
 mouths.
¹⁸Those who make them will be like
 them,
 and so will all who trust in them.

¹⁹O house of Israel, praise the LORD;
 O house of Aaron, praise the
 LORD;
²⁰O house of Levi, praise the LORD;
 you who fear him, praise the
 LORD.
²¹Praise be to the LORD from Zion,
 to him who dwells in Jerusalem.

 Praise the LORD.

Psalm 136

¹Give thanks to the LORD, for he is
 good.
  His love endures for ever.
²Give thanks to the God of gods.
  His love endures for ever.
³Give thanks to the Lord of lords:
  His love endures for ever.

⁴to him who alone does great
 wonders,
  His love endures for ever.
⁵who by his understanding made the
 heavens,

⁶who spread out the earth upon the
 waters,
  His love endures for ever.
⁷who made the great lights—
  His love endures for ever.
⁸the sun to govern the day,
  His love endures for ever.
⁹the moon and stars to govern the
 night;
  His love endures for ever.

¹⁰to him who struck down the
 firstborn of Egypt
  His love endures for ever.
¹¹and brought Israel out from among
 them
  His love endures for ever.
¹²with a mighty hand and
 outstretched arm;
  His love endures for ever.

¹³to him who divided the Red Sea*ᵃ*
 asunder
  His love endures for ever.
¹⁴and brought Israel through the
 midst of it,
  His love endures for ever.
¹⁵but swept Pharaoh and his army
 into the Red Sea;
  His love endures for ever.

¹⁶to him who led his people through
 the desert,
  His love endures for ever.
¹⁷who struck down great kings,
  His love endures for ever.
¹⁸and killed mighty kings—
  His love endures for ever.
¹⁹Sihon king of the Amorites
  His love endures for ever.
²⁰and Og king of Bashan—
  His love endures for ever.

²¹and gave their land as an
 inheritance,
  His love endures for ever.
²²an inheritance to his servant Israel;
  His love endures for ever.

²³to the One who remembered us in
 our low estate
  His love endures for ever.
²⁴and freed us from our enemies,
  His love endures for ever.
²⁵and who gives food to every
 creature.
  His love endures for ever.
²⁶Give thanks to the God of heaven.
  His love endures for ever.

ᵃ13 Hebrew Yam Suph; that is, Sea of Reeds; also in verse 15

Psalm 137

¹By the rivers of Babylon we sat and
  wept
  when we remembered Zion.
²There on the poplars
  we hung our harps,
³for there our captors asked us for
  songs,
  our tormentors demanded songs
  of joy;
  they said, "Sing us one of the
  songs of Zion!"
⁴How can we sing the songs of the
  LORD
  while in a foreign land?
⁵If I forget you, O Jerusalem,
  may my right hand forget ¸its skill¸.
⁶May my tongue cling to the roof of
  my mouth
  if I do not remember you,
  if I do not consider Jerusalem
  my highest joy.

⁷Remember, O LORD, what the
  Edomites did
  on the day Jerusalem fell.
  "Tear it down," they cried,
  "tear it down to its foundations!"
⁸O Daughter of Babylon, doomed to
  destruction,
  happy is he who repays you
  for what you have done to us—
⁹he who seizes your infants
  and dashes them against the
  rocks.

Psalm 138

Of David.

¹I will praise you, O LORD, with all
  my heart;
  before the "gods" I will sing your
  praise.
²I will bow down towards your holy
  temple
  and will praise your name
  for your love and your
  faithfulness,
  for you have exalted above all
  things
  your name and your word.
³When I called, you answered me;
  you made me bold and stout-
  hearted.

⁴May all the kings of the earth praise
  you, O LORD,
  when they hear the words of
  your mouth.
⁵May they sing of the ways of the
  LORD,
  for the glory of the LORD is great.
⁶Though the LORD is on high, he
  looks upon the lowly,
  but the proud he knows from
  afar.
⁷Though I walk in the midst of
  trouble,
  you preserve my life;
  you stretch out your hand against
  the anger of my foes,
  with your right hand you save
  me.
⁸The LORD will fulfil ¸his purpose¸ for
  me;
  your love, O LORD, endures for
  ever—
  do not abandon the works of your
  hands.

Psalm 139

For the director of music. Of David. A psalm.

¹O LORD, you have searched me
  and you know me.
²You know when I sit and when I
  rise;
  you perceive my thoughts from
  afar.
³You discern my going out and my
  lying down;
  you are familiar with all my
  ways.
⁴Before a word is on my tongue
  you know it completely, O LORD.
⁵You hem me in—behind and
  before;
  you have laid your hand upon
  me.
⁶Such knowledge is too wonderful
  for me,
  too lofty for me to attain.
⁷Where can I go from your Spirit?
  Where can I flee from your
  presence?
⁸If I go up to the heavens, you are
  there;
  if I make my bed in the depths,ᵃ
  you are there.

ᵃ8 Hebrew *Sheol*

377

⁹If I rise on the wings of the dawn,
  if I settle on the far side of the
    sea,
¹⁰even there your hand will guide
    me,
  your right hand will hold me fast.

¹¹If I say, "Surely the darkness will
    hide me
  and the light become night
    around me,"
¹²even the darkness will not be dark
    to you;
  the night will shine like the day,
  for darkness is as light to you.

¹³For you created my inmost being;
  you knit me together in my
    mother's womb.
¹⁴I praise you because I am fearfully
    and wonderfully made;
  your works are wonderful,
  I know that full well.
¹⁵My frame was not hidden from
    you
  when I was made in the secret
    place.
  When I was woven together in the
    depths of the earth,
¹⁶ your eyes saw my unformed
    body.
  All the days ordained for me
  were written in your book
  before one of them came to be.

¹⁷How precious to[b] me are your
    thoughts, O God!
  How vast is the sum of them!
¹⁸Were I to count them,
  they would outnumber the grains
    of sand.
  When I awake,
  I am still with you.

¹⁹If only you would slay the wicked,
    O God!
  Away from me, you bloodthirsty
    men!
²⁰They speak of you with evil intent;
  your adversaries misuse your
    name.
²¹Do I not hate those who hate you,
    O LORD,
  and abhor those who rise up
    against you?
²²I have nothing but hatred for them;
  I count them my enemies.

b17 Or concerning

²³Search me, O God, and know my
    heart;
  test me and know my anxious
    thoughts.
²⁴See if there is any offensive way in
    me,
  and lead me in the way
    everlasting.

Psalm 140

For the director of music. A psalm of
David.

¹Rescue me, O LORD, from evil men;
  protect me from men of violence,
²who devise evil plans in their hearts
  and stir up war every day.
³They make their tongues as sharp as
    a serpent's;
  the poison of vipers is on their
    lips.   *Selah*

⁴Keep me, O LORD, from the hands
    of the wicked;
  protect me from men of violence
  who plan to trip my feet.
⁵Proud men have hidden a snare for
    me;
  they have spread out the cords of
    their net
  and have set traps for me along
    my path.   *Selah*

⁶O LORD, I say to you, "You are my
    God."
  Hear, O LORD, my cry for mercy.
⁷O Sovereign LORD, my strong
    deliverer,
  who shields my head in the day
    of battle—
⁸do not grant the wicked their
    desires, O LORD;
  do not let their plans succeed,
  or they will become proud. *Selah*

⁹Let the heads of those who
    surround me
  be covered with the trouble their
    lips have caused.
¹⁰Let burning coals fall upon them;
  may they be thrown into the fire,
  into miry pits, never to rise.
¹¹Let slanderers not be established in
    the land;
  may disaster hunt down men of
    violence.

¹²I know that the LORD secures
    justice for the poor
  and upholds the cause of the
    needy.

¹³Surely the righteous will praise
    your name
  and the upright will live before
    you.

Psalm 141
A psalm of David.

¹O LORD, I call to you; come quickly
    to me.
  Hear my voice when I call to
    you.

²May my prayer be set before you
    like incense;
  may the lifting up of my hands be
    like the evening sacrifice.

³Set a guard over my mouth, O LORD;
  keep watch over the door of my
    lips.

⁴Let not my heart be drawn to what
    is evil,
  to take part in wicked deeds
    with men who are evildoers;
  let me not eat of their delicacies.

⁵Let a righteous man strike me—it is
    a kindness;
  let him rebuke me—it is oil on
    my head.
  My head will not refuse it.

  Yet my prayer is ever against the
    deeds of evildoers;

⁶ their rulers will be thrown down
    from the cliffs,
  and the wicked will learn that my
    words were well spoken.

⁷They will say, „As one ploughs
    and breaks up the earth,
  so our bones have been scattered
    at the mouth of the grave."ᵃ

⁸But my eyes are fixed on you, O
    Sovereign LORD;
  in you I take refuge—do not give
    me over to death.

⁹Keep me from the snares they have
    laid for me,
  from the traps set by evildoers.

¹⁰Let the wicked fall into their own
    nets,
  while I pass by in safety.

Psalm 142
*A maskilᵃ of David. When he was in the
cave. A prayer.*

¹I cry aloud to the LORD;
  I lift up my voice to the LORD for
    mercy.

²I pour out my complaint before him;
  before him I tell my trouble.

³When my spirit grows faint within
    me,
  it is you who know my way.
  In the path where I walk
    men have hidden a snare for me.

⁴Look to my right and see;
  no-one is concerned for me.
  I have no refuge;
    no-one cares for my life.

⁵I cry to you, O LORD;
  I say, "You are my refuge,
    my portion in the land of the
    living."

⁶Listen to my cry,
  for I am in desperate need;
  rescue me from those who pursue
    me,
  for they are too strong for me.

⁷Set me free from my prison,
  that I may praise your name.

  Then the righteous will gather
    about me
  because of your goodness to me.

Psalm 143
A psalm of David.

¹O LORD, hear my prayer,
  listen to my cry for mercy;
  in your faithfulness and
    righteousness
  come to my relief.

²Do not bring your servant into
    judgment,
  for no-one living is righteous
    before you.

³The enemy pursues me,
  he crushes me to the ground;
  he makes me dwell in darkness
    like those long dead.

⁴So my spirit grows faint within me;
  my heart within me is dismayed.

⁵I remember the days of long ago;
  I meditate on all your works

ᵃ7 Hebrew *Sheol*   ᵃTitle: Probably a literary or musical term

and consider what your hands
have done.
⁶I spread out my hands to you;
my soul thirsts for you like a
parched land.   *Selah*

⁷Answer me quickly, O LORD;
my spirit faints with longing.
Do not hide your face from me
or I will be like those who go
down to the pit.
⁸Let the morning bring me word of
your unfailing love,
for I have put my trust in you.
Show me the way I should go,
for to you I lift up my soul.
⁹Rescue me from my enemies, O
LORD,
for I hide myself in you.
¹⁰Teach me to do your will,
for you are my God;
may your good Spirit
lead me on level ground.

¹¹For your name's sake, O LORD,
preserve my life;
in your righteousness, bring me
out of trouble.
¹²In your unfailing love, silence my
enemies;
destroy all my foes,
for I am your servant.

Psalm 144
Of David.

¹Praise be to the LORD, my Rock,
who trains my hands for war,
my fingers for battle.
²He is my loving God and my
fortress,
my stronghold and my deliverer,
my shield, in whom I take refuge,
who subdues peoples*ᵃ* under me.

³O LORD, what is man that you care
for him,
the son of man that you think of
him?
⁴Man is like a breath;
his days are like a fleeting
shadow.
⁵Part your heavens, O LORD, and
come down;

touch the mountains, so that they
smoke.
⁶Send forth lightning and scatter the
enemies, ;
shoot your arrows and rout them.
⁷Reach down your hand from on
high;
deliver me and rescue me
from the mighty waters,
from the hands of foreigners
⁸whose mouths are full of lies,
whose right hands are deceitful.

⁹I will sing a new song to you, O
God;
on the ten-stringed lyre I will
make music to you,
¹⁰to the One who gives victory to
kings,
who delivers his servant David
from the deadly sword.

¹¹Deliver me and rescue me
from the hands of foreigners
whose mouths are full of lies,
whose right hands are deceitful.

¹²Then our sons in their youth
will be like well-nurtured plants,
and our daughters will be like
pillars
carved to adorn a palace.
¹³Our barns will be filled
with every kind of provision.
Our sheep will increase by
thousands,
by tens of thousands in our fields;
¹⁴ our oxen will draw heavy loads.*ᵇ*
There will be no breaching of
walls,
no going into captivity,
no cry of distress in our streets.

¹⁵Blessed are the people of whom
this is true;
blessed are the people whose
God is the LORD.

Psalm 145*ᵃ*
A psalm of praise. Of David.

¹I will exalt you, my God the King;

*ᵃ2 Many manuscripts of the Masoretic Text, Dead Sea Scrolls, Aquila, Jerome and Syriac; most
manuscripts of the Masoretic Text subdues my people*
ᵇ14 Or Our chieftains will be firmly established
*ᵃThis psalm is an acrostic poem, the verses of which (including verse 13b) begin with the
successive letters of the Hebrew alphabet.*

I will praise your name for ever
and ever.
[2]Every day I will praise you
and extol your name for ever and
ever.

[3]Great is the LORD and most worthy
of praise;
his greatness no-one can fathom.
[4]One generation will commend your
works to another;
they will tell of your mighty acts.
[5]They will speak of the glorious
splendour of your majesty,
and I will meditate on your
wonderful works.[b]
[6]They will tell of the power of your
awesome works,
and I will proclaim your great
deeds.
[7]They will celebrate your abundant
goodness
and joyfully sing of your
righteousness.

[8]The LORD is gracious and
compassionate,
slow to anger and rich in love.
[9]The LORD is good to all;
he has compassion on all he has
made.

[10]All you have made will praise you,
O LORD;
your saints will extol you.
[11]They will tell of the glory of your
kingdom
and speak of your might,
[12]so that all men may know of your
mighty acts
and the glorious splendour of
your kingdom.
[13]Your kingdom is an everlasting
kingdom,
and your dominion endures
through all generations.

The LORD is faithful to all his
promises
and loving towards all he has
made.[c]
[14]The LORD upholds all those who
fall

and lifts up all who are bowed
down.
[15]The eyes of all look to you,
and you give them their food at
the proper time.
[16]You open your hand
and satisfy the desires of every
living thing.

[17]The LORD is righteous in all his
ways
and loving towards all he has
made.
[18]The LORD is near to all who call on
him,
to all who call on him in truth.
[19]He fulfils the desires of those who
fear him;
he hears their cry and saves
them.
[20]The LORD watches over all who
love him,
but all the wicked he will
destroy.

[21]My mouth will speak in praise of
the LORD.
Let every creature praise his holy
name
for ever and ever.

Psalm 146

[1]Praise the LORD.[a]

Praise the LORD, O my soul.
[2] I will praise the LORD all my life;
I will sing praise to my God as
long as I live.

[3]Do not put your trust in princes,
in mortal men, who cannot save.
[4]When their spirit departs, they
return to the ground;
on that very day their plans come
to nothing.

[5]Blessed is he whose help is the God
of Jacob,
whose hope is in the LORD his
God,
[6]the Maker of heaven and earth,
the sea, and everything in them—
the LORD, who remains faithful
for ever.

[b]5 Dead Sea Scrolls and Syriac (see also Septuagint); Masoretic Text *On the glorious splendour
of your majesty / and on your wonderful works I will meditate*
[c]13 One manuscript of the Masoretic Text, Dead Sea Scrolls, Septuagint and Syriac; most
manuscripts of the Masoretic Text do not have the last two lines of verse 13.
[a]1 Hebrew *Hallelu Yah*; also in verse 10

7He upholds the cause of the
oppressed
and gives food to the hungry.
The LORD sets prisoners free,
8 the LORD gives sight to the blind,
the LORD lifts up those who are
bowed down,
the LORD loves the righteous.
9The LORD watches over the alien
and sustains the fatherless and
the widow,
but he frustrates the ways of the
wicked.

10The LORD reigns for ever,
your God, O Zion, for all
generations.

Praise the LORD.

Psalm 147

1Praise the LORD.ᵃ

How good it is to sing praises to our
God,
how pleasant and fitting to praise
him!

2The LORD builds up Jerusalem;
he gathers the exiles of Israel.
3He heals the broken-hearted
and binds up their wounds.
4He determines the number of the
stars
and calls them each by name.
5Great is our Lord and mighty in
power;
his understanding has no limit.
6The LORD sustains the humble
but casts the wicked to the
ground.

7Sing to the LORD with thanksgiving;
make music to our God on the
harp.
8He covers the sky with clouds;
he supplies the earth with rain
and makes grass grow on the
hills.
9He provides food for the cattle
and for the young ravens when
they call.

10His pleasure is not in the strength
of the horse,
nor his delight in the legs of a
man;

11the LORD delights in those who fear
him,
who put their hope in his
unfailing love.

12Extol the LORD, O Jerusalem;
praise your God, O Zion,
13for he strengthens the bars of your
gates
and blesses your people within
you.
14He grants peace to your borders
and satisfies you with the finest of
wheat.

15He sends his command to the
earth;
his word runs swiftly.
16He spreads the snow like wool
and scatters the frost like ashes.
17He hurls down hail like pebbles.
Who can withstand his icy blast?
18He sends his word and melts them;
he stirs up his breezes, and the
waters flow.

19He has revealed his word to Jacob,
his laws and decrees to Israel.
20He has done this for no other
nation;
they do not know his laws.

Praise the LORD.

Psalm 148

1Praise the LORD.ᵃ

Praise the LORD from the heavens,
praise him in the heights above.
2Praise him, all his angels,
praise him, all his heavenly hosts.
3Praise him, sun and moon,
praise him, all you shining stars.
4Praise him, you highest heavens
and you waters above the skies.
5Let them praise the name of the
LORD,
for he commanded and they were
created.
6He set them in place for ever and
ever;
he gave a decree that will never
pass away.

7Praise the LORD from the earth,
you great sea creatures and all
ocean depths,

ᵃ1 Hebrew *Hallelu Yah*; also in verse 20

ᵃ1 Hebrew *Hallelu Yah*; also in verse 14

[8]lightning and hail, snow and clouds,
stormy winds that do his bidding,
[9]you mountains and all hills,
fruit trees and all cedars,
[10]wild animals and all cattle,
small creatures and flying birds,
[11]kings of the earth and all nations,
you princes and all rulers on
earth,
[12]young men and maidens,
old men and children.
[13]Let them praise the name of the
LORD,
for his name alone is exalted;
his splendour is above the earth
and the heavens.
[14]He has raised up for his people a
horn,[b]
the praise of all his saints,
of Israel, the people close to his
heart.

Praise the LORD.

Psalm 149

[1]Praise the LORD.[a]

Sing to the LORD a new song,
his praise in the assembly of the
saints.
[2]Let Israel rejoice in their Maker;
let the people of Zion be glad in
their King.
[3]Let them praise his name with
dancing
and make music to him with
tambourine and harp.
[4]For the LORD takes delight in his
people;
he crowns the humble with
salvation.

[5]Let the saints rejoice in this honour
and sing for joy on their beds.
[6]May the praise of God be in their
mouths
and a double-edged sword in
their hands,
[7]to inflict vengeance on the nations
and punishment on the peoples,
[8]to bind their kings with fetters,
their nobles with shackles of iron,
[9]to carry out the sentence written
against them.
This is the glory of all his saints.

Praise the LORD.

Psalm 150

[1]Praise the LORD.[a]

Praise God in his sanctuary;
praise him in his mighty heavens.
[2]Praise him for his acts of power;
praise him for his surpassing
greatness.
[3]Praise him with the sounding of the
trumpet,
praise him with the harp and
lyre,
[4]praise him with tambourine and
dancing,
praise him with the strings and
flute,
[5]praise him with the clash of
cymbals,
praise him with resounding
cymbals.
[6]Let everything that has breath
praise the LORD.

Praise the LORD.

---

[b]14 *Horn* here symbolises strong one, that is, king.
[a]1 Hebrew *Hallelu Yah*; also in verse 9
[a]1 Hebrew *Hallelu Yah*; also in verse 6